COMMENTARY

ON THE

EPISTLE TO THE HEBREWS.

BY

FRANZ DELITZSCH, D.D.,

PROFESSOR OF THEOLOGY, LEIPSIC.

Translated from the German

BY

THOMAS L. KINGSBURY, M.A.

VOL. I.

Wipf & Stock
PUBLISHERS
Eugene, Oregon

Wipf and Stock Publishers
199 W 8th Ave, Suite 3
Eugene, OR 97401

Commentary on the Epistle to the Hebrews, Volume 1
By Delitzsch, Franz and Kingsbury, Thomas I.
Softcover ISBN-13: 978-1-6667-5808-5
Hardcover ISBN-13: 978-1-6667-5809-2
eBook ISBN-13: 978-1-6667-5810-8
Publication date 9/8/2022
Previously published by T&T Clark, 1878

This edition is a scanned facsimile of the original edition published in 1878.

CONTENTS.

INTRODUCTION TO THE EXPOSITION.

	PAGE
INTRODUCTION, ...	3
1. Ancient Interpreters of the Eastern Church, . .	22
2. Ancient Interpreters of the Western Church, . .	24
3. Modern Interpreters (since the Reformation), . .	25

EXPOSITION.

FIRST PART OF THE EPISTLE (CHAP. I. 1-V. 10).

THE SUPREME EXALTATION OF THE MEDIATOR OF THE NEW TESTAMENT ABOVE THE ANGELS, ABOVE MOSES AND JOSHUA, AND FINALLY ABOVE AARON.

The manifold revelations of Himself made by God through the prophets have been followed up in this last time by a revelation through the Son as accomplisher of the work of redemption; who both, *à priori*, as God of God and upholder of the Universe created by God through Him, and now, *à posteriori*, as the glorified One and Heir of all things, is exalted above the angels (Chap. i.), ... 39

Exhortation to obedience to such a revelation as this—which, as given through the Son, so far excels that given through angels—in order not to incur a so much severer punishment (Chap. ii. 1-4), ... 93

The setting forth of the divine exaltation of the Lord Jesus is continued with abandonment of the homiletic paraenesis. Not angels, but the incarnate Son, is Lord of the world to come, who for a little while was made lower than the angels, that by death He might overcome death, and being made perfect through sufferings, might be for us, His brethren and with Him children of one heavenly Father, a sympathizing high priest (Chap. ii. 5-18), ... 101

CONTENTS.

	PAGE
A second parallel, presented in the form of a renewed paraenesis, based on the preceding paragraph, and exhorting to a due regard for such a high priest, who is not only faithful as Moses was in the house of God, but so much more glorious than he, as the son is greater than a servant (Chap. iii. 1-6),	152
A fresh exhortation, based on the preceding doctrine, not to harden the heart against a Messenger of God so much greater than even Moses, and this in order not (like the generation in the wilderness) to lose an entrance into God's rest (Chap. iii. 7-19), ...	165
An invitation (subjoined as conclusion to the preceding) to enter by faith into that divine rest to which the generation of the wilderness attained not, into which Joshua likewise was unable to bring his people,—the sabbath rest of God Himself, of which His people are made partakers (Chap. iv. 1-10), ...	184
Renewed exhortation to enter into the rest of God, the intense earnestness of which is founded on the all-penetrating and all-disclosing vital energy of the divine word (Chap. iv. 11-13), ...	200
The paraenesis returns to its starting-point: how firm and joyous should our faith be in having a High Priest so gracious and so exalted! (Chap. iv. 14-16), ...	216
The high priest of Aaron's race holds, as man, on behalf of other men, his office from God: and so also Christ has been appointed priest by God His Father, after a higher order, that of Melchizedek; and though Son of God, became through suffering and prayers in the days of His flesh, the author of eternal salvation to us (Chap. v. 1-10), . . .	224

EPISODE OF EXHORTATION CONDUCTING FROM THE FIRST TO THE SECOND PART OF THE EPISTLE (CHAP. V. 11–VI. 20).

Before pursuing further the comparison of Christ with Melchizedek, the author rebukes his readers for their backwardness, in lingering on the threshold of Christian knowledge, over which he would now, with God's help, lead them onwards to perfection (Chap. v. 11-vi. 3), ...	256
He sets vividly before them the hopelessness of apostasy, in cases where a living knowledge of Christ has been once obtained. For them, however, he still persists in hoping better things, and that through stedfastness in faith they will yet inherit the promises (Chap. vi. 4-12), . . .	279

CONTENTS. vii

PAGE

Having thus expressed his confident persuasion on behalf of his readers, that they will through stedfast faith obtain the promised salvation, the sacred writer now proceeds to set before them the example of Abraham, who had also through patience entered into the possession of a promise which God had confirmed to him by an oath upon Himself. They, too, have a hope confirmed in like manner, and one reaching onwards into the innermost sanctuary, into which, as their forerunner, Jesus Himself was already entered, being made (also by the oath of God) High Priest for ever after the order of Melchizedek (Chap. vi. 13-20), ... 305

SECOND PART OR CENTRAL MAIN DIVISION OF THE EPISTLE (CHAP. VII. 1–X. 18).

THE MELCHIZEDEKIAN SUPRA-LEVITICAL CHARACTER AND DIGNITY OF OUR CELESTIAL HIGH PRIEST, WHO, AFTER ONE SELF-SACRIFICE ONCE OFFERED, IS NOW FOR EVER ROYALLY ENTHRONED.

Analysis, ... 325

SECT. I. *The* PRIEST *after the order of Melchizedek.*

Melchizedek—that old mysterious king, that priest without beginning or end, whose appearance is so enigmatical and so significant in sacred history, and whose superior dignity was acknowledged by the great ancestor of the Levitical tribe—is (here set forth as) a type of Jesus Christ, who, springing from the royal tribe of Judah, was constituted, not by a legal and temporary ordinance, but by a divine unchangeable oath, an everlasting Priest, and thus exalted far above the mortal priests of the line of Aaron (Chap. vii. 1-25), . . . 327

EXCURSUS AND NOTES.

EXCURSUS TO HEB. IV. 9, CONTAINING EXTRACTS FROM THE TALMUDIC TRACT SANHEDRIN 96*b*, 97*a*, RELATING TO THE COMING OF MESSIAH AND THE MILLENNIAL SABBATH, . . . 377

NOTES, ... 389

NOTE BY TRANSLATOR.

DELITZSCH'S *Commentary on the Epistle to the Hebrews*, one of the largest and most valuable of his exegetical works, was published eleven years ago (in 1857). Though it has now been long out of print, the author has been hitherto prevented by other engagements from putting forth a second edition, in which he purposed to have excluded or abridged many references to the writings and the controversy alluded to in his preface,—references by which, with their consequent digressions, the course of the exposition is often seriously encumbered. Under these circumstances, it was at first the translator's intention to have prepared an abridged version of the original work, excluding much of the controversial matter, with the approbation and under the superintendence of Dr. Delitzsch himself. This design has also of necessity been abandoned; but some traces of it remain in the following translation, in which many sentences, and a few paragraphs, have been transferred from the text to the notes, without detriment, it is hoped, to the original work, and certainly to the convenience of the English reader.

The translator's thanks and acknowledgments are specially due to Mr. Sinclair Manson, who, before the abandonment of the original design of a recasting of the whole work, furnished him with a rough literal version of a large part of the *Commentary* as it stands. Of this considerable use has been made in parts of the present volume.

The translator has added a few notes and elucidatory sentences, where such seemed necessary, included in brackets or signed "TR." There are also, in the early part of the volume, a few bracketed paragraphs, proceeding from Delitzsch's own pen, which, according to the plan subsequently pursued, should have been thrown into the Notes. All references to the Codex Sinaiticus are of course made by the translator, as that important MS. had not been discovered till after the publication of the original work.

PREFACE.

WHEN so much has been done recently, and so well done, for the interpretation of the Epistle to the Hebrews, I feel that in venturing to add a new commentary to those already in existence, I am bound to say a few words on the aims and motives of the present undertaking.

There is then, in the first place, one department—the theological—in the interpretation of this epistle, in which not a little still remains to be accomplished, as even those who have done the most in this line themselves (such as Bleek and Tholuck) would hardly be disposed to question. Nor would, I think, even Lünemann wish to do so, since his own performances in this respect might have been far more considerable, had he not so entirely left out of view the valuable contributions to theological exegesis furnished by Prof. v. Hofmann in his *Schriftbeweis*.[1] I have also thought that a good deal more might still be done for the interpretation of our epistle in other aspects—

---

[1] [*Der Schriftbeweis, ein theologischer Versuch.* The first section of the second half of this important publication, which treats of the person and work of Christ, and is more particularly referred to in the latter part of Prof. Delitzsch's Preface, was published in 1853. It excited, on its appearance, great attention in German theological circles. Dr. Weber, in his book on "*The Wrath of God*" (*Vom Zorne Gottes*), published at Erlangen in 1862, with Prolegomena by Delitzsch, enumerates some five-and-thirty books and essays to which this "Hofmannian Controversy concerning the Atonement" had then already given rise.—TR.]

grammatical, critical, and archæological—and that my own previous course of study has rendered me not incapable of attempting something in each of these departments likewise, especially as since 1846 (in which year I delivered at Rostock my first course of lectures on the Epistle to the Hebrews) I have several times had to go thoroughly over the same ground again. To each of these departments, therefore, I have conscientiously endeavoured to give a like attention. (1.) In questions of grammatical form and syntax I have consulted the best and latest works, down to those of Mullach and Alex. Buttmann. For parallels or illustrations in classical literature, and yet more for those in the writings of Philo, I have preferred mainly to depend on the sources opened by my own reading. (2.) All questions relating to textual criticism I have carefully examined, so far as my *apparatus criticus*—consisting, however, almost entirely of printed works—enabled me; and even these limited researches have conducted to a few textual emendations. (3.) The Talmudic literature, of such primary importance in an archæological point of view, I have everywhere consulted in its original sources. And, finally, in regard to those numerous questions concerning [rites, or documents, or customs of] the Old Testament, which the interpreter of this epistle is called on to answer, I have in many instances been able to fall back on slowly won results of previous investigation. I may therefore humbly trust that my labours with regard to this epistle were neither undertaken by me without legitimate vocation, nor are now brought to a close without some measure of success.

This work is likewise the first attempt to present, in a commentary on some considerable and integral portion of the New Testament, the whole mass of exegetical materials in living flow and combination. Herein it has been my endeavour to imitate the admirable method of v. Hofmann (in both his biblico-theological treatises), and that already so happily attempted by Luthardt (in his work on the Gospel of St.

John),—a method which, in the preface to my *Genesis*, I have called the *reproductive*, in contradistinction to the *glossatorial*. From its commencement to the end (where the epistle itself closes with a few abrupt parting communications), this commentary will be found to move on without break or lacuna; my endeavour having been to interweave all my exegetical, critical, and theological materials into one compact and continuous whole.

I was led to select this particular book for the subject of such a commentary by the force of circumstances, and not by my own independent choice or will. The second part of Dr. v. Hofmann's *Schriftbeweis* has given rise to an energetic controversy on the doctrine of the atonement; and many witnesses have already risen up against his teaching, as opposed not only to our peculiar Lutheran Confession, but also to the faith and conscientious convictions of the whole Christian church. To be silent and inactive for my own part in the midst of such a controversy, wherein the very heart and centre of Christianity itself was touched, neither my outward circumstances nor my internal sense of right permitted me. And how could I otherwise more fitly take my part therein, than in following out my immediate vocation as a professional interpreter of holy Scripture; and that the more so, as appeal was being made on either side, in a way eminently befitting evangelical theologians, to the ultimate decision of the word of God? My course, therefore, has been the following: First I sought to make myself completely familiar with the ritual and objects of Old Testament sacrifice; and then I betook myself to the exposition of the epistle, with especial regard to biblico-archæological investigations, pursued in a spirit similar to that of Keil and Ebrard. And it is my conviction now, as it was formerly, that my dear friend and colleague [von Hofmann]'s views on these essential points are not less opposed to the clear sense of the apostolic word, when impartially interpreted, than to the faith and teaching of the church, and that the latter must receive quite another development, if such doctrine is to be found compatible with it. Would that my labours might be to him of any service in the reconsideration and reconstruction of the second part of his *Schriftbeweis*, with which he is now engaged, or contribute in any way to rendering the present conflict a benefit to the church by a final victory gained for truth, to the combatants themselves by its peaceful termination.

In saying this much concerning my purposes and motives in undertaking the following Commentary, I would only justify the attempt on my part to grapple with such a theme. Before any voice as yet can reach me, whether of public or of private criticism, I feel with deepest inward shame myself how far I fall behind my own ideal of what such a Commentary ought to be. How far, indeed, does every human exposition fall short of the fulness of the unsearchable word! O that He, whose word it is, would, with His own Self-witness in the heart of every reader, supply the deficiencies, or with His own voice drown and bring to silence the feeble utterances, of my interpretation!

F. DELITZSCH.

ERLANGEN, 30*th Sept.* 1857.

INTRODUCTION.

TO THE

EXPOSITION OF THE EPISTLE TO THE HEBREWS.

Candori studendum, resque majore aut minore contentione tradendæ, prout rationum momentis parcius aut plenius sunt probatæ.

BACO DE VERULAMIS.

INTRODUCTION.

THE EPISTLE TO THE HEBREWS has not its like among the epistles of the New Testament, resembling in this uniqueness of position, as well as in tone and spirit, the great prophetic exhortation of Isa. xl.–lxvi., which in like manner stands alone among the prophetic writings of the Old Testament. The tone of thought in both these portions of Scripture has the same transcendental character; each has a threefold division of its contents; the same majestic march and flight of language characterizes each, the same Easter-morning breath from another world, and the same tantalizing veil suspended before the eyes of the vexed inquirer, now half revealing now concealing the origin and authorship of either composition. No other book of the New Testament is distinguished by such brilliant eloquence and euphonious rhythm as our epistle; and this rhetorical form is not superinduced on the subject, but is its true expression, as setting forth the special glories of the new covenant and of a new and Christ-transfigured world. Old and New Testaments are set the one over against the other, the moonlight of the Old Testament paling once and again before the sunrise of the New, and the heavenly prospect thus illumined. The language is more oratorical than dialectic, not so excited and lively as in the Epistle to the Galatians, not pressing forward with such quick triumphant step as in the Epistle to the Romans, not so unrestrained and superabundant as in that to the Ephesians, but characterized throughout by conscious repose, dignified solemnity, and majestic quietude.

We seem at first to have a *treatise* before us, but the special hortatory references interwoven with the most discursive and dogmatic portions of the work soon show us that it is really a kind of sermon addressed to some particular and well-known auditory; while at the close the homiletic form (the *Paraclesis*) changes into that of an epistle (ch. xiii. 22). The epistle has no apostolic name attached to it, while it produces throughout the impression of the presence of the original and creative force of the apostolic spirit. And if written by an apostle, who could have been its author but St. Paul? True, till towards the end it does not make the impression upon us of being of his authorship; its form is not Pauline, and the thoughts, though never un-Pauline, yet often go beyond the Pauline type of doctrine as made known to us in the other epistles, and even where this is not the case they seem to be peculiarly placed and applied; but towards the close, when the epistle takes the epistolary form, we seem to hear St. Paul himself, and no one else.

The same veil which overlies the author overlies also the recipients of this epistle. It is addressed to a Jewish Christian church, or churches, of peculiar form and history; but where are such to be sought? Inquiries have been made after these Hebrew Christians from Palestine upwards towards Syria and Asia Minor, and downwards towards Egypt, but without results of indubitable certainty or full satisfaction. No reliable conclusion has yet been reached respecting either readers or author of the epistle: one point alone stands fixed—it cannot in its present form be an immediate production of St. Paul. And even that is still disputed by some inquirers of reputation. May we not say that this epistle resembles in these respects the great Melchizedek of sacred story, of which its central portion treats? Like him it marches forth in lonely royal and sacerdotal dignity, and like him is ἀγενεάλογητος; we know not whence it cometh nor whither it goeth.[1]

Eusebius remarks (*H. E.* iii. 37), that "in the epistle which Clement addressed in the name of the Roman church to that of the Corinthians he adopts many thoughts from the Epistle to the Hebrews, and makes even some verbal citations from it, most clearly showing that it cannot be a composition of later date." "And therefore," he adds, "it was thought reasonable that it should be incorporated with the other writings of the apostle" (St. Paul). The Epistle of Clement here referred to

---

[1] From an essay of mine on Author and Readers of the Ep. to the Hebr. *Luth. Zeitschrift*, 1849, 2.

(see 1 Ep. Clem. Rom. cc. 40, 41) can hardly have been written before the destruction of Jerusalem, and was probably written long after, perhaps in the time of Domitian (A.D. 87-96).[1] The use it makes of the Epistle to the Hebrews, therefore, could only prove, what we should not doubt (on other grounds), that our epistle was already in existence when St. Clement wrote. And, moreover, its own manifest Pauline character gives us better proof of its derivation from St. Paul (in a wider sense) than any use which Clement makes of it.

That Marcion in his *Apostolicon* excluded from the canon both the Pastoral Epistles and this to the Hebrews, and that Basilides, too, rejected the latter,[2] are facts of no account; for these heretics gave little heed to external testimony in favour of writings whose contents did not please them. But not much later we are met by the far more important depreciatory opinion of the Western Church. In the *Fragmentum de Canone Sacrarum Scripturarum*, composed probably towards the end of the second century, which Muratori gives us from a codex of the Ambrosian Library, the Epistle to the Hebrews is never mentioned. For when it is there said, *Fertur enim ad Laudecenses, alia ad Alexandrinos Pauli nomine fictæ ad hæresem Marcionis, et alia plura*[3] *quæ in Catholicam Ecclesiam recipi non possunt: fel enim cum melle misceri non congruit*,—the epistle to the Alexandrians referred to cannot be this of ours to the Hebrews, for this, if for no other reason, that it is anonymous, and so could not be said to be *Pauli nomine ficta*; not to mention, that if it had been addressed to Alexandrian Jewish Christians, the remembrance of that fact would surely have been preserved in the church of Alexandria rather than in that of Rome.[4] The Epistle to the Hebrews, therefore, is here entirely ignored. Nor

---

[1] Hilgenfeld, *Apost. Väter*, pp. 83-85.
[2] *Vid.* Hieronym.: prœem. in *Ep. ad Titum; Opp.* (Vallarsi), t. vii.
[3] Jan van Gilse (*Disp. de Antiquissimo ll. N. Fœd. Catalogo Amstel.* 1852, 4to) interpunctuates: ... fictæ : ad (= apud) hæres. Marcion. et alia plura...
[4] On Wieseler's conjecture, that the author of our epistle had the temple of Onias in view, see my essay referred to above (pp. 279-281). The same conjecture was made by Frankel (*Monatschrift für Geschichte u. Wissensch. des Judenthums*, 1856, p. 390) in reference to "the Book of the Jubilees;" but none of the arguments alleged make this in either case probable. See Jost (*Gesch. des Judenth. u. seiner Secten*, i. pp. 116-120).

is it mentioned in those writings of Novatian which have come down to us. Cyprian and Victorinus Petabionensis know only of epistles of St. Paul *ad septem ecclesias*. Hippolytus (about A.D. 200) directly denied its composition by St. Paul; and Irenæus (*ob.* about A.D. 202) did the same indirectly, inasmuch as he makes hardly any allusion to our epistle.[1] And in Eusebius (*H. E.* vi. 20) we read: " There has also come to us a dialogue by Caius, a very eloquent man, delivered at Rome under Zephyrinus, against Proclus, a partisan of the Cataphrygian (Montanist) sect, in which he reproaches his opponents with their rashness and effrontery in composing new writings, and at the same time mentions only thirteen epistles of the holy apostle, not classing that to the Hebrews with the rest, as even yet some of the Romans do not allow it to be a work of the apostle." In Jerome, who (*de viris illustr.* c. 59) reproduces this testimony in Latin,[2] the concluding words read thus: *sed et apud Romanos usque hodie quasi Pauli Ap. non habetur;* and the date is thus given: *Sub Zephyrino Romanæ urbis episcopo, id est sub Antonino Severi filio* (*i.e.* Caracalla, A.D. 211–217). To the very same time belongs the testimony of Tertullian (*de pudicitia,* c. xx., according to Oehler's text):

[1] In Photius, *bibl. cod.* 232 (p. 291, ed. Bekker), among excerpts from a work of the tritheist Stephanus (surnamed ὁ Γόβαρος) we read: "Hippolytus and Irenæus say that the Epistle to the Hebrews was not by that Paul; but Clement and Eusebius, and a great choir of other godly fathers, reckon it among the other epistles, and say that the Clement spoken of translated it from the Hebrew." The word (" spoken of") εἰρημένον is probably a thoughtless addition by Photius himself. The first Clement here meant must be Clemens Alex., the second Clem. Romanus. As to Hippolytus, Photius himself confirms the statement by reference to a passage in his work "against 32 Heresies," *Bibl. cod.* 121 (p. 94, ed. Bekker): Λέγει . . . ὅτι ἡ πρὸς Ἑβρ. ἐπιστολὴ οὐκ ἔστι τοῦ Ἀπ. Παύλου. And Irenæus likewise, if he had held the epistle to be equally Pauline with the rest, would hardly have conformed to the views of the Western Church in scarcely citing it at all. Except the *verbo virtutis suæ* of c. *Hær.* ii. 30, 9, we find in his extant writings no other certain allusion. That he mentioned the epistle in his (now lost) βιβλίον διαλέξεων διαφόρων, we know from Eus. *H. E.* v. 26, but even then by no means as a Pauline epistle. Only in the second Pfaffian fragment (*Iren.* ed. Stieren, i. p. 854) is a passage quoted from ch. xiii. 15, and apparently as an exhortation of St. Paul's; but the genuineness of this fragment is disputed on good grounds. (See Höfling, *Lehre der ältest. Kirche vom Opfer*, pp. 98–107.)

[2] Photius had not seen this dialogue of Caius. *Bibl. cod.* 48.

Disciplina igitur Apostolorum proprie quidem instruit ac determinat principaliter sanctitatis omnis erga templum Dei antistitem ad ubique de ecclesia eradicandum omne sacrilegium pudicitiæ sine ulla restitutionis mentione. Volo tamen ex redundantia alicujus etiam comitis Apostolorum testimonium superducere, idoneum confirmandi de proximo jure disciplinam magistrorum. Extat enim et Barnabæ titulus ad Hebræos, a Deo satis auctorati viri, ut quem Paulus juxta se constituerit in abstinentiæ tenore [1 Cor. ix. 6] : *Aut ego solus et Barnabas non habemus operandi potestatem? Et utique receptior apud ecclesias epistola Barnabæ illo apocrypho Pastore mœchorum. Monens itaque discipulos omissis omnibus initiis ad perfectionem magis tendere, Impossibile est enim, inquit, eos qui semel inluminati sunt.* . . . *Hoc qui ab apostolis didicit et cum apostolis docuit, nunquam mœcho et fornicatori secundam pœnitentiam promissam ab apostolis norat.* Towards the commencement of this polemical treatise of Tertullian's it is said : *Pontifex scilicet Maximus quod est episcopus episcoporum, edicit: Ego mœchiæ et fornicationis delicta pœnitentia functis dimitto.* This bishop of bishops is Zephyrinus.[1] The two last mentioned testimonies, therefore, of the Western Church regarding the Epistle to the Hebrews, the anti-Montanist testimony of Caius, and the Montanist of Tertullian, belong to one and the same time, viz. that between A.D. 200 and A.D. 218. Observe, however, that while Caius denies the Pauline authorship of the Epistle to the Hebrews, Tertullian only does not venture to maintain it. Hence it is clear as day that the epistle was not traditionally handed down as Pauline in the Western Church, and that the opponents of Montanism, in rejecting our epistle, appealed to a tradition which was quite independent of the Montanistic controversy.

We find it quite otherwise in the Oriental Church. The first witness we meet with there is Clement of Alexandria (*ob.* 220), who in his Στρωματεῖς often, and without hesitation, quotes the Epistle to the Hebrews as an epistle of St. Paul's. This work being still extant, we are not on this point dependent on the reference to it in Eus. *H. E.* vi. 13. But Clement elsewhere expressed himself at length regarding this epistle in a passage, the preservation of which we owe to Eusebius, who,

---

[1] *Vid.* Gams, Art. Zephyrinus, in Wetzer and Welte's (Rom.) Cath. *Kirchenlexicon.*

H. E. vi. 14, gives us the following information: "In the *Hypotyposes*, to speak briefly, he (Clemens Alexandrinus) has given a compressed account of the whole testamentary Scripture, not omitting even the disputed books; I mean the Epistle of Jude and the other catholic epistles, as well as that of Barnabas and the so-called Apocalypse of Peter. As to the Epistle to the Hebrews, he says that it is indeed Paul's, but written to Hebrews in the Hebrew language; and that Luke having translated it carefully, published it for the Greeks. Whence there is the same colouring in respect to language and expression in this epistle as in the Acts of the Apostles. But for a good reason it is not prefaced by the expression, 'Paul the apostle.' 'For,' says he, 'addressing his epistle to Hebrews who had taken a prejudice against him and mistrusted him, he did wisely and well in not repelling them at the very outset by placing his name at the beginning.' To this he afterwards adds further: 'Now since, as the blessed presbyter' [probably Pantænus[1]] 'said, our Lord, being Himself the Apostle of the Almighty, was sent to the Hebrews, Paul out of modesty, and as having his own special mission to the Gentiles, does not here write himself down as an apostle of the Hebrews, and that both through reverence for our Lord, and because, being already a preacher and apostle of the Gentiles, he is undertaking a superfluous task in addressing a letter to the Hebrews.'"

The next and equally important testimony is that of Origen (*ob.* 254), preserved for us also by Eusebius (*H.E.* vi. 25) among extracts which he gives from some of his works concerning the canon of Scripture: "Further, he (Origen) thus expresses himself concerning the Epistle to the Hebrews in his Homilies upon it: 'The character of the diction of the epistle inscribed to the Hebrews has not the peculiar roughness (τὸ ἰδιωτικόν) which marks the style of the apostle, who himself acknowledged that he was rude in speech (ἰδιώτης), *i.e.* in style, but this epistle is in the composition of words more purely Greek; and every one able to distinguish differences of style would freely acknowledge it. But again, on the other hand, that the thoughts of the epistle are wonderful, and not inferior to the

---

[1] Pantænus taught (acc. to Jerome, *de vir. illustr.* c. 26) in the time of the Emperors Septimius Severus (193-211) and Caracalla (211-217).

acknowledged writings of the apostle, this also every one who reads the apostolic scriptures with due attention would acknowledge to be true.'[1] To this he adds further on: 'If I were to give my judgment, I should say that, while the thoughts belong to the apostle, the diction and composition of words belong to some one writing after him, as a scribe writing out notes of what has been said by the teacher. If, then, any church holds this epistle to be Paul's, let it be well thought of even on that account. For not without good reason have the ancients handed it down as Paul's. But as to who (actually)[2] wrote the epistle, God (only) knows the truth. The information which has reached us is, that by some it is said that Clement who was bishop of the Romans wrote the epistle, and by some, that Luke (was the writer) who wrote the Gospel and the Acts.'" The reader will observe that, according to Origen's statement, the Epistle to the Hebrews had been handed down from antiquity as Pauline: οὐ γὰρ εἰκῆ οἱ ἀρχαῖοι ἄνδρες ὡς Παύλου αὐτὴν παραδεδώκασι. Tradition spoke simply of St. Paul in connection with it, and therefore Origen will not have that church blamed which should regard it as directly and immediately Pauline. His position is exactly the same as that of Clemens. They both justify the witness of tradition, though the diction and anonymousness of the epistle seem to contradict it, by the assumption that the apostle wrote through the medium of another. Beside the passage preserved by Eusebius, there are only two other places in which, so far as we know, Origen takes cursory notice of the doubts in circulation respecting the Epistle to the Hebrews, viz. *Ep. ad Africanum*, c. 9, and *In Matt. XXIII.* 27, 8. Otherwise he regularly cites it as Pauline. Eusebius takes the same view. After speaking of the dependence of Clemens Romanus'

---

[1] All up to this point is extract from Origenes. Credner is mistaken in attributing the sentences ἀλλ' ἐστιν . . . and καὶ τοῦτο . . . . to Eusebius (*Einl.* p. 497).

[2] It would throw everything into confusion if we insisted on understanding ὁ γράψας here as implying full original authorship. Origen plainly attributes a certain authorship to St. Paul; ὁ γράψας therefore must denote the writer to whom it owes its present form. This is not widely different from the sense in which ὁ γράψας (τὸ Εὐαγγελ. καὶ τὰς Πράξεις) is used of St. Luke immediately afterwards. In writing both Gospel and Acts, St. Luke "worked up" materials which lay before him.

epistle on that to the Hebrews, he proceeds (*H. E.* iii. 37): "Paul having thus held written intercourse with the Hebrews in the ancestral language, some say that Luke the evangelist, others that this very Clement, translated his writing; which latter is the more probable from the resemblance of the Epistle of Clement and the Epistle to the Hebrews in the character of their phraseology, and the kindred tone of thought in both writings." But, nevertheless, so certain does Eusebius feel of the apostolicity of the epistle, that he makes no special mention of it when (at *H. E.* iii. 25) recounting the ὁμολογούμενα and ἀντιλεγόμενα of the New Testament, but only of "the epistles of Paul" in general, evidently including this epistle among them, and therefore reckoning it among the ὁμολογούμενα. The supposition, that he places it (at *H. E.* iii. 13) among the ἀντιλεγόμενα,[1] rests on a misinterpretation of his words. The view he takes of the epistle is quite the Alexandrine, or, as we may call it, the Oriental one. For not only Dionysius of Alexandria (*ob.* A.D. 264-5) and the bishops who succeeded him, but all the ecclesiastical writers of Egypt, Syria, and the whole East, cite passages from the Epistle to the Hebrews without hesitation as words of St. Paul. Even Arius and the older Arians thus acknowledged it. If i. 3 gave them trouble, they could cite on the other hand the τῷ ποιήσαντι αὐτόν of iii. 2 in their own favour. It was only the later Arians, and probably not all of these, who, to evade some controversial difficulties, declined its Pauline authorship.[2]

In the course of the fourth century the judgment of the West became gradually more favourable to the Epistle to the

[1] As Bleek, Credner, and Lünemann suppose.

[2] See Epiphanius, *Hæres.* 69, H. 37, and Theodoret in the beginning of his Preface to his Commentary on the Epistle: "It is no wonder that those who are infected with the Arian malady should rage against the apostolic writings, separating the Epistle to the Hebrews from the rest and calling it spurious." It was probably only the later Arians who did this, and not all of them. Such (among others) are chiefly referred to in the iambics attributed to Amphilochius (*ob.* after 392) and addressed *ad Seleucum*:

Τινὲς δέ φασι τὴν πρὸς Ἑβραίους νόθον
Οὐκ εὖ λέγοντες· γνησία γὰρ ἡ χάρις.

In both palimpsests of the *Bibl. Ambrosiana*, containing Ulfila's version of the Pauline Epistles, the Epistle to the Hebrews is wanting.

INTRODUCTION. 11

Hebrews. Several ecclesiastical writers indeed, as Phæbadius (*ob.* after 392), Zeno Veronensis (*cir.* 360), and Optatus (*cir.* 370), appear still to have refrained from using it; others, as Hilarius Pictaviensis (*ob.* 368), Lucifer Calaritanus (*ob.* 371), and Victorinus Afer (contemporaneous with both), make use of it rarely, yet when they do so, cite it as Pauline; while St. Ambrose (*ob.* 397) appears to have been the first, and indeed the only one of his time, who places it in every respect in the same rank with the other epistles of St. Paul. It was no longer entirely excluded as formerly from public reading in the church, though it was to be still a long time before it came to equal honour with the other *libri ecclesiastici* in general estimation. The abuse made by Arians and Novatians of several passages had prejudiced the West against the epistle, and that still more from the circumstance that no ancient Western tradition spoke in its favour. But these prejudices gradually gave way as a better exegesis showed the groundlessness of the heretical misinterpretations, and as the ever-increasing intercourse between the churches of East and West, which the Arian controversies induced, made the *consensus* of the Oriental churches in favour of the apostolic authorship better known to their Western brethren. This gradual change reflects itself in the following citation from c. 89 of Philaster or Philastrius' (*ob. cir.* 390) *Liber de Hæresibus* (Oehler, *Corporis hæresiologici,* tom. i. 1856): *Sunt alii quoque qui Epistolam Pauli ad Hebræos non adserunt esse ipsius, sed dicunt aut Barnabæ esse apostoli aut Clementis de urbe Roma episcopi, alii autem Lucæ evangelistæ. Aiunt epistolam etiam ad Laodicenses scriptam.*[1] *Et quia addiderunt in ea* (the Laodicean Epistle) *quædam non bene sentientes, inde non legitur in ecclesia, et si legitur a quibusdam, non tamen in ecclesia legitur populo, nisi tredecim epistolæ ipsius, et ad Hebræos interdum. Et in ea* (the Epistle to the Hebrews) *quia rhetorice scripsit, sermone plausibili inde non putant esse ejusdem apostoli; et quia et factum Christum dicit in ea* (iii. 2) *inde non legitur; de pœnitentia autem propter Novatianos æque. Cum ergo "factum" dicit Christum corpore non divinitate dicit "factum" cum doceat ibidem quod divinæ sit et paternæ substan-*

---

[1] So with Oehler we must read and interpunctuate, to avoid the confusions which some have made between what Philastrius here says of the TWO epistles—*ad Laodicenses* and *ad Hebræos.*

tiæ filius; (i. 3) " *Qui est splendor gloriæ,*" inquit, " *et imago substantiæ ejus.*" *Pœnitudinem etiam non excludit docendo sed diversum gradum dignitatis ostendit inter hunc qui integrum*[1] *custodivit et illum qui peccavit. Dignitatis est igitur detrimentum in eo qui peccavit non damnum salutis. Nam si fortiter quis pugnaverit per martyrium recipiet pristinam dignitatem, aut si condigne in hoc sæculo vixerit impetrat quod desiderat adipisci. Nam in ipsa epistola rebaptizatores excludit*[2] *non baptismum pœnitentiæ abnegat conferendum, quod interdum in multis fructuosum inveniatur pœnitentibus, quod postea fide, vita bono opere et in hoc sæculo a Domino collandati sunt perseverantes jam in rebus bonis et operibus fructuosis quod Dominus dixerat per prophetam* [Ezek. xxxiii. 16] : " *Non ero memor malorum ejus sed bonorum potius, si jam in bonis permanserit operibus.*"

St. Jerome contributed not a little to the change of feeling in the West towards the Epistle to the Hebrews, by making known the testimonies borne to it by the Oriental churches and Greek ecclesiastical literature. The two chief passages in his works on this subject are found in the *de viris illustribus,* c. 5 (t. ii. col. 838, ed. Vallarsi), and in *Ep.* 129 *ad Dardanum* (t. i. col. 971). The first runs thus: *Epistola autem quæ fertur ad Hebræos non ejus creditur propter styli sermonisque dissonantiam (distantiam), sed vel Barnabæ, juxta Tertullianum, vel Lucæ evangelistæ juxta quosdam, vel Clementis Romanæ postea ecclesiæ Episcopi quem aiunt* [*ipsi adjunctum*] *sententias Pauli proprio ordinasse et ornasse sermone.*[3] *Vel certe quia Paulus scribebat ad Hebræos et propter invidiam sui apud eos nominis, titulum in principio salutationis amputaverit. Scripserat ut Hebræus* [*Hebræis*] *Hebraice, id est suo eloquis disertissime, ut ea quæ eloquenter scripta fuerant in Hebræo, eloquentius verterentur in Græcam et hanc causam esse, quod a cæteris Pauli epistolis discrepare videatur.* In the second passage

---

[1] *i.e. id quod integrum est,* probably an allusion to Ps. xxxvii. 37, where the Vulgate reading is *custodi innocentiam.*

[2] See our note on τοὺς ἅπαξ φωτισθέντας, Heb. vi. 4, which was commonly interpreted = *semel baptizatos.* St. Jerome's way of escaping the difficulty is different (*adv. Jovinian,* l. ii. t. ii. col. 325).

[3] Euthalius (*cir.* 460) makes the distinction : ὡς μέν τινες, ὑπὸ Λουκᾶ, ὡς δὲ οἱ πολλοί, ὑπὸ Κλήμεντος.

INTRODUCTION. 13

Jerome says: *Illud nostris dicendum est, hanc epistolam quæ inscribitur ad Hebræos non solum ab ecclesiis Orientis sed ab omnibus retro ecclesiasticis Græci sermonis scriptoribus quasi Pauli Apostoli suspici licet plerique eam vel Barnabæ vel Clementis arbitrentur et nihil interesse cujus sit quum ecclesiastici viri sit et quotidie ecclesiarum lectionum celebretur. Quod si eam Latinorum consuetudo non recipit inter scripturas canonicas, nec Græcorum quidem ecclesiæ Apocalypsin Joannis eadem libertate suscipiunt, et tamen nos utrumque suscipimus, nequaquam hujus temporis consuetudinem, sed veterum scriptorum auctoritatem sequentes, qui plerumque utriusque abutuntur testimoniis, non ut interdum de apocryphis facere solent (quippe qui et gentilium literarum raro utantur exemplis) sed quasi canonicis et ecclesiasticis.*

These two summaries of ancient testimonies concerning our epistle leave something to be desired on the score of accuracy. For (1) it is not correct to say that in the same way as Tertullian regarded it as a work of Barnabas, so others looked on it as a work of St. Luke. Both Luke and Clement are only named by Greek writers as translators or editors of a Hebrew original. (2) Neither is it correct to say that the epistle was regarded as a work of St. Paul *ab omnibus retro ecclesiasticis Græci sermonis scriptoribus;* for Hippolytus and Irenæus were at least exceptions. (3) The expression *licet plerique eam vel Barnabæ vel Clementis arbitrentur* might lead us to imagine that Tertullian was only one of many who thought it a work of Barnabas, whereas he is the sole authority for that opinion. Evidently Jerome is here too general and positive in his assertions—perhaps in order thereby to overcome the rooted prejudices of the West. It is certainly much to his credit that he was so ready to accept the actual witnesses to the epistle outside that portion of the church to which he himself belonged, and no less praiseworthy is it in him that he did not oppose with violence and anathema the prejudices which he found himself compelled to combat. His moderation, no doubt, helped to form the bridge by which the epistle was to pass into general recognition. His manner of using it as commentator (on other parts of Scripture) is quite different from the confident assertions of Oriental theologians: he hardly ever refers to it without some restriction;—*e.g.* Ep. liii. *ad Paulin.* (t. i. col. 280) : *Paulus Ap.*

ad septem ecclesias, octava enim ad Hebræos a plerisque extra numerum ponitur;—in Jes. l. iii. c. 6 (t. iv. col. 91): *Unde et Paulus Ap. in Ep. ad Hebr. quam Latina consuetudo non recipit, "nonne omnes," inquit, "ministri sunt spiritus?"*—and again (col. 97): *Pauli quoque idcirco ad Hebr. epistolæ contradicitur, quod ad Hebræos scribens utatur testimoniis, quæ in Hebræis voluminibus non habentur;—in Jes.* l. iii. c. viii. (t. iv. col. 125): *Ceterum beatas Ap. in epistola quæ ad Hebræos scribitur docet (licet eam Latina consuetudo inter canonicas scripturas non recipiat) . . .—in Jerem.* l. vi. c. xxxi. (t. iv. col. 1072): *Hoc testimonio Ap. Paulus sive quis alius scripsit epistolam usus est ad Hebræos;—in Ezech.* l. ix. c. xxix. (t. v. col. 335): *Et Paulus Ap. loquitur si quis tamen ad Hebr. ep^m suscipit;—in Amos,* c. viii. (t. vi. 339): *Quod quicunque est ille qui ad Hebr. scripsit ep^m disserens ait. . . .—in Zach.* c. viii. (t. vi. 838): *De hoc monte et de hac civitate et Ap. Paulus (si tamen in suscipienda epistola Græcorum auctoritatem Latina lingua non respuit), sacrata oratione disputans ait. . . .—in Matth.* c. xxvi. (t. vii. 212): *nam et Paulus in ep. sua quæ scribitur ad Hebr. licet de ea multi Latini dubitent . . .—in Eph.* c. iii. (t. vii. 583): *Nescio quid tale et in alia ep. (si quis tamen eam recipit) prudentibus quibusque lectoribus Paulus subindicat dicens: Hi omnes testimonium accipientes fidei . . .—in Ep. ad Titum,* c. ii (t. vii. 714): *Relege ad Hebr. ep^m Pauli Ap. sive cujusquam alterius eam esse putas, quia jam inter ecclesiasticas est recepta.* Even the Origenist Ruffinus, though convinced himself of the Pauline authorship, yet adds to a quotation which he makes from the epistle in his *Invectiva in Hieronym.* the qualifying clause: *si quis tamen eam receperit.*

Neither does St. Augustine (*ob.* 430), although he regards the epistle as St. Paul's, venture to place it in the same line with the rest; nay, abstains on principle from so doing. In his work *de doctrina Christiana* (ii. 8) he says of the Scripture student: *Tenebit—hunc modum in scripturis canonicis ut eas quæ ab omnibus accipiuntur ecclesiis catholicis præponat eis quas quidam non accipiunt; in eis vero quæ non accipiuntur ab omnibus præponat eas quas plures gravioresque accipiunt, eis quas pauciores minorisque auctoritatis ecclesiæ tenent. Si autem alias invenerit a pluribus, alias a gravioribus haberi, quamquam hoc facile inveniri non possit, æqualis tamen auctoritatis eas habendas*

INTRODUCTION. 15

puto. Hereupon he proceeds to reckon fourteen epistles of St. Paul. He reckons the Epistle to the Hebrews among them, because the arguments against its canonicity do not appear to him convincing, and influenced by the *auctoritas ecclesiarum orientalium* (as we see from his work *de peccat. meritis et remiss.* i. 27); but he does not place it in the same rank with the undisputed epistles, and commonly cites it without naming the author. His personal conviction, then, was in favour of the Pauline authorship, and has been no doubt of great influence in the church, but was not pressed as authoritative by Augustine himself. The language of the Councils of Hippo Regius (393) and Carthage (397) is still *Pauli Ap. epistolæ tredecim ejusdem ad Hebræos una;* while that of the Council of Carthage of 419 is: *Epistolarum Pauli Ap. numero quatuordecim.* So also that of Innocent I. in his *Ep. ad Exsuperium* (405), and of Gelasius (494). Isidore of Hispalis (*ob.* 636), on the other hand, still says: *Ad Hebræos epistola plerisque Latinis ejus (Pauli) esse incerta est propter dissonantiam sermonis,* but he can hardly be thinking of his contemporaries. He recognises himself the epistle as St. Paul's, and yet, so strong is the influence still of the *Latina consuetudo* with him, that he speaks of St. Paul as having written to only seven churches.[1]

We need not pursue further the history of our epistle. The question of its authorship ceased to be stirred in the East in the fourth century. The pillars of the church in that age—Athanasius[2] (*ob.* 373), Cyril of Jerusalem (*ob.* 386), Gregory Nazianzen (*ob.* 389-90), Epiphanius (*ob.* 403)—the canon of the Council of Laodicea (364), and the 85th of the Apostolic Canons, reckon without hesitation fourteen epistles of St. Paul. All that we find about our epistle in Greek, Latin, or Syriac[3]

[1] In Cod. Erlang. 245 (of 13th cent.), containing *Isidori Etymologiæ* and *de mappa mundi,* I find in an appended dissertation concerning Dionys. Areopagita the following: *Nam exceptis iv libris quos scripsit ad Tymotheum . . . exstat hodieque ipsius Dionisii Epistola, in qua Ep^m ad Hebr. Pauli Ap. esse evidentissime confirmat.* Is that the ninth epistle in which (with allusion to Heb. v. 12 et seq.) the Pseudo-Dionysius says: ὁ θειότατος Παῦλος ἐκ τῆς σοφίας εἰληφὼς τῆς ὄντως στερεᾶς τροφῆς μεταδίδωσι?

[2] *e.g.* in the eleventh of the Paschal Epistles lately discovered in a Syriac version.

[3] *e.g.* the Syriac *proœm. in Ep. ad Hebr.* (Beelen), and *Clementis Rom. Epp. binæ de virginitate,* Lovanii 1856, p. 311.

writers after the fourth century are mere repetitions of what was said by Clemens Alex. and Origen, with additional statements as to the place of composition and the bearer, resting on no real traditional authority, and therefore often simply misleading.

The Epistle to the Hebrews has had various places assigned to it among the canonical epistles of the New Testament, corresponding to different degrees of certainty as to its authorship. Epiphanius knew of MSS. in which it stood as the fourteenth epistle of St. Paul after that to Philemon; and this was certainly its most ancient position, and assigned to it as being an appendix to the collection of which the immediate Pauline authorship was universally recognised: he knew, however, also of MSS. in which it preceded the Pastoral Epistles, and therefore occupied the tenth place in the Pauline collection.[1] This place was assigned it when no more doubts existed as to its full authenticity. It follows Philemon in Syriac and Arabic MSS.[2] and elsewhere; it precedes the Pastoral Epistles in A. B². C. H. and several cursives. In the Græco-Latin Codex Bezæ (D.) it occupies the fourteenth place, and the Latin version is there singularly negligent. It is altogether wanting in Cod. G. (Boernerianus), which is also a Græco-Latin MS.; and in Cod. F. (Augiensis) it is found in Latin, but not in Greek. From these facts Bleek concludes with reason (i. 242), that even after our epistle had gained general recognition in the West, it was still not so often multiplied in MS. copies as the other epistles. Nor, in the West, has it ever been placed between any others of the epistles of St. Paul. In the Vulgate it keeps the fourteenth place, after Philemon.[3] Luther, falling back on the ancient scruples of the Latin Church, placed it after the Epistles of Peter and John, and only honoured it so far as to give it the precedence of those of James and Jude.

The long persistent refusal of the West to receive our

---

[1] *Opp.* ed. Colon. p. 373.

[2] So in the old Arabic version brought by Tischendorf from the East (in 1853).

[3] In Cod. Erlang. 588 the order is *Rom., etc., Hebr., Actus, Epp. cathol., Apocalyps.* (as by Nic. Lyranus, and elsewhere). In Cod. Erlang. 610, 611, *Roma., Hebr., Laod., Actus, Epp. cathol., Apoc.*

epistle is still an unsolved enigma. Taking into account that the Muratorian *Fragmentum de Canone* rejects it along with the first Peter and the Epistle of James, the conjecture seems natural that the Gentile Church of the West may have rejected these three Jewish Christian epistles as not concerning her. It has been recently said on this point :[1] " The Epistle to the Hebrews remained in the East, whither it had been addressed, and was there well known and honoured; the Western Church did not receive it because addressed to a Jewish Christendom." But the Epistle of St. James was also *in the East an Antilegomenon*, and Irenæus, Tertullian, and Cyprian used the first Peter as a canonical and apostolic writing, notwithstanding its Jewish Christian address and character. These did not therefore prevent its reception; and indeed it is incredible that the universal authority of *any* apostolic writing, to whomsoever addressed, should not have been recognised. Much less could this have been the case with such an epistle as that to the Hebrews! The Western Church could never have thought meanly of it if they had had any tradition of its apostolic origin. We must therefore assume, that whatever may have been the private knowledge of Clemens Romanus, the epistle could not have become generally known in the West till much later, and at a time when the claims to apostolicity that were made on its behalf no longer received credit.

Tertullian's hypothesis that Barnabas was the author had no basis in tradition. His anxiety to bring the epistle into esteem led him to confound it with the Epistle of St. Barnabas, which perhaps he had heard of, but not seen. The Western Church, had they really believed the epistle to be even the composition of Barnabas, would not so easily have set it aside. The Oriental tradition, on the other hand, persistently declared it to be Pauline, and the private opinions which made a Luke or a Clement to have had a hand in its production rested at any rate on grounds of reason and criticism. St. Clement's connection with it was made to rest on the *grandis similitudo* between it and the style of his Epistle to the Corinthians. But this *grandis similitudo* is after all illusory—the result of direct plagiarisms from our epistle. The difference is immeasurable

[1] See essay by Hofmann, entitled *Deuterokanonisch?* in *Zeitschr. für Protestant. und Kirche*, 1857, pp. 397-400.

VOL. I.　　　　　　　　　　　　　　　B

between the originality, profundity, and nervous strength of the Epistle to the Hebrews and the simply reproductive, diffuse, and sermonizing character of the Epistle to the Corinthians. The other conjecture therefore remains, that the Epistle to the Hebrews is a work of St. Paul which owes its present form to the intervention of St. Luke. And this happens to be the first view of its origin which is presented to us in Christian antiquity. We cannot indeed assert positively that Clemens Alexandrinus, who gives this view in his *Hypotyposes* (see above), himself derived it from those before him. But one thing is noteworthy—he first states as a fact that St. Luke translated and published the epistle for the Greeks, and then by this fact explains the similarity between its diction and that of the Acts of the Apostles. He does not, as would be natural in the case of a mere conjecture, derive the fact from the observed similarity, but (as we have said) accounts for the similarity after stating the fact. His testimony therefore remains the only one well-founded statement which Christian antiquity has handed down to us concerning the origin of the epistle.

This important testimony of Clemens, therefore, we shall have chiefly to keep in view in the following exposition. For Luther's conjecture that Apollos wrote the epistle, there is no ecclesiastical tradition, and no possible means of testing its truth. At the same time, no one can deny that Apollos' (or Apollodorus') character, as drawn by St. Luke (Acts xviii. 24, etc.), very strikingly corresponds to the character of our epistle. The party names in the Church of Corinth and St. Paul's statements in 1 Cor. concerning his relations to Apollos are not directly favourable to this hypothesis; nor yet, if we take into account the continued friendly relations of the two great teachers (Tit. iii. 13), can we say that they are directly opposed to it. But it must be confessed that any strong argument in favour of Apollos' authorship has not been produced. The recognised epistles of St. Paul as well as this to the Hebrews stand in close relation to the Jewish Alexandrinism as it appears in the writings of Philo. Philo not only calls the Logos ἀρχιερεύς with the predicates ταξιάρχης τῆς φύσεως and ἁμαρτημάτων ἀμέτοχος, but he speaks also of Him as ὡσανεὶ σώματος ἡνωμένου κεφαλή (1, 640, 20), just as St. Paul does in the Epistles to the Colossians and Ephesians, Philo understanding by σῶμα the universe, St. Paul the church. Similar relations of thought may be found not only in the writings of St. Paul, but in those of St. John as well, and in other parts of the New Testament. From which it follows that the dogmatic developments of the literature of the חכמא,[1] after the cessation of prophecy, had a real place in the divine purposes and the working out the plan of redemption. Not only was the version of the Septuagint a herald to the Gentile world of that salvation which was to come forth from Israel, but Alexandrinism itself also was a real precursor of the great transformation of the religion of the Old Testament into a world-wide religion under the New. Alexandrinism was the product of an endeavour to separate the nucleus of revealed truth from its literal, national, historical, and individual encasement, and to prove that this nucleus comprised the unity of all truth among all nations, being itself the universal and objective truth and the highest form of philosophy. In this attempt to establish the worldwide character of the revealed religion this Jewish Alexandrinism became itself worldly, and too receptive in its relations to the Pythagoræo-Platonic philosophy of the Greeks. Nor was it possible anyhow that it should succeed in this endeavour. The true liberation of the revealed religion of the Old Testament from the bonds of a single nationality into which it had entered, could not be effected by a merely speculative development of doctrine, but only by a fresh and mighty fact of revelation breaking those bonds; and this was pre-announced in the word that salvation should go forth from Israel, and so also that He who should hereafter be the incarnate Author and Maintainer of this salvation was already, in His pre-historic and super-historical existence, a Person of absolute significance in His relations not to Israel only, but to all mankind. But although it was thus impossible for the religious philosophy of Alexandria to attain its goal, it was yet vouchsafed to it to create beforehand, in part at least, the forms of thought and language of which Christianity could make use in proclaiming

[1] The Chaldaic form of חכמה, the "Wisdom" or divine philosophy of the Book of Proverbs, afterwards developed in the Sapiential books of the Apocrypha and other Jewish writings subsequently to the Macedonian conquests.—TR.

the gospel of the incarnation and of universal salvation thus provided for mankind, and in basing such proclamation on the utterances of Old Testament Scripture.[1]

This being the case, and the whole New Testament, more especially the writings of St. Paul and St. John, standing in such close relations to Alexandrinism, the fact of the Epistle to the Hebrews having so strong an Alexandrian colouring does not of necessity lead us to fix on the Alexandrian Apollos as its author. Moreover, were it so, we should have expected some tradition to that effect in the Church of Alexandria, whereas all the great teachers there speak only of Paul and Luke, or Paul and Clement.

Whatever the epistle may say itself in respect to its author, or even the church to which it is addressed, belongs not to the Introduction, in which it is too commonly treated of (against all sound method), but to the exposition of the epistle itself, which begins in a certain way when we inquire the meaning of the inscription πρὸς Ἑβραίους. That, so far as ever we can go back in our inquiries, is the proper title of our epistle. So it is entitled in all MSS., except perhaps in the *Codex Arabicus* of Tischendorf, where the title is رسالة العبر انيين, *i.e.* ἐπιστολὴ τῶν Ἑβραίων.

The name Ἑβραῖοι designates in the first instance their national origin without respect to place of birth or residence. In this sense St. Paul, though born in Cilicia, is called a "Hebrew of Hebrews;" and Eusebius (*H. E.* iii. 4) says that Peter wrote his epistle "to those of the Hebrews who were in the dispersion of Pontus," etc.; Ἑβραῖοι here being used as a general antithesis of "Ἕλληνες = ἔθνη. (Comp. Euseb. *H. E.* iv. 16.) But when, in the second place, it is the antithesis of Ἑλληνισταί, as at Acts vi. 1 and ix. 29, Ἑβραῖοι designates those who adhered on principle to the Hebrew language in public worship, and to the national customs of the Hebrew fatherland;[2] and such would naturally be natives and inhabitants of Palestine. I know at least of no instance of this

---

[1] The above concerning Alexandrinism is from the Essay already referred to, Note 1, p. 4.

[2] The usage is itself *Hellenistic*. In Talmud and Midrash the word עברים or עבראין ("Hebrews") is used only as an ethnographical name, and almost confined to references to the pre-Mosaic history. Neither does the

INTRODUCTION. 21

antithesis between Ἑβραῖοι and Ἑλληνισταί out of Palestine. We should naturally conclude, therefore, that an epistle which bears the title πρὸς Ἑβραίους was addressed to Palestinians. To which we may add, that no traces are found of the existence of any such purely Jewish churches in the Diaspora as the recipients of this epistle must have been, while the Church of Jerusalem actually bore the title ἡ τῶν Ἑβραίων ἐκκλησία (Clementis *Ep. ad Jacob*. hom. xi. 35) as consisting entirely of "Hebrews"—ἐξ Ἑβραίων πιστῶν (Euseb. *H. E.* iv. 5). And further, the whole epistle gives the impression that its readers must have lived in the neighbourhood of the temple, the antithesis throughout not being that of συναγωγή and church, but of temple and ἐπισυναγωγή of Christians. These reasons are not impaired, as we shall see, by what we read in the epistle of the history and present condition of the Hebrews, and are confirmed by the circumstance that the inscription πρὸς Ἑβραίους has always from the time of Clemens Alex., and the πρεσβύτεροι before him, been traditionally interpreted as referring to Jewish Christians in Palestine. We agree, therefore, with Tholuck, that while the inscription in itself points only probably to such an interpretation, the other circumstances make out that interpretation to be certainly true.

I now proceed to give a synopsis of the literature of the exposition of our epistle, referring my readers for that of investigations concerning its author and recipients to the various "Einleitungen" to the New Testament, especially Credner's, and the very learned and satisfactory labours of Bleek and Tholuck, being content for my own part to rest in the traditional view as stated above.

The literature of the interpretation is here presented in a fuller form than elsewhere, but is far from being complete. I have for various reasons abstained from naming books which I have not had myself in hand, and so endeavoured to avoid the many errors which from this cause are wont to be propa-

---

idiom of the Talmud, though abounding in Greek words, make use of the word Ἑλληνισταί, though it does of ἑλληνιστί in the form אלכונסתין. The regulation which allowed some to recite even the Shemá ("Hear, O Israel," Deut. vi. 4 et seq.) of the morning and evening prayers in Greek, applied of course to the Hellenists.

gated in similar synopses. I am fully aware that many of the works whose titles are here given are of inferior value and importance to some of which (unwillingly or unwittingly) I have remained ignorant: the literary field is immense, and without some self-restraint one may easily lose one's way therein. My chief object has been to give my readers brief bibliographical accounts of all the works which are more or less made use of in the following Commentary. Only with regard to patristic literature I have allowed myself to make a few exceptions to my rule, in order to render the synopsis in this respect as complete as possible.

I. ANCIENT INTERPRETERS OF THE EASTERN CHURCH.

EPHRÆM SYRUS (*ob. cir.* 378). His commentaries to the Pauline epistles, written in Syriac, are (with exception of the Epistle to Philemon) preserved in an Armenian translation. *Opp.*, ed. Aucher, t. iii. Venet. 1836, 8. These I have been unable to make use of.

JOHANNES CHRYSOSTOMUS (*ob.* 407). Among his works is found a complete exposition of the Epistle to the Hebrews in thirty-four homilies, published after his death ἀπὸ σημείων (from short-hand notes) by Constantine, presbyter of Antioch; abbreviated in no very satisfactory manner by Johannes Damascenus in his 'Ἐκλογαί (*Opp.* t. ii.); translated into Latin at the instance of Cassiodorus by Mutianus Scholasticus; and published with this translation at Cologne 1487, 1530, and since frequently. (Concerning this Mutian see de Viviers, *Vie de Cassiodore*, 1695, p. 271.) Cassiodorus' own words are (*de instit. divinarum litterarum*, c. viii., *Op.*, ed. Garet, ii. 543):
"*Ad Hebræos vero epistolam, quam sanctus Joannes Constantinopolitanus triginta quatuor homiliis Attico sermone tractavit, Mutianum virum disertissimum transferre fecimus in Latinum, ne epistolarum ordo continuus indecoro termino subito rumperetur.*" The homilies of St. Chrysostom are without doubt the best exposition of the epistle which has come down to us from the primitive church, being thoroughly independent, and abounding in intelligent exegesis. It deserves to be constantly consulted, and has been much read and borrowed from by subsequent expositors.

THEODORE OF MOPSUESTIA (*ob.* 427–8) in *Theodori Episc. Mopsuest. in N. T. commentariorum quæ reperiri potuerunt.* Collegit, disposuit, emendavit Otto Fridol. Fritzsche, Turici 1847-8. Though there be somewhat of affectation in Theodore's striving after independence of thought, and something perverse in his method of exposition, yet is the loss of his suggestive commentary to be regretted as leaving a serious *lacuna* in the historical development of the interpretation of this epistle.

CYRIL OF ALEXANDRIA (*ob.* 444). A mosaic of fragments (chiefly of polemical passages against Arianism) in *Nova Patrum Biblioth.* t. iii., Romæ 1845 (small folio); other similar fragments in *Angeli Maii Collectis Nova*, t. viii. 2, p. 147. Grandiloquent, with some dogmatico-historical, but little exegetical value.

THEODORET (*ob.* 457). Complete Commentary in *Opp.*, ed Nösselt, t. iii. pp. 541–637, Halæ 1771-8. Brief, plain, clear, but meagre and unedifying.

EUTHALIUS (fifth century). His tables of contents and divisions into chapters of the *Acts* and the *Epistles*: first published by Laur. Alex. Zacagni in his *Collectanea Monumentorum veterum Ecclesiæ Græcæ et Latinæ, quæ hactenus in Vaticana Bibliotheca delituerunt*, Romæ 1698 (small folio); also in Gallandii *Biblioth.* t. x.

ŒCUMENIUS (tenth century). Complete Commentary in *Opp.*, ed. Morell, p. ii. Paris 1631, fol. A copious work, in which is gathered the whole mass of Greek exposition down to Photius.

THEOPHYLACT (since 1078 Archb. of Achris in Bulgaria). Complete Commentary in *Opp.*, ed. de Rubeis et Bonif. Fanetti, t. ii. Venet. 1755, fol. A catena in which *Œcumenius* is already made use of.[1]

(ANONYMI). *Scholia (Græca) in Ep. ad Hebr. in D. Pauli Epp. ad Hebr. et Colossenses* Græce et Lat. varias lectiones . . . . adjecit Christ. Friedr. Matthæi, Rigæ 1784-8. Much rubbish, but some pearls.

[1] A continuous commentary formed from extracts from Chrysost., Œcum., and Theophyl. is found in *Jo. Gregorii (nuper Archidiac. Glocestriensis) N. T. una cum Scholiis Græcis e Græcis scriptoribus tam ecclesiasticis quam exteris maxima ex parte desumptes* (published after the author's death by Jo. Ernst Grabe), Oxonii 1703, fol.

II. ANCIENT INTERPRETERS OF THE WESTERN CHURCH.

AMBROSIASTER. The commentary assigned to the great name of *St. Ambrose* (*Opp.* t. iii. ed. Paris 1634, fol., col. 611–656), but certainly the work of another author, extends only to the end of ch. x. A work of moderate ability, as much inferior to the speculative acuteness of Hilarius Pictaviensis as to the mystic depth of the real Ambrose. Not contained in the oldest editions of St. Ambrose by Amerbach and Erasmus, regarded commonly as a later compilation completing the Ambrosiastrian commentary on St. Paul's Epistles, and perhaps the work of Rhabanus Maurus. Omitted for these reasons by the Benedictines and Migne (*Ambrosii Opera*, Paris 1845, 4to, 4 tom.).

PRIMASIUS (Bishop of Adrumetum, sixth century). The commentary attributed to him, and first published as such by *Jo. Gagney*, Coloniæ 1538, 8, circulated also under the names of Haymo and Remigius.[1] The commentary is valuable. It is the Western counterpart to that of Theodoret, plain and clear like that, but deeper and more vigorous.

ALCUIN (*ob.* 804). In *Opp.*, ed. Frobenii, Ratisbonæ 1777, fol. (only cc. i.–x.). The commentary is chiefly from Chrysostom.

SEDULIUS SCOTUS (ninth century). *Collectanea in Epp. S. Pauli*: first published by Sichard, Basil 1528, fol.; also in t. vi. of *Bibl. Maxim. Lugdunensis*.

LANFRANCUS CANTUARIENSIS (*ob.* 1089). *Glossæ in Ep. ad Hebr.*, *Opp.*, ed. Giles, Oxon 1848, 8, t. ii. pp. 129–146. Meagre, unsatisfactory, and for us obsolete observations.

ANSELMUS CANTUARIENSIS: in *Enarrationes in omnes S. Pauli. Epp.*, attributed at any rate to the Archbishop, ed. princ. by Renatus Castaneus, and more correctly by Godofr. Hittorp, Coloniæ 1633, fol. Whether this commentary be

---

[1] The *Magna Biblioth. Patr. Coloniensis* contains this commentary in t. vi. p. ii. pp. 112–150, as *Primasii*, and t. v. p. iii. pp. 994–1037, as *Remigii Ep. Rhemensis Comm.* For the designation *Rhemensis* (of Rheims) must now be substituted (since the edition of Vilalpandus) that of *Altesiodorensis* (of Auxerre). Under the name of Haymo this commentary is contained in Cod. Erlang. 161. On this confusion about the author see Schröck's *Kirchengeschichte*, vol. xxiii. pp. 282–284.

rightly assigned to Anselm or not (some attribute it to one of his disciples, *Anselmus Laudunensis, ob.* 1117), it must rank for clearness and depth among the best exegetical works of the Scholastic period. I regret having too late become acquainted with it.

PETRUS LOMBARDUS (*ob.* 1164), in his *in omnes D. Pauli Ap. Epp., Collectanea ex DD. Augustino, Ambrosio, Hieronymo, aliisque nonnullis S. Scr. primariis interpretibus.* Composed 1140 ; first printed, Paris 1535, fol. Dry and jejune.

HUGO DE S. VICTORE (*ob.* 1141). *Quæstiones super Ep. ad Hebr.*, in *Opp.*, ed. Rothomagi, t. i. pp. 459–469, 1648, fol. Unworthy of the otherwise deep-thinking and warm-hearted man.

THOMAS AQUINAS. *Expositio super Ep. S. Pauli Ap. ad Hebr.*, in *Opp.*, ed. Cosmes Morelles, t. xvi. Antwerp 1612, fol. An ocean of thought, but full of sandbanks and perilous whirlpools.

III. MODERN INTERPRETERS (SINCE THE REFORMATION).

JAC. FABER STAPULENSIS (Doctor of the Sorbonne, *ob.* 1537). *Epp. S. Pauli cum Commentariis*, Paris 1512, 17, fol.

DESIDERIUS ERASMUS (Roterod). *In Ep. Pauli Ap. ad Hebr. Paraphrasis extrema*, Basil 1521, 8 : often published since with his other commentaries on the N. T. and with all of them together (t. ii. of his Works); to which should be added his *Adnotationes in N. T.*, Basil 1516, fol. (*Opp.* t. vi.). Not deep and yet well-conceived beginnings of the grammatical and historical exposition.

JO. BUGENHAGIUS POMERANUS. *Annotationes in Epp. Pauli ad Galat.—Philem., Hebr., ab ipso autore nuper recogn.* Nurembergæ 1525, 8.

HEINR. BULLINGERUS. *In piam et eruditam Pauli ad Hebr. Ep. Commentarius*, Tiguri 1532, 8.

JO. ŒCOLAMPADIUS. *In Ep. ad Hebr. Explanationes* (published after his death from notes taken of his Basle Lectures): Argentorati (Strassburg) 1534, 8.

JO. CALVINUS. *In Ep. ad Hebr. Comm.* (A.D. 1549), recently reprinted in *Johannis Calvini in omnes Pauli Ap. Epp. atque etiam in Ep. ad Hebr. Comm. ad ed. R. Steph, accuratissime exscripti,* Halis 1831, voll. ii. 8vo: the most distinguished (and still instructive) commentary of the sixteenth century, as learned as it is practical; the fruit of a thorough knowledge and appreciation of the original text, though the latter is somewhat limited by that dominance of the reflective understanding which is characteristic of Calvin.

JOACH. CAMERARIUS. *Notationes figurarum sermonis in scriptis apostolicis,* Lips. 1556, 8vo and fr.

JO. BRENTIUS F. (filius). *In Ep. quam Paulus Ap. ad Hebr. scripsit de persona et officio Domini nostri J. Chr. Comm.* Tubingæ 1571, 8vo.

BENEDICTUS ARETIUS (in Bern). *Commentarii in Ep. ad Hebr.* Morgiis 1581, 8vo and fr.

THEOD. BEZA, in dessen *Novum Testamentum* (2d ed. with Greek text; 3d ed. with Vulg., a translation of his own, and notes), Genevæ 1582, fol.: continuing and completing Calvin's critical and philological services.

GERH. ANDREAS HYPERIUS (in Marburg). *Commentar. in Ep. ad Hebr. nunc primum opera Jo. Mylii edit.* Tiguri 1584, fol.

EGIDIUS HUNNIUS (in Marburg). *Exegesis Ep. ad Hebr. scripta et recognita,* Francof. a. M. 1586, 8vo.

JO. JAC. GRYNÆUS (in Heidelburg, and afterwards at Basle). *Explanatio Ep. S. Pauli Ap. ad Hebr.* Basileæ 1586, 8vo.

FRANC. DE RIBERA (Jesuit). *Comm. in Ep. ad Hebr.* Salamanc. 1598, and fr.

FRID. BALDUINUS. *XV Disputationes de Ep. ad Hebr.,* in his *Comm. in omnes Epp. Pauli,* Witebergæ 1608, 4to and fr.

BENEDICTUS JUSTINIANUS (Jesuit, *ob.* 1622). *In omnes Epp. Pauli explanat.* t. ii. Lugduin (Lyons) 1612-13, fol.

GUIL. ESTIUS (Prof. in Löven, *ob.* 1613). *In omnes App. Epp. Commentar.* Duaci (Douai) 1614, Paris 1623, fol. and fr.

CORNELIUS A LAPIDE (Jesuit, *ob.* 1637). *Comm. in omnes D. Pauli Epp.* Antwerp 1614, and fr.—the most celebrated, but not the best Roman Cath. expositor of his time.

DAV. PAREUS (Prof. in Heidelberg, *ob.* 1615). *Commentar. in varios S. Script. ll.,* 2 vols. Francof. 1628, fol., and frequently in Frankf. and Geneva.

Jo. GERHARDUS. *Comm. sup. Ep. ad Hebr.* Jenæ 1641, 4to; published four years after his father's death by Jo. Ernst Gerhard, disfigured by the all-mutilating scholasticism of its arrangement, and evidently not left ripe for publication. MICHAEL WALTHER. *Der guldene Schlüssel des Alten und der süsse Kern des N.T.*, etc. (The Golden Key of the Old Testament and the Sweet Kernel of the New, etc.), Nuremberg 1646, fol. One hundred sermons preached at Aurich in East Friesland. CONR. HORNEIUS (in Helmstädt). *In Ep. S. Ap. Pauli ad Hebr. Expositio literalis*, Brunsvigæ 1655, 4to. ANONYMI. *Prælectiones in Ep. ad Hebr.* 1654-5, in Cod. Erlangen 907. On a level with the best Lutheran commentaries of the seventeenth century. JONAS SCHLICHTINGIUS A BUKOWIEC. In .t. ii. of *Jo. Crellii Franci Opp. omnia exegetica*, Eleutheropoli 1656, fol., is found a commentary on this epistle, the preface to which is by Schlichting. He speaks of the commentary as largely Crell's as well as his own : *Est vero Comm. hic vivente adhuc Jo. Crellio doctissimo litterarumque monumentis clarissimo viro, collega meo desideratissimo, a me confectus elucubratusque, ita ut in eruendis epistolæ istius sensibus omnis num Crellio sociata fuerit opera, atque ita ut ei primas hic partes merito deferre debeam.* Apart from the effects of Socinian prejudices this is an admirable work, marked by thorough attention to the text, delicacy of appreciation, and excellence of method.

ERASMUS SCHMID (*ob.* 1637 at Wittenberg). *Versio N. T. nova . . . et notæ et animadversoines. . .* Norimb. 1658, fol. An advance in philological criticism.

CRITICI SACRI, Londini 1660; Amstel. 1698; Francof. 1695; fol. The commentaries to this epistle are arranged chapterwise, being the interpretations of Laur. Valla, with notes by Jac. Revius; Erasmus Roterod; Franc. Vatablus; Sebast. Castalio; Isodorus Clarius; Nic. Zegerus; Jos. Scaliger; Is. Casaubonus; Jo. Drusius; Jo. Camero; Jac. Cappellus; Lud. Cappellus; and Hugo Grotius. (In Pole's *Synopsis Criticorum* this apparatus is increased by extracts from Cajetan, Dan. Heinsius, Piscator, Lud. de Tena, and many others.) Among these I ought to have paid more attention to Cameron (*ob.* 1625) and the brothers Cappellus (*ob.* 1624 and 1658), all the three *Coryphæi* of Protestant theology in Saumur and Sedan.

ABRAH. CALOV (*ob.* 1686). *Bibl. N. T. illustrati*, tomi iv. Francofurti a. M. 1672-76, fol. (in German Wrttenb. 1681-82).

SEBASTIAN SCHMIDT (Strassburg). *In Ep. D. Pauli ad Hebr. Comment.* Argentorati 1680, 4to, pp. (1482). The most copious, enlightened, and sensible Lutheran commentary of the seventeenth century.

SAM. SZATTMAR NEMETHUS. *Ep. S. Pauli ad Hebr. explicata*, Francqueræ 1695, 4to: the result of lectures held at Clausen in Transylvania. Excellent method, and well-considered striking judgments.

THEODOR. AKERSLOOT. *The Epistle of the Apostle Paul to the Hebrews* (from the Dutch of 1695), translated into German by Plesken, Bremen 1714, 4to.

JO. BRAUNIUS (in Groningen and Omland). *Comment. in Ep. ad Hebr.* Amstelod. 1705, 4to. Anti-Socinian and anti-Remonstrant. Pays special attention to archæology.

HENR. BENED. STARKIUS. *Notæ Select. Crit. Philolog. Exegeticæ in Ep. S. Pauli ad Ebræos*, Lipsiæ 1710, 4to. Learned, sound, and pithy.

JOH. D' OUTREIN. *The Ep. of Paul to the Hebrews dissected, etc.* (tr. into German from the Dutch of 1711), 2 vols. Frankf. 1713-18, 4to.

PHIL. A LIMBORCH (Arminian, *ob.* 1712). *Comm. in Acta Ap. et Epp. ad Rom. et ad Hebr.* Roterod 1711, fol.

JOH. CHR. WOLF. *Curæ philolog. et crit. in X posterior. Pauli epp.* Hamb. 1734, 4to, 2d ed. 1738.

JO. ALB. BENGEL, in his classical, inexhaustibly rich, and never obsolete *Gnomon N. T.*, first published at Tübingen 1742, 4to.

JO. BENEDICT CARPZOV (in Helmstädt). *Sacræ Exercitationes* in S. Pauli Ep. ad Hebr. ex Philone Alexandrio, Helmstadii 1750, 8vo.

JO. ANDR. CRAMER (*ob.* 1788 as Prof. at Kiel). *Erklärung des Br. Pauli an die Ebr.* (Exposition of St. Paul's Ep. to the Hebr.), 2 vols., Copenhagen and Leipsic 1757, 4to.

FRIEDR. CHRISTOPH. STEINHOFER. *Tägliche Nahrung des Glaubens aus der Erkenntniss Jesu nach den wichtigen Zeug-*

nissen der Ep. an die Ebr. (Daily nourishment for faith drawn from the testimonies of the Ep. to the Hebrews), 2 vols., Tübingen 1761, 8vo. Written in Bengel's spirit.

SIEGMUND JAKOB BAUMGARTEN. *Erklär. des Br. St. Pauli an die Hebr. mit Andr. Gottlieb Maschens Anm. und Paraphrasi und Joh. Sal. Semler's Beiträgen zu genauerer Einsicht dieses Briefes*, Halle 1763, 4to. (Exposition of St. Paul's Epistle to the Hebrews, with observations and paraphrase by Masch, and appendices by Semler.) Careful in showing the connection of thought, but disfigured by excessive analysis and minute tabulation.

JOHANN RUDOLPH KIESSLING (in Erlangen). *Richtige Verbindung Mosaischen Alterthümer mit der Auslegung des Sendschreibens des h. Ap. Paulus an die Hebr.*, Erster Theil, Erlangen u. Leipzig 1765, 4to. (Connection of the Mosaic Antiquities with the Exposition of the Epistle of St. Paul to the Hebrews.) An archæological commentary on the whole epistle—loquacious, superficial, unproductive.

CHRIST. FRID. SCHMID (in Wittenberg). *Observ. super Ep. ad Hebr. historicæ, criticæ, theologicæ, c. præf. Chr. A. Crusii*, Lips. 1766, 8vo.

JOH. DAVID MICHAELIS. *Erklär. des Br. an die Hebr.*, zwei Theile, Frankfurt u. Leipzig (Exposition of the Ep. to the Hebrews, 2 vols.), first published 1762-4, and subsequently in much improved form, 1780-86, 4to. It is still worth reading on account of its learning and critical acuteness.

SAM. FR. NATHAN MORUS (in Leipzig). *Der Br. an die Hebr. übers. (mit Anm.)* [The Ep. to the Hebr. translated, with observations], second ed. Leipsic 1781, 8vo. Insignificant and obsolete.

JOH. CHRISTIAN BLASCHE. *Systematischer Kommentar über den Brief an die Hebr.*, zwei Theile (Systematic Commentary on the Ep. to the Hebr., 2 vols.), Leipsic 1782-86, 8vo. Conceited and loquacious—perverse interpretations.

LUD. CASP. VALCKENAER (at Franeker, and afterwards at Leyden, *ob.* 1785). *Selecta e Schol. in Ep. ad Hebr.* in the *Selecta e Schol. Valckenarii in ll. quosdam Novi Testamenti ed. discipulo Ev. Wassenbergh*, tom. ii., Amstelodami 1817, 8vo. Much alien matter, but also much that is instructive from the mouth of the great philologer.

PETR. ABRESCH. *Paraphrasis et Adnotationum in Ep. ad Hebr. III specimina* (ch. i.-vi.), Leyden 1786-87-90, 8vo. Continued by Heringa (beginning with ch. vii.) in A.D. 1817.

GOTTLOB CHRIST. STORR (*ob.* Oberhofprediger—Court chaplain—in Stuttgart, 1805). *Pauli Br. an die Hebr. erläutert* (St. Paul's Ep. to the Hebr. explained), Tübingen 1789 (and 1809), 8vo. A meritorious work, which the learned, orthodox, and faithful author opposed as a rampart to the invasion of Rationalism. The treatise on the purpose of our Lord's death occupies as much space as the commentary itself.

JO. AUG. ERNESTI. *Prælectiones Academicæ in Ep. ad Hebr. ab ipso revisæ*, published with copious additional notes of his own by Gottlieb Imman. Dindorf, Lipsiæ 1795, 8vo. The interpretation runs frequently into dogmatic excursuses, and the dogmatic but exegetically insignificant interpolations of the editor are often disturbing.

CARL HEINRICH RIEGER (formerly Consistorial-Rath and Stiftsprediger in Stuttgart). *Betrachtungen über das N. T.*, Th. iv. Aufl. 3, Stuttgart 1847, 8vo. (Contemplations on the New Testament.) A work so full of spiritual life and interpenetrated by the spirit of prayer, that it is secured from becoming obsolete, and has an abiding blessing.

DAV. SCHULZ. *Der Br. an die Hebr., Einleitung, Uebers. und Anmerk.*, Breslau 1818, 8vo. (The Ep. to the Hebr., Introduction, Translat., and Notes.) A work full of most extraordinary assertions, *e.g.* that the writer of this epistle, from his own Christian point of view, meant to leave the sacrificial and priestly institutions of Judaism intact, and appears not to have regarded Christianity as having any independent existence as an institution upon earth.

ARCHIBALD M'LEAN (Baptist Minister). *A Paraphrase and Commentary on the Ep. to the Hebrews*, 2 vols., London 1820, 8vo. A sensible, unpretending book.

G. MENKEN. *Erkl. des elft. Cap. des Br. an die Hebr.* (Exposition of the 11th chapter), Bremen 1821, 8vo.

G. MENKEN. *Homilien über das 9te und 10te Cap. des Briefes an die Hebr. nebst einem Anhange etlicher Homilien über Stellen des 12ten Cap.*, Bremen 1831, 8vo. (Homilies on the 9th and 10th chapters, with appendix of Homilies on some parts of the 12th chapter.) Chiefly resting on Bengel, and therefore of only subordinate exegetical, but of the highest homiletical value.

Jo. Heinr. Heinrichs. (*Paulli*) *Ep. ad Hebr. græce, perpetua adnotatione illustrata*, Gottingæ 1792; ed. ii. 1823, 8vo. Forms the 8th vol. of Koppe's N. Test.

Christ. Frid. Böhme. *Ep. ad Hebr. latine vers. atque comm. instr. perpetuo*, Lips. 1825, 8vo. A work of sound scholarship, though written in a painfully affected style—acute, independent, not theologically profound, but richly suggestive.

Christ. Theoph. Kuinoel. *Comm. in Ep. ad Hebr.*, Lips. 1831, 8vo. Far inferior in originality to Böhme, but superior to his commentary in the classic simplicity of its style.

Heinr. Klee (Cath. Prof. of Theology at Bonn). *Ausl. des Br. an die Hebr.*, Mainz. 1833, 8vo. (Expos. of the Ep. to the Hebr., Mayence.) Deserves praise at any rate for its avowed endeavour to attain to what he calls "objective" exegesis, which is to be at once grammatical, historical, rational, and mystic.

Fried. Bleek. *Der Br. an die Hebr. erläutert durch Einl. Uebers. und fortlaufenden Comm.*, Abth. i. (Einl.), Berlin 1828; Abth. ii. (Capp. i.–iv. 13), 1836; Abth. iii. (Capp. iv. 14–xiii.), 1840, 8vo. (The Ep. to the Hebrews illustrated by an Introduction, Translation, and continuous Commentary, published in three divisions, in the years 1828, 1836, and 1840.) Every competent scholar will confirm the judgment of de Wette, that it is a work occupying one of the first places, if not the very first place, among the exegetical productions of our time, and as much distinguished by a clear love of truth and genuine theological spirit as by extensive learning and the proofs of most unwearied industry.

A. Tholuck. *Komm. zum Br. an die Hebr.*, Ausg. 1, Hamburg 1836 (Commentary on the Ep. to the Hebr., 1st ed. 1836); 2d ed. 1840; 3d ed. 1850, 8vo; with two appendices, on "The Old Testament in the New," and "The Citations of the O. T. in the N. T., on Sacrifice and Priesthood in Old and New Testament," 3d ed. 1849, 8vo. A commentary which has greatly improved and matured in its progress—supplements theological deficiencies in Bleek, full of rare pieces of knowledge, aims at striking the right mean between an idealistic and realistic interpretation.

KARL WILH. STEIN. *Der Br. an die Hebr. theoretisch-practisch erklärt,* u. s. w., Leipz. 1838, 8vo. Laudable on account of the attempt to combine the theoretical with the practical interpretation, and to show the connection between the parts.

CHR. F. FRITZSCHE. *Krit. Beiträge zur Erkl. des Briefes an die Hebr. mit Rücks. auf den Komm. von Tholuck,* Leipz. 1840, 8vo.

RUD. STIER. *Der Br. an die Hebr. in 36 Betrachtungen ausgelegt* (The Ep. to the Hebr. expounded in 36 meditations), 2 vols., 1842, 8vo. Thoughtful, and only too full of thought.

KARL R. KOESTLIN. *Der Lehrbegriff des Ev. und der Br. des Johannes und die verwandten neutest. Lehrbegriffe,* Berlin 1843, 8vo. (Doctrinal System of the Gospel and the Epistles of St. John, and similar Doctrinal Systems in the New Testament.) This work contains, pp. 387-472, an account of the doctrinal system of the Epistle to the Hebrews, and succeeds in showing that it occupies the mid space between that of St. Paul's later epistles (Eph. and Col.) and that of the Gospel of St. John.

DE WETTE. *Kurze Erkl. des Br. an Tit. Tim. u. d. Hebr.* Ausg. 1, 1844; Ausgab. 2, 1847, 8vo. (Short Exposit. of the Epistles to Titus, Timothy, and the Hebrews, 1st ed. 1844, 2d ed. 1847.) De Wette's merits as an interpreter, his critical tact, accuracy, clearness, and solidity, are universally recognised; but so also his undeniable prejudices, and his unfair, irreverent, and schoolmaster-like way of pretending to set right prophets and apostles.

OTTO VON GERLACH. *Das Neue Test.,* etc., Bd. 2, Berlin 1837, 8vo, and frequently since. This popular commentary is not without a scientific basis, and exhibits the exercise of an independent judgment.

L. STENGEL (Catholic Professor of Theology at Freiburg). *Erkl. des Br. an die Hebr., nach dessen Nachlass von Jos. Beck.* Karlsruhe 1849, 8vo. (Expos. of Ep. to Hebr., published from his literary remains by Jos. Beck.) Both editor and author attach themselves to the principles of historico-critical interpretation; both refer frequently to Hirscher; the doctrine of vicarious satisfaction is combated; and the views of the sacred writer as to " the pre-existence of Jesus" are supposed to have been " undefined."

JOH. HEINR. AUG. EBRARD. *Der Br. an die Hebr. erklärt*, Königsberg 1850, 8vo. (Part of the fifth vol. of Olshausen's Commentary.) Bold and combative, striving after a kind of mathematical certainty : sometimes striking out true interpretations, but not seldom self-destructive.

AUG. BISPING (Cathol. Profess. of Exegesis at Münster). *Erkl. des Br. an die Hebr.*, Münster 1854, 8vo. Among (Roman) Catholic commentaries the most connected and pleasing.

J. CHR. K. VON HOFMANN. *Der Schriftbeweis :* First half, Nördlingen 1852 (2d ed. 1857); second half, sec. 1, 1853 ; sect. 2, 1855. The same author's *Abhandl.* 2, *zur Enstehungs-geschichte der h. Schrift.—Der Br. des Jacobus und der Br. an die Hebr.* (Treatise on the History of the Composition of Holy Scripture—the Ep. of James and the Ep. to the Hebr.), *Zeitschrift für Protestantismus und Kirche*, 1856, pp. 329-350. Although this author is not seldom withdrawn from the plain sense of Scripture by his peculiar views respecting the Logos and the doctrines of sacrifice and atonement, yet nevertheless these contributions to the interpretation of our epistle, especially in the *Schriftbeweis* (ch. i.–x.), are very complete and comprehensive. Taken all together, they furnish the most valuable hints which have yet been given as to the purpose, plan, and connection of thought in the epistle, and will be recognised as doing so by every one who is more than a superficial inquirer.

GOTTLIEB LUENEMANN. *Kritisch. exegetisches Handbuch über den Hebräerbrief* (Critical and Exegetical Manual on the Ep. to the Hebr.), Göttingen 1855, 8vo. Worthy to form a part of Meyer's complete commentary on the New Testament. It is founded for the most part on Bleek, though with real independence. See the review of it in the *Allgem. Kirchenzeitung*, L. B. 1857, No. 29, by Willibald Grimm.

JO. H. R. BIESENTHAL. *Epistola Pauli ad Hebr. cum rabbinico commentario*, Berlin (Leipzig bei Dörffling und Franke), 1857, 8vo. The praise bestowed even by Jewish scholars on the same author's rabbinical commentary on the Ep. to the Romans (*vid.* Jost, *Gesch. des Judenthums u. seiner Secten*, Abth.

i. p. 416 seq. 1857) belongs also to this. It is the first Judæo-Christian interpretation of this Judæo-Christian epistle. The illustrations from Jewish sources testify to a very extensive range of reading, far overstepping the ground occupied by Schöttgen's *Horæ* (1733). It abounds also in thoughtful and delicate observations. The text on which it is founded is the Hebrew version of the New Testament published under the auspices of the London Jews' Society, which in the Ep. to the Hebrews is also not much better than the Hebrew version of Frid. Alb. Christiani, Lipsæ 1676, 4to. (This translation has been much improved in the edition of the Hebrew New Testament published by the London Society in 1866, and subsequently to Delitzsch's writing the above in 1859.—TR.)

Delitzsch proceeds to enumerate three English works which had come into his hands after the conclusion of his commentary in 1859:

1. GEORGE VISCOUNT MANDEVILLE. *Horæ Hebraicæ: An attempt to discover how the argument of the Epistle to the Hebrews must have been understood by those therein addressed; with Appendices on Messiah's Kingdom, etc.;* London 1835, large 8vo. From this work of the late Duke of Manchester Delitzsch translates a paragraph, enumerating the English works of Deering, Owen,[1] Lawson, Jones, Vaughan, Stewart, Maclean, Macknight. These Delitzsch confesses not to have seen.[2] On the other hand, he has made occasional use of H. HAMMOND (*ob.* 1660) in Latin by Jo. Clericus; DAN. WHITBY (*ob.* 1726); THOM. PYLE (1725), transl. into German by E. G. Küster; J. PEIRCE (*ob.* 1726) in Latin by J. D. Michaelis; A. A. SYKES (*ob.* 1756) in German by Semler; and S. T. BLOOMFIELD (*Recensio Synoptica Annotationis Sacræ, being a Critical Digest, etc.*, 8 vols., London 1826-7, 8vo). He regrets especially having been unable to use the Commentary of M. Stuart (first published at Andover, U.S., in 1827-8, in 2 vols.), which he characterizes as a work rivalling the scientific method of German *exegesis*.

---

[1] His *Exercitations on the Ep. to the Hebrews*, London 1668-74, fill four folios.

[2] Delitzsch says this apparently overlooking that he had included Maclean's commentary in his synopsis, with a brief criticism. See above. —TR.

2. *The Epistle to the Hebrews, with Notes,* London 1851, 8vo. "The writer's object is to prove that the whole epistle shows the acceptance of Christianity to be no loss, but in every respect a real gain for the Jews, and as such dedicates his book to Jewish readers."

3. WILLIAM TAIT. *Meditationes Hebraicæ, or a Doctrinal and Practical Exposition of the Ep. of St. Paul to the Hebrews, in a series of Lectures,* New and enlarged edition, London 1855. The writer avows his agreement with such commentators as Barnes in America and Ebrard in Germany, and has adopted improvements of the authorized English version suggested by the use of "the English *Hexapla*, the Commentary of M. Stuart, the *Horæ Hebraicæ* of the late Duke of Manchester, and the excellent translation by the Rev. Henry Craik of Bristol."

EXPOSITION

OF THE

EPISTLE TO THE HEBREWS.

When Moses put on the veil, the people looked at him; but when he took it off, they turned away their faces from him; and not understanding what they read, invented one thing after another for themselves.

ATHANASIUS, 19 *Pasch. Ep.* (Syriac).

FIRST PART OF THE EPISTLE.

CHAP. I. 1—CHAP. V. 10.

THE SUPREME EXALTATION OF THE MEDIATOR OF THE NEW TESTAMENT ABOVE THE ANGELS, ABOVE MOSES AND JOSHUA, AND FINALLY ABOVE AARON.

CHAP. I.—*The manifold revelations of Himself made by God through the prophets have been followed up in this last time by a revelation through the Son as accomplisher of the work of redemption; who both, a priori, as God of God and upholder of the Universe created by God through Him, and now, a posteriori, as the glorified One and Heir of all things, is exalted above the angels.*

VERS. 1-3 are the *proœmium* to the whole epistle as well as to this its first part, to which ver. 4 following this proœmium forms the transition: God has made a final revelation of Himself in the Son as fulfiller of the work of atonement; who being from all eternity above all things, by virtue of the essential dignity of His divine person is now exalted above all in the nature which He assumed in time.

The epistle begins, like the first Epistle of St. John, with a grandly solemn but more rhythmically rounded period, in which we find all the main thoughts of the whole treatise, and are prepared for their subsequent development. The supra-prophetical, super-angelical, and supra-levitical dignity of Christ is here briefly indicated, and at the same time regarded from that unearthly transcendental point of view which is maintained throughout the epistle.

Ver. 1. *God having spoken in the past at many times and in manifold ways unto the fathers through the prophets, hath spoken at the end of these days unto us through the Son.*

We have here at the outset the same high-sounding and significant rhythm, the same striking and beautiful collocation of words, which characterizes the whole epistle. The author begins, as Valckenaer delicately observes, with two *pæones quarti* (⏑⏑⏑–) connected by καί—πολυμερῶς καὶ πολυτρόπως —and thus with "winged words" sets forth in their contrast to each other the revelations of the Old and New Testament. The aorist λαλήσας has here (as is frequently the case with the aorist in participial and other subordinate clauses) a pluperfect signification. The first of these divine revelations is that which was given πάλαι (*i.e.* not *antiquitus*, "of old," as contrasted with what is *modern* or *new*, but rather *ante hac*, "formerly," "in the past," as contrasted with the existing present); while the second is that which has now superseded it, ἐπ' ἐσχάτου τῶν ἡμερῶν τούτων (*i.e. in the terminal period which these days constitute*, but not, "*on the last of these days*" [Winer, § 51, 9(?)], which would require the reading ἐπ' ἐσχάτης). 'Επ' ἐσχάτου is the right reading here as well as at 1 Pet. i. 20 (comp. Num. xxiv. 14, LXX.), instead of that of the *textus receptus*, ἐπ' ἐσχάτων, which was substituted for it as the easier, more intelligible form of expression, and likewise as that more usual in the LXX.—*e.g.* Gen. xlix. 1.

῎Εσχατον τῶν ἡμερῶν corresponds to the Hebrew term אחרית הימים, and expresses the notion never merely of a simple future which is to follow the present in the course of ordinary historical development, but always that of the end or final period which is to conclude all history and forms the utmost boundary of the speaker's circle of vision. It is then for our author here, as for St. Peter (1 Ep. i. 20), that "last time" which to his apprehension, looking back upon the past, is already begun and in process of unfolding itself before his eyes; and so by the word τούτων (which logically belongs to the whole term) he indicates to his readers that the present, in which they are all now living, is indeed this very ῎Εσχατον in contrast to that Πάλαι.

He proceeds to lay down what is common and what is distinctive in both revelations. (A.) What is *common:* in both

CHAP. I. 1.   41

periods it is ὁ Θεός, the One only and Most High God, who reveals Himself, and this revelation is characterized in both as a λαλεῖν, a speaking of God to men (λαλεῖν corresponding to דִּבֶּר as λέγειν to אָמַר). The very form of expression λαλήσας—ἐλάλησεν indicates that there is an historical continuity of both periods, that the revelation in both is substantially one and the same. But the stress is here laid not on what is *common*, but on (B.) what is *distinctive*. And therefore we have, on the one hand, the distinctive characteristics of the Old Testament placed at the beginning and end of the *protasis*—πολυμερῶς καὶ πολυτρόπως .... ἐν τοῖς προφήταις, and, on the other, set in contrast with them at the end of the *apodosis*, the one grand characteristic of the New Testament—ἐν υἱῷ.

The revelation of the Old Testament is characterized (*a*.) as given πολυμερῶς καὶ πολυτρόπως, *i.e.* quantitativè in successive portions, and qualitativè in various forms. A scholiast has expounded πολυμερῶς as referring to the τὸ διάφορον τῶν καιρῶν, and πολυτρόπως to the τὸ ποικίλον τῶν θείων ὀπτασιῶν; but it would be more strictly correct to say, that πολυμερῶς refers to the *truth* of revelation as given to the fathers in many distinct portions, not all at once, but piecemeal or "memberwise," and that πολυτρόπως refers to the *modes* of revelation, according to which it came to them in manifold shapes, *i.e.* not immediately, but now in one form of mediation, now in another. The next characteristic of the Old Testament revelation is, (β.) that it was made ἐν τοῖς προφήταις —that is, through a multitude of middle-persons chosen and selected by God for this instrumentality. The word προφῆται is here used in its most comprehensive sense so as to include on the one hand Moses, who was a prophet and more, and on the other David and Daniel, who officially were not "prophets" at all. All who were the ministering organs of divine revelation to ancient Israel are here called *prophets*—all, that is, *through whom*, as the sacred writer himself expresses it, *God had once spoken to the fathers*. ["Through whom," but not, as v. Gerlach renders it, "in whom." Ἐν τοῖς προφήταις has here the same sense as at 1 Sam. xxviii. 6, LXX. Λαλεῖν ἐν is "to speak by," like דבר ב׳, 2 Sam. xxiii. 2, and elsewhere frequently; ἐν answering to the Hebr. *Beth instrumenti* (a usage found in classical Greek in reference to things, but not to persons: Kühner, § 600, 3). Its use here corresponds to that of διά, ch. ii. 3 of this epistle, Luke i. 70, and Acts iii. 21.] It is then characteristic of the Old Testament to be a complex of manifold parts, modes, and instruments of revelation, held together by the unity of a common goal, the ἔσχατον τῶν ἡμερῶν, but at the same time bearing witness by its very multiplicity that this goal is not yet attained.

On this fragmentary and multiform speaking of God to the fathers follows now His speaking unto us ἐν υἱῷ. One revelation is contrasted with the many, the instrumentality of the prophets with that of the Son. To render ἐν υἱῷ, with Bleek, by "through a Son," *i.e.* "through one who is a Son," would hardly be consistent with the author's meaning. Υἱός is here, as at vii. 28, so applied to the Mediator of the New Testament as almost to be regarded as a proper name, and therefore used without the article, like βάσιλευς and μέγας βασιλεύς when applied to the Persian king. In the same way בר occurs Ps. ii. 12 without the article. This absolute use of υἱός like a proper name is just what we should expect in the Epistle to the Hebrews as one of the last of the Pauline writings.[1] Moreover, the great fundamental difference between the two revelations is clearly indicated in the simple *antithesis* of ἐν τοῖς προφήταις and ἐν υἱῷ; the term προφῆται making a relation purely accidental and official in its character, υἱός one that is essential and necessary, being grounded in the nature of the person by whom it is occupied. The author now proceeds by means of relative clauses to develop the main characteristics of that supreme exaltation by which the Son, as Mediator of this the final revelation, excels the prophets.

Ver. 2. *Whom he appointed to be heir of all things, through whom he also made the worlds.*

Ἐν υἱῷ is naturally followed in the first place by the clause

---

[1] For this use of *logically* defined substantives without the (definite) article, see Rost, § 98, 6, and the syntactic part of the collection of examples, p. 45 and foll. (second ed.). The best parallel to the New Testament use of υἱός for ὁ υἱός is perhaps the classical use of ἄνθρωπος, *e.g.* in Xenoph. *Memor.* i. 4, 11 (a passage not cited by Rost): θεοὶ μόνον τῶν ζώων ἄνθρωπον ὀρθὸν ἀνέστησαν.

ὃν ἔθηκεν[1] κληρονόμον πάντων, the notion of "son" readily suggesting that of "heir;" υἱός and κληρονόμος constitute in the Pauline system an inseparable pair of notions (Gal. iv. 7). Even because the Mediator of this final revelation is υἱός must He also be the Lord over all that pertains to His Father, and that, indeed, *jure hæreditatis*. In Him the promise made to the seed of Abraham, τὸ κληρονόμον αὐτὸν εἶναι τοῦ κόσμου (Rom. iv. 13 ; Gal. iii. 16), attains its complete fulfilment.

The next clause, δι' οὗ καὶ ἐποίησεν τοὺς αἰῶνας, is exhibited by means of the καί (which is here more than a mere expletive) in its intimate connection of thought with the preceding. God hath appointed the Son to be heir of all things, even as He also made the worlds through Him. Οἱ αἰῶνες is not equivalent here to the Old Testament העולמים, which (from עלם, to veil) signifies inscrutable periods or successions of time, but to the rabbinical post-biblical העולמים or העולמות (the *el-âlamîn* of the Koran), *i.e.* the infinite multitude of worlds which have their existence in those unlimited periods of time. It expresses in the plural form the same notion as κόσμος in the singular, *i.e.* not the systems or economies of the history of the universe, but the cosmical systems of actual creation. The word is used in the same sense, xi. 3 ; it is used in both these so closely connected meanings, 1 Tim. i. 17 ; and *here* expresses the same thing as the πάντα of the preceding clause. Creator of this universe of worlds is God (ὁ Θεός): Mediator of that creation is the Son (υἱός). And here we have no ground whatever for assuming that our author takes the name υἱός, as it were, out of its proper soteriological connection, and applies it by way of anticipation only to the Mediator in His creative capacity. The transcendent dignity, indeed, marked by this use of the word υἱός, of that essential relation in which the

---

[1] I have followed Lachmann and Tischendorf's custom of putting ν ἐφελκ. even before words beginning with a consonant, therein following the custom of the Cod. Alexandr. (retained also by Grabe) and that of most uncials. Though I do not believe that the writers of the New Testament themselves made a rule of this irregularity, it is yet more than probable that this mode of spelling may have been as common in their autographs as in the older or nearly contemporary written documents which have come down to us ; *e.g.* the perhaps Ptolemaic *Psephisma Parium*, the Turin and Vienna Papyrus edited by Peyron, the MS. rolls of Herculaneum, etc. See Thiersch, *de Pentateuch. Vers. Alexandr.* ii. §§ 10, 11.

so-Named stands to God, is set in the clearest light by that relation thus being shown not to have had its commencement in the midst of time, but to have existed before all times and all worlds, and so also to have exercised a mediatorial agency in their production. The exalted rank attained by the Son in His historical manifestation through God's appointing Him heir of all things, is only the correlative of that which He possessed already before all times, when God created the universe through Him. Between this ראשית (commencement) and that אחרית (consequence) there exists a real connection, to which the καί points. (The *antiquus verborum ordo*, as even in his time Bengel called it—δι' οὗ καὶ ἐποίησεν τοὺς αἰῶνας—rightly now preferred by Lachmann and Tischendorf, is more in accordance with this correlative character of the two clauses than that of the *text. rec.*—δι' οὗ καὶ τοὺς αἰῶνας ἐποίησεν; and moreover, such a strictly logical and rhythmical arrangement down to the smallest details in the collocation of words, is one peculiarly characteristic of the whole epistle: the Son is made the heir of All, that All too owes its origin to Him.)

We have here assumed against Baumgarten and Bleek, that the clause ὃν ἔθηκεν exclusively refers to that dignity which the Son has attained to in His historical manifestation; so that in the second verse we have a retrogression from what has been a matter of historical development to that which preceded it, and formed the commencement of all history. It must be allowed that ὃν ἔθηκεν might also refer to an eternal predestinating decree on God's part; but there is nothing to indicate such a reference here, which therefore can hardly have been present to the mind of the writer. Moreover, the "chiastic" (or cross-wise) relation in which the clauses of the following verse stand to these is against such a reference of ὃν ἔθηκεν. For *there* we have—first, in the clauses dependent upon ὤν and φέρων (taking up the δι' οὗ ἐποίησεν τοὺς αἰῶνας), some of the eternal attributes of the Son, and then, in the following clauses, His redeeming work in time, and His return thereby to God, from whom He came, and with whom henceforth, as κληρονόμος πάντων, He for ever sits enthroned.

Ver. 3. *Who, being the effulgence of his glory and express image of his substance, and upholding all things by the word of* his power, *after having by himself accomplished the purification of our sins, sat down on the right hand of Majesty in highest places.*[1] The *consequences* of this session on the right hand of God are expressed in the following verse (ver. 4). From this alone it is evident that the participial clauses which precede ἐκάθισεν must describe the *antecedents* of that exaltation. No one denies that the clause ποιησάμενος describes the work which has had that exaltation for its consequence; and the uniform impression made from the very first on all readers sharing the mind of the church on these subjects, by the preceding clauses ὤν and φέρων, was, that they describe the internal, timeless, and essential ground of the Son's personality. Nevertheless Hofmann (*Schriftbew.* i. 140-142) refuses to allow that ὤν and φέρων bear this sense, inasmuch as he insists on interpreting all the utterances of Scripture in the New Testament concerning the eternal person which has manifested itself in Jesus, solely in reference to that manifestation, thus assigning them merely an historical and dispensational significance, and throwing an impenetrable veil over the whole doctrine of the Trinity apart from those relations of inequality in which the Godhead has manifested itself in the economy of redemption. These clauses, therefore, ὤν and φέρων, tell us nothing, in his view, concerning our Lord apart from His historical manifestation; they merely express what He now is, and is able to do since, after accomplishing the purification of sin, He is set down at the right hand of God;—an interpretation which is not only opposed to the natural impression made by the words themselves, to the order of thought, and to the general construction of the sentence, but which likewise fails to find adequate support in the reasons alleged by Hofmann for main-

[1] The parallel passage to this and some of the following in the first Epistle of Clemens Romanus, c. 36, runs thus : "Ὅς ὢν ἀπαύγασμα τῆς μεγαλωσύνης αὐτοῦ τοσούτῳ μείζων ἐστὶν ἀγγέλων ὅσῳ διαφορώτερον ὄνομα κεκληρονόμηκεν. γέγραπται γὰρ οὕτως· " Ὁ ποιῶν τοὺς ἀγγέλους αὐτοῦ πνεύματα, καὶ τοὺς λειτουργοὺς αὐτοῦ πυρὸς φλόγα." ἐπὶ δὲ τῷ υἱῷ αὐτοῦ (for this ἐπὶ c. dat., see note to viii. 1) οὕτως εἶπεν ὁ δεσπότης, " Υἱός μοι εἶ σύ, ἐγὼ σήμερον γεγέννηκά σε· αἴτησαι παρ᾽ ἐμοῦ καὶ δώσω σοι ἔθνη τὴν κληρονομίαν σου καὶ τὴν κατάσχεσίν σου τὰ πέρατα τῆς γῆς." Καὶ πάλιν λέγει πρὸς αὐτὸν· " Κάθου ἐκ δεξιῶν μου ἕως ἂν θῶ τοὺς ἐχθρούς σου ὑποπόδιον τῶν ποδῶν σου."

taining it. For surely, to say that the clause ἀπαύγασμα τῆς δόξης καὶ χαρακτὴρ τῆς ὑποστάσεως αὐτοῦ, if meant to refer to our Lord apart from the incarnation, must have commenced with ὅς ἐστιν instead of ὤν, is to make an unwarrantable demand on the sacred writer, whose purpose evidently is, by the use of participial constructions here, to exhibit the eternal character and accomplished work of the now exalted Saviour as the glorious background of His exaltation. Neither does it prove anything for that position to say, that the omnipotent rule over the universe of created things expressed by φέρων forms the most complete antithesis to the humiliation of our Lord's earthly life; for Hofmann himself assumes (2, 1, 24), that even in that humiliation He could not cease to take His part in the divine government of the world, or, as we have expressed it elsewhere (*Psychologie*, 286), "the work of redemption forms the very centre of that divine energy of the Triune Godhead by which the universe is governed and preserved, and which, so far from suffering interruption when God the Son, falling back on the essential ground of His divine being, exchanged the form of God for the form of a servant, was only the more intensely manifested by that very act of self-renunciation. The 'upholding all things,' therefore, 'by the word of His power' maintained all through our Lord's humiliation its abiding truth, though under the veil of a mystery which the very angels could not penetrate, just as the human spirit maintains, without a moment's interruption, its vital energising power over the human body as much during the captivity of sleep as when in the full activity of its waking condition."

We continue, accordingly, to maintain that the clauses ὤν and φέρων do express the absolute essence and operation of the Son, which remains through all the historical developments to which by the incarnation He has committed Himself as the unchangeable and hidden basis for them all. But we do not (with de Wette for example) regard ὤν and φέρων as expressing the cause of His exaltation. Neither rendering, *utpote qui sit—ferat*, nor *quum esset—ferret*, would be the right one here. The absolute divine being of the Son does not stand in the relation of cause and effect to His exaltation. What He is in Himself belongs to the category of metaphysical necessity; what, as the result of historical developments, He has become, belongs to that of ethical freedom; and these are quite distinct categories. The ground of His exaltation must be sought in the fact, that He undertook and accomplished a certain work—the purification of our sins; and the participial clauses ὤν and φέρων tell us what in Himself He was who did this work, that is, they describe the eternal, unchangeable, and absolute background of the whole of His historical action, setting it forth in the light of its true significance. The participles might therefore be thus resolved: who while He (from eternity) is ... and (evermore) upholdeth ... did after accomplishing (or, in consequence of His having accomplished) the cleansing ... sit down on the right hand ... (Böhme, von Gerlach, and others). This interpretation makes evident why ὤν is so expressively put forward at the head of the sentence; namely, because it is the timeless being of the Son to which it refers, and which gives its infinite dignity to His historical existence. Ὤν is here used as *supra-temporally*, and so to speak *omni-temporally*, as at John i. 18, iii. 13 (comp. viii. 58 and xvii. 24). Just the same is the case with ἐστίν, Col. i. 15, as is clear from the αὐτός ἐστι (not ἦν) πρὸ πάντων of ver. 17; for there likewise Christ is called εἰκὼν τοῦ Θεοῦ τοῦ ἀοράτου not, as Hofman would have it, as the *glorified*, but as the *eternal* One. For there first going back to His eternal derivation from the supra-mundane Father, and expressing by ὅς ἐστιν εἰκών, κ.τ.λ., the relation in which He stood to the world at its first creation, the apostle proceeds, after calling Him the Head of the church (ver. 18), to designate Him (in the next clause, ὅς ἐστιν ἀρχή, πρωτότοκος ἐκ τῶν νεκρῶν) as an ἀρχή, or fresh beginning, in His relation to the same world newly redeemed. In both relations He is the mediating principle: in the first, by virtue of His divine birth antecedently to all creation (πρωτότοκος, not πρωτόκτιστος); in the second, by virtue of His birth from the dead, in which the new creation took its beginning: in the first, as the eternal Son; in the second, as the glorified God-man.

In turning our attention, then, to the clause ὢν ἀπαύγασμα τῆς δόξης καὶ χαρακτὴρ τῆς ὑποστάσεως αὐτοῦ, we both may and must assume that these words express the eternal and divine relation in which our Reconciler stands to God, a relation on which Holy Scripture does not otherwise leave us uninformed, because without such information the atoning work of Christ could neither be appreciated nor understood. Even were the question regarded merely from an historico-literary point of view, it would seem improbable that such predicates as εἰκών (ἀπεικόνισμα) Θεοῦ, ἀπαύγασμα, and χαρακτήρ (σφραγίς) should be familiarly applied to the Logos by the Jewish Alexandrinism, and not have a like application to the eternal person manifested in Christ when employed by writers of the New Testament; and least of all in the case of this epistle, which, as K. R. Köstlin (*Johanneischer Lehrbegriff*, 1843) has convincingly demonstrated, forms a link between the later Pauline epistles and the writings of St. John, and excels all other books of the New Testament in the abundance of what cannot be merely accidental resemblances to Alexandrine modes of thought and expression. To us, indeed, it seems indisputable that the Jewish theology of the last few centuries before Christ in Palestine, and more especially in Alexandria, did manifest various foregleams of that fuller light which was thrown on divine things in general, and on the triune nature of the Godhead in particular, by the great evangelical facts of redemption ; nor can the admission that so it was, prove a stumbling-block to any but those who think that the long chain of divine preparations for the coming of Christ, on which the whole outward and inward history of Israel is strung, must have been abruptly broken off with the last book of the Old Testament canon. Is it then possible that the Book of Wisdom (vii. 26) should speak of the Sophia as ἀπαύγασμα φωτὸς ἀϊδίου, Philo (*de Cherub.*) of God as ἀρχέτυπος αὐγή, and now our author of Him who was manifested in Jesus as ἀπαύγασμα τῆς δόξης αὐτοῦ, without these several terms having any internal historical connection ?

Ἀπαύγασμα is either *reflected* brightness as from an illuminated surface (of water, for example, or a mirror), or the brightness *given forth* by a shining object from itself. The first meaning is grammatically as possible as the second, and not otherwise inadmissible : the Son, as reflecting the divine glory (2 Cor. iv. 6), might be called ἀπαύγασμα ;—but the second meaning more readily suggests itself, and is more in accordance with the general use of the word : the Son is ἀπαύγασμα as the *effulgence* or eradiation of that glory. So

Philo employs the word when he speaks of the human spirit as τῆς μακαρίας καὶ τρισμακαρίας φύσεως ἀπαύγασμα; and that it must have the same meaning in Wisdom vii. 26, is evident from all the other predicates there associated with it (especially the ἀπόρροια τῆς τοῦ παντοκράτορος δόξης εἰλικρινής). All the fathers understand the word in the same way. So, for example, Origen, when he says, οὐκ οἶμαί τινα τὸ πᾶν δύνασθαι χωρῆσαι τῆς ὅλης δόξης τοῦ Θεοῦ ἀπαύγασμα, ἢ τὸν υἱὸν αὐτοῦ, and Tertullian: *ille tanquam sol, hic quasi radius a sole porrectus;* and so understood, it called forth the church's watchword, φῶς ἐκ φωτός, and its consequences rightly drawn— (1.) that the Son must be *consubstantial* with the Father, inasmuch as what emanates from light must itself have the nature of light; and (2.) that the divine generation of the Son must be at once a free and a necessary process within the Godhead, inasmuch as ἡ αὐγὴ οὐ κατὰ προαίρεσιν τοῦ φωτὸς ἐκλάμπει, κατὰ δέ τι τῆς οὐσίας συμβεβηκὸς ἀχώριστον. If this sense be attached to ἀπαύγασμα, the relation between God the Son and God the Father is similar to that between sunlight and the sun; and so Hesychius (*Glossar. Alb. in N. T. sub voce* ἀκτίν) interprets ἀπαύγασμα by ἡλίου φέγγος.[1] The unfolding by God of His own glory is the forthshining of the Son, who thereby obtains an existence which, though derived, is yet self-subsistent and divine. The divine glory here spoken of is no mere nimbus or luminous veil like the כבוד of the Old Testament theophanies in which God was pleased to exhibit Himself to human sense, but the supersensuous light and fire of His own nature thrown out for the purpose of self-manifestation to Himself; and the Son is called the ἀπαύγασμα of this glory, because it is in Him that all its powers of inward light are collected and appear as in a glorious sun shining forth in the eternal firmament of the divine nature. It is in the deepest sense the same thing when Philo

---

[1] In a kindred sense, Christ is called by Clemens Romanus (c. 16) *the outstretched sceptre of Divine Majesty* (τὸ σκῆπτρον τῆς μεγαλωσύνης τοῦ Θεοῦ). The Midrash of the Synagogue recognises also מְטֹה as a name of Messiah, *Bereshith Rabba* to Gen. xxxviii. 18. Compare further the beautiful interpretation of ἀπαύγασμα given by von Gerlach, which concludes with these words: "*As we cannot see the sun without the brightness which issues from him, so we cannot see the Father without the Only-begotten Son.*"

defines this divine glory to be the unfolding of the fulness of the divine δυνάμεις, and calls the Logos ἡνίοχος τῶν δυνάμεων; i.e. the generation of the Son is a process carried on within the Godhead, and implies an operation which, if proceeding from God, must equally react again upon Himself.

Further, the Son is styled χαρακτὴρ τῆς ὑποστάσεως αὐτοῦ. The proper signification of χαρακτήρ is undoubtedly that which makes a mark or impression, as ζωστήρ, that which girdles; but Hofmann's assertion (1, 142), that χ. never signifies the impression itself, or the thing which bears the impressed image of another thing, is against the usage of the language. Indeed, this interchange of significations is a very natural one, inasmuch as that which makes an impression must itself bear the image which it makes, to which the similar interchange of meanings, type and antitype, in εἰκών and its synonyms may be compared. When Philo calls the human *logos* χαρακτῆρα θείας δυνάμεως, he means that it is a substance on which the divine Logos has impressed its image (ὑπὸ θείου λόγου χαραχθέν); and when he speaks of the divine Logos (which he does not, as is well known, properly distinguish from the ideal Cosmos), and calls it χαρακτῆρα σφραγῖδος Θεοῦ, his meaning is, that the divine Logos is the stamp or die by which the seal or impress of God is set upon the soul of man. Hofmann admits for χαρακτήρ the significations "trait" or "outline," but these are inadequate; rather, it signifies an image or model which in all its features corresponds with the original, or with the die from which it is struck: so Eunapius expresses by βίου χαρακτήρ a complete biographical representation of the whole course of a man's life. It is this bye notion of complete similarity which distinguishes χαρακτήρ from its synonyms μίμημα, εἰκών, ἀπεικόνισμα, and the like, bringing it nearest in sense to τύπος and ἐκμαγεῖον. This notion of absolute similarity is the chief point here. A mere effluent brightness might be a μερικὸν ἀπαύγασμα, but that which shines forth and takes shape in the Son of God is a χαρακτήρ, having an absolute congruity with its divine original, and being not merely χαρακτὴρ αὐτοῦ, but χ. τῆς ὑποστάσεως αὐτοῦ.

Ὑπόστασις, according to its fundamental signification, *that which stands or is placed under*, signifies here the essence or essential ground underlying the phenomenon; in which sense

CHAP. I. 8.   51

Philo, for example, says of light : ἡ αὐγὴ καθ' ἑαυτὴν ὑπόστασιν
οὐκ ἔχει, because in his opinion fire is the substantial basis of
all light. Elsewhere also he uses ὑπόστασις as a synonym of
οὐσία. The *usus loquendi* by which ὑπόστασις (= ἡ δι' οὐσίας
περιγραφή) came to express the single persons of the Trinity
was a later one which has no place here.¹ The Vulgate renders
correctly, *figura substantiæ ejus*, and Origen more accurately
still, *figura expressa substantiæ Patris* (*de Princip.* iv. 2, 8), with
the remark that this perfect similarity of the Son implies the
" *naturæ et substantiæ Patris unitatem*."²

The participial clause ὤν is now followed by a second,
attached to it by the enclitic τε, and having a like reference
to the immutable, inward, and divine aspect of the Redeemer's
personality : φέρων τε τὰ πάντα τῷ ῥήματι τῆς δυνάμεως αὐτοῦ.
The particle τε, which, except in the writings of St. Paul,
and still more in those of St. Luke, is rarely found in the
New Testament, being abbreviated from the demonstrative τει
or τῇ, is merely an attenuated enclitic—" so," " also," " likewise " (Nägelsbach, *Anm. zur Ilias*, 1850, p. 277). Winer
makes a distinction between τε as adjunctive and καί as conjunctive ; a distinction borne out by usage, for even the correlative τε—τε is rather appositive than conjunctive, while used

¹ Lexical information concerning ὑπόστασις may be found in JULIUS
POLLUX, *hist. sacra*, p. 376, and SOCRATES, *hist. eccles.* iii. 7, p. 144 D.
We learn therefrom that IRENAIOS the grammarian (in his " Alphabetical
Atticist," τῷ κατὰ στοιχεῖον 'Αττικίστῃ) called ὑπόστασις a λέξις βάρβαρος,
that is, a non-Attic word, yet cited a passage from the *Phœnix* of SO-
PHOCLES in which ὑπόστασις had the signification of ἐνέδρα, and another
from MENANDER in which ὑποστάσεις are = καρυκεύματα, highly flavoured
dishes (pieces de resistance ?). In both cases ὑπόστασις is that *which can
be held by*, or taken as a basis, unless perhaps the meaning which it has in
Menander may have reference to the *sediment* in the dishes in question.
So the explanations given by JULIUS POLLUX, SOCRATES, and the *Onomas-
ticon* of POLLUX the elder : *jusculum densum admixto amylo densatum* (comp.
Meineke, *Fragm. Comicorum* iv. 206). Among the many definitions of the
word in its higher signification which are accumulated by Zonaras and
Suidas in their Lexicons of the twelfth century, the following seems the
best : ὑπόστασίς ἐστι πρᾶγμα ὑφεστός τε καὶ οὐσιῶδες, ἐν ᾧ τὸ ἄθροισμα τῶν
συμβεβηκότων ὡς ἐν ἑνὶ ὑποκειμένῳ πράγματι καὶ ἐνεργείᾳ ὑφίστηκεν.

² The Hebrew translation of the London Jews-Missionary Society has
וְתַמוּנַת מְצִיאוּתוֹ, but that would mean " likeness of His existence ; " Biesenthal has substituted for this the correct term יֶשְׁנוּתוֹ, " His being."

singly puts together side by side things which, if no absolutely correlative, have yet some internal connection. This single τε, which is of comparatively rare occurrence in classical prose, is here employed to combine the assertion of the Son's eternally divine co-equal majesty in His relation to God with the assertion of the same in His relation to the world. Even as He is the effluent brightness and image of God, so is He also the ground of existence to the world: *He upholds all things; i.e. God*, who is (as so often called in the dogmatic utterances of the Synagogue, *e.g. Ex. Rabba*, c. 36) "the Sustainer of the worlds" (סובל עולמות), *upholds all things by Him*: not only was the world originally created, but its government is still carried on through His mediation. Philo, moreover, sometimes speaks of God, as the Son is spoken of here, as ὁ ὄντα (πάντα) φέρων. Hermas says, in allusion to our text: *Audi, nomen filii Dei magnum et immensum est, et totus ab eo sustentatur orbis.*[1] This all-sustaining activity is exercised by the Son *by the word of His power*. In τῷ ῥήματι τῆς δυνάμεως αὐτοῦ, whether we write αὑτοῦ or αὐτοῦ,[2] the pronoun must be referred to the Son, not (as Cyrillus Alexandrinus thought) to the Father. It may, however, seem strange that *that* whereby the Son is thus said to sustain all things should be called τὸ ῥῆμα τῆς δυνάμεως αὐτοῦ, that is, *the utterance of His power,*— a *word* proceeding from and filled with His divine omnipotence;

---

[1] [Simil. ix. 14. The Greek text as now recovered reads, ἄκουε, φησί· τὸ ὄνομα τοῦ υἱοῦ τοῦ Θεοῦ μέγα ἐστὶ καὶ ἀχώρητον καὶ τὸν κόσμον ὅλον βαστάζει.—HILGENFELD, *Hermæ Pastor. Græce. e Codd. Sinait. et Lips., etc., restit.* 1866).—TR. 1867.]

[2] In this case αὑτοῦ would classically be as admissible as αὐτοῦ (Buttmann, § 127, 3, Anm. 3), and so it would be in a hundred other cases. The latest critical editors of the New Testament write throughout αὐτοῦ, αὐτῷ, αὐτόν; and indeed it would appear that the aspirated reflexive is as foreign to the idiom of the New Testament as to that of the LXX. (THIERSCH, *loc. cit.* p. 98). The matter is, however, not yet fully cleared up (WINER, p. 157). It cannot be maintained, at any rate, that the total or nearly total absence of αὑτοῦ, αὑτῷ, and αὑτόν from biblical Greek is due solely to the influence of Hebrew. For ἑαυτου, ἑαυτω, and ἑαυτον, is certainly not less in use than the unaspirated αυτου, αυτω, αυτον, referring to the subject, and the writers of MSS. of the New Testament were not under the influence of Hebraism, but of the popular idiom of their time. In this, however, the reflexive pronoun, except in cases of special emphasis, was gradually softened down from ἑαυτοῦ, through αὑτοῦ and αὐτοῦ, to the enclitic του of modern Greek.

CHAP. I. 3. 53

seeing that the Son Himself is, in accordance with a view with which the writer of the Epistle to the Hebrews must have been familiar, called *The Word, Logos*, or *Memra* (Λόγος, מימרא, דִבְּרָא), and further, that His state of humiliation, which is here referred to, would seem to have excluded the possibility of such omnipotent working in the universe. The first difficulty may be solved by the observation, that as the personal (masculine) Λόγος is understood to denote an absolute divine being, so the impersonal (neuter) ῥῆμα may be taken to signify the particular divine will or purpose in reference to the world, and a medium of working common at once to the Father and the Son; a distinction which we find even in Philo, when he says: τῷ περιφανεστάτῳ καὶ τηλαυγεστάτῳ ἑαυτοῦ λόγῳ ῥήματι ὁ Θεὸς πάντα ποιεῖ, *i.e.* God makes all things by His Logos, and through the instrumentality of the *Rhêma* (*Leg. Alleg.* lib. i.). The other difficulty is removed by the consideration, that the all-sustaining power of the Son of God, exercised through His *Rhêma*, suffered indeed a change in the *form* of its activity during His humiliation, but was by no means annulled thereby, nay, concentrated itself with intenser energy in the span of time in which the work of our redemption was accomplished.

The sacred writer, having thus described the enduring background of the Redeemer's work, as formed by the ever-equal and unchangeable glory of the Son, proceeds to that action which formed the prelude to His exaltation in time: δι' ἑαυτοῦ καθαρισμὸν ποιησάμενος τῶν ἁμαρτιῶν ἡμῶν. So reads the *Textus receptus*. But ἡμῶν is without sufficient MS. authority, and should be removed; nor is it, as Bleek rightly observes, required by the sense, the whole description of the divine Son dealing in generals (compare x. 4 and xi. 9, 26). Δι' ἑαυτοῦ is also of uncertain authority. Lachmann and Tischendorf have excluded it.[1] It is wanting in A. B. al.,[2] in several ancient versions, as the Vulgate (but not the It.) and Armenian, and in the citations of the Greek and Latin fathers. (D. reads δι' αὐτοῦ as at ver. 3, which, according to Theodoret, should be read δι' αὑτοῦ). Further, instead of καθαρισμὸν ποιησάμενος τῶν ἁμαρτιῶν (ἡμῶν), we have in A. B. D. E., and citations both Greek and Latin, the arrangement of words preferred by

---
[1] Tischendorf readmitted it in his seventh ed.—TR.
[2] Also in the Codex Sinaiticus.—TR.

Bengel and Lachmann, καθαρισμὸν τῶν ἁμαρτιῶν ποιησάμενος.[1] The participial sentence thus constructed appears to me to form a lighter and more airy transition to the ἐκάθισεν of the next clause. But I hesitate to give up δι' ἑαυτοῦ. I would rather believe that the Uffenbachian Uncial-Fragments have preserved the original reading: φέρων τε τὰ πάντα τῷ ῥήματι τῆς δυνάμεως δι' ἑαυτοῦ καθαρισμὸν τῶν ἁμαρτιῶν ποιησάμενος.[2] The middle voice is finely chosen here for the participle ποιησάμενος. It indicates what is further expressed in the δι' ἑαυτοῦ and something besides. The first reflexive meaning of the middle voice is not indeed admissible here, but ποιεῖσθαι (a favourite word both with St. Paul and St. Luke) is used in a similar sense to that which it bears in the phrases δεήσεις ποιεῖσθαι (Luke v. 33; Phil. i. 4; 1 Tim. ii. 1), κοπετὸν ποιεῖσθαι (Acts viii. 2), ἀναβολὴν μηδεμίαν ποιεῖσθαι (Acts xxv. 17), in which, with the general notion of the performance of an action, is combined that of an earnest, vigorous, energetic activity on the part of the acting subject (See Kühner, § 398, 5). Here, then, the middle voice in ποιησάμενος designates the act of cleansing as one specially and properly belonging to the Son, a notion further expressed by δι' ἑαυτοῦ. The act was done by Him, not through the instrumentality of any outward means, but by interposition and within the sphere of His own personality.

There is a reference in καθαρισμὸν ποιησάμενος to the Levitical priests of the Old Testament. The idea is further developed in the latter part of the epistle, but is already present here, and seems to have led to the choice of the word. For καθαρίζειν (Heb. טָהֵר), to cleanse or pronounce clean from impurity, is a priestly act. Καθαρισθῆναι ἀπὸ πασῶν τῶν ἁμαρτιῶν is the fruit resulting from the priest-offered sacrifices of the day of atonement (Lev. xvi. 30). The notions of טָהֵר and כִּפֶּר are so nearly related that the Septuagint sometimes renders כִּפּוּרִים by καθαρισμός. The genitive τῶν ἁμαρτιῶν is somewhat peculiar, καθαρίζειν being generally elsewhere construed with ἀπό and ἐκ. The author follows, in the construction καθ. τ. ἁμαρτ., the Septuagint at Ex. xxx. 10 (comp. 2 Pet. i. 9), and even the whole phrase ποιεῖν καθαρισμὸν τῆς ἁμαρ-

---

[1] So the Codex Sinaiticus.—TR.
[2] Tischendorf, *Anecd. Sacra et profana*, p. 177.

τίας (Sept. at Job vii. 21, העביר את עון [comp. 2 Sam. xii. 13 and xxiv. 10] = "to make sin pass away" or "disappear") he found ready to his hand. Τῶν ἁμαρτιῶν is in any case a *genitivus objecti*; and although the phrase καθαρίζονται ἁμαρτίαι is not found, yet we find in Homer καθαίρειν followed by the accusative of the impurity to be removed : we read at Matt. viii. 3 ἐκαθαρίσθη αὐτοῦ ἡ λέπρα, and καθάρισίς τινος is a classical phrase similar to ἐλευθερία τινος (Ditfurt, *Attische Synt.* § 109). Finally, the term here used so indefinitely and absolutely indicates the absoluteness of that divine cleansing from sin of which the epistle afterwards treats.

The SON, then (so and not otherwise has our author hitherto called Him), having performed this priestly act of absolute validity here below, has now entered yonder into His kingly glory—ἐκάθισεν ἐν δεξιᾷ τῆς μεγαλωσύνης ἐν ὑψηλοῖς. To which word and notion does ἐν ὑψηλοῖς[1] more properly belong? —to ἐκάθισεν, or to τῆς μεγαλωσύνης? Logically, no doubt, it belongs to both (comp. viii. 1 and Eph. i. 20). Grammatically it belongs not to τ. μεγαλωσ. (Bleek) but to εκαθ., for ἡ μεγαλωσύνη is here (as at viii. 1) equivalent to הַגְּדֻלָּה, the μεγαλοπρεπὴς δόξα of 2 Pet. i. 17, and the δύναμις of Matt. xxvi. 64, that is, it is a simple periphrasis for "God." So in post-biblical Hebrew it is not usual to say הגבורה שבשמים, but simply הגבורה: for example, מפי הגבורה שמענום, "*out of the mouth of God have we heard them*" (Buxtorf's *Lexic. Chald.* c. 385).

To sit down (*considere*) on the right hand of Majesty is the same as sitting "on the right hand of God :" ἐν δεξιᾷ is the expression here, and is common to the Epistle to the Hebrews with Rom. viii. 34, Eph. i. 20, Col. iii. 1. The Acts of the Apostles, on the other hand (as ought to be noticed [2]), uses for ἐν δεξιᾷ, τῇ δεξιᾷ (לימין), or ἐκ δεξιῶν (מימין). The question, whether the *sessio ad dexteram* was a note of fellowship in *honour*, or of fellowship in actual *dominion*, need not have been put in that dilemmatic form, for the being entitled Lord and actual ruling are in the divine glory, the world of truth and reality, quite inseparable—as the one *potentia*, the other *actus*.

---

[1] ἐν ὑψηλοῖς answers to the במרום of Ps. xciii. 4; compare ἐν ὑψίστοις = במרומים of Job xvi. 19.

[2] Namely, as being a note, so far as it goes, against the supposed authorship of the epistle by St. Luke, which Delitzsch favours.—TR.

Of real significance, on the other hand, is another question: whether the writer of this epistle conceived of this sitting at the right hand of God as a *local* or as an *illocal session*. Luthern dogmatic theology insists on the two propositions: *dextera Dei omnipotens ejus virtus* and *dextera Dei ubique est;* while for that of the Reformed Church [1] (to use the words of Schneckenburger, *Zur Kirchlichen Christologie*, p. 107) the ascension of Christ was not a flight beyond the bounds of the sensible universe, but a real *loci mutatio*, a change of actual locality. *Ideo*, says Zach. Ursinus, *Deus nos scire voluit locum in quem Christus ascenderit ut constaret Christum esse verum hominem, neque ipsum evannisse, sed mansisse.* Ebrard, too, although he regards the καθίζειν ἐν δεξιᾷ as a figurative expression for the participation of the glorified Jesus in the divine majesty and dominion, without any reference to locality or illocality, yet says elsewhere (p. 267), "*Heaven is that sphere of creation in which the will of God is perfectly done, and where no sin is found to hinder Him in a full and adequate revelation of Himself. . . . Into that sphere, that locality of the created universe, Christ ascended as the first-fruits of redeemed humanity, in order to draw us thither after Him.*" This localizing conception necessitates, as is well known, some evil consequences, but the exclusively *illocal* one, on the other hand, cannot be acquitted of the charge of onesidedness. The right combination of both views appears to be the following: The ὑψηλά (heavenly heights) into which our Reconciler has entered, and the δεξιὰ τῆς μεγαλωσύνης, where He is set down, are simply *illocal* so far as the divine being itself is concerned, but not simply *illocal* in reference to the divine self-manifestation vouchsafed to the creature. 1*st*, In reference to the divine nature itself, those ὑψηλά are the sphere of that pre- super- extra-mundane glory of God which is His own infinitely rich and glorious reflection of Himself, His own eternal, uncreated, and self-constituted heaven; and the δεξιὰ Θεοῦ is God's absolutely omnipotent, omnipresent, and throughout creation ever-working and all-

---

[1] The reference is to the once vehement *Ubiquitarian* controversy, concerning the presence of the human nature of Christ, between the Lutheran theologians on the one hand, and the "Reformed" (chiefly Swiss and French) on the other. *Ursinus*, referred to below, and one of the authors of the Heidelberg Catechism, took an active part in it."—Tr.

ruling power. Into these unimaginable heights, and to the side of this right hand, *i.e.* into the divine recesses of that inner life of God which, lying beyond and behind all creaturely existence, and all conditions of space and time, is its own illocal place (Ezek. iii. 12), thither is the incarnate Son as God-man, after accomplishing our reconciliation, Himself returned. But 2*dly,* Ever since the created universe has come into actual existence, there is *beside* and *along with* that omnipresence of God in the world, which is the necessary consequence of the absoluteness of His being, a special revealed presence confined (so to speak) to certain places and certain times, and taking either a judicial or a gracious character, according to the condition of the creature itself. And so there is (we say) within the created universe itself a real heaven of glory, the place where God vouchsafes to manifest Himself in love to the blessed among His creatures, called " *heaven,*" because exalted so far above the earth, and because the manifestation of divine love makes it *so heavenly.* That such there must be, is a necessary consequence of the *antithesis* in which all creaturely existence must ever stand to the uncreaturely and supra-mundane being of God. In this created heaven the glorified Jesus presents Himself *visibly* to those blessed ones who are deemed worthy of the sight, as He does *invisibly* to the eternal Father in the uncreated heaven; He is contemplated as *sitting,* or as St. Stephen beheld Him *standing* (Acts vii. 56), at God's right hand. Moreover, we should err if we assumed that the author of our epistle was thinking here of either of these heavens to the exclusion of the other, whether it be the supernal heaven of the Divine Nature (as the elder Frizsche maintained, *diss. de Jesu Christo ad Dei dexteram sedente,* 1843), or the lower heaven of manifested Love. Further on we shall meet with various expressions, in which one or the other of these heavenly places seem *specially* referred to: here they are combined, as it were, in one dioramatic view.

The author now advances to the discussion which is to form the main subject of the epistle. This with exquisite art he connects with his *prooemium* by means of an apposition, which in our so much less elastic language it is quite impossible adequately to render. Beginning here from the present exaltation of the manifested Son above the angels, his purpose is gradually to descend to a comparison with the human personalities who have proved most eminent in the development of the plan of salvation.

Ver. 4. *Having by so much become greater than the angels, by how much a more excellent name he hath inherited than they.* The construction of this sentence is not at all Pauline : for not only is the correlative τοσοῦτο—ὅσον (familiar to our author as to Philo[1]) nowhere found in the writings of St. Paul, but also παρά c. accusat., for the gen. *comparationis*, which is a favourite construction in this epistle, is almost unknown to St. Paul (excepting perhaps at Rom. xiv. 8), but not so to St. Luke, being found in his Gospel (iii. 13). The comparative διαφορώτερος (from διάφορος, which elsewhere, when it signifies superiority of rank, is construed with the genitive, and when mere opposition, with the dative) is, so far as the New Testament is concerned, an ἅπαξ λεγόμενον. It has been produced hitherto from no other profane author but Sixtus Empiricus. Further, κρείττων, although not an unpauline word, is yet a *special* favourite with the writer of this epistle, generally used by him in the sense of superiority in goodness, but here in that of superiority in power. Clemens Romanus (*loc. cit.*) employs for it μείζων.[2] Having assured ourselves of the abidingly present signification of the participle ὤν in ver. 3, we cannot overlook the antithetical relation to it of γενόμενος here (τοσούτῳ κρείττων γενόμενος τῶν ἀγγέλων). What the Son was in Himself before all time, and what He was and always has been and is to the world as such, His true personal being and personal manifestation, which had been for a time clouded and concealed in His self-humiliation : all this is now contrasted with that which, after the accomplishment of His atoning work, He has *become*, being seated at the right hand of God, and

[1] *e.g.* ἐφ' ὅσον δὲ κρείττων ὁ ποιῶν ἐπὶ τοσοῦτο καὶ τὸ γεγόμενον ἄμεινον. Ed. Mangey, i. p. 33 ; *De Mundi Opif.* H. 49.

[2] Which notion the fundamental signification of this comparative seems well fitted to express, as indeed it does elsewhere in our epistle. For κρατύς, the positive, is "*strong*," "*vigorous*," "*powerful*;" and κρείττων is =κρατύτερος (vid. *Etymol. Magnum*, p. 537, 17 ; *Etym. Gud.* p. 344, 23 ; and the *Scholia ad Plat.* p. 219, collected by RUHNKEN, concerning the otherwise inexplicable Oxymoron, which this derivation of κρείττων makes clear : τὸ χεῖρον κρεῖττον τοῦ ἀμείνονος).

exalted above the angels, with one of whom (Michael the *Metatron*, probably = "Mediator") Jewish theology was certainly not indisposed to identify Him. In the correlative member of the sentence, ὅσῳ διαφορώτερον παρ' αὐτοὺς κεκληρονόμηκεν ὄνομα, we find the assertion that the sublime exclusiveness of His super-angelic exaltation finds its correlative in the sublime exclusiveness of a super-angelic *name*, which He has obtained, and continues to hold for ever. (This last thought may be found in the choice of the perfect κεκληρονόμηκεν, instead of the aorist.) We *might* also find a further meaning in κεκληρονόμηκεν; but in the word κληρονομεῖν the notion of inheritance often falls into the background, and the meaning becomes simply that of possessing, *possidere, possidendum accipere*, with following *accusative*, or in the older language, *genitive*. Compare ירש and נחל.

The question remains, What "name" is here meant by the διαφορώτερον ὄνομα? Most commentators (and even Bleek, though making it the ground of a charge of ignorance against the writer) reply, "The name υἱός." For inasmuch as the angels, and even men, are not unfrequently called in the Old Testament "sons of God," Bleek supposes that the writer must have been unacquainted with the original language of Scripture, and that he was not only misled by the usual Septuagint rendering (in the recension represented by the Cod. Alex.) of בני האלהים by ἄγγελοι Θεοῦ, but also must have overlooked such passages as Ps. xxix. 1 and Ps. lxxxix. 7, where υἱοὶ τοῦ Θεοῦ is the reading in all MSS. But assuming the correctness of the answer, that υἱός IS the ὄνομα here spoken of, it would by no means be necessary to find for the sacred writer so miserable a justification. The fact is, that nowhere in the Old Testament is any single man or angel called "Son of God," or "the Son of God," or simply "the Son." The children of Israel are, as the elect people begotten of God, sometimes called Jehovah's first-born and Jehovah's children; so also the angels as a class among creaturely existences, and magistrates or rulers, as bearing the divine image, in their official or corporate capacity as God's representatives and servants here below, are called sons of (בני האלהים) Elohim or Elim (אלים, Ps. xxix. 1), or even themselves Elohim (אלהים); but in no place whatever of the Old Testament does any one single angle or man receive the name or call himself Son of Jehovah or Son of God (בן־האלהים). It is therefore true that this name בר or υἱός does appertain to the exalted Jesus as a personal name, in a way that it does not to any other being from among angels or men. But does it appertain to Him *as the exalted One?* Is it not rather (if we have rightly understood vers. 1–3) the name which has accompanied our Redeemer in all His manifestations, from eternity itself and the commencement of creation, through His work for us here below, and up again to the throne of God? Bleek himself has felt the difficulty, and accordingly explains the meaning of the writer thus : " *The dignity which He now possesses above the angels is in accordance with the name which from the beginning belonged to Him as His special prerogative above them.*" But it is only necessary to bear Phil. ii. 9 in mind, in order to see the inadmissibility of this way of evading the difficulty. Nor is it wanted. For although the name υἱός did certainly appertain to the now incarnate One even before His incarnation, yet is it also true, that at His exaltation the divine and human elements of His personality were for the first time so visibly and gloriously united, that the name υἱός may be said to have been then in all its fulness of meaning first imparted to Him. But nevertheless I cannot think that ὄνομα here is simply equivalent to υἱός, any more than that at Phil. ii. 9 the ὄνομα τὸ ὑπὲρ πᾶν ὄνομα means simply the name Κύριος. Still less at the same time should we be right in evaporating the concrete notion of the word ὄνομα into that of mere *dignitas*. What is here meant is that *heavenly name* of the glorified One, the *Shêm hammephôrêsh, nomen explicitum*, which on this side eternity no human ear has heard, no human heart conceived, no human tongue expressed—*the name which no one knoweth but Himself* (Rev. xix. 12). In the following quotations from Old Testament scriptures He is accordingly called not merely Υἱός, but also Θεός and Κύριος. These appellations belong to the ὄνομα of the glorified Jesus, as rays of light to the body of the sun. They are parts from which we infer what the whole must be. That super-angelic name which He, mounting up (be it noticed) through an earthly and historical development to the throne of God, has made eternally His own, lies above and beyond the notional fragmentariness of human speech. The following words of Scripture are but *indices*, which hint to us and help us to imagine how infinitely glorious that name must be.

The author now proceeds to enter on the discussion of the proper subject of his epistle, to which the transition has been made from the *prooemium* by ver. 4. He begins it in his rhetorical way by a question addressed to his readers, as men well acquainted with the scriptures to which he refers:

Ver. 5. *For to which of the angels hath he ever said, My son art thou, to-day have I begotten thee? And again, I will be to him a Father, and he shall be to me a son?*

The τίνι ποτε is not equivalent to *cui tandem*, but, as at ver. 13, to *cui unquam*. The question asked is therefore, Whether in the course of history God have ever so declared Himself concerning an angel? The subject (unexpressed) of εἶπε is ὁ Θεός (Clemens Romanus, δεσπότης), which the author, full of the conviction that God is the first and last originator of all Scripture (compare the usual formula of citation in the Talmud, אמר רחמנא, the Merciful One saith), is wont to omit. The note of interrogation is to be repeated at the end of the second clause, the whole verse being a twofold question, of which the last clause forms the second half. Of the two quotations from Scripture, the former is from Ps. ii. 7, repeated at chap. v. 5. (The same verse of the same Psalm is cited by St. Paul at Acts xiii. 13, the second and third verses at Acts iv. 24-26, and the ninth verse alluded to at Rev. xii. 5 and xix. 15, comp. ii. 27.) The second quotation from Scripture is 2 Sam. vii. 14 (1 Chron. xvii. 13). The former text has the latter for its historical basis. We begin, therefore, with the latter.

Jehovah is there (2 Sam. vii. 14) responding to David's high-hearted determination to build Him a house,—a determination founded on the still unfulfilled word of revelation, that the Lord should have a settled dwelling and sanctuary in the midst of Israel (Ex. xv. 17 and Deut. xii. 5), and favoured by the circumstances of the time, especially the then prevailing peace. Jehovah replies to it, through the prophet Nathan, with the promise that He will Himself build David a house; that David's seed shall hereafter possess by inheritance his royal throne, and that for ever; and finally, that this seed (not David himself), standing to Jehovah in the relation of son to father, shall build the Lord a house. This promise gave a new turn to the Messianic hopes and announcement. Prophecy had hitherto spoken of a King to rise out of the tribe of Judah (Num. xxiv. 17; 1 Sam. ii. 10, 35),[1] but left it undetermined whether David's family or some other should give birth to this King. That question is now solved. Henceforth all hopes and desires of the faithful are concentrated in *David's seed*, זרע דויד. But this seed of David is, in the first instance, not a definite individual, *i.e.* not exclusively so. The prophecy has respect to a boundless future, and has been in some measure fulfilled in all of David's race who have occupied his throne: in Solomon, therefore, who was not born at the time of its delivery, as well as in Jesus the Son of David. But the fulfilment was not exhausted in Solomon. The temple built by him was destroyed, his kingdom divided, his line ultimately deprived of the throne. It became therefore clear, as the history developed itself, that the prophecy, which could not remain unfulfilled, could only be accomplished in a descendant of David, who should at once be Son of God, build Jehovah an indestructible temple, and possess for ever an unshaken throne, no longer exposed to such vicissitudes. This descendant of David, in whom not only 2 Sam. vii. 13, etc., but also Isa. iv. 2 (Jer. xxiii. 5, xxxiii. 15) and Ps. cx., should be fulfilled, was foretold again by Zechariah (vi. 12, etc.), and appeared in Jesus, whose birth was announced by the angel with the words: δώσει αὐτῷ Κύριος ὁ Θεὸς τὸν θρόνον Δαυὶδ τοῦ πατρὸς αὐτοῦ. Καὶ βασιλεύσει ἐπὶ τὸν οἶκον Ἰακὼβ εἰς τοὺς αἰῶνας, καὶ τῆς βασιλείας αὐτοῦ οὐκ ἔσται τέλος (Luke i. 32, 33).

Our author is therefore justified in making for his special purpose this citation from 2 Sam. vii.: first, because the promise, ἐγὼ ἔσομαι αὐτῷ εἰς πατέρα, καὶ αὐτὸς ἔσται μοι εἰς υἱόν, speaks of a reciprocal relation between Jehovah and the seed of David, in which the Lord has never placed Himself with any angelic being ; and secondly, because when the prophecy is contemplated in the light thrown upon it by fulfilment, it becomes manifest that no other than Jesus Christ was the ultimate object of those words,—that without Him, as Hengstenberg has strikingly observed, the whole Davidic dynasty

---

[1] Delitzsch has omitted Gen. xlix. 10, which seems necessary to his argument.—Tr.

would be a headless trunk,—that in Him all the promises made to David's line attain their true accomplishment. It is easy to imagine how profound an influence the promise recorded in 2 Sam. vii. must have had on the Messianic element in the poetry of the Psalter, as it was indeed the one soul of all future Messianic announcements in the prophets. It is the proper theme of Pss. lxxxix. and cxxxii.: it is presupposed by, and forms the basis of, the second Psalm.

The main thought of that Psalm is the following: The obstinate rebellion of allied (Gentile) nations and their rulers against Jehovah and His Anointed will be broken in pieces by the unshaken, world-subduing power of the kingdom assigned by Jehovah to His King enthroned on the hill of Zion. It is evident that this idea of an all-conquering King, begotten of Jehovah, and named by Him His Son, rests on 2 Sam. vii. 14. The prophecy is individualized in the Psalm. It is unquestionably a member of David's family of whom the Psalm speaks. The Psalm is anonymous; and this is a presumption against the Davidic authorship not outweighed by Acts iv. 25, which adopts the ordinary formula of citation for all Psalms as "*Psalms of David.*" The psalmist, moreover, does not represent himself as the Lord's Anointed, but introduces Him as one of the speakers in the dramatic composition. But if David be not the author of the Psalm, there remain no necessary grounds for maintaining its merely typical and denying its direct prophetical character. It is, as it were, a lyrico-dramatic echo of that prophetic cycle of Isaiah, ch. vii.-xii., which, following Christian August Crusius, we would call *the Book of Immanuel.* The psalmist, living in the terrible Assyrian time, or one similar to that, and having therefore for *his* present an historical condition very fitted to prefigure the times of the end, is transported ἐν πνεύματι into the midst of those times, and contemplates the final conflict between the power of the world and Jehovah with His Christ, upborne by the conviction that all the kingdoms of the world will be theirs in the end (Rev. xi. 15, xii. 10). The Lord's Anointed, of whom the psalmist speaks, is the same as He whom Isaiah exhibits, under the name of Immanuel, as an image of terror to the enemies of David's house and people but one of unspeakable comfort to God's faithful ones. The Anointed begins at ver. 7 Himself to speak, and tells of a *decree* (חק from חקק, to engrave), an original and immutable ordinance which can never be disputed or set aside. In fearless self-conscious strength He holds forth against those who are now disputing His sovereignty a divine immutable decision. *Jehovah spake to me, My Son art Thou; Myself this day have I begotten Thee.*

The translation, υἱός μου εἶ σύ· ἐγὼ σήμερον γεγέννηκά σε, is *exact*. ילד is found elsewhere in the sense of *begetting* (not *giving birth to*), though rarely, e.g. Gen. iv. 18. It is not therefore necessary to translate, with Hupfeld, *This day have I borne Thee*; nay, inasmuch as the relation predicated is one in virtue of which He who enters it can say (Ps. lxxxix. 27) אבי אתה, such translation would be inadmissible. But what kind of *begetting* is it that is here meant? Not surely a begetting into natural existence: the child in embryo is not the proper subject of such an address. It must be, then, a begetting before and after which the man who is the object of it stands over against God his Father as a fully self-conscious person, able to perceive and know what is done to him. The matter here in hand being institution into royalty, the begetting spoken of must be a begetting into royal existence, which is the inward reality symbolized by the anointing.[1] This sense of ילדתיך, derived from a consideration of the context in the Psalm, is that also assigned to it by the sacred writer in his application of it here. He does *not* refer it to the eternal ante-mundane generation of the Son (see note to ch. v. 5), nor to the miraculous conception by the Holy Ghost in the womb of Mary which imaged forth that archetypal generation, but to the Lord's entrance into the royal estate of divine and super-mundane glory (see von Gerlach). The moment at which this entrance commenced was the resurrection. St. Paul therefore, in full accordance with our epistle, refers the γεγέννηκά σε of the Psalm to the resurrection of Jesus (Acts xiii. 33, comp. Rom. i. 4). That resurrection was a *begetting* into a new and heavenly life, over which death could have no more power. Jesus, before and for us all, became the first-born or first-begotten from the dead (Col. i. 18; Rev. i. 5).[2] The thought is fundamentally the same when, in

---

[1] The ancient synagogue interpreted the בכור (first-born) of Ps. lxxxix. 28 (27) in this *royal* sense, and regarded it as Messianic.

[2] ἀναστήσας at Acts xiii. 32 *might* be interpreted, with appeal to the

CHAP. I. 5.   65

the twelfth chapter of the Apocalypse, the historical manifestation of Christ (in the almightiness predicted by Ps. ii. 9, with the iron sceptre of world-conquering power) is viewed under the image of a birth from the midst of the church in whose bosom He has vouchsafed to dwell. The same sense of γεγέννηκά σε is here presupposed, only another point is fixed for the σήμερον, the final consummation in the general judgment. This, from the elasticity of the notion "to-day," is quite admissible. Compare σήμερον, ch. iv. 6–9, with היום in Ps. xcv. 7. The apostles did not originate this interpretation of Ps. ii., in which they all substantially agree. The Psalm was in their time universally regarded as a prophetic one. The two names for Messiah, ὁ Χριστός and ὁ υἱὸς τοῦ Θεοῦ, in the mouth of Israelites (John i. 50 ; Matt. xxvi. 63), involved a reference to it. The apostles did nothing more than *testify* that JESUS was the all-conquering Christ and Son of Jehovah of whom the Psalm had spoken. Having appeared on earth in the person of Jesus, He was now in the same Jesus enthroned in heaven. And so our author teaches here. The Atonement-maker, the exalted One of whom he speaks, bears at Ps. ii. 7 and 2 Sam. vii. 14 a name which no angel bears, and which, in that absolute sense, no other man could bear but He.

The words which follow (ver. 6), introducing a third quotation from Scripture, are difficult. On a superficial view, it would seem natural to regard πάλιν as having the same meaning as at ver. 5, *i.e.* as simply introducing the fresh quotation, and to assume that εἰσάγειν εἰς τὴν οἰκουμένην, like εἰσέρχεσθαι εἰς τὸν κόσμον (x. 5), refers to the Son's first entrance into the created universe by the incarnation. (So the Peshito, Erasmus, Luther since 1528, Calvin, Beza, Schlichting, Bengel, and many others.) But this interpretation proves, on closer inquiry, to be grammatically and exegetically untenable. It is

ἀναστήσει of Acts vii. 37, thus : *inasmuch as He raised up Jesus as a prophet.* But that it really should refer to the *resurrection* is, after Acts ii. 24, 32, just as possible, and the arrangement of the whole speech favours the assumption that it does so ; for vers. 23-25 speak of the first appearance of Jesus, vers. 26-29 of His death and burial, vers. 30, 31 of His resurrection : on which last it is natural to suppose the apostle lingering at ver. 32. Nor is the relation of ver. 34 to ver. 33 against this: ver. 33 treats of the *resurrection* as such, ver. 34 of the eternal life on which the risen One has entered, and both in words borrowed from Old Testament Scripture.

VOL. I.   E

so grammatically; (1.) because ὅταν (= ὅτε ἀν) with following aorist conjunctive cannot possibly be rendered by *cum introduxit* (Bleek). The aorist conjunctive here corresponds to the Latin *futurum exactum* (ὅταν ἴδω = *cum videro*, whereas ὅταν ὁρῶ = *cum video*), and must therefore be rendered *cum introduxerit*, "*when he shall have brought in.*" This holds good whenever a *future* (verb) stands in the *apodosis* (comp. Acts xxiii. 35), or an *imperative* (Luke xvii. 10), or even a *present* involving a *future* signification, or for which a *future* might be substituted (*e.g.* Matt. v. 11). [Compare Od. xi. 218, αὕτη δίκη ἐστὶ βροτῶν ὅτε κέν τε θάνωσιν, i.e. "Such is (*will be*) the fate of mortals when they are dead" (*shall have died*), which might indeed be rendered "when they die," but with neglect of the exact significance of the Greek expression.] The same meaning (that of the *futurum exactum*) must be assigned to ὅταν εἴπῃ in the one doubtful passage, 1 Cor. xv. 27, which expresses in the very briefest form this thought: "When it shall be said, 'All things are put under Him' (*i.e.* when the promise in Ps. viii. 7 shall have been finally accomplished), then, as is clear, He will be still an exception who shall have thus subjected all things to Him." (2.) Πάλιν, to have the meaning assigned to it above, would have to be explained by assuming a *trajection* (= πάλιν δέ, ὅταν, κ.τ.λ.); but when thus introducing a new citation, πάλιν *always* stands elsewhere in the Epistle to the Hebrews (as in the rest of the New Testament and in Philo) at the beginning of the sentence: comp. ii. 13, iv. 5, x. 30. Moreover, on *other* grounds, the rendering "*again when He bringeth in*" is untenable. For (1) the sacred writer, having already applied (in ver. 5) two passages of Scripture to the historical manifestation of the Son, would hardly with a simple δέ go on to apply a third to His first (invisible) entrance into the world; and, moreover, (2) a glance at ch. ii. shows that he regarded the Son as in His historical manifestation for a time subjected below the angels (παρ' ἀγγέλους), while *their* subjection to Him is always connected in the New Testament (Phil. ii. 9, etc.; Eph. i. 20–22; 1 Pet. iii. 21, etc.) with the *status exaltationis*. We must therefore translate :

Ver. 6. *And when he shall have again brought in the first-*

begotten into the world, he saith, And worship him let all the angels of God.

The former clause (*protasis*) thus rendered cannot be referred either to the incarnation (as, for instance, among the ancients[1] by Remigius Primasius, and among moderns by Ebrard), or to any transaction supposed to have taken place before the incarnation, but not elsewhere mentioned in Scripture (as by Bleek), or even to the resurrection (as by Brentius junior), but only to the *second advent*, the visible re-introduction of the risen One who is now hid in God. So, among moderns, Böhme, Tholuck, De Wette, Lünemann, Biesenthal, and Hofmann (*Schriftb.* i. 151). With the last (Hofmann) we here *so far* agree; without, however, being able to endorse his assertion (*Schriftb.* i. 113), that the *antithesis* in which ver. 6 stands to ver. 5 makes it certain that it is the first introduction of the Son of God into the world which is there referred to, and therefore neither the resurrection nor any other event in the Lord's life subsequent to the incarnation itself. But surely there is no real injury done to the *antithesis* which is here unquestionably made between the first and the second advent, if ver. 5 be referred (as by us) to the royal fulfilment of the filial relation of the man Christ Jesus to the heavenly Father which resulted from His resurrection, and marked the close of His first advent. The true meaning of ילדתיך at Ps. ii. 7, so convincingly established by Hofmann himself (*Weiss.* i. 160; *Schriftb.* ii. 1, 66), is, when applied to Jesus, as unfavourable as possible to the reference of ver. 5 to the commencement of our Lord's earthly life, instead of to that anointing and entrance on the kingly state which in the New Testament are always regarded as subsequent to it. But if, on the other hand, we take ver. 5 as referring to our Lord's resurrection and exaltation, how genuinely Pauline is the expression chosen to describe His second coming! The returning Saviour is here called πρωτότοκος (a term nowhere else employed so absolutely, and marking our epistle as one of the last of the Pauline epistles); and He is so called, as Hofmann himself says, chiefly because He is regarded as the first-born among many brethren, and therefore in the

---

[1] Patristic exegesis shows here (as elsewhere) how soon the church began to lose sight of the second advent, if not as an object of faith, yet as one of hope and expectation.

sense of Rom. viii. 29. That title, "first-born among many brethren," belongs to Him as the risen One, One who has been born of God into the new life of the Spirit and glorification,— the first new man who has experienced a birth out of the womb of the grave, and the founder of a new humanity, enjoying a primacy both of time and rank above His fellows. This new primacy corresponds to the dignity of the original filial relation enjoyed from eternity, and within the developments of time it impresses on Him above all creatures the divine seal (Col. i. 15). As strikingly remarked by Stier, "*the Only-begotten becomes, in His glorified humanity as the Son with many brethren, the first-born among them.*" As such a first-born or first-begotten, He appeared only now and then to His disciples during the forty days. But as *such*, and not (as before) as a man merely of our Adam kind, will *the Father* one day bring Him back into the οἰκουμένη, which He has determined to judge by Him (Acts xvii. 31). Οἰκουμένη is not to be taken here in definite universality, to express the complex of created things (Bleek), but in the same *indefinite* universality in which we use the word *world*. It is assumed thereby that the risen Jesus has gone back into a state of supra-mundane being with God, out of which He will one day come forth. The Father will then acknowledge Him, and make, by His almighty word, not only men but angels to bow down before Him.

The subject of λέγει is ὁ Θεός, not ἡ γράφη, as before ver. 5 and in all following citations from Scripture (compare v. 5 etc., viii. 5, 8). Λέγει itself is a logical future ("He will say—will command the angels to worship Him"), expressed as a present, because the future divine word of command is already signified in Scripture (Lünemann), or rather present to the writer's mind as standing fixed in the prophetic word. The quotation is here made from the additional clause added by the LXX. to Deut. xxxii. 43, from whence it is also quoted by Justin Martyr in the *Dial. c. Tryphone*. The one verse-line הרנינו גוים עמו, *Rejoice ye nations with His people*, is there expanded fourfold, thus:

εὐφράνθητε οὐρανοὶ ἅμα αὐτῷ,
καὶ προσκυνησάτωσαν αὐτῷ πάντες ἄγγελοι Θεοῦ.
εὐφράνθητε ἔθνη μετὰ τοῦ λαοῦ αὐτοῦ,
καὶ ἐνισχυσάτωσαν αὐτῷ πάντες υἱοὶ Θεοῦ.

These four lines, the third of which, corresponding to the Hebrew text, is cited by St. Paul, Rom. xv. 10, are found in all codices of the LXX.: they appear as we have given them in the Codex Vaticanus, and in the collection of Old Testament Canticles appended to the Psalter in the Codex Alexandrinus, while in the text of that Codex the second line reads,

καὶ προσκυνησάτωσαν αὐτῷ πάντες υἱοὶ Θεὸν,

and the fourth line,

καὶ ἐνισχυσάτωσαν αὐτοὺς πάντες ἄγγελοι αὐτοῦ.

The reading αὐτούς is certainly a false one; the very singularity of the expression ἐνισχυσάτωσαν proves that in this angelological expansion of the original text the LXX. must have followed some Hebrew authority (compare ver. 8, κατὰ ἀριθμὸν ἀγγέλων Θεοῦ). The whole is a mosaic from Isa. xliv. 23, Ps. xcvii. 7, and Ps. xxix. 1, with the הבו עז, *Give ye strength* (*unto the Lord*), of the latter Psalm changed into ויתנו עז; for ἐνισχυσάτωσαν αὐτῷ is correctly interpreted by Epiphanius (*Hær.* lxix.) as = ὁμολογείτωσαν τὴν ἰσχὺν αὐτοῦ. These additions and changes were probably due to the liturgical use of Moses' song, and the endeavour to give it a more hymn-like close. The sacred writer is here apparently quoting a not properly canonical portion of the Scriptures of the Old Testament. Some have sought to justify him, by assuming that he is not really quoting the passage from Deuteronomy, but from the Psalm (xcvii. 7), or at least makes his citation of it with its canonical position there in his mind. The *fact* however is, that the interpolater (whoever he was) of Deut. xxxii. 43 took the second line of his passage from the Psalm, and that our author now adopts it from him, with retention even of the καί with which he had introduced it. If, therefore, he require justification, such must be sought in a different way from that proposed above. The evasion that no citation is made at all, but that our author clothes a truth made known to him in some other way in words borrowed from the LXX., is based on self-deception. It is a real *bona fide* citation. At the same time, it cannot be maintained that he attributes anything like an equal authority to the LXX. version with that of the original text, though (it may be) a derived one; for it is certain that the writers of the New Testament (while holding the Alexandrine translation in due honour as an epoch-making providential phenomenon in the religious history of Israel) did by no means regard it in the same superstitious light as the Alexandrine Jews and the later Greek fathers. This is evident from their critical treatment of the quotations which they make from it, not unfrequently improving them, or even giving an independent version of their own. We would therefore rather say, that our author was justified in citing from the Septuagint version of Deut. xxxii. 43 the words καὶ προσκυνησάτωσαν αὐτῷ πάντες ἄγγελοι Θεοῦ, by the fact of their agreeing with what the Scripture elsewhere says of the final advent of Jehovah, and of their meaning being set in the clearest light by the connection in which they there appear at the close of the great Mosaic song.

Deut. xxxii. is a grand prophetic utterance which laid the foundation for all subsequent prophecies: it sums up in a pleasing poetic form, easily retained in memory, the contents of Moses' third sermon, ch. xxvii.-xxx., and bears a similar relation to those chapters as the third of Habakkuk to ch. i. and ii. It takes its stand in the distant future, in which its warning testimonies against Israel will be accomplished. Calling heaven and earth to witness, the great lawgiver transports himself into the time in which Israel will repay his God for the rich abundance of His mercies with apostasy to other *elohim*. At that time this song shall proclaim in his ears the word of Jehovah. Jehovah Himself is introduced speaking at ver. 20, ויאמר bearing through Moses' words His own witness. In four clearly defined and richly coloured pictures, the whole of Israel's history to the end of days is set before them: first, Israel's creation and redemption; then Israel's ingratitude and apostasy; then God's primitive judgments; and finally, Israel's ultimate salvation through the judgment-fire. These are no mere abstract commonplaces, but real concrete history-developing ideas, the actual cycles through which the history of Israel, as of the whole church of God, must run, till, after passing through the last and most decisive of them all, the reconciled but sifted people of God, the church gathered for His praise out of Jews and Gentiles, will see no other crisis or change before it but the final passing out of time into eternity. In the view of this final self-revelation of Jehovah in judgment and in mercy, the conclusion of the song, as given by the LXX., calls on the heavens to rejoice and the *elohim* to worship. This call stands in the closest relation to ver. 17, ἔθυσαν δαιμονίοις καὶ οὐ Θεῷ, θεοῖς οἷς οὐκ ᾔδεισαν, and to the strange variation from the original text at ver. 8 (to be understood by a reference to iv. 19), ἔστησεν ὅρια ἐθνῶν κατὰ ἀριθμὸν ἀγγέλων Θεοῦ. The *elohim* who are called upon to worship Jehovah are the supra-mundane cosmic powers which had been deified among the Gentiles, and by Israel in its apostasy to Gentile heathenism. And that is the exact meaning of the parallel in Ps. xcvii., the third strophe of which Psalm reads as follows:

Ver. 7. *Ashamed be all the image-worshippers*
Who boast themselves of idol-gods;
Adore Him, all ye elohim !
8. *This Zion hearing doth rejoice,*
And Judah's daughters shout for joy,
Because of these Thy judgments, O Jehovah !

The Septuagint translation here, προσκυνήσατε, is quite correct, for השתחוו is imperative, not preterite; and St. Augustine gives the sense in the fine observation : "*Adorate eum ;*" *cessat igitur adoratio angelorum qui non adorantur sed adorant: mali angeli volunt adorari, boni adorant nec se adorari permittunt, ut vel saltem eorum exemplo idololatriæ cessent.*

The next question is, With what right or with what reason does the author refer to Christ a passage which apparently simply speaks of Jehovah? The answer is a miserable one : that, being entirely unacquainted with the Hebrew text, he was misled by the Κύριος of the LXX.; and incredible is also the assertion (of Vaihinger for instance, *Ps.* ii. p. 125), that he may have regarded all Old Testament passages in which Jehovah (the LORD) is spoken of as requiring or admitting of immediate application to Christ. The explanation sometimes offered of the application in regard to this particular passage— namely, that the sacred writer was led to it by the correlative antithesis of Israel as the πρωτότοκος of whose future the prophecy (Deut. xxxii.) speaks, and of Christ as the πρωτότοκος in whom the promises will be actually accomplished—is too far-fetched a method of evading the difficulty. The principle on which the writer proceeds is a general one, namely this : that wherever the Old Testament speaks of a final and decisive advent and manifestation of Jehovah in the power and glory of the final judgment and salvation; wherever it speaks of a revelation of Jehovah which shall be the antitype and fulfilment of that typical one in the Mosaic time, of a self-presentation of Jehovah as manifested King over His own kingdom, there Jehovah = Jesus Christ; for Christ is "Jehovah manifested in the flesh,"—Jehovah Himself entering into fellowship with humankind, and taking part in our historical developments,— Jehovah rising as the Sun of righteousness, and shining on His own people. This principle is irrefragably true; it constitutes the innermost bond between the two Testaments. All writers of the New Testament are fully conscious of it. This consciousness finds an utterance on the very threshold of the evangelical history; for, as Malachi foretells that Elias is to be sent " before the day of Jehovah" (יום יהוה), so the angel and Zacharias in St. Luke speak of John the Baptist as going "before the Lord" (ἐνώπιον Κυρίου); compare Mal. iv. 5 (Heb. iii. 23) with Luke i. 17, 76. On the same principle, all psalms in which the realization of the world-subduing kingdom of Jehovah is celebrated are strictly *Messianic*, and are regarded as such by our author. The final glory of the theocracy is in God's plan of redemption no other than a Christocracy; the kingdom of Jehovah and the kingdom of Christ are one.

Having now (ver. 6) antithetically *opposed* (with δέ) the angels to the Son, the sacred writer proceeds (with another δέ preceded by μέν) to *oppose* in a similar manner the Son to the angels (ver. 7 and foll.):

Ver. 7. *And while in reference to the angels he saith, Who maketh his angels into winds, and his ministers a flame of fire, saith he in reference to the Son.*

Bengel observes, *ad angelos indirecto sermone, ad filium directo*, but not correctly; for the preposition πρός, which expresses the *direction* of an utterance to some particular object, whether that object be actually *addressed* or merely referred to, is to be understood *both* times here in the latter sense (so iv. 13, xi. 18; Luke xx. 19, xii. 41 (according to Bengel, also xix. 9); Rom. x. 21 (Winer, § 49, *h*)). The citation is from Ps. civ. 4. The Septuagint rendering is, according to the Codex Vaticanus, ὁ ποιῶν τοὺς ἀγγέλους αὐτοῦ πνεύματα, καὶ τοὺς λειτουργοὺς αὐτοῦ πῦρ φλέγον, for which the Cod. Alexandr. reads πυρὸς φλέγα, but that *secunda manu* (a fact which commentators have omitted to notice), and therefore apparently by a mere correction derived from the text of our epistle here, πυρὸς φλόγα. The Psalm celebrates the glory of Jehovah as Creator and Lord of the existing universe, with retrospective glance at the creative beginnings as recorded Gen. i. The arrangement of the Psalm is, however, not a definite one in accordance with the history in Genesis. The psalmist passes insensibly from one day's work to another, his own point of view being the now complicated and interwoven whole of the finished creative works. At the same time, it is evident that ver. 2*a* corresponds in a lyric way to the work of the first day, vers. 2*b*-4 to that of the second (firmament, upper waters, winds, and fire, *i.e.* lightnings, being the phenomena which he celebrates). This parallelism would forbid our understanding ver. 4 as referring to the creation of the angels. Yet the now prevalent view, that the rendering of the LXX. is a mistake, and that ver. 4 ought to be translated, "*who maketh winds His messengers, and flaming fire His ministers*," is not so certainly true as expositors imagine, of whom no one has of late opposed it except von Gerlach, and no one carefully examined and tested it except Hofmann (*Schriftb.* i. 282), by whom it is rejected. And that with full right. For against this view may be observed, 1*st*, That it necessitates the combination of an object in the singular with a predicate in the plural number—*He maketh a flame of fire His ministers*— instead of saying, "He maketh lightning-flashes His ministers." This remark was already anticipated by Piscator, J. H. Michaelis, and others. Then, 2*dly*, עשׂה *with double accusative signifies* (according to Hofmann) *not the making a thing into something else, but the setting up or presenting as something.* He renders accordingly: *creating His messengers like winds, and His ministers as a flame of fire.* But this needs some correction. Undoubtedly, indeed, עשׂה with double accusative *may* mean to make or exhibit as something, so that we might render the sentence either way, *making winds His messengers,* or *making His messengers winds,* without doing violence to the language. But this is all that can be said. The idiom of the language would rather require נתן or שׂים with double accusative to express this sense; or if עשׂה be employed, then that a ל should be placed before the predicate.¹ עשׂה with double accusative does not mean *to make into something*, but *to make out of something*, so that we should have to render the clause, either *making winds of His messengers*, or, *making His messengers of winds*. The latter rendering, if we must choose between the two, is undoubtedly the right one. That which is logically the second accusative after עשׂה, denoting the *materia ex qua*, may be either placed first, as at Ex. xxv. 39, xxx. 25, or second, as here; compare Ex. xxxvii. 23, xxxviii. 3, and especially Gen. ii. 7. But God's making "His messengers out of winds," "His ministers out of flaming fire," may be understood in *two* ways: 1*st*, as mere *personification*, as when the storm-wind is said to be "doing His word" (Ps. cxlviii. 8, עֹשָׂה דְבָרוֹ); or 2*dly*, as referring to *real persons*, the angels, who (Ps. ciii. 20) are likewise spoken of as עֹשֵׂי דְבָרוֹ. The meaning would then be (as Gussetius already correctly observed), that God makes His angels out of winds, His ministers out of flaming fire, *vestiendo eos substantia venti, etc., ut cum salomo "valras ligneas aurum"* (2 Chron. iv. 18–22) *fecisse dicitur, quando eas substantia auri vestivit*. Which of these thoughts the psalmist himself combined with his words cannot be positively determined; but the conception that God gives His angels, when employing them to carry out His purposes in the sensible universe, elemental bodies, as it were, of wind and fire, as *media* of manifestation, is certainly the deeper of the two, and not unsuited to such a lyrical echo as the Psalm is meant to be of the great creative beginning. In this sense, also, the rendering of the Targum must be understood when read in the light of the Midrash [on which it is based]: "*Who maketh His messengers speedy as the wind, His ministers strong as a flaming fire*" (compare the passages in Schöttgen and Wetstein). That our author here understood the text in the Psalm in this sense cannot be

---

¹ It is instructive to observe that Abraham Cohen of Zante, in his beautiful paraphrase of the Psalms (Venice 1719), following the interpretation which, since Rashi, Abenezra, Kimchi, has been among Jews the usual one of Ps. civ. 4, thus renders it:

שת רוחות היות מלאכיו ויעש
לו למשרתיו אש להט שלהבת.

doubted. He may, indeed, on that very account (as Böhme suggests) have altered the πῦρ φλέγον of the Septuagint into πυρὸς φλόγα, and perhaps have had the appearance of the angel at Ex. iii. 2, ἐν φλογὶ πυρὸς ἐκ τοῦ βάτου, in his mind, as an instance of what the psalmist was speaking of.

He now proceeds (ver. 8 and foll.) to exhibit from another passage in the Psalter how far exalted above the angels is the Son. The angels are subject to change according to the will of God, whose servants they are, while *He* is the unchangeable, ever-reigning King. The chief point of the *antithesis* is the dependent and changing service, in contrast to the divine and immutable sovereignty.

Ver. 8. (*He saith*) *in reference to the Son: Thy throne, O God, is for the ages; a sceptre of rectitude is the sceptre of thy kingdom. Thou lovest righteousness, and hatest wrong; therefore, O God, hath thy God anointed thee with oil of gladness above thy fellows.*

Πρός has here again (as frequently ל and אל in Hebrew) merely the sense of *relation* or *reference to* (Hof. *Weiss.* ii. 32); for God is not Himself addressing the Son in this passage of the forty-fifth Psalm, but (as our author understands it) speaking of Him, inasmuch as he regards the whole contents of Scripture as being the word and utterance of God Himself. The verses of the Psalm which he cites are vers. 7, 8. In the words εἰς τὸν αἰῶνα τοῦ αἰῶνος he agrees with that recension of the text which is represented by the *Codex Alex.* (the *Vaticanus* reading εἰς αἰῶνα αἰῶνος), but in ἐμίσησας ἀνομίαν he agrees with the *Codex Vaticanus* (the *Alexandrinus* only, along with some cursive MSS., reading ἀδικίας).[1] There would be a departing from both recensions, if, instead of ῥάβδος εὐθύτητος, we read with Lachmann, following A. B. 53[2] (the above-mentioned Uffenbachian Uncial-Fragments), καὶ ἡ ῥάβδος τῆς εὐθύτητος ῥάβδος τῆς βασιλείας σου. But this aimless defining of the predicate (by means of the article) no one would probably defend. Lachmann himself did afterwards strike out the article before the predicate, without placing it before the subject. On the other hand, Bleek, Lünemann, and Hofmann

---

[1] The Cod. Sinait. also reads ἀδικίαν at Heb. i. 9.—Tr.
[2] So also the Cod. Sinait.—Tr.

adopt the καί (which is also represented in the Itala *Cod. Claromont.* and the Vulgate *Cod. Amiatin.*), regarding it as introducing the second half of the passage as a fresh quotation. Hofmann finds a special reason for this καί. His words are (*Schriftbeweis*, i. 148): " *This division of the passage in the Psalm has its motive in the form it takes in the Greek translation, which the author of the epistle was compelled, as I imagine, for his readers' sake, to make use of. In that translation the first part of the passage is so rendered as necessarily to be understood as addressed to God Himself, Jehovah, while in the original text it is the King of whose throne (as being Jehovah's throne) it is affirmed that it will stand for ever. The author, cutting off from this the remaining part of his quotation, which is unambiguously* [*in the Greek as well as the Hebrew*] *an address to the King* (ὁ Θεὸς ὁ Θεός σου *being evidently opposed as subject to Him whose* μέτοχοι *are mentioned*), *leaves his reader at liberty to regard* ὁ θρόνος σου ὁ Θεός *either as addressed to Jehovah Himself, or, with a correct understanding of the connection of* כסאך אלהים, *as addressed to His anointed King.*" But ever. assuming that this καί is genuine, and that its real purpose is to divide the one well-connected passage into two citations,[1] it cannot possibly have the object which Hofmann assigns to it. The very point of the argument for the superiority of the Son above the angels, drawn from Ps. xlv. 7 and foll., lies surely in the fact that He is here twice, or at least once, addressed in the vocative as ὁ Θεός. This at least is the impression which the quotation would naturally make on every dogmatically or apologetically unprejudiced mind. It is quite impossible that it should have been the author's deliberate intention by means of that καί to take the whole point out of his argument. His meaning is, in the first place, to be gathered from his own words, and not to be measured by *our* views of theological or typological development, which we rather ought to compare with and correct by his.

To me, then, it appears quite undeniable that the author in the first place regards the forty-fifth Psalm as a not merely

---

[1] This καί has the authority of A. B. D.* E.* and some cursives and versions. If meant to divide the citation of Ps. xlv. into two halves, we should rather expect to find it placed (after the analogy καὶ πάλιν of ii. 13) before ἠγάπησας than before ῥάβδος.

CHAP. I. 8.

typico-Messianic, but as a directly prophetico-Messianic Psalm; and secondly, that he finds there that now exalted Messiah who has appeared in Jesus addressed as ὁ Θεός, God! as in Ps. ii. He is called υἱός, the Son. And indeed it really is a Messianic Psalm; for even were it not directly and prophetically Messianic in the first intention, it soon became so. In its *first intention* it appears to have been an epithalamium, and therefore entitled שיר ידידות, "a song of lovely things," or (if *ôth* be here equivalent to the abstract termination *ûth*) "a song of love," *i.e.* a bridal song. Whoever the king may have been who was thus honoured on his wedding-day, whether Solomon on his espousals with Pharaoh's daughter (as Hofmann assumes), or Joram (as I think) on his marriage with Athaliah,[1] a princess of Tyrian descent on the mother's side, in either case the Psalm is so far Messianic that it embodies the psalmist's desire to see the idea of the theocratic kingdom, and so the promise of the coming Messiah, fulfilled and realized in the then present king; a desire this which was not fulfilled, the whole line of kings from David down to Zedekiah falling miserably short of that idea and of that promise. Nevertheless the Psalm itself became a standing portion of the Psalter and (as the title למנצה indicates) of the temple liturgy. Separated from its first historical reference and occasion, and so removed from its lower and original literal sense, it became a Messianic hymn of the church of Israel, and of directly prophetical character. It underwent a spiritual metamorphosis by this practical allegorizing in the use thus made of it. For by this change the queen of the Psalm becomes the congregation of Israel espoused to the Messias; her "companions" represent henceforth the converted Gentile nations; the "children" are a spiritual offspring; and the royal marriage is the highest point of the future union of Christ with Israel and the "nations" when finally gathered into one church. This revolution in the interpretation of the Psalm is of very high antiquity, and similar to that undergone by the Song of Songs and the locusts of Joel. Its justification will be found in the sublime ideal manner in which the psalmist treats his historical materials regarding the passing events of his time—not as common history, but from a thoroughly Messianic point of view. His own heart's desire is, that the

[1] See Delitzsch's *Comm. on the Psalter in loc.*—Tr.

king whom he celebrates may indeed prove to be the long promised Messias of Israel, even as throughout the O. T. we find similar Messianic hopes and longings attaching themselves to such kings as David and Solomon, Jehoshaphat and Hezekiah, etc. etc.,—hopes and desires which, failing all in their primary objects, are finally concentrated in the person of the second David, and become yea and amen in Jesus Christ. And so the original reference of this forty-fifth Psalm to the person of a king who failed to realize it, is, after that failure, laid aside and forgotten, but the Psalm itself remains standing as a prophecy which still awaits fulfilment. As such a prophecy it was already accounted by the prophets who wrote after the times of Jehoshaphat. So Isaiah (ch. lxi. 1-3) transfers certain of its words to the servant of Jehovah, the anointed One, who gives the שֶׁמֶן שָׂשׂוֹן (oil of gladness) "for mourning," and at ch. ix. 5 combines the גבור of Ps. xlv. 4 (E.V. ver. 3) and the אלהים of ver. 7 (E.V. ver. 6) in the composite Messianic name of אל גבור (*Deus fortis*); compare also x. 21, "*The remnant shall return . . . to the* אל גבור." In a similar spirit Zechariah, at xii. 8, prophesies that in the latter day the house of David shall be "as God" (כאלהים) and "as the angel of Jehovah" (כמלאך ה') "before," or at the head of, His people. Whatever, therefore, here and there the original meaning of the Psalm may have been, the author of our epistle must be recognised as having an old prophetic basis for his interpretation of it. And however that might be, it could not be denied that he understands the vocative ὁ Θεός in ὁ θρόνος σου, ὁ Θεός, εἰς τὸν αἰῶνα τοῦ αἰῶνος, as addressed to the Messiah. The Hebrew text here admits certainly of various renderings. 1*st,* אלהים (as vocative) may be taken as addressed to God Himself, whose "throne is from generation to generation" (Lam. v. 19), and of whose divine holiness a "love of righteousness" and "hatred of iniquity" (ver. 8, E.V. ver. 7) are elsewhere spoken of as characteristics (comp. Ps. v. 5 and Isa. lxi. 8); or, 2*dly,* in order to uphold the interpretation that the whole clause is addressed to a human king, we might adopt Ewald's rendering, *Thy throne is a throne of Elohim for ever and ever;* or, 3*dly,* regarding it as an example of that idiom in the *syntaxis ornata* (of which we have instances at 2 Sam. xxii. 23 and Ezek. xvi. 27), we might render it, *Thy divine* (or glorious) *throne is for ever and ever;* while the author of our epistle, with at least equal right, has rendered it (in accordance with the first interpretation), *Thy throne, O God, is for ever and ever.*

But the question remains: Can we, thus regarding אלהים as the vocative, yet maintain the reference to the king of whom the Psalm speaks? We can, if not in its original,[1] yet at least in its prophetic sense and interpretation. We find, indeed, undeniable traces in the Old Testament of a prophetic *presentiment* that the great Messias of the future, who was destined to accomplish what had been vainly looked for in David and Solomon, etc., should also present in His own person an unexampled union of the human and divine. The mystery of the incarnation is still veiled under the Old Testament, and yet the two great lines of prophecy running through it—one leading on to a final manifestation of Jehovah, the other to the advent of a son of David—do so meet and coalesce at certain focal points, as by the light thus generated to burst through the veil. This is clear as day in the one passage, Isa. ix. 5, where the Messias is plainly called אל גבור (the Mighty God), an ancient traditional appellation for the Most High (Deut. x. 17; comp. Jer. xxxii. 18, Neh. ix. 32, Ps. xxiv. 8). And so (Jer. xxiii. 6) He is entitled "Jehovah our righteousness," following which, as Biesenthal has shown (p. 7), the ancient synagogue recognised Jehovah (יהוה) as one of the names of the Messiah. It was already part of the faith under the Old Testament, that the mighty God, the captain of Israel, the just God and the justifier, would hereafter manifest Himself in bodily form in the person of Messias; and it is therefore mere narrow-mindedness to accuse the author here of error in his interpretation of the forty-fifth Psalm. It remains a question, however, which cannot be decided, whether in the next verse (ver. 9) he understands the first ὁ Θεός as a vocative, or whether he takes it as a nominative to which the following is in apposition. *Against*

---

[1] It must be allowed, we think, that the psalmist could not have meant to address a merely human king, if the original subject of his song, as אלהים; for, 1*st*, though the ruling power as such is so entitled (Ex. xxi. 6, xxii. 8, etc.; Ps. lxxxii.), yet never a single representative of it (Ex. vii. 1 not being a case in point); and 2*d*, though the theocratic king is said to occupy *Jehovah's throne* (1 Chron. xxix. 23), all that is meant is that he is but the human instrument of Jehovah, the sole Ruler and King.

the vocative is the *usus loquendi* of the Elohim Psalms, according to which "Elohim thy Elohim" (God thy God) would be equivalent to "Jehovah thy Elohim" (the Lord thy God). But the thought itself (if "Elohim" be taken as a vocative, and we render the clause, *Therefore, O God, hath thy God anointed thee*) is not alien to the Old Testament. Isa. ix. 5 and xi. 2 come to the same thing. The King in whom all the hopes of Israel centre has already for Old Testament prophecy both a divine and a human side and character. And so He has, according to our author, in this forty-fifth Psalm. The divine side is expressed in the term Θεός, the human in His being God's Anointed. As such He is distinguished from all His μέτοχοι. Some (Lünemann, Peirce, Bleek, Olshausen) think that by these μέτοχοι are meant the angels. But the angels are not anointed ones, and therefore the μέτοχοι here must rather be all other earthly magistrates and kings, above whom this divine King is thus immeasurably raised. God, for His love of righteousness and hatred of iniquity, has anointed Him with "oil of gladness" beyond (παρά *c. acc.* as at ii. 7, and frequently after a comparative) them all, His being the most blissful and most glorious of all kingdoms. The Psalm describes that kingdom in various aspects. But the point with our author is, that its holy and righteous Sovereign is here called Θεός, and stands in the relation of kindred Godhead to God Himself. And therein we have the summit of His exaltation above the angels, those messengers of God in forms of wind and fire.

The sacred writer proceeds to unfold, in words borrowed from the Old Testament, the super-angelic name of the glorified One, by an additional citation (from Ps. cii.), introduced by καί, and occupying vers. 10-12. After καί a colon should be placed, or at any rate understood. This citation from Ps. cii. 26-28 bears the same relation to the preceding one from Ps. xlv. 7, 8, as the latter clause of ver. 2, δι' οὗ καὶ ἐποίησεν τοὺς αἰῶνας, to the former, ὃν ἔθηκεν κληρονόμον πάντων. The writer follows here also the Septuagint, but not without allowing himself some small liberties.

Ver. 10. *And thou in the beginning, Lord, didst found the earth, and works of thy hands are the heavens.*

The order of words in the Codex Vaticanus of the Septuagint

is, κατ' ἀρχὰς τὴν γῆν σύ, Κύριε, ἐθεμελίωσας; but in the Codex Alexandrinus, κατ' ἀρχὰς σύ, Κύριε, τὴν γῆν ἐθεμελίωσας. Our author here, to mark the antithesis (of *Son* and *angels*) which *he* has in mind, but which did not exist for the composer of the Psalm, brings the Σύ into prominence, by placing it at the head of the sentence. The invocation Κύριε (Jehovah!) is wanting in the Hebrew text; but the whole Psalm is in accordance with its title: "*A prayer of an afflicted one when he is fainting, and poureth out his complaint before Jehovah.*" Κατ' ἀρχάς is here used (as at Ps. cxix. 152) for backward-stretching time, in accordance with classical and even Attic usage (Kühner, § 607, 1). The plural ἔργα (τῶν χειρ. σου) represents a singular in the Hebrew text, ומעשה (ver. 26, Heb.). The αὐτοί (הֵמָּה) which follows refers to heaven and earth taken together.

Vers. 11, 12. *They shall perish, but thou abidest; and all shall wax old as a garment (doth); and as a robe shalt thou fold them, and they shall be changed: but thou art (still) the same, and thy years shall not fail.*

It is quite unnecessary, with Bleek and others (D. E.***, Uffenb., It., Vulg., *permanebis*), to accentuate διαμενεῖς; for διαμένεις, *permanes*, expresses the *Hebrew* future equally well. The original text may be thus rendered:

They perish, while Thou standest sure.
They all shall like a robe wax old,
And like a vesture changed by Thee, be changed.
But Thou the same art: Thy years have no end.

In accordance herewith, it cannot be doubted that the original reading in the Septuagint was, καὶ ὡσεὶ περιβόλαιον ἀλλάξεις αὐτούς, καὶ ἀλλαγήσονται. So indeed reads the Latin version (Vulgate), both in the Psalter and in this epistle. But in the Greek text of our epistle all MSS. (except D.* 43) have the reading ἑλίξεις, which is also the reading of *Cod. Alex.* in the Psalter. Bleek and others have already observed that this ἑλίξεις involves a reminiscence of Isa. xxxiv. 4, ἑλιγήσεται ὁ οὐρανὸς ὡς βιβλίον; but it seems not to have occurred to any one to remark, that this combination of the two passages in the translator's mind was a very natural one, inasmuch as the character of the whole Psalm (cii.) is deutero-Esaianic. The more we read it, the more strongly are we reminded of its prophetic archetype, especially in the two last strophes from ver. 24 (Heb.) and onwards. The prayer, *not to be taken away in the midst of his days*, is grounded by the psalmist on the eternity of the divine existence. God being Himself without beginning and without end, is therefore also omnipotent, able to assign to the life of His creatures what duration He will. It is in this sense that the psalmist grounds his petition for a lengthening of life on God's own eternity (ver. 25). In ver. 26 he celebrates this eternity, looking first backwards : earth and heaven, made in primeval times, are witnesses thereof. The expression is similar to Isa. xlviii. 13 (compare Isa. xliv. 24). In the 27th verse he looks forward to the future : the present condition of the universe will yield place hereafter to another (Isa. xxxiv. 4, li. 6, 16, lxv. 17, lxvi. 22); but Jehovah stands, abides (עמד, *perstare*, like Isa. lxvi. 22), in the midst of all this change (Isa. li. 6 ; comp. l. 9), which is His work, who remains for ever the same. אתה הוא (comp. Isa. xli. 4, xliii. 10, etc.), "*Thou art He*," the One who is ever like Himself, but incomparable with all others. The Psalm closes with a thought (ver. 29) which does not concern us here, namely, that God's people have in His eternity a pledge of their own continuance (Isa. lxv. 9, lxvi. 22). What we have to inquire is, What right has our author here to regard the words addressed by the psalmist to Jehovah, as the self-existent One, before and above the world, as words directly applicable to Christ ? Some say even still, " He was *misled* to make this application, chiefly by the Septuagint interpolation Κύριε, that being the common appellation of Christ in the apostolic age." It would be sad indeed were this the case. But viii. 8 and foll., xii. 6 and foll., are enough to show that our author by no means *always* understands Κύριος in the Old Testament to signify Christ. Such a perverse conception, founded on ignorance, is not for a moment to be attributed to one who has looked so deeply into the innermost character of the Old Testament. At the same time, I cannot persuade myself that the opposite is the case, and that our author does not regard the Κύριε of the Psalm as in any way addressed to Christ. Hofmann indeed says : " That passage in the Psalm is not cited by the author of the epistle to prove from Scripture what Scripture says of Jesus ;

but it only serves, like those which precede it, to express in Scripture language, what independently, and on other grounds, is the author's own faith concerning the Lord Jesus, and assumed by him as existing in the minds of his readers. If Christ, according to His own testimony concerning Himself, was *before the world with God*, then must everything said in Scripture of the eternity and supremacy of *God* be applicable also to *Him*. *Jehovah* indeed is not *Christ*, nor Christ *Jehovah*, directly as such; but the manifestation of Christ in the world has taught us to distinguish in the Divine Being (who in the Old Testament is without distinction called Jehovah) that which is God (ὁ Θεός), and that which is God (Θεός) with God (πρὸς τὸν Θεόν). All, therefore, which is said in the Old Testament of Jehovah is true not only of Him who is ὁ Θεός, but also of Him who is Θεὸς πρὸς τὸν Θεόν" (*Schriftb.* i. 150). If this be correct, the sacred writer might with equal right have applied to Jesus the passage Ps. xc. 1 and foll., or any other passage in the Old Testament in which the eternity of God as such is spoken of.[1] But against this is the fact that his other citations from Ps. ii. 7 and Ps. xlv. 7 and foll. are unquestionably Christological: both those Psalms were universally recognised in the ancient synagogue as speaking of " the King Messiah" (מלכא משיחא). The same was also the case with the conclusion of the great song (Deut. xxxii.), which likewise had received in the synagogue a Messianic interpretation: *e.g.* Targum ii. thus renders ver. 39 of that song: " *When the word of Jehovah* (the *Logos*) (מימרא דיהוה) *shall be manifested for the redemption of His people, then will He say to all nations, See now, I am He who is, and who was, and who shall be; and there is no other god beside me. I in My Word* (My Logos, במימרי) *kill, and I make alive: I have wounded the house of Israel, and I will heal them at the latter day: neither is there any* (*else*) *which can deliver them out of the hands of Gog and his companies when they shall come against them in battle array.*" Moreover, Matt. xxii. 41 and foll. shows that the Jews of that time regarded Ps. cx., from which our author presently (ver. 13) will make a citation, as a pre-eminently Messianic Psalm. Can

[1] So Theodore of Mopsuestia, for instance (p. 162, ed. Fritzsche), justifies the citation, by remarking that wherever the Old Testament speaks of God, the Father is meant, but not without the Son.

we then maintain that he referred to all these passages as merely fitly expressing his own belief concerning Jesus in scriptural language, without regard to their original significance and application? No. He unquestionably makes use of them as having a real reference to the Messiah, the Christ of Israel's future,—a reference on which tradition had already set its seal, while he in his turn now confirms and seals the tradition. Nor can it have been otherwise with his reference to Ps. cii. Our author interprets the Psalm as speaking of Christ, because he is fully assured that the advent ($\pi\alpha\rho o\upsilon\sigma\iota\alpha$) of Jehovah, for which the psalmist, as one of those servants of Jehovah who carried in their hearts the burden of the afflictions of Jerusalem and her exiled people, is there praying, is an *advent* already vouchsafed in the first coming of the Lord Jesus, though its glorious completion is still waited for. The psalmist's prayer is for the redemption of his people, the building again of Zion, the self-manifestation and glorification of Jehovah, and the conversion of all kingdoms and peoples to Him.

Ver. 13 (12). *But Thou, Jehovah, art for ever throned!*
   Thy memory shall through every age endure.
 14. *Arise wilt Thou, and mercy show to Zion:*
   The time for favouring her, the fixed, is come.
 15. *Thy servants think with kindness of her stones,*
   And take compassion on her dust.
 16. *Then shall the nations fear Jehovah's name,*
   And all the kings of earth Thy majesty,
 17. *When Jehovah buildeth Zion,*
   And in His majesty appears.
 18. *Turns to the prayer of the impoverished ones,*
   And spurneth not their prayer.
 19. *This shall be written for posterity,*
   A people not yet made shall praise Jehovah.
 20. *Because He looketh from His sacred height,*
   Jehovah from the heaven to earth looks down,
 21. *To hear the groaning of the captive,*
   And loose the doomed to death;
 22. *That they in Zion may tell Jehovah's name,*
   And at Jerusalem His praise,

CHAP. I. 13. 85

23. *When nations gather them together,*
And kingdoms, for the service of the LORD.

What the psalmist is here hoping and praying for, our author sees fulfilled in the incarnation of the Son of God, or still in the course of fulfilment. He interprets what Ps. cii. 26-28 says of the coming Jehovah as a divine word concerning the Son, in whom the promised advent of Jehovah has been accomplished.

The two former pairs of antitheses, vers. 5, 6, and vers 7-12, in which the greatness of the Son and His name was exhibited in contrast with the angels, are now followed by a third. The whole movement is crosswise (chiastic). First (vers. 5, 6), the angels were contrasted with the Son; then (vers. 7-12) the Son with the angels; now, again, the angels with the Son.

Ver. 13. *But in reference to which of the angels hath he ever said, Sit on my right hand, until I make thine enemies the footstool of thy feet?*

Δέ is here a particle of transition occupying the third instead of the second place in the sentence, as at Luke xv. 17, Acts xiv. 17, Gal. iii. 23 (Winer, § 61, 5). It might be rendered, *further in reference to*, etc. Instead of εἶπε (ver. 5), denoting what had been once spoken in the past, or λέγει (ver. 6), denoting a continuous utterance for all time, we have here εἴρηκε, that which is fixed in Scripture as having been once spoken, but in effect continuing. Πρὸς τίνα might here be equivalent in meaning to the τίνι of ver. 5, but it seems better to translate it as at vers. 7, 8 (so also Hofmann, *Weiss.* ii. 195). The citation is from Ps. cx. 1. No Psalm is so often referred to in the New Testament as this, being quoted ten times: Matt. xxii. 41-46; Mark xii. 35-37; Luke xx. 41-44 (our Lord's enigmatical question put to the Pharisees); Acts ii. 34; 1 Cor. xv. 25; Heb. i. 13 and x. 13 (all quotations of ver. 1 of the Psalm); and further, Heb. v. 6 and vii. 17, 21 (quotations from ver. 4). Moreover, all those passages in the New Testament which speak of our Lord's session on the right hand of God have an intimate relation to, and connection with this Psalm, which first gave this its scriptural expression to that great divine fact of the new dispensation. It was also regarded in the times of our Lord and His apostles as a chief Messianic Psalm. But in the ancient Midrash which lies before us it has been already expelled from that position. It is there referred by doctors of the synagogue partly to David himself (compare the Targum), partly (along with Isa. xli. ii. etc.) to Abraham. (So also by Rashi.) But the Messianic interpretation which it was thus endeavoured to conceal peeps out nevertheless in other passages: as, for example, in the Midrash "Shocher Tob" to Ps. ii. 7, where, for the purport of the divine decree (חק) addressed to the Lord's Anointed, reference is made to Ex. iv. 22 in the Thorah (*My son, my first-born, is Israel*), to Isa. lii. 13 compared with xlii. 1 in the *prophets* (*Behold, my servant shall deal prudently, he shall be exalted and be extolled;* and, *Behold my servant whom I uphold*), and to this Ps. cx. 1 in the *hagiographa* (*Thus spake Jehovah to my Lord*), which is then compared with the undoubted Messianic passage, Dan. vii. 13 (*Behold, one like the Son of man came with the clouds of heaven*). Further, in the same Midrash (to Ps. xviii. 36), Rabbi Judan says in the name (on the authority of) Rabbi Chama: "In the future the Holy One, blessed be He, will bid King Messiah sit on His right hand, according to Ps. cx. 1, and Abraham on his left," etc. This Messianic interpretation of the Psalm must in our Lord's time have been the prevalent one, as He argues from it with the Pharisees (Matt. xxii. 41, etc.) *e concessis*. And it rested, moreover, not merely on a tradition in the synagogue; it could claim the authoritative witness of Old Testament prophecy. For as Dan. vii. 13, etc. is the key to Ps. cx. 1-3, so is Zech. vi. 12 the key to Ps. cx. 4. When in that passage the prophet says, *Thus speaketh Jehovah the Lord, Behold a man, Zémach (Branch) by name: he shall spring* (or branch forth) *out of his place, and shall build the temple of Jehovah; yea,* HE *shall build the temple of Jehovah, and obtain majesty, and sit and rule upon his throne, and be a priest upon his throne; and a counsel of peace shall be between them both* (*i.e.* between the king and the priest united in his person),—he is evidently weaving the three passages together, Jer. xxiii. 5, 2 Sam. vii. 12, etc., and Ps. cx. 4, and impressing on them at the same time the stamp of Messianic interpretation. We may from this conclude further, that the Psalm is older than the prophet Zechariah, and not, therefore, as Hitzig, v. Lengerke, and Olshausen have maintained, a Maccabean psalm.

The question, however, remains: Is the Messianic reference in this Psalm (cx.) like that in Ps. xlv. or not? *i.e.* did it acquire its direct Messianic significance in the course of time, and when its original occasion and meaning had fallen into the background; or had it for its original reference at its first composition the King Messiah, to the entire exclusion of the historical David? In answer to which question, it cannot be denied that the Psalm *may* be interpreted up to a certain point with reference to the times in which it was written, and that even if it be regarded as directly Messianic, it was not without some historical motive or occasion. As in ver. 5, etc., there is a reference to the Syro-Ammonitish war, so in vers. 1–4 to the consequent return of the ark to Mount Zion; and the conjecture seems a natural one, that this Psalm is to be regarded, like Pss. xx. and xxi., as a song put by David in the mouth of his people, in which he taught them to regard the triumphant conclusion of that great war in the light of the high honour and dignity therefrom accruing to their royal master after his return with the ark of the covenant to Zion. (David, in this way, might be called אדוני in the Psalm, as elsewhere; *e.g.* 1 Sam. xxii. 12, 1 Kings i. 17; compare "*my lord the king,*" 1 Kings i. 13, 31.) Moreover, David certainly took such a part in the national service of God as neither Saul nor any of the judges had taken before him; when, for instance, he conducted with triumphant joy the sanctuary of his God to Zion, being himself clad in a linen priestly ephod. It was there then, on Mount Zion, that Jehovah, who had made the ark and its mercy-seat the place and token of His presence, now vouchsafed to take His seat by David's side; or rather, from the higher and spiritual point of view, it was David who henceforth was permitted to sit and dwell there by the side of Jehovah. And when we add the reflection that Jerusalem, in name and locality, would remind every one of the old Salem of that Melchizedek who had been at once both priest and king, it does seem a very easy transition of thought to compare with that ancient sacerdotal sovereign this present David, whose throne in this new Salem is now placed in such close proximity to the throne of Jehovah, and who is found himself among priests engrossed in priestly cares for Jehovah's sanctuary. This comparison of David with Melchizedek was connected with a reference to the prophecy of Nathan or Gad, as is evident from the נאם יהוה, *Thus spake* (as by an oracle) *Jehovah to my Lord*. It announced to the king that that same God who in the case of Uzzah had punished an irreverent approach with death, was now admitting *him*, in gracious familiarity, to a place of honour at His own right hand, and would from thence lay all his enemies at his feet, as indeed He had in a glorious manner shown by the conquest of Rabbath Ammon. The "for ever" (לעולם) in ver. 4 would have thus to be interpreted in the same way as the "for ever" elsewhere applied to David as king (2 Sam. vii., compare 1 Sam. xiii. 13); both, that is, to be realized in his children. But just as this relative everlastingness of David's kingdom was destined to merge in the absolute everlastingness of the kingdom of his son, who should be at the same time in personal subsistence the Son of God, so too was the everlasting priesthood of David destined to find its true meaning and accomplishment in that only One to whom, as the true David and true Solomon, the true priest-king and founder of God's temple, the prophecy of Zechariah pointed (Zech. vi. 12, etc.). In substantially the same way as here developed, Hofmann in both his works endeavours to establish the typical Messianic interpretation of the Psalm. I recognise elements of truth in such an interpretation. At the same time, I cannot persuade myself that our Lord's argument at Matt. xxii. 41, etc., proceeded from any other assumption than that of the direct Messianic character of the Psalm; and we should therefore, in any case, have to take for granted that He was interpreting the Psalm not in its original but in its prophetical sense, the sense assigned to it in later prophecy, and which it had acquired in the consciousness of the post-Davidic time. To this, however, there remains the great objection, that, according to our Lord's interpretation, it is *David* (not the people) who speaks of the future Christ, who was to be his son, in the spirit of prophecy as "*my Lord*" (Κύριον). This excludes the assumption that David, writing for the people, had so called himself; a difficulty which could only be removed by assuming that our Lord was making, for the purpose of His argument, the derived prophetical into the original historical sense. There is, however, no necessity for a position so dubious and extreme. Important grounds may be discovered within the Psalm itself for discarding the merely typical interpretation.

(1.) And first: If we assume the people to be the speaker in the Psalm, then would the divine oracle referred to be some well-known prophecy already uttered, as in Ps. cxxxii. 11, etc. the congregation of Israel refer to an oath of promise that had been previously vouchsafed to David. But here (*a*) history knows nothing of any prophetic oracle corresponding to Ps. cx. 1, and still less of an eternal priesthood promised by oath from Jehovah to David; and further, (*b*) God is here introduced by נאם יה׳, as speaking in the then present: the Psalm is a product of direct prophetic inspiration, and by that very circumstance the notion of the people as speaker is excluded. (2.) Again: Though David certainly combined something of a priestly with his royal character, and so might be regarded as in some degree an antitype of Melchizedek, yet (*a*) the Old Testament nowhere uses the word כהן to express this sort of princely episcopate; nor (*b*) did Melchizedek unite royalty with priesthood merely in this way. Rather he did (according to Canaanitish custom) combine both as *offices* in his single person. He was a real sacrificing priest. Such another priest-king is nowhere else spoken of in the Old Testament, and his actual existence would have been incompatible with its institutions[1] (comp. 2 Chron. xxvi. 16). (3.) Thirdly: David's throne being so near the ark of the covenant, he did in a certain way sit *by* Jehovah; but that expression is nowhere used of him. Of the king of Israel it is commonly said, not that he sits beside, but on, the throne of Jehovah, as visible representative of the invisible God.[2] (4.) Fourthly: Although vers. 5-7 un-

[1] When Hofmann maintains that Ps. cx. 4 assigns to David not the combination of an ordinary priesthood with ordinary kingship, but such a priesthood as is involved in the very idea of genuine royalty (*Weissagung*, i. 79), or that, when the מַמְלֶכֶת כֹּהֲנִים (of Ex. xix. 6) had been summed up in the person of an actual king, he possessed as such a priesthood independent of, and yet compatible with, that of Aaron (*Schriftbeweis*, ii. 1, 355), he is uttering thoughts which seem quite foreign to the Old Testament.

[2] Compare Hofmann (*Schriftbew.* ii. 1, 355): "The throne of the king of Israel is, properly speaking, God's throne on earth, for Jehovah Himself is the real King of Israel. The sublime dignity of the Anointed One con-

doubtedly refer to the war with the Ammonites—that greatest, longest, and most glorious of David's wars, into which the ark of the covenant had been carried—they yet combine the future with the past; that future being, as in Ps. lxviii., the prospect of a final victory over, and judgment upon, the hostile world-power, which, drinking from the wayside brook, would raise its head again, refreshed and ready for fresh conflicts. For if we refer ver. 7 to the king to whom the promises are made, the transition is somewhat hard from the direct address to the speaking of him in the third person; and the thought obtained thereby, that the conqueror, refreshed by a draught of water from the stream, will be enabled to go on to fresh conquests, can be scarcely said to form a suitable conclusion. The most obvious interpretation is, to make the subject of "*he shall drink*" the same as he who in the previous clause is termed "*Head over Rabbah-land*" (for ראש על, compare Ex. xviii. 25; and for Rabbah-land = Ammon, comp. Num. xxxii. 1 and Josh. x. 41). In this case the king of Ammon may be taken to represent the whole world-power, as opposed to the God of Israel and to His Anointed. So David here, the conqueror of Ammon, is contemplating in the mirror of that victory the final triumph of Jehovah over the kingdom of this world. The conqueror of that kingdom is the great King of the future, who will be at once his son and his Lord. Jehovah, at whose right hand He sits and rules, has already smitten the allied kings of Syria and Ammon, has already "wounded the head over Rabbah," and so will through him hereafter give its death-wound to that head when again uplifted.

An explanation may also be found for the complete separation made by David here of the victory won over Ammon and Syria from his own person as the conqueror; for that war synchronized with David's adulterous connection with Bathsheba, and the course of sin into which it led him. He therefore here steps down, as it were, from his own throne, and from his pinnacle of power, and yields his place to the great

sists in this, that he, sitting on his throne, is at the right hand of the King Jehovah." But this, too, is not in accordance with the Old Testament view of the matter, which speaks of Jehovah as enthroned only in heaven, or above the cherubim on earth. A co-session of the king of Israel with Jehovah on *His* throne is never thought of in the O. T. except at Ps. cx. 4.

Anointed One of the future, all-mighty in His royalty, all-holy in His priesthood, looking up to Him as from a lowly subject station, and calling Him " *Lord*" (אדוני). From the ashes, as it were, of David's typical greatness, springs the prophetic promise of Messiah. The type itself, in self-conscious humiliation, lays down its crown at the feet of the Antitype. These thoughts are suggested by the significant structure of the Psalm itself, corresponding with its mysterious purport. I have endeavoured to represent this in the following translation:

Thus spake Jehovah to my Lord:
Be seated Thou on my right hand,
Until I make Thine enemies
A footstool for Thy feet.

The sceptre of Thy might
Jehovah shall send forth from Zion:
Be ruler Thou among Thine enemies!

Thy people come forth willing to Thy muster,
In sacred festal dress,
More numerous than the drops from morning's womb:
Like dew springs forth Thy youth.

Jehovah sware, and will not rue it,
A priest art Thou for evermore,
According to the rite of Malchi-zédek.

The Lord on Thy right hand
Hath smitten on His wrath-day kings.
Judge shall He be among the heathen,
And fill the battle-field with slain.

He smote the head o'er Rabbah-land,
Who from the wayside rill shall drink,
And so again uplift his head.

The structure of the Psalm is this: a verse of four lines is thrice followed by one of three lines; God is thrice called by the name *Jehovah*, and when mentioned the fourth time, *Adonai* (ver. 5). The Psalm turns (so to speak) on two great promises (vers. 1–4) not mentioned elsewhere in the Old Testament: the inviolability and mysteriousness of these is symbolized in the threefold heptad into which the Psalm is distributed, and the whole consecrated by the thrice-repeated name Jehovah. The application, therefore, made by the author of our epistle of ver. 1 rests on a solid basis. He rightly regards the Psalm as a prophetic one, in which David consciously and objectively prophesies of the Messiah. He stands here, without being himself typical, upon a typical ground. The address, κάθου ἐκ δεξιῶν μου ἕως ἂν θῶ τοὺς ἐχθρούς σου ὑποπόδιον τῶν ποδῶν σου, is made to one who is both David's son and the Son of God; and in that lies the solution of the enigma put by the Lord Jesus to the Pharisees. Instead of καθίζειν ἐν δεξιᾷ (ver. 3), we have here καθῆσθαι ἐκ δεξιῶν, to express the communion of height and majesty which the Lord has with the Father (δεξιῶν from τὰ δεξιά, that which is on the right hand). The ἕως ἂν θῶ, *donec posuero* = *till I shall have put*, sets indeed no goal to mark an ultimate cessation of this royal session, and yet certainly does note the complete subjugation of the enemies as an expected crisis after which something else is to commence (*vid.* Heb. x. 13 and 1 Cor. xv. 28). So must עד־כי, ἕως (ἄν), be generally understood when used *inclusively*, that is, as not excluding the continuance of what is predicated beyond the assigned term. Comp. Gen. xlix. 10; Ps. cxii. 8; St. Matt. xii. 20; 1 Tim. iv. 13.

He who is thus exalted to the throne of God is taken up and away from His enemies. He at whose right hand He is seated will not rest till He has made them the ὑποπόδιον (St. Luke xx. 43, for which, at St. Matt. xxii. 41, ὑποκάτω is to be read), that is, the *footstool* on which He may place His feet. Comp. Josh. x. 24 and 1 Kings v. 17. How exalted is thus the Son above the angels!

Ver. 14. *Are they not all ministering spirits, sent forth for service on behalf of those who are to inherit salvation?*

The author closes the series of thoughts which commenced with ver. 4 by a summary statement of the subordinate relation in which the angels stand to the Redeemer, and mediately also to His redeemed, and that πάντες, *all* of them without exception, whatever differences of rank may exist among them. They are all λειτουργικὰ πνεύματα, spiritual beings engaged in God's holy service. Λειτουργεῖν (see note to viii. 2) is the Septuagint word for שָׁרֵת, used especially for *the service* of the sanctuary. The angels are consequently called in post-biblical Hebrew מַלְאֲכֵי הַשָּׁרֵת (not הַשָּׁרֵת; comp. Num. iv. 12, כלי השרת, LXX. τὰ σκεύη τὰ λειτουργικά) = angels of service. We must not, however, assume here a reference to the heavenly sanctuary, the allusion evidently being to the τοὺς λειτουργούς of ver. 7. The present participle ἀποστελλόμενα, chosen with reference to מַלְאָךְ = ἀπόστολος, proceeds to note for what service God is continually employing them. The διακονία here is not to be primarily referred to help or assistance rendered to the heirs of salvation (in which case it would be τοῖς μέλλουσι, like Acts xi. 29, 1 Cor. xv. 16), but to service rendered to God who sends them. The service, however, which they discharge towards God, has the heirs of salvation for its object: it is done for the sake of those for whom is destined the inheritance of salvation. Σωτηρία, when signifying, as here, complete and absolute deliverance, needs no article (in the passages cited by Winer, p. 109, it would be otherwise inadmissible, viz. Rom. x. 10 and 2 Tim. iii. 15): it takes the article only where, as at John iv. 22, Acts iv. 12, it denotes the salvation of the new covenant in its historical manifestation and definiteness. Here, however, also σωτηρία is, as matter of fact, the salvation of which Christ is Mediator. The angels serve in reference to that σωτηρία which the Son, thus exalted above them, has procured for man. *They* stand before God as λειτουργοί awaiting His commands, but *the Son* sits at God's right hand: *they* minister to God and man, but *the Son* rules; and everything, even against its will, must bow to His dominion.

CHAP. II. 1-4. *Exhortation to obedience to such a revelation as this—which, as given through the Son, so far excels that given through angels—in order not to incur a so much severer punishment.*

This first hortatory portion of the epistle, like those which follow, is of such form as not only to make a personal application of the doctrine previously laid down, but also at the same time to extend and develop it. The gospel would demand the obedience of faith even if it came through one of lower standing. But now, having come through Him who is divinely exalted above the angels, the moral obligation of according it attention is so much the more incumbent.

Ver. 1. *On this account is it needful that we the more earnestly give heed to the things heard, lest anyhow we lose them.* Προσέχειν τινι in the sense of προσέχειν τὸν νοῦν τινι (without its being exactly necessary to supply τὸν νοῦν) = to give attention, to keep in view, as (Acts xvi. 14) it is said of Lydia that God opened her heart προσέχειν τοῖς λαλουμένοις. To this προσέχειν, and not to δεῖ, belongs the adverb περισσοτέρως, whether with the *receptus* we read δεῖ περισσοτέρως ἡμᾶς προσέχειν, or with Lachmann and Tischendorf, δεῖ περισσ. προσεχ. ἡμᾶς. The form περισσοτέρως, which is interchangeably used (in our epistle and the other Pauline epistles) with περισσότερον, and is not foreign to extra-biblical literature,[1] though nowhere occurring in the LXX.,[2] is a more forcible μᾶλλον. The stress of the comparative lies in this, that the degree of attention to be paid to things heard is to be measured by the dignity of Him from whom they come. These things, τὰ ἀκουσθέντα (in Heb. הַשְׁמוּעַ, *the hearing*), are the N. T. message of salvation, which is nowhere called in our epistle εὐαγγέλιον, as St. Luke likewise in his writings (except Acts xv. 7 and xx. 20) prefers to express the notion of εὐαγγέλιον by various periphrases. This New Testament message, in view of the divine and super-angelic exaltation of the Son, demands increased attention from us, μήποτε παραρρυῶμεν,[3] *lest we heedlessly pass it by, or slip by and lose it.* Παραρρυῶμεν here is the subjunctive, not of the *present active*, but of the familiar 2d aorist passive (παρερρύην like ἀπερρύην, Eurip. apud Stobæum, *Flor.* 92, 3), which signifies to get or find one's self in a state of flowing or passing by; *i.e.* in reference to an object which requires close attention, to pass it by without giving due heed to it, or to lose possession of anything through failing to lay hold. In the former sense, that of not paying due heed, we find the word used by the LXX. at Prov. iii. 21, υἱὲ μὴ παραρρυῇς (*Al.*

---

[1] Against the assertion of Bleek and others (comp. Diod. xiii. 108, Athen. v. p. 192, F).

[2] περισσότερος only is found at Dan. iv. 33.

[3] Lachm. and Tisch. read παραρυῶμεν without the reduplication, which in Homer, and sometimes in the Attic poets, is omitted for metrical reasons.

παραρυῆς); and so Symmachus says of the words of Wisdom (Prov. iv. 21), μὴ παραῤῥυησάτωσαν, let them not escape (thine eyes). But here it would involve a tautology to take μὴ παραῤῥυῆναι in precisely the same sense and reference as προσέχειν above, that of giving heed to the *message* of salvation. Προσέχειν refers to the τὰ ἀκουσθέντα as the *words* spoken, and μήποτε παραῤῥυῶμεν to the salvation of which they speak. In this *sensus prægnans* we may supply after μήποτε παραρρ. the genitive τῶν ἀκουσθέντον (as Clem. Alex. speaks of παραῤῥυῆναι τῆς ἀληθείας).[1] The Son of God being thus exalted, we owe to the message of His mercy in the New Testament more and more of earnest heed, lest by any means we come to lose those good things which it announces and offers to us.

The necessity of this περισσοτέρως προσέχειν, already deduced from the preceding argument, is further confirmed by the following considerations :—

Vers. 2, 3. *For if the word spoken by angels became stedfast, and every transgression and disobedience received a fitting dispensation of reward, how shall we escape after neglecting so great a salvation?*

That ὁ δι' ἀγγέλων λαληθεὶς λόγος means the Sinaitic law, is clear from Acts vii. 53 (comp. ver. 38), where Stephen says, ἐλάβετε τὸν νόμον εἰς διαταγὰς ἀγγέλων (ye received the law upon ordinances of angels[2]), and Gal. iii. 19, where the apostle, exhibiting the differences between the law and the promise,

---

[1] Theodore of Mopsuestia's exposition is accordingly quite correct— μήποτε παρατροπήν τινα ἀπὸ τῶν κρειττόνων δεξώμεθα; and so that of Hesychius ἐξολισθῶμεν, and that of Suidas, παραπέσωμεν. Luther's "dass wir nicht dahin faren" (and earlier, "dass wir nicht verderben müssen") = *that we be not lost* or *perish*, has the same meaning. The "dahin faren" is explained by him by the striking gloss, "like a ship which, instead of coming into port, slips off and is lost." The Itala and Vulgate are here very inferior to Luther. The Vulgate has *pereffluamus* or *prætereffluamus*. In the text to the commentary attributed to Remigius and Primasius the reading is *prætereffluamus* (Remig.) and *pereffluamus* (Primas.), and in that of the identical commentary attributed to Haymo, *supereffluamus*. The exposition of all three is, *ne forte pereamus et a salute excidamus*.

[2] It might also be rendered, "Ye received the law as commandments of angels" (Hofmann, *Weiss*. i. 136). But I prefer the rendering in the text as better grammar and sense. See Winer, sec. 49, Masson's transl., p. 415.

says that the law was afterwards added " because of transgressions" (*i.e.* to illustrate their true nature in the light of God's revealed will), and " *ordained through angels*" (διαταγεὶς δι' ἀγγέλων), ἐν χειρὶ μεσίτου. Josephus likewise makes Herod say, when addressing the army he had raised against Aretas (*Ant.* xv. 5, 3), ἡμῶν τὰ κάλλιστα τῶν δογμάτων, καὶ τὰ ὁσιώτατα τῶν ἐν τοῖς νόμοις δι' ἀγγέλων παρὰ τοῦ Θεοῦ μαθόντων. Thus it was the view of the synagogue that the law of Moses was the word of angels, that is, the word of God mediated by angels. This view, perceptible in Targum, Talmud, Midrash, and Pijut,[1] is traced back to Deut. xxxiii. 2 (not to Deut. xxxiii. 3 also, as Ebrard thinks); comp. Ps. lxviii. 18, Heb., in which it is stated that Jehovah appeared on the mount on which the law was given, surrounded by myriads of holy angels. In Ex. xix. et seq., however, we read nothing of angels, but of thunder, lightning, the sound of a trumpet accompanying the very voice of Elohim speaking. This seems contradictory to the statement that the law was not only given in the presence of angels, but was spoken by angels. Meanwhile our author himself distinguishes (xii. 19) the divine φωνὴ ῥημάτων from the phenomena of nature amid which the law was given forth. The unity of these statements consists in this, that it was indeed Jehovah who spoke on Sinai, but that His speaking was mediated through angels (including also the Angel of the Lord κατ' ἐξοχήν, Acts vii. 38, comp. 30). Thus He spoke only mediately, not as in the New Testament, immediately, for the man Jesus is personally no other than the eternal Son; but the angels whose agency Jehovah made use of were personally other than Jehovah Himself. It is the same fundamental thought which (Gal. iii. 20) St. Paul grounds upon the general proposition, that a mediator, as such, is not of one (ἑνός), but stands between two parties, but that God is one; and hence only when God reveals Himself in His oneness and

---

[1] " These words, *I am the Lord thy God, thou shalt have no other gods before me*" (*i.e.* the Decalogue),—" these words alone have we received immediately from the mouth of the Almighty, but all the rest (of the law) by the mediation of an angel" (אן על ידי מל').—Maccoth; *vid.* Rashbam on Ex. xix. 11, and Biesenthal's quotations from the Pijut in his rabbinical commentary on this verse. [The Pijut are liturgical hymns, some of very ancient date, used in the services of the synagogue.—Tr.]

aloneness, have we a revelation *radio directo* without refraction. Such a revelation is the promise coming to fulfilment in the gospel, and which has for substance God's deed to mankind, and for motive God's grace; whereas the law has, in significance, character, and contents, as strongly marked a human as divine side, and accordingly its manner of revelation also was different, since it came through angels. Hence it came not immediately from God, but mediately to Moses, and through him to Israel, assuming an individual stamp, adapting itself to the character of Israel, and entering into the conditionalities of the people whose rule of life it was appointed to be. There is no deeper conception of the distinction between the law and the gospel than this Pauline one, here summarized in the designation ὁ δἰ ἀγγέλων λαληθεὶς λόγος. The law, as to the way it was revealed, which corresponds to its nature and contents, stands far behind the revelation given in the New Testament; yet the law, the word spoken through angels, was nevertheless stedfast, ἐγένετο βέβαιος (corresponding to the Aramaic שְׁרִיר וְקַיָּם); that is, after its promulgation it stood inviolable, and evinced itself as such in the course of history, the punishments threatened against violation of it being inexorably inflicted (x. 28). Μισθαποδοσία (dispensation of reward), a compound peculiar to our epistle, is formed on the analogy of the classical μισθοδοσία, pay, wages. The classical ἔνδικος occurs only here and Rom. iii. 8 (comp. δίκη, Acts xxv. 15, and especially xxviii. 4, where, in the mouths of heathen, it is the name of the goddess of avenging justice, called by the poets ὀπισθόπους Δίκη, she who tracks the footsteps of the evil deed). The ideas παράβασις and παρακοή form a descending climax. Every actual transgression of the law, nay, every non-observance of or inattention to its demands, received its appropriate and righteous reward. If then, asks the author, even the law was upheld inviolate, how shall we (we who live in the time of perfection) escape, ἐκφευξόμεθα (absol. as in xii. 25, 1 Thess. v. 3, and the future in respect to the final judgment), if we shall have neglected or despised so great a salvation? The *talis tantaque salus* is the contents of the New Testament word, which offers itself (comp. Acts xiii. 26, ὁ λόγος τῆς σωτηρίας ταύτης,—a phrase, moreover, similar to that above, τὸ ἔσχατον τῶν ἡμερῶν τούτων) in contradistinction to the imperative contents of the Old Testament word spoken by angels. The following relative clause, with ἥτις, quippe quæ, utpote quæ, as viii. 5, 6, x. 11, 35 (see Wahl, *Clavis*), proves the greatness of this salvation in one aspect—the aspect in question in the context—the loftiness of its Mediator.

Ver. 3b. *Which having begun to be spoken by the Lord, was handed on to us in a settled shape by those who had heard it.*
The phrase ἀρχὴν λαμβάνειν (Lat. *initium, primordium, exordium capere, sumore*) does not occur elsewhere in the New Testament nor in the Septuagint, but is found in Philo, etc., and before him in Plato. 'Αρχὴν λαβοῦσα λαλεῖσθαι is short for ἀρχὴν τοῦ λαλεῖσθαι λαβοῦσα ἐν τῷ λαλεῖσθαι, *i.e.* it took its beginning of being spoken by its being spoken of the Lord Himself.

The emphasis lies on διὰ τοῦ Κυρίου as antithesis to δι' ἀγγέλων, ver. 2. When, in reference to Ebrard's interpretation here, that the σωτηρία was revealed at first-hand by our Lord, and the law only at second-hand by angels, Lünemann objects, "*The author employs the preposition διά both times, thus indicating that God is the first originator as well of the Mosaic law as of the gospel, consequently both are made known to men only at second-hand,*" he destroys the antithesis, and thereby gives a wrong interpretation of the sacred author's meaning, who certainly distinguishes between law and gospel, as the one a mediate, the other an immediate, revelation of God (comp. on xii. 25). The greatness of the salvation consists in this, that He by whom it was first of all made known is the Lord, not ministering angels; ὁ Κύριος in the absolute sense, in which it was used ch. i. for יהוה, corresponding to the הָאָדוֹן of Mal. iii. 1; comp. Rom. x. 13 with ver. 9. Nevertheless the author allows himself to say διὰ τοῦ Κυρίου, having shown (ch. i.) that He who was the mediate cause, as of the creation of the world, so also of our salvation, is, as Son, of a super-angelic and divine nature. The later course of this salvation corresponds to the dignity of its source. It has been confirmed to us by them who heard the Lord Himself make known the salvation (οἱ ἀκούσαντες, as Luke i. 2, οἱ ἀπ' ἀρχῆς αὐτόπται). The phrase εἰς ἡμᾶς ἐβεβαιώθη is quite in St. Paul's style; two of his modes of expression are combined in it: (1) εἰς, of them to whom the preaching of the gospel was addressed, and to whom it came (1 Thess. i. 5 ; comp. 2 Cor. viii. 6, Col. i. 25, 1 Pet. i. 25); (2) βεβαιοῦν, of the preaching of the gospel in demonstration of the Spirit and of power (1 Cor. i. 6, comp. Phil. i. 7) But notwithstanding the Pauline turn of the phrase, St. Paul himself could not have so written, as Luther and Calvin already recognised. Hofmann is of a different opinion; for he maintains that, in reality, the only thing which is evident from these words is, that the author was not one of those who could testify that with their own ears they had heard the Lord while on earth proclaiming the salvation which now they preached (*Schriftbeweis*, ii. 2, 352). But it were improbable that St. Paul, who elsewhere lays so great stress on his having received his gospel not less immediately than the other apostles from Jesus— namely, the glorified Jesus—should here distinguish himself as not ἀκούσας from them the ἀκούσαντες. Had he wished to keep his own apostleship in the background, he would have been obliged, in order not to contradict himself, to write εἰς ὑμᾶς. For as the words run, they are the words of a disciple of the apostles to a church founded by apostles. Now, an apostle cannot include himself with them to whom the gospel came by the preaching of the apostles. Texts like Eph. ii. 20, iii. 5, where Paul speaks objectively of the apostles, do not prove the possibility of the construction here assumed, including him with the readers, in order to favour his immediate authorship. Moreover, it is the authority of the witnesses which the author has primarily in view in ἐβεβαιώθη. In addition to this warrant, which the σωτηρία proclaimed by the apostles has in itself, there is further given a divine corroboration, which the author states in a participial clause which reminds us of Mark xvi. 20.

Ver. 4. *God also bearing them witness, both with signs and wonders, and with divers powers and distributions of the Holy Ghost, according to his own will.*

Our author delights in compound verbs : συνεπιμαρτυρεῖν (occurring in like manner in Philo and Clemens Romanus) is formed like συνεπιτίθεσθαι, Acts xxiv. 9 (since Griesbach). As our Lord Himself makes a distinction (John v. 31 sqq.) between His own testimony to Himself and the testimony which the Father gave to Him in the works He had appointed

Him to do, so our author distinguishes here between the testimony of the apostles themselves in word, and the accompanying (σύν) additional (ἐπί) testimony of God in miracle. Σημεῖα τε καὶ τέρατα correspond in meaning to the Hebrew אֹתוֹת וּמוֹפְתִים (e.g. Ex. vii. 3). In the New Testament τέρατα occurs always in this connection (in Acts sometimes in the inverse order, τέρατα καὶ σημεῖα). Σημεῖον = אוֹת (from אָוָה, to make an incision, to notch), is any thing, act, or occurrence fitted to direct attention to and guarantee the truthfulness of a person or saying; τέρας = מוֹפֵת (perhaps from יָפַע, to glisten), an absolutely supernatural (παρὰ φύσιν, as the Greeks explain), astounding, and powerfully imposing fact or appearance, especially in the heavens (Acts ii. 19). Along with these (as Acts ii. 22, comp. 2 Thess. ii. 9) are ποικίλαι δυνάμεις, manifold communications and demonstrations of præter-human agency, powers higher than ordinary, and giving outward proof of their presence. The δυνάμεις, as a species of the *charismata* (1 Cor. xii. 10), lead on to πνεύματος ἁγίου μερισμοί, by which must be understood such *charismata* as, like the gift of prophecy, tongues, etc., raise the human spirit above its usual limitations. From the order of the words, there can be no doubt that πνεύματος ἁγίου is meant to be taken as *gen. obj.*, and that κατὰ τὴν αὐτοῦ θέλησιν refers to τοῦ Θεοῦ. Μερισμός does not here signify *division*, as iv. 12, but impartation. Θέλησις is an unclassical word, but usual in Hellenistic literature, as the LXX. and the Apocrypha show; βούλησις, which rather signifies inclination and endeavour than purpose and resolution (see on vi. 17), was not suitable for the author. Moreover, the more exact definition, κατὰ τὴν αὐτοῦ θέλησιν, does not belong to the whole participial clause, to which it is not appropriate, but only to μερισμοῖς. God has left nothing undone which might, in comparison with the revelation in the law, confirm with convincing power the substantial greatness of the salvation now made manifest.[1] To the apostolic word of witness, in itself trustworthy, He has added His own corroborative witness by

---

[1] "There" (*i.e.* under the law), says Theodore of Mopsuestia, "miracles were wrought in cases of necessity only, but under the gospel many heathens have been healed by us from all manner of diseases: we possess such a fulness of miraculous power, that even the dead are raised; and ofttimes, when it must be so, we bring individuals to a sense of their wrong-doing

imparted gifts from the fulness of His Spirit, vouchsafed according to His wise disposal, to some more, to others less, in differing ways, in various measures.

VERS. 5-18. *The setting forth of the divine exaltation of the Lord Jesus is continued with abandonment of the homiletic parænesis. Not 'angels, but the incarnate Son, is Lord of the world to come, who for a little while was made lower than the angels, that by death He might overcome death, and being made perfect through sufferings, might be for us, His brethren and with Him children of one heavenly Father, a sympathizing high priest.*

Great is the salvation which has come to us under the New Testament; first, through the preaching of the incarnate Lord, and then through men commissioned by Him with miraculous corroborating testimonies from God Himself. This greatness the sacred writer proceeds to unfold thus:

Vers. 5. *For not to angels hath he subjected the world to come, concerning which we speak.*

Were it necessary to regard this argumentative clause as referring either to the words τηλικαύτης σωτηρίας or to the relative clause which follows them, ἥτις ἀρχὴν, κ.τ.λ., the latter reference (to ἥτις) would be the preferable one (so Bleek). It is not the "greatness" of the salvation in itself, so much as the grandeur of its origin and mode of dissemination, which the author is striving to establish.[1] The main point in the antithesis is this, that while the Old Testament law is but a word of angels, and therefore only *mediately* the word of God, the gospel under the New Testament is, in its origin, a word of the Lord (*i.e.* spoken by Christ Himself), and therefore *immediately* the word of God. This, however, is but one aspect of

by striking them with blindness through a mere threat, or inflict sudden death on the malevolent." What an intensity of Christian consciousness at so late a period (the boundary line of the fourth and fifth centuries), and in the mouth of a Theodore!

[1] See essay of Hofmann's, *Zur Entstehungsgeschichte der h. Schrift. der Brief der Jacobus und der Brief au die Hebr.*, in *Zeitschrift für Protestantismus und Kirche*, 1856, p. 337. [The passage is quoted by Delitzsch in the text. We have ventured to omit it.—TR.]

the gospel proclamation as presented in ver. 3, from which the greatness of its salvation may be estimated. Another aspect comes into view as the writer proceeds to survey the progress of the gospel through the world. That progress is due to men who, as the Lord's disciples, bear their testimony to His salvation, while God Himself bears witness with them in gifts and miracles., As the gospel was first preached by a Lord of super-angelic dignity, who is both God and man in His own person, so has it been brought to us the church of the present by men who received it from His mouth, and were endowed with super-natural gifts and powers for its propagation. *For not to angels hath God subjected the world to come.* The antithesis to be understood is now clear : " Not to *angels*," but to *men*, and to *men* because of that One Man who is Κύριος, the Lord and Captain of the salvation which He and His messengers proclaim. " *The world to come*" (ἡ οἰκουμένη ἡ μέλλουσα, Heb. העולם הבא, Aramaic עלמא דאתי) is, according to Bleek, the new order of things which began with the first advent of Christ. But Hofmann is quite right in demanding a more concrete intelligible form of the idea (*Weiss.* ii. 23). This world of the future is the new world of life and redemption, as contrasted with the old world of creation of the present, which in consequence of sin has become subject to decay and death. This new world is called *future* (μέλλουσα), " a world yet to come," from the N. T. point of view as well as from that of the Old Testament. True, its "powers" (the δυνάμεις μέλλοντος αἰῶνος)—among which the apostolic signs and wonders above referred to must be reckoned—are already felt, and project themselves into the present (ch. vi. 5); but the new world itself to which they belong is still, even for the church of the New Testament, an object of longing, a μέλλουσα πόλις still (ch. xiii. 14). The old world, indeed, lost all its *right* to existence and continuance when Christ first came, but continues nevertheless to exist still as the outward shell of that hidden world of the future which is not yet fully formed within it, but will one day burst from its encasement as a new heaven and a new earth at Christ's second coming (comp. Isa. lxv. 17, lxvi. 22 ; 2 Pet. iii. 13; Rev. xxi. 1). According to its hidden principle and spirit, this world is already present; according to its glorified manifestation and body, it is yet future.

This new world the writer designates as being that περὶ ἧς λαλοῦμεν, speaking of himself in the plural (as at v. 11, vi. 9, xi. 13, 18), and looking back to what he has been saying (i. 6), and forward to what he is going to say, as the main subject and *cardo* of the whole exposition (compare xi. 10-13, v. 11, ix. 5, xi. 32). Not to angels, but to men, is this world made subject. The question arises, Does he then mean that the old world of creation was subject to the angels? Hardly so. [Calovius' observation is quite correct: *Utut angelos certa ratione præesse provinciis terræ admitti possit, non tamen hæc est subjectio.* Yet is this counter-observation unnecessary, as also that of De Wette and Lünemann, who go too far when they say that the sacred writer, if he had had that meaning, must have said, οὐ γὰρ τὴν μέλλουσαν, κ.τ.λ.] The Old Testament, to which he appeals throughout, says expressly that the old world of creation was subjected to man. So, for instance, in the eighth Psalm, which he proceeds to quote and turn into a proof of the subjection to man of the new world also. His citation is made from Ps. viii. 4-6, and he takes the words in the first instance in the literal and obvious sense.

Vers. 6-8a. *Nay, but one somewhere hath borne the following testimony : What is a man, that thou art mindful of him ; or a son of man, that thou regardest him? Thou hast lowered him a little beneath the angels ; with glory and honour hast thou crowned him, and placed him over the works of thy hands : all things hast thou put in subjection under his feet.*

On the δέ in the introductory clause, Hofmann remarks (*Weissagung und Erfüllung,* ii. 24; comp. *Schriftbeweis,* i. 97) that it not only meets the previous negation with the corresponding antithetical affirmative, but proceeds further to intensify the antithesis by a kind of climax. He compares, as examples, iv. 15, ix. 12, Eph. iv. 15 ; and a better parallel perhaps could hardly be found than Thucyd. iv. 86 : οὐκ ἐπὶ κακῷ, ἐπ' ἐλευθερώσει δὲ τῶν Ἑλλήνων παρελήλυθα. But could the author of the epistle really mean to say, that God has accorded so distinguished a position in the universe not merely to man as he was in the beginning, but also to him weak and feeble as he is now? This δέ after a negation frequently signifies, without any conscious intermediate thought, nothing more than "nay but," "on the other hand," or "rather" (Winer, § 53, 7). So here: *Not to angels hath God put in subjection*, etc.; *nay but* (*immo*) (*on the other hand*), *one hath somewhere borne this witness* (διαμαρτύρεσθαι, of specially frequent occurrence in St. Luke, *e.g.* Acts xx. 23, xxiii. 11), *saying*, etc. The citation is thus introduced with a special solemnity, the author naming neither the place whence he takes it nor the original speaker, but making use (as Philo frequently) of the vague term πού τις, so that the important testimony itself becomes only the more conspicuous, like a grand pictured figure in the plainest, narrowest frame. He cites accurately in accordance with the Septuagint, but (probably) with omission of the clause (not needed for his present purpose), καὶ κατέστησας αὐτὸν ἐπὶ τὰ ἔργα τῶν χειρῶν σου. (This clause, found in the *text. recept.*, is not indeed without weighty authorities[1] in its favour, but its omission in B. D.*** I. K., and elsewhere in MSS. and versions, is decisive against it.)

The eighth Psalm is also cited elsewhere in the New Testament as Christological. Our Lord Himself referred to its second verse in answer to the priests and scribes who were offended at the Hosanna-cry of the children in the temple; and His doing so proves indirectly that praise of Jesus is in fact praise of the manifested Jehovah. St. Paul appeals (1 Cor. xv. 27) to ver. 6*b* as to the place where it is said that God hath put all things under the feet of Christ. And yet this Psalm has less of a *Messianic appearance* than almost any; nor has it, so far as we know, ever been recognised as a Messianic Psalm in the synagogue.[2] Composed by night in contemplation of the starry heavens, it is, in the first place, a lyric echo of the history of creation as given in the Thorah (Gen. i.). In it David, having begun to celebrate the glorious revelation of divine power in heaven and earth, comes to a standstill before

[1] *e.g.* the Codex Ephraem. Rescript. (C.): its fragments of our epistle begin at ii. 4. The reading τίς ἐστιν (as LXX., Cod. Al.) for τί ἐστιν is only found in C., the Copt. Vers., and some MSS. of the Itala.

[2] Bleek refers (ii. 1, 241) to a passage cited by Wetstein from Midrash Tillim xxi., in which Ps. viii. 7 (Heb.) is said to be applied to the King Messias; but, with the text of this Midrash now lying before me, I find indeed in its opening words, ובמלך המשיח כתיב, an application to Him of Ps. xxi. 6 (Heb.), but not of Ps. viii. 7, or rather viii. 6, as Bleek and Wetstein suppose.

man,—a being comparatively so powerless and mean, to whom yet God condescends in love, and whom He has made the lord of all the creatures around him. It is obviously impossible for us (without attributing extreme narrowness to the New Testament exposition of Scripture) to imagine that the writer of our epistle could have intended to make an immediate application to Christ of the ἄνθρωπος and υἱὸς ἀνθρώπου of the Psalm. On the contrary, it is evident that he arrives at this application through an intermediate thought, which is introduced by νῦν δέ in ver. 8*b*, the case being substantially the same with 1 Cor. xv. 27; so that the dictum of J. H. Michaelis—*agit hic Psalmus secundum infallibilem Christi et apostoli demonstrationem de Christo homine post exinanitionem ad dextram Dei evecto*—is only true if *agit* be understood *mediately*, but untrue if it be understood *immediately*. The man of whom the Psalm speaks is for our author also, in the first instance man simply *as such*; and the three clauses— ἠλάττωσας, ἐστεφάνωσας, and ὑπέταξας—he also regards as three declarations concerning the high place of honour conferred on man *as such* in the universe. (1) *God has made him a little lower than the angels*. Βραχύ τι here expresses a *paululum* of degree. Ἐλαττοῦν corresponds to the Hebrew חָפֵר מַ (*facere ut quid quem deficiat*, as in Eccles. iv. 8): God has made that man should have but little wanting to angelic dignity and power. Apollinaris' paraphrase is in accordance with this:

μειονά μιν ποιήσας ἐπουρανίων στρατιάων.

The Targumist likewise renders מאלהים by ממלאכיא, and the Septuagint and other ancient versions represent אלהים by ἄγγελοι at Pss. xcvii. 7 and cxxxviii. 1 as well as here. The angels are called אלהים as being pure spiritual existences, which, begotten (as it were) of God (בני אלהים), are the purest images of the divine essence, and form His own immediate retinue. The translation παρ' ἀγγέλους here is not therefore unwarrantable.[1] The warrant for it must not, however (as it seems to me), be sought in the original abstract signification of the word

---

[1] Faber Stapulensis declares it to be *false*, an error of the translator of the Pauline Hebrew original of our epistle, to be excused by his dependence on the LXX. This expositor always cites the Greek text of this epistle as merely that of an *interpres Pauli*.

אלהים as denoting the Godhead, inclusive of the plurality of spiritual beings which are the *media* of divine activity in the world (so Hofmann); for, since the singulars בעל, אדון, אלוה, are already themselves *abstracta*, their plurals אדונים, אלהים, and בעלים, cannot well have fresh additional abstract significations; and, moreover, מאלהים is equivalent to מהיות אלהים (= Thou hast made him to want but little of *being* Elohim). The warrant, therefore, for this rendering lies in this, that the angels are among all creatures the most highly placed, and stand in closest proximity to Jehovah, the Incomparable, Himself (Ps. lxxxix. 6). They are in a certain way θεοί (1 Cor. viii. 5). To say, then, man wants but little of being θεός, is equivalent to saying he wants but little of being an ἄγγελος. Weak, feeble, perishable man, half body, half spirit (אנוש), the poor and helpless *child of man* (בן־אדם), takes a position in the scale of creatures only a little below the angelic one, which is next to God. Then (2) *God has crowned him with high majesty and honour*, or *dignity* (δόξῃ, καὶ τιμῇ), as a king. The כבוד of the original designates the manifestation of glory, regarded in the aspect of gravity and fulness; הדר in that of splendour, sublimity, and beauty. And (3) *He has put all things*, or *everything, under his feet*. Man, all but a divine being, like the angels, and royally crowned, is no landless king: the world is given him to rule over; the creature far and near is his dominion. The כל or πάντα of the text is so absolute in its assertion, that we cannot suppose it exhaustively developed in the seventh and eighth verses of the Psalm. It is, however, what one (τίς) from among men has testified of man. Our author now proceeds with his argumentation:

Vers. 8*b*, 9. *For, in putting all things in subjection to him, he left out nothing unsubjected to him. But now we see not yet all things subjected to him. But him who was lowered a little beneath the angels we do see, namely Jesus, crowned because of the suffering of death with glory and honour, that so he might by the grace of God have tasted death for every one.*

With ἐν γάρ the writer commences his exposition of the passage from the Psalm, and a comparison of its statement with the actual existing condition of things, which, as not corresponding to it, fails to exhaust its meaning. God, in having expressly subjected everything to man, has left no created thing not so subjected to him : this is the exegetical *propositio major*. But now we do *not yet* see everything subjected to him, *i.e.* to man in general (as the Psalmist puts it) : this is the *propositio minor* (δέ equivalent here to *atqui*). Man in his present natural state is evidently not lord of the universe ; his destiny to rule over it is not yet fulfilled. But in Jesus it is fulfilled already And therefore—this is the irrefragable consequent *conclusio*— the ἄνθρωπος and υἱὸς ἀνθρώπου of the Psalm is Jesus, as being the man in whom has really been accomplished what the Psalm says of man in general ; and therefore again—whatever the Psalm says of the putting in subjection of the universe to mankind must belong to the world of the future, since it has not been fulfilled in the world of the present. Not to angels, but to the man Jesus, and in Him to all humanity redeemed by Him, has the μέλλουσα οἰκουμένη been put in subjection. Such is the process of the argument, and of our author's irrefragable exposition ; irrefragable inasmuch as from the standpoint of the New Testament he brings to light the very mind of that Spirit who, omnisciently surveying both the present and the future, gave such form to the letter of Scripture as to make it accord with His omniscient survey.[1]

The course of thought is clear and straightforward. Yet commentators, both ancient and modern, have deranged and distorted it; the former because they always prefer the most direct Messianic interpretation to any other reached circuitously, the latter because they think *no* Messianic interpretation too forced to be attributed to a New Testament writer. It does not prepossess one in favour of the interpretation offered, when De Wette, for instance, maintains that the author was not clear in his own mind as to the meaning to be attached to the first of the verses quoted from the Psalm, or when Lünemann remarks that Ἰησοῦν, ver. 9, is only incidentally added, and might have been omitted altogether without injury to the sense,

---

[1] "The mystery of Adam," says an ancient voice from the synagogue (see Biesenthal's *Heb. Com.* p. 2), "is the mystery of Messiah;" אדם, Adam, being the anagram of אדם, דוד, and משיח, *i.e.* Adam, David, Messiah. Again, the Midrash, on Ps. civ. 1, says, "God vouchsafed to Moses הוד, 'honour,' and to Joshua הדר, 'majesty,' intending to vouchsafe both hereafter (according to Ps. xxi. 6, Heb.) to the King Messiah."

or the perspicuity of the author's meaning. Bleek, on the other hand, makes a nearer approach to the right method, when, although adhering to the direct application of the Psalm to the Son of man κατ' ἐξοχήν, he yet admits that αὐτῷ (ver. 8), while thus referring to him as such, is not therefore to be definitely applied to the person of Jesus, in which the Son of man was manifested. Among modern expositors, Hofmann is the first who has thoroughly perceived the author's train of thought. Without being able (as will appear in the sequel) to assent to every particular in the discussions of this passage in his *Weissagung u. Erfüllung*, ii. 23, etc., and the *Schriftbeweis*, i. 185–188, ii. 1, 38, etc., I hold that (speaking generally) the development there given of the train of thought is the only one which really accords with our author's meaning—namely, that God has destined man to be lord over all things, that this destination has not yet been realized in mankind in general, but that the Son of man has, in the person of Jesus, been already exalted to such universal dominion. One may agree with this, and yet widely differ in some particulars of interpretation. So at once in the clause, ἐν γὰρ τῷ (or ἐν τῷ γὰρ, Lachmann) ὑποτάξαι αὐτῷ τὰ πάντα οὐδὲν ἀφῆκεν αὐτῷ ἀνυπότακτον, the subject is God, not the Psalmist, as appears from the different mode of expression adopted by the writer, iii. 15 and viii. 13. The construction is similar to Acts xi. 15; the meaning—God, in doing the one, did at the same time the other. Αὐτῷ, of course, is now understood to be man in general, the proximate object of reference in the Psalm. A question, however, may be still raised, as to which of the two following references of the clause ἐν γὰρ τῷ, κ.τ.λ., is to be preferred. For (1) it is possible that the writer meant thereby to justify the Psalm in speaking so emphatically, as of some great thing, of God's having thus subjected all things to man, and to justify it by reminding us that this subjecting of the world to man's dominion, which followed immediately on his creation, was then intended to be without any exception. So Hofmann; but surely this view makes the process of thought somewhat tautological, and reduces the proof to one of *idem per idem*. The ὑπέταξας of the Psalm itself refers to Gen. i. 28; and so we should rather expect οὖν than γάρ here, if such were the author's meaning. For this reason I prefer what (2) is also possible, to suppose that he intended by ἐν γὰρ τῷ, κ.τ.λ., to confirm the previous assertion of ver. 5 (Bleek, Tholuck, De Wette, Winer): Not to angels hath God subjected the world to come; but it is, on the contrary, man, to whom, according to Ps. viii., *all things* have been put in subjection. This involves (as the antithetical clause διεμαρτύρετο δέ indicates) that such must be the case with the world to come; and the clause ἐν γὰρ τῷ, κ.τ.λ., sets about the proof of it. I am, at the same time, far from holding the view, which Hofmann very properly rejects, that the writer of the epistle regards the οἰκουμένη μέλλουσα as something comprehended under the general notion expressed by πάντα. For the notion " world," regarded as the complex of all created things, is simply co-extensive with that of the πάντα. The world that now is, and the world to come, are not two different things included under the wider designation of τὰ πάντα; but each is by itself the whole τὰ πάντα, which are thus presented in two different and successive forms. And so is set aside at once an objection which, on the other view, might have been pressed upon our author here, that the Psalmist is speaking of the present world, and not of that which is to come.

He proceeds to encounter another objection—that man, as he is at present, does not assert himself as lord of the universe. But in this very circumstance is found for him the deep significance of the psalmist's words, pointing onward as they do from the world of creation to that of redemption: νῦν δὲ οὔπω ὁρῶμεν αὐτῷ τὰ πάντα ὑποτεταγμένα. With νῦν δ' (which has temporal, not logical significance) the writer points to the present condition of things; with οὔπω to the ultimate destination of man, as first pronounced in Gen. i. 28, as according to Ps. viii. still existing unrepealed, but as never yet accomplished. What the Psalm attributes to man in the totality of his race we see not (he argues) realized; *but* (so he proceeds in the following ver. 9) we do see man already even as the psalmist here depicts him, and by way of anticipation, in Jesus, that One Man who has for all our sakes already passed through death, and entered into glory and world-wide dominion. This makes the antithesis clear. How much it is obscured for those who will have it that our author finds in the Psalm an immediate and direct reference to Christ, is evident from such an exposition, for instance, as Lünemann's: "Certainly we see not at present all things put under Christ's feet as Son of man; but we see Him, at any rate, crowned already with glory and honour,"— whereby a train of thought is introduced, which, although found at 1 Cor. xv. 25, etc., is here quite foreign to the argument. But even when we have mastered the leading thought of ver. 9, considerable difficulties remain to be encountered in the interpretation both of the whole sentence and of particular points. Hofmann has given two interpretations of it. Formerly (taking τὸν ἠλαττωμένον for the predicate, 'Ιησοῦν for the object, and ἐστεφανωμένον for its apposite) he rendered it thus: " One almost equal to the angels do we behold in Jesus, who has been crowned with glory and honour" (*Weissagung*, ii. 28); but now (regarding τὸν ἠλαττωμένον as the object, 'Ιησοῦν as in apposition with it, and ἐστεφανωμένον as predicate) he translates as follows: "Him who was all but equal to the angels, Jesus, we now see crowned with glory and honour" (*Schriftb.* i. 187).

There can be no doubt, from the use of the article (compare x. 25), that τὸν ἠλαττωμένον must be regarded as part of the object (or *subject*, we might say, having regard to the simple proposition which may be extracted from the sentence); but the relation in which Hofmann makes it stand to 'Ιησοῦν must, in my opinion, be reversed. Τὸν ἠλαττωμένον I would regard as antecedent apposite of the object, and 'Ιησοῦν, whose detached position shows it to be the emphatic word in this skilfully constructed sentence (compare the similar position of Χριστός, 1 Cor. v. 7), as the object proper: (as) *Him who was a little lowered beneath the angels see we Jesus* (now) *crowned with glory and honour*. And this also seems to be the sense given in the Vulgate: *Eum autem qui modico quam angeli minoratus est videmus Jesum propter passionem mortis gloria et honore coronatum.*

But further, I hold it to be impossible to apply τὸν βραχύ τι παρ' ἀγγέλους ἠλαττωμένον to "Jesus," without some modification of the sense in which the psalmist says it of man in general. For, predicated of our Lord, *all but equality with the angels* were an unsuitable expression; whereas *that He was made a little lower than the angels*, immortal spirits,[1] may just

[1] The higher position of the angels is rightly made by Cyril to consist therein, that they are καὶ ἔξω σαρκός, καὶ τοῦ τεθνάναι κρείττους, i.e. out-

as well be said of Him as of man at his first creation, although in a somewhat different sense.

Finally, it appears to me to be equally impossible to make δόξῃ καὶ τιμῇ ἐστεφανωμένον refer to the gifts of grace bestowed on Jesus on His entrance into the world, or to His vocation as Redeemer: the whole New Testament Scriptures know of no other crowning of Jesus than His exaltation, whereby God raised Him as κληρονόμον πάντων to His own right hand. And if ἐστεφανωμένον must be referred to *the exaltation of Jesus*, it becomes all the more certain that the impression hitherto made on all readers by the clause τὸν δὲ βραχύ τι παρ' ἀγγέλους ἠλαττ.—namely, that it must be referred to our Lord's *humiliation*—is not an illusive one. The writer purposely does *not* say ἐλαττωθέντα, but balances one perfect participle by another, because the antithesis which he is making is not of two past events, but of states or conditions—the *status exinanitionis* and the *status exaltationis*. Moreover, that we do not err in referring ἐστεφανωμένον to our Lord's exaltation, is made certain by the added clause—διὰ τὸ πάθημα τοῦ θανάτου. It is confessedly a thought pervading the New Testament in general, and our epistle in particular, that that exaltation was fruit and reward of suffering freely undertaken, and especially of suffering unto death. The heavenly "joy" was, according to xii. 2, that prize of victory, in prospect of which "He endured the cross." Most improbable, therefore, is the sense assumed by Hofmann for the predicate here: We see Him (who has entered into the world) raised to dominion over all things, because of the existing suffering of death; that is, He is made Ruler *for our sakes*, because *we* are still, instead of ruling, subject to mortality: so that διὰ τὸ πάθημα τοῦ θανάτου would designate the cause or occasion of our Lord's appointment to His present condition, not the meritorious ground for His exaltation into it. Nor will the want of an αὐτοῦ be felt with our interpretation. Its insertion here would be grammatically impossible (the case being different from that of the yet disputable ἐν τῇ σαρκί, Rom. viii. 3); and it would be making too great a demand on the author to say he should have written διὰ τὸ παθεῖν αὐτὸν θάνατον, inasmuch as διὰ τὸ πάθημα τοῦ side the barrier of the flesh, and by their very essence raised above the necessity of dying.

θανάτου is equivalent to διὰ τὸ παθεῖν αὐτὸν τὸ πάθημα τοῦ θανάτου. It will, moreover, soon appear that, with our view, the clause ὅπως χάριτι Θεοῦ, κ.τ.λ., is appropriately added. The author's position is this: Jesus—Him who, as Son of God, stands high above the angels, but who, becoming man, was made a little lower than they—we now see crowned with glory and honour, even because He endured the suffering of death. He who was thus lowered, is now, as the very consequence of that humiliation, put in full possession of the dominion assigned (Ps. viii.) by God to man. This interpretation is that also e.g. of Tholuck and Ebrard, with whom, however, I cannot agree in assigning a *temporal* signification to this βραχύ τι in its original place in the Psalm, or that our author insists upon so taking it there. It has *acquired* for him, as expounded by its historical fulfilment, another sense than that of its first intention in the mind of the psalmist, as indeed elsewhere history not unfrequently expounds a text of Scripture by fulfilling it in a somewhat different sense from that it bore in the consciousness of the original writer. In the case of man as first created, this βραχύ τι expresses an enduring inferiority of degree imposed by the law of his creation; but the Son of God, having condescended to human lowliness in order to exalt humanity to the height which it is destined to attain, cannot continue in that low estate; and so what in man, as such, is a *paululum* of *degree* (compare βραχύ τι, 2 Sam. xvi. 1), is changed for Him into a *paululum* of *time* (as at Isa. lvii. 17, and in Attic writers frequently). While in ordinary humanity the *paululum* of degree has "glory and honour" for its correlative in Jesus, the *paululum* of time has it for its *antithesis*. Thus βραχύ τι here undergoes a change of meaning by no means arbitrary, but necessitated by the application to *the* man, Jesus, of words originally spoken of man in general.

We turn to the clause ὅπως χάριτι Θεοῦ ὑπὲρ παντὸς γεύσηται θανάτου. Were it impossible for us to construe this otherwise than, for instance, as Tholuck, *i.e.* in connection with the preceding διὰ τὸ πάθημα τοῦ θανάτου (against which Olshausen, Ebrard, and others rightly appeal to the not less significant than skilful arrangement of the words), we should certainly have, after all, to reconsider whether ἐστεφανωμένον

CHAP. II. 8, 9. 113

must not be really referred, with Hofmann, to our Lord's first appointment as Redeemer, rather than to His present exaltation. But it may be shown, retaining our interpretation as above, that the only right construction of the clause is to make it refer to the whole participial predicate. The sacred writer would state for what end Jesus, not without mortal suffering— nay, in consequence of that suffering—has been thus exalted. That end is this: that He, through divine grace, should be found to have tasted death for the good of all and each of us, and that He should thus have entered into the lowliness of our death-subjected humanity, in order to exalt that lowliness to the high estate which the eighth Psalm declares to be our ultimate destination, and into which He is already entered Himself. The arrangement of the words is here, as throughout the epistle, beautiful and significant.

[But it certainly would not be so if we read χωρὶς Θεοῦ (instead of χάριτι Θεοῦ); for these words, however interpreted, would thus have a too prominent and consequently misleading position. The reading is not found in the MSS. to which we have now access (except Uffenb.*, 67**[1]), but from Origen downwards is witnessed to by fathers, both Greek and Latin (among the latter, by Ambrose, Fulgentius, Vigilius (*sine Deo*), and Jerome (*absque Deo*)), and most distinctly preferred by Theodore of Mopsuestia, as well as by the Nestorians,[2] because exempting the divine nature of Christ from the suffering of death; which heretical abuse of the reading is probably the

[1] These Uffenbachian fragments are parts of a MS. supposed by Tischendorf to belong to the ninth century, and are of great critical value. We have already cited from them, under ch. i. 3, a remarkable reading hitherto unnoted. [This MS., known as M. (Codex Ruber), is described by Scrivener, *Introd. to the Criticism of the New Test.* pp. 138-140.—TR.] 67 is a Vienna MS. which Tischendorf assigns to the twelfth century. It presents χωρὶς Θεοῦ as a reading *secund. man.* Sebastian Schmidt cites the reading χωρὶς Θεοῦ from *Ed. Paris. Syriaca et Mscr. Tremellii.*

[2] Nestorius, as is well known, was a disciple of Theodore, and derived his heresy from him. Theodore's interpretation of this passage is worth reading. He explains χωρὶς Θεοῦ by οὐδὲν πρὸς τοῦτο παραβλαβείσης τῆς θεότητος, and separates so widely the divine from the human nature in our Lord as to refer αὐτῷ δι᾽ ὅν, κ.τ.λ., to God the Word (*Logos*), and τὸν ἀρχηγόν, κ.τ.λ., to the man Jesus! He pours contempt on the reading χάριτι Θεοῦ, as in this connection a meaningless and objectless rhetorical ornament.

VOL. I. H

cause of its almost total disappearance from MSS. But anyhow, a sense in accordance with the context is not to be extracted from it. Hofmann formerly (*Weissagung u. Erfüllung*, i. 92) interpreted it thus: Jesus tasted death χωρὶς Θεοῦ, *i.e.* surrendered to death a life which, having a temporal beginning, was *apart from God*; but now, with the reading, has abandoned likewise this interpretation, to which, either for sense or expression, the New Testament certainly affords no parallel. Baumgarten, on the other hand, would retain χωρὶς Θεοῦ (*Zechar.* i. 359): "The death which Christ has to taste is a death *without God*, a death which from the beginning God has denounced against sin; though now it is not the world of sinners which has to endure this God-forsaken death, but even He on whom the whole world's sin makes its assault, and in accomplishing His death attains its consummation."[1] We would willingly recognise χωρὶς Θεοῦ, thus understood, as the original reading; but neither are the words themselves an adequate expression for the thought,[2] nor, if meant to be thus understood,

---

[1] Compare a sermon of Baumgarten's, entitled *How looking to Jesus makes happy in the midst of the Troubles of Life* (Brunswick 1856), p. 21. Adopting this reading χωρ. Θεοῦ, the preacher says: "It was not enough for Christ to commit merely His soul to that labyrinth of misery in which His people was involved; but He gave up Himself, both soul and body, to the full reality of the curse of divine dereliction. You know He died on the cross: there He drained the last drops of the cup of the wrath of God: the storms and billows of that wrath passed over Him, and that was His death. And yet, even when God-forsaken, and given over to the power of darkness (St. Luke xxii. 53), He did not for one moment leave hold of God: when all those billows passed over His head, His prayer was still, *My God, my God!* And that prayer shows that, even in those three hours of deepest suffering and desertion, His inward blessedness was still assured; for, wherever God is faithfully invoked, there still His Spirit dwells, and life and blessedness abide. So was it in Jesus Christ. Even though He must and would taste death upon the cross, and that 'without' or apart from 'God,' the blessedness of faith and love remained in Him still, and by its inward power of life He overcame. And so, for time and for eternity, He gained the power which still subdues all forms and agencies of death, and manifests to us that might of love of which it is written (Cant. viii. 6), that *love is strong as death, a flame from God, which waters many cannot drown.*" Our readers will thank us for quoting this passage.

[2] One might compare a citation in Athenagoras (*legat. pro Christ.* 22, p. 101 s.) from an unknown tragic poet, which speaks of those unhappy men *whom chance or some dæmonic power sinks ever deeper into hopeless*

would they occupy their right position in the sentence. The best interpretation would probably be, either that of Ebrard, following Origen and Theodoret, "that He should suffer death for all existences, with the only exception of God Himself;" or that of Bengel, "*ut omne sibi vindicaret, ut omnium rerum potestatem capesseret, excepto Deo.*" But even were it not to be conceded that χωρὶς Θεοῦ, if meant to be so understood, ought to have been placed after ὑπὲρ παντός, what purpose, we might ask, would such an exception answer here, where the point of reference (in παντός) is not the universe (as is the case with πάντα in 1 Cor. xv. 26-28), but simply mankind (and that in quite a different connection from the apostle's argument there)? Ὑπὲρ παντός here does not mean *for every thing*, but *for every one*, *i.e.* for all mankind, without an individual exception; the use of πᾶς (*i.e.* the singular where the plural would have been equally admissible) belonging to the idiomatic peculiarities of this epistle (Bleek, i. 335). We therefore adhere to the reading χάριτι Θεοῦ.]

The suffering of death was the lowest depth of our Lord's humiliation, from out of which, and because He had descended into it, Jesus now is crowned with glory and honour, and so fulfils an ordinance of grace divine, by which He has tasted the bitterness of death in a way that should have a meritorious efficacy for the human race in all its members. His being now exalted in consequence of a previous voluntary subjection to the suffering of death, is a clear manifestation of divine grace, and at the same time puts a seal upon the meritorious character of that subjection. "*He had to die for the benefit of others, a death which, for His own sake, He needed not to die, and that not through the wrath of God, but in fulfilment of His gracious will.*" This paraphrase of Hofmann's is in itself perfectly correct, but would not be so if understood to mean that our Lord's death was not, as the death of men in general, an effect of wrath, but of grace only, to the exclusion of wrath; for it was just the death of men in general, which for their benefit He undertook to die. The sting of death, we know, is sin, and the strength of sin the law (1 Cor. xv. 56); but the strength of the law is the curse against sin, and the strength of that curse

misery ἄτερ Θεοῦ. This ἄτερ Θεοῦ is used precisely as χωρὶς Θεοῦ would be used in our text were it the right reading.

the wrath of the Holy One. Had our Lord not died this death, with just this awful background to it, His death would have been a merely fantastic one. In order to overcome death, He had not merely to put His lips as it were to the bitter potion, but to taste it in the depth of its full reality. He had to taste the very savour of wrath in death, in order, by God's gracious appointment, to take that savour away for us. And so it was the grace of God which made Him thus submit to the bitter experience of death, even to the extremity of divine dereliction, the grace of God, which He Himself subserved in thus submitting.

The emphasis, therefore, in this clause, must be laid on χάριτι Θεοῦ. That Jesus, as the Son of man, must before His exaltation suffer, by a peculiar dispensation of divine grace, for the good of all mankind, is what the following verse proceeds to establish.

Ver. 10. *For it was befitting him for whose sake all things are, and through whom all things exist, in conducting many sons to glory, to make perfect the Captain of their salvation through sufferings.*

To understand the reference of the words δι' ὃν τὰ πάντα, καὶ δι' οὗ τὰ πάντα, we must first make out what and whose action is here designated as God-befitting. The action is expressed in the aorist τελειῶσαι, which is used after πρέπει, without essentially different meaning from the pres. inf. (the one regarding the befitting action as something still in progress, the other as accomplished and concluded). But what, then, is the meaning and reference of ἀγαγόντα? Winer still persists[1] in making it refer to Christ in His earthly manifestation, wherein from the very first he began to lead many to glory by His own personal ministry.[2] But to take ἀγαγόντα without the article as antecedent, apposite to τὸν ἀρχηγόν, is in itself a doubtful construction; and the motive for its adoption—namely,

---

[1] In the sixth edition of his *Grammar*, p. 307. [This was written in 1859, when Winer was still alive.—Tr.]

[2] The Hebrew version of the London (Jews) Missionary Society reads אֶת־הַמֵּבִיא, which Biesenthal interprets as having a pluperfect signification, and referring to our Lord, "*who even before His manifestation in the flesh had through their faith in Himself led many to glory.*"

that the *part. aor.* never stands for the *part. fut.*—is not cogent; for though ἀγαγόντα may not *grammatically* be equivalent to *adducturum*, it does not thence follow that it must signify *postquam adduxerat*. Hofmann likewise still insists on the pluperfect sense of ἀγαγόντα (*Schriftbeweis*, ii. 1, 39 ; comp. *Weiss*. ii. 156) : " *The God who had already brought many sons to glory—a Moses to prophetic* (iii. 3), *an Aaron to pontifical* (v. 4 et seq.), *a David to royal glory—had now to make this Son, commissioned to realize the destinies of mankind as set forth in Ps.* viii., *through sufferings perfect for His distinctive calling.*" But apart from the objectionable interpretation of δόξα, in another and lower sense than that in which it was used, ver. 7, of the destinies of mankind, and ver. 9, of the exaltation of Jesus, the whole exposition breaks down when it comes to ἀρχηγὸν τῆς σωτηρίας αὐτῶν.[1] Jesus is so styled, as both He who has acquired salvation for the race, and He from whom it is derived to them, as being at once its First Cause and First Possessor (not only αἴτιος, as Chrysostom, but also " Captain"—*Herzog*, as Luther beautifully renders it),—as One who, being placed Himself in the forefront of humanity, leads on His followers to the appointed goal. Thus understood, ἀγαγόντα plainly corresponds to ἀρχηγόν, while δόξα is used with reference to σωτηρία, as the manifestation which corresponds to the substance, or the flower which springs from the root. If Jesus, then, is " Captain of their salvation" to the " many sons" whom God is leading to " glory," that " glory" cannot be any or every kind of honour into which some of their number may have been brought before Christ's coming, but only that transcendent glory into which He, as the only Son in the absolute sense, is already entered, and to which, on the ground of the " salvation" won by Him, God will ultimately lead the " many sons."

[Πολλοὺς υἱούς here stands for humankind in its grand totality, so far as it suffers itself to be thus exalted ; πολλούς being used not in antithesis to " all," but to " few," or to the " one" by whom the " many" are led. Moreover, it is a mis-

---

[1] The word ἀρχηγός recurs, ch. xii. 2, and further in St. Luke, Acts iii. 15 and v. 31. It is a shorter form for ἀρχηγέτης, as Adam is called by Philo, i. 32, 40. [Our rendering, " *Captain of their salvation,*" was probably suggested by Luther's *Herzog ihrer Seligkeit.*—Tr.]

take to suppose that ἀγαγόντα either must be or might most naturally be taken in a pluperfect sense. When a *partic. aor.* is combined with an *aor.* or an historical *pres.*, it may designate either a synchronous action (as Rom. iv. 20; Col. ii. 13; 1 Tim. i. 12), or one in the remoter past (as λαλήσας in Heb. i. 1); and the context in each case must determine how it is to be taken (see Bernhardy, *Synt.* 383; Madvig, *Synt.* § 183, 2).[1] The grammatical construction of the sentence here resembles that of Acts xv. 22, ἔδοξε τοῖς ἀποστόλοις ... ἐκλεξαμένους ἄνδρας ... πέμψαι, the accusative in both participles being substituted for the dative; but in the Acts ἐκλεξαμένους has a pluperfect signification, while here ἀγαγόντα coincides with τελειῶσαι (so, Col. i. 19 et seq., εἰρηνοποιήσας expresses an action which coincides or synchronizes with that expressed by ἀποκαταλλάξαι). Not that the *part. aor.* has therefore in itself a present or future (!) signification : that this is not so is plain from vi. 10, ἀγάπης ἧς ἐνεδείξασθε ... διακονήσαντες καὶ διακονοῦντες. The thought in Greek is conceived thus: It became Him ... having brought many sons to glory, to have first perfected their Captain through sufferings; *i.e.* in doing the one, to do also the other. The one act being necessary as a previous condition to the other, ἀγαγόντα might be rendered *adducturum;* but that is in no sense its grammatical meaning.][2]

The emphasis in the clause governed by ἔπρεπεν ... τελειῶσαι lies on διὰ παθημάτων. In ver. 9 the Lord's passion (τὸ πάθημα τοῦ θανάτου) was regarded as the meritorious ground of His exaltation; here (διὰ παθημάτων, the last of which was the παθ. τοῦ θαν.) it is regarded as the means of His perfecting. [Τελειοῦν = τέλειον ποιεῖν signifies either to bring to a complete or final issue, as opposed to an inchoate or unfinished

---

[1] The usage whereby the *part. aor.* sometimes loses its preterite sense in reference to the main action, is well explained by Madvig (*Bemerkungen über einige Punkte der Gr. Wortfügungslehre*, p. 45). He remarks, that in such cases the action expressed by the participle is still regarded as *past*, *i.e.* as past from the point of view of the narrator, though not past in reference to the main action.

[2] Schlichting interprets rightly, *cum Deus in eo esset ut multos filios in gloriam perduceret.* Had he known (as the more learned Sebast. Schmidt already knew) that this interpretation was quite compatible with ἀγαγόντα, he would not have spoken of a *diversa lectio* ἀγόντα. It would be difficult to say what *alia exemplaria* present this reading.

action, or to make fully answerable to its purpose, as opposed to that which is defective or inoperative.]¹ God has brought the Captain of salvation by sufferings to the goal where He is made perfect by that which, as the Leader of others to the same goal, He both would and must be. That goal is the heavenly glory, and yet we should not be right in making τελειῶσαι here = δοξασθῆναι: τελειῶσαι expresses more than δοξασθ., and mainly refers to ethical perfection, the putting into a state completely answering to His destination and commission. To bring the Lord Jesus into such a state, and so to make Him perfect through sufferings, is an act worthy of God Himself (ἔπρεπεν αὐτῷ). It *became* Him, both in His relation to fallen and perishing humanity, and in His relation to Him who, as the Author of its salvation, would stand at its head, thus to do. It was, at the same time, a work of free grace (χάρις), imposed by an inward, not an outward necessity.

Instead of τῷ Θεῷ after ἔπρεπεν, the sacred writer uses the periphrasis αὐτῷ δι' ὃν τὰ πάντα καὶ δι' οὗ τὰ πάντα; "Him," *i.e.*, who to the whole universe is the end of its developments and the ground of its being. [Δι' ὅν is equivalent to the εἰς αὐτόν of Rom. xi. 36, δι' οὗ to the ἐξ οὗ of 1 Cor. viii. 6.] God is thus designated, as rightly observed by Hofmann (*Weiss*. ii. 156), in order to justify and illustrate the use of ἔπρεπεν in sole reference to the gracious will of God. The sacred writer would therewith strike down any Judaic offence-taking at the cross. No one can have any judgment as to what is God-befitting or otherwise in the work of salvation, but God Himself, the End and the Beginning, the Alpha and Omega of all created things. Yet is the question, Why must the Redeemer be perfected through sufferings? by no means one to which we have no answer. That answer is indicated in the πολλοὺς υἱοὺς ἀγαγόντα, which reminds us of the essential "Sonship" of Him in connection with whom God is raising those "many sons" to a like "glory." In order to put His creatures of mankind in a communion of glory with His only-begotten Son, God must first put Him in a communion of suffering with all

¹ *Vid.* Köstlin, pp. 421-424, who rightly starts with the assumption that τὸ τέλειον is antithesis partly of that which is only inchoate, partly of that which is imperfect, partly of the inchoate and imperfect taken together —the *unfinished* in both senses.

mankind, and let Him issue from it with "glory" and "salvation," won as a common good and possession for all. In order to raise humanity from the depths of misery, in which it is so unlike its ultimate destination, to the heights of glory for which it is destined, God must first lead up His only Son to glory through deeps of human suffering, that thus by Him, *the* Son made perfect through suffering, He might make of us also glorious sons of God. This is what was God-befitting in the work of salvation.

Ver. 11. *For he that sanctifieth, as well as the sanctified, are all of One, for which reason he is not ashamed to call them brethren.*

The ἁγιάζων here is Christ (ix. 13, 14, xiii. 12, compared with John xvii. 19), and the ἁγιαζόμενοι such men as experience His sanctifying power who was perfected Himself through suffering (x. 14, 29). [The sacred writer could not designate them as οἱ ἡγιασμένοι, for he is not thinking of particular individuals, but of mankind in general, as that in which the sanctifying powers of Christ are working.] Ἁγιάζειν signifies here, according to Hofmann, to take out of the world, and so separate for the communion of the alone self-centered God. But the fundamental meaning of קדוֹשׁ, ἅγιος, which is thus assumed, is without etymological basis. If, on the other hand, we start from the assumption that the original meaning of קדשׁ is not that which is separated to itself from the rest of the world, but that which in itself is bright, untroubled, glorious,[1] then ἁγιάζειν[2] would signify, to bring into a state of light and glory by removal of what is dark and troubled, and so make fit for communion with the bright and glorious God. Taken in this sense, ἁγιάζειν would express the inward act of which δοξάζειν

---

[1] *Vid.* Thomasius, *Dogmatik*, i. 140-143. [This etymology of קדשׁ is adopted by Fürst, who renders it, " *to be fresh, new, young*, of things; *to be pure, shining, bright*, of persons and things;" and regards it as "identical in its organic root (ק-דשׁ) with that of ח-דשׁ" (*Lexicon*, Davidson's transl. p. 1221). Delitzsch has, I believe, now abandoned this etymology, and gone back to the older one, which makes the fundamental notion of קדשׁ that of "purity" or " separation."—Tr. 1867.]

[2] Ἁγιάζειν is an Alexandr. sacerdotal term equivalent to קִדֵּשׁ, and a synonym of καθαρίζειν, Heb. טִהַר.

is the outward; "glory" being only manifested holiness, the bright forth-shining of an inward light. In order to be crowned with δόξα καὶ τιμή, Jesus Himself must first be sanctified, or, as it is expressed in ver. 10, be made perfect through sufferings, those sufferings melting away all that was incapable of heavenly exaltation,[1] that He, thus sanctified Himself, might sanctify and lead up others to glory. The close relation between Him and them is a consequence of fellowship in sufferings. What is true of the Sanctifier, is true also of the sanctified: *they are all* (πάντες) *of One*. [We might expect to read here ἀμφότεροι instead of πάντες; but the ἁγιαζόμενοι are "many" (ver. 10), and the sacred writer emphasizes the fact that all the saved are of one race with the Saviour, and therefore classes the one and the "many" together here as πάντες.]

And these "all" are ἐξ ἑνός. If we have hitherto followed correctly the author's line of thought, we cannot suppose, with Hofmann and Biesenthal, that the "One" here meant is Adam; nor that ver. 11*a* is intended to express, in the form of a general proposition, that the antithesis of sanctifying activity and passive sanctification is one which exists within the circle of a like descent of all from a common source,—that the vocation to sanctify implies community of origin and nature between the sanctifier and those on whom his function is exercised. Against all this we need only refer to the expression used by Jehovah concerning Himself which is of such frequent occurrence in the Thorah—"*I am He that sanctifieth you*"[2]—to escape from the confusion caused by the assumed generality of the proposition (ver. 11*a*), and so arrive at the true meaning of ἐξ ἑνός. And then, what weighty considerations are suggested by the very word itself, and the whole context, against assuming a reference here to Adam, and not less to Abraham,[3] or to any other human ancestor whatso-

[1] Delitzsch's words are: *indem die Leiden dasjenige, was an ihm der Erhöhung nicht fähig war hinweggeschmolzen* — "His sufferings having melted away what in Him was incapable of exaltation." The expression seems of doubtful propriety, though in a writer at once so accurate and so devout, one feels sure they are meant to bear an orthodox sense, and not in any way to impugn the all-holiness of our Lord.—Tr.
[2] *e.g.* Ex. xxxi. 13; Lev. xx. 8, xxii. 32; comp. Ezek. xxxvii. 28.
[3] So Bengel. [" *Unus* ille Abraham uti Malachias, ii. 15." Jewish

ever!¹ For, after God Himself has been designated (ver. 10) as the absolute end and cause of the whole development,—as the superior not only of them who need salvation, but of Him also who obtains it,—and as perfecting the One through sufferings that He may lead the others on to the glorious goal for which they are destined; and after they, being men, have been distinguished as πολλοὶ υἱοί from the Saviour as υἱός (not τοῦ ἀνθρώπου, but) τοῦ Θεοῦ, it does seem impossible, after all this, that the "One" of whom ver. 11 speaks, and from whom it derives both "Him who sanctifieth and them who are sanctified," can be any other than—God. To which must be added, that the bond of brotherhood here spoken of is not till ver. 14 regarded as being that of a common nature. *He is not ashamed to call them brethren*, being linked to them by a brotherhood which has two sides: 1*st*, that of a common *sanctification*, divinely wrought in the Saviour *immediately* by God Himself, and in us *mediately* through Him; 2*d*, that of a common *human nature*, which, forasmuch as the sanctification spoken of could only be attained through death, the Saviour had to assume, to take upon Him, our flesh and blood, in order to attain it. And hence, again, the "One" (of ver. 11) from whom all are derived is God, not as the God of creation (1 Cor. viii. 6), but as the God of redemption;² the sense being nearly the same as the Johannean ἐκ τοῦ Θεοῦ εἶναι (John viii. 47; 1 John iv. 6, etc.), or the Pauline πρωτότοκος ἐν πολλοῖς ἀδελφοῖς. God is the One who originally ordained the saving work of sanctification. The Sanctifier, who is Himself first sanctified, and those who are sanctified through Him, are all in this sense FROM God.

The sanctifier (ὁ ἁγιάζων), then, is Jesus, who is regarded here in His historical relation to God [*i.e.* not in His natural or

doctors, in reference to this passage of Malachi, were wont to speak of Abraham as האחד, "The One."—TR.] See Biesenthal *in loc.*

¹ Whether Bleek is correct in saying that, if the sacred writer had intended by ἑνός to designate a human parent, he must have added πατρός, or at least a verb distinctly indicating such extraction, I will not attempt to decide, but leave his remark as I find it, seeing that the right reading at Acts xvii. 26 is also perhaps ἐξ ἑνός (Lachm.), and not ἐξ ἑνὸς αἵματος (as the *receptus* and Tischendorf).

² So Böhme, Bleek, De Wette, and all later interpreters, except Hofmann.

essential one—TR.], and who, as one made perfect by God, is born of God into His present priestly and mediatorial relation to us; the sanctified, on the other hand, are men who, in virtue of their sanctification, are also " of God," inasmuch as it was God who perfected their Sanctifier, and who now imparts to them the life of sonship through Him. [Δι' οὗ and δι' ὅν are therefore equally applicable to God in the sphere of redeeming as in that of creative activity.]

The author proceeds: δι' ἣν αἰτίαν—*for which cause, on which account* (the expression occurs only thrice elsewhere in the N. T., in the pastoral epp.)—οὐκ ἐπαισχύνεται—*He is not ashamed* (like xi. 16, with ἐπί sharpening the reference to the object) *to call them His brethren*. Chrysostom and Theodoret observe correctly that the choice of the word οὐκ ἐπαισχύνεται points to the difference between His sonship and theirs. Jesus, as the eternal Son of God, is exalted infinitely above the children of men, and yet has entered into fellowship with us in our humiliation, has been therein Himself made perfect through sufferings by God, and so has become and calls Himself our brother. To prove all this, the sacred writer might have referred to recorded words of our Lord Himself in the Gospel (such as Matt. xii. 49, xxviii. 10, John xx. 17); but he prefers still to refer to prophetic words of the Old Testament as declaratory of the divine counsel, which he regards as spoken by the Saviour yet to come:

Ver. 12. *Saying, I will proclaim thy name to my brethren; in the midst of the church* (or assembly) *will I praise thee*.

The quotation is from the Septuagint version of Ps. xxii. 22 (Heb. 23), but made from memory; the διηγήσομαι (= אֲסַפְּרָה) of the LXX. being changed into ἀπαγγελῶ, which is equally suitable. It is the first of three citations from the O. T. which express, according to our author's understanding of them, the relation in which the hereafter to be manifested Son of God should stand to God's children. Does it so *typically* only, or *prophetically* also? Hofmann maintains exclusively the TYPICAL relation of the twenty-second Psalm to Christ,[1] while

[1] *e.g.* in *Weissag. u. Erfüll.* ii. 29 : " *The thing to be shown was, that, in accordance with the word of God in the Old Testament, Jesus must be one like to us—our brother. To prove this, a passage is first cited in which David*

Bakius (for instance) represents the old traditional SUPER-PROPHETICAL interpretation when he says: *Hunc psalmum ad literam primo proprie et absque ulla allegoria, tropologia et ἀναγωγῇ integrum et per omnia de solo Christo exponendum esse.* No one in the present day is likely to maintain this view from any supposed necessity arising from our Lord's use of the first verse of the Psalm as one of His seven last words upon the cross. It is (originally) a Psalm of David, dating from the time of Saul's persecution, and contains not the slightest hint that the psalmist and the mourner are different persons; but rather is throughout a lyrical expression of the psalmist's own sorrows, rising before the close into the confidence of hope and thankful vows of praise. As certainly, however, as David is the speaker in the Psalm, and no one else, not even Hengstenberg's ideal righteous One (who is a mere fiction), so certainly also is the Psalm a *typical* Psalm; and for this very reason, that David, the anointed of Jehovah (משיח), the ancestor of Jesus Christ, is the speaker in it. The way of sorrows by which David mounted to his earthly throne was a type of that *Via Dolorosa* by which Jesus *the son of David* passed, before ascending to the right hand of the Father. All Psalms are typical in which the state of humiliation, which in David preceded his exaltation, is expressed or described in accordance

calls all other Israelites his 'brethren.' Raised up by the Spirit of Jehovah to be the mediator of His power in Israel, David yet belongs by nature and origin to the mass of the people over whom he is placed as king, and representative of THE KING, *Jehovah. A fellowship in flesh and blood with Israel on the one hand, is compatible with a fellowship in the Spirit with God on the other. In this twofold relation of David to God and Israel, the author of the epistle sees a prophecy of the twofold relation in which He would stand of whom David was the type."* Again, *Schriftbew.* ii. 1, 40 : *" All this is expressed in words taken from Old Testament Scripture, not as if those words in their original meaning directly treated of the Messiah, but as illustrating the truth of the general proposition,* ὅ τε ἁγιάζων καὶ οἱ ἁγιαζόμενοι ἐξ ἑνὸς πάντες, *which is as certainly applicable to Christ as they from whose mouths the words are taken were certainly typical of Him."* These passages contain assumptions which we have already proved to be inadmissible—viz. that identity of nature is the thing which the quotations are intended to prove, and that ὅ τε ἁγιάζων, κ.τ.λ., is meant to be taken as a general proposition. The main point—the assertion that the sacred author's right to use these quotations is founded on their merely *typical* character, and nothing beyond that—must be further examined (in the text).

with the actual historical facts. But Ps. xxii. is more than that—it is in even a higher degree than Ps. xvi. typico-prophetic. For the manifest inferiority of the type to the antitype lies in the very essence of the type itself. But in Ps. xxii. David's description of personal experience in suffering goes far beyond any that he had known in his own person; his complaints descend into a lower deep than he had sounded himself; and his hopes rise higher than any realized reward. Through this hyperbolical character the Psalm became typico-prophetic. David, as the sufferer, there contemplates himself (and his experience) in Christ; and his own, both present and future, thereby acquires a background which in height and depth greatly transcends the limits of his own personality. And this was an operation of the Spirit of God which indwelt in David from the time of his anointing—that Spirit which has eternally before Him the end and the beginning of the kingdom of promise, searching the deep things of God, the counsels of eternal love, and mingling from those deeps unutterable groanings with the prayers of all believers. This Holy Spirit (so we hold with Bleek, Tholuck, and others) drew from the same deeps, and interwove the most special lineaments of the germinant future with the references to the present in David's Psalms, and especially in this twenty-second Psalm, which so exactly describes the passion of Christ, *ut non tam prophetia quam historia esse videatur* (Cassiodorus). In the midst of his complaint, the mourner rises to the confidence of being heard, and utters vows of praise and thanksgiving[1] (ver. 23 et seq. Heb.):

[1] [This becomes more evident when the immediately preceding stanza (vers. 20-22 Heb.) is compared:

But Thou, Jehovah, be not far from me:
My strength, to aid me hasten Thou!
Deliver from the sword my soul;
From hand of dog my only one!
O save me from the lion's mouth,
And from the buffaloes' horns!—Thou answerest me:

this final word עֲנִיתָֽנִי, falling out of the grammatical order (being a perfect or historical present—*Thou answerest*, or *Thou hast answered*—instead of the imperative), is a triumphant interjection, expressing a sudden assurance on the sufferer's part that an answer to his prayer has been already vouchsafed, and so leading on to the words of thanksgiving which follow.—Tr.]

*(Now) will I tell of Thy name to my brethren:
In the midst of the church will I sing Thy praise.
O ye that fear Jehovah, praise Him:
O all ye seed of Jacob, honour Him;
And tremble before Him, all Israel's seed!*

*For He hath not despised, nor hath He abhorred, the
 sufferer's passion:
Nor hath He hidden His countenance from him;
And when he cried out unto Him, He heard.*

It is those who are connected with him by bonds of nature whom David here addresses as "brethren;" but not by bonds of nature only, but those likewise of the Spirit, as the following appellation, "ye that fear Jehovah" (or, ye fearers of Jehovah), shows. It is the gospel of their salvation which is here preached to the church of Israel. This gospel begins (ver. 24 Heb.), "*Fearers of Jehovah!*" etc., and is directed to all of Israel that is capable of salvation. The glad tidings itself is contained in the following tristich (ver. 25). The author of our epistle has a perfect right to assume that David is speaking here as a type of Christ; nay, that the Spirit of Christ is speaking in him, and so Christ Himself selecting David's trials and sufferings as symbols of His own. The Psalm is therefore both typical and prophetic, and it admits of no doubt that the writers of the N. T. allow themselves to quote utterances of typical O. T. personages concerning themselves as utterances and words of Christ. Will this remark apply to the two following citations?

Ver. 13. *And again: I will put my trust in him. And again: Behold! I and the children whom God hath given me.*

The words ἐγὼ ἔσομαι πεποιθὼς ἐπ' αὐτῷ are nowhere found exactly in this form in the LXX.; but the phrase πεποιθὼς ἔσομαι ἐπ' αὐτῷ, which is identical in meaning, occurs three times—2 Sam. xxiii. 3, Isa. xii. 2, and Isa. viii. 17. The third place alone is from a strictly Messianic passage, and is therefore certainly the one here referred to.[1] The words

---

[1] The main purpose of all the discourses from Isa. viii. 5 to ch. xii. is to apply and develop the consolation involved in the prophecy of Immanuel for faithful members of the community of Israel; and this is

which immediately follow (ver. 17), ἰδοὺ ἐγὼ καὶ τὰ παιδία, κ.τ.λ., are introduced by καὶ πάλιν as a separate quotation; because the two expressions, though standing close together, exhibit the fellowship of Christ and His people in two different aspects; and further, because ἰδοὺ ἐγώ is in fact the commencement of a fresh sentence. The Septuagint translates vers. 16–18 in such a way, that vers. 17, 18 may be well understood as words of the Immanuel to come: " *Then shall be made manifest those who seal up the law that one learn it not; and* HE *will say, In God will I trust, who hath turned away His face from the house of Jacob, and will put my trust in Him. Lo! I and the children whom God hath given me.*" It was very natural to understand, by " those who seal up," etc., the scribes and Pharisees (comp. Luke xi. 52), and by the " He," who is the subject of ἐρεῖ, Messiah, as probably the Septuagint translator himself understood it.[1] Such a dependence of our author on the Septuagint as is implied in this use of Isa. viii. 17, 18, may be allowed, without altogether denying his acquaintance with the original text (comp. Bleek, ii. 321). But in this way his procedure would be only explained, not justified, and the explanation itself a somewhat doubtful conjecture, raised on a basis of conjecture. The words of vers. 17, 18 belong in the original text to the *prophet.* Can we in any better way than that suggested above account for our author's citing them as words of *Christ?* May we assume with Hofmann (*Weiss.* ii.

specially the case with the section viii. 5–ix. 6, with particular reference to the then imminent approach of a time of affliction.

[1] Hofmann takes it otherwise, making the subject of ἐρεῖ (in καὶ ἐρεῖ) one of the σφραγιζόμενοι in the preceding clause, and adopting the reading τοῦ μαθεῖν of Cod. Alex. (*Weiss.* ii. 29). But τοῦ μαθεῖν here must have a negative sense, and therefore much the same meaning as the τοῦ μὴ μαθεῖν of the Cod. Vat. [οἱ σφραγιζόμενοι τὸν νόμον τοῦ μαθεῖν = those who seal up the law from being taught (?). The Sept. rendering of the whole paragraph is remarkably Messianic and evangelical in its colouring, and seems to have been in the apostolic writer's mind already in ver. 11, when speaking of ὁ ἁγιάζων and οἱ ἁγιαζόμενοι. It commences thus : *The Lord of hosts, sanctify* (ἁγιάσατε) *ye Him, and He shall be thy fear. And if thou put thy trust in Him, He shall be unto thee for a sanctification* (ἁγίασμα); *and not as a stumbling-stone shall ye encounter Him, nor as the falling of a rock. But the house of Jacob are sitting in a snare . . . and many among them shall fall and be broken, and men in security shall be taken. Then shall be manifest they that seal up the law,* etc. (*i.e.* the Pharisees).—Tr.]

110), that whatsoever, in their vocation as prophets, the seers of the Old Testament say of themselves, is regarded in the New Testament as prophecy concerning Christ? Isaiah, on the one hand, held communion with God in the spirit of prophecy, and on the other, with those whom he addressed in a common human nature, and a like dependence of faith and hope on God (*Weiss.* ii. 30; *Schriftbeweis*, ii. 1, 40). May we lay it down as a canon, that he and every other prophet, when acting according to their vocation, were, under all circumstances, types of Christ? Not so entirely. This canon may be adopted, but only with certain limitations. It is not every utterance of any prophet concerning himself, but only certain utterances of special significance, at certain great crises of the development of the theocracy, which have a typical character. Isaiah himself, as *the* prophet κατ' ἐξοχήν, stands midway between Moses and Christ. The theme of prophetic preaching assigned him in the sixth chapter, makes a deep incision in the history of Israel, dividing it into two halves. The curse of obduration and rejection, to which the mass of Israel was henceforth given over (while a "remnant" only should be saved), the New Testament writers saw fulfilled in their treatment of the Lord Jesus as the Prophet of the kingdom (Matt. xiii. 13-15; John xii. 37-41; Acts xxviii. 25, 27; Rom. xi. 7 et seq.). Thus from the first we find existing a typical relation between Isaiah and the Lord, with not only that one awful side, in reference to the mass of unbelieving Israel, but also another side of hope and salvation, corresponding to the names of each (Isaiah—Jesus), resonant both of ישׁע or ישׁועה, and these, moreover, favourite words with the Old Testament prophet. It is just this side which, as we shall see, finds in the context of these quotations by our author its deepest and most typical expression.

After the prophet has received for himself and the faithful the divine intimation that Jehovah would embrace in guardianship, as of a sanctuary, those who should sanctify Him as Lord of lords, but would be a stone of stumbling and a rock of offence to the mass of the people of both kingdoms, it is added, ver. 16, "*Bind up the testimony, seal the law among my disciples.*" This is an ejaculatory prayer of the prophet: So may the Lord—then He entreats—deposit His testimony, which speaks of this future, and His law, which prepares for it, and both of which the mass, in their hardness of heart, understand not and despise, secure and guarded as with cords and seal in the heart of them who receive the word in the obedience of faith. For otherwise there would be an end of Israel, unless there should continue to be a congregation of believers among them, and an end of this congregation, should the word of God, the foundation of their life, depart from their hearts. And so he waits upon the Lord, supplicating and expecting an answer (ver. 17): *" And I wait upon Him that hideth His face from the house of Jacob, and I look for Him."* A time of judgment has now begun, and will continue long; but God's word is pledged for Israel's endurance in the midst of it, and for Israel's restoration to glory after it is over. Thus, then, the prophet looks for the grace which is hidden behind wrath. His spirit's home is in the future, to which he ministers with his whole house. Ver. 18. *" Behold, I and the children whom God hath given me are for signs and for wonders in Israel from the Lord of hosts, who dwelleth in Mount Zion."* He presents himself, with his children, before the Lord, committing to Him both himself and them. They are God's gifts, and for a higher purpose than ordinary domestic happiness. They serve as signs and types of the future. And Jehovah, who has appointed them, is a God who can as certainly realize that future, as He is Himself the Almighty Lord of hosts, and will as certainly realize it, as He has chosen Mount Zion for the dwelling-place of His gracious presence on earth. True, indeed, Shear-jashub and Maher-shalal-hash-baz are as much emblems of coming wrath as of coming grace; but their father's name, יְשַׁעְיָהוּ, declares that all futurity proceeds from tissues in the Lord's salvation. Thus, Isaiah and his children are figures and emblems of redemption dawning through judgment. He, his children, his wife the prophetess, and the believing disciples (לִמּוּדִים) banded around this family, composed at that time the stock of the church of the Messianic future, in the midst of the *massa perdita* of Israel by which they were surrounded. We may go further, and say that the Spirit of Jesus was already in Isaiah, and pointed, in this holy family (united by bonds of the shadow), to the New Testament church (united by bonds of the substance), which in His high-priestly prayer (John xvii.) the incarnate Word presents to God, making intercession in terms strikingly similar to those which Isaiah here employs. Thus we have the deepest typical relation to justify our author in taking the words of Isaiah as words of Jesus. Isa. viii. 17 shows, in the mirror of the type, that he whom ver. 11 styles ὁ ἁγιάζων, is in the same frame of mind towards God, namely that of confident trust, as οἱ ἁγιαζόμενοι; and Isa. viii. 18 shows in the same mirror, that he classes together in one himself and the ἁγιαζόμενοι, as the children whom God has given him. The fellowship of flesh and blood which unites him and his children is not yet brought under consideration; but in the mouth of Jesus ἅ μοι ἔδωκεν ὁ Θεός cannot possibly express a meaning different from John vi. 39 (comp. ver. 37, πᾶν ὃ δέδωκέ μοι, and xvii. 6, οὓς δέδωκάς μοι ἐκ τοῦ κόσμου). It is, in the first place, a fellowship of (spiritual) derivation, ἐξ ἑνός (from that one God, who is beginning and end of the work of salvation), which the sacred writer is illustrating by these words from the Scriptures of the Old Testament. He proceeds to speak of the community of nature, in close connection with the third quotation, continuing thus:

Vers. 14, 15. *Since, then, the children have in common blood and flesh, he also hath in like manner assumed the same, that through death he might annihilate him that holdeth the power of death, that is, the devil, and deliver those who through fear of death had been their life long held in bondage.*

The proof of the position that it befitted God to make the Captain of our salvation perfect through sufferings, is here continued, and (with the διὰ παθημάτων specially drawn into the argument) now brought to a close. The "children" here are those of the previous quotation (Böhme, Bleek, De Wette, v. Gerlach, Lünemann),[1] and are so called as given by God to Christ, not in respect to their human nature and birth from woman, but to their heavenly life and birth from God, which is mediately through Him their Saviour. That is, they are spiritual children, drawing their origin from one and the same Divine Source with Him. But this spiritual life they have in the earthen vessel of human nature. From this thought the

[1] See, against this, Hofmann, *Schriftb.* ii. 1, 40, and *Weiss.* ii. 31.

author infers, that in order to become the Saviour of such salvation-needing, the Sanctifier of such sanctification-needing men, it was necessary for Jesus to be united with them not only in the spiritual fellowship of a life from God, but also in the natural fellowship of the same bodily life. Human nature, as to its material part, is generally designated elsewhere as σὰρξ καὶ αἷμα. (בָּשָׂר וָדָם, abbreviated בּוֹר, is in post-biblical Hebrew simply a designation for "men" or "human beings.") But here (against the *text. rec.*) we must read αἵματος καὶ σαρκός,[1] —an order of the words which is found at Eph. vi. 12,[2] and is thus distinguishable from the other and more usual one, in that it makes the inward and more important element, *i.e.* the blood, which is the proximate and principal vehicle of the soul, the fluid which feeds and forms the solid parts, and is at any rate indispensable to them, precede the more visible and tangible —the flesh. There is, moreover, here undoubtedly an allusion to that gracious blood-shedding, for the sake of which the Saviour entered into the fellowship of bodily life with us.[3] Instead of the perfect κεκοινώνηκεν of the *protasis*, which expresses what is an ordinary and abiding condition, the aor. μετέσχεν stands in the *apodosis* to denote the free and once for all accomplished fact of our Lord's assumption of human nature—now a thing of the past.[4] Μετέσχεν, indeed, cannot of itself signify *participem se fecit*, but rather is equivalent to μέτοχος ἐγένετο; and yet here, being applied not to one dead (as at 2 Macc. v. 10, οὔτε πατρῴου τάφου μετέσχεν), nor to

[1] So Bengel, Griesbach, Lachmann, Tischendorf, after A. B. C. D. E., Uffenb. (M.), It., Vulg. [and now the Cod. Sin.—TR.] Αἱμ. κ. σαρκ. is also the reading of Cyril of Alex. and of Nicephorus of Constant. (ob. 828) in two places at least of his *Antirrhetica*.

[2] Without any other various reading. [See margin of the English A.V. —TR.]

[3] Compare the order in Clemens Rom. c. xlix., αἷμα, σάρξ, ψυχή: "*Jesus Christ has given His blood for us . . . His flesh for our flesh, and His soul for our soul.*"

[4] The verb κοινωνεῖν is sometimes followed by the dative of the thing or person with which or with whom communion is held, and sometimes (as here) by the gen. of the thing possessed in common with some one else, and the dative of the person who is co-possessor, *e.g.* κοινωνῶ σοι τῆς δόξης. The τῶν αὐτῶν of the *apodosis* refers, of course, to αἵματος καὶ σαρκός, and St. Jerome rightly rejected in his version the gloss preserved in D., τ. α. παθημάτων—*earundem passionum.*

one who had no previous existence before his earthly manifestation, but to an eternal Being, can have no other meaning than one virtually equivalent to that of the ecclesiastical *assumsit* (ἔλαβεν, ἀνέλαβεν).[1] That Christ, by entering into this co-partnership in human nature, became a man like other men, is expressed by παραπλησίως, which, as Hofmann quite correctly observes (*Schriftb.* ii. 1, 41), is by no means selected as being less expressive than ὁμοίως. The author indeed substitutes for it (ver. 17) κατὰ πάντα, and therefore here it must be taken to express not a merely analogous relation, in contradistinction to complete resemblance, but as preferred to ὁμοίως, because a more descriptive, and, so to speak, *pictorial* term : Christ has assumed the very same things (the flesh and blood, of which all men are partakers), and so appeared along with them in the closest relationship.

Now follows with ἵνα a statement of the twofold object of our Lord's incarnation. He both must and would become a member of our race, in order by His own death to deprive Death itself (that greatest contradiction to the glorious promises of Ps. viii.) of its power over man, by removing (1) the cause of death—the power of Satan ; and (2) its effects—the fear of death. The first motive for His atoning death was to root out the power of death, as concentrated in the devil : ἵνα διὰ τοῦ θανάτου καταργήσῃ τὸν τὸ κράτος ἔχοντα τοῦ θανάτου τουτέστιν τὸν διάβολον. The devil is here styled ὁ κράτος ἔχων τοῦ θανάτου, not as an angel of death appointed as God's messenger in all instances,[2] nor as an arbitrary lord of

[1] Comp. Thomasius, *Dogm.* ii. 125. Hofmann, on the other hand, would substitute for the ordinary expression of Catholic theology—" *The Eternal Son took human nature upon Him* (*assumsit*), *and united it to His Godhead*"—the following (as more scriptural) : "*He who is Eternal God has in the course of history made human nature to be His nature*" (*Schriftb.* ii. 1, 27). But allowing, as he does, that He did not thereby cease to be *God*, the correctness of the Catholic term remains unassailable, so long as we understand by *natura divina* all which is essential to the being of God, and by *natura humana* all which is essential to existence as man. The objection that in this sense personality is an essential constituent of human nature, falls to the ground as soon as we surrender the false distinction sometimes drawn between *assumtio* and *unitio*.

[2] Not even in Jewish angelology does Sammael (סמאל) occupy such a position. He is indeed called " Head of all the Satans" (ראש כל השטנים); says of himself, " The souls of all who are born into this world are com-

death, placed in this respect especially over man ; but as being one whose dominion is the hidden cause of all dying, having the power of death not immediately, but mediately, through sin, through which he delivers men over to the judicial punishment of death. For death is as much a judicial exercise of God's power as it is a God-hostile exercise of the devil's power by means of sin transmitted from him to men but cherished by them. The harmony of these two ways of viewing the matter is found in the fact that the wrath of God is the principle by which the devil through his fall is wholly and entirely possessed, so that he is now confined in his rule within the limits of this principle, and, as he is subordinate in his sway to the absolute will of God, must serve this principle in its judicial manifestation. *Satanæ voluntas*, says Gregory the Great on Job i. 11, *semper iniqua est sed nunquam potestas injusta quia a semetipso voluntatem habet sed a Deo potestatem*. We should overstep the function of the expositor were we here to attempt to enter further into this last-mentioned ground of the power of death concentrated in Satan, for we read nothing here of divine wrath : enough that the author cannot think of the devil as God-hating possessor of the power of death without at the same time, since all things are, as he has stated (ver. 10), διὰ τὸν Θεὸν and διὰ τοῦ Θεοῦ, thinking of his deadly power as subserving the will of God—namely, the will of His wrath.[1]

mitted to my hand;" and is even entitled "Angel of Death" (מלאך המות); but yet it is not asserted or supposed that he in every case inflicts the death-blow. See *Debarim Rabbah*, f. 302, *a*, *b*.

[1] Hofmann is perfectly right in maintaining that spiritual, bodily (temporal), and eternal death are ideas which are involved in, or intertwined with, one another, and that Satan, as the author of all that is undivine or contrary to God, is the author also of death; so that men, having lost communion with God, fall in death under the dominion of this God-opposing, death-originating power (*Schriftb*. i. 400, 431). This is quite true, but not the whole truth. When traced back to its ultimate ground, it will be seen that death is more than a falling under the sway of a God-hating power: it is subjection to something beyond all middle causes—beyond even the devil's κράτος τοῦ θανάτου—and that something is the divine wrath itself. Without the recognition of this truth, it is impossible to reconcile the statements of Scripture, or to comprehend the mystery of the atonement. The very victory of Christ over Satan is but a mysterious foreground, which has a yet more mysterious background behind it. [This note is abridged.—TR.]

The proximate design of the incarnation of the Son of God was to annihilate this God and man detested minister of the wrath of God. That action of the incarnate Son, here called καταργεῖν (= ἀργὸν (ἀεργὸν) ποιεῖν, to render inoperative[1]), is expressed 1 John iii. 8 by the periphrasis λύειν τὰ ἔργα τοῦ διαβόλου: it is that bruising of the serpent's head which was promised in the Protevangel—that swallowing up or *absorption* of death prophesied by Isaiah (xxv. 8), through the disabling (or, as we might say, to give the force of the κατά in καταργεῖν, the deposition or depotentiating) of its prince,—a victory which, in its full greatness, will not be manifested till the close of this dispensation.

The present consequence however is, that death itself, though not yet annihilated (1 Cor. xv. 26), lies henceforth under the power of the Conqueror of its prince, whereby, for all who accept the benefit, the second object of the incarnation (as stated ver. 15) is attained. Christ's action on their behalf is described here by the verb ἀπαλλάττειν, which signifies to remove from one condition to another,[2] to set free from something (with genit. case), release,[3] deliver. The object is introduced by τούτους ὅσοι: he says ὅσοι, not οἵ, in order to designate the deliverance as one embracing all individuals found in the state which he proceeds to describe. Till the time of Christ's triumph over Satan, men were through fear of death ἔνοχοι δουλείας—"subject to bondage" (Luther, before 1527, "*pflichtig der Knechtschaft*"): comp. Matt. xxvi. 66, ἔνοχος θανάτου, (he is) *guilty of death*; 1 Cor. xi. 27, ἔνοχος τοῦ

---

[1] This signification (to "deprive of force," or "bring to nothing") καταργεῖν retains elsewhere in the New Testament; *e.g.* it is used 1 Cor. xv. 24 of the final destruction of the power of all spiritual enemies, and specially 1 Cor. xv. 26 and 2 Tim. i. 10 of that of death. (It seems not to be used in the New Testament in the weaker sense, common in classical Greek, "to leave idle, or let pass unemployed," *e.g.* Eur. *Phœn.* 754, χέρα; Polyb. ap. Suid. τοὺς καιρούς.)

[2] The condition from which deliverance is here said to be vouchsafed is that of δουλεία. Consequently, with fine rhetorical art and feeling, ἀπαλλάξῃ is placed at the beginning of the sentence, δουλείας at the end.

[3] In Hofmann's *Schriftb.* "*wiederbrächte*" is probably a *lapsus* for "*losbrächte.*" Greek grammarians, lexicographers, and scholiasts explain ἀπαλλάττειν c. gen. by ῥύεσθαι καὶ λυτροῦν (ἐκλυτροῦσθαι), *e.g.* Philemon, ed. Ossan. p. 260.

σώματος τοῦ Κυρίου, guilty of (or as to) the Lord's body, i.e. (properly) held fast thereby, ἐνεχόμενος, bound therein, or under arrest of (Ditfurt, *Attische Syntaxis*, § 134). The fear of death brings a man into a perpetual state of bondage, διὰ παντὸς τοῦ ζῆν, so that the whole of his living course (τὸ ζῆν) has for its inseparable accompaniment the fear of death, making him to be neither master of himself nor capable of true enjoyment.[1] The life of men before the incarnation and the Lord's victory over death, was a perpetual fear of dying: the very psalms in which the saints of old lay bare their inmost souls are proofs of this. The contemplation of death, and of the dark and cheerless Hades in the background, was even for the faithful among Israel under the Old Testament unendurable: they sought to hide themselves from it with their faith in Jehovah, and so in that infinite bosom of love whence one day the Conqueror of death and of the prince of death should issue. Hofmann is right in requiring (*Schriftb.* ii. 1, 274) that διὰ τοῦ θανάτου be not interpreted as if it were διὰ τ. θ. αὐτοῦ.

"*Death itself as such served the Lord as the medium of His triumph over the ruler of death, the devil; and a new life for all mankind commenced in the person of Jesus Christ mightier than any power of Satan, when He had subjected His own mortal life to a death which thus became the death of death!*" This is as true as can be;[2] but in the answer to the question, How the Lord's death became the medium of His victory over Satan? I find important omissions. "*Satan*" (says Hofmann, as above), "*in exercising the power committed to him, of inflicting death on Him whom God had appointed to become the Author of life, brought to a close that form of the relation between God and Christ which was conditioned by the weakness of human nature, and in which the human life of Christ was capable of death; but*

[1] So a fragment of Æschylus says:
Τί γὰρ καλὸν ζῆν βίου ὃς λύπιας φέρει;
comp. the *locus communis* of ancient tragedy:
Τὸ μὴ γενέσθαι κρεῖσσον ἢ φῦναι βροτοῖς.
—(Clemens Alex. *Strom.* iii. p. 520.)

[2] Primasius: *Arma quæ fuerunt illi quondam fortia adversus mundum, hoc est Mors, per eam Christus illum percussit, sicut David, abstracto gladio Goliæ, in eo caput illius amputavit, in quo quondam victor ille solebat fieri.* Gregorius Magnus, on Job xl. 19: *Dominus itaque noster ad humani generis redemtionem veniens velut quemdam de se in necem diaboli hamum fecit*. . . .

this conclusion was not the end of our Lord's communion and fellowship with God, but rather the transition to a new living and glorious manifestation of that fellowship. Thus enduring to the uttermost, and so exhausting Satan's power, Jesus finally deprived him of it." But καταργεῖν here implies not only passive endurance and suffering, but at the same time an active fight and struggle: the death by which Death was overcome was a mortal combat with him that had the power of death, with life and death for its issues, a decisive termination of the war declared against Satan at the Lord's first entrance into the world. And since (as Hofm. himself expresses it, *Schutzschr.* i. 14) Satan is not a power able to impose anything upon the Son of God beyond what the Father permits to be done, and since it was in the last resort the Father Himself who put the Son under Satan's power, it follows that that wrestling of the Son of God with Satan was at the same time a wrestling with the divine wrath against sin, which, though it could not *immediately* affect Him, the Innocent and Holy One, yet *mediately* did so, because He had entered the lists ὑπὲρ παντός, on behalf of mankind in general, and of each and every one of the human race, identifying Himself therewith, and thus made "a Substitute" for it; which last view we hope hereafter to show to be the scriptural one. It was a conflict like that of Jacob at the Jabbok; for there too it was not a feigned wrath with which the divine man assailed him, but a well-merited and real displeasure, which Jacob, holding fast in faith on the divine grace behind it, overcame, and would not leave his hold till that grace had blessed him. And even in his victory he suffered loss—his thigh was put out of joint. So, in like manner, Jesus Christ suffered the storm of wrath divine (which He who had the power of death caused to burst on Him) to pass over His head

Ibi quippe inerat humanitas, quæ ad se devoratorem adduceret, ibi divinitas quæ perforaret; ibi aperta infirmitas, quæ provocaret, ibi occulta virtus quæ raptoris faucem transfigeret. The reading of the Cod. Clarom., ἵνα διὰ τοῦ θανάτου θάνατον καταργήσῃ τὸν τὸ κράτος, κ.τ.λ., and in the Lat. text, *ut per mortem mortem destrueret*, can hardly be right, but is certainly remarkable, and, considering the importance of this MS. as evidence of the oldest form and interpretation of the text, is valuable and instructive. The second and third hands (D.** and D.***) have expunged the θάνατον. [Delitzsch might have referred to the ancient eucharistic *præfatio*—" *qui mortem nostram moriendo destruxit.*"—TR.]

in order thus to dissipate it. Having become a curse (κατάρα) for all mankind, He surrendered Himself to that curse in order to absorb it; suffering His heel to be bruised by the serpent, in order to His bruising in return the serpent's head; and sinking in death into that bosom of divine love which perfected Him thus as the Captain of our salvation, in order from that bosom to uprise again to a life of endless glory. In order to accomplish this, it was needful that the Son of God should assume a nature subject to death,[1] *i.e.* the nature of man. His purpose was to overcome the power of death, and all in subjection to it. Hofmann remarks with convincing force, that ὅσοι here denotes not so much the extent of the field over which, as the limitations within which, this redeeming energy of the Lord was operative. Only one thing must be added: ὅσοι extends the intention of Christ's work to all, without exception, whom those limits comprise. His work was designed not for beings exempt from death, but for beings held in bondage by the fear of death—for these alone (τούτους), but for all these without exception (ὅσοι). And such beings are men: therefore he continues:

Ver. 16. *For not indeed of angels doth he take hold, but taketh hold of the seed of Abraham.*

Luther renders, after the Vulgate (*nusquam enim*), "*for nowhere taketh He upon Him the angels,*" etc., inexactly; for που cannot be here separated from δή (with *local* meaning), but δήπου is one word:[2] οὐ δήπου is equivalent to the German "*doch wohl nicht,*" "*doch nicht etwa*" (Eng., probably not, I trow not). Neither is Luther's rendering of ἐπιλαμβάνεται = "*assumere*" quite exact, while the *apprehendere* of the Vulgate is better. Nor can ἐπιλαμβάνεται be understood of the " *assumptio*

[1] Cyril of Alexandria says on this passage: *Christ's death became a root of life, the annihilation of destruction, the putting away of sin, an end of wrath* (πέρας τῆς ὀργῆς). *We were curse-laden, and in Adam brought under the judgment of death; but then the Word, who knew no sin, causing Himself to be called a son of Adam, delivered us from the guilt of that transgression. Human nature appeared in Christ free from fault, and His faultlessness saved us.* [Loosely rendered, not having the Greek original before us.— TR.]

[2] δήπου is not met with elsewhere in the New Testament, nor in the LXX. (δή, too, but seldom, oftenest in St. Luke). It is of frequent occur-

naturæ humanæ," for this, if for no other reason, that the author's reasoning would then be in a circle (ἐπεὶ οὖν ... οὐ γὰρ δήπου ... ὅθεν), and because the *present* tense would be unsuitable after μετέσχεν; moreover, ἐπιλαμβάνεσθαι itself does not mean *assumere*, for ἐπί does not refer, as *ad*, to the person who takes, but to the thing taken; to apply one's self to something (ἐπί), in order to take it for one's self (λαμβάνεσθαι). We might indeed in this way arrive at, or come back to, the traditional interpretation; for the phrase *apprehensio naturæ humanæ* is admissible,[1] but the other substantial grounds already indicated are against it, and the whole expression (ἀγγέλων ... σπέρματος Ἀβραάμ) does not seem to refer to a becoming or being made "man," in contrast to a becoming or being made "angel." Thomasius, therefore, has very properly given up this old text-proof of the doctrine of the *assumtio* (*Dogm.* ii. 125), which, when Castellio first ventured to do, Beza designated as an *execranda audacia*. The anathema was misplaced, and this example may be added to the proofs that exegetical tradition is not infallible. The author's real meaning may be inferred from the very mention of the σπέρμα Ἀβραάμ. By this term he designates neither the people of Israel, as writing here to Jewish Christians (Bleek, De Wette, Köstlin, Lünemann), nor all mankind (Bengel, etc.), nor in a merely spiritual sense, the faithful under the New Testament (*e.g.* Böhme); but rather the whole church of God, beginning from the Old Testament and continuing into the New, founded on the call and faithful obedience of Abraham, embracing Israel and all believers from the rest of mankind in the same fellowship, and constituting the whole of that good olive-tree which has the patriarchs for its sacred root (Gal. iii. 29;

---

rence in Philo, and in our epistle belongs to its characteristic λέξις ἑλληνικωτέρα. The που tempers without weakening the force of the δή, and is without any approach to irony, while leaving, as it were, free room for thought and reflection. Comp. Klotz on *Devarius*, p. 262; and Xen. *Cyr.* iii. 1, 17, οὐ γὰρ ἂν δήπου, εἴ γε φρόνιμον δεῖ γενέσθαι τὸν μέλλοντα σώφρονα ἔσεσθαι παραχρῆμα ἐξ ἄφρονος σώφρων ἄν τις γένοιτο, where the consciousness and convictions of the hearers or readers are confidently appealed to. Demosthenes is fond of the expression, ἴστε γὰρ δήπου τοῦτο—that you surely know!

[1] [Compare the *Tu ad liberandum suscepturus hominem* of the Te Deum, where *hominem = naturam humanam.*—TR.]

CHAP. II. 16. 139

Rom. iv. 16 and xi. 16; *vid.* Hofm. *Schriftb.* ii. 1, 42). The proof that Jesus became man to die for men, is drawn from the fact that the object of His redeeming work was not the angels, but this church of the living God, whose members are gathered from the whole family of man. This work of redemption is here expressed by ἐπιλαμβάνεται, which we must not, with Castellio, merely render by *opitulatur*, "vouchsafe assistance to."[1] Ἐπιλαμβάνεσθαι is the Septuagint word for אָחַז, הֶחֱזִיק, and תָּפַשׂ; and the form in which the author here clothes his thoughts reminds us not only of Isa. xli. 8, 9 (as compared by Hofmann), *But thou, Israel, art my servant, Jacob whom I have chosen, the seed of Abraham my friend. Thou whom I have taken from the ends of the earth* (where the Septuagint renders הֶחֱזַקְתִּיךָ by ἀντελαβόμην); but also of Jer. xxxi. 32 (which our author cites, viii. 9), where the day of Egyptian deliverance is called ἡμέρα ἐπιλαβομένου μου τῆς χειρὸς αὐτῶν. Both passages speak not of the rendering of mere assistance, but of a gracious laying hold, in order to take out of a state of bondage, as Grotius, Nemeth, Camero, and the Geneva version[2] rightly interpret here. Ἐπιλαμβάνεται, therefore, neither signifies in this place a continuous assistance on God's part now (as Bleek, De Wette, von Gerlach, Lünemann, Hofmann, and most moderns), nor does it refer to a preparatory gracious course of action under the Old Testament (as formerly Hofmann); but (the subject being the Lord's manifestation in the flesh) it denotes that gracious laying hold in order to redeem, which commenced in the incarnation, and is thence continued.[3] The objects of this laying hold were not angels, but the seed of Abraham. Nor is there any contradiction in this to Col. i. 20 (Bleek, De Wette, Lünemann). Men alone need or are capable of *redemption.* The author's meaning is: Christ became man in

---

[1] ἐπιλαμβάνεσθαί τινος is neither equivalent to ἀντιλαμβάνεσθαί τινον, to take up some one, assist him, nor to συνεπιλαμβάνεσθαι, to aid another by joining with him in his work. Hofmann seems therefore to be wrong, formerly, in entirely rejecting the sense of "*assisting*" (*Weiss.* ii. 226), while maintaining that of "laying hold upon," and now in rejecting (*Schriftbew.* ii. 1, 42) the sense of helping altogether.

[2] "*Car il n'a pas pris les Auges pour les delivrer de l'esclavage.*"—G.V.

[3] *Angelos quodammodo reliquit aliasque cœlorum virtutes ut nos apprehenderet, et ovem perditam, passionis suæ inventam humeris impositam reportaret ad cœlestem patriam.*—ALCUIN after Chrysost.

140   EPISTLE TO THE HEBREWS.

order to die for men; He layeth not hold of angels to make of them a church of His redeemed, but of Abraham's seed: these, a church gathered from among men who are living in the flesh, subject to death, and in need of redemption,—these He lays hold of, to these associates Himself, to become their Redeemer, and raise them in the end to honour above that of angels.

The logical correctness of the following deduction is now clear. After deducing (ver. 14) the necessity for our Lord's assumption of flesh and blood from the brotherly relation between sanctifier and sanctified, as taught in the Old Testament, he now deduces, from His gracious purpose on behalf of Abraham's seed in thus becoming man, the necessity for His participation in all the details of human infirmity.[1]

Ver. 17. *Whence he needed in every respect to become like unto his brethren, that so he might become a merciful and faithful high priest as towards God, to make atonement for the sins of the people.*

The colouring of the phraseology here is throughout that of St. Luke. Ὅθεν (*unde sequitur ut*) occurs six times in this epistle and Acts xxvi. 19, but nowhere in the epp. of St. Paul. Ὁμοιωθῆναι is used precisely as at Acts xiv. 11, in the cry of the men of Lystra. Ἱλάσκεσθαι has no other parallel in the N. T. but Luke xviii. 13. Κατὰ πάντα may be said to be a Lucan as much as a Pauline expression, from its occurrence Acts xvii. 22. Τὰ πρὸς Θεόν occurs again indeed only at v. 1 and Rom. xv. 17; but we find at Luke xiv. 32, xix. 42, Acts xxviii. 10,[2] τὰ πρός as a familiar turn of expression = *ea quæ attinent ad* (not adverbially, as here, *in iis quæ*). There is nothing peculiar in ὤφειλεν. The writer of set purpose uses neither ἔδει (as Luke xxiv. 26) nor ἔπρεπεν (as above, ver. 10), —ἔπρεπεν denoting harmonious conformity with the essential divine attributes, ἔδει an inward necessity arising from the

---

[1] *In the days of the son of David* (says an old Midrash with reference to Isa. xxxiii. 7) *will sinners cry from without, lamenting that they did not hearken to God's word, and the ministering angels from within, that they are not counted worthy of the blessedness of the righteous* (Elijahu Rabba, c. 5). An expression of the same thought as 1 Pet. i. 11, εἰς ἃ ἐπιθυμοῦσιν ἄγγελοι παρακύψαι.

[2] Compare Luke xiv. 28 and Acts xxiii. 30, according to the *text. rec.*

divine counsels; while ὤφειλεν expresses the duty or obligation which the task, once undertaken, brings with it. Having become man in order to our redemption, He was bound in duty to become like us, κατὰ πάντα. The incarnation itself is not included under τὰ πάντα, having been already assumed and proved, ver. 14; τοῖς ἀδελφοῖς here presupposes it, and ὅθεν draws a conclusion from its purpose, as already stated, ver. 16. By these πάντα the sacred writer probably meant not so much abstract properties of human nature, such as infirmity, liability to temptation, mortality, etc., as more concretely the manifold sufferings, toils, perils, and conflicts which, ending in death at last, becloud, weigh down, and wear away the life of man, in its present state of distance from its destined goal. In all these particulars the Lord was bound to become like His brethren, His fellow-men, ἵνα ἐλεήμων γένηται καὶ πιστὸς ἀρχιερεὺς τὰ πρὸς τὸν Θεόν.

This is the first time in the epistle that Christ is called Ἀρχιερεύς, on which De Wette remarks, "*evidently without sufficient preparation.*" But seeing that the "cleansing of sins" (i. 3), "sanctifying" (ii. 11), and mediatorial "leadership" in the work of salvation (ii. 10), are all priestly acts and offices, and that the death of Christ, as a death for every man (ii. 9), has the character of a sacrificial death, it is evident that the fact is quite otherwise than as De Wette supposes, for this, if for no other reason, that the author (as Hofmann observes against De Wette, *Schriftb.* ii. 1, 278) does nothing more than point out the significance of the death of Christ in relation to sin, the consequence of which He has experienced and endured, in such a manner as to exhibit in His death the completion of that work of God which was prepared for and foreshadowed in the church of the Old Testament.[1] That Christ is called

[1] Hofmann, correctly observing that on this view there would be as little preparation made in the preceding paragraphs for the idea of the sacrifice as for that of the high-priesthood of Christ, adds that both terms are to be regarded as mere illustrations of the nature of His redeeming work, taken from the ordinances of the Old Testament. But surely the Old Testament high-priesthood, and its sacrifices of atonement, were for the sacred writer something more than mere *illustrations;* on the contrary, they were types of a future reality, and preliminary forms of its manifestation, being as closely connected with that reality as the shadow with the body by which it is cast.

ἀρχιερεύς (LXX. only once, Lev. iv. 3, for הַכֹּהֵן הַמָּשִׁיחַ, but frequently in Philo), not simply ἱερεύς, is the necessary consequence of the divine elevation from which He came down, and up to which He returned: for this reason He is High Priest, that is, priest in sole and absolute eminence. Yet it is not His personal dignity which in itself alone makes Him High Priest, but at the same time the nature of His work intimately connected with it; which work has its most closely corresponding type in the peculiar official functions of the Levitical high priest. It was the high priest who had to offer all the sin-offerings presented for the whole congregation (Lev. iv. 13–21), especially the sin-offering for the collective sin of the whole congregation, once every year, on the great day of atonement (Lev. xvi.). Thus ἐξιλάσκεσθαι περὶ πάσης συναγωγῆς υἱῶν Ἰσραήλ, or περὶ τοῦ λαοῦ (as the LXX. translates), was the official duty incumbent upon the high priest as such. It is in reference to this that the author says at the close τοῦ λαοῦ instead of ὑμῶν. *"To make atonement for the congregation of the Lord collectively, to cancel its sins on the great day of atonement by God's appointed ordinance, on which depended its continuing to be collectively the congregation of the Lord, was the work peculiarly belonging to the high priest; and just such a high priest Jesus had to become in the antitype"* (*Schriftb.* ii. 1, 266). If the question, what in our author's view is the terminating point of this γίγνεσθαι ἀρχιερέα, and hence the commencing point of the εἶναι ἀρχιερέα, were to be answered from this passage alone, we should be obliged to answer, in accordance with Socinus, Limborch, Peirce, etc., that Christ did not attain to the dignity nor perform the work of high priest until His exaltation; for, as His dying is included in the κατὰ πάντα ὁμοιωθῆναι, the high-priesthood appears here as the goal which He had to reach through suffering, and especially the suffering of death. But further on it will become evident to us that the author looks upon our Lord's surrendering Himself to death, His offering up of Himself, as a high-priestly act; and if type and antitype are co-extensive, it cannot possibly be otherwise: for not only the presentation of the blood in the holy of holies, but also the slaying of the victim, formed part of the official duty of the Old Testament high priest. He who is in the act of offering Himself is already High Priest, and yet still in process of becoming so perfectly; for this offering of Himself first procures for Him the possibility of entering into the heavenly sanctuary.¹ His high-priesthood, εἰς τὸν αἰῶνα, rests upon His death, suffered once for all in our behalf. He had to walk the path of human suffering down to this deep turning-point, in order to acquire the requisite qualifications for the exercise of high-priestly functions extending thenceforth from heaven to earth. ῞Ινα γένηται intimates what He should become through assuming our likeness; εἰς τὸ ἱλάσκεσθαι, what He was appointed thereafter to perform. Most expositors (including Bleek, De Wette, Tholuck) take ἐλεήμων apart by itself as a predicate,

¹ It is well known that the doctrine of the old Socinians was, that our Lord's high-priesthood commenced with His exaltation, and with His entrance into the possession of the heavenly kingdom. Hence they drew the consequence, that the death of the cross corresponded to the slaying, but not to the sacrificial presentation of the victim: *Oblatio non idem est quod mactatio; mactatio est tantum antecedens oblationis et ad oblationem præparatio et sacrificii quoddam initium.* So Schlichting on Heb. i. 3, and elsewhere. That this assertion is directly contradictory, not to our epistle only, but to the whole apostolic Scriptures, scarcely requires proof: the cross is also the altar of the Lamb of God; His dying there is antitype both of the slaying (שְׁחִיטָה) and the presentation (הַקְרִיבָה, *oblatio*) of the typical sacrifice. How contrary to Scripture it was to deny this, was felt by the Socinians themselves; hence the more cautious expression of their doctrine was: *Cum Christus corpus suum gloriosum Deo obtulit, tunc demum ipsius oblatio perfecta est.* But even this is only apparently the teaching of our epistle. With the crucified Lord's "It is finished" His sacrifice and self-oblation as "*opus,*" both passive (σφαγή) and active (προσφορά), was once for all accomplished. What followed was partly a sealing and acknowledgment on God's part of the work thus done (by the raising of Christ from the dead), and partly the Saviour's own making valid or realizing this acknowledgment which gave Him right of entrance into the celestial sanctuary (by His ascension and self-presentation before God in heaven). The sacred writer recognises indeed a certain προσφέρειν of our High Priest in the heavenly world (as we shall see more particularly hereafter), but that not as a completing of a work left imperfect on earth, but simply as the presentation of that accomplished work in heaven. Whatever was done with the sin-offerings in the outer court on the day of atonement (Lev. xvi.), found once and for all a perfect antitypical accomplishment in Christ's offering of Himself here below, *i.e.* both the slaying of the victims before the altar, and their subsequent oblation upon it. Between these two actions, in the outer court took place the high-priestly carrying of the blood into the holy of holies: this, and this alone, had a heavenly antitypical fulfilment in the Lord's ascension.

translating with Luther, "*That He might be merciful, and a faithful High Priest.*" But Ebrard and Hofmann rightly translate, "*A merciful and faithful High Priest.*" Bengel's delicate perception had already guided him to the reason why the words are placed in so inverted an order: ἐλεήμων looks backwards, because sufficiently accounted in the foregoing; πιστὸς ἀρχιερεύς looks forward, because both ideas wait for their further unfolding in what follows. Moreover, there is, at least according to my feelings, something unseemly in ἵνα ἐλεήμων γένηται. If Jesus is the One whom the author teaches us to recognise in Him, ch. i., He does not need now to become ἐλεήμων; for Jehovah declares, Ex. xxii. 26, ἐλεήμων εἰμί. And although the author has hitherto made more prominent in the work of salvation the purpose and preparation of God than the self-determination of the Saviour, yet it is sufficiently clear from what has been already said, that the motive for becoming incarnate on the part of Him who became so, was compassion for men, so that He did not need to become ἐλεήμων. But it can certainly be said, that He should become a merciful High Priest, that is, that He should acquire in the path of experience the mercifulness requisite for the office of high priest as such (see iv. 15, v. 2, 7–10). He is called ἐλεήμων (formed as αἰδήμων, νοήμων, τλήμων—Lobeck, *Pathol.* 160 ; Aram. רַחְמָן) as merciful in relation to men ; πιστός (נֶאֱמָן) in relation to God as faithful, that is (as shown iii. 2), discharging faithfully the duties of His calling. It would, however, be a mistake to suppose that the adverbial clause τὰ πρὸς τὸν Θεόν qualifies only the second attribute (Klee). Neither does it refer to ἀρχιερεύς alone (Bl., Hofm.), but to the collective idea contained under ἐλεήμων καὶ πιστὸς ἀρχιερεύς. The author intends to say, that He should be a merciful and faithful high priest, merciful and faithful in that character,—namely, in affairs pertaining to the relation which they for whom He is appointed bear to God, that is, in the sphere of His office. If the author intends any distinction here, it is between the high priest as man and as office-bearer, not between the high priest as prince of holiness and as representative of the congregation (or church); for it is in the very fact that the holiness of the church culminates in Him that this High Priest mediatorially represents the church before God—His very holiness giving

Him the capacity to do so. How we are to conceive of the representation of the church in its relation to God, as here expressed by τὰ πρὸς τὸν Θεόν, we learn further from the subordinate clause εἰς τὸ ἱλάσκεσθαι τὰς ἁμαρτίας τοῦ λαοῦ. The form of this clause is similar to that of vii. 25, εἰς τὸ ἐντυγχάνειν, κ.τ.λ. The transitive construction of ἱλάσκεσθαι (= ut expiet) is the most natural and usual one.[1] Yet, on closer inspection, ἱλάσκεσθαι τὰς ἁμαρτίας is seen to be a very peculiar expression. For ἱλάσκεσθαι is undoubtedly equivalent to ἱλαὸν (ἱλεὼν) ποιεῖν; and ἵλαος being related to ἵλαρος, the verb must naturally have a *person* for its object, so that the proper construction would be ἱλάσκεσθαί τινα, aliquem propitium facere. In classical Greek the word actually occurs in this sense, and in this alone, with "the gods" for its object, and sometimes also *men* (Plutarch's ἱλάσκεσθαι ὀργήν τινος [2] is scarcely an exception). But this classical use of the word is entirely foreign to the Greek of the Bible. Neither in the LXX. nor in the New Testament is ἱλάσκεσθαι used of an action whereby man brings God into a gracious disposition, but either occurs in a middle sense, to express a gracious self-determination on the part of God, or when used transitively (as here), has sin for its object, and implies an action whereby sin ceases to make God otherwise than gracious to man.[3] The

---

[1] Ἰλάσκεσθαι occurs both as passive and deponent in Hellenistic Greek, especially in the passive and middle forms, ἱλάσθην, ἱλασθήσομαι, ἱλασάμην, ἱλάσομαι (e.g. Ps. lxxviii. 38, Sept., where the right reading is not ἱλάσκεται, but ἱλάσεται). In the here unsuitable signification of *propitium fieri*, and in classical Greek, ἱλάσκεσθαι is never found as a passive. The New Testament aor. imper. pass. ἱλάσθητι, *be gracious*, is found in Homer in the form ἵληθι.

[2] Plut. *Cat. Min.* 61.

[3] The antithesis of *medial* and *transitive* (signification) is apt to mislead. Ἰλάσκω as active verb does not occur. In the form ἱλάσκομαι it has passive and reflexive signification indiscriminately, *to be graciously disposed*, or *to suffer one's self to be made gracious*, and is sometimes found with *passive* (Ex. xxxii. 14, ἱλάσθη ὁ Κύριος), sometimes with *middle* forms (Ps. lxv. 4, τὰς ἀσεβείας ἡμῶν σὺ ἱλάσῃ). In this respect it resembles the Hebrew *Niphal* (e.g. Ex. xxxii. 14 it corresponds to וַיִּנָּחֶם). Sometimes it has an *active* sense, with an entire loss of *reflexive* reference to the subject, as here (Heb. ii. 17) and Ps. lxv. 4, where, however, several MSS. read ταῖς ἀσεβείαις. Ἰλάσκεσθαι is otherwise used in the Sept., with the dative of the thing or person for whom atonement is made, and therefore is always

same is the case with ἐξιλάσκεσθαι or ἐξιλᾶσθαι.¹ Sin may be atoned for (ἐξιλασθήσεται ἀδικία, fut. passive, 1 Sam. iii. 14); but it is nowhere said of God that He is ἐξιλασθείς, *propitiated*, nor (ἐξιλάσκεταί τις τὸν Θεόν) that *any one propitiates Him.* This is certainly not accidental, and must admit of explanation. That, in reference to the sacrifices of the Old Testament, the ἐξιλάσκεσθαι of the LXX. should never have God for its object, may be explained by the fact that the same is the case with כִּפֶּר, of which word it is the LXX. rendering. Ἱλάσκεσθαι τὰς ἁμαρτίας, therefore, is not equivalent to ἱλάσκεσθαι τὸν Θεὸν τὰς ἁμαρτίας (Winer, § 32), but thought in Hebrew while expressed in Greek, and = כַּפֵּר עֲוֹנוֹת (lit. *to atone sins*). But why cannot כִּפֶּר have God for its object? That is more easy to explain, for the fundamental meaning of כִּפֶּר is *tegere* or *abstergere;* and it would be against decorum to apply such an expression to God Himself, or His divine wrath (Bähr, *Temp.* 176). But the same is the case in Hebrew with more fitting expressions of the idea of atonement. We frequently read of a sacrifice נרצה, that it is favourably received, but never הרצה, that it makes (God) favourable. And yet does not the essence of atonement consist not merely in the covering or hiding sin or impurity from the eyes of God the Holy One, but also in His laying aside for His part His burning and consuming wrath against it? The atonement is interposed between sin and wrath (Num. xvi. 48), and seeks to effect that God *turn from His fierce wrath* (Ex. xxxii. 30, 12). The more strange, therefore, does it seem that we nowhere find an expression equivalent to *placare Deum*, to appease or propitiate the Holy One. The reason for this phenomenon may, however, be discerned. It lies in the incongruousness of the Old Testament sacrifices with their aim and object. No atoning power could reside in the offerings of animals or things without life: they were only made *media* of atonement by a provisional arrangement on God's part, and by way of accommodation. The Israelite was not to imagine vainly, like the

equivalent to *propitium fieri*, whereas ἐξιλάσκεσθαι is frequently used with the *accus.* or περί, and therefore in the sense of *expiare*.

¹ The form ἐξιλεοῦσθαι, which is found in Strabo (ἐξιλεοῦσθαι Θεόν), does not occur in the LXX. The Complutensian reading ἐξιλέωσαν, 2 Sam. xxi. 9, is a mistake for ἐξηλίασαν.

heathen, that he mollified and appeased the Divinity by his sacrifice as his own performance (*opus operatum*): rather he was to look upon the sacrifice, with its atoning blood, as a divine gift (Lev. xvii. 11), as God's ordained means of grace for him. But is it not otherwise with the antitypical sacrifice? The work of Christ is really and truly through His own power and merit, not merely a changing of man's relation to God, but also of God's to man; not merely expiation of sin, but also " of God's wrath against sinful man." The death of the Godman has not merely deprived Satan of the claim he had on sinful man; it has also " *satisfied or given satisfaction to divine justice for the sin of Adam's race.*" Hofmann (in whose doctrine of the atonement we miss some essential elements of the church's view) expresses himself thus, and thereby bears his testimony to the scripturalness of such expressions, and of what they imply. It is the more strange, then, that Scripture should nowhere so express itself. How does that happen? It were to be wished that Philippi had started and resolved this question. How accordant with those statements would have been such expressions as, ἱλάσθη ὁ πατὴρ περὶ τῶν ἁμαρτιῶν ἡμῶν διὰ τὸν θάνατον τοῦ υἱοῦ αὐτοῦ, or Χριστὸς ἱλάσατο (ἐξιλάσατο) τὸν Θεὸν (τὴν ὀργὴν τοῦ Θεοῦ) διὰ τοῦ αἵματος αὐτοῦ! But where are they to be found? It would be quite gratuitous to supply τοῦ Θεοῦ after ἱλασμός (1 John ii. 2), where Jesus Christ is called ἱλασμὸς περὶ τῶν ἁμαρτιῶν ἡμῶν. Even κατηλλάγη, or ἀποκατηλλάγη ὁ Θεός, is nowhere found. But as the New Testament confines itself to saying that our high priest atones for (ἱλάσκεται) the sins of the people, that God has set Him forth as ἱλαστήριον for us (Rom. iii. 25), that God has sent His Son as ἱλασμὸς περὶ τῶν ἁμαρτιῶν ἡμῶν (1 John iv. 10), so it calls God in Christ καταλλάξας, or ἀποκαταλλάξας, that is, He who has reconciled us to Himself (2 Cor. v. 18 sqq.; Col. i. 20; Eph. ii. 16); while it speaks of us as καταλλαγέντες, reconciled ones, but never of God as καταλλαγείς, the reconciled One. Yet, on the other hand, Scripture says that we are by nature the children of wrath (Eph. ii. 3); that only when we believe on the Son of God do we cease to be objects of divine wrath (John iii. 36); that it is the blood of Christ whereby we are saved from the wrath to come (Rom. v. 9; comp. 1 Thess. i. 10); that Christ has given Himself for us, προσφορὰν καὶ θυσίαν τῷ Θεῷ εἰς ὀσμὴν εὐωδίας (Eph. v. 2). Hence it looks upon Christ's self-offering as really an act which has rescued us from deserved wrath, and won for us the grace of God, who is gracious only in holiness; it really teaches that Christ has again made man an object of divine love, in that He, as partaking of the sin of the race to which He had joined Himself, and still more, as laden with the sin He had taken on Himself, submitted Himself to the wrath of God, and in the midst of wrath kept hold of love, and so overcame the wrath impending over us, and regained love for us. Thus Scripture teaches, without, however, expressing itself anywhere in the manner above mentioned.[1] Why does it not? As the Old Testament nowhere says that sacrifice appeases God's wrath, lest man should suppose that, by offering sacrifice, he does a thing by which, as a performance, he brings God to be graciously disposed; so the New Testament nowhere says that the self-sacrifice of Christ has appeased the wrath of God, that man may not think that it is a performance which precedes God's gracious will, and by which, while God is passive in the matter, grace instead of wrath is, without His co-operation, wrested, or, so to speak, extorted from Him. The New Testament seeks to guard against this heathen view of the work of the atonement, being replete with the consciousness that it was prepared for us by the prevenient love of the Father when we were strangers to God, that the Father hath sent His Son and given Him for us, that it was the Holy Ghost by whose agency He was incorporated with the human race, and that it is God's counsel of love which He has fulfilled. "*Sin must be annulled —made as if it had never been committed; only on that condition does God become gracious. How then shall He become gracious, unless He Himself performs something whereby sin may be thus in His sight annulled?*" (Hofmann, *Schriftb.* ii. 1, 227.) That such considerations determine the soteriological phraseology of

---

[1] Already in Clem. Rom. we find the expression ἐξιλάσκεσθαι τὸν Θεόν (*to propitiate God*, viz. by penitent prayer), c. vii.; and God is spoken of as ἵλεως γενόμενος (made propitious) and καταλλαγείς (reconciled), c. xlviii.; comp. Irenæus, iv. 8, 2. But the phraseology is unknown to Scripture; a fact which did not escape the Socinians. So Schlichting here: *Non est ergo cur quispiam ex hoc placandi voce concludat Deum a Christo nobis fuisse placatum*, etc.

Scripture is undeniable. That phraseology has a twofold character, being determined in accordance with the two poles, so to speak, of the work of the atonement,—one the eternal love which formed the plan, the other the eternal love which was drawn forth by its accomplishment. Between these two eternal things, love's beginning and love's end, the temporal realization of the eternal counsel of love is accomplished, but not without the incarnate Mediator feeling the operation of the divine wrath as merited by sin, and not without its cloud and tempest gathering and breaking on His innocent head, till He sinks in the deeps of divine dereliction.[1] The storm of wrath, however, which the holy and beloved One suffered thus to pass over Him, while holding fast by love still, and so manifesting His true nature, proved thereby to be but the unveiling of love's eternal sun ; God's fiery wrath against sin, when Christ had suffered it, proved to be God's hunger of love for our salvation, and the curse which Christ was made for us broke a pathway for the blessing which was concealed behind it. And so the work of atonement, when regarded in its totality, and beginning, middle, and end are taken together, is but the self-reconciling of the Godhead with itself. Θεὸς ἦν ἐν Χριστῷ κοσμὸν καταλλάσσων ἑαυτῷ (2 Cor v. 19). Our author, too, from ver. 11 onwards, considers the work of atonement under no other point of view than this : an arrangement of the Godhead within and at unity with itself for our salvation. All the sufferings inflicted by the will of the Father on

[1] Hofmann's remark (*Schriftb.* ii. 1, 279) in reference to Heb. ii. 9 et seq., that "it is evident from these words, that the conception of a vicarious satisfaction on our Lord's part is neither necessary to a true appreciation of the expressions of Scripture concerning His death, nor sufficiently broad to cover them," is easily answered. The doctrine of vicarious satisfaction does not pretend to such broadness as to be an exhaustive representation of the Redeemer's work; it is but a middle thing, between the beginning and the end of God's counsel of love on behalf of sinful humanity. Hofmann himself allows that the Son of God, in virtue of His high-priestly character, made satisfaction to the punitive justice of God on our behalf, *i.e.* overcame for us the wrath of God. He calls it, indeed, an act performed by man, but maintains that it was as such not performed by man of his own power, but a divine economy in man—an act of God made man. But what is this but saying that it was a *vicarious* act? And so Hofmann comes back, in the way of independent reflection, to the traditional doctrine which he had rejected. [Somewhat abridged—TR.]

the Son are means of making the Saviour of mankind, as such, perfect. In such connection of thought, the phrase ἱλάσκεσθαι τὸν Θεόν becomes impossible; and even though applied to the death of Christ, would have no meaning beyond it. For He mediates now and henceforth as high priest for a reconciled church and people, called in Old Testament phrase ὁ λαός, *the people of God;* and all His reconciling work henceforth is directed to one end, the preventing of that sin which still clings to His people from disturbing the relation of love once for all established. His work as high priest, therefore, is no ἱλάσκεσθαι τὸν Θεόν, but ἱλάσκεσθαι τὰς ἁμαρτίας, and those τοῦ λαοῦ. The seed of Abraham, to which as Redeemer He has joined Himself, still lives in the flesh, and needs therefore a high priest to assure it of the grace of God, notwithstanding its clinging infirmity and sin. Such an high priest Jesus Christ has become, after entering into fellowship with all our misery. He can do now for the church of His redeemed all that she stands in need of.

Ver. 18. *For in that he himself hath suffered, being tempted, he is able to succour them that are tempted.*

The church of the redeemed, for which He is appointed high priest, consists of πειραζόμενοι, such as are continually tempted, being placed in situations in which they are in danger of sin, and their faithfulness has to approve itself. In such situations, in which they would be overcome if left to their own strength without higher aid, He is able to succour them (δύναται construed with the *inf. aor.*, as with few exceptions is always the case in our author; comp. Luke i. 20, 22, iii. 8, v. 12, etc.). This ability He has acquired αὐτὸς πειρασθείς, that is, through His own experience of suffering. He Himself was tempted, ἐν ᾧ πέπονθεν, in that He suffered, or (what is the same thing, only retaining more consciously the radical signification of the ἐν ᾧ) in His suffering, which is now past. Thus explained, the whole is clear and consistent. All modern expositors agree in this, that ἐν ᾧ amounts to the same as ἐν τούτῳ ὅτι, Luke x. 20 (like Rom. ii. 1, viii. 3), except Bl. and Winer, even in the sixth edition (p. 144, 34*b*), who assert that ἐν ᾧ should be resolved into ἐν τούτῳ ὅ (ᾧ). But the conjunctional use of ἐν ᾧ (still retained in modern Greek) cannot be doubted; further, if ἐν were intended to point out the sphere within which aid is given, then the author would certainly have written ἐν οἷς (comp. iv. 15, κατὰ πάντα πεπειρασμένον). There seems to me less force in the objection (Böhme, *Thol. Ausg.* 3; Hofm.), that in that case it would have been necessary to use the aor. ἔπαθεν (as v. 8, xii. 13) instead of the perf. πέπονθεν; for the author could quite as well indicate the suffering within the sphere of which the exalted Redeemer can give aid to His people, by mentioning it as a matter of past experience, as by mentioning it as a definite condition. Thus also, taking our view of the ἐν ᾧ, he might, not altogether inappropriately, have written ἔπαθεν αὐτὸς πεπειρασμένος instead of πέπονθεν αὐτὸς πειρασθείς. But since the suffering to which Christ submitted Himself was hitherto the predominant idea in the discussion, it was relatively more appropriate to transfer the fact of the πειρασθῆναι into the condition of the πεπονθέναι, than to transfer the fact of the παθεῖν into the condition of the πειρασμένον εἶναι. At all events, the author comprises the one under the other.[1] Hofmann too far separates the two when he paraphrases and explains in the following manner (*Schriftb.* ii. 1, 277): "That He has passed through suffering, puts Him, after He Himself has been tempted, in a condition to succour them that are tempted. For without His suffering the church would not have been reconciled, and then He could not now give succour to the unreconciled church. Or, in other words, it is only upon the ground of His high-priestly work of atonement, that He can stand for His people in the presence of God."

On this thought, true in itself, we have here, at ver. 18, nothing further to say. The subject here is not the satisfactory and meritorious effect for us of the suffering of Christ, as basis of His high-priesthood, but its effect, as ethically fitting Him for this priesthood. It is πειρασθείς, and not ἐν ᾧ ἔπαθεν, which is given as proof of the δύναται τοῖς πειραζομένος βοηθῆσαι; and ἐν ᾧ ἔπαθεν is simply to show the truth of the πειρασθείς. Sufferings, as parallels from Luke prove, are as

---

[1] Also, in classical Greek, πειρᾶσθαι is sometimes found used as equivalent to πάσχειν. An unknown poet, cited by Plutarch, *Mor.* p. 51 E, says: *The old man is best respondent to the old man, a boy to a boy, a woman to woman.* Νοσῶν τ' ἀνὴρ νοσοῦντι καὶ δυσπραξίᾳ ληφθεὶς ἐπῳδός ἐστι τῷ πειρωμένῳ. See also Suidas, *sub voc.* πεῖρα (= βλάβη).

such πειρασμοί (Acts xx. 19), and especially our Lord's sufferings were so (Luke xxii. 28); and as this latter passage shows, not merely the sufferings beginning in Gethsemane (from which date onward, Hofmann (*Schriftb*. ii. 1, 279) would designate the πεπονθέναι here as expiatory). In His sufferings, or through His sufferings, He was tempted, and thereby put into a position to succour them that are tempted.

Reviewing all we have already gone over, we see that the author has now demonstrated the exaltation of Jesus above the angels, on the one hand, through His eternal Godhead, and on the other, through the glory He attained by becoming man, and passing through suffering for the benefit of mankind. The Hebrews, to whom the author is writing, are in danger of taking offence at the suffering form of Christ's humanity, and of thereby losing sight of His pre-eminence, which preceded and followed His temporary humiliation. The author therefore shows them, that it was necessary for the eternal Son of God to enter into the low condition of human nature, as it at present is under the dominion of death, in order to raise the human race, to which, as prophesied in the O. T., He is related as brother, with Himself to the high position assigned to it (Ps. viii.). He who is higher than the angels, was made for a little time lower than the angels, in order in and through Him to exalt humanity above the angels. The parallel between Jesus and men on the one hand, and between Him and angels on the other, this parallel revolving around Ps. viii. 5 as its axis, is now at an end. Next follows,

CHAP. III. 1-6. *A second parallel, presented in the form of a renewed parænesis, based on the preceding paragraph, and exhorting to a due regard for such a high priest, who is not only faithful as Moses was in the house of God, but so much more glorious than he, as the son is greater than a servant.*

In the former exhortation (ch. ii. 1) the sacred writer had included himself with his readers as "we;" now, after exciting earnest feelings by his solemn words, and in the full consciousness of his own fraternal sympathy, he ventures to address them directly as "brethren."

CHAP. III. 1. 153

Ver. 1. *Wherefore, holy brethren, partakers of a heavenly calling, consider ye well the apostle and high priest of our confession, Jesus.*

In these few weighty words all the preceding thoughts of our epistle recur. So it is even with the terms of the address, " holy brethren," " partakers of a heavenly calling," in which each word is an echo of something that has gone before. Ἀδελφοὶ ἅγιοι, as a vocative, has no other example in the New Testament. In the epistles of St. Paul we find " *brethren,*" " *my brethren,*" " *my beloved brethren,*" " *brethren beloved of God;*" but he nowhere addresses them as " *holy ones*" or " *saints,*" though he so often speaks of them by that designation.¹ In this epistle, too, we have elsewhere simply "brethren" (ἀδελφοί). Here the text expresses more than the relation in which the writer stands to those whom he addresses: their common brotherhood with Christ is the main thought in his mind. Of this he has already spoken (ch. ii. 11). The redeemed are with the Redeemer all children of one Father; the Sanctifier therefore stands in a brotherly relation to those whom He sanctifies: He is their ὁ ἁγιάζων; they ἅγιοι through Him, and ἀδελφοὶ ἅγιοι with Him and towards one another. The second term of the address (κλήσεως ἐπουρανίου μέτοχοι) carries us back to ch. i. 1 and ii. 3. The καλῶν thus referred to is the eternal Son, through whom God has now spoken, who came from heaven, and is returned thither. And hence the κλῆσις coming through Him, and manifested on earth, is heavenly (comp. ἡ ἄνω κλῆσις, Phil. iii. 14); that is, a call issuing from heaven and inviting to heaven: its contents, the place whence it proceeds, and that to which it invites, all heavenly. Of this heavenly calling Christians are partakers (μέτοχοι, apart from our epistle, found only Luke v. 7), and as such are united in fellowship of the same high privileges and duties. Hence they should, considering Him through whom they are what they are, adhere to Him the more firmly, and seek to be rooted and grounded in Him: κατανοήσατε τὸν ἀπόστολον καὶ ἀρχιερέα τῆς ὁμολογίας ἡμῶν Ἰησοῦν. We must in the outset reject the signification Mediator, in which Tholuck and Biesenthal, starting from the rabbinical-talmudic שָׁלִיחַ,

¹ The genuineness of the reading ἁγίοις before ἀδελφοῖς in the *text. rec.* of 1 Thess. v. 27 is doubtful.

think the designation ἀπόστολος may be taken. (שָׁלוּחַ) שָׁלִיחַ, however, never means mediator, but always merely delegate, commissioner, or representative, whether of God or the synagogue. But that Jesus should be called delegate of the church, in the way in which the high priest was called שְׁלוּחֵנוּ (our delegate[1]) by the members of the Sanhedrim, who before the day of atonement made him swear to observe the ritual of that day (with reference to Sadducean departures from tradition), is a thought unworthy of our Lord's dignity. Besides, such a reference in the time of the second temple to the above-mentioned observance is improbable: the appellation ἀπόστολος would thus give a priestly sense,[2] whereas we expect here a prophetic one. For τὸν ἀπόστολον is manifestly connected with κλήσεως ἐπουρανίου μέτοχοι, as ἀρχιερέα refers (chiastically) to ἀδελφοὶ ἅγιοι. Jesus, as the inaugurator of the heavenly calling, is our Apostle, and as Sanctifier our High Priest. To which must be added, that the title Ἀπόστολος, given once here to our Lord, and nowhere else, is evidently intended to connect Him with His own apostles, the ἀκούσαντες of ch. ii. 3, who had continued under Him the proclamation of the gospel, which is the same thing as this heavenly calling. The word, therefore, is to be understood here as equivalent to "sent of God" (comp. Luke iv. 43, ix. 48, x. 16; Acts iii. 20, 26; Gal. iv. 4; John xvii. 3, 18, and many other places, especially in the writings of St. John). Our Lord is therefore here called Apostle, as one who, as God's messenger of salvation, is above the prophets (i. 1), and higher than the angels (ii. 2); while as High Priest He has accomplished that salvation, and is still its Mediator.

Ὁμολογία[3] signifies in the New Testament the Christian confession, or profession of faith, not in the abstract, as a creed

---

[1] See my *Aufsatz über die Discussion der Amtsfrage in Mischna und Gemara*: Luth. Zeitschr. 1854, iii. pp. 446-449.

[2] The appellation שָׁלִיחַ, thus absolutely taken, could have no other than a sacerdotal sense, and signify the priest, either as God's deputy on the one hand, or that of the church on the other. Even the שליח צבור of the synagogue is the substitute of the offering priest (במקום המקריב).

[3] Tholuck has done right in abandoning his former rendering of ὁμολογία by *pactum*, for which may be compared the "*Messenger of the Covenant*" of Mal. iii. 1, and the rendering of the Itala, *constitutionis nostræ*. The word has never this meaning in the New Testament, which

or formulary, but as the act of the believing church or person, or rather both these in one. (It recurs ch. iv. 14, x. 23; and thrice in St. Paul.) The genitive τῆς ὁμολογίας depends on both substantives, ἀποστ. and ἀρχιερ. (their close combination is indicated by the omission of the article before ἀρχιερέα); the plain sense being: He who is the subject of our confession; where there is no occasion to inquire whether ὁμολογία be used subjectively (as act) or objectively (as *symbolum*), being in fact the self-utterance of the church's living faith. Ἰησοῦν[1] stands here after its appositive clause, just as it did at ch. ii. 9 (comp. note there). What we *confess* is, that we have in the man *Jesus* one sent of God, to bring us the message of salvation, and a High Priest to accomplish it. On Him, then, being such (so runs the exhortation here), keep fixed your mental gaze (the eye of faith—πίστει νοοῦμεν)—κατὰ νοήσατε. The word is a favourite one with St. Luke, for prolonged, earnest, searching consideration (comp. Luke xii. 24, 27, and especially Acts xi. 6). Ὅθεν connects this exhortation with all that had preceded it: the following clause grounds it on the Lord's faithfulness in His own divine calling:

Ver. 2. *As being faithful unto him that made him, even as was Moses in all his house.*

Πιστὸν ὄντα is the second accusative to κατανοήσατε. We are to contemplate God's Apostle and High Priest as being one who is found faithful, wherein lies a further motive for the exhortation to regard Him. He is faithful to His calling which has our salvation for its object: we have the best in every respect to look for from Him. Τῷ ποιήσαντι might be rendered " Him that created Him." The sacred writer having

here would yield a weak and unsuitable sense. Philo in one place (i. 654, 6) calls the Logos ὁ μέγας ἀρχιερεὺς τῆς ὁμολογίας; which Carpzov renders, *summus sacerdos professionis* (*quam profitemur*); Grossmann, *antistes fœderis nostri* (*De philosophiæ sacræ vestigiis nonnullis in Ep. ad Hebr. conspicuis*, p. 23). So also Wesseling. Bleek, with Mangey, regards the reading τῆς ὁμολογίας as suspicious. It is discredited, by its omission in Cod. Med.

[1] The Vulgate also reads *Jesum*. Luther's *Christi Jhesu* follows all three editions of the Greek text which he may have used: that of Gerbelius, 1521; the second edition of Erasmus' Greek Testament, 1519; and the Aldine edition of Asulanus,—all three of which presented him with Χριστὸν Ἰησοῦν.

so unambiguously testified to our Lord's pre-existence in ch. i., might, without fear of misinterpretation, so speak of God the Father here, as author of the temporal existence of the Son; and so orthodox Greeks (*e.g.* Athanasius) and Latins (Ambrose, Vigilius Taps., Primasius) do not scruple to expound ποιήσαντι here as referring to the *creatio*, *i.e. corporalis generatio*, of the man Christ Jesus. The Arians, on the other hand (as Epiphanius informs us), appealed to it in support of their position that Christ is a creature (κτίσμα). Bleek and Lünemann think it possible that ποιήσαντι may refer to the eternal generation. But this is inadmissible : ποιεῖν being so clearly used (ch. i. 2) to express the creative act by which the material and spiritual universe had been brought into being, could not be applied to the infinitely higher *genesis* of the Son. Nor could it properly express His human conception, that unique, incomparable act of divine power, by which the Eternal Word took flesh in the womb of Mary. For ποιεῖν in such a signification no parallel could be found. Neither is it admissible to supply (as most expositors have done, with appeal to Acts ii. 36) a second accusative after ποιήσαντι—*faithful to Him that made Him apostle and high priest*. De Wette's interpretation seems to be the right one, taking ποιεῖν absolutely in an ethical or historical sense, like עשה, 1 Sam. xii. 6 (*It is the Lord that made Moses and Aaron*), where *made* does not refer to natural creation, but the placing them on the stage of history. The sacred writer may, indeed (as Bleek conjectures), have had this very passage in view, when the LXX. renders thus, ὁ Κύριος ὁ ποιήσας τὸν Μωυσῆν; and afterwards at ver. 8, ἀπέστειλε ὁ Κύριος τὸν Μ. He adds (combining a reminiscence of Num. xii. 7), ὡς καὶ Μωυσῆς (Μωσῆς text. rec., as also Uffenb. [and Cod. Sinait], etc.) ἐν ὅλῳ τῷ οἴκῳ αὐτοῦ. That this last clause is part of the comparison, and that αὐτοῦ must be referred to τῷ ποιήσαντι αὐτόν, are points admitting of no doubt. We are necessitated to assume the former, by the fact that the author afterwards proceeds to contrast the vocation of Moses "*in*" the house of God, with that of Jesus "*over*" the same; while here it is a like faithfulness in what is assumed to be a like position which is the subject of consideration. The complete expression, therefore, of the thought would be : ὡς καὶ Μ. πιστὸς ἦν τῷ ποιήσαντι αὐτὸν ἐν ὅλῳ τῷ οἴκῳ αὐτοῦ. The whole sphere of Moses' work is here called, after Num. xii. 7, "the house of God" (comp. Ps. lxix. 10; Hos. viii. 1). The Greek πιστός[1] corresponds exactly to the Hebrew participle נאמן, with its twofold meaning of *fide dignus* and *fidem servans*. The witness of Jehovah concerning Moses, as received by Aaron and Miriam at the door of the tabernacle, declared that he was not, like other prophets, limited to revelations through dream or ecstasy, but that, as one found trustworthy in the whole house of God, he had free scope given him in all the details of its management here below. In Num. xii. 7 the emphasis lies on ἐν ὅλῳ τῷ οἴκῳ μου, which therefore precedes the πιστός ἐστι. Here πιστὸν ὄντα, as the main though not the only point of comparison, is placed first. Moses' faithfulness in the whole house of God corresponds to the faithfulness of Jesus to *His* vocation, which embraces the whole church (Hofmann, *Entsteh.* 339) of God, and in fulfilling which He is both apostle and high priest, that is, discharges an office at once prophetic and pontifical. Πιστόν is here predicate of ἀπόστολον as well as of ἀρχιερέα (otherwise we should have expected a comparison with Aaron rather than with Moses); and ὄντα indicates the continuance in heaven not only of the Lord's high-priesthood, but also of His apostleship or prophetic office. The comparison is now followed by a contrast, exhibiting the superior excellence of the antitype Jesus to the type Moses.[2]

Vers. 3–6 have long occasioned great perplexity to commentators. Bleek correctly apprehends the starting-point. The glory conferred on Christ surpasses that of Moses in the same

[1] De Wette needlessly finds fault with the rendering of the Sept., which is here better than his own—*mit meinem ganzen Hause ist er betrauet.* For נאמן ב׳ nowhere signifies "to be entrusted with anything;" for this *Niphal* never governs a ב, but is only occasionally followed by this preposition, signifying its sphere of action. It is used sometimes in a temporal sense, *long-continuing* (Deut. xxviii. 59); sometimes in a *local* sense, firm, unchangeable (Josh. vii. 9; 1 Sam. ii. 35, etc.); sometimes in an historical, *to be verified* (Gen. xlii. 20); sometimes in an ethical, to be approved as faithful (as here, and Ps. lxxviii. 37).

[2] This superiority is acknowledged by the Jewish Midrash (Jalkut to Isa. lii. 13). The Servant of Jehovah, the King Messiah, will be more venerable than Abraham, more exalted than Moses, and superior to the ministering angels.

proportion as the κατασκευάσας οἶκον enjoys greater honour than the οἶκος itself. But when he proceeds simply to identify Christ with the κατασκευάσας οἶκον, he renders his own further comprehension of the argument impossible, and makes ver. 4 sink down for him into a mere "parenthesis." Tholuck, von Gerlach, Ebrard, and Lünemann fail in the same way in comprehending ver. 3. They also identify the κατασκευάσας with our Lord, and so regard ver. 4 as a parenthesis—and what a parenthesis! Tholuck says: "*It might appear strange to the reader to find Christ styled the founder (κατασκευάσας) of 'the house of Jehovah,' i.e. of the theocracy, and therefore our author adds the intimation, that every family must have some founder, though God be the primary cause of all.*"[1] But the main thought of vers. 3-6 could hardly be better reproduced than it is by Hofmann (*Entst.* 339): "*The vocation of Jesus Christ is so much the more glorious, as in Him has appeared the promised Saviour, who should belong as Son to the Almighty Creator of the church, and of all things ; whereas Moses was but a part of the church himself, and therein only a servant, and giving a prophetic testimony to the gospel of the future.*" The sacred writer's purpose is, in fact, to confirm and enforce the exhortation of vers. 1, 2, while he thus continues:

Ver. 3. *For this one hath been counted worthy of more glory than Moses, inasmuch as he who established the house hath more honour than the house.*

It is quite in accordance with the chain-like development of his argument, that the author thus proceeds to enforce the exhortation (which is linked on by ὅθεν to what had gone before) by a further unfolding of the comparison between Moses and Jesus Christ. (So Bengel, Böhme, Tholuck, Lünemann, and many others.)[2] By "the glory of Moses" (δόξα) Hofmann understands that "wonderful appearance" (δόξα

[1] De Wette in his first edition left everything in obscurity (1844); in his second he has avoided the error of making κατασκευάσας refer to Christ, and judiciously altered the whole exposition (1847). Köstlin has rightly conceived the thought of the paragraph vers. 3-6 (p. 409).

[2] This simple relation of the thoughts is perverted by Bleek, who, mistakenly referring αὐτοῦ (ver. 2) to Christ, proceeds: "*He now goes on to explain in what way the house belongs to Christ, namely, that He is its builder*

from δοκεῖν), that "glory of his countenance" (2 Cor. iii. 7), of which we read (Ex. xxxiv. 35) "*that the skin of Moses' face shone*" (ἦν δεδοξασμένη ἡ ὄψις τοῦ χρωτὸς (χρώματος) τοῦ προσώπου αὐτοῦ, LXX.),—namely, after his converse with God, and when he was about to convey God's words to Israel (*Weiss.* ii. 188). That shining appearance was the effect of a temporary nearness of the "glory of Jehovah" (כבוד יה) as manifested on earth on the bodily part of Moses as mediator of the old covenant (διαθήκη γράμματος), and might be contrasted with the more excellent glory (δόξα) by which the whole corporeity of the Lord Jesus being filled and interpenetrated, has now been spiritualized and assumed into full communion with the omnipresent Godhead. This view might be taken; but it is simpler and more natural to understand the δόξα here of that official "glory" (or "honour") in which the Lord Jesus excels Moses; His glorious office being not limited, as Moses' was (a δόξα καταργουμένη, 2 Cor. iii. 7), to this lower sphere of being, but extending from it to the world above, and there, after passing through the probation of death, unfolded in all its greatness, fulness, and efficacy. The omission of κατὰ τοσοῦτο in the first member of this sentence (as correlative to the καθ' ὅσον in the second) is intentional. The first clause merely expresses the Lord's superior excellence to Moses; the second gives the measure of it, as suggested by the figure involved in the ἐν ὅλῳ τῷ οἴκῳ αὐτοῦ. Κατασκευάζειν includes the procuring of everything necessary to the erection and completion of a house: ὁ κατασκευάσας, therefore, is here the constructor, builder, architect. In the first member, the subject might be a δόξα in which Moses is surpassed by Jesus; in the second, a word of more general signification had to be chosen, allowing reference to the house as well as its builder; hence, instead of δόξα, we have here τιμή, that which is highly prized, worth, or value. *Τοῦ οἴκου* is the genitive of comparison : to

(κατασκευάσας)." De Wette likewise avoids the most obvious interpretation, for the worthless reason that it is not the author's immediate object to justify the assertion of ver. 1, that Christ is greater than Moses. He renders γάρ by *nämlich*. But surely there is nothing illogical in such a sequence of thought as this : " Contemplate earnestly the Lord Jesus, who is comparable to Moses for fidelity in the whole house of God, seeing that in glory He is incomparably his superior."

take together τιμὴν τοῦ οἴκου, honour by the house or in relation to the house (e.g. Luther, combining this meaning with that of comparison), sounds harsh, and is wholly unnecessary. The order of the words is artistically inverted in both members of the sentence: in the first member we read, with Griesb., Lchm., Tischd., πλείονος γὰρ οὗτος δόξης, instead of the rec. πλείονος γὰρ δόξης οὗτος. The sacred author has contrived to form a masterly combination of a logically strict sequence of idea, syntactical elegance, and rhythmical euphony. The following is the comparison instituted by him: Jesus stands in relation to Moses as the architect to the house. Were we thence to infer that, in the author's view, Jesus was the architect, we must also infer that, in his view, Moses was the house, which is absurd. It is, in fact, a comparison in which the relation of the first two members is compared with the relation of the other two, but in which the first two are not identified with the other two respectively. Let us, then, allow the author to speak for himself, and listen to his further explanation.

Ver. 4. *For every house is builded by some one or other; but he that built all things is God.*

Πᾶς οἶκος here does not mean the whole house in all its parts (Hofm. *Weiss.* ii. 9), but, according to the style of the epistle (comp. v. 1, 13, viii. 3), every house whatsoever. The universally known and acknowledged truth (ver. 3b) is illustrated by the likewise universally known and acknowledged proposition, that there is no house which has not some builder. This proposition, trivial as it is, serves as basis to the conclusion at which the author seeks to arrive. But to regard ὁ δὲ, κ.τ.λ., as already this conclusion, deranges the whole argument. The proposition, ὁ δὲ, κ.τ.λ., is itself only an intermediate link in the chain of argument, but still a necessary link, not a mere accessory thought, not a parenthesis to be bracketed off, as is done by Griesb., Thiele, and others. The author, in saying πᾶς οἶκος, has in view the house in which Moses was found faithful. To justify and confirm the comparison previously instituted, he is obliged to show the superiority of Jesus to Moses, in their respective relations to this house and its κατασκευάσας. He therefore, in coming to particulars, proceeds from the above-mentioned general proposition to the proposition ὁ δὲ πάντα

CHAP. III. 5, 6.   161

κατασκευάσας Θεός. Ὁ ... κατασκευάσας is manifestly the predicate (notwithstanding the article; see Winer, p. 104), Θεός the subject. Δέ sets in contrast to the τίς, that is, the builder, whoever he may be, whom a house of whatever kind must as a house have, the more definite builder, back to whom, as ultimate cause, everything,[1] and so whatever is or can be called a house, is to be traced. After this proposition stands the following parallel, containing the justification and confirmation of the comparison instituted (ver. 3b).

Vers. 5, 6a. *While then Moses (has been found) faithful in all his house, as a servant, for (bearing) testimony unto the things that should afterwards be spoken of; Christ, on the other hand, as a Son is over his house. Whose house are we.*

Jesus stands related to Moses, as one who has built a house stands related to the house itself; Moses as servant forming part of God's house, whilst Christ as Son is over it. Or, to put the chain of argument more clearly, Jesus is, as compared with Moses, what the architect is in relation to the house which he builds : every house must have some builder, and God is the supreme architect of all; Moses was faithful to God in His whole house as a servant, Christ is placed over it as a Son; *therefore* Christ is related to Moses as the architect (whose Son Christ is) is related to the house in which Moses was a servant. Both αὐτοῦ's must be referred to God, by whom all things were made at the first, Moses being called θεράπων with reference to Num. xii. 7. The LXX. purposely renders עבד here by another word than δοῦλος or παῖς (the renderings most frequently employed), in order to exclude the notion of unfree, slavish dependence contained in δοῦλος and παῖς, from which θεράπων, in the oldest Greek, is free.[2] It is evident from the context that Christ is here called Son in reference to God the builder of the house, and that the term is used in the

[1] Πάντα (Lachm., Tischend.) is to be preferred (both as better attested and as giving a better sense) to the τὰ πάντα of the *text. rec.* [The Cod. Sinait. also reads πάντα.—TR.]

[2] Comp. Passow, *Lexic. s. voce.* ["In early Greek it always differs from δοῦλος, as implying free and honourable service, and in Homer is often = ἑταῖρος, ὀπάων, *a companion in arms*, comrade, though usually inferior in rank and name; so Patroclus is θεράπων of Achilles, *Il.* xvi. 244."
—LIDDELL and SCOTT.] Greek lexicographers distinguish δοῦλος, *slave*, one

full sense which it bears in ch. i. 1. The question remains, how the sacred writer intended the clause Χριστὸς δὲ ὡς υἱὸς ἐπὶ τὸν οἶκον αὐτοῦ to be understood. The following views have been taken of its meaning : (1.) *Christ (is faithful) as a Son, (is sure to be faithful) over His house;* so Bleek and De Wette. This is inadmissible, first, because if ὡς θεράπων is equivalent to *ut famulus,* ὡς υἱός cannot be rendered by *quemadmodum filius;* and further, because this interpretation would require ἑαυτοῦ (over His own house), making the church to be here the house of Christ,—a phrase of which, as we have seen, Scripture affords no other examples. (2.) Another interpretation admits of two forms : Christ (is faithful) over His house as Son, or Christ as Son over His house (is faithful). For the former, appeal might be made to x. 21, *a great priest over* (ἐπί) *the house of God;* for the latter, to Matt. xxv. 25, *thou wast faithful over* (ἐπί) *a few things.* So Tholuck and Lünemann ; Tholuck, however, referring αὐτοῦ to Christ, Lünemann (as we have done) to God. But even in this its more acceptable form, we cannot approve of this assumption of an ellipsis of πιστός ἐστιν, forasmuch as the construction πιστὸς ἐπί would totally efface the emphatic antithesis of ἐν τῷ οἴκῳ and ἐπὶ τὸν οἶκον. According to this, the sentence is a purely *nominal* one, admitting of no other ellipsis than that of the logical copula ; and as we cannot, with Erasmus and others, refer αὐτοῦ to υἱός (*suam ipsius domum*), there remains but one other interpretation. (3.) *Christ is* (or *stands*) *as Son over (God's) house,* being not merely faithful as a servant, like Moses, employed in the house, but placed as a Son over it. In this way only the intentional antithesis of ἐν and ἐπί is brought out sharp and clear. Moses, as servant, resembles the house in this, that he, like it, stands under God who formed it, and so is employed in a household which is not his own, but only entrusted to his care : Christ, as Son, resembles the builder

politically or morally perfectly unfree, from οἰκέτης, house-servant or messenger, one who has a master but is not in bondage, and θεράπων, a ministering friend of lower rank. So Ammonius Hesychius, Thomas Magister, etc. The *usus loquendi* of Scripture has ennobled the meaning of δοῦλος, yet still the notion connected with θεράπων remains a peculiar one. Euripides, in a fragment, uses διάκονος for it : Πιστὸν μὲν οὖν εἶναι χρὴ τὸν διάκονον.— NANCK, *Tragicorum Gr. fragmenta,* p. 377.

of the house in this, that He, like the builder, stands over the house; for, by virtue of His Sonship, the house is His own: as κληρονόμος πάντων (i. 2) He stands on the same line with the κατασκευάσας πάντα; whatever is the Father's, is also His *jure hæreditatis*. We have in this not indeed a direct, but certainly an indirect, proof of the Godhead of Christ, the idea of υἱός including it. The author employs here the name Χριστός instead of Ἰησοῦς intentionally. He who was formerly called Ἰησοῦς is called Χριστός, as Lord in contradistinction to servant, as fulfiller of the law in contradistinction to him who gave testimony of future fulfilment. Most modern expositors efface the intimation here given of this typical relation, in that they understand by λαληθησόμενα the Thorah (law), which it was Moses' office to proclaim to the people (Bl., De W., Thol., Lünem.). Ebrard and Hofmann, however, decide, with good reason, in favour of the interpretation found inadmissible by Bleek and the others,—namely, that it refers to the gospel of the New Testament, and to that exclusively, and not, as Bengel says, at once to the Thorah in its prophetic aspect and the gospel. Moses held the charge of a θεράπων, " for a testimony of those things which were to be spoken after," that is, of the future perfect revelation of God through the Son (i. 2a). As he prophesied of the Son, the Apostle of the final salvation, by his position and faithfulness in his calling, so also did he by his testimony (John v. 46, 39). And equally did the Old Testament house of God, in which Moses was a servant, namely the Old Testament church, which had as centre-point the "tabernacle of *testimony*" (Acts vii. 44; Rev. xv. 5), with its typical furniture and order, prophesy of the New Testament house of God, over which Christ is set as Son, namely the New Testament, which has its centre-point in Christ, in whom God was manifested in human form; and thus the σκήνωσις (tabernacling) of God with men, prefigured in the Old Testament σκηνή (tabernacle) is realized in the antitype. In this way we have an express parallel drawn between Μωυσῆς ὡς θεράπων and Χριστὸς ὡς υἱός, and a latent parallel between εἰς μαρτύριον τῶν λαληθησομένων and οὗ οἶκος ἐσμεν ἡμεῖς; and it is not, as Lünem. calls it, "a strange perversion," when Ebrard assumes that there is an antithetical relation of these two members of the sentence. The reading ὅς οἶκος (D*,

Uffenb. 6, 67**, It., Vulg.) is an old correction, made on the supposition that αὐτοῦ should be referred to Christ. The article (οὗ οἶκος for οὗ ὁ οἶκος) is wanting, as in the passages aptly compared by Ebrard (xi. 10; Ps. cxliv. 15, LXX.). That αὐτοῦ, οὗ refers to God, is evident from x. 21; 1 Tim. iii. 15; 1 Cor. iii. 9, 16; 2 Cor. vi. 16; Eph. ii. 22; 1 Pet. iv. 17, ii. 5. The church is always called only God's house, never Christ's. The passages which Bleek quotes to the contrary (Eph. iii. 17; John xiv. 23; Rev. iii. 20) prove nothing. The house is named after its κατασκευάσας, and He is God, who is also *auctor primarius* of the work of salvation, and of the church of finished salvation, as well as of the church of preparatory salvation. The phrase οὗ οἶκος ἐσμὲν ἡμεῖς intimates the thoroughly personal, inward, and spiritual nature of the church. Attached to this there is a conditional clause, with which the tone of exhortation is resumed.

Ver. 6*b*. *So far as we hold fast the confidence and the boasting of hope* [*unshaken to the end*].

The words μέχρι τέλους βεβαίαν of text. rec., recognised already as a gloss by Mill, but now defended by Bleek, De Wette, Tholuck, Lünemann, are undoubtedly to be expunged,[1] as an interpolation from ver. 14. For, 1*st*, It is highly improbable that so rhetorically practised a writer as our author should have repeated himself in so short a space; and 2*dly*, βεβαίαν (instead of βέβαιον, or even as one MS. has it, βέβαια) is very harsh, whether we explain it as taking its gender from παρρησίαν (as most do) or from ἐλπίδος (as Stengel and Tholuck): the latter giving a better sense, but being grammatically harsher still.

If the reading were βέβαιον, the words might be considered genuine; but βεβαίαν is too sure a sign that they are supplied from ver. 14. Hence we hold with Tischendorf, that the Cod. Vat. gives the original here: ἐάν (Lucif. Calar., however, *si tamen*, thus indicating ἐάνπερ) τὴν παρρησίαν καὶ τὸ καύχημα τῆς ἐλπίδος κατάσχωμεν (according to the usual accentuation, instead of κατασχῶμεν). Thus runs the condition, on the con-

---

[1] So Tischendorf, following B, Æthiop., Lucif., Ambr. The reading is found in D (Greek and Lat.), and in the Vulgate [also in Cod. Sinait.—TR.].

CHAP. III. 7-19.   165

tinuance of which depends the reality of our being God's house (*cujus domus sumus ac porro erimus, si obtinuerimus*). The genitive τῆς ἐλπίδος pertains as well to τὴν παρρησίαν (comp. vi. 11, the kindred expression πληροφορίαν τῆς ἐλπίδος) as to τὸ καύχημα (comp. x. 23, the kindred expression ὁμολογίαν τῆς ἐλπίδος). Παρρησία is used here in a sense not essentially different from that which it has, for instance, in Acts, where it always denotes the unreserved and joyful openness or frankness of confessing and preaching the gospel: here, and iv. 16, x. 19, 35, where the only relation meant to be expressed is that of the Christian to God, not to men, it is the inward state of full and undisturbed confidence. Καύχημα, which is coupled with παρρησία, denotes the joyful opening of the mouth, which is the result of this confidence. This word καύχημα occurring elsewhere exclusively in St. Paul's epistles, is not to be taken as quite synonymous with the likewise almost exclusively Pauline καύχησις. Καύχησις signifies the act of rejoicing; καύχημα (passive) the product or object of this act. Add to this, that ἐλπίς is considered here rather with respect to the unseen riches which are its object, than as an affection of the mind (comp. Rom. viii. 24, ἐλπὶς βλεπομένη οὐκ ἔστιν ἐλπίς) : so that παρρησία τῆς ἐλπίδος is the assured confidence upon which hope in this sense is founded; and καύχημα τῆς ἐλπίδος is the noble boasting which his hope assures to the Christian, or the object of that boasting which he has in his hope. If the New Testament church of God holds fast (κατέχειν = *obtinere*, to maintain) the treasure of hope, notwithstanding all the contradictions between the present and the promised future, in the midst of all dangers of offence and falling away prepared for her by the threatenings and allurements of the enemies of the cross, then, and only then, does she continue the house of God, under the faithful and fostering care of Christ, the now exalted only Son of God, her Brother, her Apostle, and her High Priest.

VERS. 7-19. *A fresh exhortation, based on the preceding doctrine, not to harden the heart against a messenger of God so much greater than even Moses, and this in order not (like the generation in the wilderness) to lose an entrance into God's rest.*

The sacred writer gives now a turn to his exhortation, which he had already in view when instituting the comparison between Christ and Moses. Israel's self-obduration against the word of God, as given by Moses in the wilderness, had received a fearful punishment. The example of this punishment he now presents, as a mirror of warning to the readers of his epistle, that they may pay more earnest heed than Israel of old had done to the word of God, which is now proclaimed to them by the Son of God Himself, the greatest of apostles, and by His messengers, the apostles under Him. Instead of putting this reference and warning in words of his own, the sacred writer takes them from the ninety-fifth Psalm, in which the psalmist himself, referring to the Thorah, reminds the men of his own time of the judgments which had fallen on their fathers, and of the unbelief by which they had forfeited the promised inheritance.

In the original this Psalm is anonymous; but the LXX. entitles it αἶνος ᾠδῆς (שִׁיר תְּהִלַּת, which occurs in no Hebrew title of a Psalm) τῷ Δαυίδ. Our author, too, as will be seen in ch. iv., assumes it to be a Psalm of David; and if to this assumptive weight no valid objection can be raised, yet should nothing be thereby decided in an historical-critical sense regarding its authorship. In the view of the synagogue and of the New Testament, the whole Psalter is Davidic; the whole Psalm poetry is born of the Spirit that came upon David at his anointing. If we consider the Psalm in itself, it begins with a tetrastich, vers. 1, 2, containing a call to worship God and sing His praise: the grounds for this call are given in two decastichs, 3–7b, 7c–11. Jehovah (1) is God above all gods. He is (2) the Creator, in whose power are all things,—earth, hills, sea, and dry land. He is (3) Israel's God, and Israel is the sheep of His hand: His own creative hand has called them into existence. Thus the first decastich gives three grounds for the summons to kneel before the Lord and worship Him. The second founds it on an exhortation not to leave the gracious call of God unheeded, and to remember the judicial wrath which had swept away the generation in the wilderness. This second decastich our author appropriates: he not merely quotes, but appropriates it. For to connect διό, ver. 7, with βλέπετε, ver. 12, and to look on καθὼς λέγει and all that follows as a parenthesis (Böhme, Bleek, Lünemann), is inadmissible. This parenthesis is so long, that one entirely forgets the διό, ver. 7;

and the second διό, ver. 10 (no matter whether written διό or δι' ὅ, as Lünemann will have it), would look as if purposely intended to confuse both reader and hearer, especially the latter. The shorter parenthetic quotations, vii. 21, x. 20 sq., standing without causing any possibility of confusion between the major and minor propositions, cannot be compared with such a monster of a period as this would be. It would be far better to say that the author left out the applicative clause, commencing with διό, ver. 7, namely, μὴ σκληρύνητε τὰς καρδίας ὑμῶν (Thol., De Wette). Rom. xv. 3, 21, 1 Cor. i. 31, ii. 9, have been cited as parallels; but in all these passages there is no proper ellipsis. It is entirely wrong to speak of an ellipsis of the minor; it is the major that is incomplete, not the minor. The major proposition, namely, is blended into one with the subordinate proposition; and the result apparent is fundamentally the same as when, for instance, Herodotus says, iii. 14, ὡς δὲ λέγεται ὑπ' Αἰγυπτίων δακρύειν μὲν Κροῖσον for δακρύει μὲν Κροῖσος; or Cicero, *de off.* i. 7, 22, *atque ut placet Stoicis, quæ in terra gignantur, ad usum hominis omnia creari*, for *creata sunt* (see Kühner, § 857e). Thus, in the above-cited passages of St. Paul, the continuation of the main proposition begun with ἀλλά or otherwise, is contained in the subordinate proposition beginning with καθώς, and also composed of a quotation from Scripture. Now, as the words of the Psalm cited in our passage have themselves a form which fits them to serve as continuation of the main proposition commencing with διό, we can, even in the light of above Pauline parallels, come to no other conclusion than that the author intended διὸ ... σήμερον ... μὴ σκληρύνητε to be taken together, and that he thus makes the exhortation of the Psalm his own (Klee, Ebrard, and others). In taking this view, I do not find that the words of God coming in vers. 9–11 " occasion great harshness" (Lünem.): this change of speaker is derived from the Psalm itself; for there the warning of the psalmist, while meditating on the word of God in the Thorah, Num. xiv. 21–23, suddenly changes into the words of Jehovah Himself. It is the momentous truth just now expressed, that the possession of salvation is conditioned by faithfulness in keeping it, which induces the author to continue:

Ver. 7. *Wherefore, as the Holy Ghost saith, To-day, if ye will hear his voice.*

Every word of Scripture is as such a word of the Holy Ghost; for Scripture in all its parts is θεόπνευστος (2 Tim. iii. 16). It is the Holy Ghost, surveying at once all times, who forms the word applicable to the present, and at the same time meeting the exigencies of the future. In this, and in no other sense, does our author regard the Psalm, which moreover, by that sudden introduction of the Lord speaking, assumes the character of a prophetic Psalm. The σήμερον is in the first instance the present of the psalmist, not a future point of time detached from that present; and yet not a day of twenty-four hours, and, to speak in general, not a limited period under the Old Testament economy, but the second great day of salvation following the Mosaic period of redemption, and which, when our author wrote, had reached its noontide height.[1] It is generally thought that the words of the Psalm with which he

---

[1] The following in many respects remarkable Messianic *haggadah*, from T. B. *Sanhedrin* 98a, shows that by the synagogue also, the "To-day" of the Psalm was made to refer to the great second period of redemption (the times of Messiah): " *Rabbi Joshuah ben Levi once found the prophet Elijah standing at the entrance of the cave of Rabbi Simeon ben Jochai. He asked him:* ' *Shall I reach the world to come?*' *The prophet answered:* ' *If the Lord here will*' " (אדון, Lord, that is, the invisible Shechinah, which Elijah has present with him). " *Whereupon R. Joshuah went on to relate:* ' *I saw two (myself and him), but I heard the voice of Three*' " (that is, the voice of the Shechinah was added to their own). " *He asked him again:* ' *When will Messiah come?*' *Elijah answered,* ' *Go and ask Himself.*' Joshuah: ' *And whither?*' Elijah: ' *He sitteth at the gate of Rome.*' Joshuah: ' *And how is He to be recognised?*' Elijah: ' *He sitteth among poor and diseased persons, who all unbandage their wounds at once, and bandage them up again, while He unbindeth and bindeth up again one wound after another; for His thought is, Perchance I shall be called for* (summoned to manifest Himself), *and then I must not be hindered* (as would be the case if He had opened all wounds at once).' *Joshuah went to Him* (the Messiah), *and said: Peace be with Thee, my Master and Teacher!* He answered: *Peace be with the son of Levi! Joshuah asked: Lord! when comest Thou? He answered: To-day. Joshuah returned to Elijah, who inquired of him:* ' *What said He unto thee?*' Joshuah: ' *Peace be with thee, son of Levi!*' Elijah: ' *Thereby hath He assured to thee and to thy father a prospect of attaining the world to come.*' Joshuah: ' *But He hath deceived me there, in that He said to me that He would come to-day.*' Elijah: ' *Nay; for what He meant was, To-day, if ye will hear His voice.*' "

begins, must in the original be translated, " O that ye would hear His voice" (אִם as in Ps. lxxxi. 9); but a glance at the plan on which the Psalm is composed, shows us that אִם is hypothetical, and that ver. 8 is the conclusion grounded on the antecedent supposition, and this without our needing to assume " a little gap here," with Olshausen, who delights so much in enriching the Psalms with gaps. For the second of the two decastichs—which, presenting themselves unsought, follow the prologue, vers. 1, 2—begins with אִם בְּקֹלוֹ. Consequently we must adopt the interpretation which accords with such passages as Ex. xxiii. 22, and which, moreover, is on other grounds the most obvious interpretation. Thus the LXX., and also Trg. The author evidently follows the LXX., and especially the form the text has in the Cod. Alex. At the same time, it is a question whether this version has not been altered in this and other passages, from regard to the Epistle to the Hebrews. Next follows the clause dependent upon ἐὰν, κ.τ.λ., which is at the same time the continuation of the main proposition, begun with διό.

Ver. 8. *Harden not your hearts, as at the provocation, on the day of the temptation in the wilderness.*
Two instances of Israel's tempting God are cited as warnings; the first of which (Num. xx. 1-13) took place in the fortieth, the second (Ex. xvii. 1-7) in the first year after the exodus. Moses also refers to both these instances in his parting benediction (Deut. xxxiii. 8). They serve to show how Israel's self-obduration continued through the whole probation of the forty years. Moses recounts them in chronological order; *here*, with equal propriety, that order is reversed. The second occurrence gave its name to the place called *Meribah* (מי מריבה), the first to that called *Massah* (מסה ומריבה). The text in the Psalm literally rendered would be: *Harden not your hearts as at Meribah, as on the day of Massah in the wilderness.* The Septuagint translates the proper names (Meribah freely,[1] by Παραπικρασμός=*embitterment;* Massah exactly by Πειρασμός= temptation) without intending to deprive them of their appellative character, though the rendering of כיום by κατὰ τὴν ἡμέραν

[1] As if from מרי, while מי מריבה is always more accurately redered ὕδωρ ἀντιλογίας.

followed by τοῦ πειρασμοῦ has had that effect. Κατά, used of time, may sometimes be rendered by *towards*, as Acts xvi. 25, *towards midnight*; sometimes by *on* or *during*, as here, *on the day*, and Heb. ix. 9, *the time during which*. The sacred writer proceeds with οὗ in a local sense, corresponding to the Hebrew אשר, which has both local and temporal meaning, like the German *da*.

Ver. 9. *Where your fathers tempted me, proved me, and saw my works forty years.*

I have given the translation of the *text. rec.*, which runs thus: οὗ ἐπείρασάν με οἱ πατέρες ὑμῶν, ἐδοκίμασάν με. The LXX. Vat. omits the second με, Alex. the first με. Instead of ἐδοκίμασάν με, A.B.C.D.*E., Uff. 73, 137, Lucif., Clem. Alex., and likewise the Itala (*ubi temptaverunt patres vestri in experimento*) and Coptic, read ἐν δοκιμασίᾳ,—a reading which, on account of this distinguished testimony, has been accepted by Lchm., Bleek, and Tischd., who at the same time, in accordance with most of the above-named authorities, leave out the first με. The text in this way stands thus: οὗ ἐπείρασαν οἱ πατέρες ὑμῶν ἐν δοκιμασίᾳ καὶ εἶδον τὰ ἔργα μου τεσσ. ἔτη = *where your fathers tempted in proving, and saw my works forty years*; which must be thus understood: They made experiments with the divine government, trying whether it would evince itself, and so again and again were made to recognise manifestations of its providential sovereignty (τὰ ἔργα being object to ἐπείρασαν as well as to εἶδον). This reading so explained is plausible, but diverges widely from the original text, which makes not the Lord's works, but Himself, the object of the tempting and the proving. Moreover, it is quite inconceivable how the author should come to make this alteration of the LXX. For his honour, we may surely assume that he was not misled, as Bleek thinks, by an accidental error of transcription in the copy of the Septuagint he used. On the other hand, ἐν δοκιμασίᾳ becomes intelligible, provided we leave the με after ἐπείρασαν undeleted, and assume that the author wrote as Cod. Uffenb. reads,[1] and Clem. Al. (*Protrept.* c. 9, § 84) quotes, οὗ ἐπείρασάν

---

[1] We have already observed that this MS. appears to have preserved the original reading of i. 3.

με οἱ πατέρες ὑμῶν ἐν δοκιμασίᾳ.[1] For if the text stood in our author's Septuagint as in the Cod. Vat., οὗ ἐπείρασάν με οἱ πατ. ὑμῶν, ἐδοκίμασαν καὶ εἶδον τὰ ἔργα μου, then it is conceivable that he preferred to change this bare ἐδοκίμασαν, which it is slightly against the original to connect with τὰ ἔργα μου, into the ἐν δοκιμασίᾳ corresponding to a Hebrew gerundive. That he deals pretty freely with the LXX., may be seen from the fact that, in opposition to the LXX. and the Hebrew original, he connects τεσσαράκοντα (Tischd., following A.B.C. and other authorities, always has τεσσεράκοντα, τέσσερες, Alex., originally Ionic; Kühner, § 354, 1[2]) ἔτη with εἶδον, and expressly separates it by διό from what follows. The reason is evident, and has been recognised by older commentators, Schöttgen for instance (see Bleek, ii. 439). It is not as the period of the προσοχθίζειν, but as that of the ἰδεῖν τὰ ἔργα τοῦ Θεοῦ, that the forty years of the Psalm find their antitypical parallel in the history of the church of Christ which the author was reviewing. There were forty years from the first proclamation of salvation by the Lord Himself (ii. 3), that is, from the commencement of His public ministry, to the destruction of Jerusalem, the forty Messianic years; to which even the synagogue bears unwilling testimony, when it is stated in the Talmud, Pesikta, Tanchuma, and Sohar, that "the days of the Messiah shall last forty years: for it is said (Ps. xcv. 10), Forty years was I angry with this generation; and (Ps. xc. 15), Make us glad according to the days wherein Thou hast humbled us, and the years wherein we have seen evil." These forty years must have almost elapsed when our author wrote. What awful and earnest import is contained in the comparison implied between these forty years and the forty years of the exodus under Moses! The race then redeemed from Egypt persisted in their unbelief and tempting of God, notwithstanding the wondrous deeds of His condescending grace which He showed them time after time.

[1] Apollinarius' paraphrase is:

Ὡς πάρος εὖτε θεοῖο κατὰ τρηχεῖαν ἔρημον
Γμέτεροι τοπρόσθεν ἐπειρήσαντο τοκῆες.

What was the reading of his text of the Septuagint can hardly be determined from this.

[2] Compare Bredow, de dialecto Herodotea, pp. 279-281.

Ver. 10. *Wherefore I was sore vexed with that generation, and said, They do always err in their heart; but they knew not (did not recognise) my ways.*

Προσοχθίζειν is an exclusively Hellenistic word, signifying to feel (rarely to cause) annoyance, repugnance, loathing. It is formed from ὀχθίζειν, ὄχθειν, which stands in the same relation to ἄχθεσθαι as πορθεῖν to πέρθειν.¹ The Codd. vacillate between τῇ γενεᾷ ἐκείνῃ (*rec.* and LXX.) and τῇ γεν. ταύτῃ; the observation of some expositors (Böhme, Bl., De W.), that the author may have wished by ταύτῃ to make the passage apply more closely to his readers, attributes to that pronoun a sense impossible in this connection. Next follow the words in which God rebukes the self-hardening of His people, in order to bring them to a knowledge of themselves and to repentance: καὶ εἶπον (Lchm. εἶπα, as the Vatican Septuagint and the Cod. Alex. *here*, while at Ps. xcv. 10 it has εἶπον) ἀεὶ πλανῶνται τῇ καρδίᾳ. "*They always do err*" gives the sense of the participial and therefore intransitive Hebrew term. In reference to this follows αὐτοὶ δέ (so LXX. Al., whereas Vat. καὶ αὐτοὶ) οὐκ ἔγνωσαν τὰς ὁδούς μου. I can understand the δέ only as adversative: God has set their error before their eyes; but Israel has refused to recognise His ways, so as to turn back from their own way of error. The וְהֵם לֹא יָדְעוּ of the original (comp. Ps. lxxxii. 5 with the preceding context) was probably intended to be taken in the same way. God had not immediately punished the disobedience of His people with forfeiture of all the promises. He had remonstrated with them. But His call to repentance had been unavailing: they had remained without *knowledge*; they had refused to recognise the purpose of His dealings with them.

Ver. 11. *So that I sware in my wrath, Surely they shall not enter into my rest.*

It is not necessary to render, with Bleek and Lünemann, *as then I sware*; for ὡς, like אֲשֶׁר (Ew. § 337, *a*), can, as consecutive particle, signify "so that." No doubt it is, when equivalent to ὥστε, usually construed with the infinitive, but sometimes with the optative and ἄν (*e.g.* Xen. Œcon. viii. 14),

¹ Compare Eustathius, 143, 13, ἐκ τοῦ ὁμηρικοῦ ὀχθῆσαι τὸ παρὰ τοῖς ὕστερον προσοχθίζειν παρήχθη (Lobeck, Ῥηματικόν, p. 227).

and rarely, as here, with the indicative (ὥστε ὁμόσαι με); comp. Herod. ii. 135, ὡς . . . ἐξέμαθον (Winer, p. 410). On the other hand, the εἰ of the oath is a Hellenistic Hebraism. The אִם of the Psalm refers back to the אִם of the original passage, Num. xiv. 21–23. This passage (comp. Deut. xii. 9) also shows clearly that κατάπαυσις is the promised settlement in Canaan in peace and freedom, after long wandering in foreign lands. It would, however, be a superficial conception of the idea, to suppose that it meant nothing more than this outward fulfilment, which outward fulfilment was itself so imperfect as to stir the hearts of all believers to inquire after something higher which lay behind it. The warning expressed in the language of the Psalm, *Harden not your hearts*, and enforced thereby, is now followed by an exhortation to mutual, and, as it were, pastoral watchfulness over each other's souls.

Ver. 12. *See to it, brethren, that there be not in any one of you an evil heart of unfaithfulness (exhibited) in departing from the living God.*

This warning is introduced without any connecting particle, such as δέ, which is actually found in a Moscow MS. (116), but would be here unsuitable,[1] or οὖν, which is supplied by Itala and Ethiop., and would be much better. The writer rejects any such connecting particle, in order to make this warning, βλέπετε, stand out more distinctly from the dark background of the preceding paragraph, as a similar βλέπετε at xii. 25 is thrown up, so to speak, by the light background of the glorious description of Christian privileges which there precedes it. Βλέπετε μήποτε is equivalent to *curate ne forte*. The indicative after μήποτε (as Col. ii. 8, comp. Luke xi. 35 : Winer, p. 446 ; Rost, p. 660 sqq.) implies that there is urgent cause for apprehension founded on the actual state of the case. The expression is not unclassical,[2] but it is still more Hebraistic. Μήποτε ἔσται is equivalent to the Hebrew פֶּן יִהְיֶה ; εἶναι, like הָיָה, being here = *existere*. In καρδία πονηρὰ ἀπιστίας also, the

---

[1] It would be too remote to indicate the continuation of the previous warning, vers. 7, 8.

[2] Comp. Aristoph. *Eccl.* 487, περισκοπουμένη . . . μὴ ξυμφορὰ γενήσεται τὸ πρᾶγμα; and Plato, *Men.* p. 89 B. We would guard the youth, etc., ἵνα μηδεὶς αὐτοὺς διέφθειρεν.

usual mode of expression καρδία πονηρά is blended with the Hebraistic καρδία ἀπιστίας (comp. Ps. xc. 12, לבב חכמה). The question whether ἀπιστίας is the genitive of cause (*e.g.* Bleek) or of consequence (De Wette), should not be put at all: it is the genitive of quality in the widest sense (Thol.). It is quite correct to say, either that ἀπιστία (unbelief, unfaithfulness) leads to πονηρία (wickedness), or that it proceeds from it; but entirely wrong to maintain the one to the exclusion of the other: ἀπιστία is both the root and the full fruit of πονηρία. Nor is the expositor at liberty to separate ideas which mutually interpenetrate in the thought and expression of the writer. Καρδία πονηρὰ ἀπιστίας is a heart perverted through sin (*cor pravum*), which, viewed in its relation to God, has ἀπιστία for its characteristic condition. In regard also to this ἀπιστία, we have not to decide whether it signifies unbelief or unfaithfulness: the word contains both significations, which mutually involve each other, inasmuch as faith (*i.e.* true belief) and faithfulness (fidelity) (blended also in the Hebrew אמונה, an abiding [אָמַן־מִן = μέν-ειν] and a holding fast) have self-surrender or devotion as their common fundamental characteristic. That ἀπιστία combines the idea of unfaithfulness with that of unbelief, is shown by the clause ἐν τῷ ἀποστῆναι ἀπὸ Θεοῦ ζῶντος added, to describe more exactly the καρδία πονηρὰ ἀπιστίας by one of its symptoms. This clause ἐν τῷ ἀπ., κ.τ.λ., cannot be taken in connection with ἔσται, in the sense, "*lest it show itself in departing*," etc. The evil heart which keeps not faith or faithfulness, does actually announce itself in a *departing from God*, who is purposely called here *the living God*, not merely as He who *exists*, but also as one who graciously manifests Himself, and judicially punishes when His grace is unthankfully rejected, into whose hands it is a fearful thing to fall (x. 31). The Hebrews are exhorted to take good heed that not one of them call forth such judicial dealing: they must not let it come to this. And βλέπετε μήποτε involving some such negative proposition as this, the author can continue with an ἀλλά (but).

Ver. 13. *But exhort one another daily, while it is called To-day; lest any one of you be hardened through the deceitfulness of sin.*

If παρακαλεῖτε ἑαυτούς were to be understood of each one exhorting himself, the writer must have said παρακαλεῖτε ἕκαστος ἑαυτόν; but παρακαλεῖν ἑαυτόν is a phrase of which probably no example could be produced. But, inasmuch as both classical Greek and that of the New Testament (Col. iii. 16 for instance) employ ἑαυτούς for ἀλλήλους,[1] the call here addressed to the Hebrew church can only mean that she should exhort herself in all her members, that is, that they should exhort one another. This they ought to do without intermission of a single day, ἄχρις οὗ τὸ σήμερον καλεῖται. The general sense of these words is clear: *so long as the day of grace lasts*. Ἄχρι (from ἄκρος) and μέχρι (from μακρός), with their later forms ἄχρις and μέχρις,[2] are at least etymologically distinguishable; so that ἄχρι fixes the highest point of an *ascending* historical line, and μέχρι the extreme point of an *extending* line. In actual use this distinction is not observed (comp. iii. 14, μέχρι τέλους, with vi. 11, ἄχρι τέλους); and ἄχρις οὗ as well as μέχρις οὗ is used in the signification "so long as," of the whole course on one side unto the terminating point: comp. Acts xx. 6, ἄχρις ἡμερῶν πέντε, *in the course of five days*.[3]

But the question remains, whether the translation should be, "*while it is called 'To-day,'*" i.e. "*while 'To-day' is so called*" (Vulg., Bleek, Lünem.), or "*while the call 'To-day' is uttered*" (Calv., Böhme, Thol., De W.). If the rendering first given means nothing more than, So long as a present day is still spoken of, it is incorrect; for τὸ σήμερον (*the* To-day), (comp. Luke xxii. 37), undoubtedly refers to the הַיּוֹם of the

[1] The notion contained in ἑαυτούς is, of course, not quite the same as that of ἀλλήλους, and hence the Greek grammarians differ as to whether one can be used in quite the same sense as the other. (See *Tryphonis Gramm. Alex. fragmenta*, ed. de Velsen, p. 29 seq.) The distinctions made come to mere hair-splittings. But while it is maintained by some, as Philemon and Suidas, that ἀλλήλων may be substituted for ἑαυτῶν, this is with right denied by others.

[2] Attic writers (according to Moeris in his λέξεις) use ἄχρι (μέχρι), not ἄχρις (μέχρις), or (according to Thomas Magister) sometimes one, sometimes the other form, before a word beginning with a vowel; but the Attic use of the form with final ς is very doubtful. (See Jacobitz on Thomas Mag. p. 127.)

[3] Comp. Klotz on *Devarius*, p. 224 seq., according to whom ἄχρι νῦν properly signifies *up till now*, and μέχρι νῦν, *until now*.

Psalm. If this, however, be understood, then the first rendering coincides with the second, and we may translate with Luther, *So lange es Heute heisset*,[1] that is, So long as the word of earnest exhortation, "To-day," is still sounded forth (καλεῖται=is named or proclaimed). The Hebrews are exhorted to give heed to the time of grace of which the Psalm speaks, and during which they may either obtain grace or incur judgment, and to employ it in daily mutual exhortation, lest any one of them become self-hardened. The *aor*. 1 *pass*. σκληρυνθῇ of σκληρύνεσθαι (Acts xix. 9) may, especially with reference to the expression in the Psalm (harden not your hearts), be taken here also in a middle sense. But it would be scarcely possible to draw here a very sharp and conscious distinction between the reflexive and the passive sense of σκληρύνεσθαι. In actual experience, a man cannot finally and definitively harden himself, without being at the same time hardened by God. Not that God *hardens any* (to speak with our older dogmatists) *positive aut effective*, His proper will and direct work being *only* our salvation; but He may well be said to do so *occasionaliter et eventualiter*, when the energizing powers of divine grace only serve to increase the inward tumult in which they are swallowed up, and to fill up the measure of human iniquity. And further, He may be said to *harden* sinners *judicialiter*, when His judicial will comes into operation, whereby that which was ordained for their "wealth" becomes "an occasion of falling," and is so turned into judgment; and when grace ceases to work, because it has exhausted all the ways and means of showing mercy. Such a divine judicial sentence, which would at the same time be a self-condemnation, the Hebrews are exhorted to avoid by anticipatory self-discipline. Instead of τις ἐξ ὑμῶν we must read, with Griesbach, Lachmann, Bleek, and all moderns, ἐξ ὑμῶν τις. The position of ἐξ ὑμῶν *before* τις is certainly significant; but for the antithetical reference to the forefathers in the wilderness, which, since Bleek and Böhme, is commonly found therein, we should require a καί (*etiam*),—a somewhat forced ellipsis. It must therefore be thus explained: *lest of you, the highly favoured, any one should perish in that self-obduration*. By ἀπάτη τῆς ἁμαρτίας (reminding us of the ὁ ὄφις ἠπάτησέ με of Gen. iii. 13), sin, with her seductive siren voice, is personified

---
[1] Literally, "so long it is called to-day."

as at Rom. vii. 11. Ἁμαρτία is here meant in the same sense as the Sept. of Jer. xiv. 7, where it is the rendering of מְשׁוּבָה, *backsliding*, and of Dan. viii. 12, where it is the translation of פֶּשַׁע, *transgression*. So apostasy is called, as being sin in its very essence. To warn the Hebrew Christians against such sin, which is striving, now with threats and now with blandishments, to draw them back into the synagogue, and to arm them for conflict with its various temptations, is the aim of our epistle. And here already the sacred writer sets before his readers the tendency of all such sin of unfaithfulness to end in self-obduration, and shows them, as from afar off,[1] how behind it the door of repentance is shut.

He proceeds to confirm his exhortation to incessant mutual watching and guarding against the sin of apostasy, by reference to the greatness of the loss which would be thereby incurred.

Ver. 14. *For partners of Christ are we become, so far as we hold stedfast the beginning of our confidence unto the end.*

The order of the *text rec.*, μέτοχοι γὰρ γεγόναμεν τοῦ Χρ., must be changed for the μέτ. γὰρ τοῦ Χρ. γεγόναμεν of Griesbach, Lachmann, Bleek, Tischendorf,[2] which throws its proper emphasis on τοῦ Χρ. On the other hand, we cannot concede what most modern interpreters insist on, that μέτοχοι is not here = *socii*, as in the quotation from the Septuagint version of Ps. xlv., given at ch. i. 9, but = *participes*, as in iii. 1, vi. 4, xii. 8; for μέτοχοι in the sense of *socii*, and μετοχή in that of *societas*, are not unknown to St. Luke and St. Paul (Luke v. 7; 2 Cor. vi. 14). Μέτοχος signifies partner as well as partaker (through a collateral idea not contained in the word itself, but connected therewith); so that μέτοχοι τοῦ Χρ. can equally well signify those who partake of Christ, and those who partake of that of which Christ is Himself partaker. But in the whole previous discourse from ii. 5 is summed up the latter, not the former notion, as was felt even by De Wette, although he decides for the signification *participes*. The δόξα into which our ἀρχηγός has entered is, by virtue of the κλῆσις ἐπουράνιος, not merely His, but also ours, although, as respects its manifestation and completion, so only in hope. As the Anointed One in His kingly glory, He is called ὁ Χριστός. Grace has

[1] Comp. vi. 4–8, and notes there.   [2] So also Cod. Sinait.

made us His μέτοχοι (this is the force of the γεγόναμεν), or as St. Paul says (Rom. viii. 17), συγκληρονόμοι with Him. We have become so already, but continue in this fellow-holding with Christ only so far as we suffer not ourselves to be bereft of that hope which has for its substance and its aim this our common possession, the heavenly glory. This is the leading thought of the conditional clause, ἐάνπερ τὴν ἀρχὴν τῆς ὑποστάσεως μέχρι τέλους βεβαίαν κατάσχωμεν. The ancient Greek, Syrian, and Latin commentators and translators take, as also Luther does, ὑπόστασις here, with manifold modifications of the sense, in the same signification as i. 3 (*substantia, subsistentia, fundamentum*); so Theodore of Mopsuestia understands by it ὥσπερ τινὰ φυσικὴν πρὸς τὸν Χριστὸν κοινωνίαν, and many explain it by reference to xi. 1 (where faith is defined as ἐλπιζομένων ὑπόστασις): so, for instance, Remigius-Primasius (combining two interpretations, and in both the echo of earlier commentators), *fidem Christi per quam subsistimus et renati sumus, quia ipsa est fundamentum omnium virtutum*. But since ὑπόστασις stands here in the same ethical connection as ἐλπίς does (iii. 6), and is not only used in the LXX. for תּוֹחֶלֶת and תִּקְוָה, but also occurs in writers deserving special consideration for the New Testament—such as Josephus, Polybius, and Diodorus Siculus—in the signification of *perseverantia* and *fiducia*, it is now almost universally conceded that here too it must be taken as equivalent to *firm confidence*. Starting from the fundamental notion of a firm position, taken under something else, it acquires the ethical meaning of steady persistence, hope, or courage under discouragements or difficulties. In our epistle, faith comes into consideration chiefly in this aspect, as a confident expectation of the future glorious development of what it already bears in itself as an appropriated possession. This faithful hope, which takes not offence at the servant form of the crucified Saviour, nor at the church which bears His cross, but holds on its way with joy, amid all contradictions and enigmas of the present, is called ὑπόστασις. We have now to consider what the author means by ἀρχὴν τῆς ὑποστάσεως. Most modern commentators (Bleek, De Wette, Lünem.) understand by it the good beginning of firm trust which the Hebrews had once made, but were now in danger of losing. Ebrard, on the ground that the beginning of faith in the church of Palestine, the oldest of all churches, could not be thus referred to, draws the inference that this epistle must have been addressed to a "*circle of catechumens and neophytes,*" and not to the Hebrew church at large. And unquestionably the Christians of Palestine, especially those of Jerusalem, could not have been now mere beginners in Christianity; nor does our author treat his readers as such. He makes it a ground of reproach against them (v. 12), that their knowledge bears no proportion to the long time that they have already been in Christ.: he extols (vi. 10, x. 32, xiii. 7) their first love (Rev. ii. 4) and their first faith (1 Tim. v. 12), maintained in a fight of afflictions, and the exemplary walk in faith of their departed rulers. Accordingly, ἀρχὴ τῆς ὑποστάσεως refers here, not to the beginning of believing confidence as inwardly experienced by the Hebrews, but to their exhibition of it in the world,—*fiducia Christiana a lectoribus primitus exhibita*, as it is correctly explained by Böhme and Tholuck; τέλος being the antithesis to this ἀρχή, as afterwards ἀρχηγός to τελειωτής (xii. 2). They are exhorted to hold fast their believing confidence in all the intensity of its first manifestation unshaken μέχρι τέλους, *unto the end*, *i.e.* the final redemption of individuals and of the whole church. The ἐάνπερ (according to the distinction taught by Hartung between περ and γε) implies that the first proposition holds true in all its extent, provided only that the second be added. What Christ possesses belongs also to them, and will continue theirs, now concealed, but to be made manifest hereafter, provided only they remain stedfast in their confidence of faith, and so the close of their Christian course correspond to its commencement.

This conditional character of the Christian inheritance of salvation is further illustrated by the case of the Israelites, the redeemed of Moses' time: they, too, forfeited their redemption, by failing to fulfil its conditions

Vers. 15, 16. *While it is said,* " *To-day, if ye will hear his voice, harden not your hearts, as at the provocation:*" *Who then were they that, having heard, gave provocation? Was it not indeed all who, under Moses' leadership, had come forth out of Egypt?*

This passage is well fitted to strengthen the conviction that there is a real progress in the exposition of Scripture. The ancients generally[1] took τινες (ver. 16) as an *indefinitum*; so *e.g.* the Itala, whose erroneous rendering (*quidam enim*) Jerome has retained. According to this view, the οὐ πάντες would be Joshua, Caleb, and the younger generation (which, however, as Seb. Schmidt acknowledges, cannot strictly speaking be taken into account). So also Luther (following the editions of Erasmus, Asulanus, and Gerbelius) translates: "*for some, when they had heard, gave provocation; howbeit, not all that came out of Egypt by Moses.*" But that the author should call the 600,000 who came out under Moses τινάς is unimaginable; and the appeal in favour of this interpretation to 1 Cor. x. 7-10, where the apostle four times designates by τινές αὐτῶν so many subdivisions of the majority of Israel who had incurred judicial punishment, is mere perversity. On the other hand, an appeal to the τινές dictated by love of Rom. xi. 17 (comp. ἀπὸ μέρους, ver. 25), would be better, though unwarrantable in this connection. Since the time of Bengel, the accentuation τίνες has justly made way everywhere, and the exclusive authority it at present enjoys will not soon again be shaken.[2] This mistake about τινες made it impossible for the ancients to see the proper construction of the ἐν τῷ λέγεσθαι, κ.τ.λ. Even the Syrians, with their τίνες, got no further. The impossible was regarded as possible; Chrysostom, for instance, held that ver. 15 is the antecedent proposition to iv. 1, and all between a parenthesis. Scarce any one will again propound this view.[3] Since Ribera (*ob.* 1591), many (and among the rest Bengel) have connected ἐν τῷ λέγεσθαι with ver. 13, thus making ver. 14 parenthetical; in which case ver. 15 would be an awkward and quite unnecessary addition. This view, likewise, is no longer heard of Some, however, still cherish the delusion that the *apodosis* is contained in ver. 15 itself. Bloomfield translates, as Luther

---

[1] With exception of the Antiochene or Syrian school, whose traditions are preserved by the Peshito, its daughter-version edited by Erpenius, St. Chrysostom, and Theodoret.

[2] The Hebrew version of the London Jews' Miss. Society still reads כי אחדים, " for some," which Biesenthal attempts to justify by references to the 250 of Num. xvi. 35 and the 3000 of Ex. xxxii. 28.

[3] It is much to be regretted that all we know of Theodore of Mopsuestia's commentary on this text is, that he clearly discerned the absurdity of the reading τινές, but not how he construed ver. 15 (p. 165, ed. Fritzsche).

also meant to be understood, *When it is said, " To-day, if ye will hear His voice," harden not your hearts.*[1] The sacred writer could not possibly have more confused his readers than by such an ἐν τῷ λέγεσθαι, referring to only one half of the quotation from the Psalm: surely in such a case he would (instead of ἐν τῷ λέγ.) have written διό, and thus, as in ver. 7, appropriated the whole quotation. Hence Winer, in his sixth edition (p. 504, comp. 5th ed. p. 626), has, with good reason, abandoned this his former view. It would be better to suppose, with von Gerlach, that the author made the words of the Psalm, from ἐάν onwards, his own: *While it is said, " To-day," harden not your hearts when ye hear His voice.* But can we imagine such disruption of the words of the Psalm? The natural supposition, after such a formula as ε. τ. λ., is, that all the words from the Old Testament which follow belong to the quotation thus introduced. The view represented by the Peshito, Erasmus, Luther—the view which has prevailed most extensively since the Reformation—that ver. 15 is intimately connected with ver. 14, satisfies this supposition. I was formerly of opinion myself, that ver. 15, following upon ver. 14, concluded on the one hand the application of the Scripture text (made vers. 12-14), and on the other formed the transition to a further application, beginning ver. 16. In like manner, Ebrard says, "With ἐν τῷ λέγεσθαι, the author gives, in words of Scripture, proof and reason why a man must persevere in faith in order to be a μέτοχος τοῦ Χριστοῦ." But this view likewise rests on an illusion,—namely, that ἐν τῷ λέγεσθαι can signify, "*since it is said*," or "*declared*" (in Scripture itself). But to express this the author would have written either καθὼς γέγραπται, or κατὰ τὸ γεγραμμένον, or οὕτως γὰρ εἴρηκεν, or διὸ λέγει, or the like. There remains, therefore, for con-

[1] This interpretation suggested, no doubt, the various reading μὴ σκλη ρύνετε of D* and E* (?) here; for elsewhere (iii. 8 and iv. 7) we have the subj. pres. μὴ σκληρύνητε (in all MSS.) where the sacred writer is directly quoting from the Old Testament. Otherwise he follows, when writing in his own person, the classical usage of μή with the subj. aor. and indic. pres. The construction with subj. pres., which is common only in later Greek, is not without example in the classical language: *e.g.* Thuc. i. 43, μήτε δέχησθε, μήτε ἀμύνητε. The omission of ὡς before ἐν τῷ παραπικρασμῷ in the Cod. Uffenbach. (Tischend. *Anecd.* p. 183) is probably due only to an error of transcription.

sideration only the now nearly dominant view (Böhme, Klee, Tholuck, Bleek, De Wette, Lünemann), that ver. 15 really is what it purports to be—the protasis to which the interrogative clause, τίνες γὰρ, κ.τ.λ., forms the apodosis, γάρ serving to make the question more pointed (Kühner, § 833, 2, i). This use of γάρ is idiomatic in the New Testament (Winer, p. 396), found in St. Luke (Acts xix. 35, viii. 31) as well as in St. Paul (1 Cor. xi. 22). It rests originally on the omission of an intermediate clause, which the question is intended to confirm or illustrate (see Frotscher's Glossary to Xenophon's *Hiero*, under γάρ), though a conscious reference to such intermediate clause has almost entirely disappeared, if not quite so entirely as in the Latin *quisnam*? The following is the train of thought in the author's mind: When it is said in the Psalm, "To-day, if ye will hear His voice, harden not your hearts, as in the provocation," it is to be observed that these provokers to whom the Psalm refers were themselves redeemed of the Lord, and yet fell under wrath and came short of the promised rest. These considerations, whereby he seeks to stimulate the conscience of the church of the redeemed of Jesus Christ, assume with him the form of pressing questions, τίνες γάρ, τίσι δέ, τίσι δέ; and even the answers given to these questions take an interrogative form, the author thereby appealing to the conscience of his readers, which cannot deny the justness of these answers. Against thus making ver. 16 the conclusion of the period commencing with ver. 15, there is only the one objection, that in all other instances the interrogative pronoun with this γάρ stands either at the beginning of an independent interrogative clause, or after a vocative (comp. Acts xix. 35), but never, so far as I know, in a question which forms the *apodosis* to a previous proposition. This objection, however, may be met by assuming that, when the author began with ἐν τῷ λέγεσθαι, it was not in his mind to continue with these interrogations, but that the *apodosis* took involuntarily (as it were) and by *anacolouthon* this interrogatory form. "When it is said, To-day, etc. Yes, observe! who were the people that gave such provocation?[1] namely, at Meribah and elsewhere— and *that* after hearing (ἀκούσαντες) the voice of God, to which

---

[1] παρεπίκραναν is used here absolutely, as Ps. cvi. 7 and elsewhere, without any necessity for supplying τὸν Θεόν.

in faith they should have yielded obedience!" Evidently an intermediate thought is omitted—not such as that supplied by Böhme, Ebrard, and others, "Was it then *only* those who provoked at Meribah?" nor that suggested by Bleek and De Wette, "How can you ask?" but one of much more importance, suggested to the author's mind by contemplation of the high privileges vouchsafed to the church of the New Testament, "What people were they who thus provoked God?" We might think of such as had never heard the divine voice, or witnessed its attestations. "Ah! no," he replies (ἀλλ' οὐ like ἀλλ' οὐχί, Luke xvii. 7, etc.; compare ἀλλὰ τί, Matt. xi. 7-9), "was it not all whom God redeemed from Egyptian bondage through Moses?"[1] Then follows, with δέ, another question, answered as before by a fresh interrogation.

Ver. 17. *And with whom* (with what sort of persons) *was he angered forty years? was it not with them that had sinned, whose members dropped in the wilderness?*

It was then a company of redeemed persons, redeemed though fallen, who provoked the divine wrath for the forty years of wandering in the wilderness between Massah and Mo Meribah. Those years were, on the one hand, years of grace (so they are regarded, ver. 9); on the other, years of wrath, as they are regarded here, in close connection with Ps. xcv. 10, comp. Ps. xc. 7-11. With whom, it is asked, was God compelled to be wroth and not gracious (though He had been and was yet willing to become so) for all those forty years? The answer is given by another question—οὐχὶ τοῖς ἁμαρτήσασιν; (Hebr. הלא באשר פשעו בו). Ἀμαρτάνειν (like ἁμαρτία, ver. 13) is here used of such sinning as throws out of grace by a presumptuous rejection of it, and wilful renunciation of divine communion. No note of interrogation (Böhme, Bleek, De Wette, Tholuck, Lünemann) ought to be placed after ἐρήμῳ at the end of the third clause. It is rightly punctuated as an affirmative statement by Bengel, Griesbach, Lachmann, and Tischendorf—ὧν τὰ κῶλα ἔπεσεν (Lachmann

[1] Bengel, Schulz, Kuinoel, translate wrongly: "Nay, but it was simply such as," etc. This would require, in order to mark ἐξελθόντες as the predicate, the article before πάντες—ἀλλ' οὐχ οἱ πάντες, or without the article ἅπαντες or σύμπαντες.

and Bleek, ἔπεσαν, Alex. = ἔπεσον) ἐν τῇ ἐρήμῳ. It forms a strict parallel to the clause καὶ βλέπομεν of ver. 19. For vers. 18, 19 consist likewise of three clauses (in sense if not in form), *i.e.* two questions and an affirmative proposition.

Vers. 18, 19. *Unto whom, moreover, sware he that they should not enter into his rest?* unless (it were) *to those who had proved unfaithful* (disobedient)? *And we see that they were unable to enter in on account of faithlessness.* Bleek, De Wette, Lünemann, are quite in error in regarding ver. 19 as the conclusion drawn from what precedes, or, as Ebrard expresses it, " a quod erat demonstrandum." Vers. 15, etc., is not a chain of deductions in logic, but a plain development of historical matters of fact for present warning and instruction. As the affirmative clause following the second question in ver. 17 proves the fearful reality of the divine wrath against apostasy, by reference to the actual fulfilment of the divine threatening, Num. xiv. 29-33, ἐν τῇ ἐρήμῳ ταύτῃ πεσεῖται τὰ κῶλα ὑμῶν, in those who dropped memberwise (so to speak) out of the living congregation in the wilderness, and made of the whole a company (as it were) of wandering corpses; so, in like manner, the καὶ βλέπομεν of ver. 19 refers to the evident fulfilment of the divine minatory oath, Ps. xcv. 11, εἰ εἰσελεύσονται εἰς τὴν κατάπαυσίν μου (comp. Num. xiv. 21-23). The ἀπιστία of ver. 19 corresponds to the ἁμαρτῆσαι of ver. 17 and the ἀπειθῆσαι of ver. 18. They fell away in the sin of apostasy, they were disobedient to the divine word, they exhibited themselves as utterly void of faith in God. This was the reason why it became for them impossible, despite all striving and longing, to reach the promised goal. What a solemn sermon lies in this fact for the redeemed under the New Testament—for the church of Christ! Then follows ι

CHAP. IV. 1-10. *An invitation (subjoined as conclusion to the preceding) to enter by faith into that divine rest to which the generation of the wilderness attained not, into which Joshua likewise was unable to bring his people,—the sabbath rest of God Himself, of which His people are made partakers.*

After the foregoing demonstration, that the fathers through

unbelief had failed to reach the promised מנוחה (Deut. xii. 9), we naturally expect the thought: How careful should *we* be not likewise to be excluded from it! This thought, which necessitates a further declaration that the rest remains for us, is immediately added.

Ver. 1. *Let us therefore fear, lest, since there still is left a promise of entering into his rest, any of you should seem to have come short of it.*

Leaving the participial clause for the present, and taking from it only the words τῆς καταπαύσεως αὐτοῦ (τοῦ Θεοῦ) as to be supplied after ὑστερηκέναι, we have, first of all, to reject decidedly the translation, " lest any one should think or imagine that he has come too late, or has lost all opportunity of entering into it" (Bretschn., Wahl, Ebr.): the author would then be warning his readers against the disheartening notion, that now no hope at all were left of entering into the rest of God. But (1) the warning, in this case, ought to have begun with μὴ οὖν δοκῶμεν, or at least μὴ οὖν φοβηθῶμεν, not φοβηθῶμεν οὖν; (2) the spiritual state of the readers which the epistle discovers to us, shows no trace of such despondency regarding their personal salvation; and (3) the spiritual trial which such a view supposes is a pure figment of the imagination. For it were too sad a folly, even for one melancholy-mad to infer from the fact, that the Israel of Moses' time forfeited the right of entering into the promised rest, that now there is no longer *any* entering into such rest at all. Hence, although the language might bear such interpretation (δοκεῖν = imagine, as x. 29, and the perfect = the aor., cf. Acts xxvii. 13), we must altogether discard it, as not harmonizing with the φοβηθῶμεν οὖν, and as contrary to the purport and sense of the passage. We must therefore take δοκεῖν in the sense of *videri*, as synonymous with φαίνεσθαι. But as δοκεῖν, *putare*, does not always signify a groundless fancy, so neither does δοκεῖν, *videri*, always signify a deceptive appearing. It is also used of such appearance as manifests an existing reality (hence δόξα, in the scriptural sense = divine glory), and especially for that which appears in public opinion, the credit or esteem in which any one stands (Mark x. 42; Gal. ii. 9; Luke xxii. 24), and the manifestation, more or less remote, of any real existence.

Thus here: *Let us be on our guard* (φοβηθῶμεν, subjunctive of exhortation, as Philo, ii. 674; the same φοβηθῶμεν is to be understood after Phil. ii. 12), *lest any of you should seem to have remained behind* (Bl., De W., Thol., Lünem., and most others). The author addresses the church (the reading ἐξ ἡμῶν instead of ἐξ ὑμῶν, which Faber Stap. contends for, is only a correction or mistake, made for the sake of conformity), while beginning with the communicative φοβηθῶμεν, to express his anxiety for their welfare. The phrase δοκῇ ὑστερηκέναι for ὑστερήσῃ in one aspect softens the expression (Oekum., Theophyl.),[1] and in another makes it more pointed, as Parcus already remarked correctly, and not too subtly (Seb. Schmidt) expressing the sense of the word: *Verbo δοκῇ sollicitudine tanta hic opus esse innuit, ut non modo quæ revera nos frustrent sed etiam, quæ videantur frustratura, provide caveamus.* They are bound to take earnest heed that there be not even the semblance of any one of them having remained behind. Ὑστερεῖν, as frequently also in classic writers, = to remain behind something, so as not to attain to what is striven for, to fail or come short of it. The goal thus missed, which is here to be supplied in the genitive, is the rest of God.[2] When a man's life of faith, endeavour after holiness, and perseverance in his Christian profession, begin to grow languid, he seems to be a ὑστερηκώς, that is, one who has let pass by the proper time for entering in with others into the rest of God. But if, in the case of the New Testament church, we may still, as in that of the Old Testament in the time of Moses, speak of a rest of God as the goal of their pilgrimage, we must also be able to point to a promise of entering such rest. That there is such a promise, is declared by the foregoing participial clause, καταλειπομένης ἐπαγγελίας εἰσελθεῖν εἰς τὴν κατάπαυσιν αὐτοῦ. It is now universally acknowledged that this has nothing to do with the phrase καταλείπειν τὴν ἐπαγγελίαν, to leave or neglect the promise (Luther: see Acts vi. 2), and that ἐπαγγελία does not mean commandment (*mandatum*), but, as always in the New Testament (occurring most frequently in St. Paul and St. Luke), promise or pledge. It is combined with the simple

---

[1] See Frotscher's glossary to Xenophon's *Hiero*, under δοκεῖν.

[2] Comp. Philo, ii. 656, where a similar genitive follows ὑστερίζειν—ὁ νοῦς ὑστερίζει τῆς κατὰ φύσιν ὁδοῦ.

infinitive instead of τοῦ εἰσελθεῖν (comp. xi. 15 ; Acts xiv. 5 ; Winer, p. 285, § 44) : There still remains a promise of entering into God's rest. The idea is utterly false, which many commentators, especially modern ones, introduce here ; namely, that the promise of entering into God's rest was not fulfilled in the case of the generation in the wilderness, and therefore still remains open. That were a strange logic ! The older generation in the wilderness perished, indeed ; but the younger entered into Canaan, came to Shiloh (a spot in the very heart of the country, which had its name from rest, Josh. xviii. 1), and found a settled dwelling-place of their own, in which the Lord planted them, and in which He vouchsafed them long periods of peace. Nor could it follow from the fact that the generation which came out of Egypt fell short of the rest of God, that there should still be a rest remaining. That fact is indeed a warning example, but not the legitimate premiss to such a conclusion. On the contrary, the author has yet to prove that there is still a promised rest remaining, notwithstanding Joshua's having led the younger generation into the land of promise. Commentators are in grievous error when they think that this proof is contained in what has preceded ; whereas the author introduces it first in that which follows, and does so by making a use of Ps. xcv. which we should hardly have imagined unless conducted to it by his own words in iv. 2, etc. We are not therefore at liberty to carry it back to iv. 1, where we find only the unproved thesis—" We are not come too late to find a promise ; for a promise still remains, if only we be very careful not to fall short of it."

Ver. 2a. *For unto us has a gospel been preached as well as unto them ; but the word preached did not profit them.*

Ἡμεῖς (καὶ γὰρ ἡμεῖς), the omission of which has been thought inconvenient (Bleek), is here omitted intentionally. De Wette and Lünemann would place the emphasis upon ἐσμὲν εὐηγγελισμένοι, we have also a message of salvation ; not, also we have such a message ; but it is better, however, to take καὶ γάρ here in the sense of *etenim* than in that of *nam etiam*, and so make the emphasis fall on καθάπερ κᾀκεῖνοι.[1] Except in

[1] "As even they had such a message." It must be allowed that καί in this connection has sometimes intensive, sometimes only copulative force.

Acts xv. 7, xx. 24, the noun εὐαγγέλιον occurs neither in St. Luke's writings nor in our epistle (where it might have been employed, as at ii. 1-3); but εὐαγγελίζεσθαι, as used passively of the persons to whom salvation is proclaimed, is common to our epistle, with Luke vii. 22, xvi. 16. At the same time it must not be concealed, that except in our epistle καθάπερ occurs in the New Testament only in the epistles of St Paul: it is the classical word for designating perfectly similar relation. The church of Jesus Christ has a message of salvation, which is on a level with, and in nothing behind, that which promised the rest of the land to the church of the Old Testament, when redeemed from Egypt, but (how full of warning for us!) without profiting them. With allusion to the words of the Psalm, σήμερον ἐὰν τῆς φωνῆς αὐτοῦ ἀκούσητε, which are still lingering in the author's mind, this gospel message is here called ὁ λόγος τῆς ἀκοῆς, an expression already used (Sir. xli. 23) to designate the word or matter received by hearing, and applied by St. Paul (1 Thess. ii. 13) to the New Testament word of preaching. For as εὐαγγελίζειν (εὐαγγελίζεσθαι), equivalent to בִּשֵׂר, was suggested by such eschatological passages as Isa. xl. 9, lii. 7, so ἀκοή, as equivalent to שְׁמוּעָה (הִשְׁמִיעַ), was suggested by Isa. liii. 1 and lii. 7 (comp. Rom. x. 14-17). The classical use of ἀκοή (for instance, ἀκοὴν ἔχω λέγειν τῶν προτέρων, that is, a tradition of the ancients; Plato, *Phædr.* p. 274 C) does not of itself alone explain the apostolic use of the word: we must take along with it the Hebrew שְׁמוּעָה, the thing heard, the tidings (with the genitive of its contents, 2 Sam. iv. 4, or of the person that brings it, Isa. liii. 1): *that* especially is called ἀκοή which the prophet having heard from the Lord declares to the people (Isa. xxviii. 9; Jer. xlix. 14); hence there could not be a more suitable term to express what had been received mediately or immediately from the lips of the apostolic ἀκούσαντες (ii. 3), and therefore to be used to express the whole New Testament preaching, as a phrase already familiar, and well understood.[1] The idea and expression as such being not peculiar to the New Testament, might be applied to the divine word, as addressed to Israel in Moses' time, espe-

against Hartung, who makes it always "cumulative." (See Klotz on Devarius, p. 642, 8.)

[1] Comp. 2 Thess. ii. 13.

cially in its promissory aspect, without its being necessary to suppose a direct reference to such passages as Ex. xix. 5, ἐὰν ἀκοῇ ἀκούσητε τῆς φωνῆς μου. This "word of hearing" did not profit them. Why not? Because (we translate from the text. rec.)—

Ver. 2b. *Not having been mingled by means of faith with* (or *for*) *them that heard it.*

Such is the reading, as given already by Erasmus: μὴ συγκεκραμένος τῇ πίστει τοῖς ἀκούσασιν. It might also be differently rendered by taking [with the English authorized version] τῇ πίστει as a dative, governed by συγκεκραμένος (in accordance with the phrase συγκεκρᾶσθαι τινι, *commixtum*, *admixtum esse alicui*), *Not having been mingled* or *mixed with faith*. In this case the second dative, τοῖς ἀκούσασιν, would be best taken, not (1) as the dative after a passive (*e.g.* Luther, till 1527, "inasmuch as faith was not added thereto by them that heard it"[1]); nor (2) even as a *dativus ethicus* (so De Wette, *denen zu gut*, "for their benefit who heard it"); but (3) as a dative of simple relation,[2] "not having been mixed (or combined) with faith in the case of those who (then) heard it" (so finally Lünemann, and also Winer, p. 196, § 31, 10). This, too, appears to be the meaning of the rendering in the Peshito.[3] But far preferable (as not so abstractly separating faith from the word) seems to me the interpretation of Schlichting (finally adopted by Tholuck, and represented in our translation as above), whereby τοῖς ἀκούσασιν is regarded as the dative, governed by συγκεκραμένος, and τῇ πίστει as the dative of the means or instrument, faith being represented as that which unites and combines together the divine word and the human auditory, in some such way as the chyle in the human system serves to combine the nourishing particles of our food with the sustaining principle of natural life, the blood (Hedinger). But

[1] Luther's original words are: *da der glaube nicht dazu than ward von denen die es höreten*. These he afterwards changed for those of the present text of his version: *da nicht glaubeten die so es höreten.*—TR.

[2] Which dative is often used where the use of the genitive might lead to misconception (Ditfurt, § 167).

[3] מטל דלא ממזגא הות בהימנותא להנון דשמעוה. The verb מזג is construed with ב in the Peshito, when used in the sense of mixing with anything. Comp. Ps. cii. 10.

however we understand the two datives, the thought will remain much the same, and is just the thought which we should have expected, expressed as well and clearly as possible in the reading presented by the *text. receptus*. If, however, we followed no other authorities for the original form of the text than the oldest Greek manuscripts, we must have decided for another reading. For instead of the nominative συγκεκραμένος, found (incorrectly written, too, συγκεκραμμένος) in only five minuscules (enumerated by Griesbach), the manuscripts give, some συγκεκραμένους or συγκεκραμμένους (D***, E.I.K., and 60 minuscules), and others (instead of this Attic form, one interchangeable with it in later usage) συγκεκερασμένους (A.B.C.D.*, Uffenb., and some ten minuscules), from the perf. pass. κεκέρασμαι.[1] Among modern editions, the former reading is adopted by Matthai, the latter by Lachmann (and formerly by Tischd. also). With either the meaning can only be, that the word preached did not profit them, because they did not believingly associate themselves with those who obeyed it. No doubt συγκεράννυναί τινι may signify to mix in company with one; but how purposeless would such an expression be here! Can, moreover, τοῖς ἀκούσασι be thus taken absolutely in the same sense as τοῖς ὑπακούσασι? The author should at least have already drawn a distinction between believers and unbelievers in the Israel of the wilderness. This he has not done; and the aorist shows that believers in general cannot be meant. Moreover, the whole idea is a departure (discordant with the context) from the simple and obvious thought, that the word did not profit, because not received in faith. Attempts have been made to support this reading by further conjectures. Theodore of Mopsuestia proposed to read μὴ συγκεκερασμένους τῇ πίστει τοῖς ἀκουσθεῖσι (which is found in Cod. 71, as also other conjectures of the fathers have passed into manuscripts); and Bleek (following Nösselt on Theodoret), τοῖς ἀκούσμασιν. But ἄκουσμα is a word foreign to the whole

---

[1] Comp. Rev. xiv. 10. The form is found *e.g.* in Anacreon and Lucian. Comp. Creuzer on Plotin. *de pulchritudine*, p. 50, βουλόμενος αὐτῷ συγκραθῆναι, where the MSS. vary in a similar way. The reading of D. is συν- (not συγ) κεκερασμένους, and even 3a man. συνκεκραμένους. The orthography of συνκ. is Alexandrine. Comp. Sturz, *de dialecto Maced. et Alex.* p. 131 s.

range of biblical Greek; and Theodoret, like his teacher, probably read τοῖς ἀκουσθεῖσι.[1] The sense which results from this alteration coincides with that of the *text. rec.* But how much more appropriate is it to say that the word of God was commingled by means of faith with the hearers, than to say that they were commingled by means of faith with the word of God! (τοῖς ἀκουσθεῖσι being, as Theodoret explains, = τοῖς τοῦ Θεοῦ λόγοις.) We adhere, therefore, with Böhme, De W., Thol., Lünem., to the *text. rec.*, to which Tischendorf also (1849) has now returned.[2] And indeed, on closer inspection, it has in its favour not unimportant testimonies, which (as shown by Tholuck and Lünemann) have been too much undervalued by Bleek. Besides the five minuscules, it is found in the Peshito, the Vulgate, and the Arabic of Erpenius; the Itala, too (in Sabatier), *verbum auditus non temperatum fide* (in Lucifer Calar. *fidei*) *auditorum*, presupposes it, and so also Cyril of Alexandria in one citation. Of all these testimonies, the most weighty is the single one of the Peshito, the oldest translation of the New Testament.

The further development of the thought is as follows: We too have a promise (so said ver. 2), which speaks of entering into the rest of God,—a promise which others had failed to realize. For (continues ver. 3) we who have believed do enter into rest. That such entrance into rest is possible, is further proved thus: (1.) God's rest began on the completion of the work of creation; but an entering into it is further spoken of. (2.) The generation in the wilderness failed to enter into God's rest; and the exhortation to enter into it was again renewed in the time of David, making evident that the entering into Canaan under Joshua had not been the true entering into the

---

[1] S. Jerome's version, both in Cod. Amiatinus (?) and in the modern Roman edition of the Vulgate, reads: "*sed non profuit illis sermo auditus* (= *auditionis*) *non admixtus fidei ex iis quæ audierunt.*" This is derived from the reading ἀκουσθεῖσι. Mediæval and Roman Catholic commentators (Justinianus, Estius, Ribera, etc.) are at a loss how to interpret it. The Itala follows the reading τῶν ἀκουσάντων; but its form in D. (see Tischend. Cod. Claromont. p. 481) has no intelligible meaning: *non temperatus fidem auditorum*. [The Cod. Amiatin. reads *admixtis*, acc. to Tischend.—TR.]

[2] Ebrard also maintains it, but on inadmissible grounds, and in a totally unauthorized form, συγκεκερασμένος. [This form is now found in Cod. Sin.—TR.]

rest of God. Hence (ἄρα) (3.) the final entrance of the people of God into His rest, the Sabbath of the church of believers, the ultimate goal of their history, a Sabbath-keeping corresponding to God's Sabbath at the end of the work of creation, remains unaccomplished still. The first link in the chain of this argument is thus given:

Vers. 3-5. *For we are entering into rest, we who have become believers; even as he said, As I sware in my wrath, they shall not enter into my rest: although the works were finished from the foundation of the world. For he hath spoken somewhere of the seventh day thus, " And God rested the seventh day from all his works." And here again he saith, " They shall not enter into my rest."*

It is a grievous misconception to suppose, in the outset, that the first clause here, εἰσερχόμεθα γὰρ εἰς τὴν κατάπαυσιν οἱ πιστεύσαντες, is meant to confirm what was said, ver. 2b, that the word preached to the Israel of the wilderness was made profitless through their unbelief (Bleek), and that so the clause is logically connected with τῇ πίστει, ver. 2 (Lünem.). This undue emphasis laid on οἱ πιστεύσαντες, either discomposes more (Lünem.) or less (Bl.) the subsequent train of thought, or necessitates an exposition which differs radically from the author's meaning (Ebr.). And surely the clause, even taken by itself, stands as closely related to ver. 2a through εἰσερχόμεθα γὰρ εἰς τὴν κατάπαυσιν, as to ver. 2b through οἱ πιστεύσαντες. We also (he would say) have now a promise, as they once had who lost it through unbelief, for we who have believed are entering into rest; that is, the way which we walk has, like theirs of old, God's rest (הַמְּנוּחָה) for its goal, if so be that we are really a company of faithful persons. The present (εἰσερχόμεθα), instead of the future, might be explained as expressing the idea of abstract universality (Bleek, De Wette, Tholuck), or that of confident expectation (Lünem.); and the *aor. part.* οἱ πιστεύσαντες (not πιστεύοντες) as expressing the necessary condition to the εἰσέρχεσθαι (so Seb. Schmidt, and most others). But the present tense here may, I think, be better accounted for thus: the entering in of which the writer speaks is regarded as the ultimate goal of a long-continued journey, even as Israel's entrance into their land of promise was by a journey through the wilderness: consequently the οἱ πιστεύ-σαντες here will signify not those who have *given proof of* their faith, but (as this form at least more commonly signifies; see Acts iv. 32, xi. 21, xix. 2; and comp. Rom. xiii. 11) those who have *attained to* faith. This appositional οἱ πιστεύσαντες implies no doubt a conditional ἐὰν πιστεύσωμεν; and yet here it designates the church (without regard to those of its members who may ultimately fail) simply as a company of *believers*.

That this church of the New Testament, like that of the Old, has a rest for the end and aim of its journey, is now proved, or rather begun to be proved, from Ps. xcv. 11, in combination with Gen. ii. 2. "Undoubtedly," says Bleek, "the author here again alludes to Ps. xcv. 11, as implying that faith is required for entering into God's rest, but also, at the same time, as a passage from which, as indicating the non-fulfilment of the divine promise, it may be inferred that that promise still stands open." In this way Bleek's interpretation turns back from the mistaken interpretation of εἰσερχόμεθα γὰρ, κ.τ.λ., into the right road. But it is lamentable to see how many commentators have here gone wrong, partly by taking καίτοι in senses which it never has (*e.g.* Vulg. and Luther: *et quidem, und zwar*), partly by denying that τῶν ἔργων ἀπὸ καταβολῆς κόσμου γενηθέντων is the genitive absolute, and making guesses as to how it may be governed (so, latterly, Klee and Bloomfield: "and indeed" into a rest "from works already completed," etc.); or by connecting the *gen. absol.* as such with the following verse (Luther and others).[1] But even commentators who take καίτοι[2] in its proper signification (see Hartung, ii. 362), understanding also and assigning its proper connection to the participial clause (*e.g.* Böhme, *tametsi operibus a jacto mundi fundamento factis*), make nevertheless utter nonsense of what is here said: *revera introituros esse Christianos ad requiem Dei per Psalmi vaticinium promissam, quamquam hæc promissio ad antiquissimam pertineat requiem, scilicet statim post mundi primordia coeptam.* In what pitiful logic, as well as exegesis, does this

---

[1] [Luther's rendering might be thus translated: *And indeed, when the works from the beginning of the world were made, spake He in a certain place of the seventh day thus*, etc.—Tr.]

[2] καίτοι is found in some MSS. for καίτοιγε at Acts xiv. 17, and for καίγε at Acts xvii. 27.

VOL. I. N

quamquam involve the interpreter! And yet the sacred writer's treatment of the subject is as transparently true as deep, if only we examine it with a little attention to the divine law of development in the work of redemption; each step in the onward movement pointing to the final goal, which harmoniously combines a beginning in which all was contained, with an end in which all shall be unfolded. According to God's own utterance in Scripture, Ps. xcv. (εἴρηκεν, sc. ὁ Θεός), He had sworn in His wrath against the Israelites of Moses' time, that they should not enter into His rest. An entering, therefore, into God's rest is spoken of in the time of Moses, as an entrance whereby they who attained it should arrive at the destined end of their existence, although the creature works of God had reached their predestined end[1] from the time when, in the six days' work of creation, He laid the foundation of the world (ἀπὸ καταβολῆς κόσμου, a phrase not found in the LXX., but occurring Luke xi. 50, and often in the New Testament). *For He hath somewhere spoken* (Gen. ii. 2) *of the seventh day on this wise,* "*And God rested on the seventh day* (ἐν τῇ ἡμέρᾳ τῇ ἑβδόμῃ, for which our Septuagint text has simply the dative of time) *from all His works;*" *and in this place* (viz. the passage under immediate discussion, τούτῳ, neuter, like ἐν ἑτέρῳ, v. 6) *again* (πάλιν, vicissim, on the other hand, as Matt. iv. 7), "*Verily they shall not enter into my rest.*" From this comparison of two divine sayings, or (what is the same thing) of two passages of Scripture, it is evident that the end to which created things were brought at the close of creation was not a final end; that correlative to the rest into which God then entered, there remains still a rest into which all creatures have to enter before they can be perfected; and that such an entrance into rest which, on man's part in particular, is conditioned by faith, was the promised goal set before the Israelites when redeemed from Egypt, but not attained by them because of their unbelief. The chain of reasoning is now continued as follows: The end which God has set before the creature, especially mankind, and, more especially still, His own people, and of which His promise (His message) of salvation speaks, cannot remain unattained to: there must of

---

[1] γενηθέντων, originally a Doric form for γενομένων, and far the more suitable one here.

CHAP. IV. 6-9.   195

necessity be persons who really reach it, since the Israelites in the wilderness have failed to do so. This conclusion is irrefragable. But, it may be asked, although the elder generation that came out of Egypt perished in the wilderness, did not the younger generation, under Joshua, actually enter into the promised rest? To this question the author has now to reply; for it is a mistake to maintain, as most commentators do, that he at once identifies the entrance into God's rest promised by Moses, with that which is the true counterpart of the divine Sabbath after the works of creation. The entrance into rest which Moses promised was (as is expressed in a hundred passages, and as our author himself well knew) simply the taking possession of the land of Canaan. But things combined in the promise were disjoined in the fulfilment. It became manifest that the taking possession of Canaan did not cover the whole extent of the promise, and did not exhaust it. The intrinsic force of the conclusion which our author draws, is not therefore in the least affected by a reference to what had happened under Joshua. When separated from the incomplete and merely natural side of its fulfilment, the promise still continued, and awaited a far nobler fulfilment in the future. With this in view, the author continues :

Vers. 6-9. *Since therefore it remaineth still that some should enter thereinto, and they who formerly received the promise did not enter in because of their contumacy, he again fixeth a certain day, " To-day," through David speaking, after so long a time, as we have already said, " To-day, if so be ye hear his voice, then harden not your hearts." For had Jesus* (Joshua) *brought them into rest, he would not be found after these things speaking of yet another day. There remaineth therefore still a sabbath-rest for the people of God.*

In ἀπολείπεται τινὰς εἰσελθεῖν the conclusion is not drawn that participation in the rest of God is of necessity an ἀπολειπόμενον for every member of the human race. If that had been the sacred writer's meaning, he would not have written τινάς. That mankind has to enter into the divine rest, is a thought suggested by Gen. ii. 2, compared with the promises of the divine word,—a thought presupposed by the argument, but not expressly uttered. With ἐπεὶ οὖν rather a new consequence is drawn from Ps. xcv. 11 combined with Gen. ii. 2, which, as De Wette ingeniously observes, is expressed first positively and generally, then negatively and historically, in order thus to show that a fresh exhortation of the same kind was actually given in David's time. What has been said makes evident that it still remains, or is reserved,[1] in the divine counsels, for some other persons than the above mentioned to enter in; since—thus we would put it—οἱ πρότερον εὐαγγελισθέντες (εὐηγγελισθέντες), that is, those to whom in Moses' time entrance into God's rest was opened by promise, did not enter thereinto, even because they did not submit themselves with the obedience of faith to the word preached. And just because this was the case, God afterwards (*opp.* πρότερον) fixes again τινὰ ἡμέραν, *i.e.* a day of invitation, to enter into His rest (the more general idea of ἡμέρα σωτηρίας, 2 Cor. vi. 2, being here particularized), to David's contemporaries, saying by David, "*To-day*," μετὰ τοσοῦτον χρόνον, that is, after the lengthened period elapsed since Moses (the promise therefore continuing unrevoked), "*To-day, if ye will hear His voice.*" That ἐν Δαυίδ is intended to signify "in the book of Psalms" (comp. ἐν Ἠλίᾳ, Rom. xi. 2 = in the Scripture account of Elias: Bleek, De W., etc.) is improbable: in that case he must at least have said ἐν τῷ Δαυίδ; but the Psalter, although doubtless held as *à potiori* Davidic (*e.g.* Acts iv. 25), is never thus cited, and least of all here, where a Psalm is spoken of which the LXX. actually superscribes with τῷ Δαυίδ. By προείρηται (the reading to be preferred with Bg., Lchm., Tischd., etc., to the εἴρηται of the *text. rec.*[2]) the author refers to his repeated quotation from Ps. xcv. 7. The quotation is here purposely interrupted by the words introducing it, in order to bring out more distinctly the σήμερον with which it is commenced and again resumed. This fresh fixing of a time is accounted for in ver. 8, from the fact that the promise of entering into God's rest had not only remained unfulfilled in the case of the generation of the wilderness, but also had not

---

[1] This is the true meaning of ἀπολείπεται (comp. x. 26) as distinguished from καταλείπεται = *is left behind*. Luther showed a delicate perception of this distinction, when he changed his former translation "*hinterstellig*" into the later "*fürhanden.*"

[2] The Cod. Sin. also reads προείρηται.—Tr.

found its final realization in the conquest of Canaan under Joshua. And ver. 9 proceeds to draw from what has been said, and from the fact assumed, though not expressed, that even after David's time the promised rest was not attained, and that therefore the σήμερον of the Psalm must be extended to the times of the New Testament, the very obvious conclusion, ἄρα ἀπολείπεται σαββατισμὸς τῷ λαῷ τοῦ Θεοῦ. The promise is still open, its fulfilment not yet exhausted: there is still reserved for the people of God, still to be expected by them, as the church of believers, a σαββατισμός,[1] the keeping of a Sabbath, the enjoyment of a Sabbath rest. So it is, and must be; for the Sabbath of God the Creator is destined to become the Sabbath of all creation, an ἑορτὴ τοῦ παντός (to use Philo's phrase, i. 21, 35), but especially of the people of God: this is the main-spring (as it were) of all history. Our author stands not alone in this view. That "a day which shall be all Sabbath" (יום שכלו שבת) will close the great week of the world's history, is a thought expressed in manifold forms in the traditions of the synagogue, e.g. F. B. *Sanhedrim* 97a: "As the seventh year brings in a time of rest at the end of a period of seven years, so the millennial rest will close a period of seven thousand years." But the earthly millennium which is to close this world's history will not yet be (as is clear from Rev. xx. 7, etc.) a full realization of this promise of the final Sabbath. It has indeed been usual in the church to designate the millennium as the seventh day (ἡ ἑβδόμη), and the blissful eternity beyond it as the eighth (ἡ ὀγδόη).[2] But that eighth day, or octave, of eternity is in fact nothing else but the eternal continuance of the final Sabbath, as Athanasius speaks in his sermon *on the Sabbath and Circumcision* (*Opp.* ed. Bened. iii.),

---

[1] Σαββατισμός from σαββατίζειν, to keep Sabbath, as ἑορτασμός from ἑορτάζειν, to keep feast or holiday.

[2] The old Latin *brevis* to our section [*e.g.* in Cod. Amiatin. ed. Tischend. —Tr.] is, *de sacramento diei septimi et millesimi anni*. The view is not unknown even in the synagogue. See *Elijahu Rabba*, c. 2 (on Ps. xcii. 1). *The Sabbath indicated* (viz. in the title of the Psalm, which is the first verse in the Hebrew—Tr.) *is that Sabbath which will give rest from sin that now rules in the world, the seventh day of the world*('s history), *on which will follow the after Sabbath* (מוצאי שבת) *of the world to come, wherein there is no more death, nor sin, nor punishment of sin, but only enjoyment of the wisdom and knowledge of God.* Comp. Rom. xi. 33.

Τὰ μέλλοντα ἐλπίζομεν σάββατα σαββάτων. "We look for that future Sabbath of Sabbaths. The new creation will have no end, but be manifested in the enjoyment of a perpetual feast" (διόλου ἑορτάζει). The final Sabbath will not therefore be realized till time is swallowed up of eternity, and mortality of life. It will be the eternal conclusion of the week of time, as seven is the numeric symbol of perfection and rest.[1] And this is the object of our author's thought and expectation when he says, ἄρα ἀπολείπεται. Somewhat, however, still remains wanting to completely establish his conclusion. He has proved that Joshua had not brought the people of Israel into the rest of God;[2] but the question still remains unanswered, why this could not be? why the κατάπαυσις, which he in fact procured (Josh. xxiii. 1), was not the true and promised rest? This question is answered in the following verse.

Ver. 10. *For he that is entered into his* (God's) *rest, even he resteth from his works, as from his own works God* (rested).

That there still remains, then, a Sabbath-rest, is proved from its nature; the true rest being very different from that outward one of the settlement in Canaan. Like the rest of God after the work of creation, it is a rest of man from his works, that is, his daily labour here below: it is therefore a rest above in heaven. With appeal to the aor. (εἰσελθών, κατέπαυσεν), it might certainly be made to appear that ver. 10 bears the same relation to its preceding context as ii. 9 : " *Mankind has received a call to enter into the rest of God; Joshua did not bring it into that rest; the final Sabbath is to be still looked for; for Jesus, who has entered Himself into God's rest, rests there sabbatically now, as God had done before.*" So Ebrard. But if the author meant to be so understood, why not name the Lord Jesus? To this Ebrard replies, Because he had just been using the name

[1] Τῷ ὄντι, says Philo, ii. 5, 34, ὁ ἕβδομος ἀριθμὸς ἐν τῷ κόσμῳ καὶ ἐν ἡμῖν αὐτοῖς ἀστασίαστος καὶ ἀπόλεμος, ἀφιλονεικότατός τε καὶ εἰρηνικώτατος ἁπάντων ἀριθμῶν στει. Comp. my *Genesis*, ii. 198, and *Psychol.* p. 39. A modern rabbi (Hirsch, *Religions-philosophie*, p. 849) finds in the above-mentioned traditions of the synagogue nothing but echoes of Persian legends. In this shameful way is modern Judaism ever ready to surrender anything which may seem to connect it with Christianity.

[2] See Feder on the active use of καταπαύειν here, in his *Excerpta Codice Escurialensi*, p. 190.

Ἰησοῦς to designate Joshua. As if he could not have continued with ὁ γὰρ Χριστός ! But the aorist κατέπαυσεν does not compel us thus to refer this clause to Christ; there being no other indication that we must do so. The author might indeed have written καταπαύει or (more classically[1]) καταπέπαυται (*perf.* as Rom. vi. 7); but (as already remarked by Böhme, Bleek, and De Wette) he has taken up into the main proposition the κατέπαυσεν, which properly belongs (according to Gen. ii. 2) to the clause of comparison: whosoever has entered into God's rest, of him the κατέπαυσεν ἀπὸ τῶν ἔργων αὐτοῦ holds good, in the same manner as of God. He has, in retrospect of the life here, found rest. Divine and human ἔργα being thus compared, Tholuck will have it that the latter must be works of moral activity, and not outward employments; and since all active exertion does not cease in the world above, he finds the essential characteristic of these ἔργα, from which man rests in God, to consist in conflicts with moral evil. But such a limitation[2] is quite gratuitous; and seeing that the exalted Lord Himself has still to withstand and overcome the adversaries of His kingdom, the essential characteristic of those works which cease in heaven might rather be found in a cessation from labour, toil, and pain. And yet τὰ ἔργα here is not quite the same as οἱ κόποι or πόνοι at Rev. xiv. 3, xxi. 4. For when it is said, that every man who is entered into rest, rests in his own person from his works, as God the Creator has rested from His own peculiar works, the works of creation (ἀπὸ τῶν ἰδίων = ἀπὸ τῶν ἑαυτοῦ; comp. vii. 27, ix. 12, xiii. 12), τὰ ἔργα denotes in the one place the special task or business (מלאכא) assigned to Himself by God, in the other the vocation or mission assigned by God to man. *Noli ita Deo adulari* (says Tertullian, *adv. Hermog.* c. 45), *ut velis illum solo visu et solo accessu tot ac tantas substantias protulisse, et non propriis viribus instituisse.... Major est gloria ejus si laboravit. Denique septima die requievit ab operibus. Utrumque suo more.* This

[1] Καταπαύειν in classical Greek is always transitive: κατέπεσεν is here used with special reference to the Septuagint version of Gen. ii. 2. See Thiersch, *de Pentateuchi vers. Alex.* p. 39.

[2] Especially when we consider that it is the divine activity in the work of creation, and in laying the foundation of the world, with which the works of man are here compared.

utrumque suo more may be applied to the case before us. Man's daily work in this world, with all its labours, conflicts, and sorrows, corresponds to the six days' work of God. From this, the מלאכה imposed on him here, he rests in God. To share in this his Sabbath-rest with God, is the hope set before the church from the very beginning. The church of the New Testament has still the same goal placed before her; and the way to attain it is thrown open in the gospel.

CHAP. IV. 11-13. *Renewed exhortation to enter into the rest of God, the intense earnestness of which is founded on the all-penetrating and all-disclosing vital energy of the divine word.*

The exhortation with which the chapter opened, its tenor and motive being now made clear, is most earnestly resumed:

Ver. 11. *Let us therefore earnestly strive to enter into that rest, that no one may fall after the same pattern of disobedience.*

Σπουδάσωμεν οὖν, studiamus igitur[1]—σπουδάζειν, to exhibit zeal and earnest endeavour; εἰσελθεῖν εἰς ἐκείνην τὴν κατάπαυσιν, that rest which is at once the reflection and the participation of God's own Sabbath. Ἐκείνην here does not point forwards, as in the phrase ἐκείνη ἡ ἡμέρα, but backwards—that rest of which we have been speaking; to attain its blessedness the utmost diligence must be applied, lest that befall us which happened to the people in the time of Moses: ἵνα μὴ ἐν τῷ αὐτῷ τις ὑποδείγματι πέσῃ τῆς ἀπειθείας. Luther's rendering, which follows the Vulgate,[2] "that none may fall into the same example of unbelief," has been given up by all modern commentators— Lünemann only has ventured to renew it—and yet it has been mere ignorance of Greek usage which has, since Bleek, determined its rejection. Lünemann's observation is perfectly correct, that πίπτειν ἐν is as old and good Greek as πίπτειν εἰς

---

[1] This is the only true resumption of the parænesis; for the perverse reading of some copies, εἰσερχωμεθα (A.C.), *ingrediamur* (Prim.), at ver. 3, is scarcely worth mentioning.

[2] *Ut ne in id ipsum quis incidat incredulitatis exemplum* (Vulg.). *Auf dass nicht jemand falle in dasselbige Exempel des Unglaubens* (Luther).

(or as πίπτειν followed by the simple dative of direction); to which we may add, that πίπτειν ἐν is as usual in Hellenistic Greek as π. εἰς: comp. πεσεῖν ἐν τῇ παγίδι, Ps. xxxv. 8; ἐν ἀμφιβλήστρῳ, Ps. cxli. 10; ἐν καρδίᾳ θαλάσσης, Ezek. xxvii. 27 (while נָפַל בְּיַד, in the sense of falling by the hand of any one, is rendered by πεσεῖν ἐν χειρί; and in the sense of falling *into* the hand of any one, 2 Sam. xxiv. 14, by ἐμπεσεῖν εἰς χεῖρας). This notwithstanding, the old interpretation renewed by Lünemann must be rejected here. For no authority can be alleged in Hellenistic literature for πίπτειν ἐν in the sense of falling into this or that ethical condition, and scarcely any in classical Greek, except it be some places in the poets (as πεσεῖν ἐν κλύδωνι καὶ φρενῶν ταράγματι, Euripides, *Herc. fur.* 1092). In such a case, the almost exclusive usage is πεσεῖν εἰς, or *cum dativo* (to fall into or become subject to such or such a condition). Consequently πέσῃ has here an independent meaning, in determining which we must not allow ourselves to be misled by a fancied reference to ὧν τὰ κῶλα ἔπεσεν (iii. 17). The pilgrimage of the church of the New Testament out of the world, and through the world towards the final rest, corresponds antitypically to Israel's journey out of Egypt and through the wilderness towards Canaan. The church is exhorted to endeavour zealously to advance on the way to this end with steady step, lest any stumble and fall (πεσεῖν nearly as Rom. xi. 11). The people, under Moses are herein an ὑπόδειγμα (as 2 Pet. ii. 6),[1] or, as St. Paul expresses it (1 Cor. x. 6), a τύπος for us—a warning example. Should any Christian fall on the way to God's rest, it would be ἐν τῷ αὐτῷ ὑποδείγματι τῆς ἀπειθείας, he would present a like example of disobedience. The ἐν is the ἐν of state or condition, similar to the Hebrew so-called *Beth essentiæ*. Τῆς ἀπειθείας is advisedly placed at the end of the sentence, to lead on to what follows. Disobedience implies a divine *word*, here a word of promise,

---

[1] The word ὑπόδειγμα is used by Clemens Romanus, *e.g.* cc. 5 and 55. The equivalent term in the older Attic, παράδειγμα, is not found in the New Testament. A passage in Xenophon's Ἱππικός is the only one where the word ὑπόδειγμα occurs in an Attic writer. See Lobeck, *Phryn.* p. 12. A Christian grammarian in Bachmann's *Anecdota,* ii. 553, is wrong in asserting that ὑπόδειγμα is a *fore-type,* παράδειγμα a *copy:* each word combines both significations.

which demands a corresponding course of action. It is a λόγος τῆς ἀκοῆς which (according to ver. 2) is now addressed to the church of the New Testament, as formerly to that of the Old. From the nature of this word, further reasons are adduced for the exhortation.

Vers. 12, 13. *For full of life is the word of God, and full of energy, and more cutting than any two-edged sword, and penetrating even to a dividing asunder of soul and spirit, as well as of joints and marrow, and passing judgment on the thoughts and intents of the heart. Nor is any creature hidden from it: but all things are bare and exposed to the eyes of him with whom we have to do.*

We may take for granted, and as undeniable, that the only logical connection of these two verses with what precedes, as well as with what follows, is to be found in their expressing the living and inexorable energy of that word which, as it formerly brought death upon Moses' contemporaries through their disobedience to its injunctions, so now imposes on the church of Jesus Christ the duty of earnest striving after the promised salvation. It is characteristic of the word of God, that it endures no obscurity or divided allegiance : the effect of its operation in us lies open before God our Judge ; and hence the need of holding fast by the profession of this word, which is offered to our faith during the present interval between the beginning and the end of the work of redemption (Hofmann, *Entsteh.* p. 40). This is the evident connection of thought, both with that which precedes and that which follows. It would therefore be to pervert and confuse the sense to interpret, with the ancients (and with Biesenthal among moderns), ὁ λόγος τοῦ Θεοῦ as designating Christ the personal Logos, whereas both the heavenly Sabbath and Christ Himself the Saviour (comp. ver. 14 with iii. 1) are here conceived of as the subject of the Word. Nevertheless, considering the relation borne by our epistle to the writings of St. Paul on the one hand, and to those of St. John on the other, *i.e.* as forming a link between them ; and considering further the resemblance, which cannot be accidental, of what we here read of the λόγος τοῦ Θεοῦ to similar utterances of Philo, we cannot escape from the question, How are we to explain the connection of ideas in this paragraph?[1] If we compare the commencement of St. John's first epistle with that of his Gospel, there will be seen to be an evident and close connection between λόγος as designation for the personal Word, and λόγος as designation for "the Word of preaching;" and the question offers itself for solution, why the same term is applied to both, and how the idea of one passes into that of the other? This essential connection of the two ideas must be explained. Unless it be duly recognised by us, we divide into lifeless and unscriptural abstractions, ideas which very manifestly interpenetrate. And, moreover, to recognise this intimate connection is necessary in order to our understanding the historical relation in which the Palestinian Jewish, the Alexandrian Jewish, and the New Testament Christian representations of the divine Logos (דברא, מימרא די יה') stand to one another.

Hofmann recognises but misunderstands this connection when he says, that Jesus Christ may be called ὁ λόγος in a personal sense, as being the substance of the Word sent into and offered to the world, *i.e.* as He who is preached in the world, but not as one anterior in existence to it (*Schriftb.* i. 102). For such a blow levelled at a conviction deeply rooted since the days of Justin Martyr in the mind of the Christian church, and which has exercised a mighty influence on the historical development of its dogmas, the following is all that he offers us by way of compensation. We are still permitted to make the inference, that if the relation between the man Jesus and God be represented as that of Father and Son, the eternal relation between them must correspond to that which is thus manifested in time; and that if Jesus, *as* man, be the personal Word of God *to* man, He must also stand to Him who has thus sent Him in an eternal relation, which may be compared to that of

---

[1] It is a defect in Hofmann's work, that he sets aside this question in the outset by denying that the assumed influence of Philo on Jewish thought has any basis of proof, more especially in the New Testament (*Schriftb.* i. 110). When we take into account the mighty influence exercised by the Alexandrian version of the Septuagint in the New Testament era, such denial is seen to have but little internal probability; and when the full state of the case is considered, is manifestly untenable, unless for an easily apprehended process of historical development in the revelation of the divine economy of redemption, we are content to substitute an incredible supremacy of mere chance.

word and speaker (*Weiss.* ii. 8). But this is merely a concession or an inference.[1] The bond of connection between the personal Word and the word of preaching remains for Hofmann a mere metonymy, an interchange of designations, a putting of the *continens pro contento*. But surely that bond must be sought at a far greater depth than this. We shall acquire an insight into its nature, if we start from the proposition with which Hofmann concludes as a mere inference, that the eternal relation to God of the eternal Person, manifested in Jesus, may be compared to that of Word and Speaker. This we

[1] Hofmann maintains that, as an inference or deduction, the doctrine and language of the church is in this way not only admissible, but justifiable, but only as a deduction. When, for instance, St. John says (i. 18) that *no one hath seen God at any time*, but that *the only-begotten Son who is in the bosom of the Father* (ὁ ὢν εἰς τὸν κόλπον τοῦ Πατρός) *hath declared Him* as He is to us, he must (according to Hofmann) be understood to mean by ὁ ὤν, not *He who is and hath been from all eternity in His own immutable being in the Father's bosom*, but only *one who is there now, after having been assumed into it*. And so again, when he says (i. 14) that *the Word became flesh*, the evangelist's meaning would be, not, *He who from all eternity, being Himself divine, stood in the relation of Logos to God, assumed human nature*—but simply, *He who is the personal object of the preached word became man*. But seeing, in the first place, that St. Paul speaks of the author of our redemption as *the image* (εἰκών) *of the invisible God*, the πρωτότοκος πάσης κτίσεως, even as Philo in several places speaks of the Logos as ἡ τοῦ Θεοῦ εἰκών and ὁ πρεσβύτατος, or πρωτόγονος αὐτοῦ υἱός; seeing, in the second place, that our own Epistle to the Hebrews, which forms the connecting link between the later epistles of St. Paul and the writings of St. John, calls Him ἀπαύγασμα τῆς δόξης καὶ χαρακτὴρ τῆς ὑποστάσεως αὐτοῦ, even as Philo speaks of the Logos as ὁ χαοακτὴρ τῆς σφραγίδος τοῦ Θεοῦ (i. 332, and elsewhere), and as a bright emanation of the divine glory, in the beautiful metaphor ἀνθήλιος αὐγή (i. 656, *de Somniis*, § 41); seeing, in the third place, that St. John, in whose Gospel, κατὰ τὸ πνεῦμα, the apostolic doctrine reaches its highest expression, has summed up the whole apostolic testimony to the true Godhead of the man Christ Jesus in the one designation ὁ λόγος, thereby not only confirming all that was true in the previous utterances of the synagogue in Palestine and Egypt concerning the being and operations of the eternal Word, but also combining it with the hitherto unimagined and unimaginable fact of the incarnation;—seeing all this, can it possibly be maintained that the name of Logos, as given by St. John to our Lord in His pre-existent state (i. 1), and in His present exaltation (Rev. xix. 3), was nothing more than a neutral designation, transferred *per metonymiam* from "the word of preaching" (ὁ λόγος τῆς ἀκοῆς) to Him who was the sum and substance of that preached word?

maintain on other ground, viz. that the names ὁ υἱὸς τοῦ Θεοῦ and ὁ λόγος, which Hofm. asserts to be exclusively historical, belong to the eternal Person of the Lord Jesus as such. For as God in relation to the eternal Son is ὁ γεννῶν, so is He in relation to the eternal Word ὁ λέγων or ὁ λαλῶν. Scripture does not expressly say this, but it leads us by internal necessity to it,—a conception which we find expressed in Philo (*e.g.* i. 175, 34), εἰ ὁ λόγος ἔφθακε πολλῷ μᾶλλον ὁ λέγων αὐτός; i. 561, 23, ἡνίοχος μὲν τῶν δυνάμεων ὁ λόγος, ἔποχος δὲ ὁ λαλῶν; *arm.* p. 514, *primo Dicens et secundo Verbum*. We do not cite these and other parallels from Philo under the delusion that his doctrine of the Logos coincides entirely with that of the New Testament, or that the latter is derived from his writings, but because we have the dawn of truths in Philo which attained not to a noontide clearness till the obscuring elements which beset them were dispersed by the sunrise of the mystery of the Word incarnate (ὁ λόγος σὰρξ ἐγένετο). These truths thus dawning in Philo had their root not merely in Pythagoræo-Platonist ideas, but above all in the Old Testament: their natal soil, as becomes more and more manifest since Grossmann's investigations, and the light now thrown on the sources of the Cabbala, is not Alexandria, but Palestine. And if God is the Father of the eternal Son, then is He (what in meaning is essentially the same) the Speaker of the eternal Word; and if this eternal Son, this eternal Word, has within the Godhead a personal being issuing from God, and continually returning to Him (which is attested by εἰς τὸν κόλπον instead of ἐν τῷ κόλπῳ, and πρὸς τὸν Θεόν instead of παρὰ τῷ Θεῷ), then no divine *opus ad extra* could take place without the participation and mediation of the Word. He is the Mediator of creation, and is unanimously affirmed to be such by St. Paul, by the author of our epistle, and by St. John, as well as by Philo.[1] But if the Logos is Mediator of creation, the divine creative word (Fiat) by which the world was called into existence must stand in inseparable connection with Him; and this is precisely the fundamental idea, starting from which St. John begins his Gospel with a בראשית ברא of yet higher mood. The divine Logos is not indeed absolutely the same as the creative Word, nor as Philo's world-idea, nor as the divine Sophia; and yet

[1] *e.g.* ii. 225, *de Monarch.* § 5; i. 106, *Legis Alleg.* iv. § 31.

this is certain, God did not accomplish the creation of a world destined to be typical of His own divine attributes, without uttering the spoken word which should call it into existence, through and by the personal Word, in whom He has before Him His own eternal image, and in whom He had from all eternity beheld the world to be hereafter created in that typical relation to Himself (comp. the τὰ πάντα δι' αὐτοῦ καὶ εἰς αὐτόν of Col. i. 16). The author of our epistle calls the creative word by which the world is sustained, as proceeding from the Father through the Son (i. 3), τὸ ῥῆμα τῆς δυνάμεως αὐτοῦ; and Philo makes a similar distinction when he says that the world was made τῷ τοῦ Θεοῦ λόγῳ καὶ ῥήματι (i. 47, 26; comp. i. 165, 10); and when he elsewhere combines the terms λόγος καὶ ῥῆμα, he says not inaptly (i. 122, 5), that ὁ λόγος bears the same relation to ῥῆμα as the whole to the part, the universal cause to the particular operation, as the articulating mouth to the individual word proceeding from it. Moreover, as the Logos is Mediator of creation, so is He also Mediator of redemption, being the Mediator, or if that expression (though correct) be not allowed, the middle person of the triune Godhead. The plan of creation would never have been carried out, had not God at the same time conceived the plan of redemption, had not both plans been together hid from all eternity in the mind of the Creator of all things, waiting *there* for their historical manifestation (Eph. iii. 9); so that when the first was realized, all things were created in the only Son of His love, the divine Logos, destined as Redeemer to become man in the fulness of after-times (Col. i. 16). On this point, indeed, a veil hangs before Philo's eyes. And yet it would be a great mistake to suppose that the activity of the Logos exists for Philo only in the sphere of nature, and not in that of grace. The Logos, in his view, is principle and agent of all spiritual life, of all that answers to the divine ethical idea. He is the divine seed of all the virtues which the soul, as recipient, has to make her own. He gives wisdom, awakens the sleeping or dreaming soul,—enlightens, confirms, establishes it, and ever leads it on to better things. His operations are sudden and inexplicable. Through His divine compassion He rescues the soul sunk in sensuality, and makes Himself its shepherd and guide, its teacher and physician. He is the heavenly manna which feeds it, the heavenly fountain which waters it. Therefore Philo in adoring prayer beseeches Him, that he may in His moonlike milder countenance behold the sunlight of the face of God. In all this it cannot be denied that New Testament truth is seen to dawn in Philo's spirit, although so far is he from having any surmise of the incarnation, that at a time when it had already actually taken place he can say (i. 561, *de Profugis*, § 19), ὁ ὑπεράνω τούτων (τῶν Χερουβίμ) λόγος θεῖος εἰς ὁρατὴν οὐκ ἦλθεν ἰδέαν, ἅτε μηδενὶ τῶν κατ' αἴσθησιν ἐμφερὴς ὤν ἀλλ' αὐτὸς εἰκὼν ὑπάρχων Θεοῦ; and (i. 479, *Quis ver. dir. her.* § 9), τὸ πρὸς Θεὸν οὐ κατέβη πρὸς ἡμᾶς, οὐδὲ ἦλθεν εἰς τὰς σώματος ἀνάγκας. He failed to obtain an insight into the mystery of the incarnation, perhaps without his fault, and also, but not without his fault, into man's true need of redemption; nevertheless the Logos has for him an infinitely higher significance than that of an idea useful for solving a philosophical problem: it is one with whom he stands in true ethical communion; for as God, revealing Himself to Himself, has concentrated in the Logos the fulness of His own being, so is the Logos again the revealer of God. It is indeed touching to read how, in contrast with the noisy self-sufficient wisdom of the Agora, he refers the silent thirst of true philosophy to a future time, in which God should provide τὸν ἑρμηνέα ἄριστον;[1] "the best interpreter" being in Philo's sense the divine Logos, who by the prophets had called to repentance,[2] and from whom Philo would now for himself learn the true meaning of Scripture (διδάξει με ὁ ὑποφήτης αὐτοῦ λόγος, i. 58, *de Mutat. Nom.* § 3). Here it is evidently not the creative word, but another word, that of revelation, which is thus contemplated in closest union with the personal Word, the Logos.

But what Philo knows of all this is but as the gleaming of light behind a curtain,—a curtain which, having been since withdrawn for us from the mystery of the incarnation, *we* know that the relation in which the Logos as Mediator of redemption stands to the word of the gospel now, is similar to

---

[1] i. 200, *Quod det potiori insid.* § 13. Mangey remarks on this sentence: *Vide annon hæc ab auctore dicta ad spem de Messia pertineant.*
[2] i. 293, *Quod Deus immut.* § 29; comp. i. 128. *Legis Allegor.* iii. § 73, where he explains τὸ ὄνομα τοῦ Θεοῦ by ὁ ἑρμηνεὺς λόγος.

that in which as Mediator of creation He stood in the beginning to the creative word. The First Cause of both creation and redemption is God the Father, who formed the plan of each. But this His plan is carried out only through the Son, who therefore is bearer both of the word of redemption, which calls into existence the new humanity and the new world, and that of creation, which called into existence the old world and the first man. This twofold word of the Father was from all eternity in the heart of the Son, and, since the incarnation, the redeeming and new-creating word was also in His mouth; as the prophet witnesses (Isa. li. 16), "*I have put my words into thy mouth, and I have covered thee in the shadow of mine hand, to plant heavens, and lay the foundations of an earth, and say to Zion, Thou art my people;*" and as Christ Himself in His earthly manifestation testified (John viii. 26), ἃ ἤκουσα παρ' αὐτοῦ ταῦτα λέγω εἰς τὸν κόσμον, and (John xii. 50), ἃ οὖν λαλῶ ἐγὼ καθὼς εἴρηκέ μοι ὁ πατήρ, οὕτω λαλῶ.[1]

We have now reached the terminus of our inquiry. Our Lord is called ὁ λόγος as the personal Word of God, and that not as merely spoken by God into the world, but as His own eternal utterance of Himself; and again, not as being merely the personal substance of the preached word, but as One who eternally in Himself contains both words, that of creation and that of redemption, and who, in the power and by the will of His Father, has uttered both, in realizing as mediate cause or mediator the works for which they are respectively instrumental. Such at least are the lines of connection drawn by Scripture between the personal and the preached λόγος. When St. John, for instance, in the commencement of his first epistle, speaks of the word preached in the same way as in the commencement of his Gospel of the personal Logos, and when our author here speaks of the preached Logos as Philo before had done of the personal (a parallel for which we believe we have shown above just cause), the reason is, that both Words stand to each other in a relation of immanence,—a relation, however, which is not limited to the mere fact that the personal Word, the divine Logos, is the subject of the other, the λόγος τῆς ἀκοῆς and τῆς σωτηρίας, but consists in this, that every revelation of God by

---

[1] On the significance of this passage in the triuogical division of St. John's Gospel, compare my *Untersuchungen über die Evangelien*, i. 57.

word or deed is mediated through the personal Logos; that all His words from all eternity have been spoken into the heart of the Son, and from that heart flow forth to us, bearing to Him (the Word of words) the same relation as the sunbeams to the sun; that, in short, every word or utterance of God, every revelation or manifestation of Himself, has in the eternal Logos, His Son, an ever-present basis and background.[1]

This being so, we may concede to Köstlin, Olshausen, and Dorner,[2] that our present passage (Heb. iv. 12, etc.) is one of those which prepare for the thesis first distinctly enunciated by St. John, that Jesus Christ, in His own eternal pre-existence, is the Word of God; and in this way we may finally dispose of the long vacillations of exposition, whether here the personal or the preached word is that of which our author speaks. We now turn our attention to the metaphor which he proceeds to draw.

The word of God is (1) ζῶν, as God Himself is called (iii. 12, x. 31), and again His word, or "oracles," 1 Pet. i. 23, Acts vii. 38 (λόγια ζῶντα). It is living as being instinct with the life of its source, the living God, with which life it continues inseparably connected, neither hardening into a lifeless utterance divorced from its personal ground, nor subject to decay, like an effect in which the cause is no longer operative; so that if we only distinguish between the mere outward form of manifestation (letters and syllables) and its true essence, the Word of God is seen to be, not a dead reflection, but the living witness which the fulness of life divine vouchsafes of itself.

It is (2) ἐνεργής (the form become usual in later Greek for ἐνεργός), full of activity (comp. Philem. 6), whether for salvation or for judgment; never therefore without results, and those inevitable.

It is (3) τομώτερος ὑπὲρ πᾶσαν μάχαιραν δίστομον, "more cutting" (from the classic positive τομός) "above" (same construction as Luke xvi. 8) "any two-edged," literally (the

---

[1] Similarly Harnack, *Commentatio in Prologum Ev. sec. Joh.* 1843: 'Ο Λόγος verbum reale et ὑποστατικόν, ex quo omnia verba vitæ orta sunt, quia in eo tota comprehenditur realitas Divina, cujus ideo verus et unicus est ἐξηγητής.

[2] Olshaus. *Opuscula*, p. 125 ss.; Köstlin, *Johanneischer Lehrbegriff*, p. 396 ss.; Dorner, *Entwickel.* i. 100 ss.

cutting, biting edge, being regarded as the sword's mouth), "two-mouthed sword." Such a sword proceeds (Rev. xix. 15; comp. i. 16, ii. 12) from the mouth of the Logos, being (like the rod of Isa. xi. 4) a symbol of the sifting, judging, annihilating word of Him who is the Word of words. Philo, in like manner, compares the Logos to the flaming sword—φλογίνη ῥομφαία—before the gate of paradise (i. 144); and also thus interprets the πῦρ καὶ μάχαιραν of Gen. xxii. 6, saying that Abraham took fire and the knife[1] (emblems of the flaming sword, and so of the Logos), "to cut off and consume his still adherent mortality, as earnestly longing to be able to soar with freed naked spirit up to God" (i. 144). When, therefore, the Logos is elsewhere (e.g. i. 491) called by him ὁ τῶν συμπάντων τομεύς, and described under various figures as the mediate cause of all divisibility in the universe, we are not to understand him as meaning that the Logos manifests this all-penetrating, alldividing power only in the sphere of the natural world;[2] nor need we regard the comparison of such utterances in Philo with what is said here as either unwarrantable in itself or derogatory to our epistle. Indeed, it cannot be a merely accidental coincidence when Philo says (i. 491), that the Logos, whetted to the utmost sharpness, is incessantly dividing all sensuous things (ἐπειδὰν δὲ μέχρι τῶν ἀτόμων καὶ λεγομένων ἀμερῶν διεξέλθῃ, πάλιν ἀπὸ τούτων τὰ λόγῳ θεωρητὰ εἰς ἀμυθήτους καὶ ἀπεριγράφους μοίρας ἄρχεται διαιρεῖν οὗτος ὁ τομεύς); and when our author here, quite in the same way, speaks of the divine λόγος as cutting like a two-edged sword (which penetrates more irresistibly and more deeply than a one-edged weapon) through the whole man, and as dividing and intersecting his inner being even to the smallest fibre.

For it is (4) διικνούμενος ἄχρι μερισμοῦ ψυχῆς (τε) καὶ πνεύματος, ἁρμῶν τε καὶ μυελῶν. These words, if ἄχρι μερισμοῦ be taken in a purely local signification, would describe

[1] The German is "Feuer und Wasser," the latter by a curious misprint for "Messer."—TR.

[2] Compare, among others, the curious passages in which Philo likens the divine Logos as τομεύς, or divider of the six faculties of the human soul, whose harmonious subordination constitutes its δικαιοσύνη, to the midshaft of the seven-branched candlestick (i. 504); and again speaks of the soul under the same figure as destined ἄνω τὰς αὐγὰς ἀποστέλλειν πρὸς τὸ Ἐν. (i. 520.)

only the irresistibly penetrating power of the divine word, "even to the point of separation of soul and spirit" (Schlichting, Böhme, Hofm. *Weiss.* i. 22). But this passive, or rather local sense is thus assigned to μερισμός, without authority elsewhere. We must therefore first try taking the word in the active sense (which it has, *e.g.*, at ii. 4); and certainly the meaning thus obtained, that the Divine "Logos" not only penetrates to a man's inmost being, but also divides it into its component parts (ἄχρι μερισμοῦ = ἄχρις οὗ μερίσῃ), both accords more fully with the facts of the case, and answers better to Philo's manifestly cognate view of the office of the Logos as τομεύς or διαιρέτης.[1] It is not improbable, that for this very reason our author purposely uses here, not the ῥομφαία of Luke ii. 35, but μάχαιρα, which properly signifies a large knife, employed in slaughtering, carving, or dissection. And now, to come to the particulars of exposition, I hold as certain in the outset, that ἀρμοί τε καὶ μυελοί (the joints between[2] and the marrow in the bones) denotes the corporeal inward part of man, as ψυχή together with πνεῦμα the spiritual. The second τε here (ἀρμῶν τε καὶ μυελῶν) is supported by every authority; but the former (in the *text. rec.*) is to be erased, with Lachmann and Tischd., after A.B.C.H.I., and many other authorities, both mediate and immediate. The second τε seems designed to couple the later pair of terms, ἀρμῶν καὶ μυελῶν, with the former, ψυχῆς καὶ πνεύματος, and each pair to designate a whole by means of its parts: "the word of God pierces to the dividing asunder of soul and spirit, as well as of joints and marrow;" by which is meant,[3] that it pierces unto where (or, what is now not essentially different in meaning, until) it divides the two pairs respectively into their two parts, or until it separates each of the four by itself into its constituent parts—soul, spirit, joints, and marrow. Even this latter interpretation is, as parallels in Philo prove, admissible; less so, however, if the first τε be erased than if it were retained. Hofmann, how-

---

[1] See Mangey on the passage, and Dähne, *Jüdische Alexandrinisch-Religions-philosophie*, i. 193.
[2] Hesychius interprets ἀρμῶν in this sense by ἁρμονιῶν.
[3] The quotation is from Hofmann, *Schriftbew.* i. 258. His interpretation here giving μερισμοῦ its proper active sense, is much better than at *Weiss.* i. 22.

ever, feels constrained to reject this whole mode of explanation, even in this corrected form, because of what seems to him the unnatural combination of what is literally true and of what is only figurative, seeing that the Divine Word pierces and divides indeed the spiritual life of man, but not the joints and marrow of his bones. "The only way," says Hofmann (*Schriftb.* i. 259), "by which we can get rid of such an unnatural combination, is to make the genitives ψυχῆς καὶ πνεύματος dependent on ἁρμῶν τε καὶ μυελῶν, so that (the figure being retained throughout) the word of God is said to penetrate and divide 'both joints and marrow' of the inner life." But such a complicated inversion,[1] and one so liable to be misunderstood, would surely, in point of language, be most unnatural. If, therefore, to take ἁρμῶν τε καὶ μυελῶν in a literal sense, would necessarily result in an unnatural combination of two incongruous ideas, we should still prefer the interpretation and paraphrase of Bengel, Bleek, De Wette, Tholuck, Lünemann: until it divides soul and spirit (as to) both joints and marrow, *i.e.* the inner spiritual life, in its subtlest essence and most secret recesses. In support of this may be alleged, that the rhetorico-poetical expression μυελὸς τῆς ψυχῆς is found in classical writers. But what if the whole assumption on which these attempts at interpretation proceed were a mistake?

It is not true that ἁρμῶν τε καὶ μυελῶν could not be as literally meant as ψυχῆς καὶ πνεύματος, and that so what is strictly literal and what is mainly figurative are here combined. For if Philo could say that *the divine Logos, whetted to the utmost sharpness, is perpetually dividing all sensible things* (τὰ αἰσθητὰ πάντα), and so penetrating to their ultimate and "indivisible atoms," our author surely might also intend his ἁρμῶν τε καὶ μυελῶν to be taken literally, and without figure, although not exactly in Philo's sense, but in his own more deep and purely ethical application. By ψυχὴ καὶ πνεῦμα he designates the invisible and supersensuous, by ἁρμοὶ καὶ μυελοί the perceptible and sensuous part of man. Both parts are in themselves divisible into two more: the latter into ἁρμοί, which subserve bodily motion, and μυελοί, which minister to bodily sensation;[2]

---

[1] Hofmann refers indeed to vi. 1, 2 for a similar construction in βαπτισμῶν διδαχῆς; but the cases are by no means parallel. See note there.

[2] See my *Psychologie*, p. 190.

the former into ψυχή and πνεῦμα, which, after the analogy of ἁρμοὶ καὶ μυελοί, must be regarded as not merely two aspects of the immaterial part of man, but as two separable constituents of it. Into this (man's twofold substance) the word of God penetrates inquisitorially and judicially, dividing its most intimate combinations, and (what, if not expressed, is obviously implied) dissecting the whole into its several parts. Perhaps we may best arrive at the author's meaning, by presenting his thought to our minds in the following way: Πνεῦμα is the *spirit*, which proceeds immediately, though after the manner of a creature, from God Himself, and therefore carries in itself the divine image; this image, since the fall, has retired into itself, and so become for man as it were extinguished. At this point begin the operations of grace: man recalls to mind his own true nature, though shattered by sin,[1] and that heavenly nature of man reappears when Christ is formed in him. The word of God, in discovering to a man the degree in which this precious gift has been lost or recovered, marks out and separates the Πνεῦμα in him. The ψυχή, on the other hand, is a life emanating from the Πνεῦμα, when united with the body,— a life which, while it ought to be the *doxa* or effulgence of the Spirit pervading and ruling the bodily part, has through sin become an unfree and licentious disharmony of energies and passions, and a powerless plaything in the hands of material and demoniac influences. That again the word of God exhibits to the man, in showing him the breach between soul and spirit, and the abnormal monstrous condition of the soul in herself. And no less does it exhibit to him the fact, that ungodly powers are also working in his *bodily* frame, which has now in every joint, and chord, and marrow, become the seat of sin and death. The expression here, though not itself figurative, is founded on the image of the μάχαιρα. It assumes that the word of God, having completed its work of dissection in the spiritual, goes on to scrutinize the bodily part of man,

---

[1] Compare Luke xv. 17, εἰς ἑαυτὸν ἐλθών, said of the repentant prodigal. "The fall of man was a twofold process: first he fell out of God into himself, and then out of himself into nature. The process of his recovery is likewise twofold: first he returns to himself in the consciousness of sin, and then with faith and repentance to God his Saviour" (H. Klee).

or at least may easily do so if it will; and that it stops not even then (οὐ λήγει, as Philo says), but proceeds to separate the joints of the bones, with the sinews which move them, and to divide the bones themselves, so as to lay bare the marrow which they contain. The four terms (soul, spirit, joints, marrow) appear to correspond to each other *chiastically* ;[1] and the Divine Word is said to lay bare the whole man thus described, before the eyes of God and before his own, discovering by means of a strict analysis both his psychico-spiritual and his inward corporeal condition. This it does by showing that, so far as the man has not yet yielded himself to the work of grace, or so far as this work remains imperfect in him, the very marrow of the body is corrupted like the spirit, which is, as it were, the marrow of the soul; and the very framework of the body is disordered like the ψυχή, which is, as it were, the embodiment of the spirit. That μερισμοῦ is meant to be thus ethically understood, is clear from what he proceeds to say of the further operations of the Word.

It is (5) κριτικὸς ἐνθυμήσεων καὶ ἐννοιῶν καρδίας,[2] *i.e.* able and ready on all occasions to distinguish and decide, and so pass judgment on the ἐνθυμήσεις (emotions, notions, fancies) and the ἔννοιαι (self-conscious trains of thought), which have their source and operation in the heart; καρδία being here considered as the personal point of unity whence emanate all corporeo-vital and all psychico-spiritual activities of the man, and whither by reaction they return. Over the most secret occurrences of the inner life the word of God exercises a judicial scrutiny, for which it exhibits both authority and power. When, therefore, he goes on to say, καὶ οὐκ ἔστι κτίσις ἀφανὴς ἐνώπιον αὐτοῦ, it is certainly not unnatural to refer αὐτοῦ, both here and in the following clause, to ὁ λόγος (so Köstlin), but more probable that the author, in accordance with one of the most frequent forms of scriptural anthropomorphism (comp.

---

[1] ψυχή answering to the ἁρμοί, πνεῦμα to the μυελοί, and the four together designating man in his compound nature.

[2] The Codex Ephraemi Rescriptus (C) reads ἐνθυμήσεως καὶ ἐννοιῶν; Cod. Claromont. (D*), ἐνθυμήσεως ἐννοιῶν τε. Ἐνθύμησις occurs in three other places of the New Testament, viz. Acts xvii. 29, Matt. ix. 4, and xii. 25. Κριτικός nowhere else in New Testament or LXX. It takes a *genit. object.* as the adjectives in ικός generally.

Ps. xi. 4; Sir. xxiii. 10), should be thinking of the eyes of God rather than those of His Word in the expression τοῖς ὀφθ. αὐτοῦ; and inasmuch as all the attributes of the λόγος here are selected to express its connection with the supreme cause. as a mediate cause and instrument, the prevalent view now is that αὐτοῦ refers both times to God,—a view which we shall see is demanded by the concluding relative clause, πρὸς ὃν ἡμῖν ὁ λόγος. Before God (ἐνώπιον, Hellenistic = לִפְנֵי, e.g. Sir. xxxix. 19) no κτίσις, no created thing, and nothing in or pertaining to it, is ἀφανής, invisible, or non-transparent. Following this negative proposition, we have, connected with δέ instead of ἀλλά (see on ii. 6), an affirmative one, which goes beyond a mere antithesis to the foregoing; nay, rather, on the contrary, all things are for God's all-seeing eyes: (1) γυμνά, presenting themselves stript of all natural or artificial covering, as they really and truly are; and (2) τετραχηλισμένα, with head thrown back and throat exposed. This is unquestionably the literal sense of the word, the only doubt being as to what secondary meaning is here to be attached to it. Bretschneider, Bleek, De Wette, von Gerlach, and others, following Perizonius, think of the Roman custom of exposing criminals *reducto capite* (*retortis cervicibus*); but this view has no support from Greek literature. For the signification *cruciare*, to torment, which τραχηλίζειν (ἐκτραχηλίζειν) frequently has (in Josephus and Philo, *e.g.* i. 195, ii. 15, 534), is probably not derived from the treatment of delinquents, but from the conduct of a wrestler with his antagonist, whom he seizes by the throat in order to throw him (*e.g.* Philo, ii. 413). Klee supposes this to be the secondary meaning of the word here. Others (almost all the ancients) think it refers in some way or other to the manner in which victims, whether slain or about to be slain, were dealt with. But what need is there for all this? Τραχηλίζειν, which undoubtedly means to seize by the throat and throw back the head, receives here its secondary meaning from the context, without needing any archæological illustrations, and yet also without its being necessary to take τετραχηλισμένα (*resupinata*, ὕπτια), with entire loss of the image, as simply equivalent to πεφανερωμένα (Hesych., Phavor., Peshito), *aperta* (all the Latins), uncovered (Luther).[1] The meaning seems to

---

[1] Luther's word is now *entdeckt*—discovered; his former, *dargeneigt*—

be, that whatever shamefaced creature bows its head, and would fain withdraw and cloak itself from the eyes of God, has indeed the throat, as it were, bent back before these eyes, and so remains, with no possibility of escape, exposed and naked to their view. (See Oekumen. in Bleek, ii. 589). To the second αὐτοῦ is now subjoined the relative clause, πρὸς ὃν ἡμῖν ὁ λόγος. Hofmann (*Schriftb.* i. 97) thinks that the former αὐτοῦ has also a reference to it. This is possible, but the assumption is not needed to prove αὐτοῦ both times to refer to God and not to the λόγος. For if the relative clause meant nothing more than "of whom we speak" (πρὸς ὅν = περὶ οὗ, v. 11), which sense it would undoubtedly bear, we should have, whether referring both αὐτοῦ's to God or to the λόγος, a feeble and unmeaning pleonasm. Πρὸς ὃν ἡμῖν ὁ λόγος must therefore signify "to whom we have to give account" (Peshito), *cui reddituri sumus rationem actuum nostrorum* (Alcuin and others), or rather, since λόγος πρός τινα (ἀποδοτεός) is scarcely Greek, "to whom we stand in relation, *i.e.* in a relation of responsibility" (Calvin, Bengel, Böhme, Bleek, De Wette, Lünemann); as Libanius, for instance, says once, τοῖς ἀδίκως ἀποκτενοῦσι καὶ πρὸς θεοὺς καὶ πρὸς ἀνθρώπους γίνεται ὁ λόγος (that is, they find they have dealings in consequence both with gods and men). If the clause πρὸς ὅν, κ.τ.λ., has (as can scarcely be doubted) this sense, it is self-evident that αὐτοῦ is meant to refer both times to God as being our judge; and this concluding thought reveals the purpose of what might seem the somewhat episodical description of the word of God, which is given here as a reason for the σπουδάσωμεν of ver. 11. With ver. 14 the exhortation is resumed.

CHAP. IV. 14–16. *The parænesis returns to its starting-point: how firm and joyous should our faith be in having a High Priest so gracious and so exalted!*

The author having, at iii. 1, urged the contemplation of Jesus as the Sent of God, and High Priest of our profession, has now shown what we owe to Him, as God's Messenger, raised so high above Moses, and how much depends on our

bowed or bent—was more expressive. [Our English "open" suppresses also the image.—TR.]

faithfulness to Him. This he has shown by the example, so full of warning for Christendom, of the ancient people whom Moses led, and by the present activities of the word of God, searching out and exposing to view the inmost being of His creatures. On all which he proceeds to ground a further exhortation, which on the one hand concludes that commenced at iii. 1, and on the other leads to a fuller account of the office and dignity of our great High Priest.

Ver. 14. *Let us therefore, having a great high priest who hath passed through the heavens, Jesus the Son of God, hold fast by our confession.*

The latest commentators do not seem to have understood the logical connection here. The sacred writer has not been speaking immediately before this of the high-priesthood of Christ, and Bleek therefore pronounces the method of reasoning to be inexact, and somewhat incongruous. De Wette and Tholuck would connect our verse with ii. 17, iii. 1, as if nothing lay between; while Lünemann makes the οὖν refer back to the whole previous discussion (ch. i. 1–iii. 6). All these expositors lie under the illusion that this οὖν in the participial clause must also logically belong to it, whereas logically it belongs to κρατῶμεν τῆς ὁμολογίας. For what is the conclusion drawn by οὖν from the preceding context? A fresh exhortation, or the motive for one? In the first instance, certainly, a fresh exhortation. With more reason, therefore, Hofmann takes the οὖν as referring to both exhortation and motive taken together (*Schriftb.* ii. 1, 44): " *Both the existence for us of such an High Priest, and the holding fast by our profession—the former as a fact, the latter as a requirement based upon it—are already contained in the section just concluded* (iii. 1–iv. 13), *the whole contents of which section form the basis of the present exhortation; and hence the* οὖν *is justifiably employed to lead on from the former parænesis, which was founded on the contemplation of Christ as our great Apostle, the true Moses and the true Joshua, to this following one, which is based upon the fact that He is not only the true High Priest and antitype of Aaron, but also the kingly Priest, exalted now to God's right hand, and antitype of Melchizedek.*" But here likewise I feel that there is not a due recognition of the close relation in which ver. 14 stands in the first instance to vers. 12,

13. The word of God demands obedience and self-appropriation, *i.e. faith*, but faith not merely confined to inward apprehension,—a "Yea and Amen" openly pronounced,—a profession (ὁμολογία) without reserve or regard to consequences,—the echo from the mouth of the heart's belief, and of the living hope[1] which it more especially proclaims. The danger to which the Hebrew Christians were exposed from the synagogue, was that of suffering themselves to be deterred from making this profession, or even brought to abandon it. The author, therefore, sets before them the all-penetrating energy of the divine word, and the omniscience, from which there is no escape, of the Searcher of hearts, whose word it is, and to whom we are responsible. On all this he grounds the admonition, Let us therefore hold fast (*firmiter teneamus*)—properly, grasp firmly so as not to let go (*firmiter prehendamus* with the genitive, as at vi. 18)—our (Christian) profession. The participial clause (ἔχοντες, κ.τ.λ.) confirms this exhortation, by stating how glorious, consolatory, and encouraging the substance of our profession is. That substance is Jesus, an High Priest infinitely exalted above the Levitical. As our author is now beginning to treat more particularly of the special subject of the Christian profession, in the aspect indicated by τὸν ἀρχιερέα τῆς ὁμολογίας ἡμῶν—and it is, moreover, his general custom in exhortations, not merely to apply doctrines previously enounced, but to make further developments of them—we are not bound to trouble ourselves with endeavouring to show that this participial clause, in all its parts, merely recapitulates what has been said already. This much, however, is certain, that not one of the attributes here assigned to our Lord has been wholly unprepared for.[2] This is now the third time that He is styled ἀρχιερεύς (ii. 17, iii. 1), and not without its having been shown previously in what sense. Such He became through suffering and death, and so continues; for after having purged our sins,

[1] The epexegetical addition, τῆς ἐλπίδος ἡμῶν, is found in several MSS., and in Primasius, "*spei nostræ.*"

[2] We must, however, beware of finding allusions here which could hardly have been in the author's mind: *e.g.* that our Lord is called "Jesus the Son of God," in contrast with *Joshua the son of Nun*, who is also called "Jesus" at ver. 8, where, however, υἱὸς Ναυή is not found; or again, that διεληλυθότα τ. οὐρ. designated our Lord as having truly entered into God's rest, whereas again ver. 10 does not directly refer to Him.

He continues to reconcile and sanctify and represent us before God, performing always and continuously for His people, what the high priest of the Old Testament did only once a year. Because of His exaltation above this Levitical high priest the author calls Him μέγαν; and from what has preceded, we already know wherein His greatness consists: raised high above the angels, He sits crowned (in consequence of death) with glory and honour, at the right hand of Divine Majesty (τῆς μεγαλωσύνης), in highest places. Ἀρχιερεύς μέγας, a name given also by Philo to the Logos as mediator of all good in the whole sphere of creation, is used here in a sense as far above Philo's thoughts as heaven is above earth. And further, the meaning of διεληλυθότα τοὺς οὐρανοὺς here is substantially the same as that of ἐκάθισεν, κ.τ.λ., at i. 3. The throne of God is the final goal of the Lord's transit through all the heavens. We must beware of regarding this διεληλυθότα τοὺς οὐρανοὺς as parallel to the διὰ τῆς μείζονος καὶ τελειοτέρας σκηνῆς of ix. 11 (see note there); and indeed we are forbidden to do so by the addition in that passage of the epithet οὐ χειροποιήτου. The heavens here are the *created* heavens, which Christ passed through in going to the "*Place*" of God (Ezek. iii. 12). That "Place" is God's own eternal Doxa, the *uncreated* heaven (αὐτὸς ὁ οὐρανός, ix. 24) of His eternal residence and self-manifestation. We must distinguish between that highest heaven and the heaven of glory in which He vouchsafes to manifest Himself to the blessed. This latter is of necessity local, albeit not as a place expressly created for the purpose: it is the *cœlum empyreum* which our dogmatic theologians rightly call a *dulce sine somno somnium*, and the collective whole of the "many mansions" into which the blessed are received. But the uncreated heaven of God Himself is His own omnipresent glory,—omnipresent, because absolutely without any local limitations: it may be said to be *above* all the created heavens, inasmuch as it is the super-creaturely background of all creation, and to be everywhere present, yet so as resting uncomprehended by the finite in its own infinitude. And now Jesus the exalted One, being thus above all heavens in this His Doxa with God, is thereby omnipresent too. This conclusion, drawn by the dogmatic theology of our church,[1] is incontrovertible. Heb. iv. 14,

[1] [*i.e.* the Lutheran communion, especially those portions of it which

taken in connection with Eph. iv. 10, is rightly adduced as proving the "ubiquity" of Christ. Compare, besides what was said on i. 3, the passage in Philo, quoted by Dorner (*Entw*. i. 29): πάντα γὰρ πεπλήρωκεν ὁ Θεὸς καὶ διὰ πάντων διελήλυθεν καὶ κενὸν οὐδὲν οὐδὲ ἔρημον ἀπολέλοιπεν ἑαυτοῦ. Finally, the two last appellations here given to our Lord (Ἰησοῦν, τὸν υἱὸν τοῦ Θεοῦ) have also their root in what has gone before. First, we have the Son of man, who for our good passed through suffering and death to royal and priestly glory, called by His birth-name (Ἰησοῦν); and then τὸν υἱὸν τοῦ Θεοῦ, to remind us of the divine height from which He descended, in order to regain it as the reward of that suffering. And having thus on what we have in Jesus based the exhortation, to "hold fast our profession" in Him, the author proceeds to develop the statements contained in the participial clause, and from them to show how not only are we bound to obey it, but thereby enabled stedfastly and cheerfully to do so.

Ver. 15. *For we have not an high priest unable to sympathize with us in our infirmities, but one who has in all points been tempted in like manner, without sin.*

Συμπαθεῖν is used of that compassion which, by a fellow-feeling, places itself in the position of the sufferer (as x. 34); whereas συμπάσχειν is to share in one and the same experience of suffering (Rom. viii. 17; 1 Cor. xii. 26). Under ἀσθενείαι may be comprehended the various kinds of physical evil to which our frail humanity is subject (Luke v. 15, and often; comp. Matt. viii. 17); but here, in the first instance, the manifold kinds of temptation are meant to which we are exposed in the midst of this sinful world, and in which we have need of higher help, in order to stand firm. The High Priest whom we have is not one who can have no fellow-feeling with those states of suffering from which our weakness cannot defend itself, and in which this weakness often enough becomes mourn-

are committed to the dogmatic definitions of the *Formula Concordiæ*, drawn up in 1575. See § viii. *de Persona Christi*. The *extreme* Lutheran position might be expressed in the following syllogism: "Christ in His human nature is seated at the right hand of God;" God's right hand is everywhere; therefore Christ, in His human nature, is omnipresent. —Tr.]

fully manifest; "on the contrary, He is one who," etc. Δέ is here, as ii. 6 and iv. 13, adversative, while also introducing an additional thought not contained in the direct antithesis. That would simply be δυνάμενον συμπαθῆσαι; but here we have the further proposition, πεπειρασμένον δὲ κατὰ πάντα καθ' ὁμοιότητα, which shows why Jesus cannot but thus συμπαθεῖν ταῖς ἀσθενείαις ἡμῶν (Hofm. Weiss. ii. 25). Instead of the πεπειρασμένον of the text. rec.,[1] retained by Wetstein, Scholz, and Lachm. (following A.B.D.E., etc.), Mill, Bg., Kn., Tischd., have preferred the reading πεπειραμένον (C.I.K. and other authorities), prevalent in the editions before Beza, but rejected by Bleek and Lünemann, as giving, instead of the here requisite designation of our Lord as tentatus, the unsuitable one of expertus. The context would certainly lead us to expect tentatus, i.e. πεπειρασμένος, here (comp. ii. 18): πεπειραμένος might indeed (comp. πειρᾶν τινος or τινα) also bear the sense of tentatus, did not usage seem to confine it to the other of expertus, which again would require πάντων or πᾶσι instead of κατὰ πάντα. Add to which, the specially Attic forms πειρᾶν, πειρᾶσθαι, are very rare in Hellenistic Greek;[2] while πειράζειν, πειράζεσθαι, are quite common. The author therefore, in all probability, wrote πεπειρασμένον.[3] Instead of ὁμοίως, in like manner, similarly, he uses the stronger term καθ' ὁμοιότητα, after the likeness, suggesting the addition of ἡμῶν, of us; and further, the χωρὶς ἁμαρτίας serves, by making only one exception, to extend the idea of unqualified similarity to every other particular. This χωρὶς ἁμ. is appended, not to κατὰ πάντα, but to καθ' ὁμοιότητα, to imply not merely that temptation produced no sin in our Lord, but also that it found in Him no sin (Hofm. Schriftb. ii. 1, 32). It limits the similarity of His temptation and ours in this sense, in order to bring out more clearly the unlimited similarity in all other respects.[4] It is a

[1] i.e. the Elzevir edition, for R. Stephens reads πεπειραμένον.
[2] In the Septuagint it is perhaps only found at Prov. xxvi. 18; in the New Testament nowhere beyond suspicion but in Acts xxvi. 21.
[3] Or if πεπειραμένον, only as a bye-form or variation of πεπειρασμένον, in the same sense. See Winer, § 15, Obs. at the end. Cyril of Alexandria read πεπειραμένον, and explains it in the sense of expertum.
[4] Zonaras (on the word καινοτομία) appeals with effect to this καθ' ὁμοιότ. against those who taught that our Lord had a human nature of a peculiar and different kind from ours. V. Gerlach vindicates its true meaning

necessary, though here only a subordinate addition. Χωρὶς ἁμαρτίας might indeed be taken as conveying a main idea: Christ has not only experienced, but also overcome temptation. His mere experience of it would profit us nothing, unless He had under every condition and kind of temptation continued the sinless One; but this He has done, and therefore is not only disposed to help us, from having shared our experiences, but also able so to do, from having overcome in like trials to our own. But the context does not favour this more emphatic view of the meaning of χωρὶς ἁμαρτίας: it is here only a secondary consideration (Bl.). Christ has passed through a life in which He was in all points equally tempted as we are, provided only we leave out of account the sin through which our temptations find in us an innate proneness to be led astray (*Schriftb.* ii. 1, 45). Nothing is wanting to us, the author means to say, for encouragement to expect victory in the trials of our faith: we have a great, and at the same time a compassionate High Priest, who has without sin endured exactly the same temptations as ourselves,[1] so that we can supplicate divine assistance with the joyful confidence of certainly obtaining it.

Ver. 16. *Let us therefore approach with confidence to the throne of grace, that we may obtain mercy, and find grace for seasonable assistance.*

The sacred writer must not be supposed, in using the term θρόνος τῆς χάριτος, to have had in view [what we after Luther[2] are wont to call the mercy-seat] the Cappôreth of the ancient tabernacle, which in the Septuagint is always rendered ἱλαστή-

---

from the heterodoxy of Irving and Menken: "We are tempted by sin and to sin: Christ is tempted like as we are in both respects, but only externally, and therefore *without sin*, although there lay in the human nature which He assumed the abstract possibility of falling."

[1] The Logos of Philo is also a sinless high priest (i. 562, *de profugis* 20), who makes of the human soul a sanctuary, and preserves it from sin (*ib.* 21); but he knows of no incarnate sufferer descending from heaven and returning thither.

[2] [*Gnadenstuhl.* Cappôreth properly signifies the "cover," or lid of the ark. The rendering ἱλαστήριον, or *propitiatorium*, gives it a metaphorical and spiritualizing sense, which does not belong to the term as originally applied.—Tr.]

ριον, the propitiatory. Compare note on ix. 5. As in Ezekiel's vision the "firmament" over the "chariot" corresponds to the golden Cappôreth of the earthly sanctuary, so here (had this been the writer's thought) the throne of grace would be the seat of Jehovah, as worshipped by the cherubim behind the veil (Isa. vi.; Rev. xi. 19). But this supposed reference, which our translation of Cappôreth so naturally suggests to us, has no basis in the text. Θρόνος τῆς χάριτος, which would in Hebrew be כסא החסד, might (when compared with θρόνος τῆς Μεγαλωσύνης of ch. viii. 1, Hebr. כסא הגבורה; comp. note on i. 3) be taken to signify the seat on which grace is enthroned, but (comparing Ps. xlvii. 9, Heb.; Prov. xx. 8; Jer. xiv. 21) is better understood of a throne established upon grace (Isa. xvi. 5; Ps. lxxxix. 15, Heb.), or one from which grace proceeds. To this throne, from which descends the grace obtained and conveyed by the high-priestly work and office of Christ (comp. δι' αὐτοῦ, vii. 25), we are exhorted to draw near,[1] imploring aid with joyous confidence that we shall obtain it. The following clause, ἵνα λάβωμεν ἔλεον καὶ χάριν εὕρωμεν, forms a beautiful and euphonious *chiasmus*.[2] It can hardly be decided whether the author wrote ἔλεον (from the classical ὁ ἔλεος, of the occurrence of which in the New Testament we are not quite certain) or ἔλεος (the neuter form τὸ ἔλεος, used almost exclusively in Hellenistic Greek, and undoubtedly the only form found in St. Luke): the *text. rec.* has ἔλεον, but Lchm. and Tischd. prefer ἔλεος, which is better supported by MSS. It is indeed possible that the author meant to express the same thing by the classical λάβωμεν ἔλεον and the Hebraizing χάριν εὕρωμεν (= לִמְצֹא חֵן). Ἔλεος is mercy which lays to heart the unhappy situation of another, and by sympathy makes it her own; χάρις, kindly favour, which from a free

---

[1] Προσέρχεσθαι is a favourite word with our author: it is derived from the קָרַב of the Old Testament, used specially of the approach of the priest to the altar—comp. Lev. xxi. 17, etc.,—or of the levitically clean to the holy place—Lev. xxii. 3.

[2] [*Chiasmus*, χιασμός (the making of a χ or cross), is a figure of rhetoric, thus described by H. Stephens (*Thesaur. sub lit.* K, not X, p. 4660 of Valpy's edit.): "*Figura est quando quatuor propositis tertium secundo respondet et convenit quartum primo.*" Here Delitzsch seems to think there is a crosswise (chiastic) reference of the verbs and substantives, λάβωμεν more properly belonging to χάριν, and εὕρωμεν to ἔλεον.—Tr.]

internal impulse inclines to one who has no claim on its regard, and devotes itself to befriending him. In τῷ θρόνῳ τῆς χάριτος both are included under χάρις, as the general designation of God's prevenient condescending love, as sympathizing with and manifesting itself to His creatures, and more especially to sinful men. To this throne we are exhorted to draw near, as to the source of grace, that we may obtain both that mercy which is moved by the contemplation of our wretchedness, and the grace which is ever ready to give εἰς εὔκαιρον βοήθειαν. To take this as a reference to iii. 13, and by it understand a help vouchsafed in the time of grace, and before its expiration (Bleek, De Wette, Lünemann), accords, as seems to me, neither with the expression nor the context. We all are πειραζόμενοι (ii. 18), and they who received this epistle were so, as being in a special manner surrounded by temptations to apostasy. The author directs them to the throne, where the Redeemer, exalted to give help, sits at God's right hand, that (as need requires) they may thence obtain help at the right time, *i.e.* before sinking through their own infirmity. Βοήθειαν reminds us of the βοηθῆσαι of ii. 18,—the thought on which this exhortation is founded being similar to that, but here expressed with greater fulness.

The sacred writer now proceeds to speak more copiously and argumentatively of the high-priesthood of Christ, and so to provide his readers with the defensive armour of which they stand most in need.

CHAP. V. 1-10. *The high priest of Aaron's race holds, as man, on behalf of other men, his office from God: and so also Christ has been appointed priest by God His Father, after a higher order, that of Melchizedek; and though Son of God, become through suffering and prayers in the days of his flesh, the author of eternal salvation to us.*

The close internal connection of these ten verses is recognised by all modern expositors except Tholuck, who takes vers. 1-3 as explanatory supplement to iv. 15, 16, and begins the new section with ch. v. 4.[1] Older commentators, such as Beza,

[1] Tholuck regards vers. 1-3 as explanatory of iv. 15 above: "For (γάρ) there is this difference between our High Priest and every other human

Schlichting, Hammond, Limborch, Storr, and the Lutherans Balduin and Gerhard, do much better in finding the requisites for a true high priest first laid down at vers. 1–3, and then exhibited as fulfilled in Christ at vers. 7–10. They rightly regard the structure of vers. 1–10 as *chiastic*, vers. 4–6 forming the centre, from which vers. 7, 8 look back, and correspond to vers. 2, 3, and vers. 9, 10 to ver. 1, thus completing the parallelism in all particulars. As the high priest of Aaron's race was taken from among men, and could therefore sympathize with men, so also is it with Christ; and as the Aaronic high priest was made by God the mediator and offerer of sacrifice on man's behalf, so also again was Christ,—both requisites, the true humanity of the priest himself, and the divine origin of his call, being found antitypically in the Lord Jesus; yet so that, in virtue of the essential superiority of antitype to type, He is not only the antitype of Aaron, but also that of Melchizedek.

No modern expositor has evinced such a thorough understanding of this orderly arrangement of thought, the symmetry of which is not merely mechanical, but of organic growth, as Hofmann (*Schriftbeweis*, ii. 1, 280 et seq., comp. 49).[1] The γάρ, v. 1, is not merely explanatory, but demonstrative. "*From the nature of the high-priesthood of Jesus, resembling as it does* one, that while the mediatorial functions of the latter are based on fellow-feeling with their brethren, it is a fellow-feeling in the sense of guilt.*" But as the thought involved in iv. 15 was even there quite subordinate, so here too it stands in the background; and it only needs a glance at vers. 7, 8, to see that it is not points of difference, but points of agreement between Christ and the Aaronical priesthood, which the author has here in view. Bleek, De Wette, Lünemann, and others, are right in regarding vers. 1–10 as an inseparable whole; but they fail in discerning what a perfect whole it is. There is no proper application to Christ in their view of what is said of Aaron's priesthood, vers. 1–3. Bleek supposes the author to have dropped some of the threads of his argument; while De Wette and Lünemann suppose, that either such applications may be inferred from what had gone before in iv. 15, ii. 17, etc., or are supplied in what follows, vii. 27, viii. 3, ix. 11, x. 11, etc.

[1] Ebrard correctly observes, that the author of the division into chapters was guided by a happy instinct in making v. 1 the commencement of a new chapter; but he deranges the order of thought when he makes iv. 16 the *thesis* of which v. 1–9 is the exposition, and finds the enunciation of a fresh thesis at v. 10.

on the one hand the *priesthood of Aaron*, and on the other that of *Melchizedek*, the author demonstrates, v. 1-10, *that we shall not ask in vain for manifestations of the goodness and grace of God.*" This, in Hofmann's words, is the plain natural order of the thoughts. As reasons are given for the exhortation κρατῶμεν τῆς ὁμολογίας, on the one hand by ἔχοντες, κ.τ.λ., from the exaltation of our High Priest above the heavens, and on the other by οὐ γὰρ ἔχομεν, κ.τ.λ., from His human sympathy, derived from His own experience; so reasons for the exhortation προσερχώμεθα are given on the one hand from this very sympathy which suggests it, and on the other from the combination, as set forth v. 1-10, in the person of Christ, of Aaron's true humanity and Melchizedek's dignified exaltation. He is willing and He is able to help, the former as antitype of Aaron, the latter as antitype of Melchizedek; and both as the priest made perfect through deepest God-appointed sufferings, being at the same time all-prevailing King after the order of Melchizedek. The γάρ, the force of which is perhaps not clear when viewed simply with respect to v. 1, while grammatically belonging to vers. 1-3, logically governs the whole section vers. 1-10, in which a single but very significant thought is unfolded in a succession of separate propositions.

After this glance at the organic connection of the whole paragraph, without which we miss the force of the connective γάρ, we will now endeavour to explain it in detail.

Vers. 1-3. *For every high priest, being taken from among men, is appointed for men, in things relating to God, that he may offer both gifts and sacrifices for sins, as being one able to have a kindly feeling for the ignorant and erring; since he himself also is compassed with infirmity, and on that account is under obligation as for the people, so also for himself, to offer for sins.*

The author here describes the first essential characteristic of the high priest according to the ordinances of the divine laws; and doing this, proceeds on the assumption, that whatever may characterize the high priest as such, will be found also in Christ. It would not be in perfect accordance with his meaning to interpret πᾶς ἀρχιερεύς here by "every Aaronical high priest;" for the descent from Aaron, as not being an essential characteristic, is here left out of account.¹ The first essential here insisted on is, that the high priest is appointed as a representative of men in their relations to God, to offer sacrifices on their behalf; and that in order to his knowing, by personal experience, how sin-laden human beings feel, he must himself be selected from among them. Καθίστασθαι is used in accordance with the idiom which is also found in the Septuagint, καθιστάναι τινά τι = to appoint a man to something; and τὰ πρὸς τὸν Θεόν has the same meaning as at ii. 17, where it is followed by εἰς τὸ ἱλάσκεσθαι, κ.τ.λ., as here by ἵνα προσφέρῃ δῶρα τε καὶ θυσίας ὑπὲρ ἁμαρτιῶν.² Among the religious functions of the high priest, as a representative of others, the chief is that of offering sacrifices. Elsewhere our author speaks of all kinds of offerings, bloody and unbloody alike, as simply δῶρα (ch. viii. 4), and by that title designated Abel's sacrifice (ch. xi. 4); but here (as also at viii. 3 and ix. 9) δῶρα stands for all offerings made without blood-shedding, θυσίαι for those of which the slaying of a victim formed a principal part. The addition ὑπὲρ ἁμαρτιῶν must not be taken as further defining the two species of offerings,³ but rather as belonging to the verb προσφέρῃ, and meant to indicate the final purpose of every kind of sacrifice. The chief end of all sacrificial worship is, for our author, the making an atonement for sin. Such "atonement," through offering of blood, forms indeed a part of *every* animal sacrifice, even where the removal of the guilt of actual transgression may not, as in the case of the sin-offering (חטאת), be the specific object; and so too the Minchah (δῶρον, "meat-offering"), while properly⁴ a present (מנחה from מנה, to present as a gift), made

¹ Compare v. Gerlach and Ebrard, whose remarks are not quite accurately represented by Hofmann (*Schriftbew.* ii. 1, 280).
² Compare Heb. viii. 3, εἰς τὸ προσφέρειν δῶρά τε καὶ θυσίας καθίσταται.
³ Our author always speaks of the sin-offering as προσφορά or θυσία περὶ ἁμαρτιῶν (or ἁμαρτίας), and never, as the Septuagint sometimes (*e.g.* in Ezek.), ὑπὲρ ἁμ. Comp. Heb. x. 18, 26, xiii. 11, and x. 6, 8. The Thorah knows of no δῶρον, Minchah (unbloody offering), properly so called as a sin-offering, except in the one case, Lev. v. 11-13, when the poor man is unable to bring *two* turtle-doves.
⁴ Even in the one case in which the Minchah is a sin-offering (Lev. v. 11-13) there is no proper atonement, but only the need of atonement negatively expressed by the absence of the customary oil and frankincense.

in token of grateful acknowledgment for past mercies, and combined with petitions for future favours, has also for its antecedent and basis the idea of an accomplished expiation, being not an independent sacrifice in itself, but generally a mere appendage of the burnt and peace offerings. And here, too, we must bear in mind that our author is not thinking of the priestly offerings in general, but of those of the high priest in particular, and more particularly still, of those made by him on the day of atonement. The high priest's ministry on that day was most especially a προσφέρειν δῶρα[1] τε καὶ θυσίας ὑπὲρ ἁμαρτιῶν. The aim of all his sacrifices on that day was to reinstate or to secure Israel in a condition of acceptance with God, to remove or avert the hindrances made by sin; and therefore all his sacrifices on that day were specially made ὑπὲρ ἁμαρτιῶν. To discharge that office the high priest was appointed ὑπὲρ ἀνθρώπων, and was also ἐξ ἀνθρώπων λαμβανόμενος. It is now universally recognised that Luther's version here is incorrect: "Every high priest who is taken from among men." Had such been the author's meaning, he would certainly have written either πᾶς ἀρχιερεὺς ὁ λαμβανόμενος or πᾶς ... λαμβανόμενος ἀρχιερεύς. We must therefore render it: *Every high priest is, being taken from among men, appointed to act on their behalf in their relations to God.*

The design of this participial clause (which may involve a reference to Num. viii. 6) is not (as Hofmann thinks) to lay stress on the fact that the high priest is appointed to represent his equals before God, as if there were anything specially remarkable in a man being selected to stand in that relation for other men; but its purpose rather is to indicate the ground of his fitness for the office, as being one capable of sympathy with those on whose behalf he discharges it; another participial clause, μετριοπαθεῖν δυνάμενος, being also added (to bring this out more clearly) to the ἵνα προσφέρῃ.[2] The word

---

[1] The meat-offerings (Minchas) on the day of atonement were mere accompaniments of the sevenfold burnt-offering, and the so-called Musaphim (additional sacrifices). Comp. Num. xxix. 7-11.

[2] It is God's ordinance, that he who performs the atonement, making sacrifice for his brethren, should be one μετριοπαθεῖν δυνάμενος. Hofmann's remark is quite correct, that the author purposely uses not εἰς τὸ προσφέρειν, but ἵνα προσφέρῃ, in order more conveniently to introduce this μετριοπαθεῖν δυνάμενος, on which so much stress is laid.

μετριοπαθεῖν (with its cognates μετριοπάθεια, μετριοπαθής, μετριοπαθῶς) comes from the mint of Greek ethical philosophy: it was employed by Academics, Peripatetics, and Sceptics, to indicate the right mean between a slave-like passionateness and stoic "apathy,"[1] and is used by Philo[2] to describe Abraham's sober grief on the loss of Sarah (ii. 37), and Jacob's imperturbable patience under affliction (ii. 45). Transferred from the language of the schools to that of general literature, μετριοπαθεῖν signifies the disposition of mind which keeps the right mean between excessive feeling and sheer indifference, and here a judgment and feeling which is neither too severe nor too lenient, but reasonable, sober, indulgent, and kind; differing from συμπαθεῖν not simply as the higher from the lower (Tholuck), but rather as a feeling *for* others differs from a more lively sense of one's own infirmity, or as compassion roused by the contemplation of sufferings, and here specially of such as are the consequences of sin, from a fellow-feeling with them in which one's own experience has a principal share.

This μετριοπαθεῖν is followed (like other words expressing mental affections, θυμοῦσθαι, δυσχεραίνειν, χαλεπαίνειν τινι, Dittfurt, § 180) by the dative τοῖς ἀγνοοῦσιν καὶ πλανωμένοις. This definition of the nature of the sins in question is chosen to exclude those who sin "with a high hand" (בְּיָד רָמָה), that is, defiantly, of set purpose, with open contempt of God and His law. Such sin which, under the Thorah, incurred sudden destruction by a divine judgment (Num. xvi. 30), could not be an object of the high priest's μετριοπάθεια, which in such a case would fail of a due abhorrence of evil. Moreover, the sacrificial worship under the law, as in its essence an evangelical institution, did not permit the approach of such sinners, who, as so deeply fallen, could only escape utter destruction by a great and timely penitence. It would, however, be wrong to suppose that every conscious and wilful sin was one committed בְּיָד רָמָה, and as such was excluded from sacrificial atonement.[3] Sins

---

[1] Equivalent to the term μετριάζειν in older Greek.
[2] Philo in certain cases is not satisfied with μετριοπάθεια, but demands perfect ἀπάθεια. Comp. i. 113, i. 85, and i. 603.
[3] A view rightly disputed by Hofmann, *Schriftbew.* ii. 1, 158. Comp. Eichhorn, *Princip. des Mosaismus*, i. 208.

"with a high hand" were such as combined with transgression aversion to the law itself, and a determination not to be bound by it, but were not those into which a man is betrayed, when his better knowledge and conscience are overmastered by the power of appetite or passion. The assurance of pardon in the case of such sins might and was to be sought for by sacrifice, provided always that such sacrifice was preceded by sincere repentance on the part of the offender. The perjured witness who, from fear or favour, had kept back evidence he should have given, might, after his free confession before being legally convicted, clear himself by a trespass-offering (Lev. v. 1); and even the man whom carnal appetite had misled to having sexual intercourse with a betrothed bondmaid, was allowed, after having been convicted and punished by scourging for his misconduct, to cleanse himself before God by a trespass-offering (Lev. xix. 20-22). With respect, then, to the day of atonement, it was all the sins of Israel in general and without limitation which were then atoned for by the sin-offerings of that day, especially by that of the two goats, even sins not committed בִּשְׁגָגָה, and therefore excluded from atonement by sacrifice on other days of the year. All sins were on that day forgiven to Israel, on the presupposed condition of repentance; for the notion that the atonement resulted *ex opere operato*[1] is even in the Talmud itself (*Cherithoth* 7a) mentioned only to be forthwith rejected. While, therefore, τοῖς ἀγνοοῦσι καὶ πλανωμένοις certainly excludes the case of presumptuous and defiant transgressors of the law, it would be wrong to limit ἀγνοεῖν and πλανᾶσθαι here to merely unconscious and involuntary violations of the divine precepts; especially as in the LXX., ἀγνοεῖν, ἀκουσιάζεσθαι, ἀκουσίως ἁμαρτεῖν (the more usual renderings of the Hebrew שׁגג and בשׁגגה חטא), together with πλημμελεῖν (the special word for expiable transgressions), do not designate exclusively unconscious faults, or such as were the result of outward compulsion. Ἀγνοεῖν καὶ πλανᾶσθαι must therefore be taken here to denote such sin as originates in the fallible weakness and sinful inclinations of human nature, being an ἀγνοεῖν, so far as from confused moral consciousness it mistakes the divine will and so trespasses against it, and a πλανᾶσθαι, so far as by yielding to temptation

[1] Chald. כפרה ממילא אתי.

it is drawn into the path of error. Towards those involved in such mistakes and errors the high priest is able to feel kindly disposed, ἐπεὶ καὶ αὐτὸς περίκειται ἀσθένειαν, because he is himself beset with infirmity. The infirmity meant is a moral weakness, as opposed to moral perfection (i. 28, comp. iv. 15). Instead of ἐπεὶ περίκειται αὐτῷ ἀσθένεια, infirmity besets him, the author prefers to say, He is himself surrounded, or compassed with infirmity, περικεῖσθαί τι being used passively, like περιτεθεῖσσαί τι (see Kühner, § 565, 2, and the authorities collected in the fifth edition of Passow's Lexicon). This transposed construction of περικεῖσθαι, found nowhere else in the New Testament except Acts xxviii. 20, is specially appropriate here, to designate the innate weakness which hinders us from free self-decision. The high priest, himself a man, is capable of a gentle and moderate disposition of mind towards those who seek through him to obtain forgiveness of their ἀγνοήματα (ix. 7): (1) because, like them, he is conscious of besetting infirmity; and (2) because, for that reason, the very same obligation is imposed upon himself. Ver. 3 is not therefore an independent proposition (Böhme, Bleek, Ebrard, Lünemann), but, like καὶ αὐτὸς περίκειται ἀσθένειαν, from which it is an inference, dependent on ἐπεί (De Wette, Hofmann). We read with Tischd., καὶ δι' αὐτὴν ὀφείλει, καθὼς περὶ τοῦ λαοῦ οὕτως καὶ περὶ ἑαυτοῦ προσφέρειν περὶ ἁμαρτιῶν. The received reading διὰ ταύτην (ob eam ipsam) is not without support; but δι' αὐτήν[1] has weightier authorities in its favour, and is more suitable in a dependent clause. But if, with A.B.C.*D.*, we read δι' αὐτήν, we must also with these and other authorities read περί (not ὑπέρ) ἁμαρτιῶν, which, alternating with the ὑπὲρ ἁμαρτιῶν of ver. 1, which is there the reading of all mss., must be understood in the sense of xiii. 11 (where περὶ ἁμαρτίας is the reading of the text. rec.[2]) and of x. 6, 8. The περὶ ἑαυτοῦ we leave unchanged, as preferable here (where the high priest is set in contrast to the people) to Lachmann's περὶ αὐτοῦ, supported by B. and D.* The perpetual Minchah which the Levitical high priest as such had to offer daily from the day of his consecration, half every morning

---

[1] Preferred by Lachmann also. [It is that of the Cod. Sinait.—TR.]

[2] [Omitted by Tischendorf, placed by Lachmann after τὰ ἅγια. It is found in its old place in the Cod. Sinait.—TR.]

and half every night (Lev. vi. 13–16, Heb.; vers. 20–23, Eng. ver.), and which, like every pontifical Minchah, came wholly on the altar, remains here out of account. The author has the ritual of the day of atonement here exclusively in view. According to that ritual, the high priest entering the inner court commenced the chief service of the day by laying his hands on the bullock of the sin-offering, and there making confession for himself[1] and his house, standing between the temple and the altar; and this was the only occasion[2] on which the high priest, as such, concurred with the congregation of Israel, gathered together as one whole, in a common acknowledgment both of a moral and legal need of atonement. We must not define ὀφείλει here as expressing one kind of need apart from the other (*i.e.* the ethical apart from the legal, or the legal apart from the ethical), since both were doubtless inseparably combined in the thought of the sacred writer.

A sentence follows, connected by καί to the main verb in the period vers. 1–3. To the first requirement in the high priest, that he be taken from among men, is now added a second, the divine calling:

---

[1] The high priest's three confessions—the first for himself and his own family, the second for the priesthood in general, and the third for all Israel—are given and explained in my *Geschichte der jüdischen Poesie*, pp. 184–189. The first, for himself and family, ran thus: *O for Jehovah's sake* (or, *O Jehovah*, according to another reading) *do Thou expiate the misdeeds, the crimes, and the sins wherewith I have done evil, and have sinned before Thee, I and my house, as is written in the law of Moses Thy servant:* " *On that day shall he make an atonement to cleanse you; from all your sins shall ye be clean before Jehovah*" (Lev. xvi. 30). Only as one who had been himself atoned could the high priest make atonement for others, on the received principle, "An innocent man must come and make an atonement for the guilty; but the guilty may not come and make an atonement for the innocent." *Vid.* Van der Waegen, *Varia Sacra*, p. 149.

[2] The high priest might indeed have occasion, at other times in the course of the year, to offer sin-offerings for himself as well as for the congregation (Lev. iv. 3–12), and in both cases he must himself officiate and sprinkle the blood before the veil of the Most Holy; whence such offerings were called חַטָּאוֹת פְּנִימִיּוֹת, *i.e.* sin-offerings presented immediately before God; but he was never placed in such exact parallel with the people as one whole, except on the day of atonement, when the general need of expiation, arising from a common sinful state or nature, rather than from special cases of transgression, was the main thought in all these sacrifices.

Ver. 4. *And not unto himself doth one take the honour, but as being called* (thereto) *by God, even as was Aaron.*

Τὴν τιμὴν is here equivalent to τὴν τιμὴν τοῦ ἀρχιερέως, or to τὴν ἀρχιερωσύνην; and Aaron is the historical personage who, as specially appointed by God Himself (κατὰ τὰ χρησθέντα λόγια, Philo, ii. 161), is the prototype of all his successors. MSS. decide in favour of καλούμενος without the article ὁ (which is found in the *text. rec.*, and appears in the versions of the Peshito and Luther[1]), and this reading is in itself preferable. The best authorities are also in favour of 'Ααρών (not ὁ 'Ααρών); and Tischendorf's reading, καθώσπερ[2] (quite, entirely so as), is to be preferred to the καθάπερ of the *text. rec.*, or the inadequately supported καθώς of Lachmann. There is no occasion to assume, with Bleek, a kind of zeugma in the use of λαμβάνειν, when supplied in the second clause. The meaning is simply this: a man does not take this honour to himself of his own accord; but when called by God thereto he takes it *as* so called. Self-willed assumption is opposed to submissive reception. Aaron did not make himself high priest, but received a divine vocation to the office. Understanding λαμβάνειν ἑαυτῷ of self-willed assumption or usurpation, we have a perfect parallel between the case of Aaron and that of Christ.

The author now begins his proof of the fulfilment of both requirements for the discharge of the high-priesthood by our Lord *chiastically* with the second.

Vers. 5, 6. *Thus Christ also glorified not himself, to be made high priest, but he that spake unto him, My son art thou, to-day have I begotten thee. Even as he saith also in another place, Thou art a priest for ever, after the order of Melchizedek.*

The thought we naturally expect here is: as Aaron, so Christ, took not the honour to Himself. But instead of οὕτω καὶ ὁ Χριστὸς οὐχ ἑαυτῷ ἔλαβε τὴν τιμὴν (i.e. τὴν ἀρχιερωσύνην), we have οὐχ ἑαυτὸν ἐδόξασεν γενηθῆναι ἀρχιερέα. The infinitive γενηθῆναι[3] ἀρχιερέα, indicates the object implied in

---
[1] It is supported among the Uncials only by C** and I. The Cod. Sin. reads ἀλλὰ καλούμενος.

[2] For καθώσπερ, see Himerios (p. 362), Psellos, and Tzetzes. Comp. for all these forms, Sturz, *de dialecto Macedon.* pp. 74–77.

[3] Cod. A. 71, al. read γενέσθαι, in accordance with the rule given by

ἐδόξασεν, He took not to Himself the δόξα of becoming high priest. (It is an *infinitivus epexegeticus;* Winer, § 44, 1.) Hofmann, disapproving this simple explanation, proposes one more artificial : " *We need not assume that the author uses* ἐδόξασεν *here in the sense of* ἠξίωσεν (*as Böhme*), *or means nothing more than that Christ did not arrogate the high-priesthood to Himself* (*as Bleek interprets him*), *in which case certainly the infinitive* γενηθῆναι *would drag somewhat strangely; but* ἐδόξασεν *is here emphatic; and the insertion of* ὁ Χριστός *itself is significant. It was in no way of self-exaltation, but in one of suffering and sorrow, that the anointed Mediator of our redemption attained the glory in which He now reigns as High Priest after the order of Melchizedek*" (*Schriftb.* ii. 1, 282). But this antithesis of δοξάζειν and παθεῖν is needlessly brought forward from vers. 7, 8 ; whereas δοξάζειν ἑαυτόν is rather opposed here to the καλεῖσθαι or καθίστασθαι ὑπὸ τοῦ Θεοῦ of vers. 1 and 4. Neither can the infinitive be said to " drag," or be superfluous. The construction is similar to that of Luke ii. 1, Acts xiv. 25, xv. 10, and Col. iv. 6 (where there is no need to supply τοῦ). Nor does the usual explanation give a weak or superficial sense to δοξάζειν here. The οὐχ ἑαυτὸν δοξάζειν of our text has for its antithesis a δοξάζεσθαι ὑπὸ τοῦ Θεοῦ in the sense of St. John. Wherein, moreover, consists the δόξα of the God-man, but in His glory as being High Priest and King? That twofold dignity is not the consequence of, but *is* His δόξα, or at least belongs to it. We have already learned (i. 3, ii. 9 sq.) how through God's appointment He attained the δόξα of a King; and now (after hints previously given, as at ii. 17) we are told in what follows how He also attained to that of a High Priest. But the οὐχ ἐδόξασεν refers only to the end attained, without telling us anything of the way to it. It is more than a mere framework for the γενηθῆναι ἀρχιερέα; it includes the elevation to royal dignity as well. The same is also indicated in the ὁ Χριστός, which is not our Lord's special title as Priest (הכהן המשיח[1]), but rather as King (מלכא משיחא), the Messiah. What

Phrynichus (p. 108, ed. Lob.), ὁ Ἀττικίζων " γενέσθαι " λεγέτω. But our author, like Polybius, Diodorus, Dionysius, Strabo, Pausanias, etc., uses, certainly not without meaning, sometimes the passive, sometimes the middle aorist.

[1] In the time of the second temple, when the high priest was not

the sacred writer would say is : He who made not Himself a King, but was anointed to that dignity by God, in the same way took not to Himself the δόξα of High Priest, but solemnly received it from God too. The same antithesis is contained in the following ἀλλ' ὁ λαλήσας, and the two citations from Scripture which are introduced by it. The relation in which these citations stand to one another is misunderstood, when it is made a question, as by Ebrard, how far the notion of γέννησις might involve that of conferring priesthood. The two texts are not meant to be a twofold testimony to our Lord's divine installation into the pontifical office ; but after stating and confirming by the first quotation that it was not Himself, but the Father, by whom Christ was glorified in being made High Priest (for after ἀλλ' ὁ λαλήσας, κ.τ.λ., we have to supply ἐδόξασεν αὐτὸν γενηθῆναι ἀρχιερέα), the sacred writer adds the other passage introduced by καθὼς καὶ ἐν ἑτέρῳ[1] λέγει to confirm the fact already testified, as not resting on any self-assumption on our Lord's part, but on the ordinance of that God and Father by whom He is called " Son." If indeed the author understood Ps. ii. 7 of the eternal generation of the Son,[2] we might have a difficulty in discerning a reason for the paraphrase of the simple idea of ὁ Θεός, there being no proper internal connection of thought between the calling Christ " my Son," and the conferring the priesthood upon Him. And even if the author be supposed to make Ps. ii. 7 refer to the incarnation (Böhme, Hofmann), the connection between the two citations would still be a loose one, though in a less degree. " *God, who begat Him to be His Son, has also caused to be fulfilled in Him that other prophecy which calls the King of God's people a Priest after the order of Melchizedek.*" So Hofmann paraphrases our pas-

anointed, but only invested with the sacred garments, he was called but rarely כהן משוח, and generally כהן גדול.

[1] Comp. Acts xiii. 35, and Clem. Rom. cc. viii. 29, 46, ἐν ἑτέρῳ τόπῳ.

[2] It scarcely weighs anything in favour of this interpretation, that Philo occasionally understands by σήμερον an endless, ever self-renewing day (comp. i. 92 in reference to Gen. xxxv. 4, and i. 554 in reference to Deut. iv. 4) ; for, so far as we know, the passages here referred to (Ps. ii. 7 and cx. 4) are nowhere mentioned in his extant writings. Theodore of Mopsuestia's objection, however, to this the prevalent interpretation (τὸ σήμερον λέγεσθαι οὐκ ἂν δύναιτο μὴ οὔσης ἡμέρας), is also of no force : eternity might be so called, as an ever-resting, self-evolving present.

sage, ingeniously taking υἱός here as a name denoting both nature and dignity (comp. Böhme, *omnem Jesu Messiæ excellentiam uno υἱοῦ divini complecti nomine*). But if, as Hofmann grants, the σήμερον γεγέννηκά σε of the Psalm refers to David, and his inauguration into royalty by an anointing (*Weiss*. ii. 31), then the corresponding commencement of Christ's fully recognised filial relation as man to the Father, would not be the Incarnation, but the Resurrection, and His visible entrance thereupon into the royal life of divine glory. It is then that exaltation which our author understands by the σήμερον of the Psalm, as we have already shown at i. 5, and not the incarnation, for which, as antitypical of David's anointing, no clear testimony can be adduced from Scripture, whereas a comparison of Rom. i. 4 with Acts ii. 36 is sufficient to show that our view is quite in accordance with the inspired text. Taking, then, this view of Ps. ii. 7, we see a very close connection between the two citations from the Psalter. He who solemnly declares Christ to be His Son, whom " to-day" (the day of His exaltation) He has begotten into the glory of royal power (as He did with David, after lengthened suffering), is the same who has made Him High Priest (with a priesthood which, according to Ps. cx. 4, is inseparable from His Kingship),— a Priest, that is, after the order of (the king) Melchizedek.[1] It is substantially this view which Tholuck and De Wette take, when they refer Ps. ii. 7 to Christ's exaltation, in which He is at once constituted High Priest and King. They only err in thinking that the author proves from Ps. ii. 7 the reception of the high-priesthood from God; whereas he only proves from it that Christ was thereby constituted King, and afterwards from Ps. cx. 4 that He has also been inaugurated into a priesthood inseparably connected, as in the case of Melchizedek, with His royal dignity. Both are therefore inseparably united in our Lord, yet not so that His kingship and priesthood are identical, —a view of Hofmann's, already mentioned at i. 13, but destitute of all scriptural authority, unless we hold that Ps. cx. is merely typical, and take, with him, its fourth verse as fully applicable in the first instance to David. But the priesthood

---

[1] Compare Tertullian, *adv. Judæos*, c. xiv., "post resurrectionem suam indutus poderem (the ' garment down to the feet' of Rev. i. 13 ; comp. Ex. xxviii. 27, LXX.) sacerdos in æternum Dei Patris nuncupatus."

of Melchizedek was much more than what we are wont to include under the *summepiscopatus* of a Protestant sovereign ; for, according to the custom of the ancient Canaanites, he was at once a king and a sacrificing priest: his priesthood was as complete and real as that of Aaron afterwards ; and hence he united in his own person the offices both of David and of Aaron. This, at least, was the view taken by our author, who, from the very fact that there could be no such priest-king under the Old Testament institutions, infers that Melchizedek ideally belongs to the promised future now realized in Christ the anointed King, in whom the Davidic line terminates, without further succession, and who is at the same time, in virtue of the divine oath addressed to Him, not only a King, but also an eternal Ἱερεὺς κατὰ τὴν τάξιν Μελχισεδέκ. He is called ἱερεύς, not ἀρχιερεύς, it being easily understood that as the Priest-King He must occupy among all priests the highest place. The author himself explains κατὰ τὴν τάξιν, which is an exact rendering of the original, by κατὰ τὴν ὁμοιότητα, ch. vii. 15. Τάξις is not therefore here the equivalent either of succession or rank, but simply denotes position, character, manner, or kind (comp. 2 Macc. i. 19, ix. 18). After the same manner in which Melchizedek was at once both priest and king, is Christ eternally and antitypically possessor of both those dignities. The same Person whom God, addressing with בני אתה, declares to be His own anointed, world-subduing King, He also designated with אתה כהן as an eternal Priest; and so are combined in one expression two unique, divine prophetic utterances of the Psalter.

Having thus shown, in vers. 5, 6 (chiastically appended to ver. 4), that Christ possesses the first essential requisite for the office of high priest—a divine commission, the author goes on to demonstrate His possession of the second—a human personality, in which He both suffered here below, and so became the author of our salvation and High Priest in heaven. He is not only καλούμενος ὑπὸ τοῦ Θεοῦ, but also ἐξ ἀνθρώπων λαμβανόμενος. We have already observed, that as the inner members of the comparison (vers. 5, 6, and ver. 4) correspond, so do also the outer (vers. 7, 8, and vers. 1-3). We must not be misled by the relative ὅς to suppose that ver. 7 merely continues the preceding statement : ὅς connects here the two links of the argument: He who has been already exhibited as ordained of God to this priestly office, must now be shown to have attained it by a course of human obedience and suffering.

Vers. 7, 8. *Who having in the days of his flesh offered prayers and supplications to him that was able to save him from death, with strong outcry and tears, and having been heard because of his piety : though being a son, yet learned obedience from the things which he suffered.*

The sacred writer now, therefore, begins¹ to unfold the way of human sorrow, fear, and suffering, and of human submission to the divine will, by which Christ attained to His pontifical glory. It is indeed in heaven that He sits enthroned as "High Priest for ever, after the order of Melchizedek," that is, as a King seated at God's right hand, and mediating still in priestly wise for us; but all this He *became* on earth (see on ii. 17).

Excluding for the present the participial middle clauses, the main proposition will stand thus : ὃς ἐν ταῖς ἡμέραις τῆς σαρκὸς αὐτοῦ καίπερ ὢν υἱὸς ἔμαθεν ἀφ᾽ ὧν ἔπαθεν τὴν ὑπακοήν. We are warranted in thus putting it, even though we grant that ἐν ταῖς ἡμέραις, κ.τ.λ., was connected in the first instance in the author's mind with the following participial clause, δεήσεις ... προσενέγκας ; for *logically* ἐν τ. ἡμ. must be taken as defining the time in which all that is here spoken of occurred. We render, therefore, the main sentence thus :² *In the days of His flesh he learned* (that *human* virtue) *obedience.* "Days of His flesh," or better, "His days of flesh,"³ *i.e.* (comp. Phil. i. 22, 1 Pet. iv. 2) the time in which He bore about Him our human nature as weakened and made subject to death through sin (θνητὴν σάρκα, 2 Cor. iv. 11; comp. above, ii. 14). "Flesh" (σάρκα) He has indeed still now, both since His resurrection (Luke xxiv. 39) and (though Bleek denies it) since His ascension

---

¹ Hofmann deranges the order of thought here, through his mistaken interpretation of οὐχ ἑαυτὸν ἐδόξασεν noticed above.

² The construction καίπερ ... ἔμαθεν (*e.g.* Stengel), "although he had learned," is inadmissible, (1) as giving a contorted and unsuitable sense, and (2) from the consideration that καίπερ is never found with a finite verb, but in a dependent clause, and generally with a participle. Comp. vii. 5 and xii. 17.

³ In the original, "*seine Fleischestage*,"—equivalent to fleshly life (Fleischesleben) or "life in the flesh." Comp. Gal. ii. 20.—Tr.

too, and therefore in heaven, as may be inferred from the sixth of St. John, according to which the Lord's flesh and blood is the meat and drink of eternal life, albeit of a different quality now from that body of humiliation wherein He once joined in fellowship with our sinful humanity; His body now is a σῶμα τῆς δόξης (Phil. iii. 21). The author's object being to demonstrate the Lord's possession of a true humanity as the second requisite for the pontifical office, the very phrase ἐν ταῖς ἡμέραις τῆς σαρκὸς αὐτοῦ asserts his being ἐξ ἀνθρώπων λαμβανόμενος, that He *is* a man now, and once *became* a man like us. But this date, ἐν ταῖς ἡμέραις, κ.τ.λ., is but the framework for a more extended proof of his position, viz. that while here on earth, although a Son, Christ learned obedience by what He suffered. Grammatically everything is clear: τὴν ὑπακοήν has the article, because the act or habit of obedience is the thing meant. Μανθάνειν ἀπό τινος is the same as ἔκ τινος, *e.g.* Matt. xxiv. 32 (comp. Matt. xi. 29, *text. rec.*); and ἔμαθεν ἀφ᾽ ὧν ἔπαθεν is a play on the words not uncommon in other Greek writers, *e.g.* Æschylus (*Agam.* 174-178), Ζῆνα ... τὸν πάθει μάθος θέντα. A similar assonance is often found in Philo; *e.g.* i. 566, ἔμαθον ὃ ἔπαθον; p. 673, ὁ παθὼν ἀκριβῶς ἔμαθεν ὅτι τοῦ Θεοῦ ἐστιν; ii. 178, παθόντες ἔσονται τὸ ἐμὸν ἀψευδές, ἐπεὶ μανθάνοντες οὐκ ἔγνωσαν; p. 340, ἵν᾽ ἐκ τοῦ παθεῖν μάθῃ.[1]

The sentence is, as we have said, in itself grammatically clear and simple, but its further interpretation depends on the idea connected here by the commentator with the word υἱός. Hofmann proceeds on the assumption (maintained likewise very decidedly by Ebrard, p. 197) that it is always Christ as incarnate, and therefore as begotten in time, whom the author designates by υἱὸς Θεοῦ. But with this view of Sonship μανθάνειν τὴν ὑπακοήν stands by itself, and is antithetical to nothing, there being nothing extraordinary in the assertion that the human son of a heavenly Father stands to Him in the subordinate relation of ὑπακοὴ, or that the Son had once to acquire, by

---

[1] A similar paronomasia is not found elsewhere in our epistle: vii. 13 (μετέσχηκεν—προσέσχηκεν), x. 29 (ἡγησάμενος—ἡγιάσθη), xi. 9 (παρῴκησεν —κατοικήσας), etc., are instances of *assonance*, in which the first word is not without influence on the choice of the second, but in which the gnomic point essential to a true paronomasia is missing.

rendering it an experimental knowledge of what obedience is. If this view be taken, the emphasis must be laid neither on ἔμαθεν nor on τὴν ὑπακοήν, but on ἔπαθεν. " *The way in which He learned obedience, that though God's Son, He had to learn it by what He suffered, i.e. in the midst of suffering, this is the chief point here insisted on*" (Hofm.). " *The meaning is, that Christ abated nothing from the general obedience which as Son He owed and gave to the Father, even when called to evince it in the midst of the sufferings imposed on Him by the divine will*" (Ebrard). This explanation, which lays all the emphasis upon ἔπαθεν, would be admissible if the hypothesis on which it is founded were correct; but that hypothesis has been shown to be false. It is indeed true, that whenever he speaks of the "Son of God," our author always designates by that term Christ come in the flesh; but it is not true that the idea involved in the term is exhausted in Him as miraculously conceived and born of Mary. The very commencement of the epistle is a proof of this, in which our incarnate Lord is called υἱός not merely as the glorified Redeemer, but also as the Mediator of all creation. And when, a little after, the author calls Him "the effulgence of the Divine Essence," etc., which He was before and apart from time, the terms ἀπαύγασμα and χαρακτήρ must be regarded as substantive expressions of that eternal relation of the incarnate One to God which finds personal expression in the name υἱός. And a strong argument it is against this exclusive application of the idea of υἱός to the Lord's historical manifestation, that it compels us to regard such passages as Heb. i. 3, Col. i. 15, John i. 18, as speaking of that human personality which appeared in time, rather than of the eternal Person which therein was manifested. Here likewise for Hofmann, taking this view, the name υἱός awakens no remembrance of what our Lord had been before His incarnation, nor makes any allusion to the union in Him of Godhead and manhood;[1] and we are told that " *the term υἱός is so much the more incompetent to express such ideas, because it has not the article*" (Hofmann, *Schriftb*. ii. 1, 48). Surely a very futile

---

[1] De Wette, however, compares Phil. ii. 6, ἐν μορφῇ Θεοῦ ὑπάρχων; and Tholuck discerns in the καίπερ a contrast drawn between the divine elevation of the Son, and the humiliations of the suffering humanity which He assumed.

objection! Not to mention that this very epistle employs υἱός anarthrously (i. 1, vii. 28) as much in the style of a proper name as Κύριος, Θεός, Χριστός are so employed, υἱός being here predicate, needs the article as little as in the ὁρισθέντος υἱοῦ Θεοῦ of Rom. i. 4. We are therefore justified in understanding υἱός here of that *Eternal* Son, whose birth in time shadowed forth[1] by an inward necessity His γέννησις in eternity, and may so proceed to an impartial consideration of the question as to where the main emphasis of the sentence should fall. Now as to the emphasis being laid on the clause ἀφ' ὧν ἔπαθεν, of which Hofmann allows no doubt to be possible, it must be observed, that the emphatic words of a sentence are generally placed either at the beginning or at the end, and not in the middle. Accordingly, the ideas which are here made prominent are ἔμαθεν and τὴν ὑπακοήν; the learning of obedience being thus placed in contrast with the fact of Sonship: He who as " God from God" stands related to His source in an eternal community of essence and of love high raised above all relations of earthly subordination, did nevertheless as man learn obedience, and learned it through suffering, and a voluntary self-submission under the mighty hand of God. What passed between Him and His God in this suffering school of obedience, we learn from two parenthetical clauses, of which the first is δεήσεις τε καὶ ἱκετηρίας πρὸς τὸν δυνάμενον σώζειν αὐτὸν ἐκ θανάτου, μετὰ κραυγῆς ἰσχυρᾶς καὶ δακρύων προσενέγκας. The synonyms δεήσεις and ἱκετηρίας form a climax, and are also found together, Job xl. 22, LXX.[2] Ἱκετηρία (fem. of

[1] We have a striking testimony in Lipsius, *de Clement. Rom. Ep.* p. 12, to the genuine impression made by the words καίπερ ὢν υἱός, when, recognising υἱός at v. 5 as designation of the glorified Jesus, he confesses that here it must designate the eternal and consubstantial One, and adds a too hasty expression of exegetical despair, *quæ quo modo inter se conciliari possint alii viderint*. Köstlin, in like manner, finds it difficult to reconcile the human elements involved in the name υἱός with the divine, and needlessly imagines some contradiction between the doctrine of St. Paul on this point and that of our epistle. He allows, however, that nothing better illustrates the ἐκένωσεν ἑαυτόν of Phil. ii. 7 than the doctrine concerning Christ in the Epistle to the Hebrews, and especially in this place, v. 7, 8.

[2] Where the Cod. Alex. actually reads δεήσεις καὶ ἱκετηρίας, perhaps influenced by this text in our epistle.

ἱκετήριος, namely, ῥάβδος or ἐλαία) is properly the olive branch wrapped round with wool, by which a suppliant announces himself as seeking protection and help, as Orestes, for example, is represented doing in the *Eumenides* of Æschylus (43 sq.); from that it came to signify, like ἱκεσία or ἱκετεία (see Philo, i. 147, and comp. ii. 586), the supplication itself; hence we have here not only prayers, but (τε καὶ) supplicatory and urgent though humble prayers. To these ἱκετηρίας, etc., and not to προσενέγκας (Lünem.), which, however meant, would be construed with a dative (τῷ δυναμένῳ),[1] the πρὸς τὸν δυνάμενον must be referred: they are prayers addressed *to* Him "that was able to save Him from death." From which we learn, that deliverance ἐκ θανάτου was the object of those prayers and supplications. The phrase (ῥύεσθαι, ἐξαιρεῖσθαι) ἐκ θανάτου may either signify to rescue from death and make alive again one dead already (Hos. xiii. 14), or to rescue one whom death looks in the face from becoming its prey (Ps. xxxiii. 19; Jas. v. 20). Here, where the subject is not a dead person, but the prayers of one still living, σώζειν ἐκ θανάτου can be understood only in the latter sense; and we are at once reminded of our Lord's agonizing prayer in Gethsemane. He there prayed that "the cup"—that is (as is not only self-evident, but here expressly declared), *the cup of death*—might pass from Him. According to St. Mark (xiv. 36), He there confessed, beginning with the words 'Αββᾶ ὁ Πατὴρ πάντα δυνατά σοι, that God was δυνάμενος σώζειν αὐτὸν ἐκ θανάτου—Lord over life and death, and also over the prince of death and all his instruments. *There*, too, He offered up "prayers" (δεήσεις) and "supplications" (ἱκετηρίας); for, as St. Luke tells us, He prayed: and being in an agony, He prayed ἐκτενέστερον. It is indeed St. Luke who specially delineates (xxii. 39-46) that wrestling in prayer with marked details, which here press on the memory as we read the μετὰ κραυγῆς ἰσχυρᾶς καὶ δακρύων. "*His sweat ran like drops of blood to the ground*" is a part of the narrative in St. Luke which,

---

[1] Προσφέρειν in the sense of *offerre* is always followed by a *dative* in the LXX. and in the New Testament. Lünemann appeals to Polybius, προσφέρειν χάριν and προσφέρειν χάριν πρός τινα; but even here it is possible that πρός may belong more strictly to the noun than to the verb—χάριν πρός τινα, favour towards some one, rather than προσφέρειν πρός.

according to Bleek (p. 73), borders on the apocryphal, and is critically suspicious; but it is supported by Justin Martyr, Irenæus, and Hippolytus, and only occasionally omitted in some MSS. (see Tischd.), perhaps as expressing too painfully the truth of our Lord's suffering humanity. According to Epiphan. (*ancor.* 31), it includes in many copies of St. Luke a mention also of His "tears:" ἀλλὰ καὶ ἔκλαυσεν κεῖται ἐν τῷ κατὰ Λουκᾶν εὐαγγελίῳ ἐν τοῖς ἀδιορθώτοις ἀντιγράφοις; and very possible it is that St. Luke himself *did* write this ἔκλαυσεν, especially since (except John xi. 35) St. Luke alone elsewhere represents our Lord as weeping (Luke xix. 41). Evidently here the original form of the text of his Gospel has suffered from a piously intended but ignorant intermeddling. It is also allowable to suppose that' μετὰ κραυγῆς ἰσχυρᾶς καὶ δακρύων is a finishing touch to the narrative in the Gospel drawn from a vivid conception of the circumstances or from traditional knowledge, and that it thus bears the same relation to the Gospel narrative as Hosea's retrospect of Jacob's wrestling at Jabbok (Hos. xii. 4; comp. also Böhme) does to Gen. xxxii. 26. The conjecture, in itself not unnatural, that the Psalms of the passion were floating in the author's mind at the time (Bleek), is unnecessary; and that the more so, as he had doubtless here chiefly in view the scene in Gethsemane. But not that exclusively. The ἀγωνία (Luke xxii. 44) was not without prelude in our Lord's life (see John xii. 27), and was finally renewed and completed when He cried on the cross φωνῇ μεγάλῃ, *My God, my God, why hast Thou forsaken me?* or when, having cried (κράξας) φωνῇ μεγάλῃ, "He gave up the ghost" (Matt. xxvii. 46, 50; comp. Luke xxiii. 46). De Wette will not admit this part-reference to the Lord's conflicts on the cross, because our author evidently regards these "prayers and supplications" as preparatory to the ἔμαθεν and ὑπακοή, and therefore antecedent to His παθήματα. Hofmann, too (*Schriftb.* ii. 1, 47, 206), takes προσενέγκας and εἰσακουσθείς in relation to ἔμαθεν in this pluperfect sense (After having . . .). But, as Lünemann rightly observes, the force of these participles is not to be rendered here by an "after," but by a "while." In point of grammar, indeed, both renderings are equally possible; but since the main proposition is not ἐνεδείξατο ἐν οἷς ἔπαθεν τὴν ὑπακοήν, but ἔμαθεν ἀφ' ὧν ἔπαθεν τὴν ὑπακοήν, and since, what seems to me clear as day, the participial clauses represent the Son of God as the subject of this μαθεῖν, and made a disciple in this suffering school of obedience, the conclusion must be, that the aorists indicate contemporaneous occurrences, and that therefore we must not say with Hofmann that our Lord's lesson of obedience began with His betrayal into the hands of His enemies, or His passion with the arrest which followed the agony in Gethsemane. Even were it true that the author did not mean by ἃ ἔπαθεν every single experience of our Lord, but only those sufferings which were nothing but suffering, that passion-tide which ended in death (*Schriftb.* ii. 1, 48)—(though I see not why we must understand by ἃ ἔπαθεν only the Passion in the narrower sense),—still it is clear from our author's own words that the agony in Gethsemane must at all events be considered as the first stage of that final passion; and Hofmann himself elsewhere acknowledges this: " The passion begins with the agony in Gethsemane" (ii. 1, 202). Here, however, he maintains that that agony formed no part of those παθήματα to which our author now refers as being our Lord's school of obedience, but insists that his meaning is, that after being heard in those " prayers and supplications," the Lord proceeded " in a new way" to manifest His filial obedience, and so in his passion ἔμαθεν τὴν ὑπακοήν (ii. 1, 284). But not to insist upon it that we can hardly be said to " manifest" *in* learning, but rather *after* and what we have learned, these fine distinctions between different kinds of " suffering" and " manifestation" are much too subtle, and crumble in the grasp of a robust criticism.

Before entering on the question, which no expositor has hitherto so thoroughly discussed as Hofmann, " Whether προσενέγκας is here to be understood in its sacerdotal sense or not?" we will first endeavour to make clear the meaning of the second participial clause, καὶ εἰσακουσθεὶς ἀπὸ τῆς εὐλαβείας. Even the oldest versions differ here. The Vulgate (followed by Luther) translates *pro sua reverentia;* Vigilius, *propter timorem.*[1] According to both these renderings, ἀπὸ τῆς εὐλαβείας denotes the reason why the Lord was heard. On the other hand, the Itala and Ambr. give the rendering, *exauditus a metu,* equiva-

[1] So Eng. Ver.: " *in that He feared.*"—Tr.

lent to that of the Peshito ומן דחלתא;[1] thus making ἀπὸ τῆς εὐλαβείας designate the object in reference to which a hearing was vouchsafed Him, viz. the fear of death. Most modern expositors (Böhme, Klee, Stuart, Stein, Ebrard, Bloomfield, etc.) decide in favour of the latter view; Tholuck also, but somewhat irresolutely, understanding εὐλάβεια of the reluctance expressed in εἰ δυνατόν. De Wette likewise vacillates; whereas Hofmann is decisive that every interpretation of εὐλάβεια here, except that of dread of death, has against it the author's own use of the word elsewhere (xi. 7, xii. 28). On a closer view, εὐλαβής is properly one who takes a good, that is, a careful, hold of anything, and therefore one who acts with caution and wariness, as well as (it may be) from anxiety or fear; εὐλαβεῖσθαι is to take heed, to be on one's guard, or to exhibit prudence, foresight, and also reverence in one's conduct and behaviour; εὐλάβεια is caution, thoughtfulness, circumspection, and a reverent regard for that which is venerable or holy. This is both the classical and the Hellenistic usage. The LXX. has εὐλαβεῖσθαι ἀπό of fear or reverence towards God, or man, or a court of justice; εὐλαβεῖσθαι τὸν Θεόν is to fear God, to be religious; εὐλαβής is a God-fearing, pious man; εὐλάβεια is piety, "the fear of the Lord" (Isa. xi. 2), and also anxiety, solicitude (דאגה). It cannot be denied that these words sometimes signify not only a fear which is the result of caution and foresight (to which meaning Bleek and Lünemann would restrict them), but also one which springs from a naturally apprehensive and anxious disposition, or from an overpowering and alarming impression made on the mind. Thus in Philo (ii. 93) Moses is called, with reference to Ex. iv. 10, τὴν φύσιν εὐλαβής (aptly rendered by Carpzov, natura timidiusculus), and in Josephus (Ant. xi. 6) Artaxerxes lays his sceptre on Esther's neck εὐλαβείας αὐτὴν ἀπολύων. Εὐλάβεια might well, therefore, signify here "the fear of death," and is indeed once used in that sense in (a passage overlooked by Bleek and Lünemann) Ecclus. xli. 3: μὴ εὐλαβοῦ κρίμα θανάτου, which may either mean, Seek not timorously to escape the common destiny of all men; or simply, and in perfect accordance with the *usus loquendi*, Be not afraid of the sentence of death.[2]

[1] The Peshito, however, attaches the words to the following ἀφ᾽ ὧν ἔπαθεν.
[2] So the Syriac version and that of the English Bible.—TR.

Here thus also εὐλάβεια, even if understood as referring to the dreaded sentence of death, need not be taken with Tholuck in the sense of *detrectatio* or *industria declinandi*, but simply that of shrinking apprehension; and we may easily find a reason why so mild a term should be selected here, because that shrinking from death on our Lord's part was tempered by a willingness to drink its cup. But this notwithstanding, I feel constrained to decide with Bleek and Lünemann against such an interpretation of εὐλάβεια; and in the first place, for the weighty reason that our Lord's entreaty was not to be freed from the fear of death, but (as the πρὸς τὸν δυνάμενον σώζειν αὐτὸν ἐκ θανάτου shows) to be delivered from death itself, to have the cup of death removed. A freeing, therefore, merely from the fear of death could not be called an answer to His prayer, unless indeed (with Calvin and others) we understood εὐλάβεια as metonymically put for the object of fear, *i.e.* the death itself which He thus feared (a quite inadmissible exegetical *quid pro quo*). And secondly, New Testament usage (especially that of our author) does not favour this interpretation. The passages adduced in its support by Hofmann fail to afford it. For εὐλαβεῖσθαι at xi. 7 does not so much express Noah's dread of the threatened deluge, as his conscientious and wise precautions against the approaching calamity in contrast with the carnal security of the unbelievers; and xii. 28, where εὐλάβεια is combined with δέος or αἰδώς, it does not denote a fear we ought to have of God's consuming fire, but religious watchfulness over ourselves, so as to avoid whatever might displease Him. This sense of religious awe and conscientiousness is the only one which εὐλαβεῖσθαι with its derivatives may be said to carry throughout both the Epistle to the Hebrews and the writings of St. Luke,[1] which here again, as so often, characteristically agree. Εὐλαβής is in Luke ii. 25, Acts ii. 5, viii. 2, and xxii. 12,[2] synonymous with εὐσεβής.[3] So also here we may interpret εὐλάβεια as expressing that religious fear of God and anxiety not to offend Him which manifests itself in

---

[1] With the single exception of Acts xxiii. 10.

[2] 'Ανανίας . . . ἀνὴρ εὐσεβής, *text. rec.*; but Lachmann, after the best authorities [including now the Cod. Sin.], reads εὐλαβής.

[3] εὐσεβής with εὐλαβής is the regular rendering for the Hebrew 'ה ירא, God-fearing or Jehovah-fearing.

voluntary and humble submission to His will; and this without the need of supposing any ellipsis or suppressed thought, as would be more or less the case with any other interpretation. To which may be added, that in place of the always dubious *constructio prægnans*—" heard *from* the fear of death," *i.e.* so heard as to be delivered from it—we gain by our interpretation a much simpler construction, and one, moreover, quite in St. Luke's style: " *heard because of His piety ;*" ἀπό being used as in ἀπὸ τοῦ ὄχλου, Luke xix. 3 ; ἀπὸ τῆς χαρᾶς, Luke xxiv. 41, Acts xii. 14; ἀπὸ τοῦ ὕπνου, Acts xx. 9 ; ἀπὸ τῆς δόξης, Acts xxii. 11. Εὐλάβεια, as the mildest term for " the fear of the Lord," is the most suitable in this application. No other word could so adequately describe our Lord's disposition towards the heavenly Father manifested in the prayer in Gethsemane as this term, so expressive of pious resignation to God's will. A Greek scholium aptly observes : εἰ καὶ χάριτι, φησί, πατρικῇ ὡς υἱὸς εἰσακούσθη ἀλλ' ἀπὸ τῆς οἰκείας εὐλαβείας· εὐλαβείας γὰρ ἦν τὸ λέγειν· πλὴν οὐχ ὡς ἐγὼ θέλω, ἀλλ' ὡς σύ. Moreover all the Greek expositors agree in this interpretation,—an agreement which must on all accounts weigh heavily in its favour. And after all this, it is now evident that the second participial clause, with its emphatic word εὐλαβείας placed at the end, is not a mere incidental remark (Bleek, Lünemann), but one closely connected with the main proposition : " Christ Himself learned obedience by suffering, in that, having to wrestle with His God in prayer, He too was heard only because of the reverential awe with which He then submitted His own will to that of the Father. The hearing vouchsafed Him did not consist in a mere deliverance from that dread of death which made submission thereto so hard, although, no doubt, this *was* in part a fruit of that agonizing prayer (the great antitype of Jacob's wrestling) : for what Christ prayed for was a deliverance from death itself; to which the only answer could have been a real deliverance. He was heard therefore (in brief), when raised of God from the dead and exalted by Him to heavenly glory (so Bleek, Lünemann, etc.). But if His prayer before death was that, if possible, He might escape it altogether, a subsequent resurrection and exaltation, however glorious, could not be called an answer to such prayer ; for which reason Köstlin will not admit any reference here to the agony in Gethsemane. The difficulty vanishes on a closer view. If we considered Jesus as a mere man, His prayer would be to be kept from the death with which His enemies threatened Him; and in that case it would, especially the more earnest supplicatory part of it, be incomprehensible, seeing how many just men, both before and after, have met with joy the martyr's doom; to suffer for *God* being in itself a suffering most blessed. And if, as we must, we consider Jesus as the God-man and Mediator, then at first sight it would also seem almost blasphemous to suppose that He could have sought to withdraw Himself from the work of atonement, precisely when its final accomplishment was in question. But His supplication had reference to the mortal agony on the way to that end. That betrayed by His people to the Gentiles He would die, and that for the salvation of the world, was to Him well known. He had indeed announced it beforehand to His disciples with gradually increasing clearness; and yet, when death with all its terrors presented itself immediately before His soul in the garden, an anguish and a "horrible dread" overwhelmed Him, which, in the consciousness of the inevitable necessity, wrought in His mind a momentary obscuration and apparent wavering. In this state of human ἀσθένεια He prayed to One who was able to save Him from death, One who, in respect of power, *could* do so; He prayed that, if it were possible, He would let the cup of death pass from Him,—"if possible," that is, if consistent with His divine counsel and will. It was the whole abyss of death itself into which the Lord looked down when He offered this supplication; He saw there the workings not only of evil men and of the demon-prince of death, but also of the ultimate ground of death, which is no other than the wrath of God Himself.[1] And He saw that death, in this its full reality, could not be withheld from Him, who was appointed by dying to overcome death, and by being made a curse to absorb the curse for all mankind. God Himself had willed that so it should be, for He willed to love mankind, and not of necessity to be for ever wroth with them. It was the love of God, there-

---

[1] See v. Gerlach, with whom we are here in perfect agreement: "Why shrunk He back from death, except because He discerned therein the curse of God, and a conflict to be endured with all the powers of sin, and hell itself?"

fore, which sent the Son into the world, and it was the same love which gave Him up to death; but only as the ultimate cause of that condemnation which, viewed apart from its reason and purpose, was a manifestation of God's wrath, not as against the innocent One, but as against the guilty many in whose room the Mediator stood. And now, therefore, even because He, as the Representative of all mankind, did not supplicate for deliverance from death, without at the same time an obedient self-submission to everything beforehand which the determinate counsel and foreknowledge of God might demand, God heard and answered Him on account of that His $Εὐλάβεια$, i.e. He compassed Him with love in the very midst of His mortal agony, and when under the sense of divine dereliction, and therefore of divine wrath, and so translated Him through dying to a life of glory. This was the Father's answer to the awful cry, *My God, my God, why hast Thou forsaken me?* " It is because I love Thee the more, and in Thee would love and glorify mankind!" The Son was heard, not by deliverance from the necessity of dying, but by temporal death being made for Him the gate of paradise, and the cross of shame a ladder to heaven. He was heard, in that David's hope (Ps. xvi. 8–11) was in Him fulfilled (Acts ii. 24–31, xiii. 35-37),—heard, in that, though He must taste of death (ii. 9), God loosed its "pangs" (Acts ii. 24), and made it manifest that they were but the birth-throes of an endless life for Him and for the world. We view the work of atonement generally from the height of the divine plan as now revealed; and so for us it is a mystery made plain. But if we place ourselves in the midst of its mysterious development, and venture to accompany step by step the incarnate Redeemer in His suffering work of atoning love for all His brethren, and in His prayers and supplications for Himself from Gethsemane to Golgotha, then we shall not fail to see that those agonies of death so suddenly transformed into the joys of paradise were a hearing of His prayer surpassing even what as man He had asked and desired Himself. We say, surpassing what as man He had asked or desired Himself, for that almost despairing cry upon the cross, as well as the "Father, if it be possible," in the garden, presents Him before us sunk in a depth of suffering, which was at the same time the deepest obscuration of the divine light in His human consciousness and the lowest prostration of His human ἀσθένεια. Most certainly this suffering had in its greatest extremity an infinite divine power of endurance for its accompaniment and support; but that notwithstanding, the burden was no less heavy which He had and was willing to bear in order to disburden us. Had He not experienced the terrors of death Himself, He would not have been κατὰ πάντα like us, nor what it needed that our High Priest should be, ἐξ ἀνθρώπων λαμβανόμενος. Had He not been under the necessity of compelling the σάρξ, which in itself shrinks from suffering and the cross, to stand firm against it in submission to God, and as strengthened in Him, He would not have entered into the fellowship of our ἀσθένεια, nor have been the true antitype of Aaron, able to sympathize with those whose High Priest He has become, ἐπεὶ καὶ αὐτὸς περίκειται ἀσθένειαν.

We now come to the very important question (above referred to), "Whether the writer of our epistle means in ver. 7 to say that there is anything analogous in Christ to what he has laid down concerning the Levitical high priest in ver. 3, viz. that he is bound as for the people, so also περὶ ἑαυτοῦ, to offer for sins?" And here we must premise, that Christ being altogether χωρὶς ἁμαρτιῶν, the analogy, at all events, can only consist in *this*, that as in the case of the Levitical high priest it was his own actual sins, so in the case of our Lord it was only His human ἀσθένεια (connected as that was by origin with human sinfulness) that made it needful for Him to offer περὶ ἑαυτοῦ. Of modern expositors, some find no reference in the προσενέγκας of ver. 7 to the προσφέρειν of ver. 3 (De Wette); some a slight allusion, with an half conscious paronomasia, to the προσφέρειν of vers. 1 and 3 (Bleek); while others express no opinion (Tholuck, Ebrard, Lünemann). Hofmann alone has seriously raised and thoroughly entered into the question. He thinks to find a profound parallelism between the προσενέγκας here predicated of Christ, and the προσφέρειν περὶ ἑαυτοῦ to which the Jewish high priest was bound before he could offer on behalf of the congregation. His own words are as follows (*Schriftb.* ii. 1, 283; comp. also 206, etc.): "*Christ's earnest prayer that the cup of death might pass from Him, was, like the high priest's offering for himself, a pious utterance of human infirmity (only with the difference which must obtain* between the infirmity of a sinful priest and that of the sinless Saviour), and not therefore to be compared with such supplications as might be offered by any individual believer, but strictly answering to that peculiar and unique expression of the high priest's own relation to God, being as closely connected with the passion that followed as was the high priest's offering for himself with his offering for the congregation. It was the presentiment of that approaching passion which made Jesus, in the contemplation of it, 'sore amazed and heavy,' 'with loud outcry and tears;' but the outcry was the voice of prayer, the tears were those of a suppliant, and both, consequently, an offering well-pleasing to God, wherein Jesus exhibited His true relation to the Father. It was an offering, therefore, which God accepted." Ingenious as this parallel is, yet I do not believe that our author had it in his thoughts; for, 1*st*, the hypothesis on which it is founded, namely, that προσενέγκας and εἰσακουσθείς, with their dependent clauses, stand to ἔμαθεν ἀφ' ὧν ἔπαθεν τὴν ὑπακοήν in the relation of precedents in point of time, cannot be proved. We have seen, on the contrary, that according to our author's view, Christ learned obedience in doing and experiencing the things there stated. Then, 2*dly*, if we have rightly apprehended the author's meaning, such an exclusive reference of ver. 7 to the scene in Gethsemane would be unwarrantable, since it also refers to the conflict on the cross, and especially since εἰσακουσθεὶς ἀπὸ τῆς εὐλαβείας was only fulfilled in that transition from death to life when Jesus κράξας φωνῇ μεγάλῃ gave up the ghost and entered paradise, and was only made manifest in the glory of His resurrection. 3*dly*, The author does not distinguish (ver. 3) the two offerings of the high priest by a πρότερον and ἔπειτα, as, on Hofmann's hypothesis, we should expect him to do. And 4*thly*, which is the main point, when he does so distinguish (vii. 27), he knows of only one antitypical offering made by Christ, viz. the sacrifice of Himself made for us and once for all, *i.e.* an offering of the innocent for the guilty, and exclusive, therefore, of anything analogous to the ὑπὲρ τῶν ἰδίων ἁμαρτιῶν here.

It is to this offering of Himself for us that, according to Hofmann's parallel, we should have to refer the ἔμαθεν ἀφ' ὧν ἔπαθεν, κ.τ.λ., discussed above, and suppose that that clause sets forth how our Lord, after the conflict in Gethsemane, went on to manifest in a new way, *i.e.* one perfectly passive, the filial obedience which He rendered to the Father. Hofmann says: " It is not here expressly stated that this self-sacrifice was made by Christ on our behalf, the context not requiring such a comparison between the work of Aaron and that of our Lord: the point of resemblance here insisted on is, that in both cases the high priest was not exempted from such liability to temptation and suffering infirmity as rendered him more sympathetic for others, and more ready to help them." The reason here assigned for the omission of any statement that our Lord's sacrifice was made for us, is perfectly correct; not so, however, the connecting it with ἔμαθεν, κ.τ.λ., rather than with προσενέγκας. The Lord's sacrifice for us began in Gethsemane, and was already in will almost as good as accomplished when He cried, πλὴν μὴ τὸ θέλημα μοῦ, ἀλλὰ τὸ σὸν γενέσθω. It was realized in outward act upon the cross, and finished when He there cried τετέλεσται, and commended His spirit into the hand of God. But the fact, that both in Gethsemane and on the cross He made His offering not without " prayers and supplications," and " strong crying and tears," in the one case, with the *Father, if it be possible*, etc., and in the other, with *My God, my God, why hast Thou forsaken me?*—the fact, that in both cases His stedfast submission to the divine will was made in the midst of so great a conflict,—all this showed His possession of a true humanity, enabling Him to feel with and compassionate us. His " prayers and supplications," which began in the garden and were continued to the end, being poured forth in one stream from a soul troubled unto death (as the twenty-second Psalm, which gives us so deep a view into the inmost mind of the Crucified, bears witness),—these are, no doubt, all of them included and designated as a sacrifice in the word προσενέγκας. But they were not a sacrifice in and by themselves, and offered by our Lord, as Hofmann says, περὶ ἑαυτοῦ, in contradistinction from His offering of Himself περὶ τοῦ λαοῦ. They were indeed the accompaniments of that one self-oblation, or rather formed of it an integral part. We cannot distinguish in our Lord's doings and sufferings what was done for Himself and what for us, since all was done both for us as those to be redeemed, and for Himself as our representative. Being at once both High Priest and sacrifice, He was also as

CHAP. V. 9, 10.   253

Son of man the new humanity itself, which in that awful sacrifice, by conflict and submission, made its way from death and condemnation to life and peace, and in itself made all of us the objects of the Father's love. And just because the sacrifice of Christ was so intensely personal, it was not a dumb or silent offering, but one that was step by step accomplished in acts of prayer, whereby He manned Himself (so to speak) again and again for renewals of the conflict, and in the midst of the sense of divine dereliction held fast by faith in the divine love, so winning in Himself for us deliverance from the wrath divine.

The sacred writer having thus asserted for our Lord the two essential qualifications of a high priest,—1*st*, that of a divine appointment; and 2*dly*, that of being taken from among men, and able to sympathize with them from His own experience of human infirmity,—proceeds (vers. 9, 10) to exhibit Him as having reached, by that way of sorrows, the exalted station in the heavenly glory to which the same divine appointment had called Him.

Vers. 9, 10. *And being perfected, he became for all who are obedient to him the originator of eternal salvation, being solemnly addressed by God as high priest after the order of Melchizedek.*

The context proves that τελειωθείς must be referred not to our Lord's filial,[1] but to His mediatorial relation (compare also vii. 28 with ii. 10). That relation was, so long as the days of His flesh lasted, in a process of development. But after He had shown Himself *obedient* (ὑπήκοος) *unto death, even the death of the cross* (Phil. ii. 8), that process of development attained its end, the state of humiliation was exchanged for one of glory, and Christ came forth from the school of obedience made perfectly that which He was intended to become, God so putting the seal of acceptance on the sacrifice that had been made. And being thus made perfect, He who to His last breath on the cross had been obedient to the will of God, became the originator of eternal salvation for all who now on their part are obedient to Him, that is, who submit themselves in faith to the merit of His obedience (Rom. v. 19). The order of the words varies here between τοῖς ὑπακούουσιν αὐτῷ πᾶσιν

[1] So Hofmann.

(retained by Tischd. 1849) and πᾶσι τοῖς ὑπακούουσιν αὐτῷ (Lchm.). The latter order being the better attested, is to be preferred.[1] It seems also more fitting that πᾶσι, which expresses the universality of the salvation thus provided, should precede, and that τοῖς ὑπακ. αὐτῷ, which expresses the subjective condition of its attainment, should follow. This salvation is here in readiness for all who will accept it (without distinction, as is self-evident, and especially in a Pauline epistle), i.e. it is a universal salvation, and in its inward essence is eternal too (תְּשׁוּעַת עוֹלָמִים, Isa. xlv. 17),—a " saving to the uttermost" (vii. 25). And of all this Christ is now become the Mediator, yet not so as of a salvation attainable apart from Himself, but, as is implied by αἴτιος (comp. ἀρχηγός, ii. 10, Acts iii. 15, v. 31), its author and possessor, or, if the expression may be allowed, its one personal principle (ἀρχή). The phrase αἴτιος εἰμί τινί τινος, in a good sense as well as in a bad, is classical: in Josephus (Ant. iii. 3), Aaron with his family and Raguel magnify the God of Israel ὡς τῆς σωτηρίας αὐτοῖς καὶ τῆς ἐλευθερίας αἴτιον; and Philo (ii. 440) calls Noah, in relation to his sons, τὸν αἴτιον τῆς σωτηρίας πατέρα. Having thus stated what our Lord as perfected became, the author returns once more to Ps. cx. 4, προσαγορευθεὶς ὑπὸ τοῦ Θεοῦ ἀρχιερεὺς κατὰ τὴν τάξιν Μελχισεδέκ. Raised to that state of perfection, He became the personal Mediator of an all-embracing and eternal salvation, and became so in that He was solemnly addressed by God as " ἀρχιερεὺς κατὰ τὴν τάξιν Μελχισεδέκ." Observe the *part. aor.* : it is the title of honour wherewith the Son made perfect through sufferings was saluted by the Father when He raised Him from the dead and made Him sit at His own right hand (Hofmann, *Schriftb.* ii. 1, 47). The title with which God openly and solemnly received Him was not merely ἱερεὺς κατὰ τὴν τάξιν Μελχισεδέκ, but ἀρχιερεὺς κατὰ τὴν τάξιν Μελχ. Although we cannot agree with Hofmann in his view, already given, of Melchizedek's priesthood as simply identical with or involved in his royal dignity and office, yet he alone of modern expositors has rightly put and answered the question, why in this designation of the priesthood of our Lord, taken as it is from Ps. cx., His high-priestly character

---

[1] So Bleek and Lünemann. [The reading in Cod. Sin. is also πᾶσιν τοῖς ὑπακούουσιν αὐτῷ.—Tr.]

is thus expressly named (*Schriftb*. ii. 1, 285). "*From the time of His glorification onwards, Christ is the ' Priest after the order of Melchizedek.' But it was through previous suffering even unto death that He was made perfect as an High Priest. Had Bleek rightly distinguished between these two, he would not have fallen into the mistake of supposing that our author makes Christ's high-priesthood first begin with His glorification.*" This is quite true. Seated now at the right hand of God, and so raised¹ to fellowship with Him in royal glory, the perfected One is an ἱερεὺς κατὰ τὴν τάξιν Μελχ. But having also entered the heavenly sanctuary, after first making an oblation of Himself here on earth, with prayers and supplications, He is also the antitype of Aaron, and as such styled 'Ἀρχιερεύς.² Bleek himself cannot withhold the acknowledgment (ii. 1, 361), that our author assigns a high-priestly character to our Lord's own oblation of Himself upon the cross previous to His entrance into the heavenly sanctuary, but thinks that he regarded this as merely an inauguration into the dignity of the heavenly high-priesthood. Hofmann very justly contends that it was more than that—that it was an essential part of His High Priest's work performed in the outer court, that is, in this world. And therefore, when the Father in the heavenly sanctuary thus salutes the Son made perfect on His entrance there, " High Priest [art Thou], after the order of Melchizedek," we have the two great antitypical titles inwoven into one.

¹ Bearing the title, as Luther would say, of Shêblimînî (שֵׁב לִימִינִי, *Sit Thou on my right hand!*) with the inscription on His stirrup : *I will make Thine enemies Thy footstool;* and this on His diadem : *Thou art a Priest for ever.*

² While Josephus, in speaking of Melchizedek, is careful to avoid the term 'Ἀρχιερεύς, Philo calls him ὁ μέγας ἀρχιερεὺς τοῦ μεγίστου Θεοῦ. (ii. 34 ; comp. Jos. *Ant*. i. 10, 2, and *Bell*. vi. 10). Mangey is mistaken in comparing Philo ii. 586, where it is not Melchizedek but the Asmonæan high priest who is referred to : the fragment ii. 657 is more to the point, where Philo says : " The earliest kings appear to me to have been at the same time high priests, so testifying that those who rule over others are the ministers of them that fear God." In the Epistle to the Hebrews, Ἀρχιερεύς is never applied to Melchizedek, but only to the Levitical office-bearer, and to our Lord as antitype of Aaron.

EPISODE OF EXHORTATION

CONDUCTING FROM THE

FIRST TO THE SECOND PART OF THE EPISTLE.

CHAP. V. 11-VI. 20.

CHAP. V. 11-VI. 3.—*Before pursuing further the comparison of Christ with Melchizedek, the author rebukes his readers for their backwardness, in lingering on the threshold of Christian knowledge, over which he would now, with God's help, lead them onwards to perfection.*

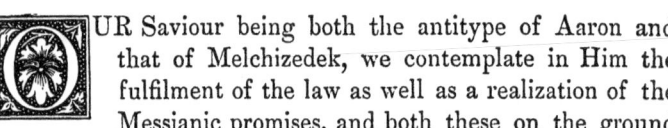UR Saviour being both the antitype of Aaron and that of Melchizedek, we contemplate in Him the fulfilment of the law as well as a realization of the Messianic promises, and both these on the ground of that suffering unto death which is still a σκάνδαλον to the persecuting and seductive synagogue, from whose threatenings and allurements the readers of the epistle are in perpetual danger. He is this, too, in consequence of a return to the Father's glory, whereby He has become our salvation and our boast; the object of a faith which apprehends the invisible, and the aim of a hope which lives in the future. Of this Aaron-like working of the glorified Jesus as the High Priest after the order of Melchizedek, begun indeed on earth but continued in heaven, the sacred writer has already commenced, after a preliminary hint (ii. 17, etc.) and a precursory admonition (iv. 14-16), expressly to treat in the preceding section (v. 1-10); but now interrupting the train of his exposition, he thus continues:

Ver. 11. *Concerning which we have much to say, and that hard to expound clearly, since ye have become dull in hearing.*
Περὶ οὗ refers neither to Christ nor to Melchizedek, but **to**

the subject of which he is treating. The reference to Christ, if we follow Bengel, who would take us back to the ὅς of ver. 7, is too remote, and that to Melchizedek (Peshito, Bleek, De Wette, Tholuck, etc.) too narrow; for the sacred writer is not treating of Melchizedek himself in his own person. Περὶ οὗ, therefore, is either = περὶ Χριστοῦ ἀρχιερέως κατὰ τὴν τάξιν Μελχ. (Lünemann), or, which I prefer, taking οὗ as a neuter, = περὶ τοῦ εἶναι Χριστὸν ἀρχιερέα κατὰ τὴν τάξιν Μελχ. So Schlichting, Böhme, Ebrard, Hofmann, and many others. The sentence which follows can hardly be rendered literally—*i.e.* word for word; the following is an attempt to do so paraphrastically: " Concerning which much or copious is the discourse which we should wish to make, and one hard to render intelligible to such as you." I cannot think, with Storr, Bleek, and Lünemann, that there is any kind of *zeugma* in the use here of ὁ λόγος, viz. that it is employed in one sense as connected with πόλυς (that of discourse, lecture, or exposition), and in another with δυσερμήνευτος (that of the subject of such discourse or exposition); ὁ λόγος in both cases is what one has to say, πολύς denotes its copiousness in regard to materials,[1] and δυσερμήν. the difficulty which besets it in respect to the method of exposition; λέγειν is a more closely defining infinitive, equivalent to the Latin supine *dictu*.

The next question is: Whether the reproach ἐπεὶ νωθροὶ, κ.τ.λ., is intended to explain and justify the second predicate (δυσερμήν.) only, or to apply to the former (πολύς) as well? Among modern commentators, Hofmann is the only one who takes the latter view (*Entst.* 341). "*In saying that Jesus, after having endured such things, is henceforth a high priest after the order of Melchizedek, the author had said all that he needed to say, had his readers understood at once what this implied, and what comfort was contained in it. But now, sensible of the necessity of entering into further details, he feels impelled to rebuke them first, for being so little advanced in knowledge as to need this.*" Against this view of Hofmann's is both the evidently intentional separation of the two predicates, and the

---

[1] Compare for a similar use of πολύς, Dionysius of Halicarnassus, *de Compos. Verbor.* § 8 : πολὺς ἂν εἴη μοι λόγος εἰ περὶ πάντων βουλοίμην λέγειν τῶν σχηματισμῶν. So again he says in the 1st book of the *Antiquities*, περὶ ὧν πολὺς ἂν εἴη λόγος εἰ βουλοίμην τὴν ἀκρίβειαν γράφειν.

nature and bearing of the subject. The author has, indeed, scarcely yet entered on the discussion (λόγος) of the high-priesthood of Christ; and his very commencement of it leads us to expect a further setting forth of the rich significance of such a theme. He cannot mean that the hints already given would suffice for this, were only the spiritual condition of the readers different; but the difficulty of dealing with so large and copious a subject of instruction brings vividly to his recollection the condition of his readers, and impels him involuntarily to make this digression. He does not, indeed, say expressly that the subject is difficult in its own nature; but every one who tries to work out for himself the thoughts compressed in the section v. 1–10 will feel that it is so. Hence, when he adds καὶ δυσερμήνευτος λέγειν, he means that it is difficult for him to find the fitting ἑρμηνεία (mode of expression, or method of exposition), in which he would have to pursue his theme;—ἐπεί—alas! that I should have to commence with this reproach!—νωθροὶ γεγόνατε ταῖς ἀκοαῖς. The adjective νωθρός (here and vi. 12)[1]—a secondary formation from νωθής, synonymous with νωχελής (νώχαλος) and νῶκαρ,[2] and connected in Clemens Romanus, c. 34, with παρειμένος—signifies *difficult to move, heavy, slow, dull, languid, indolent*.[3] It is here applied, like the following ταῖς ἀκοαῖς (a dat. instrumenti, for which also τὰς ἀκοάς were admissible), to the use of the sense of hearing, that is, *here*, of the inward ear. In the New Testament, and in classical literature as well, αἱ ἀκοαί (for ἡ ἀκοή, comp. 1 Cor. xii. 17) signifies sometimes the sense of hearing in general, sometimes the capacity of a particular individual (Mark vii. 35; comp. Luke vii. 1, Acts xvii. 20). That which characterized the

---

[1] The LXX. use the word νωθροκάρδιος.

[2] All these words are in part· compounds of the negative νή—though this is denied by Passow and Lobeck (*Pathol.* p. 107).

[3] The original notion of νωθρός is hit by Orion (ed. Sturz, col. 108) when he says: Νωθρός. νω. καὶ νη. στερητικὰ μόρια, ὁ τοῦ θορεῖν ἐστερημένος, ὃ ἐστὶν ἀξίως κινεῖσθαι. But the derivation from ὠθεῖν, proposed by other grammarians, is more probable than this from θόρειν or θρώσκειν. In a similar way they explain νωχελής and νοκελής (vid. Orion, Photius, etc.; Cramer, *Anecdota Græca*, ii. 393; Bachmann, *Anecdota*, i. 310) by δυσκίνητος, properly, μὴ κέλλων from κέλλειν = ταχέως τρέχειν. Pollux combines νώθεια, νωθρεία, ἀμβλύτης as synonyms. Luther's former rendering of νωθροί in our text was lässig, *i.e.* slothful, negligent.

later Nazarenes, a stunted growth and consequent lameness (see Dorner, *Entw.* i. 306), the author has already to lament in his Jewish-Christian readers. They are deficient in quickness of spiritual apprehension, and that, as intimated by γεγόνατε, in consequence of a falling back from their previous position to an alarming and unnatural degree.

Ver. 12. *For when ye ought for the time* (elapsed) *to be teachers, ye have again need that one should teach you how it stands with the very first elements of the word of God, and have become such as have need of milk, not solid food.*
If it be true, as Hartung maintains (see above at iv. 2), that the καί in καὶ γάρ has always a *cumulative* force, and, though placed at the commencement of a sentence, belongs properly to one of its following members, we must not leave it untranslated (as do Bleek, De Wette, and the majority of expositors), but reversing the inverted form of expression, connect it in our rendering with διδάσκαλοι (as, among others, Lünemann): *nam cum deberetis etiam magistri esse propter tempus.* I cannot, however, convince myself of the correctness of Hartung's canon, and continue, therefore, to hold, with Winer[1] and others, that καὶ γάρ is sometimes equivalent to *etenim*, sometimes to *nam etiam*. Here, with the majority, I take it in the sense of *etenim*.

Χρόνος (*period* in contradistinction to καιρός, *season* or *point* of time) is the whole time which has elapsed since these Hebrews first became believers in Christ,—a period of such length that they ought on this account to be not only far advanced in knowledge of the truth for themselves, but also to be the teachers of it to others. Nay, but—on the contrary—"ye stand again in need τοῦ διδάσκειν ὑμᾶς τινα τὰ στοιχεῖα τῆς ἀρχῆς τῶν λογίων τοῦ Θεοῦ." It has been made a question whether we should accentuate τινα here as τίνα, "which be," or τινά, "some one." All ancient versions and all patristic commentators, with Tholuck and De Wette, are in favour of τίνα, and so also reads Tischendorf. Luther, Calvin, Böhme, Bleek, Ebrard, and Lünemann adopt the meaning τινά, which is the reading of Lachmann. But this reading is maintained on grounds of no real value. For, 1*st*, it is not true that τινά

[1] *Gramm.* § 53, 8, Engl. transl. p. 468.

alone is grammatically possible, because otherwise the author must either have written διδάσκεσθαι or supplied another subject for διδάσκειν, such as ἡμᾶς, ἐμέ, or the like. So Lünemann. The truth is, that the thought "you are again in need of instruction" might be rendered equally well by διδάσκειν as by διδάσκεσθαι. Compare 1 Thess. v. 1, οὐ χρείαν ἔχετε ὑμῖν γράφεσθαι, with 1 Thess. iv. 19, οὐ χρείαν ἔχετε γράφειν ὑμῖν. And even if the argument from 1 Thess. iv. 9 be withdrawn by the other reading, οὐ χρείαν ἔχομεν,[1] being preferred, it remains beyond doubt that both constructions are equally allowable, and Winer seems to be right in supposing that the active construction may be more common than the passive.[2] One of the boldest examples is found in Euripides, *Iph. Aul.* 1477, 1478: *Bring hither wreaths; here is my hair to crown* (πλόκαμος ὅδε καταστέφειν). So here χρείαν ἔχετε τοῦ διδάσκειν ὑμᾶς is simply equivalent to "you have need of instruction." And again, it is, 2*dly,* not true that τίνα must be rejected on account of the sense, as if the reading τίνα would imply that the Hebrews are supposed to be in need of being told what points belong to the primary teaching of the gospel. De Wette rightly appeals against confining τίνα here to this very superficial meaning, to such places as Luke x. 22, xxiv. 17, Acts xvii. 19, etc. We need not interpret it as denoting a mere catalogue of the things intended. The question concerning the τί of anything goes beyond its bare name, and extends to its character and essence. We decide, therefore, in favour of τίνα, as against the weak expletive τινά. The Hebrew Christians are again in need of instructions as to the fundamental principles of Christianity, because, instead of building on them further, they have lost that very apprehension of those doctrines themselves which is necessary for any further development. In this didactic, not physical sense, στοιχεῖα (*elementa*) is also used, Gal. iv. 3, 9 and Col. ii. 8, 20, where it signifies the Old Testament cosmic beginnings in the divine education of the human race,—those legal ordinances which, too poor and weak in themselves to give inward perfection, were content with producing an outward appearance of sanctity and purity in the natural and bodily life of the individual or the people.

---

[1] So Lachmann. The Cod. Sin. reads ἔχετε.

[2] Winer, *Gramm.* § 44, Eng. transl. p. 355; Madvig, *Synt.* §§ 148*b*-150.

That the word is used in a didactic sense, is evident from those subjected to these στοιχεῖα being spoken of as in the age of νηπιότης and ὑπὸ παιδαγωγὸν. But here the distinction drawn is not between the revelations of the Old and New Testaments, as the former preparatory and the latter perfect, but one found within the New Testament revelation itself, between the elementary and the higher forms of teaching. This is clear from the τὸν τῆς ἀρχῆς τοῦ Χριστοῦ λόγον of vi. 1, in accordance with which we must interpret here. The genitive τῆς ἀρχῆς resembles a descriptive adjective—the first, fundamental elements (Luther, "the first letters," the A, B, C);[1] and τὰ λόγια τοῦ Θεοῦ (although, of course, it might be used to designate the Old Testament revelation, Acts vii. 38, Rom. iii. 2, yet here where Christians are addressed as such) is the revelation of the New Testament, the whole Word of God in relation to Jesus Christ, God's testimony to Him, and His own regarding Himself. These Hebrew Christians, instead of being able to give, have still need to receive instruction in the Word of God imparted under the New Testament (τὰ λόγια = ὁ λόγος), and this in consequence of a lamentable relapse which has brought them back to the age of childhood (needing milk), and the stage of catechumens, needing primary instruction, when they ought to be at man's estate, which requires the solid food of higher truth. In like manner, St. Paul (1 Cor. iii. 2) contrasts γάλα (milk) with βρῶμα (food); and Philo, γάλα or γαλακτώδης τροφή with that which is κραταιοτέρα, πεπηγυῖα, εὔτονος, τελεία. Solid food, in order to be transformed into chyle and blood (*in succum et sanguinem*), requires more powerful digestive organs than the babe, *ob stomachi teneritudinem* (Lactant. *Inst.* v. 4), is yet possessed of ; and hence it is used to designate such kinds of knowledge as not only require a spiritual receptivity for their appropriation, but such as can be gained only by means of an intense personal exercise of the spiritual intelligence, and that based upon an inward, experimental knowledge which has been already acquired. The older commentators ask here, What, then, are the doctrines which the author includes under the term γάλα? and without waiting for the explanation given by himself, vi. 1 sq., they make all sorts of useless suppositions on

---

[1] Germ. *die ersten Buchstaben;* or, in an earlier text of Luther's version, "*das erste Schulrecht.*"

the subject. This only is already obvious here, that the high-priesthood of Christ and its character resembling that of Aaron (by way of antitype), and that of Melchizedek (according to prophecy), is reckoned by our author among the higher subjects of Christian knowledge. Such solid food, he says, belongs not properly to them, *they* need the milk of elementary instruction. The inference drawn from this by Mynster and Ebrard, that the Epistle to the Hebrews could not have been addressed to Palestinian churches, or at least not to the original mother church as such, rests on a misunderstanding. For, though constrained thus to reproach his readers with their ignorance and incapacity, he yet goes on to speak to them of these higher things. His πάλιν χρείαν ἔχετε must not, therefore, be taken in too absolute a sense. A conclusion is drawn as to their knowledge from their conduct. Whoever suffered himself to be shaken or seduced from his Christian profession by the outward splendour of the Jewish worship, or by the offence taken at the cross, or by the Jewish rejection of the crucified and now invisible Saviour (and such cases must have been numerous in the Jewish-Christian churches of Palestine, held as they were in dangerous proximity to the unbelieving synagogue by their attachment to the ritual prescribed in the law),—whoever seemed so shaken in his allegiance to Christ showed thereby that he had lost all true and living knowledge of the elements of Christian faith, and that for him no solid food, but only milk, was a fitting nourishment.

Vers. 13, 14. *For every one that partaketh of milk is inexperienced in rightly ordered speech, for he is a child; but the solid food belongs to the perfect, to such as by reason of habit have their perceptive organs in a well-trained condition for distinguishing between good and evil.*

The author explains what was meant when he said that his readers have need of milk, not of solid food, by exhibiting the state of one who uses milk; and what, on the contrary, their condition should be for whom solid food is suitable nourishment. And this description he holds before them as a mirror, in which to view and examine themselves. Had he, as Bleek would have it, placed the first clause in the reverse order, πᾶς γὰρ ὁ ἄπειρος, κ.τ.λ., he would have directly affirmed of them that they were such ἄπειροι; but this he avoids doing by a delicate inversion, though with slight detriment to the symmetry of the members of the sentence. Μετέχειν γάλακτος is to partake of milk, as Philo (i. 440) says with reference to one who has found in the sacred Logos the home of his spirit, that *there* τὸ νηπίας καὶ γαλακτώδους τροφῆς ἀμέτοχον finds its true resting-place; comp. also St. Paul's expression (1 Cor. x. 21), τραπέζης κυρίου μετέχειν. Λόγος δικαιοσύνης is, from the wide application of both ideas, capable of various interpretations. One question is, whether λόγος here signifies doctrine or discourse? and another, whether δικαιοσύνη denotes the quality or the subject of this λόγος? Almost all moderns render the words, " doctrine of righteousness "[1] (so Bleek, Tholuck, Ebrard, Lünemann), or " doctrine which conducts to righteousness" (De Wette), understanding δικαιοσύνη of moral perfection in general, or (as for instance Lünemann) of the righteousness of faith in particular, and in the Pauline sense. I also have been wont to explain it in the same way. The author might have said, " *inexperienced in the word of God;*" but prefers to define the word, not by its Author, but by its essential contents or principal subject, viz. the δικαιοσύνη Θεοῦ revealed in the gospel (Rom. i. 17) considered as to the mode of its attainment, ἡ κατὰ πίστιν δικαιοσύνη (xi. 7). Λόγος δικαιοσύνης might be therefore regarded as like νόμος δικαιοσύνης, Rom. ix. 31, comp. διάκονοι δικαιοσύνης, 2 Cor. xi. 5, without the article, because δικαιοσ. expresses the quality or ideal character of the word in question as one which has righteousness for its contents or subject; and such a word the gospel is.[2] Against this interpretation, however, is, that it is unsupported by the context, and involves a reference so remote as to βασιλεὺς δικαιοσύνης (vii. 2). The objection is not indeed conclusive, since it is open to a writer to use expressions not related to those in the context when their meaning is otherwise known or clear. But if in this case another construction is possible, which brings λόγου δικαιοσύνης into closer connection with the context, the preference is certainly due to it.

[1] Germ. *Lehre von der Gerechtigkeit*, doctrine or teaching concerning righteousness.
[2] So " the ministry of the word" is also called, 2 Cor. iii. 9, ἡ διακονία τῆς δικαιοσύνης.

Now as νήπιος (from νη and ἔπος) signifies one incapable of speech, a babe, there is a presumption that λόγος in ἄπειρος λόγου δικαιοσύνης signifies power of speech; for λόγος is used not only for the gift of eloquence (Luke xxiv. 19, δυνατὸς ἐν λόγῳ; 2 Cor. xi. 6, ἰδιώτης τῷ λόγῳ), but also for ordinary speech; and seeing the word αἰσθητήρια occurs in the antithetical parallel clause, this meaning is so much the more probable here, as ὁ λόγος, in the meaning "speech" or "faculty of speaking," occurs in Philo innumerable times in connection with αἴσθησις, or the πέντε αἰσθήσεις (Grossmann, Quæst. Philon. ii. 13–16), the organs of which are called αἰσθητήρια (Philo, i. 123, 29; 134, 11). The genitival combination λόγος δικαιοσύνης resembles the Hebrew מאזני צדק, אבני צדק, זבחי צדק (*i.e.* stones, sacrifices, scales of righteousness), and the like, and is not without example elsewhere in the New Testament. As, 1 Cor. xii. 8 (on which see Olshausen), λόγος σοφίας signifies the gift of speaking wisely, and λόγος γνώσεως the gift of speaking with understanding, so λόγος δικαιοσύνης signifies ability to speak in accordance with righteousness,—the same which Philo frequently calls ὀρθὸς λόγος (*sermo rectus*), the Hebrew for which would be דְּבַר צֶדֶק. We regard δικαιοσύνης· therefore, as here the genitive of quality, but not as to be taken in the superficial sense in which Böhme explains it, "*Sermo iustus*, i.e. *loquela satis ad intelligendum composita.*" As τὰ αἰσθητήρια does not mean the outward organs of sense, but the inward ones of spiritual perception, so λόγος here is not natural discourse, but such as relates to spiritual things; and connected here with δικαιοσύνης, it means discourse concerning spiritual things in strict conformity with truth, examining, balancing, and harmoniously grouping all the elements which enter into the case.[1] Δικαιοσύνη is here, as צֶדֶק, יֹשֶׁר, מֵישָׁרִים, frequently, the synonym of ἀλήθεια and antithesis of ψεῦδος (comp. ψευδολογίας λόγοι, Philo, ii. 259, 30). With this interpretation the connection of ideas in ver. 13 becomes a very strict one. He who must still use milk (*i.e.* can only deal with or comprehend the first doctrines and elements of Christianity) is still

---

[1] Ἐστὶ γὰρ ἰσότης (says Philo, ii. 373) ὡς οἱ τὰ φύσεως ἀκριβοῦντες ἡμῖν παρέδοσαν, μητὴρ δικαιοσύνης· ἰσότης δὲ φῶς ἄσκιον, ἥλιος εἰ δεῖ τἀληθὲς εἰπεῖν, νοητός· ἐπειδὴ καὶ τοὐναντίον ἀνισότης, ἐν ᾧ τό τε ὑπερέχον καὶ τὸ ὑπερεχόμενον σκότους ἀρχή τε καὶ πηγή.

unskilful in rightly framed, that is, in sound or orthodox discourse, as being but a child, who just begins with stammering lips to use his unformed organs of speech. The antithesis of νήπιος, Eph. iv. 14, 1 Cor. iii. 1, is τέλειος, 1 Cor. ii. 6, which is here also used in the special sense of *adultus*, a grown man; comp. εἰς ἄνδρα τέλειον, of attainment to the ripeness of Christian knowledge, Eph. iv. 13.[1] It is not to children in understanding, but to τέλειοι, those in full manhood, that solid food belongs. The added participial clause, τῶν διὰ τὴν ἕξιν τὰ αἰσθητήρια γεγυμνασμένα ἐχόντων πρὸς διάκρισιν καλοῦ τε καὶ κακοῦ, has the article, because it further describes these so-called τέλειοι, and establishes indirectly what has been said of them (Winer, § 59). Τὰ αἰσθητήρια is object, and γεγυμνασμένα predicate, as in the similar passage in Galen, *de dign. puls.* iii.: ὃς μὲν γὰρ τὸ αἰσθητήριον ἔχει γεγυμνασμένον ἱκανῶς ... οὗτος ἄριστος ἂν εἴη γνώμων. "Perfect" men, men of full age spiritually, are those who possess developed by exercise (γεγυμνασμένα) all the capacities of spiritual apprehension,—these capacities being thus developed διὰ τὴν ἕξιν, by reason of the readiness acquired by use; ἕξις is here used in the same sense as that in which Philo (i. 45) says, that a man, to be formed for independent thinking, should in the first seven years learn to understand ordinary names and words, λογικὴν ἕξιν περιποιούμενος, so acquiring a readiness in the use of language, and familiarity with the notions with which it deals. The advantage to its possessor of a mind thus formed is indicated by πρὸς διάκρισιν καλοῦ τε καὶ κακοῦ. He is able, with independent taste and judgment, to discern what is good and wholesome, and what bad or deleterious, in the multiplicity that is offered him as spiritual food; it not being enough to have mere derived opinions imprinted on the mind: in addition to this, there must be, to speak with Philo, ii. 353, διαστολὴ τούτων καὶ διαίρεσις εἴς τε αἵρεσιν ὧν χρὴ καὶ φυγὴν τῶν ἐναντίων.

This state of τελειότης is, alas, not found in the Hebrew Christians who are here addressed, and yet is it the natural goal of all spiritual growth. The author therefore exhorts them to strive after it, offering on his part to aid them in

[1] In the same way Philo also contrasts the νήπιος with the τέλειος, i. p. 62, ed. Mangey: οὐδενὸς ... τούτων ὁ τέλειος δεῖται ... τῷ δὲ νηπίῳ παραινέσεως καὶ διδασκαλίας (ἐστι χρεία).

attaining it, if that be still possible, seeing it is now long since they had first received instruction in the elements of Christianity, and instead of advancing, had stood still, or rather retrograded:

Chap. vi. 1–3. *Therefore, leaving the first elementary doctrine of Christ, let us press on unto perfection; not laying again the foundation in repentance from dead works and faith in God, in the doctrine of baptisms and of laying on of hands, of the resurrection of the dead and of eternal judgment. And this let us do, if so be God permit.*

Some commentators regard this sentence as the sacred writer's declaration of his purpose (Klee, De Wette, Tholuck, etc.), others as an exhortation to his readers (Böhme, Bleek, Ebrard, Lünemann, Hofmann (*Schriftbeweis*, i. 553)); but no one has put the question whether we have actually to decide for the one view to the exclusion of the other. The words διὸ ἐπὶ τὴν τελειότητα φερώμεθα, taken by themselves, appear no doubt to be a communicative exhortation, in which the writer includes his readers along with himself; but the participial clauses ἀφέντες and καταβαλλόμενοι render it quite impossible for us to regard the whole passage as such. A teacher might indeed well say that he intends to leave on one side the fundamental truths of Christianity, and not to begin his present work by laying again the foundation of Christian life and doctrine; but if his intention were to exhort his fellow-Christians to strive after the maturer knowledge of spiritual manhood, and to this end he bade them neglect the fundamental truths of their religion, and lay no more the foundation in repentance, etc., that would, considering the inseparable connection between the foundation and the building, commencement and progress, surely be strange and dangerous advice, and especially so in the mouth of our author, who has readers in view in whom, as we have heard, the foundation of Christianity, laid long ago, was certainly in need of strengthening and renewal. We *must* therefore assume that the plural in this passage partly belongs to the author alone (as v. 11, ii. 5), and is partly inclusive of him and his readers, and that in the following way: Therefore, he would say (because a Christian cannot possibly remain always a child, but must, if he fall not away, grow on to ever higher and maturer knowledge), let us endeavour to arrive at the state of the τέλειοι—that is, such maturity in knowledge as is capable of a right spiritual judgment, and such fulness of age as is required for a stedfast and worthy profession; and let us do this by my imparting instructions corresponding to the state referred to, and by your seeking to follow these instructions: and this (namely, this φέρεσθαι ἐπὶ τὴν τελειότητα) let us do (ποιήσωμεν to be preferred, with Bleek and Lünemann, as a better supported reading to the ποιήσομεν retained by Lchm. and Tischendorf), so far at least as God may permit, *i.e.* permit me to help you forward, who have lingered behind by your own fault so long, and permit you to draw the intended benefit from my efforts on your behalf. In this way, then, the author includes himself with his readers in the two main propositions φερώμεθα and ποιήσωμεν. In ἐάνπερ ἐπιτρέπῃ ὁ Θεός the fear is indicated of the impossibility of helping forward to a higher stage those who had fallen back so far, or remained behind so long. On the other hand, the participial clauses are so placed, that grammatically they have the same twofold subject (the writer and his readers) with φερώμεθα and ποιήσωμεν, but logically their principal reference is to the writer,—a reference which governs and determines the choice of the terms used. There is nothing unnatural in this: it would be allowable for any of us to say, if we had to do with backward scholars, Let us think earnestly of higher knowledge, and leave aside what you ought to have gone over long ago; let us press forward, unless indeed your having stood still so long has made you incapable of doing so. Φέρεσθαι (*ferri*) is used very appropriately here with ἐπί of the mark or object aimed at: it combines the notion of an impulse from without with that of eager and onward pressing haste (comp. Acts ii. 2, where it also signifies *cum impetu ferri*). De Wette and others are mistaken in understanding φερώμεθα as said exclusively of the writer, and in consequence τελειότητα as designating merely a fully developed line of teaching; whereas it refers at once to knowledge and to life, to word and action (λόγος, ἔργα), and here especially to the fulness of spiritual knowledge manifesting itself in a Christian profession as the antithesis of νηπιότης. Ἀφιέναι is the usual word employed by an orator or writer when he declines to speak of a subject which presents itself for consideration, in order to revert to or to discuss another. What the author here intends to leave on one side is the τὰ στοιχεῖα τῆς ἀρχῆς τῶν λογίων τοῦ Θεοῦ of v. 12, which he now describes as the τὸν τῆς ἀρχῆς τοῦ Χριστοῦ λόγον. As above τὰ στοιχεῖα τῆς ἀρχῆς were the primary elements, so here ὁ λόγος τῆς ἀρχῆς is the primitive word or witness (of the gospel), and τοῦ Χριστοῦ is a *genitivus objecti* (ὁ λόγος τοῦ Χρ., like ὁ λ. τοῦ Κυρίου or τοῦ Θεοῦ[1] = τὸ εὐαγγέλιον). It is, then, that instruction regarding Christ with which a beginning is made by all preachers of the gospel that is now to be passed over, in order to advance to higher developments of divine truth.[2]

Like ἀφέντες, we have in μὴ πάλιν θεμέλιον καταβαλλόμενοι a current phrase to express the ordinary methodical procedure of the instructor, who, in teaching, first "lays the foundation," and then builds upon it. Ebrard acknowledges this, but only to adopt in its room the perverse interpretation, "not again throwing down the foundation" (as if warning against apostasy or unbelief). There being nothing new under the sun, he can, it seems, find authority for even such a strange perversion as this, and appeals to a rendering in the Itala— "*non iterum fundamentum diruentes.*" But "throwing down" (*dejicere*) would neither in itself be the proper expression for "destroying" a foundation ; nor, though καταβάλλειν has the sense of *dejicere* or *diruere*, can this be extended to the middle καταβάλλεσθαι here, especially as καταβάλλεσθαι θεμέλιον is the regular antithesis of ἐποικοδομεῖν[3] (comp. also Philo, i. 266,

[1] It has been already observed that St. Luke almost invariably employs some such *periphrasis* for εὐαγγέλιον.
[2] ὁ λόγος τῆς ἀρχῆς is a peculiar Hebraizing construction. In Hebrew, however, the word corresponding to ἀρχῆς, whether ראשׁ, ראשׁית, or תחלה, would have to take the first place, as the Peshito renders here, "the beginning of the word of Messiah"—*schurojo de-melthe da-meshicho.* The three words, ἀρχή, ἀφείς, φέρεσθαι, are found together in a place in Euripides (*Androm.* 392), first pointed out by Wetstein :

Τὴν ἀρχὴν ἀφεὶς
Πρὸς τὴν τελευτὴν ὑστέραν οὖσαν φέρῃ.

[3] Comp. Eurip. *Herc. Fur.* 1261, 1262 :

"Οταν δὲ κρηπὶς μὴ καταβληθῇ γένους
Ὀρθῶς ἀνάγκη δυστυχεῖν τοὺς ἐκγόνους.

ὑποβάλλεσθαι θεμέλιον; ii. 289, βάλλεσθαι θεμέλιον; and 1 Cor. iii. 10, τιθέναι θεμέλιον). The three following pairs of genitives are instances of the so-called *genitivus appositionis* (Winer, § 59, pp. 503, 504, Eng. transl.), indicating what the "foundation" is, or wherewith the "laying" of such foundation has to do. It is usual to speak of six points of doctrine here, but properly we have only four points of doctrine preceded by two features of Christian life— Repentance and Faith. The word διδαχῆς does not stand before μετανοίας, but only before βαπτισμῶν. The sacred writer most clearly distinguishes (says Hofmann) between what they ought no longer to have to do (*i.e.* begin again to repent and believe) and what they ought no longer to have to learn (the doctrines connected with baptism, etc.). The Christian life begins with a turning away from such a life or course of action as is destitute of life from God, and a turning to God in living faith and trust in Him. This is the μετάνοια ἀπὸ νεκρῶν ἔργων and the πίστις ἐπὶ Θεόν which is here spoken of. He who has made such a beginning, is next taught the significance of the two rites of baptism and imposition of hands which the church performs on him: he is taught what is there done to him, and what God will one day do for him, when He shall raise from the dead him who has been sealed with the Holy Spirit, and by a final judgment shall associate for ever with the blessed him who is here separated by the waters of baptism from an evil world. The author, therefore, is not here speaking of a doctrine concerning the nature of faith in contrast with higher points of doctrine, but of the commencement of the Christian life (the first "believing," Rom. xiii. 11) in contrast with its riper age (*vid.* Hofmann, *Schriftb.* i. 553). In this way Hofmann very justly refutes the false inference drawn by Ritschl and others from our passage, that faith occupies a lower position in our author's system than in St. Paul's. In a certain sense, however, it may be said that, even in our author's view, repentance and faith are the two first and fundamental doctrines of Christianity. They represent the order of development of divine grace, into which no one can enter unless taught both from law and gospel regarding the necessity and nature both of repentance and of faith; and so, accordingly, our Catechism begins with the Decalogue and the Creed. But, as we have said already, if we regard the actual form of the expression, it is certainly not instruction as to the way of salvation, but the actual entering on that way itself, which is here spoken of as the first foundation of Christianity. The laying of that foundation has to do, first (in the case of unbelievers), with repentance and faith as negative and positive commencements of the new life; and secondly (in the case of catechumens), with the doctrine of the two initiatory sacramental actions and that of the "last things," which will form the corporeo-spiritual and eternal consummation of the new life begun in repentance and faith here, and sealed, enriched, advanced by baptism, and its accompanying rite of the laying on of hands. We will now consider separately these three pairs of *fundamentalia*.

I. The first is that of *repentance from dead works and of faith towards God*—(μετανοίας ἀπὸ νεκρῶν ἔργων καὶ πίστεως ἐπὶ Θεόν). The construction μετάνοια ἀπό is found in St. Luke (Acts viii. 22); and πιστεύειν ἐπὶ (Θεόν or τὸν Κύριον), while not quite without example in St. Paul (comp. Rom. iv. 5, 24), is (with πιστ. εἰς) at least a more usual expression in St. Luke than in any other writer of the New Testament (Acts ix. 42, xi. 17, xvi. 31, xxii. 19). In substance, the τὴν εἰς Θεὸν μετάνοιαν of Acts xx. 21 is equivalent to the πίστεως ἐπὶ Θεόν here: both seem to say so little, and in truth include so much. The Word of God begins its work in a man by addressing his innermost self, his proper *Ego*. The first thing one has to do is to change or turn with the νοῦς (μετάνοια), *i.e.* the whole self-conscious, self-determined personal intelligence, away from (ἀπὸ) νεκρῶν ἔργων. The interpretation of νεκρὰ ἔργα (here and at ix. 14) given by Köstlin (*Lehrbegriff*, p. 400 seq.), as equivalent to ἔργα ἄκαρπα ("dead," *i.e.* "fruitless" works), is true so far as it goes, but not exhaustive. Hofmann's is better —though he perhaps exceeds the writer's meaning—"all such acts as belong to that death which reigns in the natural world" (*Weiss*. ii. 166). Better still is his definition referred to above: "every act or course of action in which is not inherent a life from God." So also Bleek, De Wette, Tholuck, Lünemann, and most moderns. "Dead works" are works which have not their source or motive power in a life from God, and are consequently destitute of any true worth before Him. They have no power to act for good on the world without, nor to react for good on the doer himself, and are therefore *fruitless*: they bear no abiding fruit in the kingdom of God. In this term is included all that in Hebrew is called שָׁוְא, that is, show without substance, or אָוֶן (from אין, *spirare*), lightness, vanity,— the opposite of what has any reality or true worth, and especially the *opus operatum* or pharisaical righteousness of the Jewish hypocrite, which Philo depicts in the remarkable passage concerning ceremonial worship (i. 195): "He also wanders from the path of godliness who thinks that ritual observance may take the place of true sanctity."

In contrast to this, the grace of God produces in the mind, which it has turned away from "dead works," an immediate personal relation and self-surrender to Him, as manifested in the gospel; and this is its second product, πίστις ἐπὶ Θεόν. Faith in its deepest ground is trust towards and upon the self-revealing God (*fiducia*); and the personal relation to God, which is constituted by faith, is opposed here to every other, the result of outward work or ceremonial observance. It is purposely designated as πίστις ἐπὶ Θεόν; for faith in God, the God of salvation, is not distinct from, but inclusive of, faith in our Lord Jesus Christ. So John xiv. 1, *Ye believe in God, believe also in me; i.e.* remain united, as with God the invisible by faith, so also with me, when I shall have returned to Him, and ye see me no more. In view of the scrupulous persistence of Judaism in the exclusive dogma of the unity of God (יִחוּד הַשֵׁם), it was specially necessary to insist on this point of πίστις ἐπὶ Θεόν, in reasoning with Jewish Christians not yet firmly grounded in the faith. After mentioning the two chief constituents of the foundation of Christian life, the author next speaks of the elementary doctrines to be imparted to those who have entered on the way of salvation. They follow ἀσυνδέτως, without connective particle, in order to make the living basis of all the more prominent.

II. The second pair of *fundamentalia* is βαπτισμῶν διδαχῆς ἐπιθέσεώς τε χειρῶν. The reading διδαχήν (only B.) would deserve no consideration had it not been adopted by Lchm. It shows, however, that the writer of the Vatican MS. connected βαπτισμῶν as a governed genitive with διδ. ("doctrine of baptisms"). And so far he was certainly in the right. For it is quite impossible (a) to separate βαπτισμῶν διδαχῆς by a comma, and regard διδαχῆς as standing by itself as an independent *fundamental* (so Erasmus, Luther, and many others, and in our own day De Wette and Höfling (*Sacrament der Taufe*, i. 94)). This, among other reasons, has the logical one against it, that διδαχή, whether taken to signify the necessary catechetical instruction or the contents of such instruction, would form, if regarded as a separate *fundamental*, a member of the group quite disparate from all the rest. For in the former sense διδαχή would be an independent ecclesiastical institution, *i.e.* the office or function of catechetical teaching; and in the latter it would, by the worst possible manner of dividing, be introduced into the midst of things which form parts of itself. It is equally impossible (b) to make διδαχῆς the governed genitive after βαπτισμῶν, as *e.g.* Bengel renders it—*baptisms of doctrine*—a rendering still defended by Winer (§ 30, 3, note 4, p. 205, Eng. transl.). His words are: " *The rendering of* βαπτισμοὶ διδαχῆς *by* '*baptisms upon instruction,*' *as designating the peculiarly Christian rites, and so distinguishing them from the legal baptisms or lustrations of the Jews, is supported by* Matt. xxviii. 19, βαπτίσαντες—διδάσκοντες. *The objection to this urged by Ebrard, that Christian baptism is distinguished from those lustrations, not by the special instructions connected with it, but by the remission of sins and regeneration, is of no weight,* Matt. xxviii. *saying nothing about remission of sins.*" But, in fact, βαπτισμοὶ διδαχῆς would be almost the worst possible designation of *Christian* baptisms, if meant to distinguish them from what no doubt would here be primarily referred to—the baptisms of proselytes among the Jews.[1] No Jewish proselyte would receive baptism without being previously instructed in his new religious faith and duties; and

---

[1] Baptism was held to be as indispensable as circumcision for converts to Judaism, according to the maxim לעולם אינו גר עד שימול ויטביל—He only is a proselyte who has been circumcised and baptized. After מילה (circumcision) and טבילה (baptism) a third indispensable requisite was קרבן (the offering a sacrifice—corban): a proselyte had to testify by offering a sacrifice, that he had entered into the fellowship of Israel; and even after the destruction of Jerusalem, he had to deposit a fixed sum to buy a victim when the temple service should be restored. This, however, was abolished by R. Jochanan for fear of abuse (*Talm. Babl. Cherithoth* 9a).

CHAP. VI. 1-3. 273

in any case, the author of our epistle could hardly have chosen a more ambiguous and unsuitable expression than this, which is capable of such various interpretations.[1] Had it been his purpose to define more closely the baptism of the gospel, he would have used quite a different epexegetical genitive—as, for instance, βάπτισμα παλιγγενεσίας, or the like.

We must therefore take βαπτισμῶν as dependent on διδαχῆς; and then, without violation of grammar, we may either (with the Peshito) make ἐπιθέσεώς τε χειρῶν a second dependent genitive, or adopt another construction, such as that given by Jo. Gerhard:[2] *doctrina catechumenis tradi solita, antequam baptizarentur vel manuum impositione in fide Christiana confirmarentur.* But the illogicalness of the division tells almost as much against this view as against taking διδαχῆς apart by itself. And therefore not only βαπτισμῶν, but also ἐπιθέσεως, ἀναστάσεως, and κρίματος must be construed as dependent on διδαχῆς (Bleek, Tholuck, Ebrard, Hofmann, Lünemann). Rightly understood, there is nothing strange in the syntax here. Böhme translates correctly, *baptismorum doctrinæ et (doctrinæ) impositionis manuum.* It is an instance of brachylogy: βαπτισμῶν διδαχῆς ἐπιθέσεώς τε χειρῶν for βαπτισμῶν διδαχῆς, διδαχῆς τε ἐπιθέσεως χειρῶν.[3] The question now is : What kind of doctrine is διδαχὴ βαπτισμῶν? In every other passage Christian baptism is called βάπτισμα, whereas βαπτισμοί is the name given to the Jewish washings (ix. 10; Mark vii. 4-8). Attempts are made to explain the plural here as applied exclusively to

---

[1] Bengel, for instance, explains it quite differently from Winer. His words are : " Βαπτισμοὶ διδαχῆς erant *baptismi*, quos qui suscipiebant, *doctrinæ* sacræ Judæorum sese addicebant. Itaque adjecto διδαχῆς *doctrinæ* distinguuntur a lotionibus ceteris leviticis," c. ix. 10.

[2] Which is apparently that of the Vulgate, and is so interpreted by Remiguis-Primasius, etc.

[3] The scheme is that of an imperfect χιασμός, one member of which is suppressed. It is in Latin a not unusual construction, that when the two central members of such χιασμός consist of one and the same word twice repeated, this word may, under certain circumstances, be omitted, now from the former, now from the latter member of the sentence, while the position of the remaining words remains such as to exhibit the *chiastic* character of the whole (Nägelsbach, *Lat. Stylistik*, § 167, 4). The same construction is possible also in Greek, there being also not unfrequently an inversion of the governing and governed genitive, *e.g.* Thuc. i. 143, ὀλίγων ἡμερῶν ἕνεκα μεγάλου μισθοῦ δόσεως.

Christian baptism, by referring (1) to the ancient practice of trine immersion; or (2) to the multiplicity of the candidates and of the acts of baptism performed on their behalf.[1] But of these explanations, the former is, in the outset, open to the objection that it takes for granted a custom to which the New Testament bears no witness,[2] and the second makes the plural quite objectless. The proper and now almost universally received explanation—which, however, Köstlin (p. 447) groundlessly rejects—is, that the plural βαπτισμοί denotes Christian baptism, along with the Jewish baptism of proselytes, and that of John inclusive (Böhme, Klee, Bleek, von Gerlach, Hofmann, Lünemann, Biesenthal, and many others). We must at the same time reject the particular inference drawn from this βαπτισμῶν by Tholuck and others, that the author designedly names such points of doctrine as " *do not constitute the essence of Christian faith, but were in some degree known to his Jewish-Christian readers already as Jews, and therefore might be still adhered to by those of the church who were otherwise ready to relapse into Judaism.*" The six points named were doubtless one and all recognised by the synagogue also as *fundamentalia*. Their Jewish names would be: תשובה, repentance; אמונה, faith; טבילה, baptism; סמיכה, laying on of hands; יום הדין, day of judgment; and תחיה, life everlasting, or resurrection. These six points would therefore of necessity be (not in some degree only, but) perfectly familiar to educated Jewish Christians; but yet as conditions, *media*, or issues of salvation in a Jewish sense, they could not possibly be styled the θεμέλιος of Christian life and doctrine, or " the beginning of the word of Christ" (ὁ τῆς ἀρχῆς τοῦ Χριστοῦ λόγος): such they could become only as enlarged and enriched with deeper meanings, by new relations and disclosures under the gospel.

This is precisely what the plural βαπτισμῶν indicates, as I find already observed by Schlichting, and still better by Schöttgen. The Christian catechumen coming out of Judaism

---

[1] Maintained latterly by De Wette, who hesitates between the two methods of explanation.

[2] The earliest testimony to trine immersion is in the τρία βαπτίσματα μιᾶς μυήσεως of the Apostolical Canons, on which Zonaras says: τρία βαπτίσματα ἐνταῦθα τὰς τρεῖς καταδύσεις φησὶν ὁ κανὼν ἐν μιᾷ μυήσει ἤτοι ἐν ἑνὶ βαπτίσματι. The Jewish proselyte was immersed only once.

had to be instructed how New Testament baptism in the name of Jesus, or of the Triune God, is distinguished by its sacramental, inwardly-transforming, and mysterious character from the lustrations of the law, and from the traditional טְבִילָה enjoined along with circumcision on Gentile proselytes to Judaism (or in the case of female proselytes supplying its place), as well as from the preparatory baptism of John, which paved the way for the coming kingdom, and was itself called by Josephus (xviii. 5, 2) βαπτισμός and βάπτισις. Now follows (connected with the particle τε, "as also"[1]) the second member of the second pair of *fundamentalia*—ἐπιθέσεώς τε χειρῶν. What is here referred to is (at least primarily and principally) the imposition of hands, which in the apostolic age was connected with baptism, and followed it either immediately, as at Acts xix. 5 sq., or as a later complement, as at Acts viii. 15-17. Hofmann is the first [amongst us] who has properly appreciated the distinction between baptism and imposition of hands. Baptism brings the man as a person into the state of grace, the imposition of hands qualifies him for bearing witness; the former translates him out of the world into the fellowship of Christ, the latter by means of marvellous gifts[2] enables him to serve Christ in the world; the former ministers to him the divine χάρις, the latter the manifold divine χαρίσματα (2 Tim. i. 6).

It is very significant—and, as in the case of every other apostolic word, it demands serious consideration here—that the author of our epistle reckons the doctrine of the imposition of hands among the fundamental articles of Christianity. As the purpose of the ordinance was to qualify for independent participation in the official work of the Christian church, its separation in time from baptism (with which it was not always connected even in the apostolic age) has been necessitated since the church began regularly to renew herself out of the bosom

[1] Originally identical with τεῖ or τῇ (as is generally recognised since Hartung's investigations), and from that softened down to an enclitic.

[2] [The expression in the ancient prayer for the clergy and people, *Who alone workest great marvels* (qui facis mirabilia magna solus), *send down upon our bishops*, etc., *the healthful spirit of Thy grace*, appears to refer to the miraculous gifts originally connected with the illapse of the Holy Spirit. The prayer is as old as the fifth century. Palmer, *Orig.* lib. i. p. 278.—TR.]

of the family, and so children to be ordinarily baptized; but it still continues a fundamental condition of the revival of church life that confirmation be restored to its proper place as a complement to baptism, and that the imposition of hands be regarded as the means of imparting the gift of the Holy Ghost, which the church, in virtue of being the body of Christ, and having dwelling within her the fulness of His Spirit, is empowered to dispense. It is not meant that the imposition of hands is to be regarded as a sacrament in the sense in which baptism and the Lord's supper are so: still something of a sacramental character attaches to it; for while, on the one hand, it is an apostolic ordinance in which the Lord's own example is followed, it is on the other, by virtue of the word of prayer and blessing connected with it, an effectual means of conveying heavenly (although for the time no longer extraordinary) gifts. The ancient synagogue had no סמיכה connected with its טבילה. Excepting the סמיכה of the offerer made on the head of the victim before its sacrifice, Judaism knows of no other imposition of hands but that employed in the ordination of a rabbi; and that form, moreover, is regarded as permissible only within the borders of the promised land. But Christianity, by connecting, through the employment of the same sign in both cases, the solemn ordination of the clergy to the special ministries of the church with that initiation to the general Christian service and warfare which in the form of confirmation ordinarily follows upon every baptism, has set its seal on the essential unity of the universal priesthood of all Christians with the special priesthood of the Christian ministry.

From all this it will follow that the "doctrine of the laying on of hands" here referred to will have consisted, in conjunction with that of "baptisms," first, in instruction with regard to the various operations of the Holy Ghost, given through baptism on the one hand, and through imposition of hands on the other; then in instruction regarding the right way of preparing one's self to receive by baptism the spirit of faith, and by imposition of hands the spirit of power; and finally, in instruction how to retain faithfully and employ conscientiously the justifying and sanctifying grace received in the one, and the special gifts for the benefit of the church and of the world which were ministered by the other.¹ (See Acts viii. 14–17, xix. 5 sq.; comp. x. 44 sqq., ii. 38.) It may cause surprise that the author should thus expressly mention the imposition of hands, and be totally silent regarding the Lord's supper. We cannot, of course, evade this difficulty by the hypothesis that he is naming only such "fundamentals" as required nothing more than a course of good Jewish instruction to be appreciated and understood (Bengel, Tholuck, etc.), for that hypothesis we have already found to be incorrect. It must therefore be assumed that the sacred writer gives us here only the main outlines of the instruction imparted to Christian catechumens, and that the mystery of the Lord's supper was excluded from it.² The author (it should be well observed) is not enumerating everything of fundamental importance in the great whole of Christian truth, but first those practical facts of spiritual experience with which Christian life commences, and then those instructions with which the church meets on the threshold one who, having repented and believed, asks for reception into her communion. The first point in such instruction will be regarding that baptism and imposition of hands which he is about to receive. The next follows in the third and last pair of *fundamentalia*.

III. These are ἀναστάσεώς τε νεκρῶν καὶ κρίματος αἰωνίου. These genitives are also dependent on διδαχῆς, which governs all four points of doctrine, ranged in successive order, and connected by τε... τε... καί. It may be asked, In what sense are the doctrines of the resurrection and eternal judgment connected with those of baptism and the laying on of hands? No modern expositor has entered so thoroughly into this question as Hofmann. According to him, the laying on of hands stands in the same relation to the resurrection as baptism to eternal judgment, inasmuch as that which baptism prophetically points to is fulfilled in the final judgment, and the grace which is conveyed by the laying on of hands is consummated in the

¹ See Note A at the end of this volume.
² This is also L. J. Rückert's opinion: We may conclude from this that (the apostolic writer) did not reckon the doctrine of the Lord's supper to those belonging to the first foundation, but would reserve it for the age of τελειότης. That he could have held it in small esteem, no one acquainted with the Epistle to the Hebrews could possibly imagine.

resurrection. For βαπτισμός and κρῖμα αἰώνιον, in and after this life, place a man, as a person, in the state of grace; while ἐπίθεσις χειρῶν and ἀνάστασις νεκρῶν, in and after this life, constitute his human nature a vehicle for the manifestation of grace (*Weiss.* ii. 243) : in other words, ἀνάστασις is the perfect glorification of that nature which has been fitted by the laying on of hands for the work of God; while κρῖμα αἰώνιον is the entrance on the manifestation and full enjoyment of that blessedness which was sacramentally made ours in baptism. Elsewhere, however (*Schriftbeweis*, i. 554), Hofmann states the mutual relation otherwise, and, as seems to me, less happily : in the ἀνάστασις is fulfilled that to which we have been sealed by the Holy Ghost; in the κρῖμα αἰώνιον it will be declared how we have been previously delivered from that judgment which separates eternally from God. I find these parallels less happy; because that Spirit of grace and promise which is the earnest of our final redemption, and especially of our resurrection to eternal life (2 Cor. v. 5 ; Eph. i. 14), is not first imparted through the laying on of hands, but through holy baptism. And baptism, moreover, which as a λουτρὸν παλιγγενεσίας implants in the midst of our old natural life the commencement of a new and spiritual life, stands in at least comparatively closer relation to the resurrection, in which this παλιγγενεσία will be perfected, than does the laying on of hands. Hence we conclude that such a *chiastic* relation as that supposed by Hofmann between the four points of doctrine, can hardly have been present to the mind of the author. The connection between them, as appears to us, is rather as follows : When any one has entered on the saving path of repentance and faith, the first thing is to instruct him regarding baptism, by which he is incorporated into the body of Christ, and likewise concerning the imposition of hands, which conveys the *charismata* necessary for the discharge of his Christian calling. This must be followed up by further instruction regarding the resurrection and the final judgment, since the Christian life thus begun and furnished must, in the midst of the temptations of the world, be placed under the shadow of those two great final facts in the history of redemption, which are as rich in gracious promise as they are fitted to inspire with wholesome awe. Without limitation to believers, ἀνάστασις νεκρῶν is ἀνάστασις δικαίων τε καὶ ἀδίκων (Acts xxiv. 15); and κρῖμα αἰώνιον is the final judgment, deciding for ever the blessedness of the righteous and the damnation of the wicked (Acts xxiv. 25). Both these facts, which occupy the boundary between time and eternity, are also Jewish *capita fidei*. They are here, however, conceived of as Christian facts and doctrines: the resurrection of the dead being founded on the resurrection of Christ (Acts iv. 2, xvii. 18, xxvi. 23), in which sense St. Paul calls himself especially a preacher of the ἀνάστασις νεκρῶν (Acts xxiii. 6, xxiv. 21); and the final judgment being that which is to be pronounced by the risen Saviour, as the man appointed by God to judge the world (Acts xvii. 31). This, then, is the sixfold basis of Christian life and Christian teaching, which long ere this has been deposited in the hearts and minds of these Hebrew Christians. And yet, as their wavering in presence of the synagogue too clearly shows, they are still in need of further instruction in this their A, B, C. Nevertheless the writer of the epistle will make the attempt to raise them up to the higher ground of matured intelligence, ἐάνπερ ἐπιτρέπῃ ὁ Θεός, if so be God grant His leave. With Him alone the decision rests, whether they have so far forfeited His grace already as to be incapable of making further progress. On this ἐάνπερ the whole following section (vi. 4–12) turns. The writer will do what he promises, if so be God grant him to accomplish the almost impossible. For there is a backsliding and an apostasy from which it is simply impossible to rise again, and after which the very grace of knowledge and of progress is no more.

CHAP. VI. 4-12. *He sets vividly before them the hopelessness of apostasy, in cases where a living knowledge of Christ has been once obtained. For them, however, he still persists in hoping better things, and that through stedfastness in faith they will yet inherit the promises.*

" If God permit;" for there is an apostasy from which all efforts to recover men are vain. This extreme case the apostolic writer now sets before his readers as a salutary warning.

Vers. 4–6. *For it is impossible,* [*in the case of*] *those who were once enlightened, and tasted of the heavenly gift, and became partakers of the Holy Ghost, and tasted the good word of God, and powers of the world to come, and* [*afterwards*] *fell away, to renew them again unto repentance,* [*them*] *that have crucified again unto themselves the Son of God, and exposed to an open shame.*

Whether we regard vers. 1–3 as an exhortation to his readers, or (which we think the most natural view) as a declaration of the writer's own purpose to leave the elements and advance to higher disclosures of divine truth, in either case it seems most suitable to connect vers. 4–6 with ἐάνπερ ἐπιτρέπῃ ὁ Θεός. For even if we regard vers. 1–3 as an exhortation, ἐάνπερ, κ.τ.λ., will still express something more than that pious sense of dependence for every step on the will of Divine Providence that is expressed, for instance, in the ἐὰν ὁ Κύριος ἐπιτρέψῃ of 1 Cor. xvi. 7. In either case, whether men themselves are not permitted to carry out the good resolutions to which they have been incited, or their teacher is not suffered to bring them any further on the good way, there can only be one reason for this,—namely, that grace divine itself, by way of judicial punishment, has ceased from working. This notion of there being a peremptory *terminus* beyond which renewal and progress are no longer possible, was certainly in the author's mind when he wrote ἐάνπερ, κ.τ.λ.; and it is this notion which he now proceeds (vers. 4–6) to unfold. In this view of the connection I find Tholuck and Ebrard most in accord with me.[1]

There is, I think, moreover, further evidence that vers. 1–3 expressed the author's purpose to elevate his readers' minds along with his own to Christian τελειότης in the following πάλιν ἀνακαινίζειν εἰς μετάνοιαν, on which all the participles (φωτισθέντας, γευσαμένους, and the rest) depend. For in ἀνα-

---

[1] Lünemann, on the other hand, finds in the whole paragraph the following connection of thought: "Passing by points of elementary instruction, I shall now proceed to such as demand a more profound Christian insight; for it is impossible to convert anew those who have been once enlightened, and have since then fallen away." This leaves altogether out of consideration the significant ἐάνπερ ἐπιτρέπῃ ὁ Θεός, and gives a strange and unsatisfactory meaning to the whole.

καινίζειν he expresses his own desired action as teacher and pastor, the correlative to that expressed in the ἀνακαινοῦσθαι of 2 Cor. iv. 16, Col. iii. 10. Man having fallen from his original condition as created in the image of God, needs for restoration to it, first and before all things, a "*change*" and a "*renewal*" "of the *mind*" (μετά-νοια, ἀνακαίνωσις τοῦ νοός, Rom. xii. 2). The work of grace in spiritual renovation begins with the root of our moral nature in the νοῦς, by rescuing a man's inward life, his self-conscious thinking and willing, from its degradation in God-forsaking selfishness and worldliness, and so transforming it into another and a new life. This radical transformation is here described as εἰς μετάνοιαν (resulting in an entire change of the νοῦς); and the possibility of the repetition (πάλιν) of such a change, through the human instrumentality which God usually employs (ἀνακαινίζειν), is positively denied: for, as De Wette correctly observes, the stern meaning of this ἀδύνατον is not to be meddled with.[1] Even the explanation, that what is altogether impossible with men may yet be effected "by a special operation of divine power" (Schlicht., Bengel, etc.), is inadmissible here; for it is God Himself who works through the preaching of the word. Ambrose (*de Pœnit.* ii. 3) is the first who mentions this mitigatory interpretation, but only at once to reject it, though (it must be confessed) to decide in favour of one yet far less tenable, which was the traditional exposition among Catholics of that age. Our text, as is well known, was from early times a main support of over-strict demands for church discipline. Tertullian (*de Pudicitia*, c. 20) refers to it as the testimony of a disciple of the apostles (Barnabas), that in the case of one fallen from the state of grace through gross sins of the flesh, no *secunda pœnitentia* is admissible. The Novatians appealed to it in support of their fundamental principle, that no one who

---

[1] A remarkable parallel with this ἀδύνατον, which, though not from an apostolic writer, is conceived in an almost apostolic spirit, is to be found in Philo (i. 219), where he describes the irreparable loss sustained by that soul which refuses to submit itself to the penitential discipline of the divine Logos, and overpasses those limits of humility which beseem the creature. Such a soul, he says, will not only be "widowed" in respect of all true knowledge, but will also be cast out (ἐκβεβλήσεται). Once unyoked and separated from the Logos, she will be cast away for ever, without possibility of returning to her ancient home.

had once denied Christ could be again received into church communion, but only exhorted to repent, his future destiny being left to God (Socrates, *h. Eccl.* iv. 28),—a principle the application of which they had at the time of the Council of Nice already extended (like the Montanist Tertullian) from the *lapsi* in time of persecution to all who had fallen into *peccata mortalia*. (See Hefele, *Kirchen-Lexicon*, vii. 662). This Novatian use and interpretation of Heb. vi. 4–8 was met by Catholics, since the fourth century, by an exposition which on the one hand rendered it invalid for establishing the Novatian penitential discipline, and on the other converted it into a proof passage against the Novatian practice of rebaptizing those who joined their communion (Cyprian, *Ep.* 73). This is the interpretation in favour of which St. Ambrose also gave his decision: *Sed tamen de baptismo dictum ne quis iteret vera ratio persuadet;* i.e. the words were to be interpreted not as denying the possibility of renewed repentance, but as denying the permissibility of a second baptism. So likewise Theodoret: ὁ θεῖος ἀπόστολος οὐ τὰ τῆς μετανοίας ἀπηγόρευσε φάρμακα, ἀλλὰ τοῦ θείου βαπτίσματος τὸν ὅρον ἐδίδαξε; and Sedulius Hybernus: *Sicut impossibile est Christum iterum crucifigi, ita criminosi homines non possunt iterum baptizari.* The predicative participles, ἀνασταυροῦντες, κ.τ.λ., were understood of the rebaptizers, and the guilt they thereby incurred. The appellation φωτισμός, usually given to baptism as early as the days of Justin Martyr (*Apol.* i. 62, 65), and the not less usual appellation ἀνακαινίζειν[1] for the act of baptism, favoured this interpretation; and the passage thus expounded long served to protect the objective validity of the sacrament, whether administered by Catholics or heretics, so that the form of the divine institution was adhered to. But the arbitrary character of this interpretation, invented as it was to serve a temporary controversial object, is too evident to be denied by any one. Πάλιν ἀνακαινίζειν εἰς μετάνοιαν can here by no possibility refer to the repetition of the outward act of baptism. What is meant is evidently an inward spiritual transformation; and the only questions which arise are the two fol-

[1] The author of the *Philopatris* (c. 12) uses the word in speaking of Christian baptism: ἡνίκα δέ μοι Γαλιλαίας ἐνέτυχεν, ἀναφαλαντίας ἐπίρρινος, ἐς τρίτον οὐρανὸν ἀεροβατήσας καὶ τὰ κάλλιστα ἐκμεμαθηκώς, δι' ὕδατος ἡμᾶς ἀνεκαίνισεν.

lowing: 1. Whether by the παραπεσόντες, in whom this change is declared impossible, we are to understand all in general who may have fallen through grave transgressions knowingly committed and persisted in, or only those who have lost grace through one particular form of sin; and 2. Whether, by the irredeemably lost here spoken of, we are to understand such persons as, having once been truly regenerate, afterwards fall away, or are left to infer from the fact of their apostasy that they were never truly regenerated at all. Calvin, and all predestinarian interpreters, are of necessity of the latter opinion. Bleek, too, says: " *The new life, and therefore also the new birth* (regeneration), *had made a beginning in these persons, but not yet struck such root in them as to be able to withstand all assaults from without and from within.*" And De Wette: " *We must conclude that the enlightening* (φωτισμός) *of such Christians was a merely superficial one.*" To the same purport is that expression of Schaf's in his treatise *On the Sin against the Holy Ghost* (1841) : " *Awakened, not yet fully regenerated;*" and that, too, of von Gerlach : " *Men in whom the last and most formidable opposition of the old nature had not yet been overcome.*" Julius Müller (*Sünde*, ii. 576) maintains indeed that the new life, when it really exists, can never be wholly lost again, and yet does not deny that our passage (taken, as he remarks, " from a deutero-canonical book") speaks of an apostasy of persons truly regenerate, from which recovery is impossible. This frank acknowledgment is important for us, in view of De Wette's assertion, that in the description given, vers. 4, 5, there is no manifest sign of the true regeneration of the heart and will. How groundless this assertion is, will become evident at once when we consider more closely the descriptive participles. It is impossible, says the author, to renew again unto repentance —(1) τοὺς ἅπαξ φωτισθέντας, *those who have once become light;* meaning, according as we make it refer to persons or to the faculty of sight, either *those who have been translated into a sphere of light* (Col. i. 13), or *those who have been enlightened, freed from their blindness.* If we compare x. 32 with x. 26, the latter would seem the only right view; but Ps. xxxvi. 10 (Gr.) (ἐν τῷ φωτί σου ὀψόμεθα φῶς) shows that both views may really coincide, since the enlightenment of the spirit is derived from that Divine Light by which it is encompassed, and the inward eye being thus enlightened, the whole body, the whole personality, is also made full of light (Luke xi. 34–36).[1] This enlightenment is described by ἅπαξ as an accomplished fact, which, having once taken place, subsists and continues through and from itself (comp. x. 2), but which also, if once swallowed up by the previous darkness, is incapable of renewal. A man experiences this turning from darkness to light (Eph. v. 14) only once, and no more. It is impossible to renew again unto repentance those who have returned to their old darkness.

The same is further the case with those (2) who enjoy and then lose the heavenly gift—γευσαμένους τε τῆς δωρεᾶς τῆς ἐπουρανίου. That here γεύεσθαι is not a mere superficial tasting, is plain from the emphasis implied in its very position in the sentence; the further proof derived from the *usus loquendi* is given at ii. 9. Philo speaks in a similar sense of γευσάμενοι καλοκἀγαθίας. In direct antithesis to the Calvinistic interpretation, *summis labris gustare*, the true meaning of γεύεσθαι here is, *to have a thorough experience or enjoyment* of the object which is put in the genitive; and this is fully recognised by Ebrard, who is here under no restraint from any dogmatic interest. Bleek supposes that, on account of the intimate connection (marked by the τε) between this and the preceding clause, we must assume that " the heavenly gift" is the same as the heavenly illuminating light there referred to. But the utmost we are warranted in inferring from the τε is, that the one is the result of the other. The work of grace begins with divine illumination, on which follows an apprehension and tasting of that which is thus made known.

Were we compelled to understand by "the heavenly gift" one out of many, it might be the grace of justification or remission of sins, in which all life and blessedness[2] are comprised, which

---

[1] Compare Philo's use of φωτίζειν (i. 506), and his description of the Logos as both *manna* and *light.* Comp. also i. 534, where the progressive illumination of the soul is described. There is a fine Midrash in *Pesikta rabbati* on Ps. xxxvi. 10 (Eng. ver. 9, In Thy light shall we see light): " *The light meant is that of Messiah, which was from of old hidden by God under the throne of His glory. When Satan once asked, ' Lord of the world, to whom belongs that hidden light under Thy throne?' the Holy One, blessed be He! answered him, ' It belongs to Him from whom thou once shalt flee in fear and shame.*'"

[2] [There is an allusion here to an expression in Luther's Catechism

the apostolic writer had here in view; but Tholuck, Lünemann, and other modern interpreters, rightly object to understanding by it here any one particular gift whatsoever. The δωρεὰ ἐπουράνιος, called 2 Cor. ix. 15 the " unspeakable gift," is that of *salvation in Christ*. A *gift* it is, because God has bestowed it on us, and imparts it to us in prevenient grace; a *heavenly* gift, because sent down from heaven itself, and making us partakers of celestial blessedness. In other passages St. Luke delights in calling the Holy Ghost a δωρεά (comp. ii. 4 above with Acts xi. 17); but here it is only indirectly that He is so called. The sacred writer proceeds to warn them further, as (3) καὶ μετόχους γενηθέντας πνεύματος ἁγίου. When a man has been divinely enlightened, and has tasted the supreme good, salvation in Christ and new life from God, he becomes, in the third place, a living member of the body of Christ, which is animated by the Holy Spirit. Of that Spirit he so partakes, as to carry His presence within him as an abiding possession, an impelling power, an active source of life. Μέτοχος, as already observed, is a word common to St. Luke and to this epistle ; γενηθέντες is the aorist used by the Doric and later writers, instead of γενόμενοι. It is possible that the author, in employing the word φωτισθέντος, was thinking of catechetical instruction,—in speaking of the δωρεὰ ἐπουράνιος, of the grace imparted in baptism,—and in μέτοχοι ἁγίου πνεύματος, of the imposition of hands for the gift of the Spirit. He, then, who has thus been delivered from the gloom, and poverty, and weakness of a life without God, must henceforth find his home, his source of nourishment, in the world above. The author therefore goes on to speak of such as (4) καλὸν γευσαμένους Θεοῦ ῥῆμα δυνάμεις τε μέλλοντος αἰῶνος. Considering his evident command of language, we certainly cannot regard the repetition of the verb γεύεσθαι here as to be explained by the supposition that the writer was at a loss for another appropriate word. (Bleek, Lünemann) : rather the repetition of the same term is intended to set forth more strongly the reality of the experiences referred to. The change, moreover, in the construction (γευσαμ. being now followed by an accus.) has certainly some meaning, and cannot be explained by saying that (Fifth Part, " The Sacrament of the Altar"), " *Where remission of sins is, there is also life and blessedness.*"—Tr.]

the author did not wish to accumulate more genitives dependent one on another (Böhme, Bleek, De Wette, Lünemann). The construction of γεύεσθαι with the accusative occurs but very seldom in non-biblical Greek (see Passow); in the New Testament it is found only here and John ii. 9, but more frequently in the LXX. and the Apocrypha. The two cases may be interchangeably employed elsewhere, without important difference of meaning; but here, where both constructions stand side by side, the change of regimen is certainly not without meaning. Verbs denoting enjoyment take the genitive in a partitive sense, but are followed by the accusative when the object is partaken of as a whole, or when the material of which it consists as a means of nourishment is chiefly in question (Kühner, § 526, Anmerk 3; Ditfurt, § 83). In this way are distinguished πίνειν ὕδατος, to drink some water (or take a drink of water), and πίνειν ὕδωρ, to be a water-drinker. And so here: the idea connected with γευσαμένους τῆς δωρ. τῆς ἐπουρ. is, that the heavenly gift is provided for all men, and is inexhaustible in fulness; while that suggested by καλὸν γευσαμένους Θεοῦ ῥῆμα is, that the good word of God has become, as it were, the daily bread, the ordinary spiritual food, of the persons described. The adjective καλόν is not added as a mere descriptive attribute of the divine word in general, but points more particularly to the word of promise, "the good word" or "words" of Joshua xxi. 43 (45), and Zech. i. 13 (LXX. ῥήματα καλά). Compare טוֹב (good, LXX. ἀγαθά), answering in the parallelism to יְשׁוּעָה (salvation) at Isa. lii. 7. The Christian, in the onward course of his spiritual life, has, in the midst of trials from without and within, the good, consolatory, hopeful word of God, which speaks of a glorious future and a final redemption as his daily food and refreshment by the way. And not *that* only. The world to come is with him not only as an object of promise and expectation; he tastes its marvellous powers even here. The δυνάμεις are, according to ii. 4, Gal. iii. 5, and other places, miraculous gifts, wondrous manifestations and experiences. Every miracle is an entering of the powers of the new world of redemption and eternal life into the old death-subjected world of creation. What is here meant, therefore, are those miraculous operations of the Holy Ghost, which demonstrate the wholly spiritual (or pneumatic, in antithesis to material or psychical) condition of the new divine order of things, the presence of which is thus revealed in the midst of the old order of death and sin. They are a prelude and a foretaste vouchsafed already of that future redemption which is still in progress. The "world to come" (העולם הבא or עלמא דאתי), the μέλλουσα οἰκουμένη of ii. 5, has not yet *appeared*, but is already *present* as the hidden background of "the world that now is," waiting for its manifestation, and perpetually breaking through the crust that binds it, in manifold effulgurations, which the Christian sees around him, or perceives within. He tastes the powers of the world to come.[1]

Such, then, is the description which the sacred writer gives of the previous condition of those whose apostasy he assumes as possible, and a subject of anxious warning. How can we doubt for a moment that it is the truly regenerate whom he is here describing? Can there possibly be any more sacred or more glorious manifestations of grace connected with the new birth than those which the author here names; and could he have selected any less ambiguous or more mystically profound expressions for describing it? Is it not clear as day, that what he means to say is, that the further one has penetrated into the inner sanctuary of the state of grace, the more irrecoverably is he lost if he then fall away? (Ebrard.)

Having thus with four participial clauses described the spiritual privileges of these highly favoured ones, he now with cutting brevity—with one short word—depicts the fall from such an elevation, the miserable apostasy from such grace so lovingly vouchsafed, so richly experienced, so abundantly sealed —καὶ παραπεσόντας! It is quite impossible that by παραπεσεῖν our author could have meant us to understand every kind of fall into mortal sin or out of the state of grace. Our epistle then would "contradict," as Luther says in his preface to his version of it, "all the gospels and all the epistles of St. Paul." Even Ebrard himself does not apprehend with suffi-

---

[1] Tertullian (*de Pudicitia*, c. 20) gives the false rendering here: "Qui verbum Dei dulce gustaverunt occidente jam ævo cum exciderint,"—probably occasioned (as Semler, ap. Oehler, iii. 635, suggests) by a misunderstanding of the abbreviation of δυς for δυναμεις, and the translator consequently reading δῦσαι τε μ. αἰων. Less probable explanations are given by Bleek from Mill, Matthäi, and Griesbach, iii. 187.

cient depth or clearness the thought indicated here. For the regenerate man is not therefore wholly and irrecoverably lost "who" (as he describes) "gives place to the evil one, and, growing faint in the fight, suffers himself to be entangled in some more subtle snare of Satan—some more specious lie (or, as in the case here supposed, by a seeming pious love for the institutions of the Old Testament)." Such a man is not therefore irrecoverably fallen: he may possibly, by the might of grace, regain his hold again, tear asunder the web of deceit, and again recover himself out of the snare of the devil (2 Tim. ii. 26). We must guard as much against making the apostolic warning a rack of despair, as against making it a pillow of carnal security. The brief expression παραπεσόντας is to be understood in accordance with x. 26–31, the parallel passage, by which the writer's meaning here is best illustrated, and the missing links of thought supplied.

Παραπεσεῖν (LXX. for אשם and מעל) is (like the "wilfully sinning" (ἑκουσίως ἁμαρτάνειν) of x. 26, and the ἀποστῆναι of iii. 12) intended to denote such apostasy as not only withdraws from the ethical influences of Christian truth, but renounces the truth itself; so that what was once an inward and familiar possession, is now become something merely external and alien. It was over this abyss that the Hebrew Christians were now standing. In their oscillations between church and synagogue, they might too easily be brought under the specious appearance of a return to Jehovah and the Thorah, to revile again the crucified Saviour as תָּלוּי ("the man that has been hanged"), and to change the saving name of Jesus (יֵשׁוּ) into an anagram of malediction, יִמח שמו וזכרו. That it is such apostasy as this that the author of the epistle has here in view, is evident from the two following participles—ἀνασταυροῦντας, "crucifying again," and παραδειγματίζοντας, "exposing to public derision." Their renewal to repentance is thereby rendered so impossible, that they reject the general salvation with such utter scorn and bitterness as to render it no longer a salvation for them.

First, They crucify again unto themselves the Son of God (ἀνασταυροῦντας ἑαυτοῖς τὸν υἱὸν τοῦ Θεοῦ). The verb ἀνασταυροῦν, in extra-biblical literature, always signifies "to hang up upon the pole or cross;" it may, however, equally well signify "*to crucify again*,"[1] and so was unanimously understood by the ancient Greek, Syrian, and Latin expositors, and the versions which lay before them. The apostates of whom the author speaks, repeat on Jesus, the divine Son of God, the act of crucifixion, and that ἑαυτοῖς. This ἑαυτοῖς may be variously interpreted. Stier (i. 162) unites, *more suo*, two different interpretations : "*Recrucifixion cannot, properly speaking, take place with the Son of God, who is now glorified; but rather these apostates do, 'for themselves,' crucify and reject Him again, i.e. so far as He is their Saviour; and this they do also 'in themselves,' that is, in their own hearts.*" In the latter case ἑαυτοῖς is a *dat. locativus* (Tholuck), in the former a *dat. incommodi*, for which the majority of modern expositors rightly decide,[2] though still with various modifications of the sense. Bleek suggests the right explanation by comparing Gal. vi. 14, where the apostle says that he glories only in the cross of Christ, and cannot therefore show friendship for the world in order thereby to escape its persecution : through Christ the world is crucified to him, and he to the world, *i.e.* all fellowship between him and the world is broken off : there is an antithesis between them, as between life and death. So here also the ἑαυτοῖς implies the breaking off of all fellowship with that which a man is said to crucify. "They crucify again the Son of God," repeating what their fathers had done formerly, when they gave Him over to the death of the cross, and in that way so shamefully rejected Him.

Secondly, The logical antithesis to this ἑαυτοῖς lies in παραδειγματίζοντας (as observed by Bengel, *ostentantes, scil. aliis*). They not only make Him as one dead to themselves, but also expose Him (comp. Num. xxv. 4, LXX.) to the reproach and mockery of the world. Observe, moreover, how with evident purpose present participles alternate here with the aorist participle παραπεσόντας. The aor. part. expresses the fatal change that has once for all come over them; the present participles the conduct and behaviour thereby commenced and still continued. The meaning, however, must not be taken to be, that

[1] Compare ἀναπλεῖν = (1) to sail up stream, and (2) to sail back again; and ἀναπνεῖν = (1) to take breath, and (2) to breathe again, revive.

[2] ἑαυτοῖς, if *dat. loc.* here, would require the preposition ἐν.

VOL. I.   T

persons once so highly favoured, who afterwards have fallen away, are incapable of renewal only so long as they are doing these things (Harless, *Ethik*, p. 130). This conditioned view of the ἀδύνατον, which simply amounts to the identical proposition, that "it is impossible to renew to repentance persons who have once fallen away, so long as they do not repent," is justly combated by v. Oettingen.[1] Hofmann, too (*Schriftb.* ii. 2, 316), fails to bring out the full force of ἀδύνατον, when he says: "*It is because they are crucifying the Son of God, and while they do this, not because they have done it, that it is impossible to bring them again to repentance; it is because they consciously and resolutely turn their back on the known truth, and pursue the opposite; it is for this reason, and not simply to punish them for a past apostasy, that there is for such persons no more sacrifice for sins, i.e. no other sacrifice than the one which they are rejecting, but only a judgment for its rejection.*" The element of self-punishment, which is found in the impossibility of repentance for such apostates as these, is here brought into a false antithesis. That impossibility is one-sidedly deduced from the nature of the sin, while it is at the same time a judicial punishment on account of its heinousness. Such apostates can no longer lay hold of the grace of Jesus Christ, even though they wished to do so. Von Oettingen himself does not fully recognise this aspect of God's penal sentence against them, or he would not have found Spiera's[2] case so incomprehensible a psychological enigma. For that state of irrecoverable divine dereliction does not altogether exclude remorseful anguish and longing desire for lost grace. Only such emotions come too late, and involve a sense of their own impotency. Compare the awful description of the night of despair which is to come upon obdurate Judah (Isa. viii. 21 sq.) : "*And they shall pass through it* (the land) *hardly bestead and hungry : and it shall come to pass, that, when hunger cometh upon them, they shall fret themselves, and curse their King and their God, when they shall turn their faces upwards. And when they look unto the earth, lo, distress and darkness, dimness of anguish, and a being*

---

[1] Tract. *de peccato in Sp. S. qua cum eschatologia Christiana contineatur ratione*, 1856, p. 80.

[2] [The fearful history here referred to is given at length by Herzog, *Real-Encyclopædie*, vol. xiv. art. *Spiera.*—TR.]

driven out into darkness." Here, too, there is blasphemy against Jehovah, in ascribing the results of their own apostasy to having had Him for King and God; interrupted by occasional lookings upward and vain entreaties for help, which are forthwith changed again into blasphemy, in contemplation of the ruin into which they are fallen. It cannot be but that remembrance of former intercourse with God the Saviour should at times assume the form of a desire for a communion so contemptuously broken off. But the door of repentance is now shut; and these apparently better flights of emotion have no worth or power, and soon subside again. Lamentation and blasphemy go hand in hand; and this, too, is the case even in hell, where, we are told, there is " wailing" as well as " gnashing of teeth."

Any one who has followed us thus far in our discussion of this fearful apostolic warning, will not need to be told that we regard the sin of apostasy here described (and also at ch. x.) as being substantially the same with "the sin against," or, more exactly, " the blasphemy" *of the Holy Ghost,* of which our Lord Himself speaks in the Gospels. This opinion is that also of Schaf and von Oettingen in their treatises on that sin, of Julius Müller in his classical work, and of the majority of modern expositors (Tholuck, Ebrard, Hofmann, Lünemann). It is at bottom that of Bleek too, whose observation is quite correct, that the sin against the Holy Ghost may be committed not only by those who have fallen away from faith, but by such also as may never have belonged to the Christian community; while there may also be such a fall from Christian faith as, without going so far as to become the sin against the Holy Ghost, yet bears the character of one against the Son of man. In harmony with this view, von Oettingen calls that which the Hebrews are here warned against, *exemplum horrificum apostasiæ universalis quæ est peccatum in Spiritum Sanctum.* Hofmann, moreover, calls attention to the fact that our Lord, in speaking of blasphemy against the Holy Ghost, does so in Matthew and Mark when addressing the Pharisees; but in Luke (xii. 8–10) in connection with an exhortation to His own disciples and friends, and immediately after a warning against denying Him from fear of men: so that in the Gospels also a distinction is evidently drawn between the commission of this sin by unbelievers on the one hand, who thereby harden themselves against all belief, and the commission of it by believers on the other, who thereby divest themselves of the faith of the gospel. It is also worthy of remark here, that the Epistle to the Hebrews finds its closest parallel in this respect to what among the evangelists is recorded by St. Luke. Our Lord's words in Matt. xii. 31 and Mark iii. 29 refer to the blasphemy of the Pharisees, who called the Spirit through whom Jesus performed His miracles of healing, Beelzebub, and thus calumniated the Πνεῦμα ῞Αγιον as a πνεῦμα ἀκάθαρτον. That is, they stigmatized the works of the Spirit in Jesus as works of the devil, and this knowingly and wilfully, in order to extinguish the acknowledgment of Him among the people as the Son of David. Those blasphemies of theirs were not mere insults to the Lord personally, as when they called Him "glutton," "winebibber," etc.: they were uttered against the divine and holy in Him and His working, even because it was divine and holy, and because it pressed on them and others with convicting power. Their blasphemy was directed not against the Son of man in His human manifestation, but against the Spirit of God, which wrought in Him with self-evidencing testimony. On that occasion our Lord declared that speaking against the Son of man was a pardonable sin. A man might in words express doubt of His miraculous powers, or depreciate His dignity: that would be sin, no doubt, but not sin without a possibility of forgiveness, because in Jesus Christ, though God was manifested *in* the flesh, He was also veiled *by* the flesh. But when divine actions are evidently wrought through the Spirit of God—whether by the Lord Himself, or any one else; whether in the outer world, or on the man, or in him—actions which bear in themselves the proof of their divinity, and consequently of deriving their origin from the Holy Ghost; in other words, when the divine so presents itself that it needs not to be unfolded, and so gradually recognised and more fully believed, but evinces itself at once as divine without the possibility of mistake,—then wanton blaspheming such actions and their Cause is a sin for ever excluded (οὔτε ἐν τούτῳ αἰῶνι οὔτε ἐν τῷ μέλλοντι) from all forgiveness: he who, devil-like, wilfully blasphemes the self-evidencing Spirit of God, becomes a devil himself. It is just as certain that in our Lord's meaning and that of the evangelists the Pharisees had made themselves guilty of this unpardonable sin,[1] as it is that it may be committed even now whenever the principle of all good is, in spite of its being self-evidenced by its actions, blasphemed and rejected as the principle of all evil. Here again, however (it must be observed), it is not the individual word of blasphemy in itself, or the individual deed of blasphemous opposition, but these taken in connection with the disposition of mind which is manifested in them, that constitutes the unpardonable sin. There are, moreover, *degrees* in the damnability, though the irrecoverableness—the ἀδύνατον— may admit of none. But further, blasphemy against the Holy Ghost is possible not only when God's gracious call is first vouchsafed, but also after the work of grace has already begun, and has translated the subject of its influence from darkness into light. The unpardonable sin in such a case manifests itself as a falling away from or denial of Christ, already glorified by the Spirit in the man's own soul, and of atoning grace already sealed. That even such a one may so far fall away as to pronounce what he has known and experienced by the operation of the Holy Ghost within him to be falsehood and deceit, and so root out every plant of grace within his soul by denying the truth of Christianity itself, is expressly assumed by our author as possible, and history confirms it by some terrible examples. This kind of apostasy, admitting of no further restoration, is set before the Hebrews as a solemn warning. "No more salvation," he says, "for those who, having learned by the Holy

[1] This is also Hofmann's view (*Schriftb.* ii. 2, 318): "So long as blasphemies against Christ are mere expressions of an unbelief which stumbles at the supposed contradictions between His outward humiliation and His testimony concerning Himself, they are not blasphemies against the Holy Spirit. They became so, as in the case before us, when unbelief renders itself invincible by wilfully confounding the moral impression made by the divine, which it cannot evade, with that of the satanic lie, which contradicts it." Schaf thinks the Pharisees had not yet got so far as this. Oettingen hesitates: *nostrum non est de casu hoc singulari decernere.* But when we reflect that (according to Matt. xiii. 14 seq. and other passages) the curse of obduration impending since the times of the prophet Isaiah was not resting on the mass of the Jewish people, and that that obduracy had culminated in the Pharisees, the leaders of thought and hierarchs of the age, in respect especially to Him whom Isaiah had seen in glory (John xii. 37), can we hesitate any longer?

Ghost to know Jesus as the very Son of God, assume the same position towards their Saviour as those unbelievers who brought Him to the cross." On the brink of such an abyss these Hebrews were now standing. A past—how rich in grace!—lay already behind them. If now, after such experiences, they should fall away, joining in the blasphemy of those who once crucified the Lord, or from fear of man hypocritically denying Him, in either case they would be irrecoverably lost.[1]

The sacred writer proceeds to base his warning of this special curse which awaits apostasy by reference to that general malediction which is incurred by every kind of spiritual unfruitfulness, whenever the grace of God and the means of grace have been vouchsafed and used in vain.

Vers. 7, 8. *For a land which hath drunk in the rain which cometh oft upon it, and produceth herbage meet for them on whose account it is also dressed, partaketh of blessing from God: but bearing thorns and thistles, it is rejected, and nigh unto a curse; whose end is for burning.*

The same phenomenon meets us here as in the parables of Isaiah (v. 1–vi. and xxviii. 23) and in those of the Gospels. The figurative character of the whole betrays itself by the confusion of the symbol with the thing symbolized, and expressions borrowed from the sphere of ethics being applied to that of nature. The generic term γῆ is defined in the participial clause that follows as ἡ πιοῦσα, κ.τ.λ. (Compare Xen. *Anab.* i. 10, 1, ἀποτέμνεται χεὶρ ἡ δεξιά—a hand (is cut off), namely the right hand; Gal. ii. 20, iii. 21, iv. 27. See Ditfurt, § 8.) Instead of ἐπ' αὐτήν (which would correspond to the Hebrew עליה, or even also to על־פניה) we have the genitive ἐπ' αὐτῆς,[2] which is not seldom found with ἐπί after verbs of

---

[1] See Note B at the end of the volume.

[2] ἐπ' αὐτῆς for ἐφ' αὐτῆς, as μετ' αὐτοῦ for μεθ' αὐτοῦ (Matt. xiv. 33), in accordance with Hellenistic usage, which knows nothing of the reflexive αὑτοῦ, αὑτῷ, αὑτόν, at any rate, after prepositions, the final consonant of which would require to be aspirated. Bengel long ago made this observation. (See remarks at i. 3.) Grammarians are not agreed or clear as to the difference of meaning between ἐπί c. gen. and ἐπί c. acc. after verbs of motion (Winer, § 48, Eng. tr. p. 392; Orig. p. 336; Nägelsbach, *Anmerk zur Ilias,* p. 283; Kühner, § 614). It seems to me, that when ἐπί is followed by the genitive, there is a closer connection between the notions

motion. It expresses direction towards a certain goal or object. The rain is here said to have come upon the land with the purpose of refreshing it and making it fruitful, and that frequently,[1] not once or twice only, or in short and sudden showers, where the water soon ran off and was lost, but so that the thirsty soil could "drink" it in, as Anacreon also says, ἡ γῆ μέλαινα πίνει.

In consequence of these frequent showers, the land (the mother-earth made fruitful from above) brings forth βοτάνην εὔθετον ἐκείνοις, δἰ οὓς καὶ γεωργεῖται. The adjective εὔθετος (well-put, well-placed, fitting, useful, or *useable*) is one of St. Luke's words, at xiv. 35 followed by εἰς, at ix. 62 by the dative τῇ βασιλείᾳ, in Lachmann and Tischendorf.[2] Whether, in the mind of the sacred writer, the dative ἐκείνοις belongs to τίκτουσα or to εὔθετον, can scarcely be determined. The latter appears to me most probable. The soil produces esculents (Βοτάνη from βόσκειν), useful and welcome to those on whose account (or for whom) moreover (καί) it is cultivated, *i.e.* to its owners, for whom, by producing fruit, it furnishes what they have a just right to expect from it, seeing they moreover take care to have it cultivated.[3] Soil like this, which by its fertility makes a due return to the rain of heaven and the labour of man bestowed upon it, μεταλαμβάνει εὐλογίας ἀπὸ τοῦ Θεοῦ. The expression is selected with special reference to the thing here symbolized, but admits of a direct application too. Such soil partakes of God's blessing, in that He rewards (according to the law, Matt. xiii. 12 ; comp. John xv. 2) the labour bestowed upon it with more and more abundant returns (Bleek, De Wette, Tholuck, Lünemann), or (perhaps better) in that He adds His blessing to the tender plants, and so brings them on to maturity and the harvest. But when, on the other

---

of a goal and the motion towards it. The rain (as here), the sheet (as at Acts x. 11), come down upon the earth, being sent for that very purpose.

[1] This is well brought out by the more rhythmical order of words, as given in the texts of Lachmann and Tischendorf : τὸν ἐπ' αὐτῆς ἐρχόμενον πολλάκις ὑετόν. [It is the reading also of the Cod. Sin.—TR.]

[2] In the *text rec.* εἰς τὴν βασιλ. [Cod. Sin. reads τῇ βασιλ.]

[3] For the difference between ἐργάζεσθαι τὴν γῆν and γεωργεῖν, see Philo, i. 211. Compare for καί, vii. 26, 1 Pet. ii. 8. Winer, § 53, 3, *e* (on καί used *epexegetically*, Eng. tr. p. 458).

hand, the same kind of field, under the like conditions, produces[1] thorns and thistles (ἀκάνθας καὶ τριβόλους, those products of the curse, Gen. iii. 18, LXX.), it is then ἀδόκιμος (a word used seven times elsewhere by St. Paul)—" unprobehaltig," *reprobate*,—tried and found wanting, disappointing just expectations, and proving itself unworthy of any further blessing. Nay, more; it is κατάρας ἐγγύς, nigh to a curse, which will speedily befall it, unless it change for the better.

Ἧς τὸ τέλος εἰς καῦσιν. It is a question whether the relative ἧς is to be referred to γῆ or to κατάρας. Bleek, De Wette, and Ebrard refer it to κατάρας, and Tholuck thinks such a reference at least equally fitting with the other. But Bleek's remark, that a reference to γῆ would require another form of expression, such as ἥτις εἰς τέλος εἰς καῦσιν, is incorrect. The expression is a Hebrew one, and is both rabbinical (שְׂסוֹפוֹ לְהִשָּׂרֵף) and biblical (אֲשֶׁר אַחֲרִיתוֹ לְבָעֵר, Ps. cix. 13; comp. Num. xxiv. 22). Moreover, the reference to γῆ is favoured by the strikingly similar closing words of 2 Cor. xi. 15, Phil. iii. 19. Burning, καῦσις, is the destiny of weeds, *e.g.* 2 Sam. xxiii. 7, and of the land which has incurred God's curse, Deut. xxix. 22, Heb.:
" *The whole land of Israel is brimstone, and salt, and burning: it is not sown, it beareth not, nor doth grass grow therein; it is like the overthrow of Sodom and Gomorrah, of Admah and Zeboim, which the Lord overthrew in His fierce anger, and in His burning wrath.*" Since it is not in accordance with the divine order of the natural world that ground that is or may be fruitful in any way should be under a curse,[2] we must assume the expressions were chosen here with special reference to the thing symbolized. The field which the author has in view is the Christian church; the γεωργοῦντες are the preachers of the word and ministers of its mysteries; they for whom these γεωργοῦντες labour are God the Father (1 Cor. iii. 9), and the Son who is His heir (iii. 6); the rain from heaven stands for the manifold manifestations of divine grace mentioned (ver. 4 sq.),

---

[1] Ἐκφέρουσα is in itself no ignoble word, but is intentionally substituted here for the τίκτουσα above, to mark the less natural and as it were adulterate action.

[2] The cursing of the leaf-bearing but fruitless fig-tree (Matt. xxi. 18-22) is no proof to the contrary. The action was prophetic, and typical of the fate awaiting Jerusalem.

CHAP. VI. 9. 297

and the πιεῖν τὸν ὑετὸν symbolizes the inward reception and apprehension of them; the rain often visiting this field is meant to indicate that divine grace is constantly being communicated to the church in all its members. If the church, then, gives signs of life in proportion to the grace of God and the labour of His servants, it continues to be blessed, and will be blessed more and more; in the opposite case, it is ripe for the judgment which its unworthiness has incurred. What has been hitherto said is sufficient to alarm the readers. It is now time for the author to say something to prevent the despairing impression which his communications are fitted to produce. The change of tone is already indicated in the plain and awful prose of vers. 4-6, being followed by parabolic language which in a certain measure mitigates the impression. Ἐγγύς, too, implies that the state of the readers is not yet quite hopeless, that it is not yet too late for them to repent, though it may soon be so. It is possible that the apostolic writer may have had floating in prophetic vision before his eyes the fiery judgment then impending on Jerusalem, which, along with those unbelieving Jews who had once raised the cry of "Crucify him, crucify him!" would sweep away the apostates who should have relapsed to Judaism. There is still time, he warns his friends, to escape the coming wrath. How gladly would he pluck them from it as brands from the burning!

And so the very climax of reproof and warning is interrupted by an outburst of hopeful love:

Ver. 9. *But we are persuaded better things concerning you, beloved, and pertaining to salvation, even though we thus speak.*

This is the only passage in the epistle in which the author addresses his readers as ἀγαπητοί. And certainly, if the epistle was to contain the term but once, no other place could be found in which it would be more needed or more impressive than here.[1]

Πεπείσμεθα is the plural of authorship (comp. note on ii. 5). He might have also written πεποίθαμεν ἐφ' ὑμᾶς, we rely upon you (comp. 2 Thess. iii. 4, 2 Cor. ii. 3); but prefers *persuasi sumus* to *confisi sumus* or *confidimus*, because it is not so much an inward confidence, as a conviction, the result of observation,

[1] [The Cod. Sin. reads ἀδελφοί.—Tr.]

which leads him in this case to look for better things. (The expression strongly reminds us of Rom. xv. 14.) It is hardly a fitting question here, whether τὰ κρείσσονα[1] refers to the moral condition of the persons addressed, or to their future destiny (comp. St. Chrysostom, ἤτοι περὶ πολιτείας ἢ περὶ ἀντιδόσεως), the two being so intimately connected (as Lünemann rightly observes). The author cherishes a conviction that things stand better with his beloved, than that they should come to so fearful an end as that of apostasy and ultimate malediction.

It is evident from the following ἐχόμενα σωτηρίας, which is added as it were epexegetically, that κρείσσονα does not exclude a reference to the future. In this phrase we are again reminded of St. Luke : ἡ ἐχομένη (Luke xiii. 33 ; Acts xx. 15, xxi. 26) is *the next following day* (comp. Acts xiii. 44, τῷ ἐρχομένῳ σαββάτῳ); and so τὰ ἐχόμενα σωτηρίας here are *the things which stand in immediate connection with salvation—ad salutem pertinentia*.[2] The expression is intentionally ambiguous or vague. As to what regards them, their present condition, and its issues in the future, he is persuaded that it pertains to salvation : they will in faith maintain their hold (antithesis to παραπεσεῖν), they will not ultimately forfeit it (are not ἐγγὺς κατάρας).

Of this he is assured, εἰ καί,[3] although (*notwithstanding*), he

---

[1] κρείσσομα is here (σσ instead of ττ. as elsewhere in the epistle, according to all authorities) the reading of A.B.C. [and the Cod. Sin.], etc. It is the case sometimes with other (later) writers, that the less usual form is occasionally used by way of exception. Alciphron uses κρείττων (without variation in MSS.) four times, and once κρείσσων (ii. 4, 21), perhaps to add energy to the expression. The softer form is the prevalent one in the new Attic.

[2] Compare the similar use of ὅσα ἔχεται and ἐχόμενα in Plato and Herodotus. It is to put too much meaning into this ἐχόμενα, when it is made to correspond exactly to the ἐγγύς in ἐγγὺς κατάρας, and so is rendered, *e.g.* by the Itala, *proximiora saluti*.

[3] εἰ καί is somewhat different in meaning from καὶ εἰ. The latter introduces the mention of a possible case, as a sort of climax—*even though;* the former admits a plain matter of fact, without allowing that it alters the truth of what is asserted. With εἰ καί the emphasis lies on the apodosis, with καὶ εἰ on the protasis (Hofm. *Schriftbew.* ii. 2, 388). In the present passage the emphasis lies on the apodosis πεπείσμεθα. We see this at once by an inversion which exhibits the true sense : εἰ καὶ οὕτως λαλοῦμεν (ὅμως) πεπείσμεθα.

thus speaks and sets before them such awful warnings. He has not referred to the unfruitful field with the meaning that they are already in that condition, but with the benevolent intent of warning them against a not remote danger. His favourable conviction concerning them is founded on their otherwise Christian conduct:

Ver. 10. *For not unrighteous is God* (so as) *to forget your work, and the love which ye showed towards his name, in having ministered to the saints, and yet ministering.*

Instead of καὶ τῆς ἀγάπης the *text rec.* reads καὶ τοῦ κόπου τῆς ἀγάπης; but τοῦ κόπου is now universally acknowledged to be an interpolation from the similar passage, 1 Thess. i. 3.[1] In what this work consisted, and how this love was manifested, may be learned from x. 32-34. Τὸ ἔργον (still retaining a verbal signification) is the moral conduct as a whole (as 1 Thess. i. 3, Gal. iv. 6), as distinguished from τὰ ἔργα, individual actions (comp. Rom. ii. 6 with ii. 15). Out of the general idea τοῦ ἔργου ὑμῶν, which comprehends, for instance, stedfastness under persecution, the author gives especial prominence, by means of the καί *exegeticum* (and particularly), to the love which they had shown to their poorer brethren in the faith of the gospel. This love is, however, spoken of as exhibited, in the first instance, to God Himself, since it is He whom they have honoured and loved in His people. The meaning remains the same, whether we take εἰς τὸ ὄνομα αὐτοῦ independently, *with regard to, for the sake of, His name,* or as the object of τῆς ἀγαπῆς, *love towards His name* (a very common construction, *e.g.* Rom. v. 8, 2 Cor. ii. 4, 8). The latter interpretation, as the more obvious, and giving a fuller meaning to the sentence, is rightly preferred by all modern expositors. The ultimate object of their love was that name of God in which He has revealed Himself as that whereby He would be named and known and confessed; and this love they manifested by ministering, and continuing to minister, to those by whom that name was borne and confessed and known. Διακονεῖν is the usual word for such ministering, especially as applied to the maintenance of the poorer members of the church by means of

[1] τοῦ κόπου has not only MSS. against it [including the Cod. Sin.], but also all the oldest versions (except the Coptic) and Greek patristic expositors.

collections of alms; and οἱ ἅγιοι is the special designation of Christians in Palestine, and more especially of those in Jerusalem (2 Cor. viii. 4, ix. 1 ; Rom. xv. 25, etc.), who, as forming the mother church of Christendom, were distinguished by this as a name of honour: from which it has been inferred, that our epistle could not have been directly addressed to believers in Palestine, and especially not to those of Jerusalem (Credner, Köstlin, Hofmann); but that without reason, for, irrespective of the fact that ἅγιοι is a designation of Christians in general, the reference here may still be maintained to those of Palestine; for the members of the church in Jerusalem were not all poor (Rom. xv. 26), and the history of that church begins with a magnanimous example of self-sacrificing love for the benefit of the poorer members (Acts iv. 32 sqq.). The brethren, moreover, who needed support were dispersed throughout Judea (Acts xi. 29), so that a wide field was opened for such ministrations. The closing salutation (xiii. 24) of the epistle shows that the readers themselves might very well belong to the ἅγιοι, so called κατ' ἐξ., not to mention that the τοῖς δεσμίοις συνεπαθήσατε of x. 34 was a ministry which could not be performed beyond the boundaries of the Holy Land.

It is in view of their active manifestations of Christian life, and especially in works of charity,[1] that the author takes comfort to himself concerning these Hebrew Christians, that they will be still preserved by God from the mighty spiritual perils to which they are exposed; for He is not *unjust to forget* their past and present conduct in this respect (ἐπιλαθέσθαι is epexegetical *inf. aor.* as abstract expression for the act). The language is bold, but correct. God is *just* (δίκαιος) so far as He judges and deals with the creature in accordance with the rule of His own revealed and loving will, even as He is also *faithful* (πιστός) in stedfastly carrying out and adhering to His purposes of love (comp. 1 John i. 9; 2 Thess. iii. 3). Wherever He finds in the conduct or behaviour of the creature that which corresponds to His own holiness and love, there His righteousness (or justice, δικαιοσύνη) causes Him to take this conduct into account, and to manifest a corresponding love in return ; and, on the other hand, where a contrary behaviour

---

[1] The Hebrew race were, and are still, according to an ancient saying, רחמנים בני רחמנים, *misericordes filii misericordium.*

comes under His regard, there the same δικαιοσύνη manifests itself as wrath or fiery zeal against the despisers of His love or of His representatives. That spiritual state in man which answers to this holy love of God is our δικαιοσύνη, the root of which is faith apprehending the revelation of God's love to sinful man. Faith, as a laying hold of the free unmerited grace of God, includes all kinds of merit in itself (Rom. iv. 4 sqq.); and hence it is quite unscriptural to ascribe, on the one hand, to faith *meritum de congruo*, and, on the other, to the good works which proceed from it, *meritum de condigno*. Holy Scripture, even when speaking of the rewards of the righteous (μισθός or μισθαποδοσία), allows of no legal claim to such, no acquired meritorious right on the part of man. All human service, even if it could perfectly correspond to the loving will and law of God, would be so much a matter of mere duty (Luke xvii. 10), that it would only pervert and destroy itself by setting up any claim to any other blessedness than that which would be involved in its own performance. And yet God has nevertheless ordained a certain recompense for all human conduct, whether that which is accordant with or that which runs counter to His revealed will,—a recompense over and above the reward or punishment which is involved in such conduct itself. Hence we may speak of a twofold δικαιοσύνη in God: one manifested in the natural order of creation, assigning to human actions good or evil, corresponding good or evil consequences; the other made known to us in the revelation of His word, and which, as being a free ordinance of His will, admits on the one hand of no gainsaying, and allows on the other no claim to be set up.[1] In accordance with this second δικαιοσύνη, there is and will be a divine judgment,—a preliminary one in this life, a final one hereafter,—and, as all Scripture testifies, a judgment "*according to works*" (comp. Rom. ii. 6), among which faith itself is reckoned—being an ἔργον (John vi. 29) in which our relation to God Himself is specially manifested. But at the head of these works is placed charity and kindness exhibited to those in whom Christ will have Himself loved by us on earth (St. Matt. xxv. 31 seq.); and the assigning such pre-eminence to charity is no slight done to faith. To love those who, like their Master, have on

[1] See Note C at the end of this volume.

earth no form or comeliness, and to serve them for His sake, is an exercise of that faith which contemplates the invisible. It is therefore impossible that the just and loving God, who always acts in accordance with the rules of His own holy love, should overlook acts of sympathizing charity, when exhibited by these Hebrew Christians to His friends and servants, and for His name's sake.

The author goes on to urge them to a like zeal and constancy in the maintenance of their faith and hope. Speaking the gentle language of Christian love, he puts his exhortation in the form of an earnest wish on their behalf:

Ver. 11. *But we earnestly desire that every one of you do show the same diligence with regard to the full assurance of your hope until the end.*

Τὴν αὐτὴν σπουδήν: this does not mean that he desires a continuance of their works and spirit of love, for which he has commended them,—a view of older interpreters, which is justly given up by all modern ones (except v. Gerlach). If that were all he could desire for them, there would not be much ground for censure. And yet he has indeed much to find fault with in these Hebrew Christians: first of all, a halting between two opinions, giving ground for fear of the worst consequences,— a perilous position into which they had been driven by the apparent contradiction between their present state as Christians, and the bitterly felt separation (in which it placed them) from their brethren according to the flesh, the people of the Thorah. The whole emphasis of the sentence will thus fall upon πρὸς τὴν πληροφορίαν τῆς ἐλπίδος, which the other view reduces to a mere accessory. The verb πληροφορεῖν (mistaken by the older expositors for a nautical term = *to run under full sail into harbour*) signifies to *fulfil, thoroughly accomplish* or *discharge* (as the duties of an office, 2 Tim. iv. 5, 17), *to give full satisfaction* or *full proof;* then (*pass.*) *to be fully persuaded* (Rom. iv. 21, xiv. 5; Col. iv. 12), and also *to be well attested* so as to produce full conviction (Luke i. 1). It is apparently a peculiarly Alexandrine word.[1] The noun πληροφορία is generally = full

---

[1] Comp. LXX. Eccles. viii. 11 (ἐπληροφορήθη ἡ καρδία, *the heart is fully set*); Hesychius under ἐπιστώθη; and Ptol. *Tetr.* pp. 4, 9, πληροφόρησις. The word is not certainly met with in any non-Alexandrine or non-Hellenistic

conviction, joyous assurance (comp. x. 22, 1 Thess. i. 5, Col. ii. 2),—a meaning so entirely suitable here, that we must, with most modern expositors, abide by it against Bleek and De Wette.[1] The author's earnest wish is that these Hebrews may now manifest, in reference[2] to the attainment of the unwavering and unerring confidence of Christian hope, the like care and diligence to that which they have exhibited in performing works of Christian charity. It can scarcely be decided whether he meant to connect ἄχρι τέλους with ἐνδείκνυσθαι (Böhme, Ebrard) or with πρὸς τὴν πληροφορ. τῆς ἐλπ. (De Wette, Bleek, Lünemann). In the former case, the τέλος would be the perfection or complete accomplishment of their Christian hope;[3] in the latter, he would wish them to keep that hope unshaken till the conclusion of their Christian course. The latter seems the more natural combination. In either case, however, ἄχρι τέλους is emphatic, and therefore is placed at the end of the sentence. The following clause links on with this ἄχρι τέλους :

Ver. 12. *That ye become not slothful, but imitators of them who through faith and endurance inherit the promises.*

The aspect of the present is far from exhibiting in full developed reality all the rich and glorious blessings contained in the promise. It is easy, then, to grow faint and slothful (νωθροί at v. 11 was the antithesis of vigorous increasing knowledge; here it is that of confident, unrelaxing hope). Their endeavour should be to hold fast the full assurance of this hope unto the end, *i.e.* not to let it slip ; on the contrary (δέ, same as ii. 6, iv. 13), let them be imitators (μιμηταί a classical word, and in the New Testament exclusively Pauline, except the

writer ; for πληροφορηθείς in Isocrates (*Trapez.* p. 360) is acknowledged to be an interpolation; and πληροφορήσαντες in Photius (*Biblioth.* pp. 41, 21) belongs to the epitomator, not to Ctesias himself.

[1] Who would render πληροφορία here by *perfection, completeness.* But the meaning of the noun may always be traced back to that of *full conviction, entire confidence,* which is found in the passive verb. The comparison of Philo's σπουδή, βελτίωσις, τελείωσις, is here misleading (Philo, ap. Mangey, i. 325, 48).

[2] The classical phrase would be, σπουδαίως ἔχειν πρός τι.

[3] Lünemann's rendering, "full assurance with regard to their hope," is wrong. The genitives after πληροφορία are elsewhere subjective, not objective genitives (comp. x. 22, Col. ii. 2).

doubtful passage 1 Pet. iii. 13) of those who through faith (or because of faith), which embraces the unseen as though it were visible, and the future as if present, and through long-suffering (or in consequence of patient endurance), which, without dejection or despondency (μακροθυμία here antithesis of ὀλιγοψυχία), awaits with good courage the long delaying future, obtain at last possession of the promises. Πίστις being here faith in what is promised, and μακροθυμία patient expectation of it, and κληρονομεῖν τὰς ἐπαγγελίας being represented as the result and reward of this πίστις and μακροθυμία, we cannot interpret, with Bleek, " obtain possession of the words of promise," i.e. receive the gospel, but " obtain possession," i.e. " come into the full enjoyment of the promised blessings themselves." This interpretation is moreover favoured by the notion involved in the word itself (compare use of κληρονομεῖν at ver. 17 and xi. 9), and the emphatic position in which it is placed here.

The *part. pres.* (κληρονομούντων) must not be translated as an *imperf.* (who inherited), the principal verb being no *preterite*, nor any ποτέ indicating a reference to the past (see Winer, § 45, 1). The author expresses himself thus without reference to time, and cannot therefore have had the patriarchs primarily or exclusively in his mind, in which case he would doubtless have written more explicitly κληρονομησάντων; but, on the other hand, Lünemann seems to be wrong in taking the expression as so general as to exclude any reference to the patriarchs whatsoever. It is clear from what follows, that it was from the patriarchs that the author drew the type of faith which he here sets before his readers, and indirectly therefore must have had them especially in his thoughts as being such κληρονομοῦντες. We cannot therefore evade the question, " By what right does he here ascribe a κληρονομεῖν τὰς ἐπαγγελίας to those of whom he elsewhere says that they had not received the promises, *i.e.* in their substance, xi. 13, 39?" It was this apparent contradiction which induced Bleek to understand by τὰς ἐπαγγελίας God's promises as such, and not the blessings contained in them. A glance at what follows, however, will show that this is not the proper place to answer the question, or to prove that this contradiction is one in appearance only; but this must be reserved for ver. 15, where the author expressly says that Abraham did obtain the promise, and that after patiently waiting for it. It is there proved by the example of Abraham (vers. 13-15), that the inheriting of the promises is the reward of faith and patience; while the mention of God's oath by Himself, in pledge of His own veracity, introduces a fresh element, to which is then attached a further course of thought introductory to the parallel between Christ and Melchizedek.

CHAP. VI. 13-20.—*Having thus expressed his confident persuasion on behalf of his readers, that they will through stedfast faith obtain the promised salvation, the sacred writer now proceeds to set before them the example of Abraham, who had also through patience entered into the possession of a promise which God had confirmed to him by an oath upon Himself. They, too, have a hope confirmed in like manner, and one reaching onwards into the innermost sanctuary, into which, as their forerunner, Jesus Himself was already entered, being made (also by the oath of God) High Priest for ever after the order of Melchizedek.*

The author's purpose is in the first place to show, by Abraham's example, how surely faith and patience will find their reward[1]—how certain they are to obtain the promises; and in the next place to remind his readers on what a strong foundation their Christian hope, as formerly that of Abraham, is now established:

Vers. 13-15. *For when God made a promise to Abraham, since he had no one greater to swear by, he sware by himself, saying, "Surely blessing I will bless thee, and multiplying I will multiply thee."* *And thus* (it was with Abraham, that), *having endured with patience, he obtained the promise.*

It is the transaction on Mount Moriah after the offering of Isaac which is here referred to. De Wette and Lünemann needlessly assume that ἐπαγγειλάμενος must be rendered "*having previously promised*," and therefore refer to some earlier promises made by God to Abraham, which here He repeats and by an

[1] Hofmann does not fully state the argument, when he says that the exhortation to stedfastness is based on the fact of the promise both to Abraham and ourselves being confirmed by an oath (*Entst.* 341).

VOL. I. U

oath confirms. But, as we have seen already,[1] the aorist participle in connection with an aorist verb may refer to something contemporaneous with that to which the verb refers; and this is evidently the case here. The author reasons on the very fact that the promising (ἐπαγγείλασθαι) and the oath-taking (ὀμόσαι) were thus contemporaneous. The promises, which he quotes in an abridged form, are the very ones which God gave, accompanied by an oath, on Mount Moriah; and the κατ' ἐμαυτοῦ ὤμοσα, λέγει Κύριος, constituted indeed a special introduction to them (Gen. xxii. 16–18), as being promises more gracious and more solemn than any given hitherto, and designed to reward that faith in the patriarch which his act of obedience had so gloriously attested. It is the first time in the sacred history that God is represented as taking an oath; for the promise (in Gen. viii. 21, 22, and ix. 11–16) that He would never bring again a universal deluge on the earth, though virtually, was not literally confirmed in this way.[2] No higher or more sacred guarantee of a promise can be conceived than this—κατ' ἐμαυτοῦ ὤμοσα, λέγει Κύριος.

God thus vouchsafed to swear by Himself, ἐπεὶ κατ' οὐδενὸς εἶχε μείζονος ὀμόσαι. This classical use of ἔχειν, followed by an infinitive (He *had not, i.e.* He *could not* swear), is quite in St. Luke's style (comp. Luke vii. 42, xii. 4; Acts iv. 14, xxv. 26), and it is therefore doubly worth remarking that it is in St. Luke also that we find other references to an oath-taking by God (Luke i. 73; Acts vii. 17).[3] Philo, too, expresses himself in a similar way, *Legg. Alleg.* iii. 72, p. 127 (ed. Mang.): "*Well confirming His promise by an oath, and that an oath which was worthy of God* (ὅρκῳ θεοπρεπεῖ). *Thou seest that God sweareth not by another, for there is nothing better than He, but by Himself, for He is the best of all.*"[4]

---

[1] See comment on ii. 10, pp. 117, 118, and notes 1 and 2.

[2] Comp. Isa. liv. 9. In like manner, the passing of the symbol of Jehovah's presence through the pieces of the sacrifices (Gen. xv.) was tantamount to a covenant oath—an oath upon His life (comp. Deut. xxxii. 40).

[3] [The importance attached by Delitzsch to such resemblances and coincidences between the writings of St. Luke and the Epistle to the Hebrews is derived from his conviction that St. Luke wrote the latter. See first Excursus at the end of the *Commentary*.—TR.]

[4] This oath, therefore (Philo means to say), was strictly θεοπρεπής, and

CHAP. VI. 13-15. 307

The words of the promise, as given in the LXX., are (so far as cited by our author here) literally—ἦ μὴν εὐλογῶν εὐλογήσω σε, καὶ πληθύνων πληθυνῶ τὸ σπέρμα σου. The double particle ἦ μήν (used in asseverations generally in classical Greek) is the reading of the text. rec., for which Lachmann would substitute the better attested εἰ μήν¹ of A.B.D.E. [and the Cod. Sin.]. Other authorities give εἰ μή (C.J.**D. corr.), the closest rendering of the Hebrew אִם־לֹא, which is the particle commonly used in introducing an oath (e.g. 1 Kings xx. 23); but here (Gen. xxii. 16) the introductory particle is a simple כִּי² affirmativum. We may assume that εἰ μήν, used interchangeably with ἦ μήν in the LXX., stood originally for the Hebrew אִם (in the positive) and אִם־לֹא (in the negative oath), and then for any form of asseveration. The unclassical combination εὐλογῶν εὐλογήσω is the most usual mode of representing the Hebrew method of emphasizing the verb fin. by the addition of an infin. abs. (see Thiersch, de Pentateuchi vers. Alex. iii. § 12). The abbreviation of the πληθυνῶ τὸ σπέρμα σου of the LXX. into πληθυνῶ σε here is explained by Bleek, De Wette, Lünemann, as arising from the author's looking at the promise only in its personal relation to Abraham himself, and as vouchsafed to him in recognition of his tried and approved faith; but as πληθυνῶ σε can only refer to the multiplication of Abraham's posterity, this explanation must be regarded as too subtle. The simple reason for the abbreviation is, that the author of the epistle wished to give his citation in the briefest possible form.

The second member of the period, for which the former (in vers. 13, 14) was a preparation, now follows (ver. 15), introduced by καὶ οὕτως (comp. Acts vii. 8, 27, 44, and xxviii. 14: this καὶ οὕτως is frequent also in St. Paul): καὶ οὕτως μακροθυμήσας ἐπέτυχεν τῆς ἐπαγγελίας. Bleek translates: *And so he obtained the promise in his patient enduring*. One feels at

we have no degrading anthropomorphism here, [of which the Alexandrine Jews stood so much in fear, as is evident from many paraphrastic renderings in the LXX.]

¹ εἰ μήν is the reading of the LXX. here, both in the Vatican and Alexandrine texts.
² [Correctly rendered in our English version by "*that*"—*That in blessing I will bless thee*, etc.—TR.]

once how feeble and unmeaning this rendering is. If we understand by ἐπιτυχεῖν τῆς ἐπαγγελίας the obtaining a gracious promise on Mount Moriah, not the after fulfilment of that promise (which is undoubtedly the meaning of the same term at xi. 33), and by μακροθυμία Abraham's constancy in offering up Isaac, not his patient expectation afterwards of the fulfilment of what was then promised him, we have thoughts moving in a circle, and no logical progress. Μακροθυμία, too, is hardly the word to express Abraham's act of faith in the sacrifice of his son. But if we understand ἐπιτυχεῖν τῆς ἐπαγγελίας in the sense in which it must be taken xi. 33, and is taken by all modern expositors except Bleek here, and then read over the paragraph omitting μακροθυμήσας, we become at once aware how essential is the thought involved in that word, especially after the διὰ μακροθυμίας κληρονομούντων τ. ἐπαγγ. of ver. 12. And this being the case, it seems natural to connect καὶ οὕτως with μακροθυμήσας rather than with ἐπέτυχεν (as Tholuck and Hofmann do: *Entst.* 311). God's oath (in condescension to human weakness) sealed the promise to the patriarch as an immoveable ground of hope—καὶ οὕτως μακροθ.: *and so, patiently relying on that word of God, not uttered merely, but confirmed to him by oath, he obtained at last the promised blessings of which it assured him.* This gives a more connected order of thought than taking καὶ οὕτως with ἐπέτυχεν, as is done by Bleek, De Wette, and Lünemann, with exclusion of μακροθυμήσας. But, in fact, καὶ οὕτως belongs to both words, and to the whole clause which follows it. Böhme, recognising this, paraphrases correctly: *Atque ita, hoc est, tali promisso accepto, perseverans promissum hoc Dei adeptus est.* The confirmation of the promise by that oath made perseverance easy, —made it not impossible for Abraham, in this way of perseverance, to come into possession of the blessings promised him. The *perseverans,* too, in Böhme's translation is the right word, for μακροθυμήσας stands in the same relation to ἐπέτυχεν here as ἐπαγγειλάμενος to ὤμοσεν in ver. 13. We must not therefore render " *after he had endured,*" nor even " *because he endured,*" but " *while he endured,*" or, " *while enduring, he obtained the promise;*" the two being concurrent acts—in enduring he obtained. But in what sense is it said here that Abraham received the fulfilment of the promise, when we read,

xi. 13, 39, that the patriarchs "received not the promises," but only *beheld them afar off*? De Wette answers: "*Abraham obtained it, in having Isaac his son, in whom all his hopes were centred, thus restored to him, and in him the promised continuance of his line.*" Lünemann gives the same reply. But this is certainly incorrect so far as concerns the restoration of Isaac, which did not follow, but preceded the promise. But, overlooking this objection, it might no doubt be said that Abraham, after receiving back the child of promise as from the dead, lived to witness the commencing fulfilment of the εὐλογήσω and πληθυνῶ in the birth (fifteen years before his death) of Jacob-Israel,[1] the increase of Ishmael's family, and of those of the sons of Keturah. It is not probable, however, that the author regarded this as the obtaining of the promise, which, according to xi. 12, was fulfilled in nothing less than a posterity innumerable as the stars of heaven, and as the sand of the seashore. The apparent contradiction between the two differing statements is doubtless to be solved in this way : Abraham did not obtain the promise in this life ; but persevering unto death, he obtained it, as we see, afterwards in full accomplishment. In this it is assumed that his 175th year (in which he died) was not the end of Abraham's life ; as indeed is clear from xi. 13–16, which discloses so deep a view into the pilgrim-longings of the Hebrew patriarchs, and the satisfaction they have now received in the world above. As to the fulfilment of the present promise, the author would not be much concerned to find it in Abraham's being the ancestor not of Israel only, but of Edom also, and the various Arab tribes. The apostolic view of the patriarchal promise, which is here given as εἰ μὴν εὐλογῶν εὐλογήσω σε, καὶ πληθύνων πληθυνῶ σε, was based on the בְּיִצְחָק יִקָּרֵא לְךָ זָרַע of Gen. xxi. 12, according to which that race which was properly the seed of Abraham was to have its root in no other than Isaac. So commencing, the promise is fulfilled first in Abraham's becoming through Isaac the father of the Old Testament people of promise; and then " of many nations" under the New Testament through the ingrafting of the Gentiles ; and so, finally, in his being, through the propagation of a

---

[1] [We might suspect here the accidental omission of "and Esau," who was certainly as much entitled to mention as Ishmael and the sons of Keturah.—TR.]

like blessing (which, and not a natural descent, is the main thing here), πατὴρ πάντων τῶν πιστευόντων. This view, common to all the apostolic scriptures of the New Testament, is not founded on a spiritualizing of that which had at first a different meaning (Tholuck, Phil., etc.), but calls attention to what is the really central, true, and proper fulfilment of the Old Testament promises. Hofmann is therefore right in saying (*Weiss.* ii. 226) that it is not merely a spiritual fatherhood which (at Gal. iii. 7 and Rom. iv. 11) is ascribed by St. Paul to Abraham, but a patriarchal relation to one great whole, which in the times of the Old Testament embraced and was confined to Israel, but in those of the New Testament is extended, and at the same time confined to believers in Christ Jesus, in whom the seed of Abraham attains its final development, and through whom the blessing of Abraham is extended to all nations, so that for him the original promise, " *Unto thy seed will I give* אֶת־הָאָרֶץ" (Gen. xii. 7, xxiv. 7), is extended from " the land" of Israel to the whole " earth," while he becomes with all his members κληρονόμος τοῦ κόσμου. In an epistle so thoroughly Pauline as this to the Hebrews, no other view than this of the patriarchal promise is to be thought of. The relation, then, between Heb. vi. 15 and xi. 13, 39, is similar to that between John viii. 56[1] and Matt. xiii. 17. The universal salvation of the New Testament is the joy of the patriarchs in the unseen world. The "seed of Abraham" (in the wider sense) is the church of God, which took its rise in Israel, was speedily multiplied by additions from all nations, and is still self-multiplied (see note at ii. 16). Knowing this his high position and all-glorious hopes, Abraham exhibited here below this example of μακροθυμία. God's oath-sealed word of promise is now fulfilled in Christ; and Abraham, while living on in the unseen world, is conscious of and enjoys that fulfilment, and so may be said to have " obtained the promise."

The certifying of the promise by means of a divine oath becomes now the chief point for consideration; the writer's purpose being to show that a like duty to that of the patriarchs is imposed on ourselves in reference to a word of promise, sealed for us, like theirs, by an oath of God, and pointing onwards likewise to an unseen future. We need not assume,

[1] See Luthardt *in loc.*

with Bleek and others, that what now follows (ver. 16) is not immediately connected with what has preceded. All that was previously laid down concerning the divine confirmation of the promise by an oath has been summed up in the οὕτως of ver. 15. Keeping this, the main thought, in view, the writer proceeds:

Ver. 16. *For men indeed swear by the greater, and an oath by way of confirmation is for them an end of all gainsaying.*
Lachmann, following A.B.D.*, 47, 53, strikes out the μέν of μὲν γάρ, and Bleek and Lünemann approve; but the incomplete form of the statement in ver. 16 can scarcely dispense with this index of its incompleteness. The correlative clause, which should follow with δέ, though not expressed, is virtually involved in ver. 17: "*But God sweareth by Himself, and so beareth witness to the unchangeableness of His will.*" This μέν *solitarium*, whose δέ is either omitted altogether or involved in what follows,[1] is an instance of the anacolutha which not rarely occur in both St. Luke (*e.g.* Acts i. 1) and St. Paul (*e.g.* Rom. xi. 13 sq.). Comp. Winer, § 63, i. 2, *e.*[2] In κατὰ τοῦ μείζονος, the τοῦ μείζονος both here and ver. 13 *may* be a neuter (from τὸ μεῖζον, the greater thing or Being), as is evident from vii. 7; but it is more natural to take it as masculine here, the "Greater One" by whom men swear being God. Ὀμνύειν is not first found in Polybius and Dionysius of Halicarnassus, but already occasionally occurs in Xenophon and Demosthenes in alternation with ὀμνύναι. Next follows, connected by καί, a statement of the value and efficacy attaching to an oath in ordinary human estimation, from its taking to witness the majesty of God. The author comprehends under ὁ ὅρκος both the oath of promise (*juramentum promissorium*), which clenches an agreement, and the oath of assurance (*juramentum assertorium*), which confirms the truth of an affirmation or denial; and this fixes the sense of ἀντιλογία here, which may mean either the contradiction of something affirmed, or a strife or controversy between two parties. Here we must adopt the former signification,[3] as

---

[1] For examples of this μέν without a corresponding δέ, see Rost, *Beispielsammlung Syntaktischer Theil.* p. 399 (2d edit.). [The Cod. Sin. omits this μέν.—Tr.]

[2] Eng. tr. p. 597.   [3] Comp. Heb. vii. 7, xii. 3.

the latter would not suit the parallel drawn between the human and the divine.[1] What is affirmed in Prov. xviii. 18 of the lot (whereby God is invoked to make the decision), that ἀντιλογίας παύει ὁ κλῆρος, is here in the other sense of ἀντιλογία said of the oath, that it puts an end to all gainsaying from any quarter whatsoever. Εἰς βεβαίωσιν, i.e. in consequence of the oath, the thing in question is established, cannot be shaken or disputed any more. So Philo (i. 622, 17) says of an oath in general: τὰ ἐνδοιαζόμενα τῶν πραγμάτων ὅρκῳ διακρίνεται καὶ τὰ ἀβέβαια βεβαιοῦται καὶ τὰ ἄπιστα λαμβάνει πίστιν; and (ii. 35, 36) of that at Moriah in particular: "*God, greatly rejoicing in the faithfulness of the wise man towards Him, recompensed fidelity with fidelity, confirming by an oath the gifts which He promised* (τὴν δι' ὅρκου βεβαίωσιν ὧν ὑπέσχετο δωρεῶν), *and conversing with him no longer as God with a man, but as a Friend with his familiar.*" The depth of God's condescension in that act is illustrated by another parallel in Philo to our εἰς βεβαίωσιν here: "Men, when mistrusted, have recourse to the oath to gain credence for themselves; but God when simply speaking is worthy of belief, so that His words are in themselves, by reason of their own stability (βεβαιότητος ἕνεκα), in nothing different from an oath. The case stands thus, that what we say is credited for the sake of the oath, but the oath itself for God's sake; for, so far is it from being the case that God is worthy of belief because of the oath, on the contrary, the oath is stedfast because of God (in calling upon whom and taking Him for witness it consists)." This thought is also in our author's mind. The human oath overcomes all gainsaying; and therefore God, from whom all oaths have the force of their βεβαίωσις, vouchsafed, in accommodation to human infirmity, to take an oath Himself, and so to pledge the eternity of His being for the inviolability of His promise.[2]

---

[1] The Mosaic law, moreover, recognises the oath as a legal means of proof only to a very limited extent. It knows of the adjuration of a witness, but not of a putting him on his oath; and of oaths of purgation, but only in such cases as Ex. xxii. 6 sq. and 9 sq.

[2] Comp. *Talm. Babli Berachoth* 32a, where on בָּךְ (Ex. xxxii. 13) it is observed: "*Moses spoke before the Holy One, blessed be He: Lord of the world, hadst Thou sworn to them by heaven and earth, I should have thought,*

Ver. 17. *In which behalf God, willing more abundantly to show to the heirs of promise the immutability of his counsel, intervened with an oath.*

To refer ἐν ᾧ to the immediately preceding ὁ ὅρκος is, though most natural, forbidden by the ἐμεσίτευσεν ὅρκῳ of the main sentence; it would in that case be necessary to refer it back, beyond ὁ ὅρκος, to the notion of the act itself—τὸ ὀμνύειν : " *By which irrefragable assurance God, willing to show . . . ;*" but as we certainly find ἐν ᾧ employed ii. 18 in a neuter sense, this construction is also to be preferred here, as being simpler and less forced : " *Such being the case, i.e. an oath being once for all recognised as decisive in any matter, God took that course Himself.*"[1]

With regard to the internal construction of the sentence, the same must be said of ἐν ᾧ here as of οὕτως at ver. 15. It belongs exclusively neither to the main verb ἐμεσίτευσεν (Ebrard, Lünemann), nor to the participle βουλόμενος, but to the whole sentence which follows it : because the oath was regarded as such an end of gainsaying among men, God was not content with a mere affirmation, but added an oath to confirm it. He did this περισσότερον βουλόμενος ἐπιδεῖξαι τοῖς κληρονόμοις τῆς ἐπαγγελίας τὸ ἀμετάθετον τῆς βουλῆς αὐτοῦ. The aorist after βούλεσθαι and similar verbs is the usual construction.[2] Philo also uses (speaking of God) the same term,

that as heaven and earth pass away, so also Thine oath would pass away; but Thou hast sworn to them by Thy great Name. It is so then, that as Thy great Name liveth and endureth for ever, Thine oath endureth for ever also." In the parallel *Ex Rabba*, c. 44, it is said, " *As I live and endure for ever, so also does mine oath.*"

[1] So Bleek, De Wette, Tholuck, Ebrard, Lünemann. That ἐν ᾧ may be used in this sense is undeniable. In classical authors it is found in the significations—*because* (Plato, *Rep.* v. p. 455 B), *so far as* (Thucyd. vi. 55), *while* (Soph. *Trach.* 929). For its use here, as equivalent to ἐφ' ᾧ—*in which case, the matter so standing,* etc.—no proof seems necessary. Comp. Thomasius, *Dogm.* i. p. 316 sq. Winer (§ 48, pp. 405, 406 Eng. tr., and note) speaks with needless hesitation of the similar use of ἐν ᾧ and ἐφ' ᾧ, though it must be allowed that in most of the alleged cases the proof is not absolutely stringent (compare Krüger on Thucyd. vi. 55, who punctuates and interprets differently). The use of ἐν ᾧ as a conjunction in modern Greek has been already noticed at ii. 18. Compare Mullach, *Gramm. der griech. Vulgärspr.* p. 398.

[2] In all cases where that which is willed or determined on is not of set

βουλόμενος ἐπιδεῖξαι (ii. 675). The adverb περισσότερον [1] belongs to ἐπιδεῖξαι. It is here equivalent neither to *superfluously*, nor to *more than formerly* (ἔτι μᾶλλον ἢ πρότερον, Philo, ii. 39, 43), but to *abundantius, in fuller measure*, "*more abundantly*." He willed to show by something more than a mere asseveration the unchangeableness of His will: Τὸ ἀμετάθετον,—the neuter adjective being used for a substantive, *the immutable* for *immutability*,—a usage both classical[2] and Pauline (vid. Winer, § xxxiv. 2, Eng. tr. pp. 248, 249). Philo is fond of it. He speaks, for instance, in a fragment (ii. 680) of the generation of Israel in Moses' time as μυρία μὲν εὐεργετηθεῖσα, διὰ μυρίων δὲ ἐπιδειξαμένη τὸ ἀχάριστον. So also Clemens Romanus (cc. 19, 21), to whom our epistle served as a special model. It is possible, though it cannot be maintained as certain, that βουλόμενος and βουλή are used in this sentence with conscious regard to the assonance. God's promise was an efflux of a gracious βουλή, His oath an efflux of an additional and no less gracious βούλεσθαι. Βουλή is frequently employed by St. Luke to designate the gracious will of God (Luke vii. 30; Acts ii. 23, etc. etc.), by St. Paul once only (Eph. i. 11). It is a term of more general significance than θέλημα, which is the βουλή formed into a definite purpose.[3]

Τοῖς κληρονόμοις τῆς ἐπαγγελίας we leave for the present on one side, and proceed to consider the meaning of ἐμεσίτευσεν ὅρκῳ, *interposed with an oath*. The verb μεσιτεύειν has both transitive and intransitive signification: transitive—*to mediate* or *bring about anything by mediation*; intransitive—*to act as mediator, interpose* or *intervene*. Here, where no double-sided notion as that of διαθήκη has preceded, to prepare us for the former signification, the latter is the one intended. God intervened with His oath, as it were, between Himself the Promiser and men the receivers of His promise, thus giving

purpose represented as not to be immediately performed. See Lobeck, *Phryn.* p. 747.

[1] As at vii. 15. Cod. Vat. reads περισσοτέρως, as at ii. 1, xiii. 19. [Cod. Sin. reads περισσότερον here.—Tr.]

[2] *e.g.* Xen. *fragm.* τὸ ἀμετάκλαστον σου τῆς γνώμης. Thuc. vii. 73, ὑπὸ τοῦ περιχαροῦς τῆς νίκης.

[3] See Note D at the end of this volume.

them strong assurance. The meaning is similar to that bold word of prayer in the Old Testament, עָרְבֵנִי—*Be a surety for me with Thyself* (Job xvii. 3; Isa. xxxviii. 14; compare Ps. cxix. 122). God, in thus swearing by Himself, descends, as it were, from His own absolute exaltation, in order, so to speak, to look up to Himself after the manner of men, and take Himself to witness, and so by a gracious condescension confirm the promise for the sake of its inheritors, τοῖς κληρονόμοις τῆς ἐπαγγελίας.

After what has been already said on vers. 12, 15, it is clear that by these κληρονόμοις here we are to understand not those to whom the words of the promise were given, but rather those for whom its blessings are designed. But who are these here? Tholuck answers, *The saints of the Old Testament* (comp. xi. 9); Lünemann, *Christians, and Christians only;* Bleek, De Wette, and others say, *Both these and those, the patriarchs under the Old Testament,* and *all believers under the New.* That it cannot be the patriarchs who are exclusively meant, seems clear from the following sentence. Nor can we admit that by τῆς ἐπαγγελίας we are to understand exclusively the promise made to Abraham, "I will bless and multiply thee," though it may be allowed that in its ultimate fulfilment that promise is the goal of all history. But the Hebrews, who witnessed a manifest fulfilment of it in their own time, needed not to be reminded of its having been once confirmed by an oath; nor would the author for his present purpose have quoted it in such a form to them, but rather have reminded them of the promised blessing of "all nations" through Abraham's seed, which formed a part of it. The fact is, however, that he has in view another divine utterance, also confirmed by oath, which he is about to present more particularly to their minds, as a stimulus to pusillanimous and fainting hope. A glance at what follows is enough to show that he is now making full sail towards the haven of Christian hope and confidence in the great oath-established utterance of God concerning the priesthood of His Son. And we must therefore assume that his vision is enlarged here from the contemplation of Abraham and the patriarchs to that of all the heirs of the promise in general, and down into the Christian present. With the promise made and confirmed by oath to Abraham (Gen.

xxii. 17), which indeed still awaits its complete fulfilment, and is therefore still an object of faith, he now combines another prophecy, also confirmed by oath, concerning the priesthood after the order of Melchizedek (Ps. cx. 4), which has already been on his lips at the commencement of this episode of rebuke and warning (v. 10), and on the consideration of which he is now about more fully to enter. He does not, indeed, expressly draw a parallel between the two divine utterances while he has it in his mind. The promise to Abraham of a blessing and a multiplying to be accomplished in his Seed, and that of the eternal priesthood of Christ after the order of Melchizedek, are for him in essence one and the same. In speaking, therefore, of the κληρονόμοις τῆς ἐπαγγελίας here, he combines with Abraham and the saints of the Old Testament the church of believers under the New. They form one and the same company. The μακροθυμία of those who are gone before is an example and encouragement to those that follow. For us Christians, on whom "the ends of the world" are come, the twofold promise still remains confirmed by a twofold oath of God.

Ver. 18. *That by means of two immutable things, in which it is impossible that God should lie, we may have a strong encouragement who have fled for refuge to lay hold on the hope set before us.*
Διὰ δύο πραγμάτων: δύο is here treated as indeclinable, as it always is in the New Testament, and always in Homer,[1] frequently in Herodotus, and also in the best Attic writers. Πρᾶγμα is a fact or real thing, that which has real existence, or has really been done; in Philo, and elsewhere,[2] it commonly designates a supersensuous reality, that which a ῥῆμα (especially a divine ῥῆμα) has for its subject. The two immutable πράγματα here are the promise and the oath; both results of a divine πράσσειν,—a giving of a promise on the one hand, and a meeting human infirmity and tendency to doubt by adding the confirmation of an oath on the other. In both these facts or doings (compare πράγματα at Luke i. 1), that God should lie was simply impossible. The infinitive ψεύσασθαι is, with the accusative (τὸν) Θεόν, the subject of the sentence, ἀδύνατον the predicate. The reading Θεόν is preferable to τὸν Θεόν,

[1] Who has δύω, but not δυοῖν.   [2] See Lobeck, *Aglaophamus*, p. 142.

God as such being here spoken of. The sacred author does not express the thought: It would be impossible for God to lie in making *any* affirmation, much more impossible if He vouchsafed to swear to it. Such a climax *a minori ad majus* would be almost blasphemous: the one supposition is as unimaginable as the other. Nay, God's only purpose in thus combining a promise with an oath, was thereby to give us ἰσχυρὰν παράκλησιν. Παράκλησις is a calling upon, or appeal to, in the way of exhortation, encouragement, or comfort. "Comfort"[1] is out of the question here (the context being evidently against it). We should rather think of "*the word of exhortation*" (λόγος τῆς παρακλήσεως) of xiii. 22, or of the "*exhortation*" of xii. 5 (ἐκλέλησθε τῆς παρακλήσεως). These Hebrew Christians, whose faith is stumbling at the disparity between the poor visible present and the glorious promised future, stand in need of a "strong exhortation" or encouragement to better thoughts. And this they may find in the twofold unimpeachable assurance here given them by λόγος and ὅρκος.

In οἱ καταφυγόντες believers are designated as those who have sought and found a refuge. (Compare the similar construction with οἱ πιστεύσαντες, iv. 3, and the τοὺς φρουρουμένους διὰ πίστεως εἰς σωτηρίαν of 1 Pet. i. 5.) The rendering of οἱ καταφυγόντες by "those who have fled," or "those who have taken flight," is inexact. Καταφεύγειν is not *aufugere*, but *profugere*. Compare Acts xiv. 6, συνιδόντες κατέφυγον εἰς τὰς πόλεις; and Philo, i. 95, 6, φεύγει ἀφ' ἑαυτοῦ καταφεύγει ἐπὶ τὸν τῶν ὄντων Θεόν (he fleeth from himself, and taketh refuge in the God of truth and reality); i. 560, 15, ἐφ' ὅν (the Divine Logos) καταφεύγειν ὠφελιμώτατον (with whom it is most profitable to take refuge); and ii. 677, διὰ τὴν ἐπὶ τὸν σωτῆρα Θεὸν καταφυγήν. It may be questioned whether the following clause, κρατῆσαι τῆς προκειμένης ἐλπίδος, is to be connected with οἱ καταφυγόντες or with παράκλησιν. Böhme, Klee, De Wette, Ebrard, are for the former, while Œcumenius and others (among moderns, Bleek) take the latter, as the right connection. But as οἱ καταφυγόντες appears to stand more in need than παράκλησις of an additional word or phrase to illustrate its meaning, it seems the preferable course to connect it with κρατῆσαι [as the Eng. ver., "*who have fled for refuge to lay hold*

[1] [*i.e.* consolation, as in the English version.]

upon the hope set before us"]. The arrangement of the words also favours this view; and Luther's earlier rendering (before 1527) of the clause was in accordance with it: "*die wie zugeflohen sind zu halten an der fürgesetzten Hoffnung.*" Κρατῆσαι, therefore, is the ordinary aorist infinitive, expressive of *intention*. Compare, as examples, Heb. ix. 24, Luke i. 17 (*vid.* Rost, *Gramm.* § 125, 7). He who has reached an asylum lays hold of the object which there constitutes his security; he who takes refuge in the temple lays hold of the horns of the altar (1 Kings i. 50, ii. 28). We, in like manner, have sought an asylum in laying hold of the hope set before us in the promise and oath of God. And the strongest injunction is laid upon us now to keep fast hold of that on which we have laid hold (κρατεῖν includes both meanings), in the fact that God Himself has so solemnly assured us of His gracious purposes on our behalf.

Προκεῖσθαι is the usual word for the goal of a race or contest (ἀγών), or the prizes contended for (ἆθλα): so Philo and Josephus frequently, *e.g.* Jos. *Ant.* xv. 8, 1. The competitors were drawn from all quarters: κατ' ἐλπίδα τῶν προκειμένων καὶ τῆς νίκης εὐδοξίαν. Bleek, De Wette, and Tholuck, would accordingly explain τῆς προκειμένης ἐλπίδος here as = τῆς ἐλπίδος τῶν προκειμένων. It is the Christian hope itself which is here said to lie before us, *i.e.* in the divine word of promise, which, setting forth salvation and eternal life as our future destiny, makes hope so easy and so imperative. Finding no rest or satisfaction in that which is present, visible, and earthly, we have taken refuge in the gospel, to lay hold of and appropriate the hope there set before us. Hope is here primarily the subjective affection, but not exclusively so: it includes all the glorious things that the promise warrants us to hope for. It is to hope in this sense that the following clause refers:

Ver. 19. *Which we have as an anchor of the soul, a sure and stedfast one, and passing into that* [which lieth] *within the veil.*

It should have been needless to remark that ἥν does not refer to παράκλησιν (Grotius, Seb. Schmidt, etc.), but to ἐλπίδος. The anchor, never mentioned in the Old Testament,[1]

[1] There is no Semitic name for anchor either in post-biblical Hebrew or in the Aramaic dialects. In the Talmud and Midrash it is called חוגין, עוגין, אוגין. The Peshito has here and Acts xxvii. אוקינא or אוקינוס, probably

is used also as an emblem of hope in classical writers and on coins; whereas the likening of παράκλησις (or rather ἐπαγγελία) to an anchor is an unheard-of comparison, because quite unsuitable. The transition, moreover, from the one figure to the other is not violent. We have indeed two different figures, but homogeneous ones. In κρατῆσαι, hope is represented as a safe shelter for fugitives; in ἄγκυρα, as a strong holdfast for a tossed and troubled spirit, in imminent danger of making *shipwreck of the faith* (1 Tim. i. 19). The two adjectives ἀσφαλῆ[1] τε καὶ βεβαίαν belong to the predicate ἄγκυραν;[2] and καὶ εἰσερχομένην, too, is not to be referred to ἥν as a second predicate (Böhme, Bleek, Bloomfield, etc.), but to be regarded as a third attribute of ἄγκυραν. The image is a bold and noble one, selected from natural things to portray those above nature. The iron anchor of the seaman is cast downwards into the deep of the sea; but the hope-anchor of the Christian is thrown upwards into the deep of heaven, and passing through the super-celestial waters, finds its ground and fast-holding *there*.[3] It is a similar image when the

---

Semitic corruptions of ἄγκυρα (a similar form to ὄλυρα), which is also sometimes written ἄγγυρα. *Vid.* Leutsch u. Schneidewin, *Parœmiographi Græci*, i. 257, for the proverbial use of ἄγκυρα, and especially for that of ἱερὰ ἄγκυρα = the "last anchor," or forlorn hope.

[1] The reading ασφαλην of A.C.D.* may either be accentuated ἀσφαλῆν (with Lachmann), the ν being regarded as *paragogicum*, or ἀσφαλήν if regarded as a transition from the 3d to the 1st declension (Winer, § 9, Obs. 3); the forniss, according to Chöroboscus (Bekker's *Anecdot*. p. 1233), æolic, and to be pronounced with accent on the penultima, δυσμένην, κυκλοτέρην, εὐρυνέφην, instead of δυσμενῆ, κ.τ.λ. (comp. Otto Schneider, *Nicandrea*, p. 103). We have also (besides this ασφαλην) at Rom. xvi. 11 συγγενην (in A.D.*), and at Apoc. i. 13 ποδηρην (in A.); also ασεβην, Ps. ix. 23, x. 5, xxxvi. 35, in the same Alexandrine MS. of the LXX., which abounds in such barbarisms, derived from the popular language. The best writers present some not altogether dissimilar interchanges of forms, *e.g.* Δημοσθένην and Δημοσθένη, "Αρην and "Αρη, in Thucydides, etc. Compare also ἄνδραν, γυναῖκαν, in the Hellenistic dialect, and the collection of examples in Sturz, p. 127, and the note on Heb. viii. 5.

[2] So the Greek grammarians interpret ἄγκυρα as a metaphorical term for ἀσφάλεια.

[3] The ancients, too, admired the image. Our interpretation is that of one in the *Collectanea in Ep. ad Hebr.* of Sedulius Hybernus: *Nostram anchoram sursum mittimus ad interiora cæli sicut anchora ferrea mittitur ad interiora maris*.

"hand"[1] of one in prayer is said to be "poured out" towards heaven (Ps. lxxvii. 3; Eng. ver., ver. 2). "*The soul*" (says Ebrard truly and beautifully), "*like one in danger of shipwreck, casts forth her anchor; and though she cannot see whither the rope is running, she knows that the anchor itself is fastened to a ground*[2] *within the veil which hides the future and the heavenly from her view, and feels assured that if she can only keep fast hold to the end, she will finally be drawn by a Saviour's hand upwards and inwards to the eternal sanctuary. So hope contains within itself a power which draws on its own fulfilment.*" Τὸ ἐσώτερον τοῦ καταπετάσματος is the sanctuary within the veil, the holy of holies. Τὸ καταπέτασμα (called τὸ δεύτερον καταπ. ix. 3, or ἐνδότερον (Jos.) when specially distinguished from the κάλυμμα, which hung before the holy place) is always in the New Testament (without needing other descriptive epithet: see Philo, ii. 150, 32; 148, 30) the veil that hung before the holy of holies, and is called in Hebrew the פָּרֹכֶת. Εἰς πορεύεσθαι εἰς τὸ ἅγιον ἐσώτερον τοῦ καταπετάσματος is the usual formula for the entering of the high priest into the holy of holies on the day of atonement (Lev. xvi. 2, 12, 15; comp. Ex. xxvi. 33). This liturgical use of the formula was floating in our author's mind; and De Wette (with von Gerlach) is not altogether wrong in ascribing the bold turn given to the figure of the anchor by καὶ εἰσερχομένην, κ.τ.λ., to his purpose of reverting in this way to the original theme. It certainly serves that purpose, without, I think, being wholly occasioned by it. Till now a veil still hides (in a certain sense) the holy of holies from Christian eyes. Within that veil only the anchor of our hope can penetrate; but Jesus, as the forerunner, is already entered in within it in His own person.

Ver. 20. *Whither as forerunner Jesus for our sakes entered in, having become, after the order of Melchizedek, a high priest for eternity.*

Ὅπου is here used (as frequently) for ὅποι, the notions of

---

[1] [In the English authorized version it is, "*My sore* (marg. *hand*) *ran in the night.*"]

[2] "*Spem nobis a cælo porrexit tanquam funem a throno Dei ad nos usque demissum ac pertingentem et rursus a nobis penetrantem usque ad interiora cælorum ac Dei sedem.*"—Faber Stapulensis.

the movement towards and the terminus which bounds it being combined in one term. So ὅποι (which does not occur either in the LXX. or New Testament) is elsewhere frequently used for ὅπου (comp. Kühner, § 622, Anm. 2; Winer, § liv. 7). An anchor of hope goes (we have been told) into the innermost heavenly sanctuary. The present clause explains how, there laying hold, it brings to present rest our tempest-driven souls, and enables them to outride the storms of worldly life. It is by our having Jesus there already entered in, enthroned, and working for us within the veil.

From the concluding words, ἀρχιερεὺς γενόμενος εἰς τὸν αἰῶνα, it is evident that the author intended to connect in thought ὑπὲρ ἡμῶν with εἰσῆλθεν (Bleek, De Wette, Lünemann), and not with πρόδρομος (Böhme, Thol., Ebrard, etc.). The "entrance" of Jesus into the heavenly sanctuary is plainly regarded as a high-priestly action; but the Levitical high priest entered the holy of holies " on behalf of" (ὑπέρ) the congregation, *not* as their " forerunner." The idea therefore contained in πρόδρομος (and unfolded in our Lord's own words, John xiv. 2 sq.) must be considered as one apart by itself. The Levitical high priest, after slaying in the outer court, first the bullock of the sin-offering for himself and his house, and then the goat of the sin-offering for the congregation of Israel, entered into the typical holy of holies with the blood of the victims slain (on his own behalf and theirs); in like manner Jesus, after His death of self-sacrifice on earth, and the shedding of His blood here, entered into the heavenly holy of holies ὑπὲρ ἡμῶν, that is, thereby to perfect our atonement once for all, and to continue to mediate for us, but at the same time (as is further said, x. 19-21) to prepare a place and open the way for those who are destined to be for ever with Him where He is. That He thus, in His entering in for us, is at the same time our πρόδρομος, is what distinguishes Him from the typical high priest of the law, who represented a congregation which was entirely excluded from their holy of holies. But this is not all. Christ is not only High Priest, but also King; and High Priest not merely for a time, but for eternity. The ἱερεὺς εἰς τὸν αἰῶνα of the Psalm is here transformed into ἀρχιερεὺς εἰς τὸν αἰῶνα, to designate Him who is at once the antitype of Melchizedek, and a transcendently exalted antitype of Aaron.

And κατὰ τὴν τάξιν Μελχισεδέκ is put first emphatically, in order to make prominent the absolute elevation of royal supremacy inseparably connected with His dignity as High Priest. And what an anchor-ground of hope is that for us in God's own eternal heaven, in the midst of which our Jesus now sits enthroned, who having suffered *for us*, is now *for us* so highly exalted! We see Him not; for the "place" of God into which He is gone is undiscernible by the eyes of flesh. So far, therefore, a veil still hangs between us and Him. But unrestrained by such a barrier, the anchor of our hope goes on, and has reached already those calm supernal deeps, whence He who is taken from our sight invisibly holds fast and safe our souls, amid all the tossing billows of this world's wildest sea.

Μετὰ τὴν τάξιν Μελχισεδέκ is made the first of the three members of the significant participial sentence with which this portion of the epistle closes; and that not for the sake of emphasis only, but also because it is the writer's purpose no longer to delay, in the development of his parallel between Melchizedek and Christ, and in setting forth the rich materials for the strengthening of Christian faith therein contained. He is now arrived once more at the theme already given in a similar participial sentence at ver. 10, the threshold of which he then, out of regard to the condition of his readers, hesitated to overpass. To instruct them concerning that priesthood of Jesus Christ, which, commencing in His cross and passion here below, is continued above in a glorious exaltation, as far surpassing that of the Levitical cultus and Thorah as heaven surpasses earth—this is the aim and subject of the whole epistle. By such instruction the apostolic writer seeks to arm his readers against the offence of the cross of Jesus, and the dazzling seductiveness of the outward shows of Jewish worship. He would show them not only the divine necessity for our redemption of that once-offered high-priestly sacrifice of Himself made here below, but also the divine consolation for the church, in the continuance of His high-priestly action above. He has already approached very near (so far back as ii. 17) this the main subject of his epistle. But a further preparation was still needed before he could fully enter upon it.

The antitypical grandeur of the high-priesthood of Christ cannot be understood without a serious and intelligent recognition of his transcendent elevation above all the types of the Old Testament, and of the type and prophecy fulfilling character of the whole New Testament time. After speaking, therefore, briefly (at ii. 17, 18) of " the merciful and faithful High Priest, who is able to succour them that are tempted," the author makes a first digression, to exhibit the superiority of Christ to Moses (in ch. iii. 1-6); and this is followed by a long exhortation (iii. 7-iv. 13), in which he sets before his readers the punishment inflicted on Israel in the wilderness for disobedience to the word of God, and indirectly (at the same time) represents our Jesus as the true Joshua, by whom God is finally leading us into His rest. After this warning, which is at the same time a further preparatory instruction, he returns once more (iv. 14-16) to the great theme which fills his inmost soul, and begins (v. 1-10) the formal treatment of it. But having reached the point that Christ, being perfected through sufferings, is now High Priest after the order of Melchizedek (v. 9, 10), and so the antitype not of Aaron only, but also of the mysterious king-priest, or priest-king, of the patriarchal time, and therefore a king Himself as well as a high priest, the writer again breaks off before entering on the deep significance of this twofold type, or transporting himself to the heavenly places, where Christ is now both acting as High Priest and sits enthroned as King, interrupts the flow of his discourse under an oppressive sense of the low spiritual capacity of his readers, for which, as he warns them, they are themselves to blame (v. 11-vi. 8). For them the glory of the church is growing pale before that of the synagogue. They stand on the brink of an abyss, from which one who falls therein can be rescued no more (vi. 4, 8). Yet will he not forbear from the attempt once more to lift them up, along with himself, to the heights of Christian knowledge (vi. 3). The love which hopeth all things forbids him to entertain the worst expectations on their behalf (vi. 9, 10). With that hopeful love, therefore, he now exhorts the wavering to an imitation of the stedfast faith of Abraham, as a great exemplar, to whom in the first instance God had given a word of promise, and confirmed it with an oath (vi. 11-16). On two like pillars Christian hope, as he reminds them, is founded now,—a hope directed towards that unseen heavenly world whither Jesus as forerunner is gone before, being constituted by another oath of God Himself κατὰ τὴν τάξιν Μελχισεδὲκ ἀρχιερεὺς εἰς τὸν αἰῶνα.

With these last words the apostolic writer finds himself a third time face to face with the proper theme of his great argument. All that has been said hitherto was mere preparation; but now, after passing through the vestibule, he stands with his readers before the door of the innermost shrine of Christian truth. Having cleared away, so far as possible, all obscurities which beset his relation to them as their teacher, he is in nothing hindered now from opening that door, and by unfolding the richest meanings of the great prophetic word (Ps. cx. 4), exhibiting the surpassing glory of Christianity in contrast with Judaism.

SECOND PART OR CENTRAL MAIN DIVISION OF THE EPISTLE.

CHAP. VII. 1–X. 18.

THE MELCHIZEDEKIAN SUPRA-LEVITICAL CHARACTER AND DIGNITY OF OUR CELESTIAL HIGH PRIEST, WHO, AFTER ONE SELF-SACRIFICE ONCE OFFERED, IS NOW FOR EVER ROYALLY ENTHRONED.

ANALYSIS.

HE treatise here commencing (vii. 1), and having for its subject the high-priesthood of our Lord, is continued without break or episode of exhortation to ch. x. 18; after which the sacred writer resumes once more his former hortatory tone. The treatise itself, which thus forms the central portion of the epistle, may be divided into three sections; which might be respectively entitled: the 1st, Ἱερεὺς κατὰ τὴν τάξιν Μελχισεδέκ; the 2d, Ἀρχιερεύς; the 3d, Αἷμα τοῦ Χριστοῦ. Of these,

The First Section (ch. vii. 1–25) treats of Melchizedek, with reference to what is recorded in Gen. xiv.; and of Christ, as antitype of Melchizedek, with reference to Ps. cx. 4.

The Second Section (ch. vii. 26–ix. 12) treats of the antitypical relation in which the Priest after the order of Melchizedek stands to the Aaronic high priest, above whom he is raised: (a) by His one sacrifice, once offered on behalf of His church, and incapable of repetition; (b) by the divine and heavenly sphere in which His pontifical, and at the same time kingly, office is now discharged; and (c) by the eternal validity of that new covenant, "founded upon better promises," as Mediator of which He is now entered, "*with His own blood*," into "*the holy of holies.*"

The Third Section (ch. ix. 13–x. 18) treats of the inwardly purifying and saving operation of the blood of Christ, who, having once offered Himself as a sacrifice of propitiation (whereby He has obtained a full remission of all sins, and perfectly accomplished the will of God), must henceforth reign in that same glory in which and in no other form He is destined hereafter to return, and meanwhile has abolished all sacrifices of the law, and in particular every sin-offering (comp. Hofmann, *Entsteh.* p. 342 sq.).

The first of these three sections (ch. vii. 1–25), on the exposition of which we are about to enter, evidently divides itself into two halves (ch. vii. 1–10 and ch. vii. 11–25). The first half (A) treats of the priest-king Melchizedek as an historical personage (vii. 1–10), with reference to the narrative in Gen. xiv. It may be further subdivided thus: (*a*) The personal dignity and greatness of Melchizedek as priest and king (vii. 1–3); and (*b*) his superiority to the Levitical priesthood, proved by his superiority to Abraham, Levi's ancestor (vers. 4–10).

The second half (B) treats of our Lord as the antitype or Priest after the order of Melchizedek (vii. 11–25). As such our Lord is Priest, (*a*) not of the race of Aaron (11–14); (*b*) not by carnal descent of any kind, but through the absolute dignity of His own person (15–19); (*c*) by a divine oath (20–22); and (*d*) with an unchangeable priesthood, ever living to discharge it on our behalf (vers. 23–25). From these four heads conclusions are drawn backwards and forwards as to the performances of the Levitical priesthood on the one hand, and of that of Christ on the other. The author founds his whole argument on Ps. cx., after developing and expounding the typical elements in the historical Melchizedek of Gen. xiv., to which the κατὰ τὴν τάξιν Μέλχ. of the Psalm refers. The transition from the first typical (A) to the second antitypical (B) half of this section is finely conceived. The future tribe of Levi met Melchizedek in the person of their patriarch Abraham. It is an evident proof, therefore, of the insufficiency of the Levitical priesthood, that after its institution in the law another Priest should be ordained by God, and that after the order of the great priest-king, to whom Levi in Abraham had acknowledged himself subordinate.[1]

CHAP. VII. 1–25. *Melchizedek—that old mysterious king, that priest without beginning or end, whose appearance is so enigmatical and so significant in sacred history, and whose superior dignity was acknowledged by the great ancestor of the Levitical tribe—is (here set forth as) a type of Jesus Christ, who, springing from the royal tribe of Judah, was constituted, not by a legal and temporary ordinance, but by a divine unchangeable oath, an everlasting Priest, and thus exalted far above the mortal priests of the line of Aaron.*

The writer first compresses into one single compact sentence (vers. 1–3) everything, both in the utterances and in the very silence of holy Scripture, which may be regarded as characteristic of the person of Melchizedek, so as to convey a vivid impression of his mysteriously significant and unique personality.

Vers. 1–3. *For this Melchizedek, king of Salem, priest of God Most High, who met Abraham on his return from smiting the kings, and blessed him; to whom also Abraham imparted a tithe of all; he being first, by interpretation, "King of Righteousness," and then "King of Salem," that is, "King of Peace;" without father, without mother, without genealogy, and having neither beginning of days nor end of life; but, made to resemble the Son of God, abideth a priest perpetually.*

The main sentence is, οὗτος ὁ Μελχισεδέκ . . . μένει ἱερεὺς εἰς τὸ διηνεκές.[2] The clauses which fill up the interval between subject and predicate may be thus apportioned : All between βασιλεὺς Σαλήμ and ἐμέρισεν Ἀβραάμ belongs to the *subject*, and is in apposition with Melchizedek. All between πρῶτον μέν and μένει is *complement* of the *predicate*. All before

---
[1] See Note E at the end of this volume.
[2] This view of the main sentence explains at once the γάρ as connecting this verse with vi. 20. Jesus Christ is "*after the order of Melchizedek,*" in being "*a High Priest for ever;*" "FOR *this Melchizedek abideth a priest continually,*" [ἱερεύς in the case of the typical Melchizedek answering to ἀρχιερεύς in Christ the antitype, and εἰς τὸ διηνεκές in the one to εἰς τὸν αἰῶνα in the other].

πρῶτον μέν is simple *repetition* of what is recorded in the history (Gen. xiv.). All that follows is *Christological* interpretation and application of the historical record.

I. First, then, is put together what the Scripture expressly declares concerning Melchizedek (Gen. xiv. 18 seq.) :

(1.) That he was βασιλεὺς Σαλήμ—*king of Salem.* That the sacred writer himself identified this Salem with ancient Jerusalem cannot be doubted, with the evidence before us of the older tradition in the Targums and Josephus (*Ant.* i. 10, 2; *Bell.* vi. 10); beside which, a later one must, however, have arisen at an early date, seeing that in the time of Jerome the supposed ruins of the ancient palace of Melchizedek were pointed out at Salumias, which lay about eight Roman miles south of Scythopolis, in the territory of Samaria.[1] But there are reasons of greatest weight which support the credibility of the older tradition, as follows : (*a*) The name Melchizedek is formed according to the analogy of those of other ancient kings of Jerusalem (comp. *Adoni-zedek,* Josh. x. 1); (*b*) Salem (שָׁלֵם) is actually given at Ps. lxxvi. 3 (English version, ver. 2) as a name for Jerusalem, and, if the Psalm be a late one, poetry is (especially later poetry) fond of archaisms ; (*c*) The situation of Jerusalem is perfectly suitable for what is recorded at Gen. xiv. 17 seq. Abram is said to have been already met by the king of Sodom (ver. 17) " after his return," when Melchizedek brings forth " bread and wine" (ver. 18). Abram was therefore near home at the time of this meeting, and Mamre (or Hebron), where he then lived, was much nearer Jerusalem than any place in the neighbourhood of Scythopolis ; and finally, (*d*) Ps. xxiv. and cx. set their seal on this identification of the Salem of Melchizedek with Jerusalem. In the former the gates of the fortress of Jerusalem are called (פתחי עולם) " doors

---

[1] Jerome supposed this Salumias to be identical with the Saleim (Salim) of John iii. 23. Later critics have identified it with the αὐλῶν Σαλήμ of Judith iv. 4. The modern still inhabited village of *Sâlim,* eastward of Nablûs, cannot, at any rate, be the same place with the Saleim of St. John. [A Salem or Shalem is also mentioned as near Shechem at Gen. xxxiii. 18, according to the ancient versions (LXX., Peshito, Vulgate: *transivitque in Salem urbem Sichimorum,* etc.), followed by Luther and our English Bible : *Jacob came to Shalem, a city of Shechem.* But most modern interpreters take שָׁלֵם there to be an adjective—" Jacob came in good health (or prosperously) to the city of Shechem." See Bleek *in loc.*—Tr.]

of old," *i.e.* of unknown antiquity, while the latter Psalm had undoubtedly for its historical occasion the removal of the ark of the covenant to Mount Zion.[1] The point, however, with the author here is, not where Salem the city of Melchizedek was situated, but the name of the city itself; and a controversy, therefore, on a question of locality is here completely out of place.

(2.) It is recorded of Melchizedek that he was ἱερεὺς τοῦ Θεοῦ τοῦ ὑψίστου—*priest of God Most High, the only exalted One;* for El-eljôn (אֵל עֶלְיוֹן) does not mean, " the God who is highest among a plurality of other gods," but (as is clear from Abram's identification of Him with Jehovah at Gen. xiv. 22) the God who is in Himself exalted above all creaturely existence.[2]

(3.) Melchizedek meets Abram returning from the defeat of the kings—ὁ συναντήσας Ἀβραὰμ ὑποστρέφοντι ἀπὸ τῆς κοπῆς τῶν βασιλέων (the expression is taken from the LXX., Gen. xiv. 17). This meeting is the only instance in all the sacred history in which the great priest-king appears upon the scene. Abram is now at the summit, as it were, of earthly greatness, returning from the overthrow of four, the deliverance of five kings. Of his own free-will, without delay, with heroic courage, with victorious success, and by a perfectly disinterested course of action, he had maintained the cause and vindicated the rights of the oppressed. At this very moment, when thus raised above his fellow-men in deeds of prowess and works of mercy, Abram encounters the venerable form of the king of Salem, who steps forth for an instant from his mysterious seclusion, and as speedily retires into it again, but not before Abram, at his highest exaltation, has acknowledged in Melchizedek one higher than himself. For,

[1] Lünemann maintains, against Knobel and Ewald, that the Salem of Melchizedek was that on the Mid-Jordan.

[2] Even in the Phœnician dialect of Hebrew Ἐλιοῦν (*vid.* Sanchoniathon in Eus. *Præpar.* i. 10) had not this superlative meaning, but was simply a designation of the Godhead in itself, as is evident from the *eljonim veeljonoth* [" gods and goddesses"] of Plautus. Philo gives the right interpretation when he says, " The Logos, who is shadowed forth by Melchizedek, is 'Priest of God the Most High,' not as though there were another God who is not ' most high ;' for God is as the One in heaven above and in the earth beneath, and there is none beside Him " (i. 103, 36).

(4.) Melchizedek blesses Abram (καὶ εὐλογήσας), i.e. expresses in words of priestly benediction the thanksgiving for Abram's victory, which the bringing forth of bread and wine had silently expressed before.[1] Abram, so highly blessed himself already, and the root of blessing to all nations, receives the benediction, and willingly submits himself to the priest of God. For so we read, finally:

(5.) That Abram paid him tithe of all (ᾧ καὶ δεκατὴν ἀπὸ πάντων ἐμέρισεν Ἀβραάμ). The paying the tenth represents the consecrating surrender of the whole to God, whose representative the priest is. Abram, therefore, by this action of giving to Melchizedek the tithe of the spoil, acknowledged the divine character and dignity of his priesthood. The student may observe the dactylic movement with which this attributive clause opens (- -′ ⏑ ⏑ -′ ⏑ ⏑), and the stream of inspired rhetoric with which the whole sentence rolls along, showing how the sacred writer's mind was carried away by the profound grandeur of the type which he is here unfolding.[2]

II. Now follows, in the second place, the interpretation and application of the Scripture record, and in part even of its significant silence concerning Melchizedek. And (1) as to the significance of his own name and the name of his city. Melchizedek is first of all ἑρμηνευόμενος βασιλεὺς δικαιοσύνης; i.e., when one interprets his personal name, he is "king of righteousness." Both Philo[3] and Josephus[4] translate βασιλεὺς δίκαιος, whereas the rendering of our author is at once more grammatical, and more expressive as to the typical relation. Δικαιοσύνη is intentionally put without the article. The genitive (δικαιοσύνης) expresses that this is a king who rules in righteousness, whose sphere of action is righteousness, who lives according to its laws himself, and diffuses it all around him. In

[1] Philo calls such prayers and benedictions ἐπινίκιοι εὐχαί (i. 533, 33).

[2] We are as justified in calling attention to such characteristics in an epistle so distinguished by the delicacy of its rhythm, and the artful disposition of words, as was Dionysius of Halicarnassus in making similar observations with regard to some of the finest passages in Thucydides, Plato, and Demosthenes. Comp. the 18th section of his instructive work, de Compositione verborum.

[3] Phil. Op. i. 103, 4. Philo uses ἑρμηνεύεσθαι in precisely the same sense, e.g. i. 103, 48, ἑρμηνεύεται Ἀβραὰμ πατὴρ μετέωρος.

[4] Ant. i. 10, 2; Bell. vi. 10.

the next place (ἔπειτα δέ), his name of dignity or office, מלך שלם, is, when interpreted into Greek, βασιλεὺς εἰρήνης, for שלם signifies peacefulness or peace. Jerusalem itself is the inheritance or dwelling-place of peace.[1] Righteousness and peace are, in Old Testament prophecy, characteristics of the Messianic time. In respect to both these names pointing to those stars of hope for the divine future, Melchizedek is not accidentally, but in the purpose of God (who orders and arranges the developments of history even in such seemingly trivial circumstances as these), a fore-type of Christ. Christ's kingdom—as foretold, for instance, in the 72d Psalm—is one of perfect righteousness and perfect peace. He is "the righteous Branch" (*Tsemach*) of Jer. xxiii., "the Branch of righteousness" of Jer. xxxiii. 15, the Prince of Peace of Isa. ix. 5, "who shall speak peace to the nations" (Zech. ix. 10), who shall come as the incarnation of Peace into the midst of the heathen world (Mic. iv. 5). Of Christ in these respects the name and title of Melchizedek are pre-announcing types. We pass on to (2) the attributes assigned to Melchizedek, from the way in which he appears so suddenly and so uniquely in the midst of the sacred history (ἀπάτωρ, ἀμήτωρ, κ.τ.λ.). From these the inference has been drawn, that the writer must have regarded the priest-king Melchizedek as really the incarnation of some supernatural being, of an angel (as Origen, Didymus), or of the Holy Spirit (as Hieracas,[2] etc.), or of some "great divine power" (as the Melchizedetic anti-Trinitarians[3]), or of the Son of God Himself (as some of the ancients and several moderns[4]). Finally, some have supposed that our author may have shared the unproved so-called Jewish opinion, that Melchizedek was one who in fact had been miraculously called into existence and as miraculously withdrawn, and who is now abiding ever as an eternal priest,— an opinion or conjecture which they allow has not been dogmatically developed or established. (So Bleek, and still more wildly, Nagel.[5])

---

[1] [Or, "foundation of peace." So Gesenius in *Thesaur*. The medieval interpretation *Visio pacis* was founded on a mistaken etymology.—TR.]

[2] So also the author of *Quæstiones in V. et N. T.*

[3] *Vid.* Dorner, i. 505 seq.

[4] *E.g.* Molinæus, Cunæus, [Jones of Nayland].

[5] *Vid. die Bedeutung Melchizedeks im Hebräerbrief, Studien und Kriti-*

But, as Hofmann most justly observes (*Weiss.* i. 109), from such aberrations as these men would have been preserved, had they only remembered that no person or thing in the Old Testament is ever interpreted in the New Testament as typical or prophetical of Christ, except on the ground of the express words of the Old Testament concerning them, and that the very form in which the Holy Spirit puts His narrative belongs inseparably and essentially to the prophecy. De Wette, too, remarks with equal justice, that the whole assumption breaks down when we come to the μένει ἱερεὺς εἰς τὸ διηνεκές. If that were literally true of Melchizedek, his priesthood would come in collision not only with the priesthood of Aaron, but also with that of our Lord. A mere glance even at Philo would save us from such a mistake. There is no trace of his regarding Melchizedek as a superhuman being: he is for him a type of the ὀρθὸς λόγος. On the other hand, Philo, too, regards the silence of Scripture as not less intentional and significant than its utterances (i. 76, 20). He concludes from the fact that Scripture makes no mention of the death of Cain, that it meant to signify the "immortality of evil," *i.e.* its ceaseless and tormenting self-extension. Evil for him never dies (like Scylla), κατὰ τὸ τεθνάναι, but is ever dying, κατὰ τὸ ἀποθνήσκειν (i. 224, 43); or as he elsewhere expresses it, ὁ Κάϊν οὐκ ἀποθανεῖται, τὸ κακίας σύμβολον, ἣν ἀεὶ δεῖ ζῆν ἐν τῷ θνητῷ γένει παρ' ἀνθρώποις. He also calls Sarah ἀμήτωρ,[1] doubtless, as Mangey rightly observes, *quoniam ejus mater in sacris literis non memoratur.* With similar significance the rabbinical maxim says of the Gentile proselyte that "he has no father" after his conversion to Judaism (אין אבל גוי), *i.e.* none with a recognised name and genealogy in Jewish law. Classical authors, too, sometimes speak of those who have no known or distinguished parents as fatherless and motherless: *e.g.* Cic. *de orat.* ii. 64, *Quid hoc clamoris? quibus nec pater nec mater tanta confidentia estis?* (*vid.* Bleek, iii. 309.)

In considering, therefore, the following attributes more closely, we may assume that they are not literally applicable to

---

ken, 1849, 2, reprinted under the title, *Zur Charakteristik der Auffassung der A. T. im N. T., eine biblisch-theolog. Abh.* 1850, 8.

[1] i. 365, 46, and 481, 42. *Vid.* Grossmann, *de philosophiæ judaicæ sacræ vestigiis non nullis in Ep. ad Hebr. conspicuis,* p. 22.

the person of Melchizedek as an individual, but have a typical and prophetical significance, as applied to the manner in which he is mentioned in Scripture. In this reference he is ἀπάτωρ, ἀμήτωρ, ἀγενεαλόγητος. There is nothing said in holy writ either of his father or his mother, or of his genealogical tree. He has no father belonging, as any descendant of Aaron did, to a priestly race, nor even such a mother. No genealogy establishes his right to discharge the functions of the priesthood, which is essentially the same thing as Philo means when he says (i. 533, 34) of him, that he holds " a self-acquired, self-taught priesthood," and one bestowed on him purely by divine grace, without merit or ἔργον (i. 103, 1).[1] The attributes ἀπάτωρ and ἀμήτωρ would certainly admit of a typical reference to the earthly *fatherlessness* and the heavenly *motherlessness* of the Lord Jesus; but this interpretation, how much soever a favourite in the church, is destitute of any solid scriptural foundation.[2] Further, the third attribute, ἀγενεαλόγητος, shows[3] that all three combine to express the same thing, viz. that the royal priesthood of Melchizedek is to be regarded as a dignity purely personal, and not to be traced back to any circumstances of natural descent.

It is otherwise with what follows : μήτε ἀρχὴν ἡμερῶν μήτε ζωῆς τέλος ἔχων· ἀφομοιωμένος δὲ τῷ υἱῷ τοῦ Θεοῦ. This clause is not adequately interpreted when only made to mean, that no information is given either as to the commencement of Melchizedek's official life by way of succession, or the termination of it by his death. The words are intended to express much more than this very limited sense. As Melchizedek is a type of our Lord, 1*st*, through his name and title representing Him who should unite with His priesthood a kingship of righteousness and peace; and 2*dly*, through his attributes of ἀπάτωρ, ἀμ., ἀγεν., foreshadowing Him whose priesthood should be a per-

[1] Philo's words at i. 533, 34, are : ὁ τὴν αὐτομαθῆ καὶ αὐτοδίδακτον λαχὼν ἱερωσύνην. This description of Melchizedek's priesthood is also founded solely on the silence of Scripture.

[2] Philo, not without some measure of truth, says of the Logos (i. 562, 18) : γονέων ἀφθάρτων καὶ καθαρωτάτων ἔλαχεν, πατρὸς μὲν Θεοῦ ὅς καὶ τῶν συμπάντων ἐστὶ πατήρ, μητρὸς δὲ σοφίας δι' ἧς τὰ ὅλα ἦλθεν εἰς γένεσιν.

[3] Theodore of Mopsuestia, whose interpretation of vii. 3 is otherwise excellent, is not at a loss even here : τίς γὰρ ἂν γενεαλογία τοῦ ἐκ πατρὸς ὄντος μόνον.

sonal, not an inherited dignity; so is he, 3*dly*, as μήτε ἀρχὴν ἡμερῶν μήτε ζωῆς τέλος ἔχων, an earthly image of Him who, from His eternal community of essence with the Father, has in very deed neither beginning of days nor end of life. The Melchizedek of sacred history has neither a beginning nor end of his personal existence, but rather[1] is in this respect likewise, as in the official characteristics above referred to, made to image forth the eternal Son of God. The words are here so carefully selected, that their true meaning can hardly be mistaken. It is not merely the beginning and end of Melchizedek's official dignity, but the commencement and termination of his personal existence, which is here negatived. Hofmann indeed, starting with the assumption that the title "Son of God" does not belong to our Lord in His divine pre-existence, is obliged to support that view, by making ἡμερῶν exclusively refer to the days of His priesthood, and ζωῆς to His official life. But this very passage affords a strong argument against his assumption, which we have already combated in the notes to ch. i. 1–3. The sacred writer could have had no reason for using here the appellation τῷ υἱῷ τοῦ Θεοῦ rather than τῷ Χριστῷ, except to express by that term the eternity of the incarnate One, both *a parte ante* and *a parte post*, though by no means excluding a reference to Him as made man. I would not maintain, with Bl ek or Bengel,[2] that ἀφομοιωμένος is intended to indicate that our Lord was, as the eternal Logos, the pre-existent archetype of Melchizedek; for ἀφομοιοῦν would be correctly used even in reference to a future antitype (*i.e.* here in reference to our Lord in His earthly manifestation). Ἀφομοιοῦν signifies to make one thing in such way like another thing, that its special characteristics are withdrawn, as it were, from itself, and transferred to the other. The incarnate Son, having become man, in a manner correspondent to His eternal derivation from the substance of the Father, is here regarded as that Son of God of whom, looking backwards and forwards from the days of His flesh, it may be said that He hath neither beginning of days nor end of life, and that we have of this a typical representation in the abrupt appearance of the form of this

---

[1] For this meaning of δέ, see notes to ii. 6, iv. 13, vi. 12.

[2] [*Non dicitur Filius Dei assimilatus Melchisedeko sed contra; nam Filius Dei est antiquior et archetypus.*—BENGEL.]

priestly king, whose life at both ends is shrouded in the mystery of eternity. St. Chrysostom explains it well: "made like the Son of God. Wherein doth this likeness consist? In this, that we know of no beginning and no end of either,—in the one case because they have found *no record,* in the other because they have no existence."

The expressions ἀρχὴν ἡμερῶν and ζωῆς τέλος are finely chosen: He who is simply eternal has no *beginning of days,* being before all time; and after entering into the conditions of time He still has *no end of life,* because He cannot remain subject unto death, but takes the nature which He has assumed up into the communion of His original eternity. It is to be observed, moreover, that ἀφομοιωμένος[1] is not to be referred to Ps. cx. 4, where indeed[2] Christ is likened to *Melchizedek,* but not Melchizedek to Christ. The reference is still to Gen. xiv. God Himself, who makes history take form and shape in accordance with His own eternal counsels, is here the ἀφομοιῶν. There seems to be an intention to keep asunder the two Scripture passages by the avoidance of the expression of Ps. cx., εἰς τὸν αἰῶνα, and the substitution for it of εἰς τὸ διηνεκές,[3] as the significant closing word of the period. Melchizedek "remains a priest continually" (not "for ever," as in the Psalm); because, as Hofmann excellently interprets (*Schriftb.* ii. 1, 402), his priesthood is in Scripture simply continuous, unbroken by transmission or inheritance, and inherent in himself alone as a personal prerogative. This explanation was already given by Theodore of Mopsuestia. Tholuck, following others of the ancients, gives an interpretation quite contrary to the mind of the author, when he makes εἰς τὸ

---

[1] [Delitzsch reads ἀφομοιωμένος, as do Tischendorf and Alford, with C.D.E.L. The *text. rec.* has ἀφωμοιωμ., with A.B.K. and the Cod. Sin.; so also Lachmann.]

[2] As rightly observed by De Wette.

[3] [Dean Alford denies the propriety of this distinction, translating εἰς τὸ διην. by "for ever." He says it would be absurd to render it "for life," "seeing that all priests were for life." But, 1*st,* Is it so certain that all priests were for life? The high-priesthood of the Jews, in the times of the New Testament, was certainly not a life-long office. And 2*dly,* we need not translate "for life" if we reject the rendering "for ever." The notion involved in the rendering "perpetually," "without break or change," is still much below that of eternity.—Tr.]

διηνεκές refer to the eternal continuance and absorption of the type in the antitype. Τὸ διηνεκές, which does not occur in the LXX., and in the New Testament is found only in our epistle, is combined from διά and ἠνεκές = that which holds throughout, is continuous and unending. Melchizedek being invested in Scripture with an unchangeable, intransmissible priesthood, is in that respect made to be a figure of the Son of God.[1]

The apostolic writer having thus given a general description of the nature of the priesthood of Melchizedek, derived both from the statements and the non-statements of holy Scripture, proceeds to take a closer view of the special priestly action wherein he comes into direct contact with sacred history, in order to exhibit to his readers the superior dignity and greatness of the priest-king, as excelling that of Abraham and the Levitical priesthood.

Ver. 4. *But observe how great this man* (is), *to whom Abraham gave tithe also out of the chiefest things of the spoil,* (and he) *the father of the race.*

Θεωρεῖτε may be either indicative (comp. Acts iii. 16, xix. 26, xxv. 24) or imperative. The impassioned character of the style in the whole passage makes the latter more probable. The δέ is δὲ μεταβατικόν, marking that the writer proceeds to give a new turn to his argument. " Consider further how great the man is (or must have been) whom we have described" (vers. 1-3). Πηλίκος, *quantus,*[2] applies to age, size, and (as here) to ethical grandeur.

In the relative clause beginning ᾧ καί, Luther and others

---

[1] Tholuck is mistaken in alleging the Peshito version as favourable to his interpretation. Taking ἀφομοιωμ. . . . and . . . διηνεκές together, the Peshito renders thus: " But after the likeness of the Son of God, his priesthood abideth for ever." *Ba-dmutho* is not here " *in the antitype,*" but, as we have rendered it, and like the Hebrew בִּדְמוּת, " *after the likeness,*" or " according to the likeness," " in resemblance to," etc. The Greek grammarians grope in the dark for the derivation and formation of διηνεκής (see *e.g.* Cramer, *Anecdot.* ii. 355). Their proposed derivation from διήκω would be suitable, but is impossible (Lobeck, *Pathol.* 145). The true derivation is that from ΕΝΕΚΩ· (aor. ἤνεγκον), so that διηνεκής (Attic διανεκής) is a form analogous in its origin to the Latin *perpetuus* (*perpes*).

[2] For which D.* reads ἡλίκος, the form of the relative and of the dependent interrogative. *Vid.* Kühner, § 347.

wrongly attach the καί to 'Αβραάμ (" *unto whom even the patriarch Abraham gave a tenth of the spoils* "), whereas it belongs to the whole sentence. Compare the similar use of καί in Philo, i. 532, 38, τοῦ νικηφόρου Θεοῦ τροπαιοφόρου αὐτὸν ἀναδείξαντος ᾧ καὶ τὰς δεκάτας χαριστήρια τῆς νίκης ἀνατίθησι.[1] Lachmann omits the καί,—an omission which, like the inversion found in some authorities (ἔδωκεν 'Αβρ. for 'Αβρ. ἔδωκεν), destroys the fine anapæstic movement of the rhythm (_ _ ′ ⏑ ⏑ _ ′ ⏑ ⏑ _ ′). 'Ακροθίνια, generally found in the plural, is a classical word, which is foreign to the LXX., but is here very suitable to the grandeur and pathos of the style.[2] It denotes that which lies on the top of the heap of corn (θίς), " the finest of the wheat;" and then (improperly,[3] according to the scholiast to Euripides) the chief or finest portions of the spoils of war,[4] which were dedicated to the Deity : λαφύρων ἀπαρχαί, Hesychius.[5] It is questionable whether by ἐκ τῶν ἀκροθινίων we are to understand that Abraham gave a tithe of the best portions only of the booty, *i.e.* a tithe of the so-called ἀκροθίνια, or whether it means that, offering a tithe of the whole booty, he selected it from such choice portions ; in other words, whether the ἐκ indicates " that whereof the tithe consisted," or " that of which it was the tithe."[6] Lünemann contends for the latter view ; but the phrase is best interpreted by a reference to Num. xv. 21, in accordance with which the Hebrew version[7]

[1] It should be observed, however, that while the καί in Philo is a simple copula, combining the statements of two corresponding actions, the καί in our text marks a climax.

[2] Some MSS. have here and elsewhere the incorrect spelling ἀκροθήνια, where the η represents the long ι; for which compare Æschyl. *Eum.* 834 :

Πολλῆς δὲ χώρας τῆς δ' ἔτ' ἀκροθίνια.

H for ει is frequent in inscriptions (Franz, *Epigraph.* 247).

[3] [The scholiast's term is καταχρηστικῶς. The scholion (on Eur. *Phœn.* 203) is quoted by Alford from Bleek *in loc.*]

[4] Τῆς λείας is the term used in this reference by Josephus and Philo.

[5] But not quite equivalent to λάφυρα or σκῦλα, according to the glosses of Zonaras and others.

[6] [The words between inverted commas are taken from Dean Alford (whose *Commentary* was published two years after Delitzsch's), as expressing the distinction more lucidly than a literal version of the original : "*ob ix das des Theiles oder das dei Stoffes ist.*"]

[7] [The original is here so brief as to be almost misleading : *wonach der engl. Uebers. gut;* whereupon follow the Hebrew words. Delitzsch means,

of the New Testament published by the London Society of Missions to the Jews correctly renders it : מַעֲשֵׂר מֵרֵאשִׁית הַשָּׁלָל [a tenth from the first of the spoil]. Abraham gave the tithe ἀπὸ πάντων, the whole booty, but selected to compose it such articles as seemed most worthy of the venerable priest of God— the ἀκροθίνια. The words are arranged in the most euphonious, and at the same time logical order. Δεκάτην and ὁ πατριάρχης (◡ ◡ –′ –) form the two poles of the sentence; for the greatness of Melchizedek is denoted both by what he receives, and by the dignified position of him from whom he receives it. Πατριάρχης is a Hellenistic word, used in the New Testament by St. Luke in two places (Acts ii. 29 and vii. 8, 9). Abraham is so designated here, not as the head or ancestor of a particulor πατρία (ראש אבות), but as common father of the whole race of Israel, and indeed of all believers. He was the patriarch not merely of tithe-paying Israelites, but of tithe-claiming Levites too. He was the God-blessed ancestor of all the children of the promise. And yet he paid tithe to Melchizedek. The following verses go on to point out how exalted the personal dignity of Melchizedek must have been, to exercise such power over the patriarch.

Vers. 5, 6. *And indeed, while they of the sons of Levi receiving the priesthood have commandment to take tithes from the people, according to the law, that is, from their own brethren, although issued, like themselves, from the loins of Abraham, he, on the other hand, who hath no part in their genealogy, hath received tithes of Abraham himself, and bestowed his blessing on the possessor of the promises.*

The sacred writer proceeds with καί, atque (*and indeed*), to a further development of the greatness of Melchizedek, by an antithetical contrast of him with the Levitical priesthood, the germ of which already existed at that time in the person of Abraham. Bleek, De Wette, Lünemann, and others, translate wrongly: "those of the sons of Levi who obtain the priestly commission" [as if the priests were here expressly distinguished from the other Levites, which is not the author's meaning]. The ἐκ in ἐκ τῶν υἱῶν Λευί is not partitive, but of course, "the English translator into Hebrew," or, "the author of the Hebrew version published in England."]

causal, and indicative of origin. The meaning is: "those who, being of the sons of Levi, and by virtue of their descent from him, not by any inherent personal qualification, obtain the priesthood" (Hofmann); the point of importance in their case being not personal merit, but genealogical descent. Ἱερατεία¹ is used here only, and by St. Luke, i. 9. Elsewhere he uses ἱερωσύνη. The latter word signifies *priesthood* proper, *i.e.* priestly office or dignity; the former priestly service, or the sacerdotal constitution (*jus sacerdotale*). [Comp. Ecclus. xlv. 7, "*he gave him the priesthood among the people*," ἱερατείαν, with ver. 24, "*that he and his posterity should have the dignity of the priesthood*," ἱερωσύνης μεγαλεῖον.] The two notions, however, are frequently confounded. The LXX. uses ἱερατεία as the equivalent of כְּהֻנָּה in both significations.

We must not, however, in any case, take ἱερατεία here in the general sense of *any kind of sacred service*, so as to include the ministering Levites along with the priests proper, the Aaronidæ. There is indeed some temptation to attempt to do this, in order to avoid a serious difficulty, which most interpreters pass over in silence. The right of levying tithe belonged to the Levites in general, and was not confined to the Levitical priesthood. [The Levites alone, in fact, took tithe *of the people*, and then paid a tithe of their tithe *to the priests*.²] But here it is not the Levites in general, but only the Levitical priesthood, who, as tithe-takers from their brethren the people, are set in contrast with Melchizedek. Bleek proposes the following solution of the difficulty: It is not probable, he thinks, that the old arrangement continued after the exile, or that tithe was levied by any Levites who did not belong to the sacerdotal caste themselves, in order thus to be further tithed for the benefit of the priests. On the contrary, he supposes that all

---

¹ The accentuation is not ἱεράτεια. Abstract nouns from verbs in εύω are *paroxytona*. Arcadius (*de Accentibus*, p. 98, ed. Barker) cites as examples, ἑρμηνεία, βασιλεία, δουλεία, κολακεία, παιδεία. The most similar cases are those of the words πολιτεία, πραγματεία, and the like.

² Ebrard would meet the difficulty by laying the emphasis on the two words Λευί and λαμβάνοντες, translating, "those who, being of the sons of Levi, *receive* the priesthood," *i.e.* those descendants of Levi who, in virtue of their descent, are admitted to the priesthood. But this would require the author to have written οἱ υἱοὶ Λευὶ οἱ τὴν ἱερατείαν λαμβάνοντες.

tithe which came in would be taken by the priests for their own use, and for the general maintenance of the temple service; so that beside the priests, those Levites only who were actually engaged in the service of the sanctuary would receive any portion of the tithe, and that this they would do from the priests' hands, as a necessary means for their support. In this way he thinks it might become strictly true of the priests themselves, that they were ἀποδεκατοῦντες τὸν λαόν.[1] But the profound theologian and inquirer is here at fault. What he thinks so probable, is not only highly improbable in itself, but we read the direct contrary to it recorded at Neh. x. 38 seq., xii. 44, xiii. 10, and Tobit i. 6-8. These passages evidently show that the Levites, even after the exile, and not those Levites only who were engaged in the temple service at Jerusalem, but those also who were dispersed throughout the land, received their tithe (the so-called first tithe) themselves from the people, and then paid up the further tithe which was due from themselves to the priests.[2]

The facts of the case are as follows: The Israelite had first of all to pay to the Levites all the tithe of the produce of the soil, whether seed or fruit (Lev. xxvii. 30; Num. xviii. 21-24), this tithe being regarded as a therumah or heave-offering to the Lord, which He then made over to the Levites. "*For the tithe* (אֶת־מַעֲשַׂר) *of the children of Israel, which they heave as a heave-offering to Jehovah* (אשר ירימו לה' תרומה), *have I given unto the Levites for an inheritance: therefore have I said unto them* (or *of them*), *Among the children of Israel they shall have no inheritance*" (Num. xviii. 24). Out of this tithe, when paid over to them, the Levites had to raise (or "heave") a therumah on their own account for the Lord; and this "tithe of tithe" they had to give to the priests (Num. xviii. 26-28). The tithe paid by the people to the Levites was called מַעֲשֵׂר רִאשׁוֹן, "the first tithe;" and the tithe paid out of this by the Levites to the priests was called מַעֲשֵׂר מִן־הַמַּעֲשֵׂר, "the tithe from the tithe," or

---

[1] [Dean Alford apparently assumes this conjecture of Bleek's to be historical matter of fact. His words are: "*The writer speaks of the custom, whereby not all the Levites, but the priests only, received tithes.*" Bleek gives no authority for his conjecture; but see Note F, at the end of this volume.—Tr.]

[2] See Note F.

simply מעשר המ׳ (Neh. x. 39), "the tithe of the tithe," or the *tithe-therumah,* תְּרוּמַת הֹמ׳.[1] It must be to this second or priestly tithe, taken from the Levites, that the author of our epistle is here alluding; [and his manner of speaking of it seems to be inexact, when he says that the priests (not the Levites in general, but the priests in particular) " have commandment to take tithes of the people," their brethren, descendants with themselves of the patriarch Abraham]. A threefold solution only of this difficulty is possible: 1*st,* That of Thomas Aquinas, that the sacerdotal institute being the proper basis and object of all tithe-paying, the priests proper might be said to levy tithe *par excellence,* because they alone paid none. To which add, 2*dly,* that of Ribera, that the Levites (from whom the priests took the tithe of the tithe, the Levite therumah) are here comprehended under the term τὸν λαόν; and 3*dly,* that of Drusius, Seb. Schmidt, and others, that ἀποδεκατοῦν may be said of the priesthood, in reference to the whole people, because they actually took a tithe of the people's tithe-offerings.

By this last solution we may be content to abide. The parallel indeed is being drawn, not between Melchizedek and the Levites at all as such, but between Melchizedek and the priests under the Levitical law; and these last are here so expressly designated as οἱ ἐκ τῶν υἱῶν Λευὶ τὴν ἱερατείαν λαμβάνοντες, *i.e.* as הכהנים הלוים ("the priests the Levites"), to point out their office as limited by their origin.[2] The combination of τὸν λαόν with κατὰ τὸν νόμον—as expressing the idea, *those who according to the law constitute "the people"*—is a wrong one (Böhme and others). Not indeed that such a notion must have been expressed by τὸν λαὸν τὸν κατὰ τὸν νόμον; but here certainly it would be an awkward expression, and one of aimless particularity. Κατὰ τὸν νόμον must undoubtedly be taken with ἀποδεκατοῦν = they have commandment under the special provisions of the Mosaic law (comp. ix. 19) to impose tithe on the people, to take tithe of them. This

[1] [A paragraph, with two notes attached to it, follows in the text, in which Delitzsch puts together several apparent instances of the Jewish priests receiving tithes. This paragraph, with the notes incorporated, will be found in Note G, at the end of this volume.]

[2] For a very ingenious conjecture of the great Hebrew scholar Dr. Biesenthal of Berlin, see Note H at the end of this volume.

is the meaning here of ἀποδεκατοῦν, a verb not found in Josephus or Philo, and of the use of which no instance is alleged in classical literature. It occurs in this sense 1 Sam. viii. 15-17, but elsewhere in that of *paying tithe*. Tischendorf, following B.D.*, reads ἀποδεκατοῖν (as, according to the same authorities, κατασκηνοῖν at Matt. xiii. 32). It is not a dialectic[1] form: στεφανοῖν is found in an inscription (Krüger, i. 1, § 32, Anm. 7). Τὸν λαὸν receives the additional explanation (important for bringing out the antithesis), τοῦτ' ἐστιν τοὺς ἀδελφοὺς αὐτῶν, καίπερ ἐξεληλυθότας ἐκ τῆς ὀσφύος Ἀβραάμ (a Hebrew mode of expression, like Acts ii. 30), which Bleek, following Böhme, supposes to mean, that although it was descendants of Abraham the honoured patriarch who are thus tithed by the Levitical priesthood, yet that these nevertheless were their brethren, members of the same community,—a circumstance not so strange in itself as that Abraham should pay tithes to Melchizedek, a foreigner who had no legal rights over him. But this meaning can only with difficulty be fitted to the words—the objects must be turned into subjects; and the epexegetical clause ought to have been, τοῦτ' ἐστιν, ἐξ. μὲν ἐκ τῆς ὀσφύος Ἀβραάμ, ἀλλ' (or ὅμως μέντοι) ἑαυτῶν ἀδελφούς. But, in fact, the centre of gravity of the antithesis is a quite different one,—namely, the *Levitical* origin of the Jewish priests, and with that the *legal* determination of their powers. The sentence τοῦτ' ἐστιν means that nothing but positive law could make this difference between those who are otherwise equals; while the meaning of the antithesis in vers. 5, 6a is as follows: The priests of Israel have, by a divine ordinance of the law, and in virtue of their derivation from Levi, the pre-

---

[1] [*i.e.* not one of the four great dialects.] The Doric form of this infinitive would be ἀποδεκατῶν, the Æolic ἀποδεκάτοις (not ἀποδεκατοῖς), the Ionic ἀποδεκατοῦν and ἀποδεκατεῦν, but never ἀποδεκατοῖν. Nevertheless the existence of such a form both here and at Matt. xiii. 32 is made certain by its appearance in the MSS. B. and D. Lachmann would certainly have adopted it here, had he known that it is supported not only by the Vatican MS. (B.), but also by Cod. Claromontanus, *prim. man.* (D.*). Tischendorf, in his edition of the Codex Claromontanus (p. xviii.), reckons ἀποδεκατοῖν among Alexandrine forms; compare the various reading ζηλοῖν, Dressel, *Patres apostol.* p. 322, No. 4. Maittaise, Sturz, Schäfer on Gregor. Cor., and Ahrens, make no allusion to this form. [It is received by Alford into his text.]

rogative of levying tithe on their brethren, the other Abrahamidæ; but Melchizedek *received* tithes from Abraham himself, the forefather both of tithe-payers and tithe-imposers, without being empowered by any law to demand them of Abraham, or Abraham being so obliged to pay. Melchizedek therefore stands far more above Abraham, and in him above the Levitical priests, than these stand above their brethren : they do so in virtue of their birthright, and by legal prerogative; he, needing neither of these, in virtue of full inherent personal priestly power. The point of the argument is evidently indicated by the ὁ δὲ μὴ γενεαλογούμενος : " This man, however, although not" (or, without being) " recorded" (*i.e.* in Scripture[1]) " as deriving his descent from them" (the sons of Levi), " has (nevertheless) tithed Abraham." That is, Melchizedek, without being descended from Levi, and so without taking any part in that relation of super- or sub-ordination which the law has constituted between the Levites and other Israelites now, is found to have received tithes from Abraham himself, and that at a time when he ancestrally contained in his own person both Levi and Israel. Melchizedek, therefore, is exhibited as raised far above any subsequent distinction between the descendants of Abraham. And more than that, he has not only received tithe from the ancestor of the tithe-taking Levites : he has also bestowed a blessing on τὸν ἔχοντα τὰς ἐπαγγελίας, the possessor of the promises, the one who at that time was holding them (comp. ch. xi. 7).[2] It will be observed, moreover, that in Gen. xiv. Melchizedek's act of blessing precedes that of receiving the tithe. It was, indeed, his bestowal of the blessing which revealed to Abraham, and led him practically to recognise, Melchizedek's divine and sacerdotal prerogatives. But the writer here reverses the order of these two actions, their

---

[1] The μὴ γενεαλογούμενος here reflects a clear light on the meaning of the ἀγενεαλόγητος of ver. 3. Μή is here used (not οὐ), [" on the principle that in antitheses (comp. ver. 5), in which a peculiarly strong and emphatic negation is intended, the Greeks use μή in order to deny the very supposition itself" (Winer, § lv. p. 508, Eng. tr.)]. See also Rost, § 135, 5 (Winer, *Germ.* p. 431).

[2] Some MSS., among them A.C., read here εὐλόγησεν (ηὐλόγησεν). This substitution of the aorist for the perfect is an objectless change of tense. The two perfects δεδεκάτωκεν and εὐλόγηκεν express two finished actions, which continue even before our eyes on the face of the Scripture record.

historical connection being for him of less importance than their internal significance. The act of blessing is the exercise of a yet subliner privilege than that of receiving tithe. Melchizedek bestows a blessing on one to whom the promises are come down, in whom all their fulness is concentered, and in whom hereafter all generations will be blessed:

Ver. 7. *Now, beyond all contradiction, it is the less* (or the inferior) *which is blessed by the better* (or superior).

The relation of blessing and being blessed is that of giving and receiving. The giver of the blessing is always raised above the receiver, over whom he spreads or on whom he lays the benedictory hand, and pronounces the blessing over him in the power of God. The neuter τὸ ἔλαττον is used here to indicate the universality of the proposition (comp. vii. 19, xii. 13. And so Philo frequently: comp. i. 485, 27, and ii. 670 *ult.*). The reader is left to draw the conclusion himself. Melchizedek is greater than Abraham, the heir of so many promises. As he stands above the law in taking tithe from the ancestor of Levi, so also above the promise (so far at least as it is tied to the covenant line and people) in giving yet one benediction more to him who seemed to have the whole inheritance. The mysterious stranger vouchsafes a further blessing to one who by all men and for all men is already so richly blessed. And then, moreover, his priesthood is based neither on hereditary succession nor on positive law, but has a divine foundation, excelling in its unique and personal greatness all other greatness (whether bestowed by law or promise) under the Old Testament, and that exhibited even in the exalted personality of the founder and head of the covenant people.

Up to this point the writer has been engaged in proving Melchizedek's superiority to *Abraham immediately*, and only *mediately* his superiority to Abraham's descendants, the Levitical priesthood; now he gives another turn to the comparison, and sets forth the Levitical priesthood and that of Melchizedek in direct opposition one to the other.

Ver. 8. *And here indeed it is dying men that receive tithes, but there one of whom the witness is that he liveth.*

"Here"—ὧδε—refers, of course, not to Melchizedek, though

the last spoken of, but to the whole Levitical period, reaching down to the author's time, and so nearer to his view; and ἐκεῖ—"there"—to the occasion of which he is immediately speaking, but which, as belonging in fact to the distant past, is for him the more remote. "Here," he says then, tithes[1] are received year after year by ἀποθνήσκοντες (not θνητοί) ἄνθρωποι—"dying men"—those who, one after another, pass away in death. Single Levites owe all their dignity, not to any personal qualifications, but solely to their position for the time being as members of the tribe of Levi, the family of Aaron, to which certain privileges, summed up and symbolized in tithe-taking, are here attached.[2] It is otherwise in the case to which we are referring. THERE one receives tithes who is μαρτυρούμενος ὅτι ζῇ, of whom this witness is borne, that he abides in life. Μαρτυρεῖσθαι—to receive witness—is an expression frequent both in this epistle and in the Acts of the Apostles (cf. Acts vi. 3, x. 22, xvi. 2, xxii. 12). Of course the witness here referred to is that of Scripture. But where does Scripture testify this of Melchizedek? Some moderns are disposed to assume a double reference to Gen. xiv. and Ps. cx. 4 (so Bleek, De Wette, Lünemann). But in Ps. cx. 4 it is not Melchizedek himself, but his antitype, of whom it is said, *Thou art a Priest* εἰς τὸν αἰῶνα. It is a false consequence that Melchizedek's own priesthood is there said to be a never-ending one.[3] The witness of Scripture, moreover, according to our text, is

---

[1] Bleek observes here: "The plural (δεκάτας) is quite suitable in this place, both in reference to the various *kinds* of tithe received by the priests, and the oft-repeated *payment* of it." So also De Wette. The former part of the sentence would be more correctly worded, if for "kinds of tithe" we substituted "objects from which the tithe was taken." So Böhme. The priests (Cohanim), as we have seen (comp. Note G), received no other kind of tithe than the tithe therumah from the Levites.

[2] Hofmann, *Weiss.* i. 110.

[3] In this case we should have to say with Tholuck, following Œcumenius, "Melchizedek's typical priesthood lives on in the antitype;" or better, with Ebrard, "It is not Melchizedek as an individual man who has this testimony ὅτι ζῇ, but Melchizedek as a typical figure or picture presenting itself to the mind of the psalmist (Ps. cx.) in the historical framework assigned to it in Genesis (ch. xiv.)." But we have already declined to avail ourselves of this mode of solving the difficulty. It has the wording of the text against it, which says nothing of Melchizedek's office living on, but of the continuance in life of himself as a person.

NOT that Melchizedek's *office endures*, but that he himself, in his own person, "*liveth*,"—an expression to which Hofmann does full justice when he says, "Melchizedek acts as a person —as one who lives or exists: his priestly action is simply an action of his own personal life" (*Schriftb*. ii. 1, 402). It is, as I would express it, the discharge of an office which he holds, not as connected with any race or family, but which is rooted, so to speak, in his own personal being. What he does, he does as *from himself*, not as a link in a chain, or as a transient wave among other waves of individual existences. We must take ζῆν here, as before we took μήτε ἀρχὴν ἡμ., κ.τ.λ., as simply meaning that Scripture defines Melchizedek's life neither before nor after—assigns it no natural boundaries of birth or death [birth had nothing to do with his priesthood, death is not alluded to as depriving him of it; he passes it on to no one else]: the witness of Scripture concerning him is simply that he LIVETH. The actual historical Melchizedek no doubt died, but the Melchizedek of the sacred narrative does nothing but LIVE— fixed, as it were, in unchangeable existence by the pencil of inspiration, and so made the type of the Eternal Priest, the Son of God. The sacred writer has here still only Gen. xiv. in view: the abrupt and absolute way in which Melchizedek is there introduced is for him a Scripture testimony *that he liveth*.

This life without dying is the first point in which Melchizedek towers above the Levitical priesthood as constituted by the law. A second follows: Levi has himself paid tithe to Melchizedek, and so acknowledged his superiority.

Vers. 9, 10. *And, so to speak, in Abraham hath also Levi, who now receiveth tithes, been tithed (himself); for yet he was in the loins of his father when Melchizedek met him.*

Theodoret remarks that there would be this obvious answer for Jewish readers to make to the preceding argument: Nay, but Abraham was no priest himself, and it is therefore natural that he should pay tithes to Melchizedek, and receive his blessing. Aaron and his family were the first we know of the race of Abraham who were raised to sacerdotal rank and dignity. The author of the epistle anticipates such a retort here by a paradoxical but not less true assertion. Levi himself,[1] he says—he who now, in those of his posterity who are selected for the service of the sanctuary, receives tithe—did formerly, when Melchizedek met Abraham, being then *in lumbo patris*, in and by his father Abraham (διὰ 'Aβραάμ[2]), submit to be tithed. When the sacred writer thus speaks of Levi (both patriarch and tribe) as being then contained in the person of his ancestor, his words must be understood as expressing not only a physical, but also an ideal truth. Levi pre-existed in Abraham not only in the way of nature (*ratione seminis*, as Augustine says), but by the counsels of God. The justification of the author's position rests not only on the organic connection between all the individual members of the same family, but also on the divinely ordered connection of all the developments of the sacred history itself (in accordance with which Abraham was the ancestor by promise of the twelve patriarchs, and among them of Levi), and on the preformative and typical significance of every event in the personal history and experiences of Abraham. When these three considerations are put together, we have at once a justification of the statement, that in Abraham bowing down before Melchizedek, the whole race of the Abrahamidæ—and so, of course, the Levites among them—recognised the existence of a priesthood beyond the limits of the legal dispensation, and of the promises as tied to the covenant line. The objection that Christ, too, was a descendant of Abraham, might have been easily met with the reply, that the development of the divine purposes, which began with the patriarch, has reached its final goal in Jesus Christ, and is in Him no longer restrained by the limitations of its commencement—that in Him all particulars of type and prophecy have found a complete and personal fulfilment—that He is at once the true Melchizedek, and the promised seed of

---

[1] Lachmann and Tischendorf read Λευίς with A.B.C.* here, but Λευί (genitive) at ver. 5. [The Cod. Sin. reads λευει in both places.]

[2] διὰ 'Aβραάμ = διὰ τοῦ 'Aβραάμ, per Abr. (Syr., Vulg.). The ὁ δεκάτας λαμβάνων would be in Hebrew הַמְקַבֵּל מַעֲשֵׂרוֹת. The δεδεκάτωται must be paraphrastically rendered הוּצְרַךְ לְעַשֵׂר—one of the hundred proofs that the epistle was thought in Greek, not Hebrew. The *hithp.* הִתְעַשֵּׂר, to be tithed, and the *pual* עֻשַּׂר, to have been tithed (both of frequent occurrence in Mishnah and Gemara), have for their subject always the things from which the tithe is taken, never the persons on whom payment of it is imposed.

Abraham. But the truth of the statement is at once inverted, and turned into its opposite, when subjected to any materialistic interpretation, as when Levi or the Levites are assumed in such wise to have pre-existed in Abraham, as to take part as individuals in his actions and experiences.[1] To anticipate and avoid the offence of such perverse misinterpretation, the sacred writer adds a formula, unknown elsewhere to the language of the New Testament, but familiar in classical Greek and in the writings of Philo—ὡς ἔπος εἰπεῖν.[2] The formula in this connection may either mean, that the author wishes to give his thought the plainest possible expression—to say the whole in one word—or that his purpose is to moderate the roughness or audacity of a particular expression, by a " so to speak," or " so to say," before venturing to use it. The latter meaning is the one to be preferred here, and is that adopted by all modern interpreters. It is indeed, both for matter and for

[1] See Note I, at the end of the volume.
[2] In like manner, ὡς ἔπος φάναι, ὡς εἰπεῖν, ὡς φάναι, are also met with (vid. Bachmann, Anecdota, i. 422). The formula ὡς ἔπος εἰπεῖν was used in two ways: (1) When a speaker, breaking off, or not wishing to go more fully into a subject, summed up what he had to say as briefly as possible. So, for instance, Philo, i. 159. 23, 205. 37, along with (ὡς) συνελόντι φράσαι, i. 159. 15, 298. 32, ii. 23. 31 ; beside which, such other phrases as ὡς εἰπεῖν λόγῳ, ὡς ἁπλῷ λόγῳ, occur. This sense of ὡς ἔπος εἰπεῖν is not the suitable one for our text. The author is there not summing up a previous discussion, nor could he be said to have incurred any danger of being too diffuse. But the formula was quite as frequently employed (2) to introduce some strange or paradoxical statement. So again Philo, i. 3. 22, 353. 7, 364. 41, along with εἰ χρὴ τὸν πρόπον εἰπεῖν τοῦτον, i. 550. 48. So Thucydides, the abbreviated form ὡς εἰπεῖν (i. 1, ii. 51, iii. 39, vi. 72, vii. 18, 67, viii. 5 ; see Krüger and Poppo), while Plato and Demosthenes use the complete formula. In these cases, the writer or speaker is either urging himself on to say plainly out what he means, or is minded to claim only a relative and approximate validity for what he is uttering, like the Ciceronian " ut ita dicam" (e.g. Cic. de orat. iii. 41, Atque etiam si vereare, ne paullo durior translatio (i.e. the metaphorical expression) videatur mollienda est præposito sæpe verbo. Ut si olim M. Catone mortuo " pupillum senatum" quis relictum diceret, paullo durius ; sin " ut ita dicam pupillum" aliquanto mitius esset). Sometimes ὡς ἔπος εἰπεῖν is employed when a writer would indicate that he is speaking not exactly, but popularly, in conformity with the ordinary mode of expression. Comp. Ælian, n. a. iv. 36, λευκὴν οὐκ ὡς ἔπος εἰπεῖν ἀλλὰ καὶ χίονος καὶ γάλακτος πλέον λευκήν (vid. Lobeck, Paralipomena, p. 59).

manner, a hard saying, a σκληρὸς λόγος, to which utterance is about to be given, and one which needs the limitation which by this ὡς ἔπος εἰπεῖν it thus receives. The sacred writer having thus exhibited, on the basis of Gen. xiv., the superior station occupied by Melchizedek, within the bounds of sacred history, above that of Abraham and the Levitical priesthood, proceeds now, on the basis of Ps. cx., and the prophecy therein contained as to a new priest that should afterwards arise after the order of Melchizedek, to draw conclusions from its fulfilment in Jesus Christ, as to the relation in which this new priesthood of prophecy now stands to the old priesthood of the law, and to the ancient law itself. The insufficiency both of the Levitical priesthood, and the law established on it, is on all sides assumed by the prophetic word, and proved by its fulfilment. The first proof of this is contained in vers. 11-14. The author concludes from the proved subordination of Levi to Melchizedek, and the prophecy contained in the 110th Psalm, that the appearance of a new Priest, after the order of Melchizedek, implies the abrogation of the Levitical priesthood, and assumes the insufficiency of the law connected with it.

Ver. 11. *If then there was a perfecting through the Levitical priesthood—for the people has been legally constituted thereupon—what further need was there that, after the order of Melchizedek, a different priest should rise, and not be called " after the order of Aaron ?"* The interrogative τίς ἔτι χρεία is equivalent to τίς ἔτι χρεία ἦν, and that again equivalent to οὐκ ἔτι χρεία ἦν (there was no need), not οὐκ ἂν ἦν ἔτι χρεία, in whch case the meaning of the whole sentence would be somewhat different (comp. viii. 4). With ἄν in the *apodosis* we should have to render it: " *If there were perfection, there would be no need ;*" but without ἄν: " *If there was perfection, there was no need.*" It might also be rendered : " *If there had been perfection* (or a *perfecting*), *there would have been no need ;*" but the thought in Greek is a different one : the author speaks in both clauses from a standing-point in the past. Comp. for example, Plato, *Critias,* p. 52, E, ἐξῆν σοι ἀπιέναι ἐκ τῆς πόλεως, εἰ μὴ ἤρεσκόν σοι οἱ νόμοι (*It was in your power to leave the city, if the laws did not please you*);

or Antiph. *de cæde Herod.* § 13, ἐμοὶ εἰ μηδὲν διέφερε στέρεσθαι τῆσδε τῆς πόλεως, ἴσον ἦν μοι καὶ προσκληθέντι μὴ ἐλθεῖν, ἀλλ' ἐρήμην ὀφλεῖν τὴν δίκην (If it was a matter of indifference to me to be unable to live in this city, it was needless for me to trouble myself about appearing when summoned. I might just as well have let the judgment go by default). (*Vid.* Rost, § 121, 10, *c.*) The thought is similar in our text: If the Levitical priesthood was able to bring about perfection, what need was there to look any further? The author of the epistle thinks himself back into the time in which the prophetic oracle was given in the 110th Psalm, and speaks as objectively and as definitely as possible.

Τελείωσις, moral and religious perfection (or perfecting), is the establishment of complete, unclouded, and enduring communion with God, and the full realization of a state of peace with Him, which, founded on a true and ever-valid remission of sins, has for its consummation eternal glory: in one word, it is complete blessedness. That the Levitical priesthood had not accomplished this, is indicated already in the μέν of εἰ μὲν οὖν, provided it have in the author's mind an unexpressed correlative οὐδεμία δὲ ἦν. The analogy of μὲν γάρ, vi. 16, favours this view; and an example could scarcely be adduced in which the μέν of μὲν οὖν bears (not a correlative, but) that confirmative sense for which Hartung has now obtained general recognition.[1]

Διὰ τῆς λευιτικῆς ἱερωσύνης has attached to it the parenthetic clause ὁ λαὸς γὰρ ἐπ' αὐτῇ νενομοθέτητο. So it stands in the *text. rec.;* but instead of the pluperfect (without augment as frequently), the perfect νενομοθέτηται (found in A.B.C.D.* and other authorities) is now justly preferred, as is also (on the same testimony) ἐπ' αὐτῆς instead of ἐπ' αὐτῇ. The sense remains essentially the same; for as ἐπί *c. gen.* cannot be meant (as Grotius and Bleek would have it) in the sense "concerning," to apply to the object of the legal arrangement (in which case the parenthetic clause would be reduced to an almost meaningless observation), the meaning both times is, that the people had received the law on the ground of the

---

[1] See Klotz zu Devarius, p. 523: εἰ μὲν οὖν . . . εἰ δὲ μή occurs not unfrequently, sometimes with omission of the apodosis of the former sentence.

Levitical priesthood; that the Levitical priesthood had been made the foundation of their civil order; that the law rested entirely and altogether on the assumed existence of this priesthood, and was conditioned in its execution thereby. So De Wette, Tholuck, Ebrard, Lünemann, Hofmann. The design of the parenthetic clause is to set forth the central importance of the Levitical priesthood for the constitution of Israel under the law: the people, in their striving and longing after τελείωσις, were directed to that priesthood. If, then, it accomplished what, following the indications given by the law, men were seeking from it, what need was there of going any further?

The combination of ἀνίστασθαι, λέγεσθαι (Faber, Stap., Luther, and some others), "*what need was there of its being said that there should arise*," etc.? will now be scarcely to the taste of any one, and certainly could never have been to that of the author.[1] What he would say is: It was not needful that, after the order of Melchizedek, another kind of priest should be set up, and one of set purpose designated, as not being after the order of Aaron. 'Ανίστασθαι, to be placed on the theatre of history, *i.e.* by God, Acts iii. 22, vii. 37 (and also according to the current view, Acts xiii. 32, Gr.). Ἕτερον is used intentionally instead of ἄλλον, and in the second infinitive clause οὐ, not μή, because οὐ κατὰ τὴν τάξιν 'Ααρών is simply antithetical to κατὰ τὴν τάξιν Μελχ.

The author proceeds to prove his position, that had the Levitical priesthood accomplished a τελείωσις, the appointment of another priest, " not after the order of Aaron," would have been unnecessary, nay, inadmissible. This he proves from the consequences of such an innovation.

Ver. 12. *For the priesthood undergoing a change, there takes place of necessity a change also of the law.*

The view, that the parenthetical remark ὁ λαὸς γὰρ ἐπ'

---

[1] To prove the possibility of such a combination, Tholuck refers to the *Second Philippic* of Demosthenes (§ 2, p. 66), where the orator says, the more decidedly and openly any one declares himself against Philip, τοσούτῳ τὸ τί χρὴ ποιεῖν συμβουλεύσαι χαλεπώτερον εἶναι. A gentler, more pleasing flow of speech could hardly be imagined, with such an accumulation of infinitives;, but what Tholuck imagines our author to say would be a caricature of it.

αὐτῆς νενομοθέτηται of ver. 11 is here confirmed, should not have been revived by Lünemann. It is rather a confirmation of the τίς ἔτι χρεία, in a way for which that parenthesis prepares us (Bleek, De Wette). A μετάθεσις or transference (*translatio*, Vulg.) is at the same time nothing less than a transference and change of the law itself. The author purposely makes use of a word which implies a change, not accidental merely, but essential; the point in question being the actual transference of the priesthood from one tribe to another, —a *translatio*, as J. Cappellus has well observed, *non veluti a ramo ad ramum, sed ab arbore ad arborem*. By νόμου (= τοῦ νόμου; comp. on i. 1) is not meant any constitutional law whatsoever, but the law of Sinai. And although the ceremonial part of the Thorah is here specially thought of, the political and moral is included along with it. As the great saying (Matt. v. 17) holds good of the law in all its parts, which, while the Lord abolished it as to its temporal form in the Old Testament, He yet fulfilled as to its true eternal essence,[1] so a change of the priesthood affects and transforms not only the outward legal order of things, but also the ethical relation to God thereby constituted, in its various bearings. "*The change of the ritual law necessitates also that of the moral*" (Tholuck).

Hitherto the author has been contemplating past and future from the standpoint of the prophecy, Ps. cx. 4: he now places himself on that of its fulfilment. He illustrates the inevitable and far-reaching results of the setting up of a Priest "not after the order of Aaron," by directing attention to the person of Him who has appeared as Priest after the order of Melchizedek.

Ver. 13. *For he of whom these things are spoken belongeth to another tribe, from which no one hath given attendance at the altar.*

Ταῦτα refers to the words of Ps. cx. 4. Ἐπί c. acc. is used as at Mark ix. 12 sq. and Rom. iv. 9; in like manner it is often used by the Greek grammarians to denote that to which a word or thing refers—its significance or application.[2] He to whom

---

[1] See Delitzsch, *Untersuchungen über das Matthäus-Ev.* p. 76.
[2] *E.g. Etym. M.* 169, 10, αὐδήεσσαν, ἔνδοξον ὀνομαστὴν ὁμοιόφθογγον, ἐπὶ Λευκοθέαν ἢ πρόμαντιν, ἢ οὐδήεσσαν, ἐπίγειον, ἐπὶ κίρκην Φαρμακίδα. *Schol.*

CHAP. VII. 14. 353

these words of the Psalm refer, has become the member of another tribe (which circumstance the perfect expresses as an absolute existing fact), a tribe of which no one has ever performed the service of the altar—never, that is, in accordance with the divine law: any self-willed action contrary to the law is not here taken into account. Προσέχειν τινί is to bestow attention or labour upon something, *operam dare*, as 1 Tim. iv. 13; comp. Acts xx. 28. The perfect προσέσχηκεν (A.C. προσέσχεν) denotes what from of old until now has been thus, and not otherwise. The reading προσέστηκε (Erasm., Colin.) is a patristic gloss, destitute of support from manuscripts. Neither προσέχειν τῷ θυσιαστηρίῳ nor προσστῆναι is found in the Septuagint. Both expressions are good Greek. The first is here historically the more exact.

Not to the tribe of Levi, but to another tribe, which has never been, in any one of its members, called to the sacrificial service of the priesthood, does He belong of whom the 110th Psalm prophesies.

Ver. 14. *For it is evident that our Lord is sprung from Judah, in reference to which tribe Moses spake nothing concerning priesthood.*

The author can appeal to our Lord's descent from the house of David (Rom. i. 3), and consequently from the tribe of Judah (Rev. v. 5), as to something evident—a well-known and publicly recognised fact[1]—a πρόδηλον. [The word is Pauline (comp. 1 Tim. v. 24, 25), and a special favourite with Clemens Romanus. Πρόδηλον is a strong antithesis of ἄδηλον or ἀγνοούμενον, with προ as in *propalam*.] " *Our Lord is sprung or arisen out of Judah*"—ἀνατέταλκεν. How are we to understand the image involved in this verb? Does it refer to the springing forth of a shoot or branch, or to the uprising of the sun? (The word ἀνατέλλειν itself unites both meanings, that of צמח and that of זרח.) As the reference is here to a

---

Aristid. 317, 15, ἐγένετο δὲ αὕτη ἡ ἀνακήρυξις ἐπὶ τοὺς νικῶντας ἐν ταῖς ἱππηλασίαις. In such cases ἐπί τινος is the more common, ἐπί τινι the more rare construction. The idea presented is somewhat different, according as we use the one case or the other. See Lehrs, *Herodian*, pp. 449-453.

[1] See Note J at the end of the volume.

VOL. I. Z

genealogy, and the sacred writer had probably in his mind the Septuagint rendering of the Messianic title צֶמַח, Branch, by 'Ανατολή[1] (Jer. xxiii. 5, xxxiii. 15 ; Zech. iii. 8 (Eng. ver. iv. 2), vi. 12), it is most natural to take ἀνατέταλκεν as a figure drawn from the vegetable kingdom (Tholuck). But the other figure also, taken from the rising of the sun, or of a star (Ebrard), commends itself, through its close relation to Num. xxiv. 17 (ἀνατελεῖ ἄστρον ἐξ 'Ιακώβ), compared with Isa. lx. 1 and Mal. iii. 20 (Eng. ver. iv. 2) ; for which reason De Wette and Lünemann have pronounced no decision, while Bleek inclines to assume a combination of both images (as, according to his view, there is a similar combination in Luke i. 78, ἀνατολὴ ἐξ ὕψους). The two figures, however, are so different in kind, that the author must have connected the idea of either the one or the other with the word; and it remains, therefore, more probable that he here imaged to himself our Lord as a noble branch, springing up out of the stock of Judah. ['Aνατέλλειν, according to Eustathius on *Il.* v. 777, is a σεμνοτέρα καὶ θειοτέρα λέξις for φύεσθαι.] " With respect to the tribe of Judah," however (εἰς as Acts ii. 25, Eph. v. 32), " Moses," the mediator of the law, " spake" οὐδὲν περὶ ἱερωσύνης, that is, nothing about the priesthood being conferred upon it. Οὐδὲν π. ἱερωσ. is probably a gloss which has taken the place of the original and now with justice generally preferred reading περὶ ἱερέων οὐδέν (A.B.C.*, D.*, E., It., Vulg., Copt., *al.*),[2] which would mean that Moses had said nothing in reference to the members of this tribe being priests. The generic plural here (ἱερέων) tends to the abstract meaning of ἱερωσύνης. Thus terminates the first of the four links in the chain of inferences which occupy vers. 11–25. Without a change of the law itself, a priest after the order of Melchizedek is inconceivable : that is proved by

---

[1] It must be observed that Philo understands this ἀνατολή of the Logos as " *Lumen de Lumine :*" τοῦτον μὲν γὰρ πρεσβύτατον υἱὸν ὁ τῶν ὄντων ἀνέτειλε πατήρ (i. 414, 22). But here he comes in direct conflict with the inspired word of holy Scripture [knowing nothing as he does of the incarnation of the Logos] ; for Scripture distinctly speaks of a " man" as being that 'Ανατολή—ἰδοὺ ἄνθρωπος, ᾧ ὄνομα ἀνατολή. In this [as in so many other cases] the spiritualistic and unhistorical character of Philo's system betrays itself.

[2] [Cod. Sin. reads, περὶ ἱερέων Μωϋσῆς οὐδέν.]

the fact of fulfilment, in addition to the original word of prophecy. The Levitical priesthood, and the law in general, is thereby declared inadequate or incompetent to bring about perfection. This concluding thought may be considered as the δέ to the μέν of ver. 11. Next follows a second proof that the Levitical priesthood, and consequently the law too, which stands and falls with it, was incapable of giving us the needed perfecting.

Vers. 15–17. *And in yet greater measure is this evident: if, after the similitude of Melchizedek, there ariseth another priest, who hath become this, not after the law of a carnal commandment, but after the power of indissoluble life. For this witness is borne, " Thou art a priest for ever, after the order of Melchizedek."*

That which, from what follows, is become περισσότερον κατάδηλον, is not a change of the law as a consequence of the change of the priesthood (Bleek, De Wette, Tholuck, Lünem.), but the fact that τελείωσις οὐκ ἦν διὰ τῆς λευϊτικῆς ἱερωσύνης (Bengel; Hofmann, *Schriftbeweis*, ii. 1, 403). The proposition that the μετάθεσις of the priesthood is a μετάθεσις of the law itself, is not the author's main proposition, but only helps him to confirm it; to show, namely, that the Levitical priesthood does not accomplish what we need, and that this observation may be extended to the whole law. The insufficiency of the Levitical priesthood has been proved (vers. 11–14) from the setting up of a priest after another order than that of Aaron; and this insufficiency is yet more evident, he proceeds to say, when the priest so set up is not only distinguished by descent from the Levitical priests, but one essentially different from them, as being a priest after the similitude of Melchizedek, and in that his priesthood belongs to Him not in a legal, but in a purely personal way. What was evident as matter of fact was called πρόδηλον (ver. 14); what is evident is by way of inference called κατάδηλον here.[1] Proceeding from difference of descent to dissimilarity of nature, the sacred writer employs κατὰ τὴν ὁμοιότητα Μελχ. (placed emphatically at the commencement of the clause) instead of κατὰ τὴν τάξιν Μελχ.

[1] Comp. the similar αὐτόδηλος, "self-evident," in Æschylus and (probably also in) Aristophanes.

The relative clause expresses that wherein this difference in kind consists: ὃς γέγονεν (namely ἱερεύς), οὐ κατὰ νόμον ἐντολῆς σαρκικῆς, ἀλλὰ κατὰ δύναμιν ζωῆς ἀκαταλύτου. The Old Testament commandment respecting the priesthood is called ἐντολὴ σαρκική, because it entrusted carnal (i.e. flesh-clothed), and hence dying men, with the office, and connected that office with a carnal descent (comp. xii. 9), and in general with conditions relating to the σάρξ in its changeableness, impurity, and liability to perish. Instead of σαρκικῆς, however, we have, with Griesbach, Lachmann, and Tischendorf (following the decisive testimony of A.B.C.*, D.*, I., al.[1]), to read σαρκίνης. The adjectives in ινος are so-called μετουσιαστικά, that is, they designate things from the materials of which they consist (e.g. ἀκάνθινος, ἅλινος, αἱμάτινος, ἀέρινος, αἰθέρινος, τράγινος, Lobeck, Pathol. p. 200 ss.); whereas the noun-derived adjectives in ικός (as e.g. ἁλικός, ἀνθρωπικός, τραγικός) designate things according to their kind, or some special characteristic. Σάρκινος, therefore, signifies that which is *made of flesh* (*carneus*), or *fleshy* (*carnosus*), while σαρκικός denotes that which is of the nature of flesh—*fleshly, carnal* (*carnalis*). According to this distinction, the sacred writer should in strictness have written σαρκικῆς, and it is indeed possible that so he did write himself; but that here, as at Rom. vii. 14 and 1 Cor. iii. 1, σαρκινής early crept into the text, through the non-biblical Greek knowing only the form σάρκινος, and not that of σαρκικός.[2] It is also possible that the apostolic idiom permitted itself, when minded to express very strongly, and so to speak massively, the notion of carnality or fleshliness, to use σάρκινος for σαρκικός; and it is indeed the case elsewhere also, that adjectives in ινος (as ἀνθρώπινος[3]) combine with their own the signification of the corresponding forms in ικός (see Winer, p. 89 sq.). The latter seems to me the more probable view. Ἐντολὴ σαρκίνη is a commandment which has flesh for the matter it deals with,

---

[1] [So now also Cod. Sin.]

[2] Σάρκινος as a various reading for σαρκικός is found also in D.* F. G. at 1 Cor. iii. 3, and in F.G. at 2 Cor. i. 12.

[3] Thomas Magister's insisting on ἀνθρωπεία φύσις being used, and not ἀνθρωπίνη, is a piece of self-willed purism. In Plato we read once τὸ ἀνθρώπειον γένος, and in Antoninus ἀνθρωπικὴ φύσις. The latter is probably also an affectation.

or one exclusively relating to that which is earthly and natural. Νόμος is the more comprehensive expression of the two; and neither here nor Rom. vii. 21, 23, has it any other signification than the usual one. The תורה (νόμος) is a body of מצות (ἐντολαί) with legal validity (Eph. ii. 15); the תורת כהנים (the law of priests) is here called an ἐντολή, as being part of the whole תורה.[1] Κατὰ νόμον ἐντολῆς σαρκίνης signifies in conformity with a law, and that comprised in a precept having sole reference to the outward affairs of man in the present life. The antithesis of this literal, outward νόμος, anticipating the will of man, and therefore not in subjection to his free-will, is the inward living δύναμις which impels and strengthens from within. This spiritual energy, in contradistinction to the νόμος of an ἐντολή conditioned by the σάρξ of our human nature, and therefore presupposing a ceaseless change of the bearers of the priestly office, is described here as δύναμις ζωῆς ἀκαταλύτου, i.e. the power of a life which, because indissoluble, makes him who once has obtained and holds its priesthood, in his own person (not as member of this or that tribe), the bearer of such priestly office for evermore. The sacred writer means of course the Lord Jesus, and is thinking (as Hofmann with perfect justice remarks, Schriftb. ii. 1, 403) not of His life as commencing with His miraculous conception, but of that which began with His resurrection to glory. The subject here is not the Lord's priesthood, as it commenced in His passion and death, the antitype of Aaron's priesthood, but that priesthood after the order of Melchizedek, with which He is invested now in consequence of His return to God. The author, however, speaks hypothetically (ver. 15 sq.); and the "*other priest*," whose priesthood rests not on the natural ground of fleshly descent, character, and an external law, but on the spiritual basis (ix. 14) of His own absolute personality and its inward living power, is in the first instance the ἱερεύς prophesied of in the Psalm from which these characteristics are borrowed. And therefore, in order to prove that that "other priest" who should hereafter be is one so entirely different from those of Aaron's line, he proceeds to notice in ver. 17 how the Psalm bears witness to Him as a "priest for eternity," and "after the order

[1] The LXX. renders כל־התורה (2 Kings xxi. 8) by πᾶσα ἡ ἐντολή, and תורת מׁשה (2 Chron. xxx. 16) by ἡ ἐντολὴ Μωϋσῆ.

of Melchizedek." [The *text rec.* reads μαρτυρεῖ (*i.e.* ὁ Θεός), but the weight of authority is in favour of μαρτυρεῖται.[1] "Ὅτι is the ὅτι of citation, as at x. 8, xi. 18.] The sacred writer proceeds further to show what conclusion is to be drawn from this, as to the imperfection not only of the Levitical priesthood, but also of the law itself:

Vers. 18, 19. *For while there taketh place, on the one hand, a disannulling of the foregoing commandment because of its weakness and insufficiency*[2] (*for the law had perfected nothing*), *there is, on the other hand, a bringing in over and above of a better hope: through which we draw nigh to God.*

In the 110th Psalm it is not a merely non-Levitical, but an altogether different kind of priest who is the subject of the prophecy. For (such is our author's connection of thought) what there takes place is nothing less than this, that on the one hand (μέν) there is an annulling of the former law of priesthood, and on the other (δέ) a wide door opened to a better hope, by which that law of priesthood is done away. It is a complete misunderstanding on the part of some interpreters (Faber Stapulensis, Erasmus, Calvin, Hunnius, Jac. Cappellus, etc.), when they make of ἐπεισαγωγὴ δὲ κρείττονος ἐλπίδος an independent proposition, whereas it is merely a second subject to γίνεται. So Ebrard, who alone among modern interpreters takes this view, and gives the following paraphrase of the text: "*There taketh place, indeed, a disannulling of a preceding commandment, on account of its inherent weakness and inutility. The law, indeed, left everything imperfect, but served as (subaud.* ἦν *vel* ἐγένετο δι' αὐτοῦ) *a leading on towards a better hope.*" Without urging that μὲν γάρ must mean something beyond a mere "indeed,"[3] wê would ask further, What becomes of the ἐπί in ἐπεισαγωγή? Ebrard ignores it. And again, why at least did not the author write ἦν δὲ ἐπεισαγωγή . . . ? Ebrard con-

---

[1] The reading of Erasmus, Lachmann, Tischendorf, and recommended by Bengel and Griesbach. [It is also that of the Cod. Sin.]

[2] [Delitzsch by an oversight omits to translate here, διὰ τὸ αὐτῆς ἀσθενὲς καὶ ἀνωφελές.—TR.]

[3] Μὲν γάρ, without correlative δέ following, may be rendered by "for indeed." (*denn freilich*), or "for at least" (*denn wenigstens*), either of which would be unsuitable here.

tents himself with observing that he may for once have written " a little less accurately." And, in the third place, when did **εἰσαγωγή** (thus shorn of its ἐπί) acquire the meaning of " a leading towards?" That it has any such meaning is a mere fiction. And so all that the text is said [by Ebrard] to assert of the pedagogical character of the law, falls like a house of cards with its own weight to the ground. Ἐπεισαγωγὴ δὲ κρείττονος ἐλπίδος could only be maintained as an independent sentence on the interpretation given by Beza, Castalio, Pareus [the English version], and many others of the older expositors, among whom finally Heinrichs : " *the law made nothing perfect, but the bringing in of a better hope did,*" viz. accomplish such perfection. This is so far right [in contradistinction to Ebrard's interpretation], that it conceives of ἐπεισαγωγή as a characteristic of the new dispensation, which has succeeded to the impotence of the law. But it is awkward, in requiring the repetition of ἐτελείωσεν after ἐπεισαγωγή, to describe the operation of Christian Ἐλπίς ; moreover, ἐπεισαγωγή as the antithesis to ὁ νόμος ought to have the article ; and all that is essential in the thought is preserved and expressed in a simpler manner, if we regard οὐδὲν γὰρ ἐτελείωσεν ὁ νόμος as a parenthetical remark, like ὁ λαὸς γὰρ ἐπ' αὐτῆς νενομοθέτηται in ver. 11. Luther's rendering is excellent : " *For therewith is the former law abrogated (even because it was too weak and of no profit, for the law was able to perfect nothing), and a better hope is brought in, whereby we draw near to God.*" But his earlier rendering was still better, more literal, and more correct in defining the parenthesis : " *For therewith taketh place an abrogation of the former law, on account of its weakness and unprofitableness; and a bringing in of a better hope*" (vid. Bindseil-Niemeyer).[1] We must first of all observe here what Luther means to indicate by his " *damit*" (therewith)—namely, that the occurrence expressed by γίνεται (ἀθέτησις, κ.τ.λ.) as

---

[1] [Luther's German, as cited by Delitzsch, is (earlier version) : " *Denn es geschicht damit eine Aufhebung des vorigen Gesetzes um seiner Schwachheit und Unnutzes willen (denn das Gesetz hat nichts vollendet) und ein Einfurt einer besseren Hoffnung.*" Later (*i.e.* present) version : " *Denn damit wird das vorige Gesetz aufgehoben (darum dass es zu schwach und nicht nütz war, denn das Gesetz konnte nichts vollkommen machen) und wird eingeführet eine bessere Hoffnung durch welche wir zu Gott nahen.*"]

being involved in the setting up of the "other" Melchizedekian "priest," is referred to the Psalm as the prophetic word which brings it about. The wondrous consequences thus secured are expressed first negatively with μέν, and then positively with δέ. Therewith is accomplished, 1*st*, the abolition of a previous commandment,—that, namely, of the old law regarding priests (old in relation to the promise contained in the Psalm, the entire reference of which is to the future). As ἀκυροῦν signifies to invalidate, and καταργεῖν to make inefficient, so ἀθετεῖν is to bring to nought what is established, or completely to deny it (Lev. vii. 30), and is here used for the objective abrogation of a law. Προαγούσης ἐντολῆς is not exactly the same as τῆς προαγ. ἐντ.; the expression is left quite general, and the reader has to fill in the picture for himself : προάγειν (comp. 1 Tim. i. 18) denotes priority of time. An older commandment, *i.e.* the Levitical or Mosaic ordinance concerning priests, is in the Psalm abolished, διὰ τὸ αὐτῆς ἀσθενὲς καὶ ἀνωφελές. Διὰ τὴν αὐτῆς ἀσθένειαν καὶ ἀνωφέλειαν might also have been said ; but the author, who elsewhere prefers such neuters to the abstract (see on vi. 17[1]), uses them here probably as the gentler and more becoming mode of expression : it would have been too harsh to ascribe to the Levitical law, as such, and *à priori* in its very nature, these qualities of weakness and inutility. Τὸ αὐτῆς ἀσθενὲς καὶ ἀνωφελές is that weak and unprofitable aspect of the law which adheres to it as the concrete result of experience. Experience shows that the law is too weak to bring about perfection, and inadequate for securing real good ; for—as the author explains himself in the parenthetic clause— to speak generally, the law perfected nothing with which it had to do, whether person or thing (see ix. 23). We are here reminded of Gal. iv. 9, where the apostle speaks of the Mosaic law first as τὰ στοιχεῖα τοῦ κόσμου, that is, the outward and cosmical commencements of divine revelation ; and then as τὰ ἀσθενῆ καὶ πτωχὰ στοιχεῖα, *i.e. weak* as producing no new life, and *poor* as being unable to confer true blessedness on man ; *weak* in comparison with the gospel, which is a salvation-bringing "power of God" (Rom. i. 16), and *poor* in comparison

---

[1] Compare the Euripidean

τὸ δ' ἀσθενές μου καὶ τὸ θῆλυ σώματος
κακῶς ἐμίμφθης (NAUCK, *Tragic. Græc. fragmenta*, p. 333).

with the unsearchable riches of Christ, whom the gospel reveals for our acceptance.[1] We are also not less reminded of Rom. viii. 3, where it is said that God, by the mission of His Son, accomplished what the law could not, inasmuch as it was *weak* (ἠσθένει) through the flesh. The flesh, which contradicted and opposed the law, had been the cause of its showing itself powerless, *i.e.* unable to effect what it commanded, or (as I should prefer to say, on account of the antithesis of δικαίωμα to κατακρίνειν) unable to come to its proper verdict, assuring of righteousness and life. We soon feel, however, that the circle of ideas in which we find ourselves here in the Epistle to the Hebrews, is, although a substantially allied, yet a somewhat different one from that of the other two Pauline epistles. The author sums up all expectations which might be cherished in respect to a revelation of grace, from the first reconcilement of the conscience up to complete apprehension of the divine glory in the idea of τελείωσις; so that in this way the ἀσθενές of the law consists in its not being able to lead up to that highest end, and its ἀνωφελές in its conferring only in a shadowy and unsubstantial manner the good things which constitute the state of perfection. He says οὐδὲν ἐτελείωσεν, as looking back on the law from the historical standing-point of the Psalm, and therefore I have rendered his aorist by a pluperfect. And, moreover, since the Psalm has also brought in another and eternal priest after the order of Melchizedek, there is thereby accomplished, 2*dly*, the bringing in of a better hope, additional (ἐπί) to the commandment, and abolishing it; the hope, namely, of a better priesthood, which not only accomplishes *more* than the law, but also does that in truth and reality which the law had done only in type and shadow. The preposition ἐπί retains its proper force in ἐπεισάγειν, ἐπεισαγωγή, ἐπείσακτος, ἐπεισαγώγιμος,[2] signifying the addition or superinduction of one thing upon another, which it either continues to be associated with or (as here) supersedes.

Moreover, we are not to infer from κρείττονος ἐλπίδος, that

---

[1] See Note K at the end of this volume.

[2] *E.g.* to bring in new gods or objects of worship is called ἐπεισάγειν (where ἐπί = πρὸς τοῖς προϋπάρχουσι, Alciphron, iii. 11, 1), nearly synon. with παρεισάγειν. Imported wares are called by Demosthenes and Plato ἐπείσακτα, being additions made to the products of the country.

while the law furnished one kind of hope, that which is introduced by the prophecy in the Psalm is hope of a "better" kind. No, the κρείττων ἐλπίς here spoken of as laying hold of and possessing the promised τελείωσις, in that heaven to which its anchor has already penetrated (vi. 19), is simply contrasted with the ἐντολή, and its present unsatisfying practical effect. Nor is it spoken of as a hope as already finished and fulfilled in the manifestation of Jesus Christ. His manifestation upon earth sealed, but did not exhaust, "the better hope:" for He is described in the Psalm as "a priest for ever, after the order of Melchizedek;" that is, as one who for ever reigns as king as well as mediates as priest. Such a kingly priest our Lord first became on His entrance into the eternal sanctuary, after his high-priestly sacrifice made here below, and on His majestic session at the right hand of God (compare the γέγονεν of ver. 16). And such a priest (ἱερεύς) He continues now and evermore. The sanctuary whence our religious perfecting is now derived, has been, through abolition of the earthly and typical economy of the law, transferred to the unseen heavenly world; and hope, therefore, still remains in operation—that hope which passes through the veil which hides the invisible from our view, and is able thus constantly to pass through it, because now that free and full communion with the Holy One, in which the essence of our Christian τελείωσις consists, is no longer a mere matter of expectation, but has been already realized.

All this is indicated in the concluding words: δι᾽ ἧς ἐγγίζομεν τῷ Θεῷ. The priests under the law are those who are privileged to approach God (קרובים לה׳) (ἐγγίζοντες τῷ Θεῷ); comp. Lev. x. 3 with Ezek. xlii. 13. But now and henceforth no *cultus* connected with animal sacrifices, and no sacerdotal order of men bound by natural and mundane conditions, stand any longer between us and our God. The access to Him is free to all believers: the holy of holies, so far as it is invisible to eyes of flesh, has still a veil suspended before it; but inasmuch as Jesus our Forerunner has already entered it, it has for the eye of faith no veil.

This is the second proof for the superiority of the Melchizedek Priest of promise over the priesthood of the law—the second justification of the depreciatory judgment thus passed on the Levitical sacerdotal constitution, and the law of which it forms a part. But the author has by no means yet exhausted his text, Ps. cx. 4. A third proof for his position is thus derived from it in the words that follow.

Vers. 20-22. *And inasmuch as* (it is) *not without an oath— for they are priests who have become so without an oath, but he with an oath, through him who saith unto him, The Lord sware, and will not repent, Thou art a priest for ever, after the order of Melchizedek—of a so much better covenant hath Jesus become surety.*

Not a few of the older commentators (Chrysostom, Theodoret, Erasmus, Calvin, Erasmus Schmid, and others) combine καὶ καθ' ὅσον οὐ χωρὶς ὁρκωμοσίας with the preceding clause : " and inasmuch as it" (this " better hope") " was introduced not without oath." None now perhaps could be found who would not regard καὶ καθ' ὅσον, κ.τ.λ., as the *protasis* to an *apodosis*, which follows in κατὰ τοσοῦτο, κ.τ.λ. The only question is how to supply the ellipsis, which in any case must be assumed after ὁρκωμοσίας. Ebrard, with some others, would go for this purpose to the end of the sentence, supplying it thus : " And forasmuch (Jesus) not without oath is become a surety,"—a *prolepsis* so far-fetched as to be scarcely possible, and least of all to be credited to our author. The other interpretation commends itself much more : " And inasmuch not without an oath *he was made priest*" (supplying ἱερεὺς γέγονεν or ἱερεύς ἐστι γεγονώς). (So [the English version], Œcumenius, Gerhard, Bengel, Böhme.) Lünemann maintains that this is the only way of supplying the ellipsis which the context will allow. That it would be agreeable to the context, is of course evident from the fact that the thought itself is suggested by the mere reference to Ps. cx. 4 involved in the very words οὐ χωρὶς ὁρκωμοσίας, and is, besides, clearly expressed in the following parenthesis. But such a mode of supplying the ellipsis seems on this very account the less necessary. We can well do without ἱερεὺς γέγονεν here, and so escape the inconvenience of having still to look for its nominative case, Ἰησοῦς, in the remote *apodosis*. Nothing, in fact, seems more obvious than to supply γίνεται from vers. 18, 19 : " Not without oath is this accomplished," *i.e.* the bringing in of a better hope. So, with this interpretation in view, the Syriac translator in the Peshito, unable in his language to imitate such a period as that of vers. 20-22, makes the elliptical clause into an independent sentence, thus : " And He hath confirmed it" (this hope) " with an oath." The version of the Latin Vulgate may also be understood in the same sense : *Et quantum est* (*est* for our γίνεται) *non sine jurejurando ... in tantum melioris testamenti sponsor factus est Jesus.*[1]

The older commentators have been partly unable, partly unwilling, to find themselves in the long parenthesis that follows,[2] where the priests of the law are antithetically contrasted by οἱ μὲν ... ὁ δὲ with the Priest of promise. Of the former it is said : χωρὶς ὀρκωμοσίας εἰσὶν ἱερεῖς γεγονότες.[3] The *consecutio*

---

[1] Bleek and Tholuck are undoubtedly wrong in regarding the *et quantum* of the Vulgate as a *question* or an *exclamation*, herein partly following Justinianus and Faber Stapulensis, who certainly punctuate, "et quantum: non jurejurando?" But there can be no doubt that *quantum* (= *in quantum*, which is sometimes met with) is the correlative of *in tantum*, which follows. So Sabatier and Tischendorf (Cod. Amiatinus) interpunctuate ; and Remigius, Primasius, Estius, and other Latin commentators, explain it. This can hardly have escaped Luther, who, however, probably followed Erasmus here. Luther's rendering is similar to that of the Peshito. He turns the relative clause (the protasis) into a simple sentence, and attaches it to the foregoing sentence, thus : " *Und wird eingeführt eine bessere Hoffnung durch welche wir zu Gott nahen, und dazu, das viel ist, nicht ohne Eid.*"

[2] There is a similarly constructed sentence in Philo (i. 485, 26), ἐφ' ὅσον ... ἐπὶ τοσοῦτο, but with a shorter parenthesis. Bleek (i. 327) compares ch. xii. 18-24 of our epistle ; but Winer (p. 499, Germ.) is right in maintaining that xii. 20, 21 is not a proper parenthesis. That at Rom. ii. 12-16 κριθήσονται ... ἐν ἡμέρᾳ belongs together, and that all between is parenthesis, as Winer assumes, is a stylistic impossibility.

[3] Ὀρκωμοσία (not found in classical literature) occurs in the LXX. at Ezek. xvii. 18, 19, and in 1 Esdras viii. 95 (Eng. ver., ver. 96). Like ἀπωμοσία and ἀντωμοσία and similar nouns, it is formed from ὀμνύναι. As ὀρκομοτεῖν is a classical word, it is probable that ὀρκωμοσία is so too, though our present remains of classical literature do not happen to present it. Yet we meet with τὰ ὀρκομόσια as syn. of τὰ ὅρκια in Photius and Hesychius. Zonaras has our ὀρκωμοσία, but as derived only from the present passage. Pollux (though it seems scarcely worth mentioning) places ὀρκωμοσία between ὀρκωμοτεῖν and ὀρκωμότας, without citing any authority. The reading ὀρκωμοσία, in the scholia to the *Lysistrata* of Aristophanes (vol. ii. p. 89, ed. Dindorf), could only be appealed to through ignorance that the real author of those scholia is the French editor Bisset.

verborum in this first clause is exact and euphonious. Yet it would be wrong to say that εἰσὶ γεγονότες is only chosen here for γεγόνασι on account of the rhythm (Bleek, De Wette, Lünemann). The *conjugatio periphrastica* has indeed sometimes, especially in Herodotus, no particular significance; but here it undoubtedly serves to mark and fix the attention on the fact of the Aaronidæ having become and being priests without the intervention of an oath; and this is the translation we have endeavoured to indicate. It is, on the other hand, "*with oath*" that the Priest of promise has become what He is,— through Him, namely, who said unto Him . . . (πρὸς αὐτόν). . . . Then follow the two halves of Ps. cx. 4, in both of which David speaks *in the Spirit* with reference to the great "Son of David" of the future; and both, therefore, are really words of that God who everywhere speaks in such Scriptures. Both are spoken OF the great High Priest: the former half of the verse is said "concerning," the latter half directly addressed "to" Him; and both therefore πρὸς αὐτόν. The divine appointment of this eternal Priest is made by oath, that is, by the most binding form of obligation known among men: the divine satisfaction in the absolute assurance thus given will never fail.

The words κατὰ τὴν τάξιν Μελχ. are wanting in B.C., 17, 80, and in the Vulgate and other ancient versions. Tischendorf therefore excludes them from the text, and with good reason: their insertion by copyists is more intelligible than their omission. The author, too, elsewhere repeats quotations from Scripture in an abbreviated form (compare x. 16 seq. with viii. 8-12, x. 8 seq. with x. 5-7); and the length of the parenthesis here would recommend such abbreviation, if possible without injury to the force of the argument. The omission, indeed, of κατὰ τὴν τάξιν Μελχ. is every way an advantage, making the transition to the *apodosis* less abrupt, and the whole sentence to run more smoothly. To καθ' ὅσον in the *protasis* corresponds κατὰ τοσοῦτο, or, following another reading, κατὰ τοσοῦτον, in the *apodosis*. Both forms are (as is well known) equally admissible, the τοσοῦτον of the *textus receptus* being perhaps the more usual of the two. But our author probably wrote τοσοῦτο (Lachmann, Tischendorf), which is more euphonious here.[1] Καθ' ὅσον not being followed

---

[1] See Poppo, *Prolegomena* to his *Thucydides*, p. 225.

by a comparative in its own clause, must not be rendered "*by how much*," but "in," or "forasmuch." Compare Herod. viii. 13 (the night was so much the more terrible, ὅσῳ ἐν πελάγει φερομένοισι ἐπέπιπτε). Κατὰ τοσοῦτο, on the other hand, *is* followed by a comparative, with which it closely coheres, as indeed the *protasis* also might easily take a comparative form in accordance with the sense, which is, that the new διαθήκη is so much the more excellent by how much its surety, as a priest constituted by oath, stands higher than a priest who is not so constituted.

The development of meanings in the word διαθήκη takes a different course from that of the word בְּרִית, but both words ultimately agree in combining two different ideas. For (1.) בְּרִית (from ברה = ברא, to cut), with allusion to the old custom in concluding a covenant, to which Jehovah condescends in Gen. xv., signified originally a mutual agreement or contract made by two parties; but when applied to the relations of God and man, it came to denote sometimes a gracious dispensation of promised mercy on God's part towards man, and sometimes a votive self-surrender or devotion of himself by man as towards God,—the twofold character of the relation being never quite lost sight of, but for the most part thrown into the shade by the disparity of rank between the parties, and the relative inadequateness of that which is respectively required of either of them. The word is most frequently used of God's covenant with Abraham, and through him with Israel and all the faithful. This covenant is on Jehovah's part a work of free prevenient grace—one in which the faithfulness of Jehovah is not made dependent on that of man. The two-sidedness implied in the notion of covenant is here, therefore, not indeed unrecognised, but in great measure overborne; and so ברית, as designating a divine and gracious dispensation or arrangement on man's behalf, comes to coincide very nearly with the Aramaic קְיָם and the Greek διαθήκη, which both originally signified a *settlement* or *disposition* (*e.g.* of property). (2.) Διαθήκη, on the other hand, having for its fundamental signification that of a disposition or arrangement made by one side only (generally by last will or testament) on behalf of another, came also in process of time to be used in the sense of a two-sided contract or agreement between equals, and that as early as Aristophanes (*Ar.* 439, διατίθεσθαί τινι διαθήκην = *pactionem facere cum aliquo*). Thus both words, by opposite processes, acquired the same double meaning of first *pactio* and then *dispositio* in the case of בְּרִית, and of first *dispositio* and then *pactio* in that of διαθήκη. It is a mistake when Hofmann (like Dav. Schulz before him) endeavours to make out the same fundamental notion for both terms, viz. that of constitution or arrangement. Neither etymology nor the *usus loquendi* allows us to assume such a meaning for ברה as "fix," "constitute," "define" (= חקק), while διαθήκη has itself the double meaning which is found also in ברית.[1]

We shall have to return to this point in commenting on ch. ix., where both notions involved in the Hellenistic use of διαθήκη are present to the mind of the sacred writer, each of them having something corresponding in the matter of fact there dealt with. So also at Gal. iii. 15–18, διαθήκη is used ver. 15 only in the sense of a testamentary settlement (דיתיקי), and ver. 17 of the *covenant* of promise made with *Abraham*.[2] Luther's version here is against the author's meaning: "*Thus Jesus has been made executor of a much better testament.*"

Ἔγγυος is not the word for the executor of a will, but for one who pledges or offers himself as surety for anything—ὁ ἐγγυώμενός (ἐγγεγυηκώς) τι, much the same as ἀνάδοχος (Hesychius and the *Glossarium Alb.*). That, for the validity or carrying out of which surety is here said to be given, is the new testament covenant of grace, here called—in contrast to the covenant of the law, which was incapable of attaining or giving *perfection—κρείττων διαθήκη*. Of this covenant Jesus is

---

[1] See Hofm. *Weiss.* i. 138, and *Schriftb.* ii. 1, 94, who adheres to his opinion that ברית properly signifies a *disposition* or *arrangement*, and only improperly and derivatively a *covenant*, and that as being a *disposition* agreed upon between two parties. The Midrash (Lamentat. *Rabbathi* Introd.) is more right in deriving ברית from ברה, to separate or select (1 Sam. xvii. 8). That ברה ever means to dispose, fix, determine, is a pure fiction. On the view of those who insist on the meaning "covenant" in all cases, see what is said at ch. ix. (Davidson maintained this last view against M. Stuart in his *Introduction to the New Testament*, vol. iii. p. 284.)

[2] Philo also understands διαθήκη (Gen. xvii. 2) of a testamentary disposition (i. 586, 5), and similarly at Gen. xvii. 21 (*arm.* ii. 234): *Quemadmodum in hominum testamentis quidam inscribuntur heredes et aliqui donis digni adscribuntur, quæ ab heredibus accipiunt, sic et in divino testa-*

ἔγγυος, having pledged Himself as surety for its maintenance, and 'for the fulfilment of its promises. It would introduce confusion of thought to say that this means that our Lord gave Himself as surety of "the better covenant" when He gave Himself to death; for that covenant did not exist before our Lord's passion, but was established after and in consequence of it. If, then, He be said to have died as the ἔγγυος of any covenant, that covenant would be the law which man had broken and incurred its curse. But even so the expression would be incorrect. It is a mere assumption, that when God made the covenant of the law, or gave the commandment to our first parents as a test of their fidelity, that then also Christ took upon Himself the suretyship for its fulfilment, and, in case of non-fulfilment, the endurance of its penalty (*Christum vadem se dedisse Deo pro nobis ad mortem*, as the thought might be expressed in terms of old Roman law). All this is mere assumption, without any basis in the Scriptures. It is not Jesus as the incarnate Sufferer, but Jesus as the eternal Priest after the order of Melchizedek, as the risen and exalted One, who is here spoken of as an ἔγγυος. And He is so called because that new relation between God and man, which is the result of His great self-offering here, has now in Him, as our Forerunner in the heavenly sanctuary (vi. 20), and there royally crowned with glory and honour (ii. 9), its personal security for continuance and completion. As truly as He is Priest and King, so assuredly will the promises of the covenant be fulfilled in us,—a covenant which, in distinction from the impotence of that of Sinai, has for its objects true perfection

mento heres inscribitur ille, etc. The inheritor receives what he has neither earned nor merited, and Philo therefore regards διαθήκη as a symbol of the divine grace and its gifts—χάρις and χάριτες (i. 172, 47); and the Holy One Himself he regards as a διαθήκη (the Well-spring of all Graces) in the highest sense (i. 587, 10). (So completely has the Greek conception of the meaning of διαθήκη expelled or overshadowed in Philo's mind the Old Testament conception of a compact or covenant, though this be the literal rendering of ברית.) It is much to be regretted that Philo's περὶ διαθήκων πράξεις β′, to which he frequently refers, are lost. They would doubtless have afforded us a deeper insight into the interchange of notions in the Hellenistic (Hebrew-Greek) use of διαθήκη. In κρείττονος διαθήκης ἔγγυος, the ἔγγυος is against the purely Greek sense of the word, as observed above.

and eternal realities—free, unclouded communion with God—eternal glory. Our hope rises upwards continually to Him; in Him it sees itself accomplished. The oath in the Psalm which makes Him Priest is the sign of a promise, not of a commandment. His everlasting priesthood is not a mere office committed to Him, but a solemnly-recognised possession obtained in the way of suffering. And all He has obtained was obtained for us. He exists and lives for us eternally. His indissoluble life as Priest and King is the indissoluble bond which unites us with God, and assures us of the endurance of this blissful fellowship.

A fourth proof follows, vers. 23-25, that it is not the law, with its Levitical priesthood, which has brought in perfection, but the new covenant, with its one eternal Priest after the order of Melchizedek. The priests of the law, one after the other, are removed from their office by death, while the high-priestly, salvation-bringing work of Christ is of imperishable efficiency.

Ver. 23. *And they are in numbers constituted priests, because they are hindered by death from continuing.*

The order of words (in Lachmann), καὶ οἱ μὲν πλείονες εἰσὶν ἱερεῖς γεγονότες, is clearer and more rhythmical than the γεγονότες ἱερεῖς of the *textus receptus*[1] (wrongly restored by Tischendorf in his edition of '49),—clearer, inasmuch as ἱερεῖς is the predicate, and πλείονες the complement of the predicate, or used in apposition with it, and prefixed for the sake of emphasis: "*these have become priests as a plurality;*" the construction being exactly like that of ver. 20, where οὐ χωρὶς ὁρκωμοσίας occupies grammatically the same position as πλείονες here. Almost all interpreters, one after another, explain πλείονες in this place as expressing a plurality not simultaneous, but successive. But this is a mistake. The reference of εἰσὶν γεγονότες is evidently to the act of institution and consecration recorded Ex. xxviii. and xxix., where not Aaron only, but his sons with him, were chosen and consecrated priests. And why? In order that, when one should die, another should be ready at once to take his place (as we see shortly after, in the transference of the office from Aaron to Eleazar); and because, as is said here, no one could continue in the priestly office by

[1] [The Cod. Sin. supports the *text. rec.*—TR.]

reason of human mortality. Here again the explanation given by most modern interpreters is, *that they were hindered by death from continuing in life,* apparently not feeling how absurd and jejune would be the sense thus obtained. Bleek, indeed, seeks to support it, by observing that παραμένειν ἱερέα is a scarcely admissible formula, and one for which no authority can be cited. The reply is, that we are not to supply ἱερέα here, but τῇ ἱερατείᾳ or ἱερωσύνῃ. Compare for this dative after παραμένειν, Phil. i. 25.

There are then always many Levitical priests at one and the same time, because only so could the continuity of their office be secured. In the new covenant it is otherwise.

Ver. 24. *But he, because he remaineth "for ever," holdeth as unchangeable his priesthood.*

The simple μένειν has not precisely the same meaning as παραμένειν: the contrast is between the Levitical priests, who are prevented by death from retaining office, and one whose endless life stretches out into eternity; as the people rightly said, St. John xii. 34, though led thereby to take offence at the cross: ὁ Χριστὸς μένει εἰς τὸν αἰῶνα. For even as His life, for whom the lifting up upon the cross has been changed for a lifting up into glory, is henceforth a life absolute and without end, even so He holds His priesthood as something ἀπαράβατον, inviolate, interminable, unchangeable. Theodoret is followed by Œcumenius and Theophylact, along with Tholuck, Ebrard, Hofmann, etc., in taking ἀπαράβατον in an intransitive sense = μὴ παραβαίνουσαν (εἰς ἄλλον), that which passeth not over to another, and so is non-transferable (ἀδιάδοχον). But this is grammatically inadmissible. For (1) παραβαίνειν is not thus used of the passing over of an office by way of succession. (2.) The *verbalia* in ατος, especially those from βαίνειν, e.g. βατός, ἄβατος, ἔμβατος, ἐπίβατος, etc., have generally a passive signification, according to which it seems ἀπαράβατος must mean *that which cannot be overstepped.* So (3) even in Josephus, *c. Ap.* ii. 41 (τί γὰρ εὐσεβείας ἀπαραβάτου κάλλιον), and *Antiq.* xviii. 8, 2 (εἰς νῦν ἀπαράβατοι μεμενηκότες), ἀπαράβατος is not to be taken (though that is assumed by Lobeck, *Phryn.* p. 313) in an active sense (*non transgrediens leges*), but still passively (*transgressionis expers*), being formed not from the verb παραβαίνειν, but from the substantive παράβασις, after the analogy of ἀγήρατος, ageless. And even granting that *verbalia* in βατος may sometimes have an active signification, or that ἀπαράβατος, as derived from the noun, might be rendered *transitionless*, and so obtain the meaning of " non-transferable," it would yet be adventurous to assume this against the *usus loquendi* in respect to this word, especially when the ordinary signification is quite suitable to the context, and comes in the end to the same thing. For if our Lord possesses His priesthood, as something which cannot be overstepped or invaded, nor is subject to change, it is equally evident that it cannot pass away from Him to another. Our eternal Priest then holds, as ever living, an unchangeable, ever-enduring priesthood.

Ver. 25. *Wherefore he also is able to save unto the uttermost those who approach God through him, ever living to interpose on their behalf.*

The adverbial εἰς τὸ παντελές betrays the hand of St. Luke here, in whose Gospel it appears again, ch. xiii. 11, and nowhere else in the New Testament. It is not precisely equivalent to the other phrase peculiar to this epistle—εἰς τὸ διηνεκές—though confounded with it in the rendering of the Peshito, Vulgate, and Luther. Εἰς τὸ διην. signifies *continuously, perpetually*; εἰς τὸ παντ., *perfectly, completely, to the very end*, but without necessarily any reference to time, as is evident from such passages as Philo, ii. 567, 3, and Joseph. *Ant.* i. 18, 5, where it is used of *total* destruction, *complete* blindness. Belonging here to σώζειν, it includes the eternity of the σωτηρία; but its meaning is by no means exhausted by such reference: Christ is able to save in every way, in all respects, *unto the uttermost;* so that every want and need, in all its breadth and depth, is utterly done away. This all-embracing salvation is vouchsafed to those who through Him approach to God, *i.e.* those who in faith make use of the way of access which He has opened, and which remains open in Him; nay more, this very access to free and joyous communion with God, made by the removal of the barrier of sin, is in itself the all-including commencement of that perfect σωτηρία. Then follows a repetition of the previous thought, " He ever liveth," from which ὅθεν in this verse draws the conclusion, in order to a further development of the argument. Christ is able to effect this great redemption, even because He is πάντοτε ζῶν; and the whole energy of that endless and unbroken life is expended, as it were, in mediatorial interposition on our behalf. (After ἐντυγχάνειν ὑπὲρ ἡμῶν we must supply in thought τῷ Θεῷ, as at Rom. viii. 26, 34; comp. also Rom. viii. 27, where κατὰ Θεόν means, after a manner that is pleasing to God.) It is in this *intercessio pro nobis* that the whole life's activity of the exalted Jesus, so far as it is of a priestly nature, is comprised (*vid.* Hofmann, *Schriftb.* ii. 1, 396 seq.). In the same sense St. Paul finds the triumphant negative reply to the question, τίς ὁ κατακρίνων; (Rom. viii. 34), in the fact that Christ who died, nay rather, who is risen again, yea, and is exalted to the right hand of God, is there engaged in making continual intercession on our behalf.[1] This ἔντευξις will last so long as the final redemption of God's people—that is, the utter effacement of sin, and death, and sorrow—remains unaccomplished. Its foundation of right is the atoning sacrifice once for all made here upon the cross; its continual motive is that communion of sympathy into which incarnate love has vouchsafed to enter with our infirmities and sorrows; its method of procedure is not a mere silent presentation of Himself by the Redeemer before God, but an eloquent intercession on our behalf in reference to each individual among His redeemed, and every single case of need; and finally, its fruit is a perpetual maintenance of our relation of grace towards God, and a perpetually-renewed removal of every hindrance and shadow cast by sin. This priestly work of Christ now carried on in the unseen world bears the same relation to His redeeming work formerly accomplished for us on earth, as the world-preserving energy of God bears now to His creative activities in the beginning. And inasmuch as the work of redemption accomplished here consisted (as we see in the baptism of our Lord by St. John) in various intertwining acts of the triune God, so we need not wonder if we find the same mysterious reciprocity of inwardly divine but outwardly manifested activities continued to the time of final redemption. The Medium and Mediator in the whole work of divine love is the incarnate

[1] See Note L.

Son, who now, after His great sacrifice completed here, remains a Priest for ever in the sanctuary of God, being raised above the Levitical, earthly-conditioned, legally-constituted, and, on account of human mortality, ever shifting priesthood of the law, as the one great royal Priest and priestly King after the order of Melchizedek.

The author has now [in this first section of the second main division of his epistle], on the ground of an Old Testament history (vii. 1–3), first exhibited the superiority assigned to Melchizedek over Abraham, and over the whole Levitical priesthood as ancestrally comprised in him; and then pointed the antithesis in which the priesthood after the order of Melchizedek promised to Messiah in Ps. cx., and now realized in Jesus Christ, stands to the priesthood of the law and all its performances: (1) It is not derived from the tribe of Levi, but from that of Judah; (2) it is not bound by earthly and natural conditions, nor is it conferred or transferred by legal enactments, but founded on the power of an absolute personality; (3) it has been conferred with the solemnity of an oath; (4) and is for ever incapable of transference or change. The very fact of the prophecy that there should be such a non-Aaronical priesthood proves or presupposes the incapacity of the Levitical to bring about perfection; still more does its inadequacy become manifested when put in contrast with the different nature and the different performances of the promised priesthood of Melchizedek. Jesus, as such a Priest, is the foundation and the goal of a better hope, Surety of a nobler covenant, the eternal and all-perfect Helper, and ever-living Representative of those who enter into communion with God through Him. Throughout the whole passage (vii. 1–25) we nowhere meet with the word ἀρχιερεύς, though perpetually (and for the sense confusingly) introduced by the commentators. Only Hofmann has discerned the set design with which the author uses ἱερεύς alone up to this point, and then proceeds, τοιοῦτος γὰρ ἡμῖν καὶ ἔπρεπεν Ἀρχιερεύς, and shown how important this observation is for the understanding of the whole context.[1] Melchizedek may indeed have been a high

---

[1] The Vulgate is here faithful to the original rendering ἀρχιερεύς throughout by *pontifex*, and ἱερεύς by *sacerdos*. The Itala, on the contrary, helps the confusion of thought by rendering ἀρχιερεύς sometimes by

priest, and a sacrificing priest; but the Scripture says nothing about him in either capacity. It is only the combination of royalty with priesthood, and the high but purely personal dignity unconferred by law, and independent of conditions of time and natural descent, which form the traits of typical importance in the scriptural and historical figure of Melchizedek. But for all that relates to the *sacrifice* of Christ, and to His *service* in the heavenly sanctuary, the typical correspondences must be sought, not in Melchizedek the priest-king, but in Aaron the HIGH priest, and his successors in the office, and especially in the high-priestly functions of the day of atonement. In His high-priestly sacrifice of Himself on earth, in His high-priestly entrance after that into the eternal sanctuary, and in His work for His redeemed ones there, Christ is NOT the *antitype* of Melchizedek, but the *antitype* and *antithesis* of AARON.

The progress of the argument, then, is this: The antitypical relation of Christ to Melchizedek having been first described (vii. 1–25), there will next be introduced into the image thus obtained, the antitypical and antithetical relations of Christ to Aaron (*Schriftb.* ii. 1, 285, 404); the result of the two combined being a complete representation of the idea of the great " High Priest after the order of Melchizedek " (v. 10, vi. 20). [" HIGH PRIEST," therefore ('Ἀρχιερεύς), might be selected for the title, as it would best express the subject, of the following section, ch. vii. 26–ix. 12.]

summus sacerdos, sometimes simply by *sacerdos* (iv. 14 seq., v. 1, vi. 20, vii. 26, viii. 1), and once (iii. 1) by *princeps.* In Tertullian likewise *pontifex* is equivalent to ἀρχιερεύς when he calls our Lord (*adv. Marcion,* v. 9) *præputiati sacerdotii pontifex*—that is, a High Priest exalted above the priesthood of the circumcision.

EXCURSUS AND NOTES.

EXCURSUS.

EXCURSUS TO HEB. IV. 9, CONTAINING EXTRACTS FROM THE TALMUDIC TRACT SANHEDRIM 96*b*, 97*a*, RELATING TO THE COMING OF MESSIAH AND THE MILLENNIAL SABBATH.

[THE translation which follows is made directly from the text of the Gemara. The translator, having the assistance of Dr. Schiller-Szinessy (Teacher of Talmudical and Rabb. Literature in the University of Cambridge), has been enabled to correct a few oversights, and fill up some lacunæ in Prof. Delitzsch's otherwise excellent version. For the notes which seemed necessary, as helps to an intelligent perusal of these obscure passages by the general reader, the translator is responsible.]

"R. *Nachman* said to R. *Isaac:* Is it the case that thou ever hast heard when Bar-Naphli ('son of the fallen') cometh?

"R. *Isaac.* Who, then, is Bar-Naphli?

"R. *Nachman.* Messiah.

"R. *Isaac.* Messiah! Callest thou then *Him* Bar-Naphli?

"R. *Nachman.* Certainly I do; for it is written[1] (of Him): *In that day will I raise up the tabernacle of David that is fallen* (*han-nophéleth*) (Amos ix. 11).

"[R. Nachman continues, still addressing R. Isaac.[2]] Thus

[1] It is interesting to observe the recognition by these very ancient Jewish doctors of the Messianic character of a passage significantly referred to as such by St. James at the council of the apostles, Acts xv. 16.

[2] The original is ambiguous, being merely אמר ליה, "he said to him." Delitzsch assumes that what follows is R. Isaac's reply; but it seems better to suit the character of R. Nachman. The formula א' ל' (like ויאמר ל') in biblical Hebrew) is often used in the Talmud as introductory to the continuation of a speech (after a pause) by the same person.

spake R. Jochanan: The generation in which the Son of David (Messiah) cometh, therein shall the disciples of the wise grow fewer and fewer; and as to the rest, their eyes shall fail (or be consumed) in sorrow and sighing and many troubles; and severe decrees will be perpetually renewed. While the first is still in operation, the second speedeth hither.[1]

"*The Rabbis have delivered:* In the WEEK (Dan. ix. 25–27) in which the Son of David cometh, in its first year shall be fulfilled this Scripture: '*I will cause it to rain on one city, and on another city I will not cause it to rain*' (Amos iv. 7); in the second year the arrows of famine shall be sent forth (*i.e.* there shall be scarcity); in the third year there shall be a *great* famine,[2] and men, women, and children shall die, saints and wonder-workers,[3] and the Thorah[4] shall pass into forgetfulness from her students; in the fourth year there shall be plenty, and yet no plenty; in the fifth year there shall be great plenty, and they shall eat and drink, and rejoice, and the Thorah shall return to her students; in the sixth year there shall be voices;[5] in the seventh year there shall be wars;

---

[1] It is noteworthy that all these Jewish traditions of the coming of Messiah speak (in accordance with Scripture) of times of great trouble as preceding His advent—the so-called חבלי המשיח, αἱ ὠδῖνες τοῦ Χριστοῦ.

[2] With this year of scarcity, followed by a year of famine, compare Rev. vi. 5, 6, and 7, 8, where scarcity under the "black horse" (see Hengstenberg's note *in loc.*) is followed by famine (λίμος) under the "pale horse."

[3] "Saints" (חסידים), pious persons: "wonder-workers" (אנשי מעשה), *i.e.* lit. "men of work," not "men of good works" (as Delitzsch renders it); for these would not be distinguishable from the חסידים, but "Thaumaturgs," religious persons possessed of miraculous or semi-miraculous powers: comp. Matt. vii. 22, "*In Thy name we cast out devils, and in Thy name did many wonderful works*"—δυνάμεις.

[4] The Thorah (Pentateuch) is that part of the word of God which is the special object of Jewish reverence and study. That this should be neglected by its own disciples, is a portentous sign of overwhelming misery, or utter evil and unbelief.

[5] "Voices," Heb. קולות; Delitzsch, *Posaunenstösse*. It might be equally well rendered "thunderings." The word occurs twice in Ex. xix. 16; first "voices and lightnings," and then (in the singular) "voice of a trumpet." Comp. Rev. xvi. 18, βρονταὶ καὶ ἀστραπαὶ καὶ φωναί. We might also compare the πόλεμοι καὶ ἀκοαὶ πολέμων of Matt. xxiv. 6, Mark xiii. 7. So the rabbinical commentators explain here קולות as "*rumours* of the coming of Messiah."

EXCURSUS. 379

in the goings out of the seventh year the Son of David shall come.

"R. *Joseph*. Nay, but how many heptads have already passed, in which the like of this hath happened, and yet He is not come!"[1]

"*Abaji* (answering him). 'In the sixth year voices, in the seventh wars:' hath it been so yet? And further, have the other events happened in the order here laid down? *How have Thine enemies reproached, O Lord! reproached the footsteps of Thy Messiah!*[2] (Ps. lxxxix.)

"*Thanja* [*i.e.* It is a Boraitha]."[3]

---

[1] R. Joseph speaks here the language of scepticism. Comp. 2 Pet. iii. 3, 4: *There shall come in the last days scoffers, saying, Where is the promise of His coming? for all things continue as they were from the beginning of the creation.* Rab Joseph and Abaji were both (in succession) rectors of the school of Sora. Abaji's proper name was Abba bar Nachmeni, or Nachmeni bar-Nachmeni (since, as being a posthumous child, he took his father's name). He is commonly called "Abaji" (אביי), which was his "Notrikon" (= Notaricon), from his favourite text, Hos. xiv. 4 (Heb.), אֲשֶׁר־בְּךָ יְרֻחַם יָתוֹם, *In thee the fatherless findeth mercy.*

[2] Delitzsch, following the Rabbinical Commentary to the Gemara, says of this quotation, "Here follows in the Gemara a quite isolated citation from Ps. lxxxix. 52," and makes no attempt to account for the insertion of it here. The difficulty was felt of old, and the text is bracketed in the printed editions of the Talmud. Might not, however, the right explanation be suggested by the reference to 2 Pet. iii. 3, 4, in the preceding note? In accordance with that, I would regard this quotation from the Psalm as a sorrowful interjection of Abaji in reply to the desponding doubts expressed by R. Joseph. The devout doctor, whose adopted name symbolized his constant trust in the divine mercy (see last note), would gently rebuke his friend and master, and remind him that such questions are in fact "reproaches of the footsteps of Messiah," and more befitting the *enemies* of the Lord than one of His servants.

Another explanation has been offered, viz. that the text from the Psalm is simply a heading to the following "Boraitha," in which the terrible wickedness of the pre-Messianic time is dwelt upon. The impudence and unbelief of that evil age will be a "slandering" or "reproaching" of "Messiah's footsteps." Compare our Lord's own words: *When the Son of man cometh, shall He find faith upon the earth?* This explanation is ingenious; and in a parallel passage (Sota, p. 49, *b*) the very phrase occurs: "On the approach (lit. in the footsteps) of Messiah, impudence shall abound." But the interpretation suggested above is (I think) preferable, though it seems not to have occurred to any of the Jewish commentators.

[3] *Boraitha*, Chaldee for the Hebrew *Chitsônith* (חיצונית = ברייתא),

"R. *Jehudah.* In the generation wherein the Son of David shall come, the House of Assembly[1] shall be for harlots, and Galilee shall be in ruins, and Gablan laid waste, and men of the border shall wander about from city to city, and not find favour, and the wisdom of the scribes shall be ill-savoured, and they that fear sin shall be despised, and the face of that generation shall be (shameless) as the face of a dog, and *truth shall be driven away* (or *fail,* Isa. lix. 15), as it is said : *And it shall come to pass that truth shall be driven away, and he that departeth from evil shall go out of mind.*[2] What is the meaning of that, *Truth shall be driven away? The men of the house of Rab say :* That she shall be made into droves or flocks [*i.e.* divided among opposing schools and parties], and so betake herself away. What is the meaning of *He that departeth from evil shall go out of mind? They of the house of R. Shila say :* Every one that departeth from evil shall be counted mad[3] (or, *as one gone out of his mind*) by the world."

[A rabbinical myth follows concerning a place called Kushta, where everybody spoke the truth, and no one died before his time.]

"*Thani* R. *Nehhorai* said: In the generation wherein the

is a tradition (Mishnah or Mathnitha) taught *outside* the school-house (בית־המדרש) of R. Jehudah han-Nasi (the original editor of the Mishnah) : a Boraitha, consequently, is a tradition of inferior authority to a Mishnah proper.

[1] "*House of Assembly,*" בית הוועד, the place in which the doctors assembled for discussion. The gross profanation of such a place would be a sign that the end of the world was nigh. This speech of R. Jehudah contains a series of antitheses which are not easily reproduced in an English translation : *e.g.* בית־הוועד—זונות ; גליל—יחרב ; גבלן—יאשם ; יסובבו—אנשי גבול ; and חכמת הסופרי—תסרח. With this last compare our Lord's words : " *If the salt have lost his savour,*" etc.

[2] I have endeavoured to represent the paronomasia in the use here made of Isa. lix. 15. Delitzsch's explanation of the עדרים עדרים given in the text (viz. that it means that party strife is injurious to truth, so that when divided among various " *droves*" she is in fact " *driven*" away) is ingenious, and suggestive of a good thought, but one which, perhaps, hardly entered the mind of the Jewish doctor.

[3] It is the very sum of wickedness when men think that those who eschew it must be beside themselves. This passage in Isaiah is similar to the one subsequently cited from the Song of Moses. Both are Messianic, and represent the Lord as interposing on Israel's behalf when all other help has failed.

son of David shall come, the young men shall make ashamed the countenances of the elders, and the elders shall stand up in the presence of the young men; and the daughter shall arise against her mother, and the daughter-in-law against her mother-in-law; and the face of that generation shall be as the face of a dog, and the son shall have no reverence for his father.[1]

"*Thanja* (*i.e.* another Boraitha).

"R. *Nehemiah* saith: In the generation wherein the Son of David shall come, impudence shall increase, and that which is reverend shall do perversely;[2] and though the vine yield its fruit, the wine shall be dear, and the whole kingdom shall turn to the doctrine of the Sadducees, and there shall be none to gainsay it.

"This supports R. *Isaac*, who said: The Son of David shall not come till the whole kingdom is turned to the doctrine of the Sadducees.[3]

"*Raba* said: Where is that said (in Scripture)?

"(Answer.) (When) *it is all turned white* (*i.e.* leprous), the man *is clean*[4] (Lev. xiii. 13).

"*Our doctors have delivered* (as follows): *For the Lord shall judge* (*i.e.* avenge) *His people, and repent on behalf of His servants, when He seeth that power is gone* (from them), *and that there is none reserved* (bound up) *and left*[5] (Deut. xxxii. 36). [*Some explain this to mean*]: The Son of David cometh not till informers increase. *Others:* Till disciples diminish (become fewer and fewer). *Others:* Till the farthing disappears from

---

[1] Failing reverence to parents and elders is another mark of the last time, and of the reign of "the lawless one" (2 Thess. ii. 8). Compare the work assigned to the prophet Elijah in Mal. iv. 5, 6.

[2] Or, *they shall pervert reverence.* Delitzsch, *die Ehrerbietung wird sich verkehren*—everything shall be turned as it were upside down.

[3] That is, there shall be universal heresy and scepticism.

[4] The full manifestation of evil is the sign of the approach of better things. When the leprosy has fully broken out, it is about to pass away.

[5] For the Messianic character of the latter part of the Song of Moses see Heb. i. 6, and Delitzsch's commentary thereon. The text Deut. xxxii. 36 is laid down as the subject of the following remarks by different doctors. The two first explanations refer evidently to the clause, *when He seeth that power is gone.* Nothing so shakes ecclesiastical authority in a politically dependent people like the Jews, as the abundance of informers

the purse.[1] *Others*: Till men begin to give up all hope of redemption;[2] for it is said: *There is none reserved and left*;[3] ... *there is none that upholdeth and aideth Israel.*

"This (last interpretation) is like that (saying) of R. Zera, who, when he found the doctors busied with that question (viz. of Messiah's coming), said to them, I pray you put not the time further back,[4] for we have a tradition: Three things come unawares—Messiah, a find or godsend, and a scorpion.

"R. *Ketina* said: The world lasts six thousand years, and for one (thousand) it shall lie in ruins (or be withered); for it is said: *The Lord* ALONE *shall be exalted in that day* (Isa. ii. 11).

"*Abaji* said: For the space of two shall it be withered; for it is said: *From* (or out of) *the two days shall He revive us, and on the third day He shall raise us up, and we shall live before Him*[5] (Hos. vii. 2).

(*delatores*)—traitors in the camp—on the one hand, and the falling off of disciples in the schools on the other.

[1] Poverty is another cause or sign of weakness (אָזְלַת יָד) in an individual or a community. This interpretation may, however, (more probably) refer to the following אפס עצור = there is "*nothing bound up*" (viz. in the purse).

[2] Despair of God's mercy is the acme of sin in His people. "*God shall forgive thee all but thy despair.*" We are again reminded of our Lord's saying: *When the Son of man cometh, shall He find faith upon the earth?*

[3] The original is so concise as to be very obscure, and the meaning of the word כביכול, which I have left untranslated, is doubtful. It is commonly taken as a name of God = *The Almighty* or *all-gracious One*. If this be so, the meaning might be, "*There is none or nothing kept in reserve, and* (*Israel*) *is deserted* (forsaken) *of his God. The Almighty no longer upholdeth and aideth Israel.*" (For which compare Ps. xxii. 2, Heb., where the same word עזב is used as here.) But כביכול might be rendered "*if it were possible*," and then the meaning would be, "(*Israel*) *is deserted, and, if it be possible* (or lawful to say so), *there is none that upholdeth and aideth Israel.*" This passage is omitted by Delitzsch.

[4] R. Zera's meaning is, that if Messiah is to come when least expected ("as a thief in the night"), our thinking and talking about His coming is the way to delay it. A similar thought is familiar to the rabbinical commentators on the Song of Songs; *I charge you, daughters of Jerusalem, that ye stir not up Love until it please,* being interpreted as a warning against too impatiently praying for the final manifestations of divine mercy.

[5] Another Messianic text, but applied here not (as by the church) to our Lord's resurrection, but to His advent

"*Thauja* [*i.e.* there is a Boraitha which] supports R. Ketina: As the heptad (of years) *releaseth* (or causeth to lie fallow) one year in seven, so the world releaseth (or leaveth without culture) one period of a thousand years in seven thousand. As it is said: *The Lord* ALONE *shall be exalted in that day.* And said again: *A psalm or song for the Sabbath-day* (Ps. xcii. 1, Heb.),—that 'day,' namely, which shall be all Sabbath. And again it saith: *A thousand years in Thy sight are but as the day of yestreen when it is past* (Ps. xc.).[1]

"*Thenâ. It is a tradition of the house (school) of Elijah:* The world exists 6000 years : 2000, confusion ;[2] 2000, Thorah (Mosaic law) ; 2000, the days of Messiah. But on account of our sins, which have so multiplied, there have elapsed of them so many as have elapsed already (without Messiah appearing).

"*Elijah said to R. Judah, brother of R. Salla the Pious:* The world cannot stand less than eighty-five jubilees, and in the last jubilee the Son of David cometh.

"R. *Judah.* At the beginning or the end of it?

"*El.* I know not.

"R. *Judah.* Will (the whole time) have already passed or no (*i.e.* when Messiah cometh)?

"*El.* I know not.

"R. *Ashê said that he had thus spoken to him:* Until that time, expect Him not; from that time onwards thou mayest expect Him.

"R. *Chanan, son of Tachalipha, sent to R. Joseph* (this message) : I found (or met) a man with a roll in his hand, written

[1] The two quotations from Ps. xcii. and xc. are made to justify the interpretation of "the day" in Isa. ii. 11 as referring to the millennial Sabbath, in which the Lord alone will be exalted, while the world will be judged and laid waste. The quotation from Ps. xcii. is the title of the Psalm, which the Jews reckon as its first verse, and regard as an integral part of the Psalm. The quotation from Ps. xc. proves that Scripture speaks of a millennium as being but one day with God. Compare 2 Pet. iii. 8.

[2] "Confusion" or "lawlessness" (comp. Rom. v. 13, 14, and Gal. iii. 19, 23). The Hebrew word here rendered "confusion" is "Thohu," which, along with "Bohu," is used Gen. i. 2 to describe the primeval chaos. As *natural* order in the visible universe is due to the presence of the Creator-Spirit moving on the face of the chaotic waters, so *moral* order in the rational creation is produced by submission to the Thorah as the revealed law and will of God.

in Assyrian[1] and in the holy language (Hebrew). I said to him, Whence hast thou this? He answered me, I had enlisted myself in the Persian army, and among the Persian treasures I found it. Therein was written: After 4291 years from the creation of the world, the world shall draw towards its end; there shall be in part wars of sea-monsters, in part wars of Gog and Magog, and what follows shall be the days of Messiah; and the Holy One—blessed be He!—shall not renew His world till after 7000 years.

"R. *Acha, son of Raba.* 'After 5000 years:' so runs our tradition.

"*Thauja.* [There is another traditional report.]

"R. *Nathan* said: This Scripture penetrateth down into the abyss (*i.e.* is of deepest import): '*For yet is the vision for an appointed time: then shall He* (God) *softly call up* (lit. "breathe" or "whistle for") *the end, and will not be untrue to His word* (lit. "will not lie"); *though it* (the vision) *linger* (or, though He (God) seem to delay), *yet wait thou for Him, for it shall surely come: He will not keep it back*' (Hab. ii. 3). [This promise we must take heed to, and] not (be) like [those of] our doctors who were inquiring concerning [and reckoning by], '*Until a time, and times, and the dividing of a time*' (Dan. vii. 25); nor like R. Simlai, who was inquiring [and reckoning] concerning [that other Scripture], *Thou feedest them with the bread of tears; Thou makest them drink of weeping in a threefold measure*[2]

---

[1] "Assyrian characters" are the square (or so-called Chaldaic) characters in which Hebrew is always written and printed now. The original Hebrew alphabet was (as is well known) what we call the Samaritan (Heb. כְּתָב לִבּוֹנָאָה).

[2] The mistake of these doctors, according to R. Nathan, was in attempting to *calculate* the times of the end, and so by their failures and disappointments producing despondency and scepticism. The calculations founded on Dan. vii. 25 and Ps. lxxx. 6 coincided in making out "the times of expectation" to be exactly or a little over fourteen centuries. Thus Israel's first and prototypal captivity, that of Egypt, lasted (according to Gen. xv. 13) 400 years. This is assumed as the basis of the calculation, Daniel's "time" being reckoned as = 400 years, and consequently his "time, times, and a half" (*i.e.* $1 + 2 + \frac{1}{2}$) $= 400 + 800 + 200$ years, *i.e.* exactly fourteen centuries. A similar result was produced by the calculation made from "the threefold measure" of Ps. lxxx. 6. Thus Israel's first captivity multiplied by three (400×3) would give 1200 years, and Israel's second captivity (that of Babylon) thrice told (70×3) would give 210

(Ps. lxxx. 6); nor [finally] like R. Akiba,[1] who was [also fond of] inquiring [and reckoning] by [that saying], '*Yet one little one* [*i.e. time*, or, as R. Akiba seems to have taken it, *kingdom* or *dynasty*], *and I will shake the heavens and the earth*' (Hag. ii. 6); but [wrongly, for, as we have seen], the first kingdom [that of the Maccabees] was of seventy years' [duration], the second kingdom [that of Herod] of fifty-two years, and the kingdom of Ben Coziba (the 'son of a lie') two years and a half.[2]

"[Query.] What meaneth, then, *He shall breathe forth for the end, and will not lie*?

"R. *Samuel, son of Nachmeni*, answered: So said [and explained it].

"R. *Jonathan*: Let the very life of them breathe forth (or expire),[3] who are thus for reckoning *the times of the end* [lit. 'the ends'], because when the end approaches [which they have been predicting], and He cometh not, they say, He is not coming any more, [and so lie]; but *wait thou for Him*, for it is said, *Though He tarry* (or linger), *wait for Him* (or *for it*). But perchance thou sayest: '*We* are waiting, but *He* (God) doth not wait.' For that very reason is it said [in Scripture, Isa. xxx. 18]: *And therefore will the Lord wait* (namely) *to be*

---

years; and these numbers added together (1200 + 210) make a total of 1410 years.

[1] R. Akiba, perhaps the most honoured of all the ancient doctors among the Jews, ended his long, laborious student's life as an adherent of the impostor Bar-Cochba alluded to below. At the age, it is said, of 120 years, he was Bar-Cochba's standard-bearer. Taken prisoner at the fall of Bether, he suffered death under the most exquisite tortures from the hands of the Romans.

[2] R. Akiba's interpretation of Hag. ii. 6, as indicated by this criticism upon it, appears to have been, that "a little" (or short-lived) monarchy (in Israel) was immediately to precede the coming of Messiah. It is possible that with this expectation he joined the revolt of Bar-Cochba, regarding him as the forerunner of Messiah, not as the Messiah Himself.

[3] It is difficult to represent in a translation the play upon words on which many of these rabbinical interpretations of Scripture turn. R. Jonathan interprets the clause ויפח לקץ ונו as if it meant, *Let him breathe forth his life* (or more correctly, *Let his life be breathed forth*), *who is for the end* (*i.e.* who is always for calculating when the end will come), *and let him not* (or, *for indeed he ought not to*) *utter or make a lie* (and so bring himself and others into peril of apostasy).

gracious unto you, and therefore will He rise up (namely) *to be merciful unto you [for the Lord is a God of judgment: blessed are all that wait for Him]*;[1] but now, seeing that both we are waiting and He waiteth, what is it that hindereth [the 'end' from coming]? The (divine) quality of *judgment* (or justice) hindereth. But now, seeing that it is the 'quality of justice' that hindereth, why do we still wait? [*i.e.* what is the good of our waiting?] [Answer.] In order to receive reward (comp. Phil. i. 21, 22), for it is said again: *Blessed are all that wait for Him.*"

[A cabbalistic speculation follows, founded on the last quoted words, *Blessed are all they that wait for Him*, concerning the number of righteous persons in each generation. (Heb. לו (for Him) = ל, 30 + ו, 6 = 36.) This passage is omitted by Delitzsch.]

"*Abaji* said: The world hath not less than thirty-six just persons in every generation, who receive the face (the full effulgence) of the divine glory (Shekhinah); for it is said, *Blessed are they that wait*—לו. Now לו in Gematria is thirty-six.

"[Objection.] But it is not so, for Raba said: The generation of them which stand before the Holy One—blessed be He!—are 18,000;[2] for it is written, *The compass* (of the city) *is* 18,000 [2] (Ezek. xlviii. 35).

"[Solution.] There is no real difficulty here. On the one hand are those who look in the shining mirror; on the other, those who look in the mirror which is not shining.[3] [The first

---

[1] The clause in brackets is not cited in the text of the Gemara, but is afterwards referred to and argued from.

[2] The text of the Gemara adds in brackets "parasangs," and our English version in italics *measures*. Raba, giving the text a spiritual interpretation, seems to understand "persons." According to the following solution, the statements of the two doctors may be thus reconciled: The *inner circle* of God's servants, who compose the holy city, are only 36 persons, the outer 18,000 persons (or, as some explain Raba to mean, persons who would occupy a circuit of 18,000 parasangs). Compare the concentric circles in Rev. iv. and vii.: the twenty-four elders, the 144,000 of the tribes of Israel, the innumerable multitude of Gentile "candidates," and the outer circle of the ministering angels.

[3] This is especially interesting, as reminding us of St. Paul's ἀνακεκαλυμμένῳ προσώπῳ τὴν δόξαν Κυρίου κατοπτριζόμενοι (2 Cor. iii. 18), and βλέπομεν . . . ἄρτι δι' ἐσόπτρου ἐν αἰνίγματι (1 Cor. xiii. 12). The "shining mirror" here is what Christian mystics have called the "*speculum Trinitatis.*"

being the thirty-six of whom Abaji spoke, the others the 18,000 reckoned by Raba.]

"[Further objection.] But are there, then, so many as these?[1] Lo, Hezekiah hath reported that R. Jeremiah reported to him, in the name of R. Simeon Ben Jochai: I have looked out for the children of elevation (*i.e.* persons of exalted piety, or those to whom God has vouchsafed such elevation), and found them to be very few: if they be a thousand, I and my son are of them; if they be a hundred, I and my son are of them; if they be two (only), I and my son are those two.[2]

"[Solution.] This is again no real difficulty. Those on the one hand go in with permission, and those on the other go in without permission.[3]

"*Rab* said: All the (calculated) 'ends' have passed, and the whole matter now depends on repentance and good works [on the part of Israel].

"*Samuel* said: It is enough that the [Divine] Mourner remain in His mourning." [The meaning is, that the final deliverance will not be brought about by Israel's good works or penitence, but by the sole mercy of that God who mourns in and with His people. A noble thought, which Delitzsch,

---

[1] One may be pardoned for referring to a beautiful parallel in Mr. Myer's recent poem, *St. Paul:*

"Look, what a company of constellations!
Say, can the sky *so many lights* contain?
Hath the great earth these endless generations?
Are there so many purified through pain?"

[2] The offensive self-righteousness of this *dictum* is considerably diminished, if not altogether removed, by reference to the historical circumstances under which it was uttered. When Hadrian, after the fall of Bar-Cochba, had forbidden the study of the Thorah under the severest penalties, this Ben Jochai (who is the reputed author of the mystical book Zohar) is said to have retired with his son to a cave, and there pursued the study for thirteen years, submitting patiently to the greatest privations, which became proverbial as the type or *ne plus ultra* of endurance, and were referred to as the צער מערה, "the sufferings of the cavern." Ben Jochai's speech, therefore, is like that of Elijah, "*I, I only am left,*" or may be interpreted as referring to the visions with which the book of Zohar teems.

[3] The meaning of this is similar to that of our Lord's saying: *The kingdom of heaven suffereth violence, and the violent take it by force.* Many obtain what men have called "uncovenanted mercies."

following another and inferior rabbinical interpretation, has missed; his translation and gloss being, "It is enough that the mourner remain in his mourning (in order to move God to deliver him)." Delitzsch has overlooked what is evident from the following context (and from R. Alexandri's first interpretation, *Sanhedr.* 99a), that the "mourner" here is God Himself, not Israel.]

One thing very remarkable in this passage from the Talmud, is the witness it bears as to the ancient Jewish views of the character of the millennium, so different from those in vogue amongst ourselves in modern times. These Jewish doctors evidently regarded it not as a time of general peace and prosperity, but as one of judgment and desolation for the whole world, in which the righteous only should escape. Might not this be also the meaning of what is said of the millennium in Rev. xx. 1-5, where two notes are given of that time—1*st*, the binding of Satan in the abyss; and 2*d*, the reign of the souls of martyrs with Christ—but nothing is said of the happiness or conversion of the world as such? It is not till the following chapter (xxi. 24-26) that the redeemed world enters the New Jerusalem.

NOTES.

Note A, to Heb. vi. 3. P. 277.

On the Apostolic Rite of the Imposition of Hands.

HOFMANN clearly recognises (in some places) the integral significance of this rite, both in confirmation and ordination; *e.g. Weiss.* ii. 243 : *" He who lays on hands prays to God that the power and faculty of doing Christian service and bearing Christian testimony may pass over, as it were, through the mediation of his person and ministry, to the person of him for whom he prays."* Again, in the excellent review of Kliefoth's *Theory of Public Worship,* in the Mecklenburg *Kirchenblatt* for 1844, p. 135 seq., he says : *" If we seriously consider and accept the proposition, that confirmation consecrates the candidate for active service in the Christian community, it will follow that such consecration will not take place without the commencement of a new work of the Spirit in him who receives the imposition of hands; and it will also follow that, with limitations similar to those implied, when we say of the sacrament of baptism that it is generally necessary to salvation, we may also say of the laying on of hands that it is necessary as a preparation for any service in the church."* So again, in a paper (in the *Zeitschrift für Protestantismus und Kirche* for July 1849), " On the Right Administration of Confirmation," he thus speaks, with special reference to Heb. vi. 2 : *" By baptism the believer is separated from the world, and brought into communion or fellowship with Christ; by the laying on of hands he is, as it were, while still in the world, inwardly glorified, and wondrously provided with strength for conflict and for service."* But in the *Schriftbeweis,* even where one would most expect to find it (*e.g.* ii. 2, 235), I miss this recognition of the intimate connection between baptism and the imposition of hands. Opposition to recent exaggerations on the ministerial office, and the sacramental character of ordination, has led Hofmann to a depreciatory view of the apostolic rite, which is quite inconsistent with his former statements, but reminds one of the similar position of Höfling in the third edition of his *Kirchenverfassung,* p. 94 seq.: " *The imposition of hands,*" says Höfling, " *is but a general form for making personal application of public ecclesiastical intercessory prayer, which, when seriously made on behalf of a rightly disposed candidate, will surely not remain without effect and operation, but which, in reference to ordination, has no special divine command or divine promise attached to it, so as to be legitimately made the ground for expecting the bestowal of specific grace.*" Compare Hofmann, *Schriftbeweis,* ii. 2, 254. Kliefoth's view is substantially the same (" *Confirmation,*" p. 150) : " *Confirmation,*" he says, " *has no legitimate claim to be regarded as a quasi-sacramental action, conferring grace. The cases commonly referred to in the Acts of the Apostles for this purpose, are first of all merely historical instances of the fact that the apostles laid on hands ; but we, having no command to follow their example, and no promise that the effects in our case would be the same, can hardly be justified in doing as they did.*" He goes on to urge, in support of his position, the cessation of miraculous gifts, and thus to repeat that *testimonium paupertatis* which the church is so sadly ready at all times, without shame or sorrow, to present against herself. But surely the argument so commonly used, that the apostolic imposition of hands conferred *only* these miraculous gifts, is not consistent with those various testimonies of Scripture which speak of the *charismata,* without distinguishing miraculous or extraordinary gifts from such as were ethical and common to all Christians, *e.g.* Rom. xii. 4–8. [Compare also St. Paul's language to Timothy, 2 Tim. i. 6, 7, where the χάρισμα, which had been bestowed on him through imposition of hands, is described as (not a power of working miracles, but) a πνεῦμα—δυνάμεως καὶ ἀγάπης καὶ σωφρονισμοῦ.] How can we imagine that the apostolic writer here (Heb. vi. 3) would have reckoned the ἐπίθεσις χειρῶν along with baptism among the *fundamentals* of Christianity, if he had not regarded it as a sacred ordinance, with a promise of grace attached to it? And even if it be urged that earnest prayer, as accompanied by the laying on of hands, and not a quasi-sacramental ceremony, is here the chief matter, we may point to St. James v. 14, 15 as attaching special importance, under similar circumstances, to the " prayer of faith." Alas! alas! The church of the present falls already far enough below that of the primitive time, not to need to make the matter still worse, by creating dogmas about her own deficiencies. [There is a paronomasia in the original, which the English translator would find difficult or impossible to reproduce: " *Leider fehlt Kirche der Gegenwart viel im Vergleich mit der Kirche der erster Jahrhunderte, ihr Deficit wird aber immer grösser werden wenn sie daraus Lehrsätze um nicht zu sagen Leersätze formt.*"]

NOTE B (HEB. VI. 4-6). P. 294.

On the Unpardonable Sin, and the " Sin against the Holy Ghost."

BLASPHEMY against the Holy Ghost is the title of a class or order of sins, of which the unconverted as well as the converted may render themselves guilty. It includes, therefore, at least two kinds of sin, and is itself to be included under the more general designation of the ἁμαρτία πρὸς θάνατον of 1 John v. 16, the sin which finally excludes the possibility of obtaining or re-obtaining the grace of life. Julius Müller draws a rational conclusion, but one, nevertheless, not warranted by Scripture, when he says: " *Blasphemy of the Holy Ghost is not to be regarded as a particular kind or species of unpardonable sins, but is itself the only unpardonable sin, in contradistinction to all others. We are not to think of human sinfulness as coming to a head, and reaching the condition of unpardonableness, as it were, by different routes, of which one or two only among many would, unchecked, end in this sin against the Spirit. Rather must we say, that all sinful development of every kind, unless controlled by grace redeeming, has a tendency to complete itself in the blasphemy of the Holy Ghost*"

(*Die Sünde*, ii. 569). The same thoughts are the foundation of v. Oettingen's view, as developed in his essay, *de Peccato in Sp. S.* He also maintains, that the sin against the Holy Spirit is the final development of all sin, and that no one is finally lost in whom sin of any kind has not attained the climax which excludes all penitential sorrow, all desire for grace, all further possibility of moral renovation. But the scriptural designation of the sin against the Spirit, as ἡ τοῦ πνεύματος βλασφημία, and that again interpreted as an εἰπεῖν κατὰ τοῦ πν. τοῦ ἁγ., and finally, the description given of this sin in our epistle, is unfavourable to the generalization of the idea; and the inference that, because all sins will be forgiven on repentance, therefore every sin which entails ultimate condemnation must be the sin against the Holy Ghost, is a false one. There are three kinds of sins: 1*st*, Sins which may be forgiven, and actually are so, through apprehension of redeeming grace; 2*dly*, Sins which might have been forgiven, but remain unforgiven because the grace of forgiveness has not been timely laid hold of; and 3*dly*, Sins which, though an occasional desire may arise in the mind to be delivered from them, yet remain irremoveably resting on it still, because they are combined with a self-hardening, and a judicial hardening too from the divine hand. To this kind belong the twofold sin of blasphemy against the Holy Ghost; and to it also belongs that determined closing of the heart to the operation of convincing or admonitory grace, which finally results in an impossibility of conversion.

To regard all whom our Lord condemns (Matt. vii. 22 seq., xxv. 41-46, and elsewhere) to eternal fire, as blasphemers of the Holy Ghost, would be a purely arbitrary proceeding; and if there were no other means of refuting the doctrine of universal redemption (*apocatastasis*) than the assumption that all who go to hell will have attained to that eminence of sin which by natural necessity is incapable of reformation, my conviction is,* that any refutation of the doctrine would simply be impossible. I would indeed rather accept universalism at once than this other theory, involving consequences not a whit less dangerous, both from a dogmatic and an ethical point of view.

NOTE C (HEB. VI. 10). P. 301.

On the Doctrine of Scripture concerning Reward.

THE view expressed in the Commentary is similar to that of B. Weiss, in his interesting discussion of the biblical doctrine concerning reward, in the *Deutsche Zeitschrift für christliche Wissenschaft und christliches Leben*, 1843, Nos. 40-42 ("*Abh. über die Lehre Christi vom Lohne*"). " There is a relation," says Weiss, " between God and man, in which the notion of reward has place; but that relation is an economical one, *i.e.* it is the result of a positive appointment made by God for the carrying out of His plan of salvation." And accordingly, no good work done on the basis of this relation is really *good*, if done for the sake of a simply outward reward : every good work (properly so called) has for its object a reward, which primarily consists in the good of its own perfection. Moreover, in the Christian economy there is none of that equivalence between reward and work, which elsewhere is essentially involved in the very notion itself : the bestowal of reward is an act of grace, which excludes all legal claim of merit or deserving. The rewards of grace are earned, not merited, and bestowed, not of necessity, but of free good-will. They cannot be demanded, though they may be looked for. On this point it must not be ignored, that even the Roman dogma of *meritum de condigno* is professedly derived *ex justitia fundata in præmiantis pacto*, and that the Council of Trent expressly lays down as the basis of its teaching (vi. 16) : *Domini tanta est erga homines bonitas, ut eorum velit esse merita quæ sunt ipsius dona*. If only the consequences drawn from this seemingly so innocent proposition did not show how dangerous is any such emphasis laid on the merit of good works, how easily misunderstood, and therefore how unsuitable, the very notion of our meriting and deserving any good in our relation to God must be !

Note D (Heb. vi. 17). P. 314.

On the Difference of Meaning in θέλειν and βούλεσθαι.

ACCORDING to Ammonius (*de differentia adfinium vocc.* ed. Valckenaer, pp. 31, 70), θέλειν denotes natural, unconscious, spontaneous desire; βούλεσθαι that which is self-conscious, self-determined, and rational. The distinction is a mistaken one, and the definitions should be rather inverted; βούλεσθαι denoting *inclination*, and θέλειν *purpose.* Comp. Phil. i. (*Olynth.* i.), p. 9, προσήκει προθύμως ἐθέλειν ἀκούειν τῶν βουλομένων συμβουλεύειν, where ἐθέλειν might be rendered by *velle*, βουλομένων by *cupientes* (see F. Franke in his school edition of the *Nine Philippics*). This distinction was first formulated by Buttmann. It is recognised by Döderlein (*Lat. Synon.* v. 56), and is confirmed by the usage of the whole of classical and biblical literature. It was a retrograde step, therefore, in Pillon (*Synonymes Grecs*, Paris 1847), to return to the distinction made by Ammonius,—an error into which he was led by *Il.* xxi. 366 and John iii. 8, where a certain θέλειν is ascribed to water and to wind, the wayward and forceful actings of those elements impressing the imagination with the idea of conscious self-determined volition.

Note E (Heb. vii. 11-25). P 327.

HOFMANN [recognising the fourfold division of this paragraph—(*a*) vers. 11-14, (*b*) vers. 15-19, (*c*) vers. 20-22, and (*d*) vers. 23-25] assumes, in *Weiss.* ii. 198, that (*a*) corresponds to (*c*), as (*b*) to (*d*). The correspondence of (*b*) to (*d*) is patent, the absolutely *personal* dignity (*b*) being also an abiding one (*d*): not so that of (*a*) to (*c*), for the priesthood after the order of Melchizedek (*a*) is not necessarily a priesthood constituted by oath (*c*). This parallelism of the four pieces is abandoned by Hofmann himself, in *Schriftb.* ii. 1, 402-404. He there places (*a*) the negative, *i.e.* non-Aaronical, character of our Lord's Melchizedek priesthood on one side, and (*b*) (*c*) (*d*) its positive characteristics on the other.

Note F (Heb. vii. 5, 6). P. 340.

On Tithe and Therumah.

An ancient tradition is thus reported by Maimonides (*Hilcoth Maaser*, Sett. ix. hal. 1): *In the days of Jochanan the high priest, who lived after Simon the Just, an inquiry was made by* [order of] *the great Beth-dîn* [court of justice, which sat in Jerusalem], *throughout the land of Israel, which resulted in their discovering that, while every one was conscientious in separating and paying the great therumah* [*i.e.* the heave-offering due to the priests], *the common people* [אנשי הארץ, lit. "the people of the land,"—a term seldom used without an under tone of contempt; comp. John vii. 49] *were* [*found to be*] *lax in making their payments,* [*whether*] *of the first tithe* [due to the Levites], *or of the second tithe,* [which could only be consumed by the owner in Jerusalem], *or* [*thirdly*] *of the poor-tithe* [which was given to the poor]. *The Beth-dîn therefore made a decree, that in questions concerning tithe no declaration should be taken but that of trustworthy persons, while the fruits* [gathered in by or belonging to] *the common people* [*i.e.* " the men of the land," as above] *should be regarded as doubtful* [Heb. סָפֵק, *saphêk*,—an epithet applied here to those products of the soil concerning which it was "*doubtful*" whether they had been tithed (and so made fit for ordinary use) or not], *and that the declaration of such persons that they had been properly tithed was not to be accepted. Fruits in this condition were called dĕmāi* [Heb. דמאי, explained by rabbinnical authorities as = דא, *this?* מאי, *what is it?*].

This witness affords no support to Bleek's hypothesis [referred to in the text]. To understand it, one must bear in mind that the great *therumah* and the tithe of service might be paid in any part of the country. The Israelite might pay his *therumah* to any priest whom he might choose, and his tithe to *any* Levite [his poor-tithe also to *any* poor man]. What the priests in Jerusalem lost in this way was made up to them by other emoluments, *e.g.* the first-born of cattle (בכורות) and the first-fruits (בכורים), which could only be paid at the temple. The learned old sacred antiquary Jo. Lundius is here somewhat at fault. See his *Jüd. Alterthümer*, iv. 32-35.

Note G (Heb. vii. 5, 6). P. 341.

On some apparent Claims of the Levitical Priesthood to take Tithes of the People.

We have seen that the tithe paid by the people to the Levites (Num. xviii. 20-24), and called the "first tithe," was again tithed by them as a payment to the priests, and called "*the tithe from the tithe*," and "*the Lord's therumah*" (Num. xviii. 26). By this ordinance the Levites were subordinated to the priests, and the priests made at the same time dependent in some measure for their subsistence on the conscientiousness of the Levites (compare Neh. x. 39, and Saalschütz, *Mos. Recht*, ix. 9). In addition to this "first tithe," which was of general and standing obligation, there were, according to an ancient traditional exposition of the law, two other kinds of tithe which every Israelite had to impose on himself, viz. the so-called "second tithe" (מַעֲשֵׂר שֵׁנִי, Deut. xiv. 22-27) in the first, second, fourth, and fifth years, and the "poor-tithe" or "third tithe" (מַעֲשֵׂר עָנִי or מַעֲשֵׂר שְׁלִישִׁי, Deut. xiv. 28) in the third and sixth years. Of these the former was to be consumed by the owner in conjunction with the Levites, the latter with the Levites and the poor. The priests proper (כהנים) partook of this second and third tithe only as Levites, and when specially invited by the owner so to do, except in the one case when it was consumed at Jerusalem along with the firstlings of the herd and flock (Deut. xiv. 23). But besides those "firstlings," and the Levite "tithe from the tithe" mentioned above, the priests had two other sources of income of a somewhat similar nature; viz. (*a*) the great therumah (see last note), consisting of the firstfruits of oil, wine, and corn (Num. xviii. 11-13), and including (Deut. xviii. 4) the first products of a sheep-shearing (ראשית גז צאנך); and (*b*) the "the cake-therumah" of the first of the dough (Num. xv. 18-21), which was to be offered to the Lord, and then through Him to come to the priest (Neh. x. 38). But as these offerings could not properly have been reckoned as tithes, and as the priests' share even in the "second" and "third" tithes was occasional only, and in their character of Levites, not of priests, we may not assume that the writer of this epistle had such offerings in view when he spoke of the priests as tithing their brethren. He must have been thinking mainly of the "tithe from the tithe" which they took of the Levites, and so indirectly only received from the people. Tobit, in a passage referred to in the text (i. 7, 8), distinguishes the first or Levitical, as well as the second and third tithe, [and speaks of paying the "first" to "the sons of Levi." Another reading, followed by our English version ("*the first tenth I gave to the sons of Aaron*"), seems to favour Bleek's conjecture, though he does not himself refer to it.—TR.]. Josephus speaks cursorily of the "first" tithe (as that paid to priests and Levites, and more particularly of the two other kinds) (*Ant.* iv. 8, viii. 22). Every seventh or sabbatical year the land lay fallow, and was then tithe-free. A fourth kind of tithe known to tradition—the so-called מעשר הבהמה—being consumed like the paschal lamb by the owners at the holy city, is hardly worth mentioning here, as neither priests nor Levites had any legal claim to share it.

Philo refers to the tithe paid by the Levites to the priests thus : "*The law suffereth them not to make use of the tithes they receive, before they have in their turn raised other tithes from them as from their own possessions, and paid them over to the priests of the better order. Then, and not before, may they* (the Levites) *enjoy their tithe themselves*" (Phil. *de Sacerdot. hon.* § 6, tom. ii. 336, 39). He seems here to regard the Levites as in a certain sense "priests of the second order," but he avoids directly calling them ἱερεῖς.

NOTE H (HEB. VII. 5). P. 341.

Dr. Biesenthal's conjectural Reading.

THE *text rec.* reads (Heb. vii. 5): Καὶ οἱ μὲν ἐκ τῶν [υἱῶν] Λευὶ τὴν ἱερατείαν λαμβάνοντες, ἐντολὴν ἔχουσιν ἀποδεκατοῦν τὸν ΛΑΟΝ κατὰ τὸν νόμον, τουτέστι, τοὺς ἀδελφοὺς αὐτῶν. ... Dr. Biesenthal, who is now engaged in preparing his Hebrew commentary on this epistle, writes to me under date 5th February of this year (1857), from London, to propose what seems to him a complete solution of the difficulty contained in this verse. For ΛΑΟΝ he would simply substitute ΛΕΥΙΝ; and the meaning would then be (in strict accordance with Num. xviii. 25-32), that *those of the sons of Levi who attain the dignity of the priesthood, take tithe of (the very tribe of) Levi, that is, of their own brethren.* It is a pity that this undoubtedly ingenious conjecture has no MS. authority in its favour. If we might assume its truth, we should refer to the term ἱερατεία applied (Num. xviii. 1) to the family of Aaron, and to the τοὺς ἀδελφούς σου φυλὴν Λευί of ver. 2, as interesting parallels in the text of the LXX.; and we should observe, that while the ὁ δεκάτας λαμβάνων of Heb. vii. 9 refers to the Levites tithing the people, the ἀποδεκατοῦν of ver. 5 is more appropriate to the action of the priests, as expressing in brief a λαμβάνειν ἐπιδέκατον ἀπὸ τοῦ ἐπιδεκάτον (Num. xviii. 26, LXX.). We feel bound, at any rate, not to withhold from our readers this very ingenious and radical mode of solving the difficulty.

NOTE I (HEB. VII. 9, 10). P. 348.

On the Relation in which all Mankind stands to the Sin of Adam.

THE sacred writer's assertion here concerning Levi's being tithed *in lumbis Abrahami*, has an important bearing on the doctrine of the fall. That *in Adam we have all sinned*, though not asserted in Rom. v. 12 [where the Vulgate reads *in quo omnes peccaverunt—in quo* having been by some referred to Adam], is a strictly scriptural proposition, and finds irrefragable support in Heb. vii. 9, 10. But here, 1*st*, two distinctions must be made: we must regard Adam not merely as the natural progenitor, but as at the same time the ethical inaugurator of the human race — *principium repræsentativum in natura et gratia;* and 2*dly*, we must bear in mind that the deed of Adam can only so far be regarded as that of all men, as the whole vast many-branched tree of humanity was potentially and radically contained in him. Though there works individual existences of human souls in Adam [as some have dreamed], yet he carried us all in himself as *in massa,* or *in chao,* out of which each individual human existence proceeds, bearing in itself the stamp of the original creative beginning, and the self-determinating act of the common father of mankind.

Note J (Heb. vii. 14). P. 353.

On the Genealogy of our Lord.

Πρόδηλον γὰρ ὅτι ἐξ 'Ιούδα ἀνατέταλκεν ὁ Κύριος. This manifest certainty would rest, in the first instance, not on the descent of Mary, but on that of Joseph, from the house of David. The having a Davidic mother would not constitute one at once a Ben-David; for Jewish law never reckoned a child's descent by the mother (משפחת אם אינה קרויה משפחה, *i.e.* the mother's genealogy is not called a genealogy). It is in accordance with this maxim that the two genealogies of our Lord must be interpreted. It is evident that St. Matthew regarded Him as Ben-David because Joseph was so. Though not Joseph's actual, He was (so to speak) his *matrimonial* Son, born *to* him, as it were (the Son of David), in his wedlock with the blessed Virgin, and so by birth attached to the house of David, and proceeding from it. Nor is the case otherwise with the genealogy of St. Luke. Literally, and according to the natural sense of the words, he gives likewise the genealogy of Joseph; for τοῦ 'Ηλί (Luke iii. 23) must in the first instance be understood as designating Joseph's father. Nevertheless, I believe it to be quite possible that St. Luke's genealogy does really give the descent of Mary. Joseph's father, in St. Matthew, is called Jacob; and Mary, according to a tradition which has found its way into the Talmud, was the daughter of Eli (בת־עלי). One might represent the matter to one's self thus: that most probably Jacob (Joseph's real father) died early, and that Eli (Mary's father), a near relation of Joseph, may have taken him into his house, and that so brought up with his cousin, the blessed Virgin, he was afterwards espoused to her. In this way our Lord, reckoned as Joseph's son, would through Jacob belong to the line of Solomon, and through Eli (Joseph's foster-father and Mary's real father) to the line of Nathan. The belief that Mary was a daughter of the house of David is primitive, and found in St.

Justin Martyr, Irenæus, and Tertullian. It was only the Manichæans who held her to have belonged to the tribe of Levi. Moreover, it must be confessed that such passages as Heb. vii. 14, Acts ii. 30, Rom. i. 3, 2 Tim. ii. 8, can only be taken in their full sense when we regard our Lord as belonging, not by a matrimonial relation only, but also by natural descent, to the house of David. The way to an impartial consideration of this vital question was first opened by Hofmann, *suum cuique*. [The English reader will find the whole subject excellently treated by Lord Arthur Hervey in his " *Genealogies of our Lord*," especially ch. iii. Prof. Delitzsch, in assuming that Jacob was descended from David through Solomon, and that Eli was so descended through Nathan, seems to have overlooked two facts: *first*, that both lines pass through Salathiel and Zerubbabel; and *secondly*, that Jeconiah was in prophecy most emphatically written " childless" (Jer. xxii. 29, 30): consequently we have but one *real* genealogy (at any rate from David to Salathiel),—that, namely, which is given by St. Luke.]

Note K (Heb. vii. 18). P. 361.

On Gal. iv. 3, 8, 9.

In Gal. iv. 3 the apostle speaks *communicative* of himself and Israel, " *We were once in bondage under the cosmic elements;*" while in ver. 8 he reminds the Gentile Galatians that *they* had once been in more grievous bondage still, serving with vain worship unreal gods (ἐδουλεύσατε τοῖς μὴ φύσει οὖσι θεοῖς),— a bondage out of which they had been delivered by mere grace, being brought to the knowledge of the true God without the intermediate discipline of those " cosmic elements" by which the Jews were trained. He proceeds in ver. 9 to put the question: How then is it that ye are now for falling back into the condition in which we Jews once found ourselves, by returning to those " *weak and poverty-stricken elements*," and that state of servitude and outward discipline which, with [the true] Israel, is already come to an end, outlived and outworn?

NOTE L (HEB. VII. 25). P. 372.

THOUGH possibly disturbing to some minds, it must not be concealed that Philo also regards the Logos in some places as a Mediator-Paraclete, or heavenly intercessor; *e.g.* ii. 155, 25 (*Vit. Mos.* iii. 14), where, explaining the high priest's breastplate (τὸ λόγιον), he says: "*It was necessary that one who was to serve as priest the Father of the cosmos, should have as His Paraclete* [Advocate or Intercessor] *the (in virtue) all-perfected Son,* [*i.e.* the Logos symbolized in the λόγοιν], *so as to obtain both forgiveness of sins and a supply (in abundant measure) of all good.*" Again, ii. 501, 44 [*Quis. rer. div. her.* § 42,] speaking of the cloud which stood between Israel and the Egyptians (Ex. xiv. 19), he thus applies it to the Logos: "*The all-producing Father vouchsafed to His Logos, as leader of the angelic host* (ἀρχαγγέλῳ) *and eldest of all existences* (πρεσβυτάτῳ), *that He should stand as the boundary between created things and the Creator. And He* (the Logos) *is Himself an intercessor for mortality in its longings after the incorruptible, and an ambassador from the Lord of all to that which is His subject.*" In this way the Logos exhibits Himself as μεσίτης (so He is frequently styled by Philo), or as the personal διαθήκη (i. 960, 12, *De Somn.* ii. 36), and συναγωγός between God and man (i. 144, 3, *Lib. de Cherub.* § 9). Surely in all this we must recognise dawnings of New Testament light. And when the "*condescension in love and pity to our race,*" which Philo ascribes (i. 643, 6, *De Somn.* § 23) to God and His Logos, had reached its consummation in "*the Word made flesh,*" that surely was the rising of the longed-for Sun.

END OF VOL. I.

www.ingramcontent.com/pod-product-compliance
Lightning Source LLC
Chambersburg PA
CBHW050610300426
44112CB00012B/1442